KANNAN

SO-AWP-035

PRIMER PLUS

SECOND EDITION

Teach Yourself Object-Oriented Programming

Stephen Prata

Waite Group Press™
Corte Madera, CA

Publisher **Mitchell Waite**
Editor-in-Chief **Scott Calamar**
Editorial Director **Joel Fugazzotto**
Managing Editor **Joanne Miller**
Content Editors **Harry Henderson, Heidi Brumbaugh**
Technical Reviewer, Second Edition **Michael Radtke**
Copy Editor **Judith Brown**
Production Director **Julianne Ososke**
Designer/Project Coordinator **Sestina Quarequio**
Cover Design **Cecile Kaufman**
Production **Michele Cuneo**
Illustrations **Pat Rogondino**

© 1995 by The Waite Group, Inc. Published by Waite Group Press, 200 Tamal Plaza, Corte Madera, CA 94925

SECOND EDITION

All rights reserved. No part of this manual shall be reproduced, stored in a retrieval system, or transmitted by any means, electronic, mechanical, photocopying, desktop publishing, recording, or otherwise, without written permission from the publisher. No patent liability is assumed with respect to the use of the information contained herein. While every precaution has been taken in the preparation of this book, the publisher and author assume no responsibility for errors or omissions. Neither is any liability assumed for damages resulting from the use of the information contained herein.

All terms mentioned in this book that are known to be trademarks or service marks are listed below. In addition, terms suspected of being trademarks or service marks have been appropriately capitalized. Waite Group Press cannot attest to the accuracy of this information. Use of a term in this book should not be regarded as affecting the validity of any trademark or service mark.

Turbo C++ and Borland C++ are registered trademarks of Borland International.
Sun is a registered trademark of Sun Microsystems.
Zortech C++ is a trademark of Zortech. Inc.
AT&T is a registered trademark of American Telephone and Telegraph.
IBM is a registered trademark of International Business Machines Corp.
MS-DOS is a registered trademark of Microsoft Corporation.
UNIX is a registered trademark of AT&T Bell Laboratories.
Macintosh is a registered trademark of Apple Computer.
The Waite Group is a registered trademark of The Waite Group, Inc.
Primer Plus is a registered trademark of The Waite Group, Inc.
CodeWarrior is a trademark of Metrowerks, Inc.

The Waite Group's C++ Primer Plus, Second Edition is distributed to bookstores and book wholesalers by Publishers Group West, Box 8843, Emeryville CA 94662, 800-365-3453 (in California, 415-658-3453).

Printed in the United States of America

96 97 • 10 9 8 7 6 5 4 3 2

Prata, Stephen.
    C++ primer plus : teach yourself object-oriented programming / Stephen Prata ; the Waite Group. -- 2nd ed.
       p. cm.
    Includes index.
    ISBN 1-878739-74-3 : $32.95
    1. C++ (Computer program language)   I. Waite Group. II. Title.
    QA76.73.C153P73 1995
    005.13'3—dc20
                                       94-23514
                                       CIP

Dedication

To my colleagues and students at the College of Marin, with whom it is a pleasure to work.

Stephen Prata

ABOUT THE AUTHOR

Stephen Prata teaches astronomy, physics, and computer science at the College of Marin in Kentfield, California. He received his B.S. from the California Institute of Technology and his Ph.D. from the University of California, Berkeley. Stephen has authored or coauthored over a dozen books for The Waite Group, including *UNIX Primer Plus*, *Microsoft Quick C Programming*, *Microsoft Quick Basic Primer Plus*, and *Artificial Life Playhouse*. He also wrote The Waite Group's *New C Primer Plus*, which received the Computer Press Association's 1990 Best How-to Computer Book Award and The Waite Group's *C++ Primer Plus*, nominated for the Computer Press Association's Best How-to Computer Book Award in 1991.

TABLE OF CONTENTS

	Preface to the Second Edition	xvi
	Preface to the First Edition	xviii
	Note to Instructors	xx
	How This Book Is Organized	xxi
Chapter 1	Getting Started	1
Chapter 2	Setting Out to C++	21
Chapter 3	Dealing with Data	53
Chapter 4	Derived Types	93
Chapter 5	Loops and Relational Expressions	149
Chapter 6	Branching Statements and Logical Operators	195
Chapter 7	Functions—C++'s Programming Modules	229
Chapter 8	Adventures in Functions	281
Chapter 9	Objects and Classes	345
Chapter 10	Working with Classes	393
Chapter 11	Classes and Dynamic Memory Allocation	443
Chapter 12	Class Inheritance	505
Chapter 13	Reusing Code in C++	565
Chapter 14	Friends, Exceptions, and More	627
Chapter 15	Input, Output, and Files	687
Appendix A	Number Bases	773
Appendix B	C++ Keywords	777
Appendix C	The ASCII Character Set	779
Appendix D	Operator Precedence	785
Appendix E	Other Operators	789
Appendix F	Selected Readings	801
Appendix G	Answers to Review Questions	803
Index		823

CONTENTS

Chapter 1 **Getting Started**. 1
Learning C++. 2
A Little History 2
  The C Language 3
  Object-Oriented Programming 5
  C++. 6
Portability and Standards. 7
The Mechanics of Creating a Program 9
  Creating the Source Code 10
  Compilation and Linking 11
Conventions Used in This Book. 17
Our System 18

Chapter 2 **Setting Out to C++**. 21
C++ Initiation 22
  The main() Function 23
  C++ Comments. 26
  The C++ Preprocessor and the iostream.h File. 27
  C++ Output with cout. 27
  C++ Source-Code Formatting 30
More About C++ Statements 32
  Declaration Statements and Variables 33
  The Assignment Statement 34
  New Trick for cout 35
More C++ Statements 36
  Using cin. 37
  Function Call Statements. 37
  More cout 39
  A Touch of Class 39
  Statement Summary 41
Functions 41
  Using a Function with a Return Value 41
  User-Defined Functions. 44
  User-Defined Function with a Return Value. 47

Summary 50
Review Questions 50
Programming Exercises 51

Chapter 3   Dealing with Data 53
Simple Variables 54
   Names for Variables 54
   Integer Types 55
   The short, int, and long Integer Types 56
   Unsigned Types 60
   Which Type? 62
   Integer Constants 64
   The char Type: Characters and Small Integers 66
   The New bool Type 72
The const Qualifier 73
Floating-Point Numbers 74
   Writing Floating-Point Numbers 74
   Floating-Point Types 76
   Floating-Point Constants 78
   Floating-Point Advantages and Disadvantages 79
C++ Arithmetic Operators 79
   Which Order: Operator Precedence and Associativity 81
   Division Diversions 82
   The Modulus Operator 84
   Type Conversions 84
Summary 89
Review Questions 90
Programming Exercises 91

Chapter 4   Derived Types 93
Introducing Arrays 94
Strings 98
   String Concatenation 100
   Using Strings in an Array 100
   Adventures in String Input 102
   Mixing String and Numeric Input 108
Introducing Structures 109
   Other Structure Properties 113
Enumerations 115
   Setting Enumerator Values 116
Pointers and the Free Store 117
   Declaring and Initializing Pointers 121
   Pointers and Numbers 124

Allocating Memory with new. 125
Using new to Create Dynamic Arrays 127
Pointers, Arrays, and Pointer Arithmetic 129
Pointers and Strings 134
Using new to Create Dynamic Structures. 138
Freeing Memory with delete 140
Automatic Storage, Static Storage, the Free Store. 143
Summary. 145
Review Questions 146
Programming Exercises 147

Chapter 5   **Loops and Relational Expressions** 149
Introducing the for Loop 150
for Loop Parts 151
Back to the for Loop 157
Changing the Step Size 159
Inside Strings with the for Loop 159
The Increment (++) and Decrement (--) Operators 160
Combination Assignment Operators 162
Compound Statements, or Blocks 162
The Comma Operator (or More Syntax Tricks) 164
Relational Expressions 167
The Mistake You'll Probably Make 168
Comparing Strings 170
The while Loop 172
for vs. while 175
Just a Moment 176
The do while Loop 178
Loops and Text Input. 180
Using Unadorned cin for Input 180
cin.get() to the Rescue. 182
The End-of-File Condition 183
Yet Another cin.get() 185
Nested Loops and Two-Dimensional Arrays. 189
Initializing a Two-Dimensional Array. 190
Summary. 192
Review Questions 193
Programming Exercises 194

Chapter 6   **Branching Statements and Logical Operators** . . . 195
The if Statement 195
The if else Statement 197

Formatting Your if else Statements 199
The if else if else Construction. 200
Logical Expressions 201
The Logical OR Operator: ||. 202
The Logical AND Operator: && 203
The Logical NOT Operator: !. 207
Logical Operator Facts. 209
The ctype.h Library of Character Functions. 210
The ?: Operator 212
The switch Statement 214
switch and if else. 218
The break and continue Statements. 219
Number-Reading Loops. 221
Summary. 224
Review Questions 225
Programming Exercises 227

Chapter 7   **Functions—C++'s Programming Modules** 229
Function Review 230
Defining a Function. 231
Function Prototyping and Function Calls 233
Function Arguments and Passing by Value. 237
Multiple Arguments. 239
Another Two-Argument Function 241
Functions and Arrays. 243
Arrays and Pointers (Again). 244
Implications of Using Arrays As Arguments. 245
More Array Functions 248
Pointers and const. 253
Functions and Strings 256
Functions That Return Strings. 258
Functions and Structures. 259
Passing and Returning Structures 260
Another Example 262
Passing Structure Addresses 266
Recursion 268
Pointers to Functions. 271
Function Pointer Basics. 271
Summary. 275
Review Questions 276
Programming Exercises 277

Chapter 8   **Adventures in Functions** 281

Inline Functions 281

Reference Variables 285

     Creating a Reference Variable 285

     References As Function Parameters 288

     Reference Properties and Oddities 291

     Using References with a Structure 295

Default Arguments 300

Function Polymorphism (Function Overloading) 303

     An Overloading Example 305

     When to Use Function Overloading 308

Function Templates 308

     Overloaded Templates 310

     Specializations 312

     Which Function? 316

Separate Compilation 318

Storage Classes, Scope, and Linkage 322

     Scope and Linkage 322

     Automatic Variables 323

     The Static Storage Class 327

     The static Modifier (Local Variables) 331

     Linkage and External Variables 332

     Storage Class Qualifiers: const, volatile, and mutable 336

     Storage Classes and Functions 337

     Storage Classes and Dynamic Allocation 338

Summary 339

Review Questions 340

Programming Exercises 342

Chapter 9   **Objects and Classes** 345

Procedural and Object-Oriented Programming 346

Abstraction and Classes 347

     What's a Type? 347

     The Class 348

     Implementing Class Member Functions 353

     Using a Class 357

     Our Story to Date 361

Class Constructors and Destructors 362

     Declaring and Defining Constructors 363

     Using a Constructor 364

     The Default Constructor 364

     Destructors 366

Improving the Stock Class. 366
Constructors and Destructors in Review 373
Knowing Your Objects: The this Pointer 374
An Array of Objects. 380
Class Scope 382
An Abstract Data Type 384
Summary. 388
Review Questions 389
Programming Exercises 390

Chapter 10   Working with Classes 393
Operator Overloading 394
A Vector Class with Operator Overloading 395
Friends and Operator Overloading 404
Overloading Restrictions 412
Overloading the << Operator 413
Improving the Class by Adding a State Member 417
Automatic Conversions and Type Casts for Classes 426
Conversion Functions 432
Conversions and Friends. 435
Summary. 438
Review Questions 439
Programming Exercises 440

Chapter 11   Classes and Dynamic Memory Allocation 443
Dynamic Memory and Classes. 444
Review Example and static Class Members 444
Trouble in String City 454
Implicit Member Functions. 456
The New, Improved String Class 465
When Using new in Constructors 471
Using Pointers to Objects 474
Reviewing Techniques 478
A Queue Simulation 479
A Queue Class. 480
The Customer Class 490
The Simulation 493
Summary. 498
Review Questions 499
Programming Exercises 501

Chapter 12 Class Inheritance 505
An Array Base Class 506
    Class Declaration 508
    The Class Methods 510
    Using the Class 519
Inheritance — An Is-a Relationship 522
    Declaring a Derived Class 524
    Implementing the Derived Class 527
    Using the Derived Class 534
    Deriving Another Class 538
Virtual Member Functions 542
    Activating Dynamic Binding 543
    Why Two Kinds of Binding? 545
    How Virtual Functions Work 545
    Virtual Things to Know 546
Class Design Review 550
    Member Functions That the Compiler Generates for You . . 550
    Other Class Method Considerations 552
    Public Inheritance Considerations 555
    Class Function Summary 560
Summary 561
Review Questions 561
Programming Exercises 563

Chapter 13 Reusing Code in C++ 565
Classes with Object Members 566
    The Student Class Example 568
Private Inheritance 572
    The Student Class Example (New Version) 572
Class Templates 580
    Defining a Class Template 580
    Using a Template Class 583
    A Closer Look at the Template Class 585
    An Array Template Example 590
    Using the Template with a Family of Classes 592
    Template Versatility 600
    Template Specializations 602
Multiple Inheritance 603
    How Many Workers? 605
    Which Method? 610
    Multiple Inheritance Synopsis 618
Summary 619
Review Questions 620

Programming Exercises 622

Chapter 14   **Friends, Exceptions, and More** 627
Friends 628
Friend Classes 628
Friend Member Functions. 633
Other Friendly Relationships. 637
Nested Classes. 640
Nested Classes and Access. 641
Nesting in a Template 643
Exceptions. 646
The Exception Mechanism 649
Uncaught Exceptions 653
Exception Versatility 653
Exceptions and Classes 660
Exceptions and Inheritance 666
Exceptions and the Future. 670
RTTI 670
What's It For? 670
How Does It Work?. 671
Namespaces. 679
Traditional C++ Namespaces 679
New Namespace Features 680
Namespaces and the Future 683
Summary. 683
Review Questions 684
Programming Exercises 685

Chapter 15   **Input, Output, and Files** 687
An Overview of C++ Input and Output 688
Streams and Buffers. 688
Streams, Buffers, and the iostream.h File. 691
Redirection 693
Output with cout. 694
The Overloaded << Operator 695
The Other ostream Methods 698
Flushing the Output Buffer 700
Formatting with cout. 701
Input with cin 717
How cin >> Views Input 719
Stream States. 721
Other istream Class Methods. 723

Other istream Methods 730
File Input and Output 734
Simple File I/O 735
Opening Multiple Files 737
Stream Checking 741
File Modes 742
Random Access 753
Incore Formatting 764
What Now? 767
Summary 768
Review Questions 769
Programming Exercises 770

Appendix A   **Number Bases** 773

Appendix B   **C++ Keywords** 777

Appendix C   **The ASCII Character Set** 779

Appendix D   **Operator Precedence** 785

Appendix E   **Other Operators** 789

Appendix F   **Selected Readings** 801

Appendix G   **Answers to Review Questions** 803

Index   823

ACKNOWLEDGMENTS TO
THE FIRST EDITION

Many people have contributed to this book. In particular, I wish to thank Mitch Waite for his work in developing, shaping, and reshaping this book, and for reviewing the manuscript. I appreciate Harry Henderson's work in reviewing the last few chapters and in testing programs with the Zortech C++ compiler. Thanks to David Gerrold for reviewing the entire manuscript and for championing the needs of less experienced readers. Also, thanks to Hank Shiffman for testing programs using Sun C++ and to Kent Williams for testing programs with AT&T *cfront* and with G++. Thanks to Nan Borreson of Borland International for her responsive and cheerful assistance with Turbo C++ and Borland C++. Thank you, Ruth Myers and Christine Bush, for handling the relentless paper flow involved with this kind of project. Finally, thanks to Scott Calamar for keeping everything on track.

ACKNOWLEDGMENTS TO
THE SECOND EDITION

I'd like to thank Mitchell Waite and Scott Calamar for supporting a second edition and Joel Fugazzotto and Joanne Miller for guiding the project to completion. Thanks to Michael Marcotty of Metrowerks for dealing with my questions about their beta version CodeWarrior compiler. I'd also like to thank the following instructors for taking the time to give us feedback on the first edition: Jeff Buckwalter, Earl Brynner, Mike Holland, Andy Yao, Larry Sanders, Shahin Momtazi, and Don Stephens. Finally, I wish to thank Heidi Brumbaugh for her helpful content editing of new and revised material.

PREFACE TO THE

SECOND EDITION

Learning C++ is not a simple task. Not only is it a very full-featured language, but it also supports a programming style (object-oriented programming) that may require you to learn new ways of thinking about programming. Furthermore, C++ has rules of practice that aren't built into the language. For example, to use the language feature called inheritance correctly, you have to learn the proper language rules so that the compiler will accept your program, but you also have to learn conceptual rules about when it is and isn't appropriate to use inheritance. Also, C++ is a moving target, and it has evolved significantly since the first edition of this book.

This book aims to make learning C++ manageable, even pleasurable. It follows the precepts outlined in the Preface to the First Edition. In addition, the new edition does the following:

- ◥ It presents additions to C++, such as templates, exceptions, RTTI, and namespaces.

- ◥ It tracks changes in C++, such as in the rules governing reference arguments.

- ◥ It reflects the developing draft ANSI/ISO C++ standard.

- ◥ It provides more conceptual guidance about when to use particular features, such as using public inheritance to model what are known as *is-a* relationships.

- ◥ It illustrates common C++ programming idioms and techniques.

- ◥ It has programming exercises at the end of each chapter to provide practice in applying new ideas.

- ◥ It devotes greater attention to organizing and explaining C++ classes, dividing the original presentation into more chapters, and revising and expanding the discussion.

Like the first edition, this book practices generic C++. That means you should be able to use it with any contemporary C++ implementation. Towards that end we tested the examples with a variety of compilers, including Borland C++ 3.1, Borland C++ 4.0, GNU C++ 2.0, Metrowerks CodeWarrior CW 3.5, Microsoft Visual C++ 1.0, Symantec C++ 6.0 (PC), and Symantec C++ 7.0 (Mac). Ideally, C++ is C++ is C++, but compilers do differ in how closely they track the draft standard. For example, many of these compilers don't yet support templates or exceptions; naturally, they won't run examples using those features. Aside from that, however, we ran into only a few minor differences, which the book notes. In general, C++ implementations are more consistent with each other now than they were at the time of the first edition, which is good news for programmers.

Learn and enjoy!

PREFACE TO

THE FIRST EDITION

When the Waite Group first released *C Primer Plus* in 1984, the C language had been around for about a decade but was just beginning to boom. We take pride in the important role that our book played in introducing programmers to C. Today the C++ language, which derives from C, has reached a similar stage in its evolution. It's booming because it offers a new paradigm—object-oriented programming, or OOP—well-suited to modern programming needs. Thus AT&T is rewriting UNIX in C++ because C++ improves the reliability, maintainability, and reusability of the code. Apple is using C++ to develop system software for its Macintosh line for the same reasons and because OOP techniques are a natural match to program features such as windows and dialog boxes. Individual programmers are turning to C++ because its new features bring the thrill back to programming. Naturally, it's time to release *C++ Primer Plus* and help this new boom along.

One difference between now and then is that many more books have been written about C++ than were written about C when it was new. However, none of the new C++ books plays the role that a Waite Group "primer" does. Many C++ books assume that you already know C and know it well. That's of little help to those who wish to move to C++ from, say, Pascal or BASIC, or to those who have enjoyed C recreationally without acquiring expert status. Most of the other C++ books present the full language, not just the new elements, but still assume you are fairly knowledgeable in C and in programming in general. Some C++ books make excellent references but can be rather tough sledding for learning the language. A few C++ titles were rushed out the door. They merely tack on a few new chapters to an old C book and don't fully integrate the new material or really do justice to C++'s exciting new object-oriented features.

Enter *The Waite Group's C++ Primer Plus*. We don't assume you know C, and we integrate discussing the basic C language with presenting the C++ features. We do assume you've had some programming experience, but we don't skip over the basics. We've tried to present C++ in a book instilled with traditional Waite Group primer virtues:

- A primer should be an easy-to-use, friendly guide.

- A primer doesn't assume that you already are familiar with all relevant programming concepts.

- A primer emphasizes hands-on learning with brief, easily typed examples that develop your understanding a concept or two at a time.

◀ A primer clarifies concepts with illustrations.

◀ A primer provides exercises to let you test your understanding, making the book suitable for self-learning or for the classroom.

C++ Primer Plus presents C++ fundamentals and illustrates them with short, to-the-point programs that are easy to copy and to experiment with. The book is not intended to provide encyclopedic coverage of all features and nuances of the C++ language, but it does present the most important aspects while laying the foundation for further study. You'll learn about input and output, how to make programs perform repetitive tasks and make choices, the many ways to handle data, and how to use functions. You'll learn about the important object-oriented programming concepts of information hiding (lots of fun), polymorphism (not as bad as it sounds), and inheritance. Besides learning basic techniques, you'll learn about the OOP philosophy. Meanwhile, we'll do our best to keep the presentation short, simple, and fun. Our goal is that by the end you'll be able to write solid, effective programs and enjoy yourself doing so.

NOTE TO INSTRUCTORS

One of the goals of the second edition is to provide a book that can be used either as a teach-yourself book or as a textbook. Here are some of the features that support using *C++ Primer Plus Second Edition* as a textbook:

- This book describes generic C++, so it isn't dependent upon some particular implementation.

- The contents have been brought up to date and include discussions of templates, exceptions, RTTI, and namespaces.

- It doesn't assume prior knowledge of C, so it can be used without a C prerequisite.

- Topics are arranged so that the early chapters can be covered rapidly as review chapters for courses that do have a C prerequisite.

- Chapters have review questions and programming exercises.

- The book introduces several topics appropriate for computer science courses, including abstract data types, stacks, queues, simple lists, simulations, and using recursion to implement a divide-and-conquer strategy.

- Individual chapters are short enough to cover in a week or less.

- The book discusses *when* to use certain features as well as *how* to use them. For example, it links public inheritance to *is-a* relationships and composition and private inheritance to *has-a* relationships, and it discusses when to use virtual functions and when not to.

HOW THIS BOOK IS

ORGANIZED

This book is divided into 15 chapters and 7 appendices summarized here.

Chapter 1: Getting Started

This chapter relates how Bjarne Stroustrup created the C++ programming language by adding object-oriented programming support to the C language. You'll learn the distinctions between procedural languages, such as C, and object-oriented languages, such as C++. You'll read about the joint ANSI/ISO work to develop a C++ standard. The chapter discusses the mechanics of creating a C++ program, outlining the approach for several current C++ compilers. Finally, it describes the conventions used in this book.

Chapter 2: Setting Out to C++

Chapter 2 guides you through the process of creating simple C++ programs. You'll learn about the role of the *main()* function and about some of the kinds of statements that C++ programs use. You'll use the predefined *cout* and *cin* objects for program output and input, and you'll learn about creating and using variables. Finally, you'll be introduced to functions, C++'s programming modules.

Chapter 3: Dealing with Data

C++ provides built-in types for storing two kinds of data: integers (numbers with no fractional parts) and floating-point numbers (numbers with fractional parts). To meet the diverse requirements of programmers, C++ offers several types in each category. This chapter discusses these types, including creating variables and writing constants of various types. You'll also learn how C++ handles implicit and explicit conversions from one type to another.

Chapter 4: Derived Types

C++ lets you construct more elaborate types from the basic built-in types. The most advanced form is the class, discussed in Chapters 9, 10, 11, 12, and 13. This chapter discusses other forms, including arrays, which hold several values of a single type; structures, which hold several values of unlike types; and pointers, which identify locations in memory. You'll also learn how to create and store text strings and to handle text input and output. Finally, you'll learn some of the ways C++ handles memory allocation, including the *new* and *delete* operators for managing memory explicitly.

Chapter 5:   Loops and Relational Expressions

Programs often need to perform repetitive actions, and C++ provides three looping structures for that purpose: the *for* loop, the *while* loop, and the *do while* loop. Such loops need to know when they should terminate, and the C++ relational operators enable you to create tests to guide such loops. You'll also learn how to create loops that read and process input character-by-character. Finally, you'll learn how to create two-dimensional arrays and how to use nested loops to process them.

Chapter 6:   Branching Statements and Logical Operators

Programs can behave intelligently if they can tailor their behavior to circumstances. In this chapter you'll learn how to control program flow by using the *if, if else,* and *switch* statements and the conditional operator. You'll learn how to use logical operators to help express decision-making tests. Also, you'll meet the *ctype.h* library of functions for evaluating character relations, such as testing whether a character is a digit or a nonprinting character.

Chapter 7:   Functions—C++'s Programming Modules

Functions are the basic building blocks of C++ programs. This chapter concentrates on features that C++ functions share with C functions. In particular, you'll review the general format of a function definition and examine how function prototypes increase the reliability of programs. Also, you'll investigate how to write functions to process arrays, character strings, and structures. Next you'll learn about recursion, which is when a function calls itself, and see how it can be used to implement a divide-and-conquer strategy. Finally, you'll meet pointers to functions, which enable you to use a function argument to tell one function to use a second function.

Chapter 8:   Adventures in Functions

This chapter explores the new features C++ adds to functions. You'll learn about inline functions, which can speed program execution at the cost of additional program size. You'll work with reference variables, which provide an alternative way to pass information to functions. Default arguments let a function automatically supply values for function arguments that you omit from a function call. Function overloading lets you create functions having the same name but taking different argument lists. All these features have frequent use in class design. Also, you'll learn about function templates, which allow you to specify the design of a family of related functions. You'll learn about putting together multifile programs. Finally, you'll examine storage classes, scope, and linkage, which determine what parts of a program know about a variable.

Chapter 9: Objects and Classes

A class is a user-defined type, and an object is an instance of a class, such as a variable. This chapter introduces you to object-oriented programming and to class design. A class declaration describes the information stored in a class object and also the operations (class methods) allowed for class objects. Some parts of an object are visible to the outside world (the public portion), and some are hidden (the private portion). Special class methods (constructors and destructors) come into play when objects are created and destroyed. You will learn about all this and other class details in this chapter, and you'll see how classes can be used to implement abstract data types (ADTs), such as a stack.

Chapter 10: Working with Classes

In this chapter you'll further your understanding of classes. First, you'll learn about operator overloading, which lets you define how operators such as + will work with class objects. You'll learn about friend functions, which can access class data that's inaccessible to the world at large. You'll see how certain constructors and overloaded operator member functions can be used to manage conversion to and from class types.

Chapter 11: Classes and Dynamic Memory Allocation

Often it's useful to have a class member point to dynamically allocated memory. If you use *new* in a class constructor to allocate dynamic memory, you incur the responsibilities of providing an appropriate destructor, of defining an explicit copy constructor, and of defining an explicit assignment operator. This chapter shows you how and discusses the behavior of the member functions generated implicitly if you fail to provide explicit definitions. You'll also expand your experience with classes by using pointers to objects and studying a queue simulation problem.

Chapter 12: Class Inheritance

One of the most powerful features of object-oriented programming is inheritance, by which a derived class inherits the features of a base class, enabling you to reuse the base class code. This chapter discusses public inheritance, which models *is-a* relationships, meaning that a derived object is a special case of a base object. For instance, a physicist is a special case of a scientist. Implementing *is-a* relationships necessitates using a new kind of member function called a virtual function. This chapter discusses these matters, pointing out when public inheritance is appropriate and when it is not.

Chapter 13: Reusing Code in C++

Public inheritance is just one way to reuse code. This chapter looks at several other ways. Containment is when one class contains members that are objects of another class. It can be used to model *has-a* relationships, in which one class has components of another class. For instance, an automobile has a motor. You also can use private and protected inheritance to model such relationships. This chapter shows you how and points out the differences among the different approaches. Also, you'll learn about class templates, which let you define a class in terms of some unspecified generic type, then use the template to create specific classes in terms of specific types. For instance, a stack template enables you to create a stack of integers or a stack of strings. Finally, you'll learn about multiple public inheritance, whereby a class can derive from more than one class.

Chapter 14: Friends, Exceptions, and More

This chapter extends the discussion of friends to include friend classes and friend member functions. Then it presents several new developments in C++, beginning with exceptions, which provide a mechanism for dealing with unusual program occurrences, such as inappropriate function argument values or running out of memory. Then you'll learn about RTTI (runtime type information), a mechanism for identifying object types. Finally, you learn about the namespaces, a mechanism for avoiding name conflicts.

Chapter 15: Input, Output, and Files

This chapter reviews C++ I/O and discusses how to format output. You'll learn how to use class methods to determine the state of an input or output stream and to see, for example, if there has been a type mismatch on input or if end-of-file has been detected. C++ uses inheritance to derive classes for managing file input and output. You'll learn how to open files for input and output, how to append data to a file, how to use binary files, and how to get random access to a file. Finally, you'll learn how to apply standard I/O methods to read from and write to strings.

Appendix A: Number Bases

This appendix discusses octal, hexadecimal, and binary numbers.

Appendix B: C++ Keywords

This appendix lists C++ keywords.

Appendix C: The ASCII Character Set

This appendix lists the ASCII character set along with decimal, octal, hexadecimal, and binary representations.

Appendix D: Operator Precedence

This appendix lists the C++ operators in order of decreasing precedence.

Appendix E: Other Operators

This appendix summarizes those C++ operators, such as the bitwise operators, not covered in the main body of the text.

Appendix F: Selected Readings

This appendix lists some books that can further your understanding of C++.

Appendix G: Answers to Review Questions

This appendix contains the answers to the review questions posed at the end of each chapter.

CHAPTER 1

GETTING STARTED

You will learn about the following in this chapter:

◇ How C++ adds object-oriented concepts to the C language

◇ The history and philosophy of C

◇ Procedural versus object-oriented programming

◇ The history and philosophy of C++

◇ Programming language standards

◇ The mechanics of creating a program

◇ Conventions used in this book

Welcome to C++! This exciting language, blending the C language with support for object-oriented programming, has become one of the most important programming languages of the 1990s. Its C ancestry brings C++ the tradition of an efficient, compact, fast, and portable language. Its object-oriented heritage brings C++ a fresh programming methodology designed to cope with the escalating complexity of modern programming tasks. This dual heritage is both a blessing and a bane. It makes the language very powerful, but it also means there's more to learn. In this chapter we'll explore C++'s background further, then go over some of the ground rules for creating C++ programs. The rest of the book teaches you to use the C++ language, going from the modest basics of the language to the glory of object-oriented programming (OOP) and its supporting cast of new jargon—objects, classes, encapsulation, data hiding, polymorphism, genericity, and inheritance. (Of course, as you learn C++, these terms will be transformed from buzzwords to the necessary vocabulary of cultivated discourse.)

Learning C++

C++ joins two separate programming traditions—the procedural language tradition, represented by C, and the object-oriented language tradition, represented by the enhancements C++ adds to C. This chapter will look into those traditions shortly. But first, let's consider what this dual heritage implies about learning C++. The main reason to use C++ is to avail yourself of its object-oriented features. To do so, you need a sound background in standard C, for that language provides the basic types, operators, control structures, and syntax rules. So, if you already know C, you're poised to learn C++. But it's not just a matter of learning a few more keywords and constructs. Going from C to C++ involves about as much work as learning C in the first place. Also, if you know C, you need to unlearn some programming habits as you make the transition to C++. If you don't know C, you have to master both the C and the OOP components to learn C++, but at least you may not have to unlearn programming habits. If you are beginning to think that learning C++ may involve some mind-stretching effort on your part, you're right. This book will guide you through the process in a clear, helpful manner, one step at a time, so the mind-stretching will be sufficiently gentle to leave your brain resilient.

C++ Primer Plus approaches C++ by teaching both its C and its OOP components, so it assumes no prior knowledge of C. You'll start by learning C. Even if you know C, you may find this part of the book a good review. Also, it points out concepts that will become important later, and it indicates where C++ differs from C. Once well-founded in C basics, you'll add the C++ superstructure. At that point you'll learn about objects and classes and how C++ implements them.

This book is not intended to be a complete C++ reference; it won't explore every nook and cranny of the language. But you will learn all the major features of the language, including some, like multiple inheritance, templates, and exceptions, that are recent additions.

Now let's take a brief look at some of C++'s background.

A Little History

Computer technology has evolved at an amazing rate during the last few decades. Today a laptop computer can compute faster and store more information than the mainframe computers of thirty years ago. (Quite a few programmers can recall bearing offerings of decks of punched cards to be submitted to a mighty, room-filling computer system with a majestic 100 KB of memory—not enough memory to run a good personal computer game today.) Computer languages have evolved, too. The changes may not be as dramatic, but they are important. Bigger, more powerful computers spawn bigger, more complex programs which, in turn, raise new problems in program management and maintenance. In the 1970s, languages like C and Pascal helped usher in an era of structured programming, a philosophy that brought some order and discipline to a field badly in need of these qualities. Besides providing the tools for structured programming, C also produced compact, fast-running programs along with the ability to address hardware matters, such as managing communication ports and disk drives. These gifts helped make C the dominant programming language in the 1980s. Meanwhile, the 1980s witnessed the growth of a new programming paradigm: object-oriented programming, or OOP, as embodied in languages such as Smalltalk and C++. Let's examine these two developments (C and OOP) a bit more closely.

The C Language

In the early 1970s, Dennis Ritchie of Bell Laboratories was working on a project to develop the UNIX operating system. (An operating system is a set of programs that manages a computer's resources and handles its interactions with users. For example, it's the operating system that puts the system prompt onscreen and that runs programs for you.) For this work Ritchie needed a language that was concise, that produced compact, fast programs, and that could control hardware efficiently. Traditionally, programmers met these needs by using assembly language, which is closely tied to a computer's internal machine language. However, assembly language is a *low-level* language, that is, it is specific to a particular computer processor. So if you want to move a program to a different kind of computer, you may have to completely rewrite the program using a different assembly language. It was a bit as if each time you bought a new car, you found that the designers decided to change where the controls went and what they did, forcing you to relearn how to drive. But UNIX was intended to work on a variety of computer types (or platforms). That suggested using a *high-level* language. A high-level language is oriented towards problem-solving instead of towards specific hardware. Special programs called *compilers* translate a high-level language to the internal language of a particular computer. Thus you can use the same high-level language program on different platforms by using a separate compiler for each platform. Ritchie wanted a language that combined low-level efficiency and hardware access with high-level generality and portability. So, building from older languages, he created C.

C Programming Philosophy

Because C++ grafts a new programming philosophy onto C, we should first take a look at the older philosophy that C follows. In general, computer languages deal with two concepts—data and algorithms. The data constitute the information a program uses and processes. The algorithms are the methods the program uses. See Figure 1-1. C, like most mainstream languages to date, is a *procedural* language. That means it emphasizes the algorithm side of programming. Conceptually, procedural programming consists of figuring out the actions a computer should take, then using the programming language to implement those actions. A program prescribes a set of procedures for the computer to follow to produce a particular outcome, much as a recipe prescribes a set of procedures for a cook to follow to produce a cake.

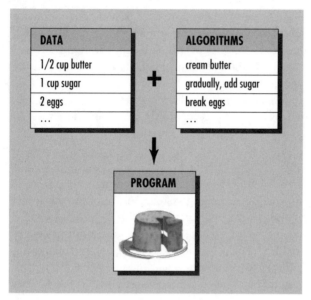

Figure 1-1 Data + algorithms = program

Earlier procedural languages, such as FORTRAN and BASIC, ran into organizational problems as programs grew larger. For example, programs often use branching statements, which route execution to one or another set of instructions depending upon the result of some sort of test. Many older programs had such tangled routing (called "spaghetti programming") that it was virtually impossible to understand a program by reading it, and modifying such a program was an invitation to disaster. In response, computer scientists developed a more disciplined style of programming called *structured programming*. C includes features to facilitate this approach. For instance, structured programming limits branching (choosing which instruction to do next) to a small set of well-behaved constructions. C incorporates these constructions (the *for loop,* the *while loop,* the *do while* loop, and the *if else* statement) into its vocabulary.

Top-down design was another of the new principles. The idea is to break a large program into smaller, more manageable tasks. If one of these tasks is still too broad, divide it into yet smaller tasks. Continue with this process until the program is compartmentalized into small, easily programmed modules. (Organize your study. Aargh! Well, organize your desk, your table top, your filing cabinet, and your bookshelves. Aargh! Well, start with the desk and organize each drawer, starting with the middle one. Hmmm, perhaps I can manage that task.) C's design facilitates this approach, encouraging you to develop program units called *functions* to represent individual task modules. As you may have noticed, the structured programming techniques reflect a procedural mind-set, thinking of a program in terms of the actions it performs.

Object-Oriented Programming

Although the principles of structured programming improved the clarity, reliability, and ease of maintenance of programs, large-scale programming still remains a challenge. Object-oriented programming (OOP) brings a new approach to that challenge. Unlike procedural programming, which emphasizes algorithms, OOP emphasizes the data. Rather than trying to fit a problem to the procedural approach of a language, OOP attempts to fit the language to the problem. The idea is to design data forms that correspond to the essential features of a problem. In C++, a *class* is a specification describing such a new data form, and an *object* is a particular data structure constructed according to that plan. For instance, a class could describe the general properties of a corporation executive (name, title, salary, unusual abilities, for example), while an object would represent a specific executive (Guilford Sheepblat, vice president, $325,000, knows how to use a *CONFIG.SYS* file). In general, a class defines what data are used to represent an object *and* the operations that can be performed upon that data. For example, suppose you were developing a computer drawing program capable of drawing a rectangle. You could define a class to describe a rectangle. The data part of the specification could include such things as the location of the corners, the height and width, the color and style of the boundary line, and the color and pattern used to fill the rectangle. The operations part of the specification could include methods for moving the rectangle, resizing it, rotating it, changing colors and patterns, and copying the rectangle to another location. If you then use your program to draw a rectangle, it will create an object according to the class specification. That object will hold all the data values describing the rectangle, and you can use the class methods to modify that rectangle. If you draw two rectangles, the program will create two objects, one for each rectangle.

The OOP approach to program design is to first design classes that accurately represent those things with which the program deals. A drawing program, for example, might define classes to represent rectangles, lines, circles, brushes, pens, and the like. The class definitions, recall, include a description of permissible operations for each class, such as moving a circle or rotating a line. Then you proceed to design a program using objects of those classes. The process of going from a lower level of organization, such as classes, to a higher level, such as program design, is called *bottom-up* programming.

There's more to OOP programming than the binding of data and methods into a class definition. OOP, for example, facilitates creating reusable code, and that eventually can save a lot of work. Information hiding safeguards data from improper access. Polymorphism lets you create multiple definitions for operators and functions, with the programming context determining which definition is used. Inheritance lets you derive new classes from old ones. As you can see, object-oriented programming introduces many new ideas and involves a different approach to programming than does procedural programming. Instead of concentrating on tasks, you concentrate on representing concepts. Instead of taking a top-down programming approach, you sometimes take a bottom-up approach. This book will guide you through all these points with plenty of easily grasped examples.

Designing a useful, reliable class can be a difficult task. Fortunately, OOP languages make it simple to incorporate existing classes into your own programming. Vendors provide a variety of useful class libraries, including libraries of classes designed to simplify creating programs for environments such as Windows or the Macintosh. One of the real benefits of C++ is that it lets you easily reuse and adapt existing, well-tested code.

C++

Like C, C++ began its life at Bell Labs, where Bjarne Stroustrup developed the language in the early 1980s. In his own words, "C++ was primarily designed so that the author and his friends would not have to program in assembler, C, or various modern high-level languages. Its main purpose is to make writing good programs easier and more pleasant for the individual programmer." (Bjarne Stroustrup, *The C++ Programming Language*. Second Edition. Reading, MA: Addison-Wesley Publishing Company, 1991) Stroustrup is more concerned with making C++ useful than in enforcing particular programming philosophies or styles. Real programming needs are more important than theoretical purity in determining language features. Stroustrup based C++ on C because of C's brevity, its suitability to system programming, its widespread availability, and its close ties to the UNIX operating system. C++'s OOP aspect was inspired by a computer simulation language called Simula67. Stroustrup added OOP features to C without significantly changing the C component. Thus C++ is a superset of C, meaning that any valid C program is a valid C++ program, too. There are some minor discrepancies, but nothing crucial. C++ programs can use existing C software libraries. Libraries are collections of programming modules that you can call up from a program. They provide proven solutions to many common programming problems, thus saving you much time and effort. This has helped the spread of C++.

The name C++ comes from the C increment operator ++, which adds 1 to the value of a variable. The name C++ correctly suggests an augmented version of C.

A computer program translates a real-life problem into a series of actions to be taken by a computer. While the OOP aspect of C++ gives the language the ability to relate to concepts involved in the problem, the C part of C++ gives the language the ability to get close to the hardware. See Figure 1-2. This combination of abilities also has helped the spread of C++. It may also involve a mental shift of gears as you turn from one aspect of a program to another. (Indeed, some OOP purists regard adding OOP features to C akin to adding wings to a pig, albeit a lean, efficient pig.) Also, because C++ grafts OOP onto C, you can ignore C++'s object-oriented features. But you'll miss a lot if that's all you do.

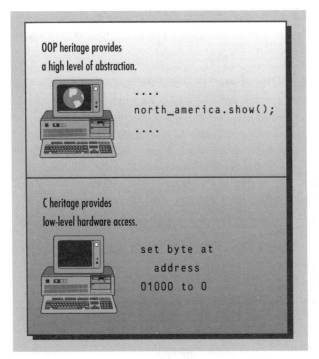

OOP heritage provides
a high level of abstraction.

```
....
north_america.show();
....
```

C heritage provides
low-level hardware access.

```
set byte at
address
01000 to 0
```

Figure 1-2 C++ duality

Portability and Standards

You've written a handy C++ program for the elderly 286 PC AT computer at work when management decides to replace the machine with a Sun workstation, a computer using a different processor and a different operating system. Can you run your program on the new platform? Of course, you'll have to recompile the program using a C++ compiler designed for the new platform. But will you have to make any changes to the code you wrote? If you can recompile the program without making changes and it runs without a hitch, we say the program is *portable*.

There are a couple of obstacles to portability. One is hardware. A program that is hardware-specific is not likely to be portable. One that takes direct control of an IBM PC VGA video board, for instance, will be speaking gibberish as far as a Sun is concerned. We will avoid that sort of programming in this book. (The Waite Group's *Object-Oriented Programming in Turbo C++* by Robert Lafore covers more hardware-specific issues.)

The second obstacle to portability is language divergence. Certainly, that can be a problem with spoken languages. A Yorkshireman's description of the day's events may not be portable to Brooklyn, even though English is spoken in both areas. Computer languages, too, can develop dialects. Is the IBM PC C++ implementation the same as the Sun implementation? Although most implementors would like to make their versions of C++ compatible with others, it's difficult to do so without a published standard describing exactly how the language works. Therefore, the American National Standards Institute (ANSI) created a committee (ANSI X3J16) to develop a standard for C++. (ANSI already has developed a standard for C.) The International Standards Organization (ISO) soon joined the process with its own committee (ISO-WG-21), so now there is a joint ANSI/ISO effort to develop the C++ standard. These committees meet jointly three times a year, and we'll simply lump them together notationally as the ANSI/ISO committee. ANSI/ISO's decision to create a standard emphasizes that C++ has become an important and widespread language. It also indicates C++ has reached a certain level of maturity, for it's not productive to introduce standards while a language is developing rapidly. Nonetheless, C++ has undergone significant changes since the committee began its work.

The ANSI/ISO C++ standard is still under development at the time of this writing. The committee is taking *The Annotated C++ Reference Manual*—ARM, for short—by Stroustrup and Ellis (Addison-Wesley Publishing Company, Reading, MA. 1990), as the base for developing the standard. The 19th chapter of the ARM is revised each printing to reflect changes and additions that the ANSI/ISO committee has approved. Also, as described in Appendix F, you can purchase a copy of the current draft standard.

The ANSI/ISO C++ standard additionally draws upon the ANSI C standard, since C++ is supposed to be, as far as possible, a superset of C. That means any valid C program ideally should also be a valid C++ program. There are a few differences between ANSI C and the corresponding rules for C++, but they are minor. Indeed, ANSI C incorporates some features first introduced in C++, such as function prototyping and the *const* type qualifier.

Prior to the emergence of ANSI C, the C community followed a de facto standard based on the book *The C Programming Language,* by Kernighan and Ritchie (Addison-Wesley Publishing Company Reading, MA. 1978). This standard often was termed K&R C; with the emergence of ANSI C, the simpler K&R C now sometimes is called classic C.

The ANSI C standard not only defines the C language, it also defines a standard C library that ANSI C implementations must support. C++ also uses that library; this book will refer to it as the *standard C library* or the *standard library*. In addition, the ANSI/ISO C++ committee will provide a standard library of C++ classes.

Before the ANSI/ISO committee began its work, many people accepted the most recent Bell Labs version of C++ as a standard. For instance, a compiler might describe itself as compatible with Release 2.0 or Release 3.0 of C++.

Before getting to the C++ language proper, let's cover some of the groundwork about creating programs and about using this book.

The Mechanics of Creating a Program

Suppose you've written a C++ program. How do you get it running? The exact steps depend upon your computer environment and the particular C++ compiler you use, but they will resemble the following steps. (Also see Figure 1-3.)

❧ Use a text editor of some sort to write the program and save it in a file. This file constitutes the *source code* for your program.

❧ Compile the source code. This means running a program that translates the source code to the internal language, called *machine language,* used by the host computer. The file containing the translated program is the *object code* for your program.

❧ Link the object code with additional code. C++ programs, for example, normally use *libraries.* A C++ library contains object code for a collection of computer routines, called *functions,* to perform tasks such as displaying information on the screen or calculating the square root of a number. Linking combines your object code with object code for the functions you use and with some standard startup code to produce a runnable version of your program. The file containing this final product is called the *executable code.*

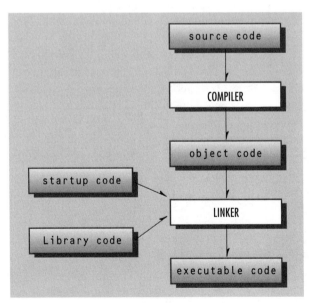

Figure 1-3 Programming steps

You will encounter the term *source code* throughout the book, so be sure to file it away in your personal random-access memory.

The programs in this book are generic and should run in any system supporting C++ as described in the ARM. (However, at the time of this writing, many compilers don't support all features. For instance, only some support exceptions and templates.) The steps for putting a program together may differ. Let's look a little further at these steps.

Creating the Source Code

Some C++ implementations, such as Microsoft Visual C++, Borland C++ (various versions), Symantec C++, and Metrowerks CodeWarrior, provide integrated development environments (IDEs) that let you manage all steps of program development, including editing, from one master program. Other implementations, such as AT&T C++ or GNU C++ on UNIX, just handle the compilation and linking stages and expect you to type commands on the system command line. In such cases, you can use any available text editor to create and modify source code. On UNIX, for example, you can use *vi* or *ed* or *ex* or *emacs*. On a DOS system, you can use *edlin* or any of several available program editors. You can even use a word processor, providing you save the file as a standard DOS ASCII text file instead of in a special word processor format.

In naming a source file, you must use the proper suffix to identify the file as a C++ file. This not only tells you the file is C++ source code, it tells the compiler that, too. (If a UNIX compiler complains to you about a "bad magic number," that's just its endearingly obscure way of saying that you used the wrong suffix.) The suffix consists of a period followed by a character or group of characters called the *extension*. See Figure 1-4.

The extension you use depends on the C++ implementation. Table 1-1 shows some common choices. For example, *spiffy.C* is a valid AT&T C++ source code file name. Note that UNIX is case-sensitive, meaning you should use an uppercase *C* character. Actually, a lowercase *c* extension also works, but standard C uses that extension. So, to

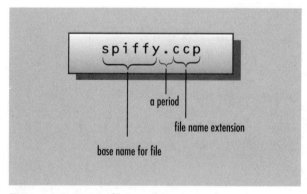

spiffy.ccp

a period

file name extension

base name for file

Figure 1-4 Source file extension

avoid confusion on UNIX systems, use *c* with C programs and *C* with C++ programs. If you don't mind typing an extra character or two, you can also use *cc* and *cxx* extensions with some UNIX systems. DOS, being a bit simple-minded compared to UNIX, doesn't distinguish between uppercase and lowercase, so DOS implementations use additional letters, as shown in Table 1-1, to distinguish between C and C++ programs.

C++ Implementation	Source Code Extension
UNIX AT&T	C, cc, cxx, c
GNU C++	C, cc, cxx, c
Symantec	cxx, cpp, cp
Borland C++	cpp
Microsoft Visual C++	cpp, cxx
CodeWarrior	cp, cpp

Table 1-1 Source code extensions

Compilation and Linking

Originally, Stroustrup implemented C++ with a C++-to-C compiler program instead of developing a direct C++-to-object code compiler. This program, called *cfront* (for C front end), translated C++ source code to C source code, which then could be compiled by a standard C compiler. This approach simplified introducing C++ to the C community. Other implementors have used this approach to bring C++ to other platforms. As C++ has developed and grown in popularity, more and more implementors have turned to creating C++ compilers that generate object code directly from C++ source code. This direct approach speeds up the compilation process and emphasizes that C++ is a separate, if similar, language.

Often the distinction between a *cfront* translator and compiler is nearly invisible to the user. For instance, on a UNIX system the *CC* command may first pass your program to the *cfront* translator, then automatically pass the translator's output on to the C compiler, which is called *cc*. Henceforth, we'll use the term "compiler" to include translate-and-compile combinations. The mechanics of compiling depend upon the implementation, and the following sections outline a few common forms. These summaries outline the basic steps, but they are no substitute for consulting the documentation for your system.

UNIX Compiling and Linking

Suppose, for instance, that you are on a UNIX system using the current AT&T Release 3.0 C++. Use the *CC* command to compile your program. The name is in uppercase letters to distinguish it from the standard UNIX C compiler *cc*. The *CC* compiler is a command-line compiler, meaning you type compilation commands on the UNIX command line.

For instance, to compile the C++ source code file *spiffy.C*, you would type this command at the UNIX prompt:

```
CC spiffy.C
```

If, through skill, dedication, or luck, your program has no errors, the compiler generates an object code file with an *o* extension. In this case, the compiler would produce a *spiffy.o* file.

Next, the compiler automatically passes the object code file to the system linker, a program that combines your code with library code to produce the executable file. By default, the executable file is called *a.out*. If you used just one source file, the linker also deletes the *spiffy.o* file, for it's no longer needed. To run the program, just type the name of the executable file:

```
a.out
```

Note that if you compile a new program, the new *a.out* executable file replaces the previous *a.out*. (That's because executable files take a lot of space, so overwriting old executable files helps reduce storage demands.) But if you develop an executable program you want to keep, just use the UNIX *mv* command to change the name of the executable file.

In C++, as in C, you can spread a program over more than one file. (Many of the programs in this book from Chapter 8 on do so.) In that case, you can compile a program by listing all the files on the command line:

```
CC my.C precious.C
```

In this case, the compiler does not delete the object code files. That way, if you just change the *my.C* file, you can recompile the program with this command:

```
CC my.C precious.o
```

This recompiles the *my.C* file and links it with the previously compiled *precious.o* file.

You may have to identify some libraries explicitly. For instance, to access functions defined in the math library, you may have to add the *-lm* flag to the command line.

```
CC usingmath.C -lm
```

The Free Software Foundation supplies the GNU C++ compiler called g++ that works much like the standard UNIX compiler:

```
g++ spiffy.C
```

Some versions may require that you link in the C++ library:

```
g++ spiffy.C -lg++
```

Turbo C++ 2.0 and Borland C++ 3.1 (DOS)

In DOS versions of Turbo C++'s and Borland C++'s integrated environment, which includes a built-in editor, you use a menu bar, accessible through a mouse or through **ALT**-key combinations, to make your desires known. For example, the File menu lets you create, save, and open files. The Edit menu assists in editing your source file. The Compile menu offers several compiling options, and the Run menu presents choices for running the program. Once you've used the built-in editor to write a program, the simplest choice is to select Run from the Run menu. This causes Borland C++ or Turbo C++ to compile, link, and run your program. If the compiler catches errors, of course, it won't run the program, but it will display a list of errors and highlight the offending lines in your source code. Also, the integrated environment includes a debugger that lets you step through the program a line at a time and examine any values you wish to see.

If you develop a program using more than one source code file, use the Project menu to open a new project. Then you can use further menu options to add the relevant files to a project list. The project file lets Borland C++ or Turbo C++ keep track of what's going on. If you change one of the files in the project list, the compiler knows it should update the executable program. In Borland C++ or Turbo C++ you can have several source code files, each in its own window onscreen simultaneously and you can easily switch from one file to another.

Both Borland C++ and Turbo C++ come with a tutorial program that shows you the ins and outs of the Borland C++ or Turbo C++ environment. And, of course, you can read the manuals.

Turbo C++ 3.0 for Windows

The interface for Turbo C++ 3.0 for Windows is similar to that of the DOS version. However, you need to create a project list even for single-file programs. When you run a compiled program, it runs in its own window. When a program completes running, you need to close its window (now labeled inactive) before you can modify and recompile the source code.

The system comes with a handy debugger.

Borland C++ 4.0

The Borland 4.0 IDE differs from that of its DOS cousins. First, you need a project file for every program, even those with a single file. You can use the integrated editor to create a source code model. Next you select the New project from the Project menu. You then can use the Browse button to select a directory for your project. You also have to choose a target type, a platform, and a target model. For the examples in this book, you can choose one of the two following combinations:

DOS Choice:
> Application in the Target Type menu

DOS Standard in the Platform scroll box
Small in the Target Model scroll box

EasyWin Choice:
EasyWin in the Target Type menu
Windows 3.x(16) in the Platform scroll box
Small in the Target Model scroll box

The DOS choice creates programs that run in the standard character-based DOS mode. The EasyWin choice creates programs that emulate the character-based DOS mode, but which run in a graphics window under Windows. For either choice, Small indicates using the Small memory model, which is sufficient for the programs in this book. You need to select a project name. The New Project dialog box suggests a default name, but you may wish to use the same base name you used for your source code. Also, while in the New Project dialog box, you can click the Advanced button and select the *.cpp* Node option.

After accepting the New Project settings, you need to add your source code file(s) to the project list, which should appear in the Project window. There's an icon in the icon bar for adding files. (It looks like a small page with text with a plus sign next to it.) Click on the icon to get a list of files, then add the files of your choice. Make sure that the executable file name in the project file is highlighted when you add files. You can remove mistakes from the project file by highlighting them, then pressing the (DELETE) key.

To compile a program, select Build All from the Project menu. To run a program, select Run from the Debug menu. Or, as a one-step shortcut, just click the lightning bolt icon to build and run. An EasyWin program will run in its own window, which you should close when the program finishes. A DOS program will run in a temporary DOS window that closes when the program finishes. To see what's onscreen, you may have to pause the program. A simple way is to add the following code at the end of the program:

```
        cin.get();     // add this statement
        cin.get();     // and maybe this, too
        return 0;
}
```

You can read the screen, then press the (ENTER) key to continue. (Whether you'll need one or two input statements depends upon which preceding input statement the program used.)

You should learn to use the debugger that comes with this program.

Microsoft Visual C++ (MVC++)

Begin by using the built-in editor to create your source code. Then create a project file by selecting New from the Project menu. Use the Browse button to select a directory for the project file, then type in a project name in the Project Name box. In the Project Type scroll box, choose either MS-DOS application or QuickWin application. An MS-DOS program runs in the standard DOS character-based mode. A QuickWin application uses the standard DOS character-based I/O, but runs under Windows. When you accept the New Project dialog box choices, MVC++ opens a new dialog box called Edit that lets you add source code files to your project. Select the file or files that belong. You can always select Edit from the Project menu later to call up the Edit dialog box and modify the project list. Close the dialog box when you finish selecting source code files. Select Build from the Project menu to compile your program, and select Execute from the Project menu to run it.

If you choose an MS-DOS application, MVC++ will open a DOS window and run the program in it, returning to Windows when the program completes. To keep the program output in view, you need to place some code at the end of the program to pause it. One approach is to add the following:

```
cin.get();    // add this statement
cin.get();    // and maybe this, too
return 0;
}
```

You can read the screen, then press the (ENTER) key to continue. (Whether you'll need one or two input statements depends upon which preceding input statement the program used.)

If you choose QuickWin, your program will run in a graphics window entitled Stdin/Stdout/Stderr. You should close this window when your program finishes running.

The QuickWin choice is more convenient, but it doesn't completely emulate a DOS session. That's an issue for only a few of the examples in this book.

You should learn to use the debugger that comes with this program.

Symantec C++ for the PC

Symantec acquired Zortech, and the Symantec C++ compiler descends from the Zortech C++ compiler. Like Borland C++ 4.0 and Microsoft Visual C++, Symantec C++ provides a project-based integrated development system. Here's one way to proceed. Select New from the File menu to create a new source code file. Enter the source code, then save the file, using the File menu in the source code window, not the File menu from the top-level Symantec C++ menu. Next, from the top-level menu, select New from the Project menu. After you enter a name for the project and accept it, the compiler opens an Edit Project window. From the file list, select the source file(s) that belong to the project, add it (them) to the project list, and click OK. Next, you need to decide upon a project type. Select Project from the Options menu. The DOS EXE type works best with this book's programs. However, this mode causes the computer to switch from a Windows graphic display mode to the DOS character display mode when running a program, then back when it completes. To see the DOS screen display, you need to pause the program before it terminates. The simplest way is to add a statement or two expecting keyboard input just before the end of the program:

```
cin.get();     // add this statement
cin.get();     // and maybe this, too
return 0;
}
```

You can read the screen, then press the (ENTER) key to continue. (Whether you'll need one or two input statements depends upon which preceding input statement the program used.)

To compile and run a project, select Execute Program from the Run menu. You should learn how to use the built-in debugger.

Symantec C++ for the Macintosh

The Symantec C++ compiler for the Macintosh merges the Think C compiler and the Zortech C++ compiler. Once you have started Symantec C++ for the Macintosh, select New Project from the File menu. (Or, to resume work on a previous project, select Open Project.) You'll see a project box. Begin by providing a list of libraries needed for your project. Select Add files from the Source menu to add files to the project list. The examples in this book work with the following selection of libraries:

❧ CplusLib

❧ ANSI++

❧ IOStreams

You can find them in the Standard Libraries folder in the Symantec C++ for Macintosh folder. (Version 7 shows an additional New Project dialog box when you select New Project. It lets you select the type of project. The C++ IOStreams Project corresponds to the choices listed above, so select it.)

Next, use Open from the File menu to open a new file to hold your source code. Use a proper suffix, such as *.cpp*. Add this file, too, to the project list. Macintosh code goes into 32 KB memory segments, so you have to organize the project code into segments, each of which mustn't exceed that limit. You can move libraries into different segments by selecting and dragging them in the project window. When you are ready, select Run from the Project menu.

TIP

Hint: To save time, you can use just one project for all the sample programs. Delete the previous example source code file from the project list and add the current source code. This saves having to enter the library files into a new list.

The compiler includes a debugger to help you locate the causes of runtime problems.

Metrowerks CodeWarrior C++ for the Macintosh

Metrowerks provides compilers for the traditional 680x0 family of processors as well as for the new Power PC processors. (The examples in this book were tested with a beta version.) You can begin either by opening a new source code file (New under the File menu) or opening a new project file (New Project under the File menu). Suppose you open a new source code file first. Enter your code and save it in a file with a *cpp* or a *cp* extension. Use the Add Window or the Add File selection under the Project menu to add your source code to the project list. Next, add libraries to the project list. The examples in this book work with the following combination libraries:

- CPlusPlus.lib
- ANSI(2i)C++.68K.Lib
- ANSI(2i)C.68K.Lib

Other combinations are possible. Macintosh code goes into 32 KB memory segments, so you have to organize the project code into segments, each of which mustn't exceed that limit. You can move libraries into different segments by selecting and dragging them in the project window. When you are ready, select Run from the Project menu.

TIP

Hint: To save time, you can use just one project for all the sample programs. Delete the previous example source code file from the project list and add the current source code. This saves having to enter the library files into a new list.

The compiler includes a debugger to help you locate the causes of runtime problems.

Conventions Used in This Book

To help distinguish between different kinds of text, we've used a few typographic conventions. Italics can denote any of the following:

- Names or values used in a program, such as *x*, *starship*, and *3.14*
- Important words or phrases used for the first time, such as *structured programming*
- Language keywords, such as *int* and *if else*
- File names, such as *iostream.h*
- Functions, such as *main()* and *puts()*

C++ source code is presented as follows:

```
#include <iostream.h>
int main(void)
{
        cout << "What's up, Doc!\n";
        return 0;
}
```

Sample program runs use the same format, except user input appears in boldface:

Please enter your name:
Plato

Since this book is about object-oriented programming, we've used geometric objects along the way to help you identify various elements of the book. All program listings are indicated by a computer. Tips, rules, and notes are marked with light bulbs, pointing hands, and pencils.

You'll find an occasional rule or suggestion in the following format:

TIP

You learn by doing, so try the examples and experiment with them.

By the way, you've just read a real and important suggestion, not just an example of what a rule or suggestion looks like.

Finally, when you enter program input, you normally have to press the (RETURN) key or the (ENTER) key to send the input to the program. Some keyboards use one and some the other; this book uses (ENTER).

Our System

This book describes the ARM definition of C++, so the examples should work with any C++ implementation compatible with the ARM, and with ANSI C. (At least, this is the vision and hope of portability.) However, C++ is still new, and you may find a few discrepancies. For example, at the time of this writing, some C++ compilers, including Visual C++ 1.5, have not yet implemented templates. Systems that use the Release 2.0 (or later) *cfront* translator may then pass the translated code to a C compiler that is not fully ANSI compatible, resulting in some language features being left unimplemented and in some standard ANSI library functions and header files not being supported. Also, some things, such as the number of bytes used to hold an integer, are implementation-dependent. For the record, the examples in this book were developed using Borland

C++ 3.1 or 4.0 on an IBM-compatible 486 PC with a hard disk and running under Windows 3.1 and MS DOS 6.2. Programs were checked using Symantec C++ 6.0 and Microsoft Visual C++ 1.0 compilers on the same machine, GNU g++ 2.0 on a Tatung running UNIX, Symantec C++ 7.0 and Metrowerks CodeWarrior DR3 on a Macintosh SE/30 under system 7.1. We'll mention any differences we've found.

CHAPTER 2

SETTING OUT TO C++

You will learn about the following in this chapter:

- ◇ Creating a C++ program
- ◇ The *#include* directive
- ◇ The general format for a C++ program
- ◇ The *main()* function
- ◇ Using the *cout* object for output
- ◇ Placing comments in a C++ program
- ◇ The newline character \n

- ◇ Declaring and using variables
- ◇ Using the *cin* object for input
- ◇ Defining and using simple functions

When constructing a simple home, you start with the foundation and the framework. If you don't have a solid structure to begin with, you'll have trouble later filling in the details, such as windows, door frames, observatory domes, and parquet ballrooms. Similarly, when you learn a computer language, you should start with learning the basic structure for a program. Only then can you move on to the details, such as loops and objects. This chapter, then, will serve to bring you an overview of the essential structure of a C++ program. While doing so, it will preview some topics—notably functions and classes—that we'll cover in much fuller detail later in the book. (The idea is to introduce at least some of the basic concepts gradually en route to the great awakenings that come later.)

C++ Initiation

Let's begin with a simple C++ program that displays a message. Listing 2-1 uses the C++ *cout* (pronounced *cee-out*) facility to produce character output. The source code includes several comments to the reader; these lines begin with //, and the compiler ignores them. C++ is case-sensitive, that is, it discriminates between uppercase characters and lowercase characters. This means that you must be careful to use the same case as in the examples. For instance, our program uses *cout*. If you substitute *Cout* or *COUT*, the compiler will reject your offering, accusing you of using unknown identifiers. (The compiler also is spelling-sensitive, so don't try *kout* or *coot*, either.) The *cpp* filename extension is a common way to indicate a C++ program; you may have to use a different extension, as described in Chapter 1.

Listing 2-1 *myfirst.cpp*

```
// myfirst.cpp--displays a message
#include <iostream.h>                              // a PREPROCESSOR directive
int main(void)                                     // heading summarizes function
{                                                  // start of function body
        cout << "Come up and C++ me some time."; // message
        cout << "\n";                              // start a new line
        return 0;                                  // terminate main()
}                                                  // end of function body
```

> ### COMPATIBILITY NOTE
>
> If you're using an older compiler, you may have to use *#include <stream.h>* instead of *#include <iostream.h>* in this and subsequent programs. On the other hand, the draft standard replaces *<iostream.h>* with *<iostream>*. Usually, that will be the only change you need to make as far as input and output go.

Once you've used your editor of choice to copy this program, you then use your C++ compiler to create the executable code, as Chapter 1 outlined. Here's the output from running the compiled program:

```
Come up and C++ me some time.
```

> ### C INPUT AND OUTPUT
>
> If you're used to programming in C, seeing *cout* instead of the *printf()* function may come as a minor shock. C++ can, in fact, use *printf()*, *scanf()*, and all the other standard C input and output functions, providing you include the usual C *stdio.h* file. But this is a C++ book, so we'll use C++'s new input facilities, which improve in many ways upon the C versions.

You construct C++ programs from building blocks called *functions*. Typically, you organize a program into major tasks, then design separate functions to handle those tasks. The first example is simple enough, as a first example should be, to consist of a single function named *main()*. The *myfirst.cpp* example has the following elements:

- Comments, indicated by the // prefix

- A preprocessor *#include* directive

- A function heading: *int main(void)*

- A function body, delimited by { and }

- A statement using the C++ *cout* facility to display a message

- A return statement to terminate the *main()* function

Let's look at these various elements in more detail now.

The *main()* Function

Stripped of the trimmings, the example program has the following fundamental structure:

```
int main(void)
{
    statements
    return 0;
}
```

These lines state that we have a function called *main()*, and they describe how the function behaves. Together they constitute a *function definition*. This definition has two parts: the first line, *int main(void)*, is called the *function heading,* and the portion enclosed in braces ({ and }) is the *function body*. See Figure 2-1. The function heading is a capsule summary of the function's interface with the rest of the program, and the function body represents your instructions to the computer about what the function should do. In C++ each complete instruction is called a *statement*, and each statement must be terminated by a semicolon, so don't omit the semicolons when you type the examples.

The final statement in *main()*, called a *return* statement, terminates the function. You'll learn more about the *return* statement later.

STATEMENTS AND SEMICOLONS

A statement represents a complete instruction to a computer. To understand your source code, a compiler needs to know when one statement ends and another begins. Some languages use a statement separator. FORTRAN, for instance, uses the end of the line to separate one statement from the next. Pascal uses a semicolon to separate one statement from the next. In Pascal, you can omit the semicolon in certain cases, such as after a statement just before an END, when you aren't actually separating two

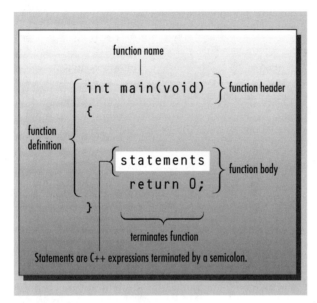

Figure 2-1 The *main()* function

statements. (Pragmatists and minimalists will disagree about whether *can* implies *should.*) But C++, like C, uses a *terminator* rather than a separator. Therefore, the semicolon that marks the end of the statement is part of the statement rather than a marker between statements. The practical upshot is that in C++ you can never omit the semicolon.

The Function Heading As Interface

Right now the main point to remember is that C++ syntax requires that you begin the definition of the *main()* function with this heading: *int main(void).* This chapter will go into details later, but, for those who can't put their curiosity on hold, here's a preview.

In general, a C++ function is activated, or *called,* by another function, and the function heading describes the interface between a function and the function that calls it. The part preceding the function name is called the function *return type,* and it describes information flow from a function to the function that called it. The part within the parentheses following the function name is called the *argument list,* and it describes information flow from the calling function to the called function. This general format is a bit confusing when applied to *main()* because you don't normally call *main()* from other parts of your program. Typically, however, *main()* is called by startup code that your compiler adds to your program to mediate between the program and the operating system (UNIX, DOS, or whatever). In effect, you can think of the function header as describing the interface between *main()* and the operating system.

Let's look at the interface for *main()*, beginning with the *int* part. A C++ function called by another function can return a value to the activating (calling) function. That value is called a *return* value. In this case, *main()* can return an integer value, as indicated by the keyword *int*. Next, consider the word *void*. In general, one C++ function can pass information to another function when it calls that function. The portion of the function heading enclosed in parentheses describes that information. In this case, *void* means that the *main()* function takes no information, or, in the usual terminology, *main()* takes no arguments. (Saying *main()* takes no arguments doesn't mean that *main()* is an unreasonable, authoritarian function. Rather, *argument* is the term computer buffs use to refer to information passed from one function to another.)

In short, the heading

```
int main(void)
```

states that the *main()* function can return an integer value *to* the function that calls it and that *main()* takes no information *from* the function that calls it.

Many programs use the classic C heading instead:

```
main() // original C style
```

Under both C and C++, omitting the return type is the same as saying the function is type *int*. Under C++ (but not C), leaving the parentheses empty is the same as using *void* in the parentheses. So, by default, the old style is equivalent to the new.

Some programmers use this heading

```
void main()
```

and omit the return statement. This is logically consistent, for a *void* return type means the function doesn't return a value. This variant works on many systems, but, because it isn't mandated as an option under current standards, it may not work on all systems.

At the time of this writing, the ANSI/ISO C++ committee has decided that a

```
return 0;
```

statement will be implicitly understood to come at the end of the *main()* function (but of no other function) if you don't explicitly provide it.

Why *main()* by Any Other Name Is Not the Same

There's an extremely compelling reason to name the function in the *myfirst.cpp* program *main()*: you have to. Every C++ program has to have a function called *main()*. (And not, by the way, *Main()* or *MAIN()* or *mane()*. Remember, case and spelling count.) Since the *myfirst.cpp* program has only one function, that function must bear the responsibility of being *main()*. When you run a C++ program, execution always begins at the beginning of the *main()* function. Therefore, if you don't have *main()*, you don't have a complete program, and the compiler will point out that you haven't defined a *main()* function.

C++ Comments

The double slash (//) introduces a C++ comment. A comment is a remark from the programmer to the reader, and usually it identifies a section of a program or explains some aspect of the code. The compiler ignores comments. After all, it knows C++ at least as well as you do, and, in any case, it's incapable of understanding comments. So, as far as the compiler is concerned, Listing 2-1 looks comment-free like the following:

```
#include <iostream.h>
int main(void)
{
        cout << "Come up and C++ me some time.";
        cout << "\n";
        return 0;
}
```

C++ comments run from the // to the end of the line. A comment can be on its own line or it can be on the same line as code. Incidentally, note the first line in Listing 2-1:

```
// myfirst.cpp -- displays a message
```

In this book we'll start all our programs with a comment giving the file name we're using for the source code and a brief program summary. As we mentioned in Chapter 1, the file name extension for source code depends on your C++ system. Some systems would use *myfirst.C* or *myfirst.cxx* for names.

TIP

You should use comments to document your programs. The more complex the program, the more valuable comments become. Not only do they help others to understand what you have done, they help you understand what you've done, especially if you haven't looked at the program for a while.

C-STYLE COMMENTS

C++ also recognizes C comments, which are enclosed between /* and */ symbols:

```
#include <iostream.h> /* a C-style comment */
```

Because the C-style comment is terminated by */ rather than by the end of a line, it can be spread over more than one line. You can use either or both styles in your programs. We'll stick to the C++ style. That way, a C programmer glancing over your shoulder will know you've advanced to a higher level of programming.

The C++ Preprocessor and the *iostream.h* File

C++, like C, uses a *preprocessor.* This is a program that processes a source file before the main compilation takes place. (Some C++ implementations, you may recall from Chapter 1, use a translator program to convert a C++ program to C. The translator also is a form of preprocessor, but we're not talking about *that* preprocessor; we're talking about the one that handles directives whose names begin with #.) You don't have to do anything special to invoke this preprocessor. It operates automatically when you compile the program.

Our listing uses the *#include* feature:

```
#include <iostream.h>     // a PREPROCESSOR directive
```

This directive causes the preprocessor to add the contents of the *iostream.h* file to your program. This is a typical preprocessor action—adding or replacing text in the source code before it's compiled.

This raises the question, why add the contents of the *iostream.h* file to the program? The answer concerns communication between the program and the outside world. The *io* in *iostream.h* refers to *input,* which is information brought into the program, and to *output,* which is information sent out from the program. C++'s input/output scheme involves several definitions found in the *iostream.h* file. The program needs these definitions to use the *cout* facility. The *#include* directive causes the contents of the *iostream.h* file to be sent along with the contents of your file to the compiler. In essence, the *#include <iostream.h>* line in the program is replaced by the contents of the *iostream.h* file. Your original file is not altered, but a composite file formed from your file and *iostream.h* goes on to the next stage of compilation.

RULE

Programs that use *cin* and *cout* for input and output must include the *iostream.h* file.

Prior to C++ Release 2.0, C++ programs used a header file called *stream.h* instead of *iostream.h.* The *iostream.h* file reflects improvements in C++ input/output handling. This books sticks to the newer version, so if you use an older implementation of I/O, you may have to make some adjustments to the examples. The draft ANSI/ISO C++ standard provides that the header file should be called *iostream* instead, reserving the *.h* suffix for regular ANSI C header files.

C++ Output with *cout*

Now let's look at how you display a message. The *myfirst.cpp* program used the following C++ statement:

```
cout << "Come up and C++ me some time.";
```

The part enclosed within the double quotation marks is the message to print. In C++, any series of characters enclosed in double quotation marks is called a *string,* presumably because it consists of several characters strung together into a larger unit. The << notation indicates that the statement is sending this string to *cout;* the symbols point the way the information flows. And what is *cout?* It's a predefined object that knows how to display a variety of things, including strings, numbers, and individual characters. (An object, as you may remember from Chapter 1, is the embodiment of a class definition that describes how data is stored and used.)

Well, this is a bit awkward. We won't be in a position to explain objects for several more chapters, yet here we have to use it. Actually, this reveals one of the strengths of objects. You don't have to know the innards of an object in order to use it. All you need to know is its interface—that is, how it's used. The *cout* object has a simple interface. If *string* represents a string, then do the following to display the string:

```
cout << string;
```

This is all you need to know to display a string, but let's see how the C++ conceptual view represents the process. In this view, the output is a *stream,* that is, a series of characters flowing from the program—a rather bucolic image. The *cout* object, whose properties are defined in the *iostream.h* file, represents that stream. The object properties for *cout* include an *insertion operator* (<<) that inserts the information on its right into the stream. So the statement (note the terminating semicolon)

```
cout << "Come up and C++ me some time.";
```

inserts the string *"Come up and C++ me some time."* into the output stream. Thus, instead of saying that our program displays a message, we can say that it inserts a string into the output stream. Somehow, that sounds more impressive. See Figure 2-2.

If you're coming to C++ from C, you probably noticed that the insertion operator (<<) looks just like the bitwise left-shift operator (<<). This is an example of *operator overloading,* by which the same operator symbol can have different meanings. The compiler uses the context to figure out which meaning is intended. C itself has some operator overloading. For instance, the & symbol represents both the address operator and the bitwise AND operator. And the * symbol represents both multiplication and dereferencing a pointer. The important point here is not the exact function of these operators but that the same symbol can have more than one meaning, with the compiler determining the proper meaning from the context. (You do much the same when you determine the meaning of "shoot" in "shoot the breeze" versus "shoot the piano player.") C++ extends the operator overloading concept by letting you redefine operator meanings for the user-defined types called classes.

The Newline Character (\n)

Now let's examine an odd-looking notation that appeared in the second output statement:

```
cout << "\n";
```

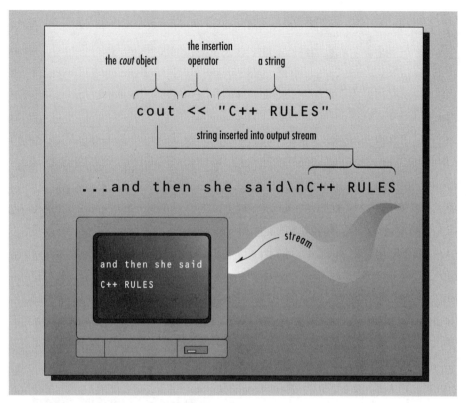

Figure 2-2 Displaying a string with *cout*

The \n is a special C++ (and C) notation representing an important concept dubbed the *newline character*. Although you type the newline character by using two characters (\ and n), it counts as a single character. Note that you use the backslash (\), not the regular slash (/). Displaying a newline character moves the screen cursor to the beginning of the next line, and sending the newline character to a printer moves the print head to the beginning of the next line. So the newline character earns its name.

Note that the *cout* facility does not move to the next line automatically when it prints a string, so the first *cout* statement in Listing 2-1 leaves the cursor positioned just after the period at the end of the output string. To move the cursor to the beginning of the next line, you must send a newline character to the output. Or, practicing C++ lingo, you must insert a newline character into the output stream.

You can use the newline character just like any ordinary character. Listing 2-1 used it in a separate string, but the listing could have used it in the original string. That is, you can replace the original two output statements with the following:

```
cout << "Come up and C++ me some time.\n";
```

You can even place the newline character in the midst of a string. For instance, consider the following statement:

```
cout << "I am a mighty stream\nof lucid\nclarity.\n";
```

Each newline character moves the cursor to the beginning of the next line, making the output as follows:

```
I am a mighty stream
of lucid
clarity.
```

By leaving out newlines, you can make successive *cout* statements print on the same line. For instance, the statements

```
cout << "The Good, the";
cout << "Bad, ";
cout << "and the Ukelele\n";
```

produce the following output:

```
The Good, theBad, and the Ukelele
```

Note that the beginning of one string comes immediately after the end of the preceding string. If you want a space where two strings join, you have to include it in one of the strings. (Keep in mind that to try out these output examples, you have to place them in a complete program, with a *main()* function heading and opening and closing braces.)

C++ Source Code Formatting

Some languages, such as FORTRAN, are line-oriented, with one statement to a line. For these languages the carriage return serves to separate statements. But in C++, the semicolon marks the end of each statement. This leaves C++ free to treat the carriage return the same as a space or a tab. That is, in C++, you usually can use a space where you would use a carriage return, and vice versa. This means you can spread a single statement over several lines or place several statements on one line. For instance, you could reformat *myfirst.cpp* as follows:

```
#include <iostream.h>
        int
main
(void) { cout
            <<
"Come up and C++ me some time.";
        cout << "\n"; return 0; }
```

This is ugly, but valid, code. You do have to observe some rules. In particular, in C and C++ you can't put a space, tab, or carriage return in the middle of an element such as a name nor can you place a carriage return in the middle of a string.

```
int ma  in(void)      // INVALID -- space in name
re
turn 0; // INVALID -- carriage return in word
cout << "Behold the Beans
 of Beauty!"; // INVALID -- carriage return in string
```

The indivisible elements in a line of code are called *tokens*. See Figure 2-3. Generally, you must separate one token from the next by a space, tab, or carriage return, which collectively are termed *white space*. However, C++ recognizes some special tokens, such as parentheses, without the need of separating white space.

```
return0;        // INVALID, must be return 0;
return(0);      // VALID, white space omitted
return (0);     // VALID, white space used
int main(void)  // VALID, white space omitted
int main ( void )      // ALSO VALID, white space used
```

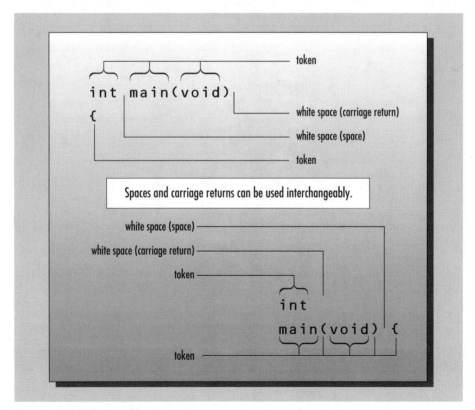

Figure 2-3 Tokens and white space

C++ Source Code Style

Although C++ gives you much formatting freedom, your programs will be easier to read if you follow some sensible style. Having valid but ugly code should leave you unsatisfied. Most programmers use the style of Listing 2-1, which observes these rules:

❧ One statement per line

❧ An opening and a closing brace for a function, each on its own line

❧ Statements in a function indented from the braces

❧ No white space around the parentheses associated with a function name

The first three rules have the simple intent to keep the code clean and readable. The fourth helps to differentiate functions from some built-in C++ structures, like loops, that also use parentheses. We'll mention other rules as we come across them.

● More About C++ Statements

A C++ program is a collection of functions, and each function is a collection of statements. C++ has several kinds of statements, so let's see some of the possibilities. Listing 2-2 provides two new kinds of statements. First, a *declaration statement* creates a *variable*. Second, an *assignment statement* provides a value for that variable. Also, the program shows a new ability for *cout*.

Listing 2-2 *fleas.cpp*

```
// fleas.cpp -- display the value of a variable
#include <iostream.h>
int main(void)
{
        int fleas;         // create an integer variable

        fleas = 28;         // give a value to the variable
        cout << "My cat has ";
        cout << fleas;          // display the value of fleas
        cout << " fleas.\n";
        return 0;
}
```

A blank line separates the declaration from the rest of the program. This practice is the usual C convention, but it's somewhat less common in C++. Here is the program output:

```
My cat has 28 fleas.
```

We will study this program in the next few pages.

Declaration Statements and Variables

Computers are precise, orderly machines. To store an item of information in a computer, you need to identify how much memory storage space is required for that information, and you need a way to identify the storage location. One relatively painless way to do this in C++ is to use a declaration statement to indicate the type of storage and to provide a label for the location. For example, our program has this declaration statement (note the semicolon):

```
int fleas;
```

This statement declares that the program will use enough storage to hold what is called an *int*. The compiler takes care of the details of allocating and labeling memory for that task. C++ can handle several kinds, or *types*, of data, and the *int* is the most basic data type. It corresponds to an *integer*, a number with no fractional part. The C *int* type can be positive or negative, but the size range depends on the implementation. Chapter 3 provides the details on *int* and the other basic types.

Besides giving the type, the declaration statement declares that henceforth the program will use the name *fleas* to identify the value stored at that location. We call *fleas* a *variable* because we can change its value. In C++ you must declare all variables. If you were to omit the declaration in *fleas.cpp*, the compiler would report an error when the program attempts to use *fleas* further on. (In fact, you might want to try omitting the declaration just to see how your compiler responds. Then, if you see that response in the future, you'll know to check for omitted declarations.)

 WHY MUST VARIABLES BE DECLARED?

Some languages, notably BASIC, create a new variable whenever you use a new name, without the aid of explicit declarations. That may seem friendlier to the user, and it is—in the short run. The problem is that by mistyping the name of a variable, you can inadvertently create a new variable without realizing it. That is, in BASIC, you can do something like the following:

```
CastleDark = 34
...
CastleDank = CastleDank + MoreGhosts
...
PRINT CastleDark
```

Because *CastleDank* is mistyped, the changes made to it leave *CastleDark* unchanged. This kind of error can be hard to trace because it breaks no rules in BASIC. But in C++, the equivalent code breaks the rule about using a variable without declaring it, so the compiler catches the error and stomps the potential bug.

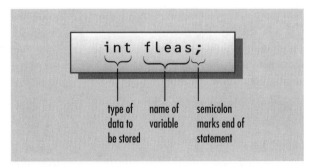

Figure 2-4 A variable declaration

In general, then, a declaration indicates the type of data to be stored and the name we'll use for the data that's stored there. In this particular case, we create a variable called *fleas* in which we can store an integer. See Figure 2-4.

The declaration statement in our program is called a *defining* declaration statement, or *definition,* for short. That means its presence causes the compiler to allocate memory space for the variable. In more complex situations, you can also have *reference* declarations. These tell the computer to use a variable that has already been defined elsewhere. So, in general, a declaration need not be a definition, but in our example, it is.

If you're familiar with C or Pascal, you're already familiar with variable declarations. You also may have a modest surprise in store for you. In C and Pascal, all variable declarations normally come at the very beginning of a function or procedure. But C++ has no such restriction. Indeed, the usual C++ style is to declare a variable just before it is first used. That way, you don't have to rummage back through a program to see what the type is. You'll see an example later in this chapter. This style does have the disadvantage of not gathering all your variable names in one place; thus you can't tell at a glance what variables a function uses.

TIP

The C++ style for declaring variables is to declare a variable as close as possible to its first use.

The Assignment Statement

An assignment statement assigns a value to a storage location. For instance, the statement

```
fleas = 28;
```

assigns the integer 28 to the location represented by the variable *fleas.* The = symbol is called the *assignment* operator. One unusual feature of C++ (and C) is that you can use the assignment operator serially. That is, the following is valid code:

```
int steinway;
int baldwin;
int yamaha;
yamaha = baldwin = steinway = 88;
```

The assignment works from right to left. First, *88* is assigned to *steinway;* then the value of *steinway,* which is now *88,* is assigned to *baldwin;* then *baldwin's* value of *88* is assigned to *yamaha.* (C++ follows C's penchant for allowing weird-appearing code.)

New Trick for *cout*

Prior to now we've given *cout* strings to print. Listing 2-2 additionally gives *cout* a variable whose value is an integer:

```
cout << fleas;
```

The program doesn't print the word *fleas;* instead, it prints the integer value stored in *fleas,* which is *28.* Actually, this is two tricks in one. First, *cout* has to replace *fleas* with its current numeric value of *28.* Second, it has to translate the value to the proper output characters.

As you see, *cout* works both with strings and with integers. This may not seem particularly remarkable to you, but keep in mind that the integer *28* is something quite different from the string *"28".* The string holds the characters with which we write the number; that is, a 2 character and an 8 character. Internally, the program stores the code for the 2 character and the code for the 8 character. To print the string, *cout* simply prints each character in the string. But the integer *28* is stored as a numeric value. Instead of storing each digit separately, the computer stores *28* as a *binary* number. (Appendix A discusses this representation.) The main point here is that *cout* has to translate a number in integer form into a character form before it can print it. Furthermore, *cout* is smart enough to recognize that *fleas* is an integer requiring conversion.

Perhaps the contrast with old C will indicate how clever *cout* is. To print the string *"28"* and the integer *28* in C, you could use C's multipurpose output function *printf():*

```
printf("Printing a string: %s\n", "28");
printf("Printing an integer: %d\n", 28);
```

Without going into the intricacies of *printf(),* note that you have to use special codes (*%s* and *%d*) to indicate whether you are going to print a string or an integer. And if you tell *printf()* to print a string but give it an integer by mistake, *printf()* is too dumb to notice your mistake. It just goes ahead and displays garbage.

The intelligent way in which *cout* behaves stems from C++'s object-oriented features. In essence, the C++ insertion operator (<<) adjusts its behavior to fit the type of data that follows it. This is an example of operator overloading. In later chapters, when we take up function overloading and operator overloading, you'll learn how to implement such smart designs yourself.

cout and printf()

If you are used to C and *printf()*, you may think *cout* looks odd. You may even prefer to cling to your hard-won mastery of *printf()*. But *cout* is really no stranger in appearance than *printf()* with all its conversion specifications. More important, *cout* has significant advantages. Its ability to recognize types reflects a more intelligent and foolproof design. Also, it is extensible. That is, you can redefine the << operator so that *cout* can recognize and display new data types you develop. And if you relish the fine control *printf()* provides, you can accomplish the same effects with more advanced uses of *cout* (See Chapter 15).

 # More C++ Statements

Let's look at a few more examples of statements. The program in Listing 2-3 expands on the preceding example by allowing you to enter a value while the program is running. To do so, it uses *cin* (pronounced *cee-in*), the input counterpart to *cout*. Also, the first two examples didn't illustrate how a function like *main()* can call another function, so this time we have *main()* call the *puts()* function. This function is from the standard C library, which C++ has inherited, and it displays a string. Finally, the program shows yet another way to use that master of versatility, the *cout* object.

Listing 2-3 *yourcat.cpp*

```
// yourcat.cpp -- input and output
#include <iostream.h>
#include <stdio.h>      // used for old C I/O functions
int main(void)
{
        int fleas;

        puts("How many fleas does your cat have?"); // Old C
        cin >> fleas;                               // C++ input
// next line concatenates output
        cout << "Well, that's " << fleas << " fleas too many.\n";
        return 0;
}
```

Here is a sample output:

```
How many fleas does your cat have?
112
Well, that's 112 fleas too many.
```

The new features in this program are using *cin* to read keyboard input, calling a function *puts()*, and combining three output statements into one. Now let's examine these new features.

Using *cin*

As the output demonstrates, the value we typed in at the keyboard (*112*) wound up being assigned to the variable *fleas*. Here is the statement that performed that wonder:

```
cin >> fleas;
```

Looking at this statement, you can practically see information flowing from *cin* into *fleas*. Naturally, there is a slightly more formal description of this process. Just as C++ considers output as a stream of characters flowing out of the program, it considers input as a stream of characters flowing into the program. The *iostream.h* file defines *cin* as an object representing this stream. For output, the << operator inserts characters into the output stream. For input, *cin* uses the >> operator to *extract* characters from the input stream. Typically, you would provide a variable to the right of the operator to receive the extracted information. (The symbols << and >> were chosen to suggest the direction that information flows.)

Like *cout, cin* is a smart object. It converts input, which is just a series of characters typed from the keyboard, into a form acceptable to the variable receiving the information. In this case, we've declared *fleas* to be an integer variable, so the input is converted to the numerical form the computer uses to store integers.

Function Call Statements

The second new feature of the *yourcat.cpp* program is calling a library function. C++ programs often use statements that *call* functions to perform various feats and tasks. Functions come from two sources: you and function libraries. You'll soon see some examples of user-supplied functions. Library functions come in library files that the compiler accesses when compiling a program. The compiler joins (*links*) your code with the relevant library code to produce the final program. The *puts()* function in Listing 2-3 is a standard library function available in both C and C++. The *stdio.h* header file contains information relating to this function, just as *iostream.h* contains information relating to *cout* and *cin*. The *puts()* function displays a string, then moves the cursor to the next line. It's a simple function to use, but it is limited. For example, it doesn't print integers. We used *puts()* because it is a simple example of a function, but we'll stick with *cout* in the future.

Let's look at the mechanics of calling a function. Listing 2-3 calls the *puts()* function:

```
puts("How many fleas does your cat have?");
```

Here's what happens. When the program begins execution, the computer goes along, happily executing the statements in *main()*. When it reaches the function call, the computer temporarily abandons *main()* and executes the statements in *puts()*. When it finishes with *puts()*, the computer then resumes executing statements in *main()*. Because the function call for *puts()* is in *main()*, we term *main()* the *calling function* and *puts()* the *called function*. See Figure 2-5.

To call a function, use the function name followed by parentheses. Many functions require information from the calling function. The *puts()* function, for example, requires a string, which it then displays. To pass such information to a function, place it within the parentheses. We call this passed information an *argument*. See Figure 2-6. An argument can be a string, integer, or other data type. Or there can be no argument at all. In that case, you still need to use parentheses:

```
showtime();   // calling a function with no arguments
```

Multiple arguments in C++ are separated by commas:

```
add_em_up( x, y, z, q, r); // function with list of arguments
```

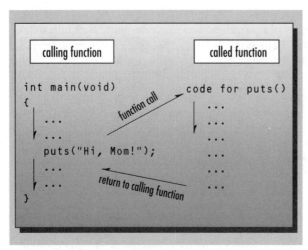

Figure 2-5 Calling a function

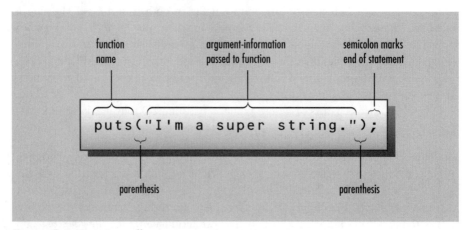

Figure 2-6 Function call statement

More *cout*

The third new feature of *yourcat.cpp* is combining three output statements into one. The *iostream.h* file defines the << operator so that you can combine (*concatenate*) output as follows:

```
cout << "Well, that's " << fleas << " fleas too many.\n";
```

This lets us combine string output and integer output in a single statement. The resulting output is the same as what the following code produces:

```
cout << "Well, that's ";
cout << fleas;
cout << " fleas too many.\n";
```

While you're still in the mood for *cout*ish advice, you also can rewrite the concatenated version this way, spreading the single statement over three lines:

```
cout    << "Well, that's "
        << fleas
        << " fleas too many.\n";
```

That's because C++'s free format rules treat newlines and spaces between tokens interchangeably. This last technique is convenient when the line width cramps your style.

A Touch of Class

You've seen enough of *cin* and *cout* to justify exposing you to a little object lore. In particular, let's talk some more about the notion of *classes*. Classes are one of the core concepts for object-oriented programming in C++.

A class is a data type defined by the user. To define a class you describe what sort of information it can represent and what sort of actions you can perform with that data. A class bears the same relationship to an object that a type does to a variable. That is, a class definition describes a data form and how it can be used, while an object is an entity created according to the data form specification. Or, in noncomputer terms, if a class is analogous to a category such as famous actors, then an object is analogous to a particular example of that category, such as Kermit the Frog. To extend the analogy, a class representation of actors would include definitions of possible actions relating to the class, such as Reading for a Part, Expressing Sorrow, Projecting Menace, Promoting, and the like. If you've been exposed to different OOP terminology, it may help to know that the C++ class corresponds to what some languages term an *object type,* and the C++ object corresponds to an *object instance* or *instance variable.*

Let's get a little more specific. Recall this declaration of a variable:

```
int fleas;
```

This creates a particular variable (*fleas*) that has the properties of the *int* type. That is, *fleas* can store an integer and can be used in particular ways—for addition and subtraction, for instance. Now consider *cout*. It is an object created to have the properties of the *ostream* class. The *ostream* class definition (another inhabitant of the *iostream.h* file) describes the sort of data an *ostream* object represents and the operations you can perform with and to it, such as insert a number or string into an output stream. Similarly, *cin* is an object created with the properties of the *istream* class, also defined in *iostream.h*.

RULE

The class describes all the properties of a data type, and an object is an entity created according to that description.

We've said that classes are user-defined types, but as users we certainly didn't design the *ostream* and *istream* classes. Just as functions can come in function libraries, classes can come in *class libraries*. That's the case for the *ostream* and *istream* classes. Technically, they are not built into the C++ language, but are examples of classes that happen to come with the language. The class definitions are laid out in the *iostream.h* file and are not built into the compiler. You can even modify these class definitions if you like, although that's not a good idea. The *iostream.h* family of classes and the related *fstream.h* (or file I/O) family are the only sets of class definitions that come with all early implementations of C++. However, the ANSI/ISO C++ committee is adding a few more classes to the standard. Also, most implementations provide additional class definitions as part of the package. Indeed, much of the current appeal of C++ is the existence of useful class libraries supporting UNIX, Macintosh, and Windows programming.

The class description specifies all the operations that can be performed on objects of that class. To perform such an allowed action on a particular object, you send a *message* to the object. For instance, if you want the *cout* object to display a string, you send it a message that says, in effect, "Object! Display this!" C++ provides a couple of

```
#include <iostream.h>
int main(void)
{
                                        ──── print message
    ...                                 ──── message argument
    ...
    cout << "Trust me";
    ...
    ...
}
    cout object    ───────►    Trust me
          object displays argument
```

Figure 2-7 Sending a message to an object

ways to send messages. One way, called using a *class method,* essentially boils down to a function call like the ones we've seen. The other, and the one used with *cin* and *cout,* is to redefine an operator. Thus the statement

```
cout << "I am not a crook."
```

uses the redefined << operator to send the "display message" to *cout.* In this case, the message comes with an argument, which is the string to be displayed. See Figure 2-7.

Statement Summary

We've used and discussed several kinds of C++ statements, so let's summarize them now.

> ◁ Declaration statements announce the name and the kind of variables used in a function.

> ◁ Assignment statements use the assignment operator (=) to assign a value to a variable.

> ◁ Function calls activate a function. When the called function terminates, the program returns to the statement in the calling function immediately following the function call.

> ◁ Message statements send a message to an object, initiating some sort of action.

Functions

Because functions are the modules from which C++ programs are built and because they are essential to C++ OOP definitions, you should become thoroughly familiar with them. Since some aspects of functions are advanced topics, the main discussion of functions comes later, in Chapters 7 and 8. However, by dealing with some basic characteristics of functions now, you'll be more at ease and more practiced with functions later. The rest of this chapter introduces you to these function basics.

C++ functions come in two varieties: those with return values and those with none. You can find examples of each kind in the standard C++ library of functions, and you can create your own functions of each type. We'll look at a library function that has a return value, and then we'll examine how you can write your own simple functions.

Using a Function with a Return Value

A function having a return value produces a value that can be assigned to a variable. For instance, the standard C++ library includes a function called *sqrt()* that returns the square root of a number. Suppose, for instance, you want to assign the square root of 6.25 to a variable *x.* You could use the following statement in your program:

```
x = sqrt(6.25); // returns the value 2.5 and assigns it to x
```

The expression *sqrt(6.25)* calls the *sqrt()* function and passes it the value *6.25* as an argument. The function calculates the answer to be *2.5* and returns that value to the calling program. You can think of the return value as being substituted for the function call in the statement.

That's practically all there is to it, except that before using a function, the C++ compiler must know what kind of arguments the function uses and what kind of return value it has. That is, does the function return an integer? A character? A number with a decimal fraction? A guilty verdict? Or something else? Lacking this information, the compiler won't know how to interpret the return value. The C++ way for conveying this information is using a *function prototype* statement.

RULE

A C++ program should provide a prototype for each function used in the program.

A function prototype does for functions what a variable declaration does for variables—it tells what types are involved. For instance, the C++ library defines the *sqrt()* function to take a number with (potentially) a fractional part (like 6.25) as an argument and to return a number of the same type. Some languages refer to such numbers as *real* numbers, but the name C++ uses for this type is *double*. (You'll see more of *double* in Chapter 3.) The function prototype for *sqrt()* looks like this:

```
double sqrt(double);    // function prototype
```

The initial *double* means *sqrt()* returns a type *double* value. The *double* in the parentheses means *sqrt()* requires a *double* argument. So this prototype describes *sqrt()* exactly as we used it. By the way, the terminating semicolon identifies this line of text as a statement, making it a prototype instead of a function heading. If you omit the semicolon, the compiler will interpret the line as a function heading and expect you to follow it with a function body defining the function.

When you use *sqrt()* in a program, you also need to provide the prototype. You can do this in either of two ways:

❚ You can type the function prototype into your source code file yourself.

❚ You can include the *math.h* header file, which has the prototype in it.

The second way is better, for the header file is even more likely than you to get the prototype right. Every function in the C++ library has a prototype in one or more header files. Just check the function description in your manual or with online help, if you have it, and the description tells you which header file to use. For instance, the description of the *sqrt()* function should tell you to use the *math.h* header file.

Don't confuse the function *prototype* with the function *definition*. The prototype, as you've seen, only describes the function interface. The definition includes the code for the function workings. C and C++ divide these two features—prototype and definition—

for library functions. The library files contain the compiled code for the functions, while the header files contain the prototypes.

A function prototype should be placed ahead of where the function is first used. The usual practice is to place prototypes just before the definition of the *main()* function. Listing 2-4 demonstrates using the library function *sqrt()*; it provides a prototype by including the *math.h* file.

Listing 2-4 *sqrt.cpp*

```
// sqrt.cpp -- use a square root function
#include <iostream.h>
#include <math.h>                    // use with math functions
int main(void)
{
        double cover;                // use double for real numbers

        cout << "How many square feet of sheets do you have?\n";
        cin >> cover;
        double side;          // create another variable
        side = sqrt(cover);   // call function, assign return value
        cout << "You can cover a square with sides of " << side;
        cout << " feet\nwith your sheets.\n";
        return 0;
}
```

USING LIBRARY FUNCTIONS

C++ library functions are stored in library files. When the compiler compiles a program, it has to search the library files for the functions you've used. Compilers differ on which library files they search automatically. If you try to run Listing 2-4 and get a message about *_sqrt* being an undefined external (sounds like a condition to avoid!), chances are that your compiler doesn't search the math library automatically. (Compilers like to add an underscore prefix to function names—another subtle reminder that they have the last say about your program.) If you get such a message, you'll have to check your compiler documentation to see how to have the compiler search the correct library. The usual UNIX implementations, for example, require that you use a *-lm* option (for *library math*) at the end of the command line:

```
CC sqrt.C -lm
```

Merely including the *math.h* header file provides the prototype but does not necessarily cause the compiler to search the correct library file.

Here's a sample run:

```
How many square feet of sheets do you have?
123.21
```

continued on next page

continued from previous page

```
You can cover a square with sides of 11.1 feet
with your sheets.
```

Because *sqrt()* works with type *double* values, we made our variables that type. Note that declaring a type *double* variable uses the same form, or syntax, as declaring a type *int* variable:

typename variablename;

Being type *double* allows the variables *cover* and *side* to hold values with decimal fractions, such as *123.21* and *1.1*. As you'll see in Chapter 3, type *double* encompasses a much greater range of values than type *int*.

C++ does allow you to declare new variables anywhere in a program, so *sqrt.cpp* didn't declare *side* until just before using it. C++ also allows you to assign a value to a variable when you create it, so you could also have done this:

```
double side = sqrt(cover);
```

We'll return to this process, called *initialization,* in Chapter 3.

Note that *cin* knows how to convert information from the input stream to type *double,* and *cout* knows how to insert type *double* into the output stream. As we've said, these objects are smart.

User-Defined Functions

The standard C library provides over 140 predefined functions. If one fits your needs, by all means use it. But often you'll have to write your own, particularly when you design classes. Anyway, it's a lot more fun to design your own functions, so let's examine that process. You've already used several user-defined functions, and they all have been named *main().* Every C++ program must have a *main()* function, which the user must define. Let's see how to add a second user-defined function. Just as with a library function, you can call a user-defined function by using its name. And, as with a library function, you need to provide a function prototype before using the function, typically by placing the prototype above the *main()* definition. The new element is that you also have to provide the source code for the new function. The simplest way is to place the code in the same file following the code for *main().* Listing 2-5 illustrates these elements.

Listing 2-5 *ourfunc.cpp*

```
// ourfunc.cpp -- defining your own function
#include <iostream.h>
void simon(int);      // function prototype for simon()
int main(void)
{
    simon(3);   // call the simon() function
    cout << "Pick an integer: ";
    int count;
    cin >> count;
```

```
    simon(count);      // call it again
    return 0;
}

void simon(int n)      // define the simon() function
{
    cout << "Simon says touch your toes " << n << " times.\n";
}                      // void functions don't need return
```

The *main()* function calls the *simon()* function twice, once with an argument of 3, once with a variable argument *count*. In between, the user enters an integer that's used to set the value of *count*. We didn't use a newline character in the *cout* prompting message. This results in the user input appearing on the same line as the prompt. Here is a sample run:

```
Simon says touch your toes 3 times.
Pick an integer: 512
Simon says touch your toes 512 times.
```

Function Form

The definition for the *simon()* function follows the same general form as the definition for *main()*. First, there is a function header. Then, enclosed in braces, comes the function body. We can generalize the form for a function definition as follows:

```
type functionname(argumentlist)
{
        statements
}
```

Note that the source code defining *simon()* follows the closing brace of *main()*. Like C, and unlike Pascal, C++ does not allow you to embed one function definition inside another. Each function definition stands separately from all others; all functions are created equal. See Figure 2-8.

Function Headings

The *simon()* function has this heading:

```
void simon(int n)
```

The initial *void* means that *simon()* has no return value. So calling *simon()* doesn't produce a number that you can assign to a variable in *main()*. Thus the first function call looks like this:

```
simon(3);        // ok for void functions
```

Because poor *simon()* lacks a return value, you can't use it this way:

```
simple = simon(3);    // not allowed for void functions
```

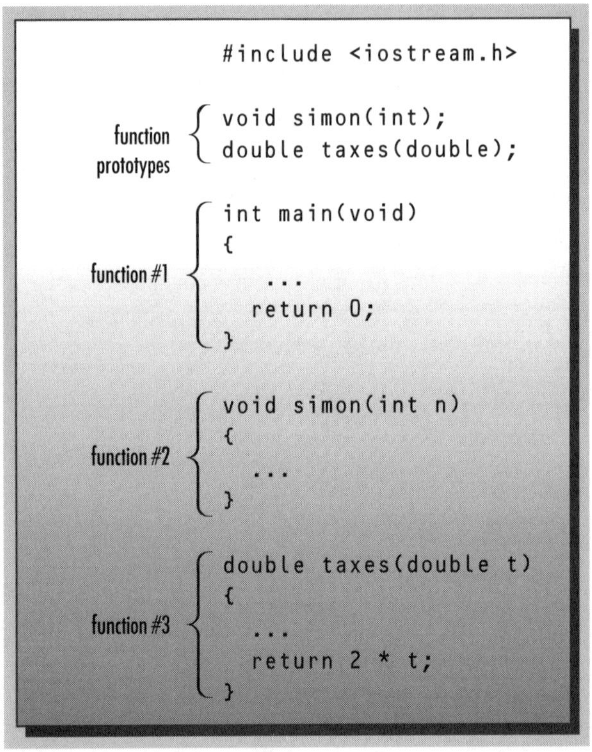

```
                       #include <iostream.h>

              ⎧ void simon(int);
function      ⎨ double taxes(double);
prototypes    ⎩

              ⎧ int main(void)
              ⎪ {
function #1   ⎨    ...
              ⎪    return 0;
              ⎩ }

              ⎧ void simon(int n)
              ⎪ {
function #2   ⎨    ...
              ⎪
              ⎩ }

              ⎧ double taxes(double t)
              ⎪ {
function #3   ⎨    ...
              ⎪    return 2 * t;
              ⎩ }
```

Figure 2-8 Function definitions occur sequentially in a file

The *int n* within the parentheses means that you are expected to use *simon()* with a single argument of type *int*. The *n* is a new variable to which is assigned the value passed during a function call. Thus the function call

```
simon(3);
```

assigns the value *3* to the *n* variable defined in the *simon()* heading. When the *cout* statement in the function body uses *n*, it uses the value passed in the function call. That's why *simon(3)* displays a *3* in its output. The call to *simon(count)* in our sample run caused the function to display *512* because that's the value we gave to *count*. In short, the heading for *simon()* tells us that this function takes a single type *int* argument and that it doesn't have a return value.

Let's review *main()*'s function header:

```
int main(void)
```

This header reverses the roles that *int* and *void* play in *simon()*. The initial *int* means that *main()* returns an integer value. The *void* means that *main()* has no arguments. Functions that have return values should use the keyword *return* to provide the return value and to terminate the function. That's why we've been using the following statement at the end of *main()*:

```
return 0;
```

This is logically consistent: *main()* is supposed to return a type *int* value, and we have it return the integer *0*. But, you may wonder, to what are we returning a value? After all, nowhere in any of our programs have you seen anything calling *main()*:

```
squeeze = main();    // absent from our programs
```

The answer is that you can think of your computer's operating system (UNIX, say, or DOS) as calling your program. So *main()*'s return value is returned not to another part of the program but to the operating system. Many operating systems can use the program's return value. For example, UNIX shell scripts and DOS batch files can be designed to run programs and test their return values, usually called *exit values*. The normal convention is that an exit value of zero means the program ran successfully, while a nonzero value means there was a problem. Thus you can design your C++ program to return a nonzero value if, say, it fails to open a file. Then you can design a shell script or batch file to run that program and to take some alternative action if the program signals failure.

KEYWORDS

Keywords are the vocabulary of a computer language. In this chapter, we've used four C++ keywords: *int, void, return,* and *double*. Because these keywords are special to C++, you cannot use them for other purposes. That is, you can't use *return* as the name for a variable or *double* as the name of a function. But you can use them as part of a name, as in *painter* or *return_aces*. Appendix B provides a complete list of C++ keywords. Incidentally, *main* is not a keyword, for it's not part of the language. Rather, it is the name of a required function. So you could use *main* as a variable name. (That could cause a problem in circumstances too esoteric to describe here, and it would be confusing in any case, so you'd best not.) Similarly, other function names and object names are not keywords. However, using the same name, say *cout,* for both an object and a variable in a program will confuse the compiler. That is, you can use *cout* as a variable name in a function that doesn't use the *cout* object for output, but you can't use *cout* both ways in the same function.

User-Defined Function with a Return Value

Let's go one step further and write a function that uses the *return* statement. The *main()* function already illustrates the plan for a function with a return value: give the return type in the function heading and use *return* at the end of the function body. We'll use this form to solve a weighty problem for those visiting the United Kingdom. In the U.K., many bathroom scales are calibrated in *stone* instead of in familiar U.S. pounds. The word stone is both singular and plural in this context. (The English language does lack the internal consistency of, say, C++.) One stone is 14 pounds, and the program in Listing 2-6 uses a function to make this conversion.

Listing 2-6 *convert.cpp*

```
// convert.cpp -- converts stone to pounds
#include <iostream.h>
int stonetolb(int);    // function prototype
int main(void)
{
        int stone;
        cout << "Enter the weight in stone: ";
        cin >> stone;
        int pounds = stonetolb(stone);
        cout << stone << " stone are ";
        cout << pounds << " pounds.\n";
        return 0;
}

int stonetolb(int sts)
{
        return 14 * sts;
}
```

Here's a sample run:

```
Enter the weight in stone: 14
14 stone are 196 pounds.
```

In *main()*, we use *cin* to provide a value for the integer variable *stone*. This value is passed to the *stonetolb()* function as an argument and is assigned to the variable *sts* in that function. Then we use the *return* keyword to return the value of *14 * sts* to *main()*. This illustrates that you aren't limited to following *return* with a simple number. Here, by using a more complex expression, we avoided the bother of creating a new variable to which to assign the value before returning it. The program calculates the value of that expression (*196* in our example) and returns the resulting value. If returning the value of an expression bothers you, you can take the longer route:

```
int stonetolb(int sts)
{
        int pounds = 14 * sts;
        return pounds;
}
```

Either version produces the same result, but the second version takes slightly longer to do so.

In general, you can use a function with a return value wherever you would use a simple constant of the same type. For instance, *stonetolb()* returns a type *int* value. This means you can use the function in the following ways:

```
int aunt = stonetolb(20);
int aunts = aunt + stonetolb(10);
cout << "Ferdie weighs " << stonetolb(16) << " pounds.\n";
```

In each case, the program will calculate the return value, then use that number in these statements.

As these examples show, the function prototype describes the function *interface,* that is, how it interacts with the rest of the program. The argument list shows what sort of information goes into the function, and the function type shows the type of value returned. Programmers sometimes describe functions as *black boxes* (a term from electronics) specified by the flow of information into them and out of them. The function prototype perfectly portrays that point of view. See Figure 2-9.

The *stonetolb()* function is short and simple, yet it embodies a full range of functional features:

❧ It has a heading and a body.

❧ It accepts an argument.

❧ It returns a value.

❧ It requires a prototype.

You can consider *stonetolb()* a template for function design. We'll go further into functions in Chapters 7 and 8. In the meantime, the material in this chapter should give you a good feel for how functions work and how they fit into C++.

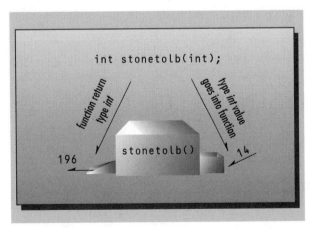

Figure 2-9 The function prototype and the function as a black box

Summary

A C++ program consists of one or more modules called functions. Programs begin executing at the beginning of the function called *main()*, so you should always have a function by this name. A function, in turn, consists of a heading and a body. The function heading tells us what kind of return value, if any, the function produces and what sort of information it expects to be passed to it by arguments. The function body consists of a series of C++ statements enclosed in paired braces: {} .

C++ statement types include declaration statements, assignment statements, function call statements, object message statements, and return statements. The declaration statement announces the name of a variable and establishes the type of data it can hold. An assignment statement gives a value to a variable. A function call passes program control to the called function. When the function finishes, control returns to the statement in the calling function immediately following the function call. A message instructs an object to perform a particular action. A return statement is the mechanism by which a function returns a value to its calling function.

A class is a user-defined specification for a data type. This specification details how information is to be represented and also the operations that can be performed with the data. An object is an entity created according to a class prescription, just as a simple variable is an entity created according to a data type description.

C++ provides two predefined objects (*cin* and *cout*) for handling input and output. They are examples of the *istream* and *ostream* classes, which are defined in the *iostream.h* file. These classes view input and output as streams of characters. The insertion operator (<<), which is defined for the *ostream* class, lets you insert data into the output stream, and the extraction operator (>>), which is defined for the *istream* class, lets you extract information from the input stream. Both *cin* and *cout* are smart objects, capable of automatically converting information from one form to another according to the program context.

Now that you have an overall view of simple C++ programs, we can go on in the next chapters to fill in detail and expand horizons.

Review Questions

You'll find the answers to these and subsequent review questions in Appendix G.

1. What are the modules of C++ programs called?

2. What does the following preprocessor directive do?
   ```
   #include <iostream.h>
   ```

3. What statement would you use to print the phrase "Hello, world" and then start a new line?

4. What statement would you use to create an integer variable with the name *cheeses*?

5. What statement would you use to assign the value *32* to the variable *cheeses?*

6. What statement would you use to read a value from keyboard input into the variable *cheeses?*

7. What statement would you use to print "We have X varieties of cheese", where *X* will be replaced with the current value of the *cheeses* variable?

8. What does the following function header tell you about the function?

   ```
   int froop(double t)
   ```

9. When do you not use the keyword *return* when defining a function?

Programming Exercises

1. Write a C++ program that displays your name and address.

2. Write a C++ program that asks for a distance in furlongs and converts it to yards (one furlong is 220 yards).

3. Write a C++ program that uses three user-defined functions (counting *main()* as one) that produces the following output:

   ```
   Three blind mice
   Three blind mice
   See how they run
   See how they run
   ```

   One function, called twice, should produce the first two lines, and the remaining function, called twice, should produce the remaining output.

4. Write a program that has *main()* call a user-defined function that takes a Celsius temperature value as an argument and then returns the equivalent Fahrenheit value. The program should request the Celsius value as input from the user and display the result, as shown below:

   ```
   Please enter a Celsius value: 20
   20 degrees Celsius is 68 degrees Fahrenheit.
   ```

   For reference, here is the formula for making the conversion:

   Fahrenheit = 1.8 x Celsius + 32.0

CHAPTER 3

DEALING WITH DATA

You will learn about the following in this chapter:

- ◇ Rules for naming C++ variables
- ◇ C++'s built-in integer types: *unsigned long, long, unsigned int, int, unsigned short, short, char, unsigned char, signed char*
- ◇ The *limits.h* file, representing system limits for various integer types
- ◇ Numeric constants of various integer types
- ◇ Using the *const* qualifier to create symbolic constants

- ◇ C++'s built-in floating-point types: *float, double, long double*
- ◇ The *float.h* file, representing system limits for various floating-point types
- ◇ Numeric constants of various floating-point types
- ◇ C++'s arithmetic operators
- ◇ Automatic type conversions
- ◇ Forced type conversions (type casts)

The essence of object-oriented programming is designing and extending your own data types. Designed types represent an effort to make a type match the data. If you do this properly, you'll find it much simpler to work with the data later. But before you can create your own types, you need to know and understand the types built into C++, for these types will be your building blocks.

The built-in C++ types come in two groups: fundamental types and derived types. In this chapter we'll look at the fundamental types, which represent integers and floating-point numbers. That may sound like just two types; however, C++ recognizes that no one integer type and no one floating-point type match all programming requirements, so it offers several variants on these two data themes. The next chapter follows up by covering several types derived from the basic types; these additional derived types include arrays, strings, pointers, and structures.

Of course, a program also needs a means to identify stored data. You'll examine one method for doing so—using variables. Next, you'll look at how to do arithmetic in C++. Finally, you'll see how C++ converts values from one type to another.

Simple Variables

Programs typically need to store information—perhaps the current price of IBM stock, perhaps the average humidity in New York City in August, perhaps the most common letter in the Constitution and its relative frequency, perhaps the number of available Elvis imitators. To store an item of information in a computer, the program needs to keep track of three fundamental properties:

- Where the information is stored
- What value is kept there
- What kind of information is stored

The strategy we've been using so far is to declare a variable. The type used in the declaration describes the kind of information, and the variable name represents the value symbolically. For instance, suppose Chief Lab Assistant Igor uses the following statements:

```
int braincount;
braincount = 5;
```

These statements tell the program that it is storing an integer and that the name *braincount* represents the integer's value, 5 in this case. These statements don't tell us (or Igor) where in memory the value is stored, but the program does keep track of that information, too. Indeed, you can use the & operator to retrieve *braincount's* address in memory. We'll take up that operator in the next chapter when we investigate a second strategy—using pointers—for identifying data.

Names for Variables

C++ encourages you to use meaningful names for variables. If a variable represents the cost of a trip, call it *costoftrip* or *costOfTrip*, not just *x* or *cot*. You do have to follow a few simple C++ naming rules:

- The only characters you may use in names are alphabetic characters, digits, and the underscore (_) character.
- The first character in a name cannot be a digit.
- Uppercase characters are considered distinct from lowercase characters.
- You can't use a C++ keyword for a name.
- C++ places no limits on the length of a name, and all characters in a name are significant.

The last point makes C++ different from ANSI C, which guarantees only that the first 31 characters in a name are significant. (In ANSI C, two names having the same first 31 characters would be considered identical, even if the 32nd characters differed.) However, note that while the language standard may pose no length limits, some implementations may.

Here are some valid and invalid C++ names:

```
int poodle;      // valid
int Poodle;      // valid and distinct from poodle
int POODLE;      // valid and even more distinct
Int terrier;     // invalid -- has to be int, not Int
int my_stars3    // valid
int _mystars3;   // valid -- can start with underscore
int 4ever;       // invalid because starts with a digit
int double;      // invalid -- double is a C++ keyword
int begin;       // valid -- begin is a Pascal keyword
int the_very_best_variable_i_can_be_version_112;  // valid
int honky-tonk;          // invalid -- no hyphens allowed
```

Although you can begin a variable name with an underscore, as with _mystars3, you're better off if you don't. That's because C and C++ implementations and libraries use identifiers beginning with one or two underscore characters for their own purposes.

If you want to form a name from two or more words, the usual practice is to separate the words with an underscore character, as in my_onions, or to capitalize the initial character of each word after the first, as in myEyeTooth. (C veterans tend to use the underscore method in the C tradition, while Pascalians prefer the capitalization approach.)

Some C++ implementations have more restrictive rules for naming a variable if that variable is shared by more than one file in a multifile program. That's because some operating systems, such as PC DOS, have their own rules about variable names shared among files. For instance, PC DOS limits such shared names (called external identifiers) to eight characters and doesn't discriminate between uppercase and lowercase. Language designers regard such limitations as pathetic irritations.

Integer Types

Integers are numbers with no fractional part, such as 2, 98, -5286, and 0. There are lots of integers, assuming you consider an infinite number to be a lot, so no finite amount of computer memory can represent all possible integers. Thus a language can only represent a subset of all integers. Some languages, such as Standard Pascal, offer just one integer type (one type fits all!), but C++ provides several choices. That gives you the option of choosing the integer type that best meets a program's particular requirements. This concern with matching type to data presages the designable data types of OOP.

The various C++ integer types differ in the amount of memory they use to hold an integer. A larger block of memory can represent a larger range in integer values. Also, some types (signed types) can represent both positive and negative values, while others (unsigned types) can't represent negative values. C++'s basic integer types, in order of increasing size, are called *char, short, int,* and *long.* Each comes in both signed and unsigned versions. That gives you a choice of eight different integer types! Let's look at these integer types in more detail. Because the *char* type has some special properties (it's most often used to represent characters instead of numbers), we'll discuss the other types first.

The *short, int,* and *long* Integer Types

Computer memory is organized into units called bytes. (See the Bits and Bytes note.) By using different numbers of bytes to store values, the C++ types of *short, int,* and *long* can represent up to three different integer sizes. It would be convenient if each type were always some particular size for all systems, for example, if *short* were always 2 bytes, *int* always 4 bytes, and so on. But life is not that simple. The reason is that no one choice is suitable for all computer designs. So C++ offers a flexible standard with some guaranteed minimum sizes. Here's what you get:

❧ A *short* integer is at least 2 bytes.

❧ An *int* integer is at least as big as *short.*

❧ A *long* integer is at least 4 bytes and at least as big as *int.*

BITS AND BYTES

Memory capacity is measured in bytes. A byte consists of 8 bits, where a bit is the smallest unit of memory. You can think of a bit as an electronic switch that can be set to either off or on. Off represents the value 0, and on represents the value 1. The 8-bit byte can be set to 256 different combinations. The number 256 comes from the fact that each bit has two possible settings, making the total number of combinations for 8 bits 2 x 2 x 2 x 2 x 2 x 2 x 2 x 2, or 256. Thus a byte can be used to represent, say, the values 0 through 255 or the values from -128 through 127. Each additional bit doubles the number of combinations. This means a 2-byte unit can be set to 65,536 different values, and a 4-byte unit can be set to 4,294,672,296 different values.

Many systems currently use the minimum guarantee, making *short* 2 bytes and *long* 4 bytes. This still leaves several choices open for *int.* It could be 2, 3, or 4 bytes in size and meet the standard. Typically, *int* is 2 bytes (the same as *short*) for IBM PC implementations and 4 bytes (the same as *long*) for Macintosh, VAX, and many other minicomputer implementations. Some implementations give you a choice of how to handle *int.* (What does your implementation use? The next example will show you how to determine the limits for your system without opening a manual.) The differences between implementations for type sizes can cause problems when you move a C++

program from one environment to another. But a little care, as discussed later, can minimize those problems.

You use these type names just like *int* to declare variables:

```
short score;        // creates a type short integer variable
int temperature;    // creates a type int integer variable
long position;      // creates a type long integer variable
```

Actually, *short* is short for *short int* and *long* is short for *long int,* but hardly anyone uses the lengthier forms.

The three types *int, short,* and *long* are signed types, meaning each splits its range approximately equally between positive and negative values. For example, a 2-byte *int* might run from -32768 to +32767.

If you want to know how your system's integers size up, C++ offers tools to let you investigate type sizes with a program. First, the *sizeof* operator returns the size, in bytes, of a type or a variable. (An operator is a built-in language element that operates on one or more items to produce a value. For instance, the addition operator, represented by +, adds two values.) Second, the *limits.h* header file contains information about integer type limits. In particular, it defines symbolic names to represent different limits. For instance, it defines *INT_MAX* to be the largest possible *int* value. Listing 3-1 demonstrates how to use these facilities. The program also illustrates *initialization,* which is using a declaration statement to assign a value to a variable.

Listing 3-1 *limits.cpp*

```
// limits.cpp -- some integer limits
#include <iostream.h>
#include <limits.h>               // defines limits for types
int main(void)
{
        int n_int = INT_MAX;      // initialize n_int to max int value
        short n_short = SHRT_MAX;  // symbols defined in limits.h file
        long n_long = LONG_MAX;

        // sizeof operator yields size of type or of variable
        cout << "int is " << sizeof (int) << " bytes.\n";
        cout << "short is " << sizeof n_short << " bytes.\n";
        cout << "long is " << sizeof n_long << " bytes.\n\n";

        cout << "Maximum values:\n";
        cout << "int: " << n_int << "\n";
        cout << "short: " << n_short << "\n";
        cout << "long: " << n_long << "\n\n";

        cout << "Minimum int value = " << INT_MIN << "\n";
        return 0;
}
```

COMPATIBILITY NOTE

The *limits.h* header file is an ANSI C addition. Some C++ implementations don't yet provide full ANSI C support and thus may not provide the *limits.h* header file. If you're using such a system, you'll have to limit yourself to experiencing this example in spirit only.

Here is the output for our base system (Borland C++ 3.1):

```
int is 2 bytes.
short is 2 bytes.
long is 4 bytes.

Maximum values:
int: 32767
short: 32767
long: 2147483647

Minimum int value = -32768
```

Here is the output for a second system (Symantec C++ 7.0 for the Mac):

```
int is 4 bytes.
short is 2 bytes.
long is 4 bytes.

Maximum values:
int: 2147483647
short: 32767
long: 2147483647

Minimum int value = -2147483648
```

Program Notes

Let's summarize the chief programming features for this program.

The *sizeof* operator reports that *int* is 2 bytes on our base system. You can apply the *sizeof* operator to a type name or to a variable name. When you use the *sizeof* operator with a type name, such as *int*, you enclose the name in parentheses. But if you use the operator with the name of the variable, such as *n_short*, parentheses are optional:

```
cout << "int is " << sizeof (int) << " bytes.\n";
cout << "short is " << sizeof n_short << " bytes.\n";
```

The *limits.h* header file defines symbolic constants (see the Symbolic Constants note) to represent type limits. As mentioned, *INT_MAX* represents the largest value type *int* can hold; this turned out to be 32767 for our system. The compiler manufacturer provides a *limits.h* file that reflects the values appropriate to that compiler. For instance, the *limits.h* file for a system using a 4-byte *int* would define the *INT_MAX* to represent 2147483647. Both C++ and ANSI C use the *limits.h* file, so it's designed to be compatible with both languages. Table 3-1 summarizes the symbolic constants defined in this file; some pertain to types we have not yet discussed.

Symbolic Constant	Represents
CHAR_BIT	number of bits in a *char*
CHAR_MAX	maximum *char* value
CHAR_MIN	minimum *char* value
SCHAR_MAX	maximum *signed char* value
SCHAR_MIN	minimum *signed char* value
UCHAR_MAX	maximum *unsigned char* value
SHRT_MAX	maximum *short* value
SHRT_MIN	minimum *short* value
USHRT_MAX	maximum *unsigned short* value
INT_MAX	maximum *int* value
INT_MIN	minimum *int* value
UINT_MAX	maximum *unsigned int* value
LONG_MAX	maximum *long* value
LONG_MIN	minimum *long* value
ULONG_MAX	maximum *unsigned long* value

Table 3-1 Symbolic constants from *limits.h*

Initialization combines assignment with declaration. For instance, the statement

```
int n_int = INT_MAX;
```

declares the *n_int* variable and sets it to the largest possible type *int* value. You can also use regular constants to initialize values. You can initialize a variable to another variable, providing the other variable has been defined first. You can even initialize a variable to an expression, providing all the values in the expression are known at compilation time:

```
int uncles = 5;                    // initialize to 5
int aunts = uncles;                // initialize to 5
int chairs = aunts + uncles + 4;   // initialize to 14
```

Moving the *uncles* declaration to the end of this list of statements would invalidate the other two initializations, for then the value of *uncles* wouldn't be known at the time the compiler tried to initialize the other variables.

RULE

If you don't initialize a variable defined inside a function, the variable's value is undefined. That means the value will be whatever happened to be sitting at that memory location prior to creating the variable.

If you know what the initial value of a variable should be, initialize it. True, separating the declaring of a variable from assigning it a value can create momentary suspense:

```
short year;        // what could it be?
year = 1492;       // oh
```

But initializing the variable when you declare it protects you from forgetting to assign the value later.

SYMBOLIC CONSTANTS THE PREPROCESSOR WAY

The *limits.h* file contains lines similar to the following:

```
#define INT_MAX 32767
```

The C++ compilation process, recall, first passes the source code through a preprocessor. Here *#define*, like *#include*, is a preprocessor directive. What this particular directive tells the preprocessor is this: look through the program for instances of *INT_MAX* and replace each occurrence with *32767*. So the *#define* directive works like a global search-and-replace command in an editor or word processor. The altered program is compiled after these replacements occur. The preprocessor looks for independent tokens (separate words), skipping embedded words. That is, the preprocessor doesn't replace *PINT_MAXIM* with *P32767IM*. You can use *#define* to define your own symbolic constants, too. (See Listing 3-2.) However, the *#define* directive is a C relic. C++ has a better way for creating symbolic constants (the *const* keyword, discussed in a later section), so we won't be using *#define* much. But some header files, particularly those designed to be used with both C and C++, do use it.

Unsigned Types

Each of the three integer types we just discussed comes in an unsigned variety, which can't hold negative values. This has the advantage of increasing the largest value the variable can hold. For instance, if *short* represents the range -32768 to +32767, then the unsigned version can represent the range 0 to 65535. Of course, you should use unsigned types only for quantities that are never negative, such as populations, inventory counts, and happy face manifestations. To create unsigned versions of the basic integer types, just use the keyword *unsigned* to modify the declarations:

```
unsigned short change;     // unsigned short type
unsigned int rovert;       // unsigned int type
```

```
unsigned quarterback;        // also unsigned int
unsigned long gone;          // unsigned long type
```

Note that *unsigned* by itself is short for *unsigned int*.

Listing 3-2 illustrates using unsigned types. It also shows what may happen if your program tries to go beyond the limits for integer types. Finally, it gives you one last look at the preprocessor *#define* statement.

Listing 3-2 *exceed.cpp*

```cpp
// exceed.cpp -- exceeding some integer limits
#include <iostream.h>
#define ZERO 0        // makes ZERO symbol for 0 value
#include <limits.h>   // defines INT_MAX as largest int value
int main(void)
{
        int sam = INT_MAX;     // initialize a variable to max value
        unsigned sue = sam;    // okay if variable sam already defined

        cout << "Sam has " << sam << " dollars and Sue has " << sue;
        cout << " dollars deposited.\nAdd $1 to each account.\nNow ";
        sam = sam + 1;
        sue = sue + 1;
        cout << "Sam has " << sam << " dollars and Sue has " << sue;
        cout << " dollars deposited.\nPoor Sam!\n";
        sam = ZERO;
        sue = ZERO;
        cout << "Sam has " << sam << " dollars and Sue has " << sue;
        cout << " dollars deposited.\n";
        cout << "Take $1 from each account.\nNow ";
        sam = sam - 1;
        sue = sue - 1;
        cout << "Sam has " << sam << " dollars and Sue has " << sue;
        cout << " dollars deposited.\nLucky Sue!\n";
        return 0;
}
```

COMPATIBILITY NOTE

Listing 3-2, like Listing 3-1, uses the *limits.h* file, which may not be available on C++ systems not providing full ANSI C support.

Here's the output:

```
Sam has 32767 dollars and Sue has 32767 dollars deposited.
Add $1 to each account.
Now Sam has -32768 dollars and Sue has 32768 dollars deposited.
Poor Sam!
Sam has 0 dollars and Sue has 0 dollars deposited.
Take $1 from each account.
Now Sam has -1 dollars and Sue has 65535 dollars deposited.
Lucky Sue!
```

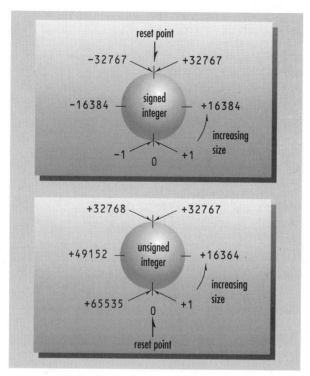

Figure 3-1 Typical overflow behavior for integers

The program sets an *int* variable (*sam*) and an *unsigned int* variable (*sue*) to the largest *int* value, which is 32767 on our system. Then it adds 1 to each value. This causes no problems for *sue*, for the new value is still much less than the maximum value for an unsigned integer. But *sam* goes from *32767* to *-32768!* Similarly, subtracting 1 from 0 creates no problems for *sam*, but it makes the unsigned variable *sue* go from 0 to 65535. As you can see, these integers behave much like an odometer or a VCR counter. If you go past the limit, the values just start over at the other end of the range. See Figure 3-1. C++ doesn't guarantee that integer types can exceed their limits (overflow and underflow) without complaint, but that is the most common behavior on current implementations.

Which Type?

With this richness of C++ integer types, which should you use? Generally, *int* is set to the most "natural" integer size for the target computer. Natural size means the integer form the computer handles most efficiently. If there is no compelling reason to choose another type, use *int*.

Now let's look at reasons you might use another type. If a variable represents something that never is negative, such as the number of words in a document, you can use an unsigned type; that way the variable can represent higher values.

If you know that the variable may have to represent integer values too great for a 2-byte integer, use *long*. This is true even if *int* is 4 bytes on your system. That way, if you transfer your program to a system with a 2-byte *int*, your program won't embarrass you by suddenly failing to work properly. See Figure 3-2.

Using *short* can conserve memory if *short* is smaller than *int*. Most typically, this will be important only if you have a large array of integers. (An array is a data structure that stores several values of the same type sequentially in memory.) If it is important to conserve space, you should use *short* instead of *int* even if the two are the same size.

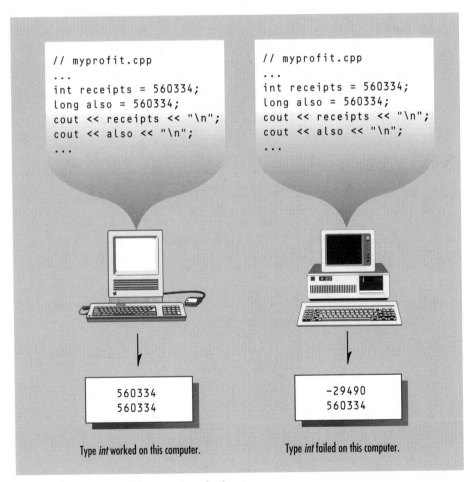

Figure 3-2 For portability, use *long* for big integers

Suppose, for example, you move your program from a 2-byte *int* PC system to a 4-byte *int* VAX system. That will double the amount of memory needed to hold an *int* array, but it won't affect the requirements for a *short* array. Remember, a byte saved is a byte earned.

If you need only a single byte, you can use *char.* We'll examine that possibility soon.

Integer Constants

An integer constant is one you write out explicitly, such as 212 or 1776. C++, like C, lets you write integers in three different number bases: base 10 (the public favorite), base 8 (the old UNIX favorite), and base 16 (the hardware hacker's favorite). Appendix A describes these bases; here we'll look at the C++ representations. C++ uses the first digit or two to identify the base of a number constant. If the first digit is in the range 1–9, the number is base 10 (decimal); thus 93 is base 10. If the first digit is 0 and the second digit is in the range 1–7, the number is base 8 (octal); thus 042 is octal and equal to 34 decimal. If the first two characters are 0x or 0X, the number is base 16 (hexadecimal); thus 0x42 is hex and equal to 66 decimal. For hexadecimal values, the characters a–f and A–F represent the hexadecimal digits corresponding to the values 10–15. So 0xF is 15 and 0xA5 is 165 (10 sixteens plus 5 ones). Listing 3-3 is tailor-made to show the three bases.

 ## Listing 3-3 *hexoct.cpp*

```
// hexoct.cpp -- shows hex and octal constants
#include <iostream.h>
int main(void)
{
        int chest = 42;        // decimal integer constant
        int waist = 0x42;      // hexadecimal integer constant
        int inseam = 042;      // octal integer constant

        cout << "Monsieur cuts a striking figure!\n";
        cout << "chest = " << chest << "\n";
        cout << "waist = " << waist << "\n";
        cout << "inseam = " << inseam << "\n";
        return 0;
}
```

By default, *cout* displays integers in decimal form, regardless of how they are written in a program, as the following output shows:

```
Monsieur cuts a striking figure!
chest = 42
waist = 66
inseam = 34
```

Keep in mind that these notations are merely notational conveniences. For instance, if you read that the CGA video memory segment is B000 in hexadecimal, you don't have to convert the value to base ten 45056 before using it in your program. Instead, simply use 0xB000. But whether you write the value ten as 10, 012, or 0xA, it's stored the same way in the computer—as a binary (base two) value.

By the way, if you want to display a value in hexadecimal or octal form, you can use some special features of *cout*. We really don't want to get into that now, but you'll find the information in Chapter 15. (You can just skim the chapter for that information and ignore the explanations.) On input, *cin* recognizes the C++ notation for different number bases. So if you type **0x20**, *cin* will interpret that as a hex value, the equivalent of 32.

How C++ Decides What Type a Constant Is

A program's declarations tell the C++ compiler the type of a particular integer variable. But what about constants? That is, suppose you represent a number with a constant in a program:

```
cout << "Year = " << 1492 << "\n";
```

Does the program store *1492* as an *int*, a *long*, or as some other integer type? The answer is that C++ stores integer constants as type *int* unless there is a reason to do otherwise. Two such reasons are if you use a special suffix to indicate a particular type or if a value is too large to be an *int*.

First, let's look at the suffixes. These are letters placed at the end of a numeric constant to indicate the type. A l or L suffix on an integer means the integer is a type *long* constant; a u or U suffix indicates an *unsigned int* constant; and ul (in any combination of orders and uppercase and lowercase) indicates a type *unsigned long* constant. (Because a lowercase l can look much like the digit 1, we recommend using the uppercase L for suffixes.) For example, on a system using a 2-byte *int* and a 4-byte *long*, the number 22022 is stored in 2 bytes as an *int*, and the number 22022L is stored in 4 bytes as a *long*.

Next, let's look at size. C++ has slightly different rules for decimal integers than it has for hexadecimal and octal integers. (Here decimal means base 10, just as hexadecimal means base 16; the term does not necessarily imply a decimal point.) A decimal integer without a suffix is represented by the smallest of the following types that can hold it: *int, long, unsigned long*. On a computer system using a 2-byte *int* and a 4-byte *long*, 20000 is represented as type *int*, 40000 is represented as *long*, and 3000000000 is represented as *unsigned long*. A hexadecimal or octal integer without a suffix is represented by the smallest of the following types that can hold it: *int, unsigned int, long, unsigned long*. So the same computer system that represents 40000 as *long* represents the hexadecimal equivalent 0x9C40 as an *unsigned int*. That's because hexadecimal frequently is used to express memory addresses, which intrinsically are unsigned. So *unsigned int* is more appropriate than *long* for a 2-byte address.

The *char* Type: Characters and Small Integers

It's time to turn to the final integer type, type *char*. As you probably suspect from its name, the *char* type was designed to store characters, such as letters and digits. Now, while storing numbers is no big deal for computers, storing letters is another matter. Programming languages take the easy way out by using a number code for letters. Thus the *char* type is really another integer type. It's guaranteed to be large enough to represent the entire range of basic symbols—all the letters, digits, punctuation, and the like—for the target computer system. In practice, most systems support fewer than 256 kinds of characters, so a single byte can represent the whole range. Therefore, while *char* most often is used to handle characters, it also can be used as an integer type typically smaller than *short*.

The most common symbol set in the United States is the ASCII (pronounced *askey*) character set described in Appendix C. A numeric code (the ASCII code) represents the characters in the set. For example, 65 is the code for the character A. For convenience, we'll use ASCII code in our examples. However, a C++ implementation will use whatever code is native to its host system, for instance, EBCDIC (pronounced *ebse-dik*) on an IBM mainframe. Neither ASCII nor EBCDIC serve international needs that well, and C++ supports a wide-character type that can hold a larger range of values. We'll discuss this development soon.

Let's try the *char* type in Listing 3-4.

Listing 3-4 *chartype.cpp*

```
// chartype.cpp -- the char type
#include <iostream.h>
int main(void)
{
        char ch;       // declare a char variable

        cout << "Enter a character:\n";
        cin >> ch;
        cout << "Holla! ";
        cout << "Thank you for the " << ch << " character.\n";
        return 0;
}
```

As usual, the \n notation is the C++ representation of the newline character. Here's the output:

```
Enter a character:
M
Holla! Thank you for the M character.
```

The interesting thing is that we type an **M**, not the corresponding character code of 77. And the program prints an M, not a 77. Yet if you were to peer into memory, you'd find that 77 is the value stored in the *ch* variable. The magic, such as it is, lies not in the *char* type, but in *cin* and *cout*. These worthy facilities make conversions on our behalf. On input, *cin* converts the keystroke input M to the value 77. On output, *cout* converts the value 77 to the displayed character of M; *cin* and *cout* are guided by the type of variable. If we placed the same value of 77 into an *int* variable, then *cout* would display it as 77. (That is, *cout* will display two 7 characters.) Listing 3-5 illustrates this point. It also shows how to write a character constant in C++: enclose the character within two single quotation marks, as in 'M'. (Note that we didn't use double quotation marks. C++ uses single quotation marks for a character and double quotation marks for a string. As you'll see in Chapter 4, the two are quite different.) Finally, the program introduces a *cout* offshoot, the *cout.put()* function.

Listing 3-5 *morechar.cpp*

```
// morechar.cpp -- the char type and int type contrasted
#include <iostream.h>
int main(void)
{
        char c = 'M';          // assign ASCII code for M to c
        int i = c;             // store same code in an int
        cout << "The ASCII code for " << c << " is " << i << "\n";

        cout << "Add one to the character code:\n";
        c = c + 1;
        i = c;
        cout << "The ASCII code for " << c << " is " << i << '\n';

        // using the cout.put() member function to display a char
        cout << "Displaying char c using cout.put(c): ";
        cout.put(c);

        // using cout.put() to display a char constant
        cout.put('!');

        cout << "\nDone\n";
        return 0;
}
```

Here is the output:

```
The ASCII code for M is 77
Add one to the character code:
The ASCII code for N is 78
Displaying char c using cout.put(c): N!
Done
```

Program Notes

The notation 'M' represents the numeric code for the M character, so initializing the *char* variable *c* to 'M' sets *c* to the value 77. The program then assigns the identical value to the *int* variable *i*. So both *c* and *i* have the value 77. Then *cout* displays *c* as M and *i* as 77. As we said, *cout* is guided by a value's type when choosing how to display it—just another example of smart objects.

Because *c* is really an integer, we can apply integer operations to it, such as adding 1. This changes the value of *c* to 78. Then the program resets *i* to the new value. Again, *cout* displays the *char* version of that value as a character and the *int* version as number.

The fact that C++ represents characters as integers is a real convenience. It makes it easy to manipulate character values. You don't have to use awkward conversion functions to convert characters to ASCII and back.

Finally, the program uses the *cout.put()* function to display both *c* and a character constant.

A Member Function: *cout.put()*

Just what is *cout.put()*, and why does it have a period in its name? The *cout.put()* function is our first example of an important C++ OOP concept, the *member* function. A class, you may remember, defines how to represent data and how to manipulate it. A member function belongs to a class and describes a method for manipulating class data. The *ostream* class, for instance, has a *put()* member function designed to output characters. You can use a member function only with a particular object of that class, such as the *cout* object, in this case. To use a class member function with an object like *cout*, you use a period to combine the object name (*cout*) with the function name (*put()*). The period is called the *membership* operator. The notation *cout.put()* means to use the class member function *put()* with the class object *cout*. Of course, we'll go into more detail when we reach classes. Meanwhile, the only classes we have are the *istream* and *ostream* classes, and we can experiment with their member functions to get more comfortable with the concept.

The *cout.put()* member function provides an alternative to using the << operator to display a character. At this point you may wonder why there is any need for *cout.put()*. Much of the answer is historical. Prior to Release 2.0 of C++, *cout* would display character *variables* as characters but display character *constants*, such as 'M' and '\n', as numbers. The problem was that earlier versions of C++, like C, stored character constants as type *int*. That is, the code 77 for 'M' would be stored in a 2-byte or 4-byte unit. Meanwhile, *char* variables typically occupied 1 byte. A statement like

```
char c = 'M';
```

copied 1 byte (the important byte) from the constant 'M' to the variable *c*. Unfortunately, this meant that 'M' and *c* looked quite different to *cout*, even though both held the same value. So a statement like

```
cout << '$';
```

would print the ASCII code for the $ character instead of simply displaying $. But

```
cout.put('$');
```

would print the character, as desired. Now, after Release 2.0, C++ stores single character constants as type *char*, not type *int*. That means *cout* now correctly handles character constants. C++ always could use the string *"\n"* to start a new line; now it also can use the character *'\n'*:

```
cout << "\n"; // using a string
cout << '\n'; // using a character constant
```

A string is enclosed in double quotation marks instead of single quotation marks and can hold more than one character. Strings, even one-character strings, are *not* the same as type *char*. We'll come back to strings in the next chapter.

The *cin* object has a couple of different ways of reading characters from input. These are more easily explored using a program that uses a loop to read several characters, so we'll go into the matter when we cover loops in Chapter 5.

char Constants

You have several options for writing character constants in C++. The simplest choice for ordinary characters such as letters, punctuation, and digits is to enclose the character in single quotes. This notation stands for the numeric code for the character. For instance, an ASCII system has the following correspondences:

```
'A' is 65, the ASCII code for A
'a' is 97, the ASCII code for a
'5' is 53, the ASCII code for the digit 5
' ' is 32, the ASCII code for the space character
'!' is 33, the ASCII code for the exclamation mark
```

Using this notation is better than using the numeric codes explicitly. It's clearer, and it doesn't assume a particular code. If a system uses EBCDIC, then 65 is not the code for A, but *'A'* still represents the character.

Some characters can't be entered into a program directly from the keyboard. For instance, you can't make the newline character part of a string by pressing the (ENTER) key; instead, the program editor interprets that keystroke as a request for it to start a new line in your source code file. Other characters have difficulties because the C++ language imbues them with special significance. For instance, the double quote character delimits strings, so you can't just stick one in the middle of a string. C++ has special notations, called *escape sequences,* for several of these characters, as shown in Table 3-2. For instance, \a represents the alert character, which beeps your terminal's speaker or rings its bell. And \" represents the double quotation mark as an ordinary character instead of a string delimiter. You can use these notations in strings or in character constants:

```
char alarm = '\a';
cout << alarm << "Don't do that again!\a\n";
cout << "Ben \"Buggsie\" Hacker was here!\n";
```

The last line produces the following output:

```
Ben "Buggsie" Hacker was here!
```

Note that you treat an escape sequence such as \a just like a regular character, such as Q. That is, you enclose it in single quotes to create a character constant and don't use single quotes when including it as part of a string.

Character name	ASCII symbol	C++ code	ASCII decimal code	ASCII hex code
newline	NL (LF)	\n	10	0xA
horizontal tab	HT	\t	9	0x9
vertical tab	VT	\v	11	0xB
backspace	BS	\b	8	0x8
carriage return	CR	\r	13	0xD
alert	BEL	\a	7	0x7
backslash	\	\\	92	0x5C
question mark	?	\?	63	0x3F
single quote	'	\'	39	0x27
double quote	"	\"	34	0x22

Table 3-2 C++ escape sequence codes

Finally, you can use escape sequences based on the octal or hexadecimal codes for a character. For instance, (CTRL)-(Z) has an ASCII code of 26, which is 032 in octal and 0x1a in hexadecimal. You can represent this character by either of the following escape sequences: \032 or \x1a. You can make character constants out of these by enclosing them in single quotes, as in '\032', and you can use them as parts of a string, as in "hi\x1a there".

TIP

When you have a choice between using a numeric escape sequence or a symbolic escape sequence, as in \0x8 versus \b, use the symbolic code. The numeric representation is tied to a particular code, such as ASCII, but the symbolic representation works with all codes and is more readable.

Listing 3-6 demonstrates a few escape sequences. It uses the alert character to get your attention, it uses the newline character to advance the cursor (one small step for a cursor, one giant step for cursorkind), and it uses the backspace character to back the cursor one space to the left. (Houdini once painted a picture of the Hudson River using only escape sequences; he was, of course, a great escape artist.)

Listing 3-6 *bondini.cpp*

```cpp
// bondini.cpp -- using escape sequences
#include <iostream.h>
int main(void)
{
    cout << "\aOperation \"HyperHype\" is now activated!\n";
    cout << "Enter your agent code:_____\b\b\b\b\b\b\b\b";
    long code;
    cin >> code;
    cout << "\aYou entered " << code << "...\n";
    cout << "\aCode verified! Proceed with Plan Z3!\n";
    return 0;
}
```

COMPATIBILITY NOTE

Some C++ systems based on pre-ANSI C compilers don't recognize \a. You can substitute \007 for \a on systems that use the ASCII character code. Microsoft Visual C++ processes the \b and \a characters normally if the program is compiled as an MS-DOS application, but displays them as filled rectangles if the program is compiled as a QuickWin application. For CodeWarrior 3.5 and Borland 4.0 C++ EasyWin applications, the backspace character erases the character it backs over.

When you start the program, it puts the following text on the screen:

```
Operation "HyperHype" is now activated!
Enter your agent code:_____
```

After printing the underscore characters, the program uses the backspace character to back up the cursor to the first underscore. Then you can enter your secret code and continue. Here's a complete run:

```
Operation "HyperHype" is now activated!
Enter your agent code:42007007
You entered 42007007...
Code verified! Proceed with Plan Z3!
```

signed char and *unsigned char*

Unlike *int, char* is not signed by default. Nor is it unsigned by default. The choice is left to the C++ implementation in order to allow the implementor to best fit the type to the hardware properties. If it is vital to you that *char* has a particular behavior, you can use *signed char* or *unsigned char* explicitly as types:

```cpp
char fodo;           // may be signed, may be unsigned
unsigned char bar;   // definitely unsigned
signed char snark;   // definitely signed
```

These distinctions are particularly important if you're using *char* as a numeric type. The *unsigned char* type typically represents the range 0 to 255, and *signed char* typically represents the range -128 to 127. For example, suppose you want to use a *char* variable to hold values that may be as large as 200. That will work on some systems but fail on others. But you can use *unsigned char* successfully for that purpose on any system. On the other hand, if you're using a *char* variable to hold a standard ASCII character, it doesn't really matter whether *char* is signed or unsigned, so you can simply use *char*.

wchar_t

Programs may have to deal with character sets that don't fit within the confines of a single byte, for instance, the Japanese kanja system. The *wchar_t* type (for *wide charac-ter*) is an integer type with more space than *char*. Initially, this type was defined in the *stddef.h* header file in terms of existing types. For example, the header file might include a line like this:

```
#define wchar_t short
```

However, the ANSI C++ committee has moved to make *wchar_t* a basic, built-in type.

You can indicate a wide-character constant or string by preceding it with an L:

```
wchar_t bob = L'BP';        // a wide-character constant
wchar_t ken[3]= L"tall";    // a wide-character string
```

Here we've used two ordinary characters to compose a single wide character. We won't be using the wide-character type in this book, but you should be aware of it, particularly if you become involved in international programming.

The New *bool* Type

The ANSI/ISO C++ standards committee has accepted a new type, called *bool*. It's named in honor of the English mathematician George Boole, who developed a mathematical representation of the laws of logic. In computing, a Boolean variable means one whose value can be either true or false. In the past, C++, like C, has not had a Boolean type. Instead, as you'll see in greater detail in Chapters 5 and 6, C++ has interpreted nonzero values as true and zero values as false. In ANSI/ISO C++, however, you'll be able to use the *bool* type to represent true and false, and the predefined literals *true* and *false* will represent those values. That is, you'll be able to make statements like the following:

```
bool isready = true;
```

The literals *true* and *false* can be converted to type *int* by promotion, with *true* converting to *1* and *false* to *0*:

```
int ans = true;          // ans assigned 1
int promise = false;     // promise assigned 0
```

Also, any numeric or pointer value can be converted implicitly (that is, without an explicit type cast) to a *bool* value. Any nonzero value is converted to *true,* while a zero value converts to *false:*

```
bool start = -100;    // start assigned true
bool stop = 0;        // stop assigned false
```

At the time of this writing, the *bool* type has yet to be commonly implemented. Later in this book, you'll see several examples where such a type would be handy.

The *const* Qualifier

Let's return to the topic of symbolic names for constants. The symbolic name can suggest what the constant represents. Also, if the program uses the constant in several places and you need to change the value, you can just change the single symbol definition. The note about *#define* statements earlier in this chapter (Symbolic Constants the Preprocessor Way) promised that C++ had a better way to handle symbolic constants. That way is to use the *const* keyword to modify a variable declaration and initialization. Suppose, for instance, that you want a symbolic constant for the number of months in a year. Enter this line:

```
const int Months = 12;  // Months is symbolic constant for 12
```

Now you can use *Months* in a program instead of *12.* (A bare 12 in a program might represent the number of inches in a foot or the number of donuts in a dozen, but the name *Months* tells you what it represents.) Once *Months* has been initialized, its value is set. The compiler will not let you subsequently change the value *Months.* For instance, Borland C++ will give an error message stating that an Lvalue is required. This is the same message you'll get if you try, say, to assign the value *4* to *3.* (An *Lvalue* is a value, such as a variable, that can appear on the left side of the assignment operator.) The keyword *const* is termed a *qualifier* because it qualifies the meaning of a declaration.

Capitalizing the name helps remind you that *Months* is a constant. This is by no means a universal convention, but it helps separate the constants from the variables when you read a program. Another convention is using all capital letters for a constant name. We'll follow the usual C convention and reserve all caps for constants created using *#define,* such as *INT_MAX.* Yet another convention is to begin constant names with the letter *k,* as in *kmonths.*

The general form for creating a constant is this:

```
const type name = value;
```

If you omit the type, C++ uses *int.*

If your background is in C, you might feel that the *#define* statement, which we discussed earlier, already does the job adequately. But *const* is better. For one thing, it lets you specify the type explicitly. Second, you can use C++'s scoping rules to limit the definition to particular functions or files. (Scoping rules describe how widely known a name is to different modules; we'll go into more detail in Chapter 8.) Third, you can use *const* with more elaborate types, such as the arrays and structures coming up in the next chapter.

> **TIP**
>
> If you are coming to C++ from C and you are about to use *#define* to define a symbolic constant, use *const* instead.

ANSI C also uses the *const* qualifier. If you're familiar with the ANSI C version, you should be aware that the C++ version is slightly different. One difference relates to the scope rules, and Chapter 8 will cover that point. The other main difference is that in C++ (but not in C) you can use a *const* value to declare the size of an array. We'll show examples in the next chapter.

Floating-Point Numbers

Now that you have seen the complete line of C++ integer types, let's look at the floating-point types, which compose the second major group of fundamental C++ types. These numbers let you represent numbers with fractional parts, such as the gas mileage of an M1 tank (0.56 MPG). They also provide a much greater range in values. If a number is too large to be represented as type *long,* for instance, the number of stars in our galaxy (an estimated 400,000,000,000), you can use one of the floating-point types.

With floating-point types, you can represent numbers like 2.5 and 3.14159 and 122442.32, that is, numbers with a fractional part. A computer stores such values in two parts. One part represents a value, and the other part scales that value up or down. Here's an analogy. Consider the two numbers 34.1245 and 34124.5. They're identical except for scale. We can represent the first one as 0.341245 (the base value) and 100 (the scaling factor). We can represent the second as 0.341245 (the same base value) and 100000 (a bigger scaling factor). The scaling factor serves to move the decimal point, hence the term *floating-point.* C++ uses a similar method to represent floating-point numbers internally, except it's based on binary numbers, so the scaling is by factors of 2 instead of by factors of 10. Fortunately, you don't have to know much about the internal representation. The main points are that floating-point numbers let you represent fractional values, they let you represent very large and very small values, and they have an internal representation much different from that of integers.

Writing Floating-Point Numbers

C++ has two ways of writing floating-point numbers. The first is to use the standard decimal-point notation you've been using much of your life:

```
12.34          // floating-point
939001.32      // floating-point
```

```
0.00023        // floating-point
8.0            // still floating-point
```

Even if the fractional part is 0, as in 8.0, the decimal point ensures that the number will be stored in floating-point format and not as an integer.

The second method for representing floating-point values is called *E notation*, and it looks like this: 3.45E6. This means that the value 3.45 is multiplied by 1,000,000; the E6 means 10 to the 6th power, which is 1 followed by 6 zeros. Thus 3.45E6 means 3,450,000. The 6 is called an *exponent*, and the 3.45 is termed the *mantissa*. Here are more examples:

```
2.52e+8        // can use E or e, + is optional
8.33E-4        // exponent can be negative
7E5            // same as 7.0E+05
-18.32e13      // can have + or - sign in front
2.857e12       // US public debt, 1989
5.98E24        // mass of Earth in kilograms
9.11e-31       // mass of an electron in kilograms
```

As you may have noticed, E notation is most useful for very large numbers and for very small numbers.

E notation guarantees that the number is stored in floating-point format, even if no decimal point is used. Note that you can use either E or e, and the exponent can have a positive or negative sign. See Figure 3-3. You can't have spaces in the number, however: 7.2 E6 would be invalid.

Using a negative exponent means to divide by a power of 10 instead of multiplying by a power of 10. So 8.33E-4 means $8.33 \div 10^4$, or 0.000833. Similarly, the electron mass of 9.11e-31 kg means:

0.000000000000000000000000000000911 kg

Take your choice. (Incidentally, note that 911 is the usual emergency telephone number in the United States and that telephone messages are carried by electrons.

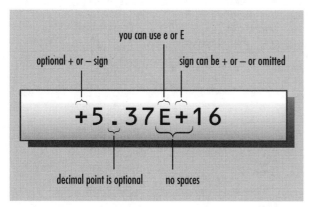

Figure 3-3 E notation

Coincidence or scientific conspiracy? You be the judge.) Note that -8.33E4 means -83300. A sign in front applies to the number value, while a sign in the exponent applies to the scaling.

RULE

The form *d.dddE+n* means move the decimal point *n* places to the right, and the form *d.dddE-n* means move the decimal point *n* places to the left.

Floating-Point Types

Like ANSI C, C++ has three floating-point types: *float, double,* and *long double.* These types are described in terms of the number of significant figures they can represent and the minimum allowable range of exponents. Significant figures are the meaningful digits in a number. For example, writing the height of Mt. Shasta in California as 14,162 feet uses five significant figures, for it specifies the height to the nearest foot. But writing the height of Mt. Shasta as about 14,000 feet tall uses two significant figures, for the result was rounded to the nearest thousand feet. In this case, the remaining three digits are just place holders. The number of significant figures doesn't depend on the location of the decimal point. For instance, we can write the height as 14.162 thousand feet. Again, this uses five significant digits because the value is accurate to the fifth digit.

In effect, the C and C++ requirements for significant digits amount to *float* being at least 4 bytes, *double* being at least 6 bytes and certainly no smaller than *float,* and long *double* being at least as big as *double*. All three can be the same size. Typically, however, *float* is 4 bytes, *double* is 8 bytes, and *long double* is 10, 12, or 16 bytes. Also, the range in exponents for all three types is at least -37 to +37. You can look in the *float.h* file to find the limits for your system. Here, for example, are some annotated entries from the *float.h* file for Borland C++:

```
// the following are the minimum number of significant digits
#define DBL_DIG     15     // double
#define FLT_DIG      6     // float
#define LDBL_DIG    19     // long double

// the following are the number of bits used to represent
// the mantissa
#define DBL_MANT_DIG 53
#define FLT_MANT_DIG 24
#define LDBL_MANT_DIG 64

// the following are the maximum and minimum exponent values
#define DBL_MAX_10_EXP      +308
#define FLT_MAX_10_EXP      +38
#define LDBL_MAX_10_EXP     +4932
```

```
#define DBL_MIN_10_EXP        -307
#define FLT_MIN_10_EXP        -37
#define LDBL_MIN_10_EXP       -4931
```

COMPATIBILITY NOTE

Some C++ implementations based on pre-ANSI C compilers don't provide a *float.h* header file.

Listing 3-7 examines types *float* and *double* and how they can differ in the precision to which they represent numbers (that's the significant figure aspect). The program previews an *ostream* method called *setf()* from Chapter 15. This particular call forces output to stay in fixed-point notation so that we can see the precision better. It prevents the program from switching to E notation for large values, and it causes the program to display six digits to the right of the decimal.

Listing 3-7 *floatnum.cpp*

```
// floatnum.cpp -- floating-point types in Microsoft VC++ 1.0
#include <iostream.h>
int main(void)
{
        cout.setf(ios::fixed, ios::floatfield);        // force fixed-point display
        float tub = 10.0 / 3.0;       // good to about 6 places
        double mint = 10.0 / 3.0;     // good to about 15 places
        const float million = 1.0e6;

        cout << "tub = " << tub;
        cout << ", a million tubs = " << million * tub;
        cout << ",\nand ten million tubs = ";
        cout << 10 * million * tub << "\n";

        cout << "mint = " << mint << " and a million mints = ";
        cout << million * mint << "\n";
        return 0;
}
```

Here is the output:

```
tub = 3.333333, a million tubs = 3333333.250000,
and ten million tubs = 33333332.000000
mint = 3.333333 and a million mints = 3333333.333333
```

COMPATIBILITY NOTES

By default, older versions of C++, when displaying floating-point values, display six digits to the right of the decimal, as in 2345.831541. Newer versions, by default, display a total of six digits (2345.83), switching to E notation once values reach a million or greater (2.34583E+06).

However, the nondefault display modes, such as *fixed* in the example, display six digits to the right of the decimal in both old and new versions.

The default setting also suppresses trailing zeros, displaying 23.4500 as 23.45. Implementations differ in how they respond to using *setf(ios::fixed, ios::floatfield)* to override the default settings. Older versions, such as Borland C++ 3.1, will suppress trailing zeros in this mode, also. Newer versions, such as Microsoft Visual C++ and Borland C++ 4.0, show them, as seen in Listing 3-7.

Program Notes

Normally *cout* drops trailing zeros. For example, it would display 3333333.250000 as 3333333.25. Our call to *cout.setf()* overrides that behavior, at least for new implementations. The main thing to note here is how *float* has less precision than *double*. Both *tub* and *mint* are initialized to *10.0 / 3.0*. That should evaluate to 3.33333333333333333...(etc.). Since *cout* prints six figures to the right of the decimal, we can see that both *tub* and *mint* are accurate that far. But, after the program multiplies each number by a million, we see that *tub* diverges from the proper value after the seventh 3. We describe this by saying *tub* is good to seven significant figures. (Our system guarantees six significant figures for *float*, but that's the worst-case scenario.) The type *double* variable, however, shows thirteen 3s, so it's good to at least thirteen significant figures. The system guarantees fifteen, so we shouldn't be surprised. Also note that multiplying a million *tubs* by ten didn't quite result in the correct answer, again pointing out the limitations of *float* precision.

The *ostream* class to which *cout* belongs has class member functions that give you precise control on how the output is formatted—field widths, places to the right of the decimal point, decimal form or E form, and so on. Chapter 15 outlines those choices. This book's examples keep it simple and usually just use the << operator. Occasionally, this practice displays more digits than necessary, but that causes only esthetic harm. If you do mind, you can skim through Chapter 15 to see how to use the formatting methods. Don't, however, expect to fully follow the explanations at this point.

Floating-Point Constants

When you write a floating-point constant in a program, in which floating-point type does the program store it? By default, floating-point constants like 8.24 and 2.4E8 are type *double*. If you want a constant to be type *float*, use an f or F suffix. For type *long double*, use an l or L suffix.

```
1.234f          // a float constant
2.45E20F        // a float constant
2.345324E28     // a double constant
2.2L            // a long double constant
```

Floating-Point Advantages and Disadvantages

Floating-point numbers have two advantages over integers. First, they can represent values between the integers. Second, because of the scaling factor, they can represent a much greater range of values. On the other hand, floating-point operations are slower than integer operations, at least on computers without math coprocessors, and you can lose precision. Listing 3-8 illustrates the last point.

Listing 3-8 *fltadd.cpp*

```
// fltadd.cpp -- precision problems with float
#include <iostream.h>
int main(void)
{
        float a = 2.34E+22;
        float b = a + 1;

        cout << "a = " << a << "\n";
        cout << "b - a = " << b - a << "\n";
        return 0;
}
```

The program takes a number, adds 1, then subtracts the original number. That should result in a value of 1. Does it? Here is the output for one system:

```
a = 2.34e+22
b - a = 0
```

The problem is that 2.34E+22 represents a number with 23 digits to the left of the decimal place. By adding 1, we are attempting to add 1 to the 23rd digit in that number. But type *float* can represent only the first 6 or 7 digits in a number, so trying to change the 23rd digit has no effect on the value.

C++ Arithmetic Operators

Perhaps you have warm memories of doing arithmetic drills in grade school. You can give that same pleasure to your computer. C++ uses operators to do arithmetic. It provides operators for five basic arithmetic calculations: addition, subtraction, multiplication, division, and taking the modulus. Each of these operators uses two values (called *operands*) to calculate a final answer. Together, the operator and its operands constitute an *expression*. For instance, consider the following statement:

```
int wheels = 4 + 2;
```

The values *4* and *2* are operands, the + symbol is the addition operator, and *4 + 2* is an expression whose value is *6*.

Here are C++'s five basic arithmetic operators:

- The + operator adds its operands. For instance, 4 + 20 evaluates to 24.

- The – operator subtracts the second operand from the first. For instance, 12 – 3 evaluates to 9.

- The * operator multiplies its operands. For instance, 28 * 4 evaluates to 112.

- The / operator divides its first operand by the second. For instance, 1000 / 5 evaluates to 200.

- The % operator finds the modulus of its first operand with respect to the second. That is, it produces the remainder of dividing the first by the second. For instance, 19 % 6 is 1, since 6 goes into 19 three times with a remainder of 1. Both operands must be integer types. If one of the operands is negative, the sign of the result depends on the implementation.

Of course, you can use variables as well as constants for operands. Listing 3-9 does just that. Because the % operator works with integers only, we'll save it for a later example.

Listing 3-9 *arith.cpp*

```
// arith.cpp -- some C++ arithmetic
#include <iostream.h>
int main(void)
{
        float hats, heads;

        cout << "Enter a number: ";
        cin >> hats;
        cout << "Enter another number: ";
        cin >> heads;

        cout << "hats = " << hats << "; heads = " << heads << "\n";
        cout << "hats + heads = " << hats + heads << "\n";
        cout << "hats - heads = " << hats - heads << "\n";
        cout << "hats * heads = " << hats * heads << "\n";
        cout << "hats / heads = " << hats / heads << "\n";
        return 0;
}
```

Here's sample output for Borland C++ 3.1. As you can see, you can trust C++ to do simple arithmetic:

```
Enter a number: 50.25
Enter another number: 11.17
hats = 50.25; heads = 11.17
hats + heads = 61.419998
hats - heads = 39.080002
hats * heads = 561.29248
hats / heads = 4.498657
```

Well, maybe you can't trust it completely. Adding *11.17* to *50.25* should yield *61.42*, but the output reports *61.419998*. This is not an arithmetic problem; it's a problem with the limited capacity of type *float* to represent significant figures.

Remember, C++ guarantees just six significant figures for *float*. If you round 61.419998 to six figures, you get 61.4200, which is the correct value to the guaranteed precision. The moral is that if you need greater accuracy, use *double* or *long double*.

Which Order: Operator Precedence and Associativity

Can you trust C++ to do complicated arithmetic? Yes, but you need to know the rules C++ uses. For instance, many expressions involve more than one operator. That can raise questions about which operator gets applied first. For example, consider this statement:

```
int flyingpigs = 3 + 4 * 5;   // 35 or 23?
```

The 4 appears to be an operand for both the + and the * operators. C++ uses *precedence* rules to decide which operator goes first. The arithmetic operators follow the usual algebraic precedences, with multiplication, division, and taking the modulus being done before addition and subtraction. Thus *3 + 4 * 5* means *3 + (4 * 5)*, not *(3 + 4) * 5*. So the answer is 23, not 35. Of course, you can use parentheses to enforce your own priorities. Appendix D shows the precedences for all the C++ operators. In it, you'll note that *, /, and % are all in the same row. That means they have equal precedence. Similarly, addition and subtraction share a lower precedence.

Sometimes the precedence list is not enough. Consider the next statement:

```
float logs = 120 / 4 * 5;     // 150 or 6?
```

Once again 4 is an operand for two operators. But the / and * operators have the same precedence, so precedence alone doesn't tell the program whether to first divide 120 by 4 or to first multiply the 4 by 5. Since the first choice leads to a result of 150 and the second to a result of 6, the choice is an important one. When two operators have the same precedence, C++ looks at whether the operators have a left-to-right *associativity* or a right-to-left associativity. Left-to-right associativity means that if two operators acting upon the same operand have the same precedence, apply the left-hand operator first. For right-to-left associativity, apply the right-hand operator first. The associativity information, too, is in Appendix D. There you'll see that multiplication and division associate left-to-right. That means we use 4 with the leftmost operator first. That is, we divide 120 by 4, getting 30, then multiply the result by 5 to get 150.

Note that the precedence and associativity rules come into play only when two operators share the same operand. Consider the following expression:

```
int dues = 20 * 5 + 24 * 6;
```

Operator precedence tells us two things: the program must evaluate *20 * 5* before doing addition, and the program must evaluate *24 * 6* before doing addition. But neither precedence nor associativity says which multiplication takes place first. You might think that associativity says to do the leftmost multiplication first, but in this case, the two * operators do not share a common operand, so the rules don't apply. In fact, C++ leaves it to the implementation to decide which order works best on a system. For our example, either order gives the same result, but there are circumstances in which the order can make a difference. You'll see one when Chapter 5 discusses the increment operator.

Division Diversions

You have yet to see the rest of the story about the division operator. The behavior of this operator depends on the type of the operands. If both operands are integers, C++ performs integer division. That means any fractional part of the answer is discarded, making the result an integer. If one or both operands are floating-point values, then the fractional part is kept, making the result floating-point. Listing 3-10 illustrates how C++ division works with different types of values. Like Listing 3-8, this invokes the *setf()* member function to modify how the data are displayed.

Listing 3-10 *divide.cpp*

```
// divide.cpp -- integer and floating-point division
#include <iostream.h>
int main(void)
{
        cout.setf(ios::fixed, ios::floatfield);        // force fixed-point display
        cout << "Integer division: 9/5 = " << 9 / 5  << "\n";
        cout << "Floating-point division: 9.0/5.0 = ";
        cout << 9.0 / 5.0 << "\n";
        cout << "Mixed division: 9.0/5 = " << 9.0 / 5  << "\n";
        cout << "double constants: 1e7/9.0 = ";
        cout << 1.e7 / 9.0 <<  "\n";
        cout << "float constants: 1e7f/9.0f = ";
        cout << 1.e7f / 9.0f <<  "\n";
        return 0;
}
```

COMPATIBILITY NOTES

Some C++ implementations based on pre-ANSI C compilers don't support the f suffix for floating-point constants. If you find yourself facing this problem, you can replace *1.e7f / 9.0f* with *(float) 1.e7 /(float) 9.0*.
Some implementations will suppress trailing zeros.

Here is the output for one implementation (Metrowerks CodeWarrior for the Macintosh):

```
Integer division: 9/5 = 1
Floating-point division: 9.0/5.0 = 1.800000
Mixed division: 9.0/5 = 1.800000
double constants: 1e7/9.0 = 1111111.111111
float constants: 1e7f/9.0f = 1111111.125000
```

The first output line shows that dividing the integer 9 by the integer 5 yields the integer 1. The fractional part of 4 / 5 (or 0.8) is discarded. You'll see a practical use for this kind of division when we discuss the modulus operator. The next two lines show that when at least one of the operands is floating-point, you get a floating-point answer of 1.8. Actually, when you try to combine mixed types, C++ converts all the concerned types to the same type. We'll discuss these automatic conversions later in the chapter. The relative precisions of the last two lines show that the result is type *double* if both operands are *double* and that it is *float* if both operands are *float*. Remember, floating-point constants are type *double* by default.

A GLIMPSE OF OPERATOR OVERLOADING

In Listing 3-10, the division operator represents three distinct operations: *int* division, *float* division, and *double* division. C++ uses the context, in this case the type of operands, to determine which operator is meant. The process of using the same symbol for more than one operation is called *operator overloading*. C++ has a few examples of overloading built into the language. C++ also lets you extend operator overloading to user-defined classes, so what we've seen here is a precursor of an important OOP property. See Figure 3-4.

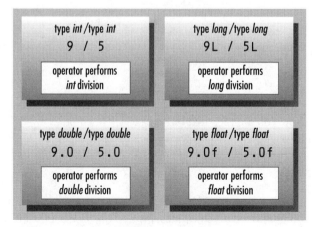

Figure 3-4 Different divisions

The Modulus Operator

Most people are more familiar with addition, subtraction, multiplication, and division than with the modulus operator, so we'll take a moment to illustrate the latter operator in action. The modulus operator, recall, returns the remainder of an integer division. In combination with integer division, the modulus operator is particularly useful in problems that require dividing a quantity into different integral units, such as converting inches to feet and inches or converting dollars to quarters, dimes, nickels, and pennies. In Chapter 2, we converted weight in British stone to pounds. Listing 3-11 reverses the process, converting weight in pounds to stone. The stone, you remember, is 14 pounds, and most British bathroom scales are calibrated in this unit. The program uses integer division to find the largest number of whole stone in the weight, and it uses the modulus operator to find the number of pounds left over.

Listing 3-11 *modulus.cpp*

```
// modulus.cpp -- uses % operator to convert lbs to stone
#include <iostream.h>
int main(void)
{
        const int Lbs_per_stn = 14;
        int lbs;

        cout << "Enter your weight in pounds: ";
        cin >> lbs;
        int stone = lbs / Lbs_per_stn;      // whole stone
        int pounds = lbs % Lbs_per_stn;     // remainder in pounds
        cout << lbs << " pounds are " << stone;
        cout << " stone, " << pounds << " pound(s).\n";
        return 0;
}
```

Here is a sample run:

```
Enter your weight in pounds: 191
191 pounds are 13 stone, 9 pound(s).
```

In the expression *lbs / Lbs_per_stn*, both operands are type *int*, so the computer performs integer division. With a *lbs* value of *191*, the expression evaluates to *13*. The product of 13 and 14 is 182, so the remainder of dividing 14 into 191 is 9, and that's the value of *lbs % Lbs_per_stn*. Now you are prepared technically, if not emotionally, to respond to questions about your weight when you travel in Great Britain.

Type Conversions

C++'s profusion of types lets you match the type to the need. It also complicates life for the computer. For instance, adding two *short* values may involve different hardware instructions than adding two *long* values. With four integer types (counting *char*) and three floating-point types, the computer can have a lot of different cases to handle, especially if you start mixing types. To help deal with this potential mishmash, C++ makes many type conversions automatically:

❬ C++ converts values when you assign a value of one type to a variable of another type.

❬ C++ converts values when you combine mixed types in expressions.

❬ C++ converts values when you pass arguments to functions.

If you don't understand what happens in these automatic conversions, you may find some program results baffling, so we'll outline the rules. C++ also lets you force type conversions, and we'll look at that process, too.

Conversion on Assignment

C++ is fairly liberal in allowing you to assign a numeric value of one type to a variable of another type. Whenever you do so, the value is converted to the type of the receiving variable. For instance, suppose *so_long* is type *long,* that *thirty* is type *short,* and you have the following statement in a program:

```
so_long = thirty;      // assigning a short to a long
```

The program will take the value of *thirty* (typically a 2-byte value) and expand it to a *long* value (typically a 4-byte value) upon making this assignment.

Assigning a value to a type with a greater range usually poses no problem. For instance, assigning a *short* value to a *long* variable doesn't change the value; it just gives the value a few more bytes in which to laze about. However, assigning a large *long* value like 2111222333 to a *float* variable will result in losing some precision. Because *float* may have just six significant figures, the value may be rounded to 2.11122E9. Table 3-3 points out some possible conversion problems.

Assigning floating-point values to integer types poses a couple of problems. First, converting floating-point to integer results in truncating the number (discarding the fractional part). Second, a *float* value may be too big to fit in a cramped *int* variable. In that case, C++ doesn't define what the result should be; that means different implementations can respond differently. Listing 3-12 shows what happens in Borland C++.

Conversion	Potential Problems
bigger floating-point type to smaller floating-point type, such as *double* to *float*	loss of precision (significant figures)
	original value may be out of range for target type, in which case result is undefined
floating-point type to integer type	loss of fractional part

continued on next page

continued from previous page

Conversion	Potential Problems
	value may be out of range for target type, in which case result is undefined
bigger integer type to smaller integer type, such as *long* to *short*	original value may be out of range for target type, typically just the low-order bytes are copied

Table 3-3 Potential conversion problems

Listing 3-12 assign.cpp

```
// assign.cpp -- type changes on assignment
#include <iostream.h>
int main(void)
{
        float tree = 3;        // int converted to float
        int guess = 3.9832;    // float converted to int
        int debt = 3.0E12;     // result not defined in C++
        cout << "tree = " << tree << "\n";
        cout << "guess = " << guess << "\n";
        cout << "debt = " << debt << "\n";
        return 0;
}
```

Here is the output:

```
tree = 3
guess = 3
debt = 0
```

Here *tree* is assigned the floating-point value *3.0*. However, because *cout* drops trailing zeros on output, it displays *3.0* as *3*. Assigning *3.9832* to the *int* variable *guess* causes the value to be truncated to *3*; C++ uses truncation (discarding the fractional part) and not rounding (finding the closest integer value) when converting floating-point types to integer types. Finally, note that the *int* variable *debt* is unable to hold the value *3.0E12*. This creates a situation in which C++ doesn't define the result. On our system, *debt* wound up with the value *0*. Well, that's a novel way to solve massive indebtedness!

Some compilers will warn you of possible data loss for those statements that initialize integer variables to floating-point values. Also, the value displayed for *debt* varies from compiler to compiler.

Conversions in Expressions

Next, let's consider what happens when you combine two different numeric types in one expression. C++ makes two kinds of automatic conversions in that case. First, some types are converted automatically whenever they occur. Second, some types are converted when they are combined with other types in an expression.

First, let's examine the automatic conversions. When evaluating expressions, C++ converts *char, unsigned char, signed char,* and *short* values to *int*. This is called *integral promotion*. For instance, consider the following fowl statements:

```
short chickens = 20;                  // Line 1
short ducks = 35;                     // Line 2
short fowl = chickens + ducks;        // Line 3
```

To execute the statement on line 3, a C++ program takes the values of *chickens* and *ducks* and converts both to *int*. Then the program converts the result back to type *short* because the answer is assigned to a type *short* variable. You may find this a bit round-about, but it does make sense. The *int* type generally is chosen to be the computer's most natural type, which means the computer probably does calculations fastest for that type.

There's one more integral promotion: *unsigned short* type is converted to *int* if *short* is smaller than *int*. If the two types are the same size, *unsigned short* is converted to *unsigned int*. This rule ensures that there's no data loss in promoting *unsigned short*.

Then there are the conversions that take place when you combine different types arithmetically, such as adding an *int* to a *float*. When an operation involves two types, the smaller is converted to the larger. For instance, the program in Listing 3-10 divided *9.0* by *5*. Because *9.0* is type *double*, the program converted *5* to type *double* before doing the division. More generally, the compiler goes through a checklist to determine which conversions to make in an arithmetic expression. Here's the list—the compiler goes through it in order:

1. If either operand is type *long double,* the other operand is converted to *long double.*

2. Otherwise, if either operand is *double,* the other operand is converted to *double.*

3. Otherwise, if either operand is *float,* the other operand is converted to *float.*

4. Otherwise the operands are integer types and the integral promotions are made.

5. In that case, if either operand is *unsigned long,* then the other operand is converted to *unsigned long.*

6. Otherwise, if one operand is *long int* and the other is *unsigned int,* the conversion depends on the relative sizes of the two types. If *long* can represent possible *unsigned int* values, *unsigned int* is converted to *long.*

7. Otherwise, both operands are converted to *unsigned long.*

8. Otherwise, if either operand is *long,* the other is converted to *long.*

9. Otherwise, if either operand is *unsigned int,* the other is converted to *unsigned int.*

10. If the compiler reaches this point in the list, both operands should be *int*.

ANSI C follows the same rules as C++, but classic K&R C had slightly different rules. For instance, classic C always promoted *float* to *double* even if both operands were *float*.

Conversions in Passing Arguments

Normally, C++ function prototyping controls type conversions for argument passing, and we'll discuss that in Chapter 7. However, it is possible, although usually unwise, to waive prototype control for argument passing. In that case, C++ applies the integral promotions to the *char* and *short* types (signed and unsigned). Also, to preserve compatibility with huge amounts of code in classic C, C++ promotes *float* arguments to *double* when passing them to a function unless the argument has been prototyped as type *float*.

Type Casts

C++ also empowers you to force type conversions explicitly via the *type cast* mechanism. (C++ is such a masterful language.) The type cast comes in two forms. For example, to convert an *int* value stored in a variable called *thorn* to type *long,* you can use either of the following expressions:

```
(long) thorn    // makes the value of thorn type long
long (thorn)    // makes the value of thorn type long
```

More generally, you can do the following:

```
(typename) value    // converts value to typename type
typename (value)    // converts value to typename type
```

The first form is straight C. The second form is pure C++. The idea behind the new form is to make a type cast look like a function call. This makes type casts for the built-in types look like the type conversions you can design for user-defined classes.

Listing 3-13 gives a short illustration of both forms. Imagine that the first section of this listing is part of a powerful ecological modeling program that does floating-point calculations that get converted to integral numbers of birds and animals. The results you get depend on when you convert. The calculation for *auks* first adds the floating-point values, then converts the sum to *int* upon assignment. But the calculations for *bats* and *coots* first use type casts to convert the floating-point values to *int,* then sum the values. The final part of the program shows how you can use a type cast to display the ASCII code for a type *char* value.

Listing 3-13 *typecast.cpp*

```
// typecast.cpp -- forcing type changes
#include <iostream.h>
```

```
int main(void)
{
        int auks, bats, coots;

        // the following statement adds the values as double,
        // then converts the result to int
        auks = 19.99 + 11.99;

        // these statements add values as int
        bats = (int) 19.99 + (int) 11.99;      // old C syntax
        coots = int (19.99) + int (11.99);     // new C++ syntax
        cout << "auks = " << auks << ", bats = " << bats;
        cout << ", coots = " << coots << '\n';

        char ch = 'Z';
        cout << "The code for " << ch << " is ";     // print as char
        cout << int(ch) << '\n';                     // print as int
        return 0;
}
```

Here is the result:

```
auks = 31, bats = 30, coots = 30
The code for Z is 90
```

First, adding *19.99* to *11.99* yields *31.98*. When this value is assigned to the *int* variable *auks*, it's truncated to *31*. But using type casts truncates the same two values to *19* and *11* before addition, making the *bats* result and the *coots* result both *30*. The final *cout* statement uses a type cast to convert a type *char* value to *int* before displaying the result. This causes *cout* to print the value as an integer rather than as a character.

The program illustrates two reasons for using type casting. First, you may have values that are stored as type *double* but are used to calculate a type *int* value. For instance, you may be fitting a position to a grid or modeling integer values, such as populations, with floating-point numbers. You may desire that calculations treat the values as *int*. Type casting lets you do so directly. Notice that you get a different result, at least for these values, when you convert to *int* and add than you do when you add first, then convert to *int*.

The second part of the program shows the most common reason for using a type cast—compelling data in one form to meet a different expectation. In this listing, for instance, the *char* variable *ch* holds the code for the letter Z. Using *cout* with *ch* displays the character Z, because *cout* zeros in on the fact that *ch* is type *char*. But by type casting *ch* to type *int* we get *cout* to shift to *int* mode and print the ASCII code stored in *ch*.

Summary

C++'s basic types fall into two groups. One group consists of values that are stored as integers. The second group consists of values that are stored in a floating-point format. The integer types differ from each other in the amount of memory used to store values and in whether they are signed or unsigned. From smallest to largest, the integer types are *char, signed char, unsigned char, short, unsigned short, int, unsigned int, long,* and *unsigned long.* C++ guarantees that *char* is large enough to hold any member of the system's character set, that *short* is at least 2 bytes, that *int* is at least as big as *short,* and that *long* is at least 4 bytes and at least as large as *int.* The exact sizes depend on the implementation.

Characters are represented by their numeric codes. The I/O system determines whether a code is interpreted as a character or as a number.

The floating-point types can represent fractional values and values much larger than integers can. The three floating-point types are called *float, double,* and *long double.* C++ only guarantees that *float* is no larger than *double,* and that *double* is no larger than *long double.* Typically, however, *float* uses 4 bytes of memory, *double* uses 8 bytes, and *long double* uses 10 to 16 bytes of memory.

By providing a variety of types in different sizes and in both signed and unsigned varieties, C++ lets you match the type to particular data requirements.

C++ uses operators to provide the usual arithmetic support for numeric types: addition, subtraction, multiplication, division, and taking the modulus. When two operators seek to operate on the same value, C++'s precedence and associativity rules determine which operation takes place first.

C++ converts values from one type to another when you assign values to a variable, when you mix types in arithmetic, and when you use type casts to force type conversions. Many type conversions are "safe," meaning they can be made with no loss or alteration of data. For instance, you can convert an *int* value to a *long* value with no problems. Others, such as converting floating-point types to integer types, require more care.

At first, you may find the large number of basic C++ types a little excessive, particularly when you take the various conversion rules into account. But most likely you'll eventually find occasions when one of the types is just what you need at the time, and you'll thank C++ for having it.

 Review Questions

1. Why does C++ have more than one integer type?

2. Define the following:

    a. A *short* integer with the value 80

    b. An *unsigned int* integer with the value 42110

    c. An integer with the value 3000000000

3. What safeguards does C++ provide to keep you from exceeding the limits of an integer type?

4. What is the distinction between 33L and 33?

5. Consider the two C++ statements that follow. Are they equivalent?
```
char grade = 65;
char grade = 'A';
```

6. How could you use C++ to find out which character the code 88 represents? Come up with at least two ways.

7. Assigning a *long* value to a *float* can result in round-off error. What about assigning *long* to *double?*

8. Evaluate the following expressions as C++ would:

   a. 8 * 9 + 2

   b. 6 * 3 / 4

   c. 3 / 4 * 6

   d. 6.0 * 3 / 4

   e. 15 % 4

9. Suppose x1 and x2 are two type *double* variables that you want to add as integers and assign to an integer variable. Construct a C++ statement for doing so.

 # Programming Exercises

1. Write a short program that asks for your height in integer inches and then converts your height to feet and inches. Have the program use the underscore character to indicate where to type the response. Also use a *const* type.

2. Write a program that asks how many miles you have driven and how many gallons of gasoline you used, then reports the miles per gallon your car got. Or, if you prefer, the program can request distance in kilometers, petrol in litres, and report the result European style, in litres per 100 kilometers.

CHAPTER 4

DERIVED TYPES

You will learn about the following in this chapter:

◇ Creating and using arrays

◇ Creating and using strings

◇ The *getline()* and *get()* methods for reading strings

◇ Mixing string and numeric input

◇ Creating and using structures

◇ Creating and using enumerations

◇ Creating and using pointers

◇ Managing dynamic memory with *new* and *delete*

◇ Creating dynamic arrays

◇ Creating dynamic structures

◇ Automatic, static, and dynamic storage

You've developed a computer game called User-Hostile in which players match wits with a cryptic and abusive computer interface. Now you need to write a program that keeps track of your monthly game sales for a five-year period. Or you want to inventory your accumulation of hacker-hero trading cards. You'll soon conclude you need something more than C++'s simple basic types to meet these data requirements, and C++ offers something more—*derived* types. These are types built from the basic integer and floating-point types. The most far-reaching derived type is the class, that bastion of OOP towards which we are progressing. But C++ also supports several more modest derived types taken from C. The *array*, for example, can hold several values of the same type. A particular kind of array can hold a *string*, which is a series of characters. *Structures* can hold several values of differing types. Then there are *pointers*, which are variables that tell a computer where data is placed. We'll examine all these derived forms (excepting classes) in this chapter and also take a first look at *new* and *delete* and how they can be used to manage data.

Introducing Arrays

An array is a data form that can hold several values all of one type. For instance, an array can hold 60 type *int* values to represent five years of game sales data. Or an array can hold 12 *short* values representing the number of days in each month. Or an array can hold 365 *float* values indicating your food expenses for each day of the year. Each value is stored in a separate array *element,* and the computer stores all the elements consecutively in memory.

To create an array, you use a declaration statement. An array declaration should indicate three things:

- ❧ The type of value to be stored in each element
- ❧ The name of the array
- ❧ The number of elements in the array

For example, the declaration

```
short months[12];     // creates array of 12 short
```

creates an array named *months* having 12 elements, each able to hold a type *short* value. Each element, in essence, is a variable that can be treated like a simple variable.

The general form for declaring an array is this:

typename arrayname[*arraysize*];

The expression *arraysize,* which is the number of elements, must be a constant, such as 10 or a *const* value; or a constant expression, such as 8 * *sizeof (int),* for which all values are known at the time compilation takes place. In particular, *arraysize* cannot be a variable whose value is set while the program is running. However, later this chapter will show you how to use the *new* operator to get around that restriction.

THE ARRAY AS DERIVED TYPE

An array is called a derived type because it is based on some other type. You can't simply declare that something is an array; it always has to be an array of some particular type. So there is no generalized array type. Instead, there are many specific array types, such as array of *char* or array of *long.* For example, consider this declaration:

```
float loans[20];
```

The type for *loans* is not "array"; rather, it is "array of *float.*" This emphasizes that the *loans* array is derived from the *float* type.

Much of the usefulness of the array comes from the fact that you can access the array elements individually. The way to do this is to use a *subscript,* or *index,* to number the elements. C++ array numbering starts with 0. (This is nonnegotiable; you have

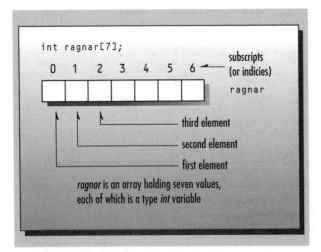

Figure 4-1 Creating an array

to start at 0. Pascal and BASIC users will have to adjust.) C++ uses a bracket notation with the index to specify an array element. For example, *months[0]* is the first element of the *months* array, and *months[11]* is the last element. See Figure 4-1. Thus an array declaration lets you create a lot of variables with a single declaration, and you then can use an index to identify individual elements.

The yam analysis program in Listing 4-1 demonstrates a few properties of arrays, including declaring an array, assigning values to array elements, and initializing an array.

Listing 4-1 *arrayone.cpp*

```
// arrayone.cpp -- small arrays of integers
#include <iostream.h>
int main(void)
{
        int yams[3];    // creates array with three elements
        yams[0] = 7;    // assign value to first element
        yams[1] = 8;
        yams[2] = 6;

        int yamcosts[3] = {20, 30, 5}; // create, initialize array
// NOTE: If your C++ compiler or translator can't initialize
// this array, use static int yamcosts[3] instead of
// int yamcosts[3]

        cout << "Total yams = ";
        cout << yams[0] + yams[1] + yams[2] << "\n";
        cout << "The package with " << yams[1] << " yams costs ";
        cout << yamcosts[1] << " cents per yam.\n";
        int total = yams[0] * yamcosts[0] + yams[1] * yamcosts[1];
```

continued on next page

continued from previous page

```
        total = total + yams[2] * yamcosts[2];
        cout << "The total yam expense is " << total << " cents.\n";

        cout << "\nSize of yams array = " << sizeof yams;
        cout << " bytes.\n";
        cout << "Size of one element = " << sizeof yams[0];
        cout << " bytes.\n";
        return 0;
}
```

COMPATIBILITY NOTE

C++ Release 2.0, as well as ANSI C, allows you to initialize ordinary arrays defined in a function. However, in some implementations that use a C++ translator instead of a true compiler, the C++ translator creates C code for a C compiler that is not fully ANSI C compliant. In that case you can get an error message like the following example from a Sun C++ 2.0 system:

```
"arrayone.cc", line 10: sorry, not implemented: initialization of
yamcosts (automatic aggregate) Compilation failed
```

The fix is to use the keyword *static* in the array declaration:

```
// pre-ANSI initialization
static int yamcosts[3] = {20, 30, 5};
```

The keyword *static* causes the compiler to use a different memory scheme for storing the array, one that allows initialization even under pre-ANSI C. Chapter 8 discusses *static* in the section about storage classes.

Here is the output:

```
Total yams = 21
The package with 8 yams costs 30 cents per yam.
The total yam expense is 410 cents.

Size of yams array = 6 bytes.
Size of one element = 2 bytes.
```

Program Notes

First, the program creates a three-element array called *yams*. Because *yams* has three elements, the elements are numbered from 0 to 2, and *arrayone.cpp* uses index values of 0–2 to assign values to the three individual elements. Each individual *yam* element is an *int* with all the rights and privileges of an *int* type. So *arrayone.cpp* can, and does, assign values to elements, add elements, multiply elements, and display elements.

The program uses the long way to assign values to the *yam* elements. C++ also lets you initialize array elements within the declaration statement. Listing 4-1 uses this shortcut to assign values to the *yamcosts* array:

```
int yamcosts[3] = {20, 30, 5};
```

Simply provide a comma-separated list of values (the *initialization list*) enclosed in braces. The spaces in the list are optional. If you don't initialize an array that's defined inside a function, the element values remain undefined. That means the element takes on whatever value previously resided at that location in memory.

Next, the program uses the array values in a few calculations. This part of the program looks cluttered with all the subscripts and brackets. The *for* loop, coming up in Chapter 5, provides a powerful way for dealing with arrays and eliminates the need to write each element explicitly. Meanwhile, we'll stick to small arrays.

The *sizeof* operator, you recall, returns the size, in bytes, of a type or data object. Note that if you use the *sizeof* operator with an array *name,* you get the number of bytes in the whole array. But if you use *sizeof* with an array *element,* you get the size, in bytes, of the element. This illustrates that *yams* is an array, but *yams[1]* is just an *int.*

More on Array Initialization

C++ has several rules about initializing an array. They restrict when you can do it, and they determine what happens if the number of array elements doesn't match the number of values in the initializer. Let's examine these rules.

You can use the initialization form only when defining the array. You cannot use it later, and you cannot assign one array wholesale to another:

```
int cards[4] = {3, 6, 8, 10};      // okay
int hand[4];                       // okay
hand[4] = {5, 6, 7, 9};            // not allowed
hand = cards;                      // not allowed
```

However, you always can use subscripts and assign values to the elements of an array individually.

When initializing an array, you can provide fewer values than array elements. In that case, just the first part of the array is initialized. For example, the following statement initializes only the first two elements of *hoteltips:*

```
float hoteltips[5] = {5.0, 2.5};
```

If you partially initialize an array, the compiler will set the remaining elements to zero.

If you leave the square brackets empty when you initialize an array, the C++ compiler will count the elements for you. Suppose, for instance, you make this declaration:

```
short things[] = {1, 5, 3, 8};
```

The compiler will make *things* an array of four elements.

 LETTING THE COMPILER DO IT

Normally, letting the compiler count the number of elements is poor practice, for its count may be different from what you think it is. However, this approach may be safer for initializing a character array to a string, as you'll see soon. And if your main concern is that the program, not you, know how large an array is, you can do something like this:

```
short things[] = {1, 5, 3, 8};
int num_elements = sizeof things / sizeof (short);
```

Whether this is useful or lazy depends on the circumstances.

 Strings

A string is a series of characters stored in consecutive bytes of memory. This implies that you can store a string in an array of *char*, with each character kept in its own array element. Strings provide a convenient way to store text information such as messages to the user (*"Please tell me your secret Swiss bank account number: "*) or responses from the user (*"You must be joking"*). C++ strings, like C strings, have a special feature: the last character of every C++ string is the *null* character. This character, written \0, is the character with ASCII code 0, and it serves to mark the string's end. For instance, consider the following two declarations:

```
char dog [5] = { 'b', 'e', 'a', 'u', 'x'};   // not a string!
char cat[5] = {'f', 'a', 't', 's', '\0'};   // a string!
```

Both arrays are arrays of *char*, but only the second is a string. The null character plays a fundamental role in C++ strings. For example, C++ has many functions that handle strings, including those used by *cout*. They all work by processing a string character-by-character until they reach the null character. If you ask *cout* to display a nice string like *cat* above, it displays the first four characters, detects the null character, and stops. But if you are ungracious enough to tell *cout* to display the *dog* array above, which is not a string, *cout* would print the five letters in the array, then keep marching through memory byte-by-byte, interpreting each byte as a character to print, until it reached a null character. Since null characters, which really are bytes set to zero, tend to be common in memory, the damage usually is contained quickly; nonetheless, you should not treat nonstring character arrays as strings.

The *cat* array example makes initializing an array to a string look tedious—all those single quotes and then having to remember the null character. Don't worry. There is a better way to initialize a character array to a string. Just use a quoted string, called a *string constant* or *string literal*, as in the following:

```
char bird[10] = "Mr. Cheep"; // the \0 is understood
char fish[] = "Bubbles";     // let the compiler count
```

Quoted strings always include the terminating null character implicitly, so you don't have to spell it out. See Figure 4-2. Also, the various C++ input facilities for reading a string from keyboard input into a *char* array automatically add the terminating null character for you. (If, when running the program in Listing 4-1, you discovered you had to use the keyword *static* to initialize an array, you'll have to use it with these *char* arrays, too.)

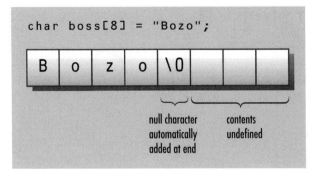

Figure 4-2 Initializing an array to a string

Of course, you should make sure the array is large enough to hold all the characters of the string, including the null character. Initializing a character array with a string constant is one case where it may be safer to let the compiler count the number of elements for you. There is no harm, other than wasted space, in making an array larger than the string. That's because functions that work with strings are guided by the location of the null character, not by the size of the array. C++ imposes no limits on the length of a string.

RULE

When determining the minimum array size needed to hold a string, remember to include the terminating null character in your count.

Note that a string constant (double quotes) is not interchangeable with a character constant (single quotes). A character constant such as *'S'* is a shorthand notation for the code for a character. So, on an ASCII system, *'S'* is just another way of writing *83*. Thus the statement

```
char shirt_size = 'S';        // this is fine
```

assigns the value *83* to *shirt_size*. But *"S"* represents the string consisting of two characters, the *S* and the *\0* characters. Even worse, *"S"* actually represents the memory address at which the string is stored. So a statement like

```
char shirt_size = "S";        // illegal type mismatch
```

attempts to assign a memory address to *shirt_size!* Because an address is a separate type in C++, a C++ compiler won't allow this sort of nonsense. (We'll return to this point later, after we've discussed pointers.) But C, which is more lenient about checking type agreement, will let this statement pass with a warning, and the result will be garbage.

String Concatenation

Sometimes a string may be too long to conveniently fit on one line of code. C++ lets you *concatenate* string constants, that is, combine two quoted strings into one. Indeed, any two string constants separated only by white space (spaces, tabs, and newlines) automatically are joined into one. Thus all the following output statements are equivalent to each other:

```
cout << "I'd give my right arm to be" " a great violinist.\n";
cout << "I'd give my right arm to be a great violinist.\n";
cout << "I'd give my right ar"
   "m to be a great violinist.\n";
```

Note that the join doesn't add any spaces to the joined strings. The first character of the second string immediately follows the last character, not counting \0, of the first string. The \0 character from the first string is replaced by the first character of the second string.

Using Strings in an Array

The two most common ways of getting a string into an array are to initialize an array to a string constant and to read keyboard or file input into an array. Listing 4-2 demonstrates these approaches by initializing one array to a quoted string and using *cin* to place an input string in a second array. The program also uses the standard library function *strlen()* to get the length of a string. The standard *string.h* header file provides declarations for this and many other string-related functions.

Listing 4-2 *strings.cpp*

```
// strings.cpp -- storing strings in an array
#include <iostream.h>
#include <string.h>  // for the strlen() function
int main(void)
{
        const int ArSize = 15;
        char name1[ArSize];        // empty array
        char name2[ArSize] = "C++owboy"; // initialized array
// NOTE: some implementations may require the static keyword
// to initialize the array name2

        cout << "Howdy! I'm " << name2;
        cout << "! What's your name?\n";
        cin >> name1;
        cout << "Well, " << name1 << ", your name has ";
        cout << strlen(name1) << " letters and is stored\n";
        cout << "in an array of " << sizeof name1 << " bytes.\n";
        cout << "Your initial is " << name1[0] << ".\n";
        name2[3] = '\0';       // null character
```

```
        cout << "Here are the first 3 characters of my name: ";
        cout << name2 << "\n";
        return 0;
}
```

Here is a sample run:

```
Howdy! I'm C++owboy! What's your name?
Basicman
Well, Basicman, your name has 8 letters and is stored
in an array of 15 bytes.
Your initial is B.
Here are the first 3 characters of my name: C++
```

Program Notes

What can you learn from this example? First, note that the *sizeof* operator gives the size of the entire array—15 bytes. But the *strlen()* function returns the size of the string stored in the array and not the size of the array itself. Also, *strlen()* counts just the visible characters and not the null character. Thus it returns a value of *8,* not *9,* for the length of *Basicman.* So if *cosmic* is a string, the minimum array size for holding that string is *strlen(cosmic) + 1.*

Because *name1* and *name2* are arrays, you can use an index to access individual characters in the array. For instance, the program uses *name1[0]* to find the first character in that array. Also, the program sets *name2[3]* to the null character. That makes the string end after three characters even though more characters remain in the array. See Figure 4-3.

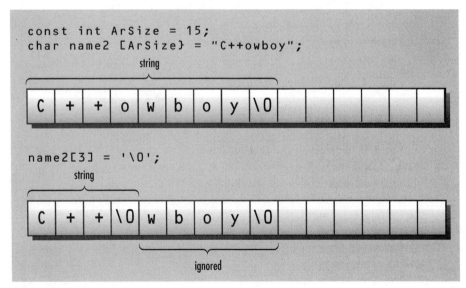

Figure 4-3 Shortening a string with \0

Adventures in String Input

The *strings.cpp* program has a blemish that was concealed through the often useful technique of carefully selected sample input. Listing 4-3 removes the veils and shows that string input can be tricky.

Listing 4-3 *instr1.cpp*

```
// instr1.cpp - reading more than one string
#include <iostream.h>
const int ArSize = 20;
int main(void)
{
        char name[ArSize];
        char dessert[ArSize];

        cout << "Enter your name:\n";
        cin >> name;
        cout << "Enter your favorite dessert:\n";
        cin >> dessert;
        cout << "I have some delicious " << dessert;
        cout << " for you, " << name << ".\n";
        return 0;
}
```

The intent is simple: read a user's name and favorite dessert from the keyboard, then display the information. Here is a sample run:

```
Enter your name:
Alistair Dreeb
Enter your favorite dessert:
I have some delicious Dreeb for you, Alistair.
```

We didn't even get a chance to respond to the dessert prompt! The program showed it, then immediately moved on to display the final line.

The problem lies with how *cin* determines when you've finished entering a string. You can't enter the null character from the keyboard, so *cin* needs some other means for locating the end of a string. The *cin* technique is to use white space—spaces, tabs, and newlines—to delineate a string. This means *cin* reads just one word when getting input for a character array. Once it reads this word, *cin* automatically adds the terminating null character when placing the string into the array.

The practical result in our example is that *cin* reads *Alistair* as the entire first string and puts it into the *name* array. This leaves poor *Dreeb* still sitting in the input queue. When *cin* searches the input queue for the response to the favorite dessert question, it finds *Dreeb* still there. Then *cin* gobbles up *Dreeb* and puts it into the *dessert* array. See Figure 4-4.

Another problem, which didn't surface in the sample run, is that the input string might turn out to be longer than the destination array. Using *cin* as we did offers no protection against placing a 30-character string in a 20-character array.

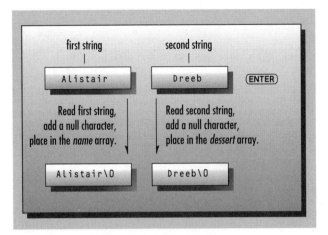

Figure 4-4 The *cin* view of string input

Many programs depend on string input, so it's worth our while to explore this topic further. We'll have to draw upon some of the more advanced features of *cin,* as described in Chapter 15.

Line-Oriented Input: *getline()* and *get()*

To be able to enter whole phrases instead of single words as a string, you need a different approach to string input. Specifically, you need a line-oriented method instead of a word-oriented method. You are in luck, for the *istream* class, of which *cin* is an example, has some line-oriented class member functions. The *getline()* function, for example, reads a whole line, using the newline character transmitted by the (ENTER) key to mark the end of input. You invoke this method by using *cin.getline()* as a function call. The function takes two arguments. The first argument is the name of the array destined to hold the line of input, and the second argument is a limit on the number of characters to be read. If this limit is, say, 20, the function will read no more than 19 characters, leaving room to automatically add the null character at the end. The *getline()* member function stops reading input when it reaches this numeric limit or when it reads a newline, whichever comes first.

For example, suppose you want to use *getline()* to read a name into the 20-element *name* array. You would use this call:

```
cin.getline(name,20);
```

This would read the entire line into the *name* array, providing that the line consisted of 19 or fewer characters. (The *getline()* member function also has an optional third argument, which we leave to Chapter 15 to discuss.)

Listing 4-4 modifies Listing 4-3 to use *cin.getline()* instead of a simple *cin.* Otherwise, the program is unchanged.

Listing 4-4 *instr2.cpp*

```
// instr2.cpp -- reading more than one word with getline
#include <iostream.h>
int main(void)
{
        const int ArSize = 20;
        char name[ArSize];
        char dessert[ArSize];

        cout << "Enter your name:\n";
        cin.getline(name, ArSize);    // reads through newline
        cout << "Enter your favorite dessert:\n";
        cin.getline(dessert, ArSize);
        cout << "I have some delicious " << dessert;
        cout << " for you, " << name << ".\n";
        return 0;
}
```

COMPATIBILITY NOTE

Some early C++ versions didn't fully implement all facets of the current C++ I/O package. In particular, the *getline()* member function wasn't always available. If this affects you, just read about this example and go on to the next one, which uses a member function that predated *getline()*. Also, early releases of Turbo C++ implemented *getline()* slightly differently so that it did store the newline character in the string.

Here is some sample output:

```
Enter your name:
Melanie Ploops
Enter your favorite dessert:
Raspberry Torte
I have some delicious Raspberry Torte for you, Melanie Ploops.
```

The program now reads complete names and delivers the user her just desserts! The *getline()* function conveniently gets a line at a time. It reads input through the newline character marking the end of the line, but it doesn't save the newline character. Instead, it replaces it with a null character when storing the string. See Figure 4-5.

Let's try another approach. The *istream* class has another member function, called *get()*, which comes in several variations. One variant works much like *getline()*. It takes the same arguments, interprets them the same way, and reads to the end of a line. But instead of reading and discarding the newline character, *get()* leaves that character in the input queue. In Listing 4-5, we replace *getline()* with *get()*. (Some older C++ implementations have *get()* but no *getline()*.)

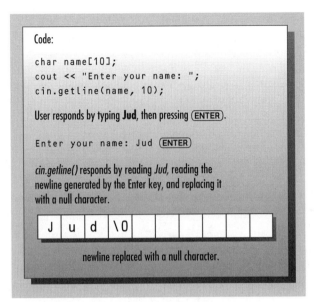

Figure 4-5 *getline()* reads and replaces the newline

Listing 4-5 *instr3.cpp*

```
// instr3.cpp - reading more than one word with get
#include <iostream.h>
int main(void)
{
        const int ArSize = 20;
        char name[ArSize];
        char dessert[ArSize];

        cout << "Enter your name:\n";
        cin.get(name, ArSize);          // reads to newline
        cout << "Enter your favorite dessert:\n";
        cin.get(dessert, ArSize);
        cout << "I have some delicious " << dessert;
        cout << " for you, " << name << ".\n";
        return 0;
}
```

Here is a sample run:

```
Enter your name:
Sparky Bandersnoot
Enter your favorite dessert:
I have some delicious  for you, Sparky Bandersnoot.
```

Darn! The program gets the name correctly, but it seems to have lost the dessert. Because *cin.get()* reads up to, but not including, the newline character, the newline character is still in the input queue after the first call to *cin.get()*. The second call to *cin.get()* then sees this lone newline as marking an empty line, so it reads the null string into the dessert array. The null string is a string consisting of one character—the null character. So poor Sparky winds up with the null dessert.

At this point, we seem to have taken a minor step backwards in our tasteful efforts at dessert distribution, although it's quite educational to see how *cin.get(name, ArSize)* differs from its *cin.getline()* sibling. As you have seen, *cin.getline()* reads a line, including the newline, which it discards, while *cin.get(name, ArSize)* reads just up to the newline, which it leaves in the input queue for the next input operation. Nonetheless, you can use *cin.get()* to get past the pesky newline by dipping further into the *istream*'s bag of member functions (discussed fully in Chapter 15). The way to success is to use another variant of *cin.get()*. If you use this function with *no* arguments, it reads the next character in the input queue and discards it. This is exactly what we want now. We can use *cin.get(name, ArSize)* to read all the first line of input except for the newline character. Then we can use *cin.get()* to read and discard the newline character. That will cause the call to *cin.get(dessert, ArSize)* to begin at the start of the next line.

There are two ways to add the argument-free *cin.get()* call to the program. The first is as a separate statement:

```
cin.get(name, ArSize); // read line
cin.get();             // read, discard next character
```

The second is to concatenate, or join, the two class member functions as follows:

```
cin.get(name, ArSize).get(); // concatenate member functions
```

What makes this possible is that *cin.get(name, ArSize)* returns the *cin* object, which then is used as the object invoking the *get()* function. Similarly, the statement

```
cin.getline(name1, ArSize).getline(name2, ArSize);
```

will read two consecutive input lines into the arrays *name1* and *name2*; it's equivalent to making two separate calls to *cin.getline()*.

We use concatenation in Listing 4-6. And when we develop classes, we'll show you how to incorporate this feature into your class definitions.

Listing 4-6 *instr4.cpp*

```
// instr4.cpp - reading more than one word with get() & get()
#include <iostream.h>
int main(void)
{
    const int ArSize = 20;
    char name[ArSize];
    char dessert[ArSize];

    cout << "Enter your name:\n";
    cin.get(name, ArSize).get();    // read string, newline
```

```
        cout << "Enter your favorite dessert:\n";
        cin.get(dessert, ArSize);
        cout << "I have some delicious " << dessert;
        cout << " for you, " << name << ".\n";
        return 0;
}
```

COMPATIBILITY NOTE

Some older C++ versions didn't implement the *get()* variant having no arguments. They do, however, implement yet another *get()* variant, one that takes a single *char* argument. To use it instead of the argumentless *get()*, you need to declare a *char* variable first:

```
int ch;
cin.get(name, ArSize).get(ch);
```

You can use this code instead of what is found in Listing 4-6. Chapters 5 and 15 further discuss the *get()* variants.

Here is a sample run:

```
Enter your name:
Mai Parfait
Enter your favorite dessert:
Chocolate Mousse
I have some delicious Chocolate Mousse for you, Mai Parfait.
```

One thing to note is how C++ allows multiple versions of functions providing they have different argument lists. If you use, say, *cin.get(name, ArSize)*, the compiler notices you're using the form that puts a string into an array and sets up the appropriate member function. If, instead, you use *cin.get()*, the compiler realizes you want the form that reads one character. We'll explore the feature, called *function overloading*, in Chapter 8.

Why use *get()* instead of *getline()* at all? First, older implementations may not have *getline()*. Second, *get()* lets you be a bit more careful. Suppose for example, you've used *get()* to read a line into an array. How can you tell if it read the whole line rather than stopping because the array was filled? Look at the next input character. If it is a newline, then the whole line was read. If it is not a newline, then there is still more input on that line. Chapter 15 will investigate this method.

ANSI/ISO C++ DRAFT UPDATE

What happens after *getline()* or *get()* reads an empty line? The standard practice is that the next input statement picks up where the last *getline()* or *get()* left off. At the time of this writing, however, the draft standard says the effect of reading an empty line with these functions is to set something called the *failbit*. The implications of this act are that further input is blocked but that you can restore input with the following command:

```
cin.clear();
```

Some oppose this new behavior, so it remains to be seen if the final standard will sanction it. Chapter 15 has more details.

Mixing String and Numeric Input

Mixing numeric input with line-oriented string input can cause problems. Consider the simple program in Listing 4-7.

Listing 4-7 *numstr.cpp*

```
// numstr.cpp -- following number input with line input
#include <iostream.h>
int main(void)\
{
        cout << "What year was your house built?\n";
        int year;
        cin >> year;
        cout << "What is its street address?\n";
        char address[80];
        cin.getline(address, 80);
        cout << "Year built: " << year << "\n";
        cout << "Address: " << address << "\n";
        return 0;
}
```

Running this program would look something like this:

```
What year was your house built?
1966
What is its street address?
Year built: 1966
Address:
```

You never get the opportunity to enter the address. The problem is that when *cin* reads the year, it leaves the newline generated by the (ENTER) key in the input queue. Then *cin.getline()* reads the newline as an empty line and assigns a null string to the *address* variable. The fix is to read and discard the newline before reading the address. This can be done several ways, including using *get()* with no argument or with a *char* argument, as described in the preceding example. This call can be made separately:

```
cin >> year;
cin.get();   // or cin.get(ch);
```

Or you can concatenate the call, making use of the fact that the expression *cin >> year* returns the *cin* object:

```
(cin >> year).get();  // or (cin >> year).get(ch);
```

If you make one of these changes to Listing 4-7, it will work properly:

```
What year was your house built?
1966
```

```
What is its street address?
43821 Unsigned Short Street
Year built: 1966
Address: 43821 Unsigned Short Street
```

C++ programs frequently use pointers instead of arrays to handle strings. We'll take up that aspect of strings after learning a bit about pointers. Meanwhile, let's take a look at another derived type, the structure.

Introducing Structures

Suppose you want to store information about a basketball player. You might want to store his or her name, salary, height, weight, scoring average, free-throw percentage, assists, and so on. You'd like some sort of data form that could hold all this information in one unit. An array won't do. Although an array can hold several items, each item has to be the same type. That is, one array can hold twenty *ints* and another can hold ten *floats*, but a single array can't store *ints* in some elements and *floats* in other elements.

The answer to your desire (the one about storing information about a basketball player) is the C++ *structure*. The structure is a more versatile data form than an array, for a single structure can hold several kinds of data. This enables you to unify your data representation by storing all the related basketball information in a single structure variable. If you want to keep track of a whole team, you can use an array of structures. The structure type also is a stepping-stone to that bulwark of C++ OOP, the class. So learning a little about structures now takes us that much closer to the OOP heart of C++.

A structure is a user-definable type, with a template serving to define the type's data properties. Once you define the type, you can create variables of that type. Thus creating a structure is a two-part process. First, you define a *structure description*. It describes and labels the different types of data that can be stored in a structure. Then you create a *structure variable,* or, more generally, a *structure data object,* that follows the description's plan.

For example, suppose that Bloataire, Inc., wants to create a type to describe members of its product line of designer inflatables. In particular, the type should hold the name of the item, its volume in cubic feet, and its selling price. Here is a structure description meeting those needs:

```
struct inflatable   // structure description
{
        char name[20];
        float volume;
        double price;
};
```

The keyword *struct* indicates that the code defines the layout for a structure. The identifier *inflatable* is the name, or *tag,* we'll use for this form; that makes *inflatable* the name for the new type. Thus you now can create variables of type *inflatable* just as you create variables of type *char* or *int*. Next, between braces, comes the list of data types to be held in the structure. Each list item is a declaration statement. You can use any of the C++ types here, including arrays and other structures. We've used an array of *char,* suitable for storing a string, and a *float* and a *double.* Each individual item in the list is called a structure *member,* so the *inflatable* structure has three members. See Figure 4-6.

Once you have the template, you can create variables of that type:

```
inflatable hat;          // hat is a structure variable of type inflatable
inflatable woopie_cushion;   // type inflatable variable
inflatable mainframe;        // type inflatable variable
```

If you're familiar with C structures, you'll notice (probably with pleasure) that C++ allows you to drop the keyword *struct* when declaring structure variables:

```
struct inflatable goose;     // keyword struct required in C
inflatable vincent;          // keyword struct not required in C++
```

In C++, the structure tag is used just like a fundamental type name. This change emphasizes that a structure declaration defines a new type. It also removes omitting *struct* from the list of curse-inducing errors.

Given that *hat* is type *inflatable,* you use the membership operator (.) to access individual members. For instance, *hat.volume* refers to the *volume* member of the structure, and *hat.price* refers to the *price* member. Similarly, *vincent.price* is the *price* member of a *vincent* variable. Because the *price* member is declared as type *double, hat.price* and *vincent.price* both are equivalent to type *double* variables and can be used in any manner an ordinary type *double* variable can. So *hat* is a structure but *hat.price* is a *double.* By the way, the method we used to access class member functions like *cin.getline()* has its origins in the method used to access structure member variables like *vincent.price.*

Listing 4-8 illustrates these points about a structure. Also, it shows how to initialize one.

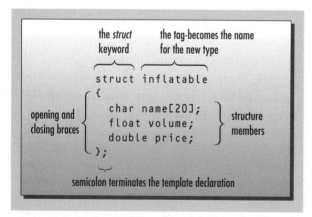

Figure 4-6 Parts of a structure description

Listing 4-8 *structur.cpp*

```
// structur.cpp -- a simple structure
#include <iostream.h>
struct inflatable    // structure template
{
        char name[20];
        float volume;
        double price;
};

int main(void)
{
        inflatable guest =
        {
                "Glorious Gloria", // name value
                1.88,           // volume value
                29.99           // price value
        };    // guest is a structure variable of type inflatable
                // It's initialized to the indicated values
        inflatable pal =
        {
                "Audacious Arthur",
                3.12,
                32.99
        }; // pal is a second variable of type inflatable
// NOTE: some implementations require using
// static inflatable guest =

        cout << "Expand your guest list with " << guest.name;
        cout << " and " << pal.name << "!\n";
    // pal.name is the name member of the pal variable
        cout << "You can have both for $";
        cout << guest.price + pal.price << "!\n";
        return 0;
}
```

COMPATIBILITY NOTE

Just as some implementations have not yet implemented the ability to initialize an ordinary array defined in a function, they also haven't implemented the ability to initialize an ordinary structure defined in a function.
Again, the solution is to use the keyword *static* in the declaration.

Here is the output:

```
Expand your guest list with Glorious Gloria and Audacious Arthur!
You can have both for $62.98!
```

Program Notes

One important matter is where to place the structure declaration. There are two choices for *structur.cpp*. We could have placed the declaration *inside* the *main()* function, just after the opening brace. The second choice, and the one we made, is to place it *outside* of *main()* and preceding it. When a declaration occurs outside of any function, it's called an *external* declaration. For this program, there is no practical difference between the two choices. But for programs consisting of two or more functions, the difference can be crucial. The external declaration can be used by all the functions following it, while the internal declaration can be used only by the function in which the declaration is found. Most often, you will want an external structure declaration so that all the functions can use structures of that type. See Figure 4-7.

Variables, too, can be defined internally or externally, with external variables being shared among functions. (Chapter 8 will look further into that topic.) C++ practices discourage using external variables but encourage using external structure declarations.

```
                                    #include <iostream.h>
external declaration—can be         struct parts
used in all functions in file       {
                                        unsigned long part_number;
                                        float part_cost;
                                    };
                                    void mail (void);
                                    int main(void)
                                    {
local declaration—can be                struct perks
used only in this function              {
                                            int key_number;
                                            char car[12];
                                        };
type parts variable                     parts chicken;
type perks variable                     perks mr_blug;
                                        ...
                                        ...
                                    }
                                    void mail(void)
                                    {
type parts variable                     parts studebaker;
can't declare a type                    ...
perks variable here                     ...
                                    }
```

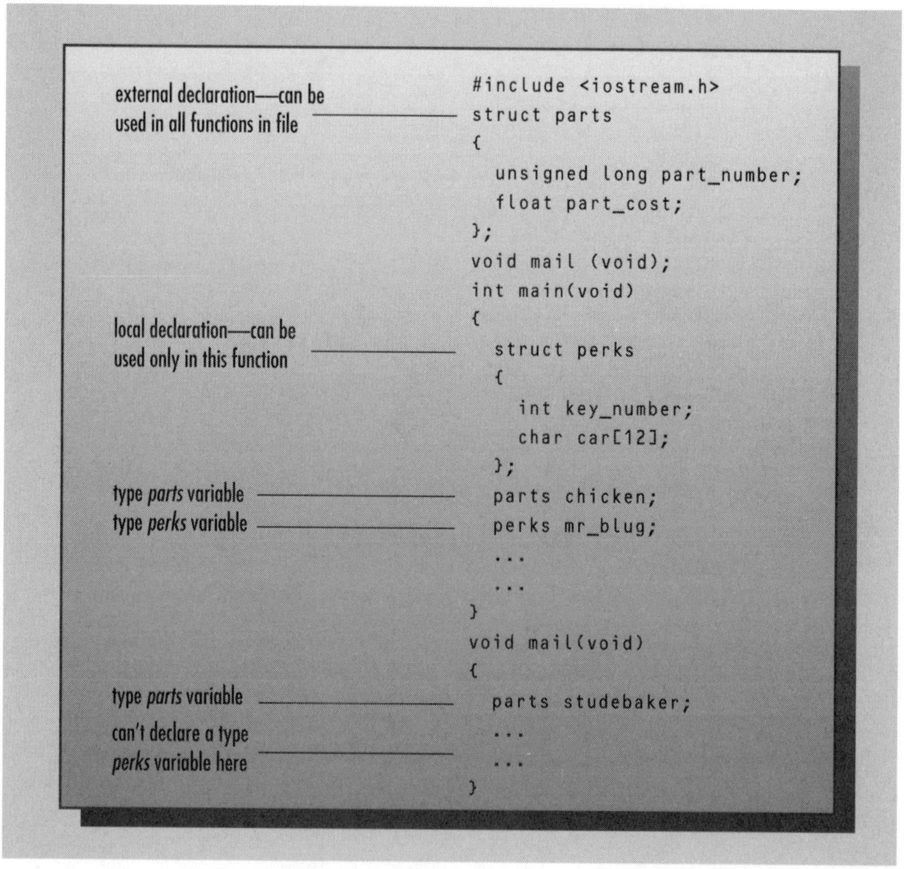

Figure 4-7 Local and external structure declarations

Next, notice the initialization procedure:

```
inflatable guest =
{
        "Glorious Gloria", // name value
        1.88,          // volume value
        29.99          // price value
};
```

As with arrays, you use a comma-separated list of values enclosed within a pair of braces. The program places one value per line, but you can place them all on the same line. Just remember to separate items with a comma:

```
inflatable duck = {"Daffny", 0.12, 9.98};
```

Each member of the structure can be initialized to the appropriate kind of datum. For instance, the *name* member is a character array, so we can initialize it to a string.

Each structure member is treated as a variable of that type. Thus *pal.price* is a *double* variable and *pal.name* is an array of *char*. And when the program uses *cout* to display *pal.name*, it displays the member as a string. By the way, because *pal.name* is a character array, we can use subscripts to access individual characters in the array. For example, *pal.name[0]* is the character A. But *pal[0]* is meaningless, since *pal* is a structure, not an array.

Other Structure Properties

C++ attempts to make using user-defined types as similar as possible to using built-in types. For example, you can pass structures as arguments to functions, and you can have a function use a structure as a return value. Also, you can assign one structure to another of the same type by using the assignment operator (=). Doing so causes each member of one structure to be set to the value of the corresponding member in the other structure, even if the member is an array. We'll defer passing and returning structures until we discuss functions in Chapter 7, but we can take a quick look at structure assignment now. Listing 4-9 provides an example.

Listing 4-9 *assgn_st.cpp*

```
// assgn_st.cpp -- assigning structures
#include <iostream.h>
struct inflatable
{
        char name[20];
        float volume;
        double price;
};
int main(void)
{
        inflatable bouquet =
        {
```

continued on next page

continued from previous page

```
                    "sunflowers",
                    0.20,
                    12.49
            };
// NOTE: some implementations may require using
//       static inflatable bouquet =

            inflatable choice;
            cout << "bouquet: " << bouquet.name << " for $";
            cout << bouquet.price << "\n";

            choice = bouquet;  // assign one structure to another
            cout << "choice: " << choice.name << " for $";
            cout << choice.price << "\n";
            return 0;
}
```

Here's the output:

```
bouquet: sunflowers for $12.49
choice: sunflowers for $12.49
```

As you can see, the *choice* structure has its members assigned the same values that were stored in the *bouquet* structure. This kind of assignment is called *memberwise assignment*.

You can combine defining a structure form with creating structure variables. To do so, follow the closing brace with the variable name or names:

```
struct perks
{
        int key_number;
        char car[12];
} mr_smith, ms_jones; // two perks variables
```

You even can initialize a variable you create in this fashion:

```
struct perks
{
        int key_number;
        char car[12];
} mr_glitz =
{
        7,              // value for mr_glitz.key_number member
        "Packard"       // value for mr_glitz.car member
};
```

However, keeping the structure definition separate from the variable declarations usually makes a program easier to read and follow.

Another thing you can do with structures is create a structure with no type name. You do this by omitting a tag name while simultaneously defining a structure form and a variable:

```
struct     // no tag
{
```

```
    int x;  // 2 members
    int y;
} position;  // a structure variable
```

This creates one structure variable called *position*. You can access its members with the membership operator, as in *position.x,* but there is no general name for the type. So you can't subsequently create other variables of the same type. We won't be using this limited form of structure.

Aside from the fact a C++ program can use the structure tag as a type name, C structures have all the features we've discussed so far for C++ structures. But C++ structures go further. Unlike C structures, for instance, C++ structures can have member functions in addition to member variables. But these more advanced features most typically are used with classes rather than structures, so we'll discuss them when we cover classes. For now, let's continue our survey of derived types.

Enumerations

The C++ *enum* facility provides an alternative means to *const* for creating symbolic constants. It also lets you define new types, but in a fairly restricted fashion. The syntax for using *enum* resembles structure syntax. For instance, consider the following statement:

```
enum spectrum {red, orange, yellow, green, blue, purple, indigo};
```

This statement does two things:

❧ It makes *spectrum* the name of a new type; *spectrum* is termed an *enumeration,* much as a *struct* variable is called a structure.

❧ It establishes *red, orange, yellow,* and so on, as symbolic constants for the integer values 0–6. These constants are called *enumerators.*

By default, enumerators are assigned integer values starting with *0* for the first enumerator, *1* for the second enumerator, and so forth. You can override the default by explicitly assigning integer values. We'll show you how later.

You can use an enumeration name to declare a variable of that type:

```
spectrum band;
```

An enumeration variable has some special properties, which we'll examine now.

The only valid values that can be assigned to an enumeration variable are the enumerator values used in defining the type. Thus we have the following:

```
band = blue;   // valid, blue is an enumerator
band = 2000;   // invalid, 2000 not an enumerator
```

Thus a *spectrum* variable is limited to just seven possible values. Some compilers issue a compiler error if you attempt to assign an invalid value, while others issue a warning. For maximum portability, you should regard assigning a non-*enum* value to an *enum* variable as an error.

Only the assignment operator is defined for enumerations. In particular, arithmetic operations are not defined:

```
band = orange;         // valid
++band;                // not valid
band = orange + red;   // not valid
...
```

However, some implementations do not honor this restriction. That may make it possible to violate the type limits. For example, if *band* has the value *violet*, or *6*, then *++band*, if valid, increments *band* to *7*, which is not a valid value for a *spectrum* type. Again, for maximum portability, you should adopt the stricter limitations.

Enumerators are of integer type and can be promoted to type *int*, but *int* types are not automatically converted to the enumeration type:

```
int color = blue;      // valid, spectrum type promoted to int
band = 3;              // invalid, int not converted to spectrum
color = blue + red;    // valid: blue, red converted to int
...
```

Note that even though 3 corresponds to the enumerator *green*, assigning 3 to *band* is a type error. (However, read about the draft standard's revised rules below.) But assigning *green* to *band* is fine, for they both are type *spectrum*. Again, some implementations do not enforce this restriction. In the expression *blue + red*, addition isn't defined for enumerators. However, both enumerators are converted to type *int*, and the result is type *int*. So, although addition is not defined for enumerations, you can use enumerations in arithmetic expressions.

You can assign an *int* value to an *enum* providing that the value is valid and that you use an explicit type cast:

```
band = color(3);       // typecast 3 to type color
```

What if you try to type cast an inappropriate value? The result is undefined, meaning that the attempt won't be flagged as an error but that you can't rely upon the value of the result:

```
band = color(40003);   // undefined
```

As you can see, the rules governing enumerations are fairly restrictive. In practice, enumerations have been used more often as a way of defining related symbolic constants than as a means of defining a new type. For instance, you might use an enumeration to define symbolic constants for a *switch* statement. (See Chapter 6 for an example.) If you plan to use just the constants and not create variables of the enumeration type, you can omit an enumeration type name:

```
enum {red, orange, yellow, green, blue, purple, indigo};
```

Setting Enumerator Values

You can set enumerator values explicitly by using the assignment operator:

```
enum bits{one = 1, two = 2, four = 4, eight = 8};
```

The assigned values must be integers. You also can define just some of the enumerators explicitly:

```
enum bigstep{first, second = 100, third};
```

In this case *first* is 0 by default. Subsequent uninitialized enumerators are larger by one than their predecessors. So *third* would have the value *101*.

Finally, you can create more than one enumerator with the same value:

```
enum {zero, null = 0, one, numero_uno = 1};
```

Here, both *zero* and *null* are *0,* and both *one* and *numero_uno* are *1*. In earlier versions of C++, you could assign only *int* values (or values that promote to *int)* to enumerators, but the proposed standard allows you to use type *long* values.

ANSI/ISO Update

Recently, the ANSI/ISO committee has refined the concept of which values can be assigned validly by type cast to an enumeration variable. Each enumeration has a *range,* and any integer value in the range, even if it's not an enumerator value, can be assigned, using a type cast, to an enumeration variable. For instance, suppose *myflag* is a type *bits* (as defined above) variable. Then the following is valid:

```
myflag = bits(6);     // valid, because 6 is in bits range
```

Here 6 is not one of the enumerations, but it lies in the range defined by the enumerations.

The range is defined as follows. First, to find the upper limit, take the largest enumerator value. Find the smallest power of two greater than this largest value, subtract one, and that is the upper end of the range. For example, the largest *bigstep* value, as defined above, is *101*. The smallest power of two greater than this is *128,* so the upper end of the range is *127*. Next, to find the lower limit, find the smallest enumerator value. If it is zero or greater, the lower limit for the range is zero. If the smallest enumerator is negative, use the same approach as described for finding the upper limit, but toss in a minus sign. For example, if the smallest enumerator is *-6,* the next power of two (times a minus sign) is *-8,* and the lower limit is *-7*.

The idea is that the compiler can choose how much space to hold an enumeration. It might use 1 byte, or less, for an enumeration with a small range, and 4 bytes for an enumeration with type *long* values.

Pointers and the Free Store

At the beginning of Chapter 3 we mentioned three fundamental properties that a computer program must keep track of when storing data. To save the book the wear and tear of your thumbing back to that chapter, here are those properties again:

◀ Where the information is stored

◀ What value is kept there

◀ What kind of information is stored

You've used one strategy for accomplishing these ends: defining a simple variable. The declaration statement provides the type and a symbolic name for the value. It also causes the program to allocate memory for the value and to keep track of the location internally.

Let's look at a second strategy now, one that becomes particularly important in developing C++ classes. This strategy is based on *pointers,* which are variables that store addresses of values rather than the values themselves. But before discussing pointers, let's see how to find addresses explicitly for ordinary variables. Just apply the address operator, represented by &, to a variable to get its location. Listing 4-10 demonstrates this operator.

Listing 4-10 *address.cpp*

```
// address.cpp - using the & operator to find addresses
#include <iostream.h>
int main(void)
{
        int donuts = 6;
        double cups = 4.5;

        cout << "donuts value = " << donuts;
        cout << " and donuts address = " << &donuts << "\n";
// NOTE: you may need to use unsigned (&donuts)
//    and unsigned (&cups)
        cout << "cups value = " << cups;
        cout << " and cups address = " << &cups << "\n";
        return 0;
}
```

COMPATIBILITY NOTE

cout is a smart object, but some versions are smarter than others. Thus, some implementations may fail to recognize pointer types. In that case, you have to type cast the address to a recognizable type, such as *unsigned int.* The appropriate type cast depends on the memory model. The default DOS memory model uses a 2-byte address, hence *unsigned int* is the proper cast. Some DOS memory models, however, use a 4-byte address, which requires a cast to *unsigned long.*

Here is the output:

```
donuts value = 6 and donuts address = 0x8566fff4
cups value = 4.5 and cups address = 0x8566ffec
```

When displaying addresses, *cout* uses hexadecimal notation because that is the usual notation used to describe memory. Our implementation stores *cups* at a lower memory location than *donuts*. The difference between the two addresses is 0x8566fff4 -0x8566ffec, or 8. This makes sense, for *cups* is type *double*, which uses 8 bytes. (In case you're interested, these particular representations of addresses reflect the PC method of describing an address by a segment value and by an offset. The segment value, 8566 in this case, identifies the block of memory being used to store the data; it's the actual address divided by 16. The offsets, *ffec* and *fff4* in this case, represent memory position relative to the beginning of the segment. PC programs can use 2-byte pointers holding just the offset if all the data is in one segment. Or they can use 4-byte pointers, with the first 2 bytes holding the segment value and the second 2 bytes holding the offset. Borland C++ displays the 4-byte form even if a program internally uses the 2-byte form.

Using ordinary variables, then, treats the value as a named quantity and the location as a derived quantity. Now let's look at the pointer strategy, one that is essential to the C++ programming philosophy of memory management. (See the note on Pointers and the C++ Philosophy.)

POINTERS AND THE C++ PHILOSOPHY

Object-oriented programming differs from traditional procedural programming in OOP's emphasis on making decisions during run time instead of compile time. Run time means while a program is running, and compile time means when the compiler is putting a program together. A runtime decision is like, when on vacation, choosing what sights to see depending on the weather and your mood at the moment, while a compile-time decision is more like adhering to a preset schedule regardless of the conditions. Runtime decisions provide the flexibility to adjust to current circumstances. For instance, consider allocating memory for an array. The traditional way is to declare an array. To declare an array in C++, you have to commit yourself to a particular array size. Thus the array size is set when the program is compiled, so it is a compile-time decision. Perhaps you think an array of 20 elements is sufficient 80% of the time, but that occasionally the program will need to handle 200 elements. So to be safe, you use an array with 200 elements. This results in your program wasting memory most of the times it's used. OOP tries to make a program more flexible by delaying such decisions until run time. That way, once the program is running, you can tell it you'll need only 20 elements one time or that you need 205 elements another time. In short, you make the array size a runtime decision. To make this approach possible, the language has to allow you to create an array—or equivalent—while the program runs. The C++ method, as you'll soon see, involves using the keyword new to request the correct amount of memory and using pointers to keep track of where the newly allocated memory is found.

The new strategy for handling stored data switches things around by treating the *location* as the named quantity and the *value* as a derived quantity. A special type of variable—the pointer—holds the address of a value. Thus the name of the pointer represents the location. Applying the * operator, called the *indirect value* or the *dereferencing* operator, yields the value at the location. (Yes, this is the same * symbol used for multiplication; C++ uses the context to determine whether you mean multiplication or dereferencing.) Suppose, for example, that *manly* is a pointer. Then *manly* represents an address, and *manly represents the value at that address. The combination *manly becomes equivalent to an ordinary type *int* variable. Listing 4-11 demonstrates these points. It also shows how to declare a pointer.

Listing 4-11 *pointer.cpp*

```
// pointer.cpp -- our first pointer variable
#include <iostream.h>
int main(void)
{
        int updates = 6;      // declare a variable
        int * p_updates;      // declare pointer to an int

        p_updates = &updates; // assign address of int to pointer

// NOTE: some users may need to type cast the addresses
//    in cout statements to unsigned or unsigned long

        // express values two ways
        cout << "Values: updates = " << updates;
        cout << ", *p_updates = " << *p_updates << "\n";

        // express address two ways
        cout << "Addresses: &updates = " << &updates;
        cout << ", p_updates = " << p_updates << "\n";

        // use pointer to change value
        *p_updates = *p_updates + 1;
        cout << "Now updates = " << updates << "\n";
        return 0;
}
```

Here is the output:

```
Values: updates = 6, *p_updates = 6
Addresses: &updates = 0x85b0fff4, p_updates = 0x85b0fff4
Now updates = 7
```

As you can see, the *int* variable *updates* and the pointer variable *p_updates* are just two sides of the same coin. The *updates* variable represents the value as primary and uses the & operator to get the address, while the *p_updates* variable represents the address as primary and uses the * operator to get the value. See Figure 4-8. And because *p_updates* points to *updates*, *p_updates and *updates* are completely equivalent. So we

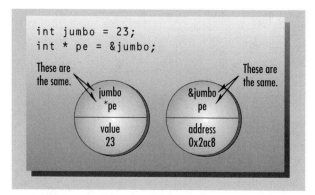

```
int jumbo = 23;
int * pe = &jumbo;
```

These are
the same.

jumbo
*pe

value
23

These are
the same.

&jumbo
pe

address
0x2ac8

Figure 4-8 Two sides of a coin

can use *p_updates* exactly as we would use a type *int* variable. As the program shows, we can even assign values to *p_updates*. Doing so changes the value of the pointed-to value, *updates*.

Declaring and Initializing Pointers

Let's examine the process of declaring pointers. A computer needs to keep track of the type of value a pointer refers to. For instance, the address of a *char* looks the same as the address of a *double*, but *char* and *double* use different numbers of bytes and different internal formats for storing values. Therefore, a pointer declaration must specify what type of data the pointer points to.

For example, our program has this declaration:

```
int * p_updates;
```

This states that the combination * *p_updates* is type *int*. Because the * operator is used by applying it to a pointer, the *p_updates* variable itself must be a pointer. We say that *p_updates* points to type *int*. We also say that the type for *p_updates* is pointer-to-*int* or, more concisely, *int* *. To repeat: *p_updates* is a pointer (an address), and *p_updates* is an *int* and not a pointer. Also see Figure 4-9.

Incidentally, the uses of space around the * operator are optional. Traditionally, C programmers have used this form:

```
int *ptr;
```

This accentuates the idea that the combination *ptr* is a type *int* value. Many C++ programmers, on the other hand, use this form:

```
int* ptr;
```

This emphasizes the idea that *int** is a type, the type pointer-to-*int*. Where you put the spaces makes no difference to the compiler. Be aware, however, that the declaration

```
int* p1, p2;
```

creates one pointer (*p1*) and one ordinary *int* (*p2*). You need an * for each pointer variable name.

RULE

In C++, the combination *int* * is a derived *type name*, the type pointer-to-*int*.

You use the same syntax to declare pointers to other types:

```
double * tax_ptr; // tax_ptr points to type double
char * str;    // str points to type char
```

Because we declare *tax_ptr* as a pointer-to-*double*, the compiler knows that **tax_ptr* is a type *double* value. That is, it knows that **tax_ptr* represents a number stored in floating-point format and occupying (on most systems) 8 bytes. A pointer variable is never simply a pointer. It is always a pointer to some type. So *tax_ptr* is type pointer-to-*double* (or type *double* *) and *str* is type pointer-to-*char* (or *char* *). Although both are pointers, they are pointers of two different types. Thus, like arrays, pointers are derived from other types.

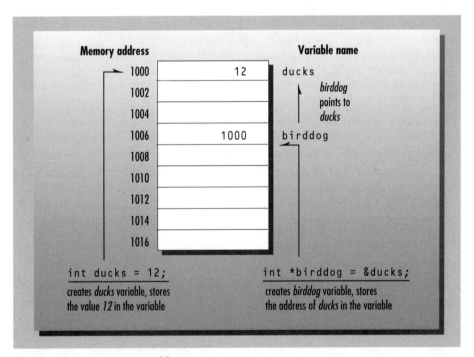

Figure 4-9 Pointers store addresses

Note that while *tax_ptr* and *str* point to data types of two different sizes, the two variables *tax_ptr* and *str* themselves typically are the same size. That is, the address of a *char* is the same size as the address of a *double*, much as 1016 might be the street address for a department store while 1024 could be the street address of a small cottage. The size or value of an address doesn't really tell you anything about the size or kind of variable or building found at that address. Usually, addresses require 2 or 4 bytes, depending on the computer system. (Some systems may have larger addresses, and a system could use different address sizes for different types.)

You can use a declaration statement to initialize a pointer. In that case, the pointer, not the pointed-to value, is initialized. That is, the statements

```
int higgens = 5;
int * pi = &higgens;
```

set *pi* and not **pi* to the value *&higgens*.

Listing 4-12 demonstrates initializing a pointer to an address.

Listing 4-12 *init_ptr.cpp*

```
// init_ptr.cpp -- initialize a pointer
#include <iostream.h>
int main(void)
{
        int higgens = 5;
        int * pi = &higgens;

// NOTE: Some users may need to type cast the addresses
//    in cout statements (&higgens and pi) to unsigned

        cout << "Value of higgens = " << higgens
          << "; Address of higgens = " << &higgens << "\n";
        cout << "Value of *pi = " << *pi
                << "; Value of pi = " << pi << "\n";
        return 0;
}
```

Here is the output:

```
Value of higgens = 5; Address of higgens = 0x8fa0fff4
Value of *pi = 5; Value of pi = 0x8fa0fff4
```

You can see that the program initializes *pi*, not **pi*, to the address of *higgens*.

Danger awaits those who use pointers incautiously. One extremely important point is that when you create a pointer in C++, the computer allocates memory to hold an *address*, but it does not allocate memory to hold the *data* that will be pointed to. Creating space for the data involves a separate step. Omitting that step, as in the following, is an invitation to disaster:

```
long * fellow;      // create a pointer-to-long
* fellow = 223323;  // place a value in never-never land
```

Sure, *fellow* is a pointer. But *where* does it point? The code failed to assign an address to *fellow.* So where is the value 223323 placed? We can't say. Because *fellow* wasn't initialized, it could have any value. Whatever that value is, the program interprets it to be the address at which to store 223323. If *fellow* happens to have the value *1200,* then the computer attempts to place the data at address *1200,* even if that happens to be an address in the middle of your program code. Chances are that wherever *fellow* points, you don't want to put the number 223323 there. This kind of error can produce some of the most insidious and hard-to-trace bugs around.

RULE

Pointer Golden Rule: ALWAYS initialize a pointer to a definite and appropriate address before applying the dereferencing operator (*) to it.

Pointers and Numbers

Pointers are not integer types, even though computers typically handle addresses as integers. Conceptually, pointers are distinct types from integers. Integers are numbers you can add, subtract, divide, and so on. But a pointer describes a location, and it doesn't make sense to, say, multiply two locations times each other. So, in terms of the operations you can perform with them, pointers and integers are different from each other. Consequently, you can't simply assign an integer to a pointer:

```
int * pi;
pi = 0xB8000000;  // type mismatch
```

Here the left-hand side is a pointer to *int,* so it can be assigned an address. But the right-hand side is just an integer. You may know that 0xB8000000 is the combined segment-offset address of video memory on your system, but nothing in the statement tells the program that this number is an address. C will let you make assignments like this. But C++ enforces type agreement more stringently, and the compiler will give you an error message saying you have a type mismatch. So if you want to use a numeric value as an address, you should use a type cast to convert the number to the appropriate address type:

```
int * pi;
pi = (int *) 0xB8000000; // types now match
```

Now both sides of the assignment statement represent addresses of integers, so the assignment is valid. Note that being the address of a type *int* value doesn't mean that *pi* itself is type *int.* For instance, in the large memory model on an IBM PC, type *int* is a 2-byte value, while the addresses are 4-byte values.

Pointers have some other interesting properties that we'll discuss as they become relevant. Meanwhile, let's look at how pointers can be used to manage runtime allocation of memory space.

Allocating Memory with *new*

Now that you have some feel for how pointers work, let's see how they can implement that important OOP technique of allocating memory as a program runs. So far, we've initialized pointers to the addresses of variables; this is *named* memory allocated during compile time, and the pointers merely provided an alias for memory you could access directly by name anyway. The true worth of pointers comes into play when you allocate *unnamed* memory during run time to hold values. In this case, pointers become the only access to that memory. In C, you could allocate memory with the library function *malloc()*. You can still do so in C++, but C++ also has a better way, the *new* operator.

Let's try out this new technique by creating unnamed, runtime storage for a type *int* value and accessing the value with a pointer. The key is the C++ *new* operator. You tell *new* what data type you want memory for; *new* finds a block of the correct size and returns the address of the block. Assign this address to a pointer, and you're in business. Here's a sample of the technique:

```
int * pn = new int;
```

The *new int* part tells the program we want some new storage suitable for holding an *int*. The *new* operator uses the type to figure out how many bytes are needed. Then it finds the memory and returns the address. We assign the address to *pn*, which is declared to be of type pointer-to-*int*. So now *pn* is the address and **pn* is the value stored there. Compare this with assigning the address of a variable to a pointer:

```
int higgens;
int *pi = &higgens;
```

In both cases (*pn* and *pi*) we assign the address of an *int* to a pointer. In the second case, we also can access the *int* by name: *higgens*. In the first case, our only access is via the pointer. That raises a question: Since the memory to which *pn* points lacks a name, what do you call it? We say that *pn* points to a *data object*. This is not "object" in the sense of "object-oriented programming"; it's just "object" in the sense of "thing." The term "data object" is more general than the term "variable," for it means any block of memory allocated for a data item. Thus a variable is also a data object, but the memory that the *pn* points to is not a variable. The pointer method for handling data objects may seem more awkward at first, but it offers greater control over how your program manages memory.

The general form for obtaining and assigning memory for a single data object, which can be a structure as well as a fundamental type, is this:

type pointer_name = **new** *type;*

You use the data type twice, once to specify the kind of memory requested and once to declare a suitable pointer. Of course, if you've already declared a pointer of the correct type, you can use it instead of declaring a new one. Listing 4-13 illustrates using *new* with two different types.

Listing 4-13 *use_new.cpp*

```
// use_new.cpp -- using the new operator
#include <iostream.h>
int main(void)
{
        int * pi = new int;    // allocate space for an int
        *pi = 1001;            // store a value there

// NOTE: Some users may need to type cast the addresses
//   in cout statements (pi and pd) to unsigned

        cout << "int ";
        cout << "value = " << *pi << ": location = " << pi << "\n";

        double * pd = new double;   // allocate space for a double
        *pd = 10000001.0;           // store a double there

        cout << "double ";
        cout << "value = " << *pd << ": location = " << pd << "\n";
        cout << "size of pi = " << sizeof pi;
        cout << ": size of *pi = " << sizeof *pi << "\n";
        cout << "size of pd = " << sizeof pd;
        cout << ": size of *pd = " << sizeof *pd << "\n";
        return 0;
}
```

Here is the output:

```
int value = 1001: location = 0x857011ec
double value = 10000001: location = 0x857011f4
size of pi = 2: size of *pi = 2
size of pd = 2: size of *pd = 8
```

Program Notes

The program uses *new* to allocate memory for a type *int* data object and for a type *double* data object. This occurs while the program is running. The pointers *pi* and *pd* point to these two data objects. Without them, you cannot access those memory locations. With them, you can use **pi* and **pd* just as you would use variables. Assigning values to **pi* and **pd* assigns values to the new data objects. Similarly, printing **pi* and **pd* displays those values.

The program also demonstrates one of the reasons you have to declare the type a pointer points to. An address in itself reveals only the beginning address of the object stored, not its type nor the number of bytes used. Look at the addresses of the two values. They are just numbers with no type or size information. Also, note that the size of a pointer-to-*int* is the same as the size of a pointer-to-*double*. Both are just addresses. But because *use_new.cpp* declared the pointer types, the program knows that **pd* is a *double* value of 8 bytes, while **pi* is an *int* value of 2 bytes. So when *use_new.cpp* prints the value of **pd*, *cout* can tell how many bytes to read and how to interpret them.

The sharp-eyed among you may be wondering how the program manages to store a number like *0x857011ec*, which appears to be 4 bytes long, in a 2-byte variable. The system on which we ran the program (IBM PC compatible) divides memory into segments of 64K (a K is 1024 bytes), and the program uses a 2-byte pointer to hold the offset of a memory location from the beginning of the segment used for data. But *cout* was implemented to print both the 2-byte segment value (*0x8570*) and the 2-byte offset (*0x11ec*) as a single 4-byte value (*0x857011ec*).

OUT OF MEMORY?

It's possible that the computer may not have sufficient memory available to satisfy a *new* request. When that is the case, *new* returns the value *0*. In C++, a pointer with the value *0* is called the *null pointer*. C++ guarantees that the null pointer never points to valid data, so it often is used to indicate failure for operators or functions that otherwise return usable pointers. Once you learn about *if* statements (Chapter 6), you can check to see if *new* returns the null pointer and thus protect your program from attempting to exceed its bounds.

Using *new* to Create Dynamic Arrays

If all a program needs is a single value, you may as well declare a simple variable, for that is simpler, if less impressive, than using *new* and a pointer to manage a single small data object. More typically, you use *new* with larger chunks of data, such as arrays, strings, and structures. This is where *new* gets useful. Suppose, for example, you're writing a program that may or may not need an array, depending on information given to the program while it is running. If you create an array by declaring it, the space is allocated when the program is compiled. Whether or not the program finally uses the array, the array is there, using up memory. This is called *static binding*, meaning the array is built into the program at compilation time. But with *new*, you can create an array during run time if you need it and skip creating the array if you don't need it. Or you can select an array size after the program is running. This is called *dynamic binding*, meaning the array is created while the program is running, and the array is called a *dynamic array*. With static binding, you must specify the array size when you write the program. With dynamic binding, the program can decide upon an array size while the program runs.

For now, we'll look at two basic matters concerning dynamic arrays: how to use C++'s *new* operator to create an array, and how to use a pointer to access array elements.

Creating a Dynamic Array with *new*

It's easy to create a dynamic array in C++; you tell *new* the type of array element you desire and how many elements you want. The syntax requires that you follow the type name with the number of elements in brackets. For instance, if you need an array of ten *ints,* do this:

```
int * psome = new int [10]; // get a block of 10 ints
```

The *new* operator returns the *address* of the first element of the block. In this example, that value is assigned to the pointer *psome.* Note that *psome* is a pointer to a single *int,* the first element of the block. It's your responsibility to keep track of how many elements are in the block. That is, the compiler doesn't keep track of the fact that *psome* points to the first of *ten* integers, so you have to write your program so the program keeps track of the number of elements.

Actually, the program does keep track of the amount of memory allocated so that it can be correctly freed at a later time if you use the *delete []* operator discussed later. But that information isn't publicly available; you can't use the *sizeof* operator, for example, to find the number of bytes in a dynamically allocated array.

The general form for allocating and assigning memory for an array is this:

type_name pointer_name = **new** *type_name* [*num_elements*];

Invoking the *new* operator secures a block of memory large enough to hold *num_elements* elements of type *type_name,* with *pointer_name* pointing to the first element. As you're about to see, you can use *pointer_name* in many of the same ways you can use an array name.

Using a Dynamic Array

Once you create a dynamic array, how do you use it? First, think about the problem conceptually. The statement

```
int * psome = new int [10]; // get a block of 10 ints
```

creates a pointer *psome* that points to the first element of a block of ten *int* values. Think of it as a finger pointing to that element. Suppose an *int* occupies 2 bytes. Then, by moving your finger 2 bytes in the correct direction, you can point to the second element. Altogether, there are ten elements, and that tells the range over which you can move your finger. Thus, the *new* statement supplies you with all the information you need to identify every element in the block.

Now think about the problem practically. How do you access one of these elements? The first element is no problem. Because *psome* points to the first element of the array, **psome* is the value of the first element. That leaves nine more elements to access. The simplest way may surprise you if you haven't worked with C: just use the pointer as if it were an array name. That is, you can use *psome[0]* instead of **psome* for the first element, *psome[1]* for the second element, and so on. So using a pointer to access a dynamic array turns out to be very simple, even if it may not be immediately obvious why the method works. The reason you can do this is that C and C++ handle arrays internally by using pointers anyway. This near equivalence of arrays and pointers is one of the beauties of C and C++. We'll elaborate on this equivalence in a moment. First, Listing 4-14 shows how you can use *new* to create a dynamic array and then use array notation to access the elements. It also points out a fundamental difference between a pointer and a true array name.

Listing 4-14 *arraynew.cpp*

```
// arraynew.cpp -- using the new operator for arrays
#include <iostream.h>
int main(void)
{
        double * p3 = new double [3]; // space for 3 doubles
        p3[0] = 0.2;                  // treat p3 like an array name
        p3[1] = 0.5;
        p3[2] = 0.8;
        cout << "p3[1] is " << p3[1] << ".\n";
        p3 = p3 + 1;                  // increment the pointer
        cout << "Now p3[0] is " << p3[0] << " and ";
        cout << "p3[1] is " << p3[1] << ".\n";
        return 0;
}
```

Here is the output:

```
p3[1] is 0.5.
Now p3[0] is 0.5 and p3[1] is 0.8.
```

As you can see, *arraynew.cpp* uses the pointer *p3* as if it were the name of an array, with *p3[0]* being the first element, and so on. The fundamental difference between an array name and a pointer shows in the following line:

```
p3 = p3 + 1; // okay for pointers, wrong for array names
```

You can't change the value of an array name. But a pointer is a variable, hence you can change its value. Note the effect of adding 1 to *p3*. The expression *p3[0]* now refers to the former second element of the array. Thus adding 1 to *p3* caused it to point to the second element instead of the first. The actual addresses of consecutive *ints* typically differ by 2 or 4 bytes, so the fact that adding 1 to *p3* gives the address of the next element suggests that there is something special about pointer arithmetic. There is.

Pointers, Arrays, and Pointer Arithmetic

The near equivalence of pointers and array names stems from pointer arithmetic and how C++ handles arrays internally. First, let's check out the arithmetic. Adding 1 to an integer variable increases its value by 1. But adding 1 to a pointer variable increases its value by the number of bytes of the type it points to. So adding 1 to a pointer to *double* adds 8 to the numerical value on systems with 8-byte *double*, while adding 1 to a pointer-to-*short* adds 2 to the pointer value if *short* is 2 bytes. Listing 4-15 demonstrates this amazing point. It also shows a second important point: C++ interprets the array name as an address.

Listing 4-15 *addpntrs.cpp*

```cpp
// addpntrs.cpp -- pointer addition
#include <iostream.h>
int main(void)
{
        double wages[3] = {10000.0, 20000.0, 30000.0};
        short stacks[3] = {3, 2, 1};


// NOTE: Some users may need to type cast the addresses
//    in cout statements (ps and pw) to unsigned

// Here are two ways to get the address of an array
        double * pw = wages;      // name of an array = address
        short * ps = &stacks[0]; // use address operator
                          // with array element
        cout << "pw = " << pw << ", *pw = " << *pw << "\n";
        pw = pw + 1;
        cout << "add 1 to the pw pointer:\n";
        cout << "pw = " << pw << ", *pw = " << *pw << "\n\n";

        cout << "ps = " << ps << ", *ps = " << *ps << "\n";
        ps = ps + 1;
        cout << "add 1 to the ps pointer:\n";
        cout << "ps = " << ps << ", *ps = " << *ps << "\n\n";

        cout << "access two elements with array notation\n";
        cout << stacks[0] << " " << stacks[1] << "\n";
        cout << "access two elements with pointer notation\n";
        cout << *stacks << " " << *(stacks + 1) << "\n";

        cout << sizeof wages << " = size of wages array\n";
        cout << sizeof pw << " = size of pw pointer\n";
        return 0;
}
```

Here is the output:

```
pw = 0x7c87ffd8, *pw = 10000
add 1 to the pw pointer:
pw = 0x7c87ffe0, *pw = 20000

ps = 0x7c87fff0, *ps = 3
add 1 to the ps pointer:
ps = 0x7c87fff2, *ps = 2

access two elements with array notation
3 2
access two elements with pointer notation
3 2
24 = size of wages array
2 = size of pw pointer
```

Program Notes

In most contexts, C++ interprets the name of an array as the address of its first element. Thus the statement

```
double * pw = wages;
```

makes *pw* a pointer to type *double*, then initializes *pw* to *wages*, which is the address of the first element of the *wages* array. For *wages*, as with any array, we have the following equality:

```
wages = &wages[0] = address of first element of array
```

Just to show that we aren't jiving you, we used the address operator explicitly in the expression &*stacks[0]* for initializing the *ps* pointer to the first element of the *stacks* array.

Next, the program inspects the values of *pw* and **pw*. The first is an address and the second is the value at that address. Because *pw* points to the first element, the value displayed for **pw* is that of the first element, *10000*. Then the program adds 1 to *pw*. As promised, this adds 8 (d8 + 8 = e0 in hexadecimal) to the numeric address value because *double* on our system is 8 bytes. This makes *pw* equal to the address of the second element. Thus **pw* now is *20000*, the value of the second element. See Figure 4-10. (The address values in the figure are adjusted to make the figure clearer.)

After this, the program goes through similar steps for *ps*. This time, because *ps* points to type *short* and because *short* is 2 bytes, adding 1 to the pointer increases its value by 2. Again, the result is to make the pointer point to the next element of the array.

RULE

Remember, adding 1 to a pointer variable increases its value by the number of bytes of the type to which it points.

Now consider the array expression *stacks[1]*. The C++ compiler treats this expression exactly as if you wrote it as **(stacks + 1)*. The second expression means calculate the address of the second element of the array, then find the value stored there. The end result is precisely what we mean by *stacks[1]*. (Operator precedence requires using the parentheses. Without them, 1 would be added to **stacks* instead of to *stacks*.)

The program output demonstrates that **(stacks + 1)* and *stacks[1]* are the same. Similarly, **(stacks + 2)* is the same as *stacks[2]*. In general, wherever you use array notation, C++ makes the following conversion:

```
arrayname[i] becomes *(arrayname + i)
```

And if you use a pointer instead of an array name, C++ makes the same conversion:

```
pointername[i] becomes *(pointername + i)
```

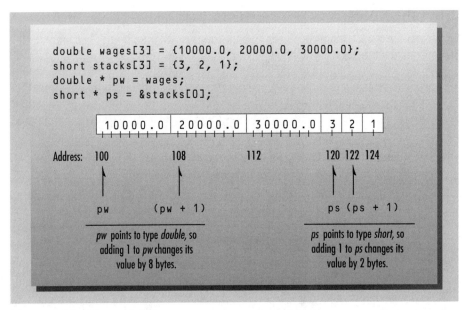

```
double wages[3] = {10000.0, 20000.0, 30000.0};
short stacks[3] = {3, 2, 1};
double * pw = wages;
short * ps = &stacks[0];
```

| 10000.0 | 20000.0 | 30000.0 | 3 | 2 | 1 |

Address: 100   108   112   120 122 124

pw   (pw + 1)   ps (ps + 1)

pw points to type *double,* so
adding 1 to *pw* changes its
value by 8 bytes.

ps points to type *short,* so
adding 1 to *ps* changes its
value by 2 bytes.

Figure 4-10 Pointer addition

Thus in many respects you can use pointer names and array names the same way. You can use array notation with either. You can apply the dereferencing operator (*) to either. In most expressions, each represents an address. One difference is that you can change the value of a pointer while an array name is a constant:

```
pointername = pointername + 1; // valid
arrayname = arrayname + 1;     // not allowed
```

The second difference is that applying the *sizeof* operator to an array name yields the size of the array, but applying *sizeof* to a pointer yields the size of the pointer, even if the pointer points to the array. For instance, in Listing 4-15, both *pw* and *wages* refer to the same array. But applying the *sizeof* operator to them produced the following results:

```
24 = size of wages array ← displaying sizeof wages
2 = size of pw pointer ← displaying sizeof pw
```

This is one case in which C++ doesn't interpret the array name as an address.

In short, using *new* to create an array and using a pointer to access the different elements is a simple matter. Just treat the pointer as an array name. Understanding why this works, however, is an interesting challenge. If you really wish to understand arrays and pointers, you should review their mutual relationships carefully. In fact, you've been exposed to quite a bit of pointer knowledge lately, so let's summarize what's been revealed about pointers and arrays to date.

Summarizing Pointer Points

Declaring Pointers: To declare a pointer to a particular *type,* use this form:

typename ***** *pointername;*

Examples:

```
double * pn;        // pn points to a double value
char * pc;          // pc points to a char value
```

Here *pn* and *pc* are pointers and *double ** and *char ** are the C++ notations for the types pointer-to-*double* and pointer-to-*char.*

Assigning Values to Pointers: A pointer should be assigned a memory address. You can apply the & operator to a variable name to get an address of named memory, and the *new* operator returns the address of unnamed memory.

Examples:

```
double bubble = 3.2;
pn = &bubble;         // assign address of bubble to pn
pc = new char;        // assign address of newly allocated
                      // char memory to pc
```

Dereferencing Pointers: Dereferencing a pointer means referring to the pointed-to value. Apply the dereferencing, or indirect value, operator (*) to a pointer to dereference it. Thus if *pn* is a pointer to *bubble,* as in the last example, then **pn* is the pointed-to value, or 3.2 in this case.

Examples:

```
cout << *pn;          // print the value of bubble
*pc = 'S';            // place the value 'S' in the memory location
                      // whose address is pc
```

Distinguishing Between a Pointer and the Pointed-to Value: Remember, if *pi* is a pointer-to-*int,* that **pi* is not a pointer-to-*int;* instead, **pi* is the complete equivalent to a type *int* variable. It is *pi* that is the pointer.

Examples:

```
int * pi = new int;   // assigns an address to the pointer pi
*pi = 5;              // stores the value 5 at that address
```

Array Names: In most contexts, C++ treats the name of an array as being equivalent to the address of the first element of an array.

Example:

```
int tacos[10]; // tacos is the same as &tacos[0]
```

One exception is when you use the name of an array with the *sizeof* operator. In that case, *sizeof* returns the size of the entire array, in bytes.

Pointer Arithmetic: C++ allows you to add an integer to a pointer. The result of adding 1 equals the original address value plus a value equal to the number of bytes in the pointed-to object.

Examples:

```
float fog = 2.2;
float * pf = &fog;      // suppose pf and &fog are the address 3000
pf = pf + 1;            // now pf is 3004 if a float is four bytes
int tacos[10];          // suppose tacos, or &tacos[0], is 4000
                        // then tacos + 1 is 4002 if int is two bytes
```

Dynamic Binding and Static Binding for Arrays: Use an array declaration to create an array with static binding, that is, an array whose size is set during compilation time:

```
int tacos[10]; // static binding, size fixed at compile time
```

Use the *new* operator to create an array with dynamic binding (a dynamic array), that is, an array that is allocated and whose size can be set during run time:

```
int size;
cin >> size;
int * pz = new int [size];    // dynamic binding, size set at
                              // run time
```

Array Notation and Pointer Notation: Using bracket array notation is equivalent to dereferencing a pointer:

```
tacos[0] means *tacos means the value at address tacos
tacos[3] means *(tacos + 3) means the value at address tacos + 3
```

This is true both for array names and for pointer variables, so you can use either pointer notation or array notation with pointers and with array names.

Examples:

```
int * pi = new int [10];      // pi points to block of 10 ints
*pi = 5;                      // set zero element to 5
pi[0] = 6;                    // reset zero element to 6
pi[9] = 44;                   // set tenth element to 44
int tacos[10];
*(tacos + 4) = 12;            // set tacos[4] to 12
```

Pointers and Strings

The special relationship between arrays and pointers extends to strings. Consider the following code:

```
char flower[10] = "rose";
cout << flower << "s are red\n";
```

The name of an array is the address of its first element, so *flower* in the *cout* statement is the address of the *char* element containing the character *r*. The *cout* object assumes that the address of a *char* is the address of a string, so it prints the character at that address, then continues printing characters until it runs into the null character (\0). In short, if you give *cout* the address of a character, it prints everything from that character to the first null character following it.

The crucial element here is not that *flower* is an array name but that *flower* acts as the address of a *char*. This implies that you can use a pointer-to-*char* variable as an argument to *cout,* also, since it, too, is the address of a *char.* Of course, that pointer should point to the beginning of a string. We'll check that out in a moment.

But first, what about the final part of the above *cout* statement? If *flower* really is the address of the first character of a string, what is the expression *"s are red\n"*? To be consistent with *cout's* handling of string output, this quoted string also should be an address. And it is, for in C++ a quoted string, like an array name, serves as the address of its first element. So the code above doesn't really send a whole string to *cout,* it just sends the string address. This means strings in an array, quoted strings, and strings described by pointers are all handled equivalently. Each is really passed along as an address. That's certainly less work than passing each and every character in a string.

RULE

With *cout* and with most C++ expressions, the name of an array of *char,* a pointer-to-*char,* and a quoted string constant all are interpreted as the address of the first character of a string.

Listing 4-16 illustrates using the different forms of strings. It uses two functions from the string library. The *strlen()* function, which we've used before, returns the length of a string. The *strcpy()* function copies a string from one location to another. Both have function prototypes in the *string.h* header file. The program also showcases some pointer misuses that you should try to avoid.

Listing 4-16 *pntstr.cpp*

```
// pntstr.cpp -- using pointers to strings
#include <iostream.h>
#include <string.h>        // declare strlen(), strcpy()
int main(void)
{
        char animal[20] = "bear"; // animal holds bear
        char * bird = "penguin";  // bird holds address of string
        char * ps;        // uninitialized

        cout << animal << " and "; // display bear
        cout << bird << "\n";      // display penguin
        cout << ps << "\n";        // blunder - display garbage

        cout << "Enter a kind of animal: ";
        cin >> animal;     // ok if input < 20 chars
        cout << "Enter a kind of bird: ";
        cin >> bird;         // not recommended, may work on
                             // some systems, but behavior
                             // is undefined
        // cin >> ps; Too horrible a blunder to try; ps doesn't
```

continued on next page

continued from previous page

```
//                      point to allocated space

        ps = animal;       // set ps to point to string
        cout << ps << "s!\n";    // ok, same as using animal
        ps = bird;               // reassign pointer
        cout << ps << "s!\n";    // risky, same as using bird

        ps = new char[strlen(animal) + 1]; // get new storage
        strcpy(ps, animal);     // copy string to new storage
        cout << "Now ps points to " << ps << "!\n";
        return 0;
}
```

Here is a sample run:

```
bear and penguin
```
                              ← output from *cout << ps << "\n";*
```
Enter a kind of animal: sloth
Enter a kind of bird: parrot
sloths!
parrots!
Now ps points to sloth!
```

Program Notes

The program in Listing 4-16 creates one *char* array (*animal*) and two pointers-to-*char* variables (*bird* and *ps*). The program begins by initializing the animal array to the *"bear"* string, just as we've initialized arrays before. Then the program does something new. It initializes a pointer-to-*char* to a string:

```
char * bird = "penguin"; // bird holds address of string
```

Remember, *"penguin"* really represents the address of the string, so this statement assigns the address of *"penguin"* to the *bird* pointer. (Typically, a compiler sets aside an area in memory to hold all the strings used in the program source code, associating each stored string with its address.) This means you can use the pointer *bird* just as you would have used the string *"penguin"*, as in *cout << "A concerned " << bird << " speaks\n"*. Finally, the pointer *ps* remains uninitialized, so it doesn't point to any string. (This, you recall, is usually a bad idea, and this example is no exception.)

Next, the program illustrates that you can use the array name *animal* and the pointer *bird* equivalently with *cout*. Both, after all, are the addresses of strings, and *cout* displays the two strings (*bear* and *penguin*) stored at those addresses. When we made the error of attempting to display *ps*, we got a blank line. Creating an uninitialized pointer is a bit like distributing a blank signed check; you lack control over how it will be used. We were a little lucky here, for *ps*, being uninitialized, may have accidentally pointed to some awkward location. As it was, it pointed to a location containing a zero, so nothing was displayed. Otherwise, you might get some garbage output.

For input, the situation is a bit different. It's safe to use the array *animal* for input as long as the input is short enough to fit into the array. Using the *bird* pointer to the string constant *"penguin"*, however, can cause problems. In our case it worked, for the original string was big enough to hold the input. But there are a couple of reasons it might fail:

> Some compilers treat string literals as read-only constants, leading to a run-time error if you try to write new data over them.

> Some compilers use just one copy of a string literal to represent all occurrences of that literal in a program.

Let's amplify the second point. C++ doesn't guarantee that string literals are stored uniquely. That is, if you use a string literal *"penguin"* several times in the program, the compiler might store several copies of the string or store just one copy. If it does the latter, then setting *bird* to point to one *"penguin"* makes it point to the only copy of that string. So reading a value into one string could affect what you thought was an independent string elsewhere.

Worse yet is trying to read information into the location pointed to by *ps*. Because *ps* is not initialized, we don't know where the information will wind up. It might even overwrite information already in memory. Fortunately, it's easy to avoid these problems—just use a sufficiently large *char* array to receive input. Don't use string constants to receive input and don't use uninitialized pointers to receive input.

RULE

When reading a string into a program, you should always use the address of previously allocated memory. This address can be in the form of an array name or of a pointer that has been initialized using *new*.

The end of a program shows a common string-handling trick for conserving memory. It also lets us bring *new* back into the discussion.

```
ps = new char[strlen(animal) + 1]; // get new storage
strcpy(ps, animal);                // copy string to new storage
```

The string *"sloth"* doesn't completely fill the *animal* array, so we're wasting space. This bit of code uses *strlen()* to find the length of the string; it adds 1 to get the length including the null character. Then the program uses *new* to allocate just enough space to hold the string. Finally, it uses the *strcpy()* function to copy the string in *animal* to the newly allocated memory. The *strcpy()* function takes two arguments. The first is the destination address, and the second is the address of the string to be copied. It's up to you to make certain that the destination really is allocated and has sufficient space to hold the copy. We accomplished that here by using *strlen()* to find the correct size and using *new* to get free memory.

By the way, don't use the following code to copy a string:

```
ps = animal; // this does NOT copy a string
```

All this does is reset *ps* to the address of the *animal* array. This makes both *ps* and *animal* refer to the same storage location; all you get are two names for the same thing. But using *strcpy()* copies a string from one location to a second location, giving you two separate, but identical, strings. Of course, we haven't really saved space because *animal* is still there, but this technique is the starting point for more sophisticated memory management.

Using *new* to Create Dynamic Structures

You've seen how it can be advantageous to create arrays during run time instead of compile time. The same holds true for structures. You must allocate space for only as many structures as a program needs during a particular run. Again, the *new* operator is the tool to use. With it, you can create dynamic structures. Again, "dynamic" means the memory is allocated during run time, not during compilation. Incidentally, because classes are much like structures, you'll be able to use the techniques you learn for structures with classes, too.

Using *new* with structures has two parts: creating the structure and accessing its members. To create a structure, use the structure type with *new*. For example, to create an unnamed structure of the *inflatable* type and to assign its address to a suitable pointer, you can do the following:

```
inflatable * ps = new inflatable;
```

This assigns to *ps* the address of a chunk of free memory large enough to hold a structure of the *inflatable* type. The syntax, you'll note, is exactly the same as it was for C++'s built-in types.

The tricky part is accessing members. When you create a dynamic structure, you can't use the dot membership operator with the structure name because the structure has no name. All you have is its address. C++ provides an operator just for this situation: the arrow membership operator (->). This operator, formed by typing a hyphen, then a greater-than symbol, does for pointers to structures what the dot operator does for structure names. For instance, if *ps* points to a type inflatable structure, then *ps->price* is the *price* member of the pointed-to structure. See Figure 4-11.

RULE

Sometimes new users become confused about when to use the dot operator and when to use the arrow operator to specify a structure member. The rule is simple. If the structure identifier is the name of a structure, use the dot operator. If the identifier is a pointer to the structure, use the arrow operator.

A second, uglier, approach is to realize that if *ps* is a pointer to a structure, then **ps* represents the pointed-to value, the structure itself. Then, because **ps* is a structure, *(*ps).price* is the *price* member of the structure. C++'s operator precedence rules require that we use parentheses in this construction.

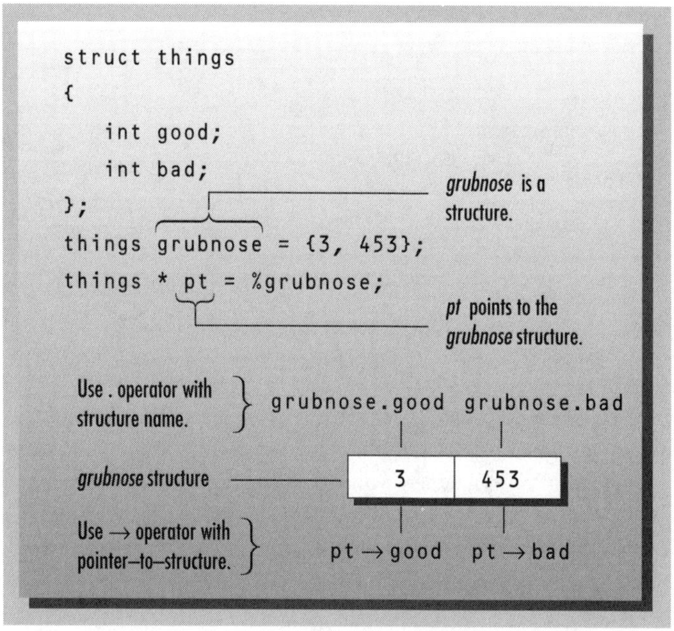

```
struct things
{
    int good;
    int bad;
};
things grubnose = {3, 453};
things * pt = %grubnose;
```

grubnose is a
structure.

pt points to the
grubnose structure.

Use . operator with
structure name.
}   grubnose.good   grubnose.bad

grubnose structure ——————

| 3 | 453 |

Use → operator with
pointer–to–structure. }   pt → good   pt → bad

Figure 4-11 Identifying structure members

Listing 4-17 uses *new* to create an unnamed structure and demonstrates both pointer notations for accessing structure members.

Listing 4-17 *newstrct.cpp*

```cpp
// newstrct.cpp - using new with a structure
#include <iostream.h>
struct inflatable   // structure template
{
        char name[20];
        float volume;
        double price;
};
int main(void)
{
        inflatable * ps = new inflatable;// allot structure space

        cout << "Enter name of inflatable item: ";
        cin.get( (*ps).name, 20); // method 1 for member access
        cout << "Enter volume in cubic feet: ";
        cin >> ps->volume;         // method 2 for member access
        cout << "Enter price: $";
        cin >> ps->price;
        cout << "Name: " << ps->name << "\n";
        cout << "Volume: " << ps->volume << " cubic feet\n";
```

continued on next page

continued from previous page

```
        cout << "Price: $" << ps->price << "\n";
        return 0;
}
```

Here is a sample run:

```
Enter name of inflatable item: Fabulous Frodo
Enter volume in cubic feet: 1.40
Enter price: $17.99
Name: Fabulous Frodo
Volume: 1.4 cubic feet
Price: $17.99
```

Freeing Memory with *delete*

Using *new* to request memory when you need it is just the more glamorous half of the C++ memory-management package. The other half is the *delete* operator, which lets you return memory to the memory pool when you are finished with it. That is an important step for making the most effective use of memory. Memory that you return, or *free,* then can be reused by other parts of your program. You use *delete* by following it with a pointer to a block of memory originally allocated with *new:*

```
int * ps = new int; // allocate memory with new
delete ps;      // free memory with delete
```

This removes the memory that *ps* points to; it doesn't remove the pointer *ps* itself. So you can reuse *ps* to, say, point to another *new* allocation.

You should not attempt to free a block of memory that's already been freed. Also, you cannot use *delete* to free memory created by declaring variables:

```
int * ps = new int;    // ok
delete ps;...........// ok
delete ps;...........// not ok now
int jugs = 5;       // ok
int * pi = & jugs;    // ok
delete pi;           // not allowed, memory not allocated by new
```

RULE

Use *delete* only to free memory allocated with *new*. However, it is safe to apply *delete* to a null pointer.

Note that the critical test for using *delete* is that you use it with *memory* allocated by *new*. This doesn't mean you have to use the same *pointer* you used with *new*; instead, you have to use the same *address:*

```
int * ps = new int;    // allocate memory
int * pq = ps;       // set second pointer to same block
delete pq;           // delete with second pointer
```

Ordinarily, you won't create two pointers to the same block of memory, for that raises the possibility of mistakenly trying to delete the same block twice. But, as you'll soon see, using a second pointer does make sense when you work with a function that returns a pointer.

If you use *new* to create an array, you should use an alternative form of *delete* that indicated that you are freeing an array:

```
double * pfees = new double [20]; // create a dynamic array
delete [] pfees;                  // free a dynamic array
```

The presence of the brackets tells the program that it should free the whole array, not just the element pointed to by the pointer. Note that the brackets are between *delete* and the pointer. Thus, if you use *new* without brackets, use *delete* without brackets. If you use *new* with brackets, use *delete* with brackets. Earlier versions of C++ may not recognize the bracket notation. With current versions, however, the effect of mismatching *new* and *delete* forms is undefined, meaning you can't rely upon some particular behavior.

```
int * pi = new int;
short * ps = new short [500];
delete [] pi;  // effect is undefined, don't do it
delete ps;     // effect is undefined, don't do it
```

In short, observe these rules when using *new* and *delete*:

- Don't use *delete* to free memory that wasn't allocated by *new*.
- Don't use *delete* to free the same block of memory twice in succession.
- Use *delete []* if you used *new* to allocate an array.
- Use *delete* (no brackets) if you used *new* to allocate a single entity.
- It's safe to apply *delete* to the null pointer (nothing happens).

A *new* and *delete* Example

What new and marvelous things can you accomplish by using *new* and *delete*? Listing 4-18 shows some of the possibilities. The program defines a function that returns a pointer to an input string. This function reads the input into a large temporary array, then uses *new* to create a chunk of memory sized to fit to the input string. Then the function returns the pointer to the block. This approach could conserve a lot of memory for programs that read in a large number of strings.

Suppose your program had to read 1000 strings, that the largest string might be 79 characters long, but that most of the strings would be much shorter. If you used *char* arrays to hold the strings, you'd need 1000 arrays of 80 characters each. That's 80,000 bytes, and much of that block of memory would wind up unused. Alternatively, you could create an array of 1000 pointers to *char*, then use *new* to allocate only the amount of memory needed for each string. That could save tens of thousands of bytes. Instead of having to use a large array for every string, you fit the memory to the input. Even better, you also could use *new* to find space to store only as many pointers as needed. Well, that's a little too ambitious for right now. Even using an array of 1000 pointers is a little too ambitious for right now, but Listing 4-18 illustrates some of the technique. Also, just to illustrate how *delete* works, the program uses it to free memory for reuse.

Listing 4-18 *delete.cpp*

```
// delete.cpp - using the delete operator
#include <iostream.h>
#include <string.h>
char * getname(void); // function prototype
int main(void)
{
        char * name;          // create pointer but no storage

// NOTE: some users may need to type cast name to
//    unsigned instead of to (int *)

        name = getname();     // assign address of string to name
        cout << name << " at " << (int *) name << "\n";
        delete [] name;       // memory freed

        name = getname();     // reuse freed memory
        cout << name << " at " << (int *) name << "\n";
        delete [] name;
        return 0;
}
char * getname(void)  // return pointer to new string
{
        char temp[80];

        cout << "Enter last name: ";
        cin >> temp;
        char * pn = new char[strlen(temp) + 1];
        strcpy(pn, temp);     // copy string into smaller space
        return pn;                    // temp lost when function ends
}
```

Here is a sample run:

```
Enter last name: Fredeldumpkin
Fredeldumpkin at 0x85b30dd6
Enter last name: Pook
Pook at 0x85b30dd6
```

Note that freeing memory in this particular example for one particular implementation resulted in the program using the same address for both names.

Program Notes

First, consider the function *getname()*. It uses *cin* to place an input word into the *temp* array. Next, it uses *new* to allocate new memory to hold the word. Including the null character, the program needs *strlen(temp) + 1* characters to store the string, so that's the value given to *new*. Once the space is available, *getname()* uses the standard library function *strcpy()* to copy the string from *temp* to the new block. The function doesn't check to see if the string will fit or not, but *getname()* covers that by requesting the right number of bytes with *new*. Finally, the function returns *pn*, the address of the string copy.

In *main()*, the return value (the address) is assigned to the pointer *name*. This pointer is defined in *main()*, but it points to the block of memory allocated in the *getname()* function. The program then prints the string and the address of the string. Here we have used a small bit of trickery. The variable *name* is a pointer, and *cout* normally prints pointers as hexadecimal addresses. But *cout* processes a pointer to *char* differently from other pointers. Instead of printing the address value of a pointer-to-*char*, *cout* prints the string stored at the address. Therefore, to print the address itself, *main()* uses C++'s type casting facility to convert the *name* pointer to another type: pointer-to-*int*. That type *cout* prints as an address.

Next, after freeing the block pointed to by *name*, *main()* calls *getname()* a second time. C++ doesn't guarantee that newly freed memory is the first to be chosen the next time *new* is used, but in our sample run the same block of memory wound up being used for the next input.

To appreciate some of the more subtle aspects of this program, you should know a little more about how C++ handles memory. So let's preview some material that's covered more fully in Chapter 8.

Automatic Storage, Static Storage, the Free Store

C++ has three ways of managing memory for data, depending on the method used to allocate memory: automatic storage, static storage, and the free store. Data objects allocated in these three ways differ from each other in how long they remain in existence. We'll take a quick look at each type.

Automatic Variables

Ordinary variables defined inside a function are called *automatic* variables. They come into existence automatically when the function containing them is invoked, and they expire when the function terminates. For example, the *temp* array in Listing 4-18 exists only while the *getname()* function is active. When program control returns to *main()*, the memory used for *temp* is freed automatically. So if *getname()* had returned the address of *temp,* the *name* pointer in *main()* would have been left pointing to a memory location that soon would be reused. That's one reason we had to use *new* in *getname().*

Actually, automatic values are local to the block containing them. A block is a section of code enclosed between braces. So far, all our blocks have been entire functions. But, as you'll see in the next chapter, you can have blocks within a function. So if you define a variable inside one of those blocks, it exists only while the program is executing statements inside the block.

Static Storage

Static storage is storage that exists throughout the execution of an entire program. There are two ways to make a variable static. One is to define it externally, outside a function. The other is to use the keyword *static* when declaring a variable:

```
static double fee = 56.50;
```

Under K&R C, only static arrays and structures could be initialized, while C++ Release 2.0 (and later) and ANSI C allow you to initialize automatic arrays and structures, too. However, as some of you may have discovered, some C++ implementations have not yet implemented initialization for automatic arrays and structures.

Chapter 8 takes up static storage in more detail. The main point here about automatic and static storage is that these methods rigidly define the lifetime of a variable. Either the variable exists for the entire duration of a program (the static variable) or else it exists only while a particular function is being executed (the automatic variable).

The Free Store

The *new* and *delete* operators, however, provide a more flexible approach. They manage a pool of memory, which C++ refers to as the *free store.* This pool is separate from the memory used for static and automatic variables. As Listing 4-18 shows, *new* and *delete* let you allocate memory in one function and free it in another. Thus the lifetime of the data is not tied arbitrarily to the life of the program or the life of a function. Using *new* and *delete* together gives you much more control over how a program uses memory than does using ordinary variables.

NOTE

Pointers are among the most powerful of C++ tools. They also are the most dangerous, for they permit computer-unfriendly actions, such as using an uninitialized pointer to access memory or attempting to free the same memory block twice. Furthermore, until you get used, through practice, to pointer notation and pointer concepts, pointers can be confusing. This book will return to pointers several more times in the hopes that each exposure will make you more comfortable with them.

Summary

The array, the structure, and the pointer are three C++ derived types. The array can hold several values all of the same type in a single data object. By using an index, or subscript, you can access the individual elements in an array.

The structure can hold several values of different types in a single data object, and you can use the membership operator (.) to access individual members. The first step in using structures is creating a structure template defining what members the structure holds. The name, or tag, for this template then becomes a new type identifier. You then can declare structure variables of that type.

Pointers are variables designed to hold addresses. We say a pointer points to the address it holds. The pointer declaration always states what type of object a pointer points to. Applying the dereferencing operator (*) to a pointer yields the value at the location to which the pointer points.

A string is a series of characters terminated by a null character. A string can be represented by a quoted string constant, in which case the null character is implicitly understood. You can store a string in an array of *char*, and you can represent a string by a pointer-to-*char* that is initialized to point to the string. The *strlen()* function returns the length of a string, not counting the null character. The *strcpy()* function copies a string from one location to another. When using these functions, include the *string.h* header file.

The *new* operator lets you request memory for a data object while a program is running. The operator returns the address of the memory it obtains, and you can assign that address to a pointer. The only means to access that memory is to use the pointer. If the data object is a simple variable, you can use the dereferencing operator to indicate a value. If the data object is an array, you can use the pointer as if it were an array name to access the elements. If the data object is a structure, you can use the pointer dereferencing operator (->) to access structure members.

Pointers and arrays are closely connected. If *ar* is an array name, then the expression *ar[i]* is interpreted as *(ar + i)*, with the array name being interpreted as the address of the first element of the array. Thus the array name plays the same role as a pointer. In turn, you can use a pointer name with array notation to access elements in an array allocated by *new*.

The *new* and *delete* operators let you control explicitly when data objects are allocated and when they are returned to the memory pool. Automatic variables, which are those declared within a function, and static variables, which are defined outside a function or with the keyword *static*, are less flexible. An automatic variable comes into being when the block containing it (typically a function definition) is entered and expires when the block is left. A static variable persists for the duration of a program.

Review Questions

1. How would you declare each of the following?

    a. *actors* is an array of 30 *char*.

    b. *betsie* is an array of 100 *short*.

    c. *chuck* is an array of 13 *float*.

    d. *dipsea* is an array of 64 *long double*.

2. Declare an array of 5 *ints* and initialize it to the first 5 odd integers.

3. Write a statement that assigns the sum of the first and last elements of the array in question 2 to the variable *even*.

4. Write a statement that displays the value of the second element in the *float* array *ideas*.

5. Declare an array of *char* and initialize it to the string *"cheeseburger"*.

6. Devise a structure declaration that describes a fish. The structure should include the kind, the weight in whole ounces, and the length in fractional inches.

7. Declare a variable of the type defined in question 6 and initialize it.

8. Use *enum* to define a *Boolean* type whose possible values are *False* and *True*. *False* should be 0, and *True* should be 1.

9. Suppose *ted* is a *double* variable. Declare a pointer that points to *ted* and use the pointer to display *ted*'s value.

10. Suppose *treacle* is an array of 10 *floats*. Declare a pointer that points to the first element of *treacle* and use the pointer to display the first and last elements of the array.

11. Write a code fragment that asks the user to enter a positive integer and then creates a dynamic array of that many *ints*.

12. Is the following valid code? If so, what does it print?

    ```
    cout << (int *) "Home of the jolly bytes";
    ```

13. Write a code fragment that dynamically allocates a structure of the type described in question 6 and then reads a value for the *kind* member of the structure.

14. Listing 4-7 illustrates a problem with the following numeric input with line-oriented string input. How would replacing

    ```
    cin.getline(address,80);
    ```

    with

    ```
    cin >> address;
    ```

    affect the working of this program?

Programming Exercises

1. Write a C++ program that requests and displays information as shown below. Note that the program adjusts the grade downward, that is, up one letter. Assume the user requests an A, B, or C so that you don't have to worry about the gap between a D and an F.

```
What is your first name? Betty Sue
What is your last name? Yew
What letter grade do you deserve? B
What is your age? 22
Name: Yew, Betty Sue
Grade: C
Age: 22
```

2. William Wingate runs a pizza-analysis service. For each pizza, he needs to record the following information:

- The name of the pizza company, which may consist of more than one word

- The diameter of the pizza

- The weight of the pizza

Devise a structure that can hold this information and write a program using a structure variable of that type. The program should ask the user to enter each of the items of information listed above, then the program should display that information. Use *cin* (or its methods) and *cout*.

3. Do programming exercise 2, but use *new* to allocate a structure instead of declaring a structure variable. Also, have the program request the pizza diameter before it requests the pizza company name.

CHAPTER 5

LOOPS AND RELATIONAL EXPRESSIONS

You will learn about the following in this chapter:

- ◇ The *for* loop
- ◇ Expressions and statements
- ◇ The increment and decrement operators: ++ and --
- ◇ Combination assignment operators
- ◇ Compound statements (blocks)
- ◇ The comma operator

- ◇ Relational operators: >, >=, ==, <=, < , and !=
- ◇ The *while* loop
- ◇ The *typedef* facility
- ◇ The *do while* loop
- ◇ The *get()* character input method
- ◇ The end-of-file condition
- ◇ Nested loops and two-dimensional arrays

C omputers do more than store data. They analyze, consolidate, rearrange, extract, modify, extrapolate, synthesize, and otherwise manipulate data. Sometimes they even distort and trash data, but we'll try to steer clear of that kind of behavior. To perform their manipulative miracles, programs need tools for performing repetitive actions and for making decisions. C++, of course, provides such tools. Indeed, it uses the same *for* loops, *while* loops, *do while* loops, *if* statements, and *switches* that regular C employs, so if you know C, you can zip through this and the next chapter. (But don't zip too fast—you don't want to miss how *cin* handles character input!) These various program control statements often use relational expressions and logical expressions to govern their behavior. This chapter discusses loops and relational expressions, and the next chapter follows up with branching statements and logical expressions.

Introducing the *for* Loop

Circumstances often call upon a program to perform repetitive tasks, such as adding together the elements of an array one by one or printing some paean to productivity twenty times. The C++ *for* loop makes such tasks easy to do. Let's look at a loop in Listing 5-1, see what it does, then discuss how it works.

Listing 5-1 *forloop.cpp*

```
// forloop.cpp -- introducing the for loop
#include <iostream.h>
int main(void)
{
        //   initialize; test ; update
        for (int i = 0; i < 5; i++)
                cout << "C++ knows loops.\n";
        cout << "C++ knows when to stop.\n";
        return 0;
}
```

Here is the output:

```
C++ knows loops.
C++ knows loops.
C++ knows loops.
C++ knows loops.
C++ knows loops.
C++ knows when to stop.
```

This loop begins by defining an integer i and setting it to 0:

```
int i = 0
```

This is the *loop initialization* part of the loop. Then, in the *loop test,* the program tests to see if i is less than 5:

```
i < 5
```

If so, the program executes the following statement, which is termed the *loop body:*

```
cout << "C++ knows loops.\n";
```

Then the program uses the *loop update* part of the loop to increase i by 1:

```
i++
```

We've used the ++ operator, called the *increment operator.* It increments the value of its operand by 1. (The increment operator is not restricted to *for* loops. For instance, you can use

```
i++;
```

instead of

```
i = i + 1;
```

as a statement in a program.) Incrementing *i* completes the first cycle of the loop.

Next, the loop begins a new cycle by comparing the new *i* value with 5. Because the new value (1) also is less than 5, the loop prints another line and then finishes by incrementing *i* again. That sets the stage for a fresh cycle of testing, executing a statement, and updating the value of *i*. The process continues until the loop updates *i* to 5. Then the next test fails, and the program moves on to the next statement after the loop.

for Loop Parts

A *for* loop, then, provides a step-by-step recipe for performing repeated actions. Let's take a more detailed look at how it's set up. The usual parts of a *for* loop handle these steps:

- Setting a value initially
- Performing a test to see if the loop should continue
- Executing the loop actions
- Updating value(s) used for the test

The C++ loop design positions these elements so that you can spot them at a glance. The initialization, test, and update actions constitute a three-part control section enclosed in parentheses. Each part is an expression, and semicolons separate the expressions from each other. The statement following the control section is called the *body* of the loop, and it is executed as long as the *test-expression* remains true:

```
for (initialization; test-expression; update-expression)
        body
```

C++ syntax counts a complete *for* statement as a single statement, even though it may incorporate one or more statements in the *body* portion.

The loop evaluates *initialization* just once. Typically, programs use this expression to set a variable to a starting value, then use the variable to count loop cycles. If you're coming to C++ from C, you may be a little surprised that our example *declares* the variable *i* in the *for* loop control section. C doesn't allow you to use a declaration there, but C++ does. The C++ programming style is to declare variables near the location they're first used. This program first uses *i* inside the loop, so we declared *i* in the initialization part of the control statement. Of course, you could instead declare the variable before the loop, if you wanted to.

The *test-expression* determines whether the loop body gets executed. Typically, this expression is a *relational* expression, that is, one that compares two values. Our example, for instance, compares the value of *i* to 5, checking to see if *i* is less than 5. If the comparison is true, the program executes the loop body. Actually, C++ doesn't limit *test-expression* to true-false comparisons. You can use any expression. If the expression evaluates to zero, the loop terminates. If the expression evaluates to nonzero, the loop continues. Listing 5-2 demonstrates this by using the expression *i* as the test condition. (In the update section, *i--* is similar to *i++* except that it *decreases* the value of *i* by 1 each time it's used.)

Listing 5-2 *num_test.cpp*

```
// num_test.cpp -- use numeric test in for loop
#include <iostream.h>
int main(void)
{
        cout << "Enter the starting countdown value: ";
        int limit;
        cin >> limit;
        for (int i = limit; i; i--)         // entry-condition test
                cout << "i = " << i << "\n";
        cout << "Done now that i = " << i << "\n";
        return 0;
}
```

Here is the output:

```
Enter the starting countdown value: 4
i = 4
i = 3
i = 2
i = 1
Done now that i = 0
```

Note that the loop terminates when *i* reaches 0. Relational expressions, such as $i < 5$, fit into this framework by evaluating to *1* if true and to *0* if false. (This will change as implementations incorporate the new ANSI/ISO C++ *bool* type; we'll discuss this a little later.) Also note that the *i* variable is not confined to the loop; we're free to display its value after the loop completes.

The *for* loop is an *entry-condition* loop. This means the test expression is evaluated *before* each loop cycle. The loop never executes the loop body when the test expression is false. For instance, suppose we rerun the program in Listing 5-2 but give *0* as a starting value. Because the test condition fails the very first time it's evaluated, the loop body never gets executed:

```
Enter the starting countdown value: 0
Done now that i = 0
```

This look-before-you-loop attitude can help keep a program out of trouble. The *update-expression* is evaluated at the end of the loop, after the body has been executed. Typically, it's used to increase or decrease the value of the variable keeping track of the number of loop cycles. However, it can be any valid C expression, as can the other control expressions. This makes the *for* loop capable of much more than simply counting from 0 to 5, the way our first loop did. You'll see some examples later.

The *for* loop body consists of a single statement, but you'll soon see how to stretch that rule. Figure 5-1 summarizes the *for* loop design.

The declaration of i in the *for* loop initialization section takes place before the looping process starts, so it is not inside the loop body. C++ does let you use a declaration statement inside the loop body itself. However, that's a poor idea, for it leads to multiple declarations of the same variable. Each instance of the variable would exist for one loop cycle, then be tossed away.

A *for* statement looks something like a function call because it uses a name followed by paired parentheses. However, *for*'s status as a C++ keyword prevents the compiler from thinking *for* is a function. It also prevents you from naming a function *for*.

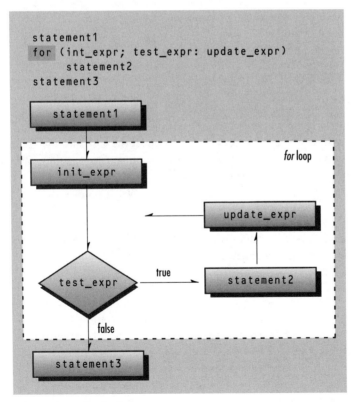

Figure 5-1 The *for* loop

TIP

Common C++ style is to place a space between *for* and the following parentheses and to omit space between a function name and the following parentheses:

```
for (int i = 6; i < 10; i++)
    smart_function(i);
```

Other control statements, such as *if* and *while*, are treated similarly to *for*. This serves to reenforce visually the distinction between a control statement and a function call. Also, common practice is to indent the body of a *for* statement to make it stand out visually.

Expressions and Statements

A *for* control section uses three expressions. Within its self-imposed limits of syntax, C++ is a very expressive language. Any value or any valid combination of values and operators constitute an expression. For example, *10* is an expression with the value *10* (no surprise), and *28 * 20* is an expression with the value *560*. In C++, every expression has a value. Often the value is obvious. For instance, the expression

```
22 + 27
```

is formed from two values and the addition operator, and it has the value *49*. Sometimes the value is less obvious. For example,

```
x = 20
```

is an expression because it's formed from two values and the assignment operator. C++ defines the value of an assignment expression to be the value of the left-hand member, so the expression above has the value *20*. The fact that assignment expressions have values permits statements such as the following:

```
maids = (cooks = 4) + 3;
```

The expression *cooks = 4* has the value *4*, so *maids* is assigned the value *7*. However, just because C++ permits this behavior doesn't mean you should encourage it. But the same rule that makes this peculiar statement possible also makes the following useful statement possible:

```
x = y = z = 0;
```

This is a fast way to set several variables to the same value. The precedence table (Appendix D) reveals that assignment associates right-to-left, so first *0* is assigned to *z*, then the value of *z = 0* is assigned to *y*, and so on.

Finally, as we mentioned, relational expressions evaluate to *1* if true and to *0* if false. The short program in Listing 5-3 illustrates some points about expression values. The << operator has higher precedence than the operators we're using in the expressions, so we've used parentheses to enforce the correct order.

Listing 5-3 *express.cpp*

```
// express.cpp -- values of expressions
#include <iostream.h>
int main(void)
{
        int x;

        cout << "The expression x = 100 has the value ";
        cout << (x = 100) << "\n";
        cout << "Now x = " << x << "\n";
        cout << "The expression x < 3 has the value ";
        cout << (x < 3) << "\n";
        cout << "The expression x > 3 has the value ";
        cout << (x > 3) << "\n";
        return 0;
}
```

Here is the output:

```
The expression x = 100 has the value 100
Now x = 100
The expression x < 3 has the value 0
The expression x > 3 has the value 1
```

RULE

A C++ expression is a value or a combination of values and operators, and every C++ expression has a value.

To evaluate the expression *x = 100*, C++ must assign the value *100* to *x*. When the very act of evaluating an expression changes the value of data in memory, we say the evaluation has a *side effect*. Thus evaluating an assignment expression has the side effect of changing the assignee's value. You may think of assignment as the intended effect, but from the standpoint of how C++ is constructed, evaluating the expression is the primary effect. Not all expressions have side effects. For instance, evaluating *x + 15* calculates a new value, but it doesn't change the value of x. But evaluating *++x + 15* does have a side effect, since it involves incrementing x.

From expression to statement is a short step; just add a semicolon. Thus

```
age = 100
```

is an expression, while

```
age = 100;
```

is a statement. Any expression can become a statement by adding a semicolon, but the result may not make programming sense. For instance, if *rodents* is a variable, then

```
rodents + 6;   // valid, but useless, statement
```

155

is a valid C++ statement. The compiler will pass it, but the statement doesn't accomplish anything useful. The program merely calculates the sum, does nothing with it, and goes on to the next statement.

Of course, what makes rules interesting are the exceptions. Note that C++ syntax causes the two semicolons in a *for* control section to act as expression separators, not as statement makers, so the three parts of the control section really are expressions, not statements, and the entire loop counts as a single statement.

Nonexpressions and Statements

Some concepts, such as knowing the structure of a *for* loop, are crucial to understanding C++. But there are also relatively minor aspects of syntax that can suddenly bedevil you just when you think you understand the language. We'll look at a couple of them now.

While it is true that adding a semicolon to any expression makes it a statement, the reverse is not true. That is, removing a semicolon from a statement does not necessarily convert it to an expression. Of the kinds of statements we've used so far, *return* statements, declaration statements, and *for* statements don't fit the statement = expression + semicolon mold. For instance, while

```
int toad;
```

is a statement, the fragment *int toad* is not an expression and does not have a value. This makes code like the following invalid:

```
eggs = int toad * 1000;     // invalid, not an expression
cin >> int toad;            // can't combine declaration with cin
```

Similarly, you can't assign a *for* loop to a variable:

```
int fx = for (int i = 0; i< 4; i++)
        cout >> i;   // not possible
```

Here the *for* loop is not an expression, so it has no value, so it can't be assigned.

At this point you may have noticed an apparent inconsistency. If the semicolons in a *for* statement control section separate expressions from each other and if dropping the semicolon from a declaration statement doesn't produce an expression, then what do we call the *int i = 0* initialization in a *for* loop like this?

```
for (int i = 0; i< 4; i++)
        cout >> i;
```

As we said, *int i = 0* is not an expression. Nor is it a declaration statement, since the semicolon is not part of it. Because C didn't allow this form at all, C++ had to come up with a new term: the *declaration-statement expression*. What it boils down to is that C++ programmers want to be able to declare and initialize a variable in a *for* loop initialization, and they'll do whatever is necessary to C++ syntax and to the English language to make it possible.

Back to the *for* Loop

Let's be a bit more ambitious with loops. Listing 5-4 uses a loop to calculate and store the first 16 factorials. Factorials, which are handy for computing odds, are calculated the following way. Zero factorial, written as 0!, is defined to be 1. Then 1! is 1 * 0!, or 1. Next, 2! is 2 * 1!, or 2. Then 3! is 3 * 2!, or 6, and so on, with the factorial of each integer being the product of that integer with the preceding factorial. (One of the pianist Victor Borge's best-known monologues features phonetic punctuation, in which the exclamation mark is pronounced something like phffft pptz, with a moist accent. The author has been assured by Professor Mark McConnell, Department of Mathematics, Oklahoma State University, in a personal communication, after reading the author's comment in the first edition of this book, that no reputable organization of mathematicians has denied that mathematicians, when in private, use Borge's pronunciation, however, that this is not the preferred pronunciation among mathematicians.) The program uses one loop to calculate the values of successive factorials, storing them in an array. Then it uses a second loop to display the results. Also, the program introduces using external declarations for values.

 ## Listing 5-4 *formore.cpp*

```
// formore.cpp -- more looping with for
#include <iostream.h>
const int ArSize = 16;          // example of external declaration
int main(void)
{
        double factorials[ArSize];
        factorials[1] = factorials[0] = 1.0;
        for (int i = 2; i < ArSize; i++)
                factorials[i] = i * factorials[i-1];
        for (i = 0; i < ArSize; i++)
        {
                cout << i << "! = ";
                cout << factorials[i] << "\n";
        }
        return 0;
}
```

Here is the output:

```
0! = 1
1! = 1
2! = 2
3! = 6
4! = 24
5! = 120
6! = 720
7! = 5040
8! = 40320
```

continued on next page

continued from previous page
```
9! = 362880
10! = 3.6288e+06
11! = 3.99168e+07
12! = 4.790016e+08
13! = 6.227021e+09
14! = 8.717829e+10
15! = 1.307674e+12
```

Factorials get big fast!

Program Notes

The program creates an array to hold the factorial values. Element *0* is *0!,* element *1* is *1!,* and so on. Since the first two factorials equal 1, the program sets the first two elements of the *factorials* array to *1.0.* (Remember, the first element of an array has an index value of *0.*) After that, the program uses a loop to set each factorial to the product of the index with the previous factorial. The loop illustrates that we can use the loop counter as a variable in the body of the loop.

Once the program declares *i* in the initialization for the first loop, it can use *i* again in the second loop. The *i* variable is no different from any other variable; it just happens to be declared in a loop initialization. The *i* variable can be used anywhere subsequently in the *main()* function.

The program demonstrates how the *for* loop works hand in hand with arrays by providing a convenient means to access each array member in turn. Also, *formore.cpp* uses *const* to create a symbolic representation (*ArSize*) for the array size. Then it uses *ArSize* wherever the array size came into play, such as in the array definition and in the limits for the loops handling the array. Now, if you wish to extend the program to, say, 20 factorials, you just have to set *ArSize* to *20* in the program and recompile. By using a symbolic constant, you avoid having to manually change every occurrence of *16* to *20.*

TIP

It's usually a good idea to define a *const* value to represent the number of elements in an array. Use the *const* value in the array declaration and in all other references to the array size, such as in a *for* loop.

The limit *i < ArSize* reflects the fact that subscripts for an array with *ArSize* elements run from *0* to *ArSize - 1,* so the array index should stop 1 short of *ArSize.* You could use the test *i <= ArSize - 1* instead, but it looks awkward in comparison.

One program sidelight is that we declared the *const int* variable *ArSize* outside the body of *main().* As the end of Chapter 4 mentioned, this makes *ArSize* external data. The two consequences of declaring *ArSize* in this fashion are that *ArSize* exists for the duration of the program and that it can be used by all the functions in the program file. In this particular case, the program has just one function, so declaring *ArSize* externally has little practical effect. But multifunction programs often benefit from sharing external constants, so we'll practice using them now.

Changing the Step Size

So far our loops have increased the loop counter by 1 each cycle. We can change that by changing the update expression. The program in Listing 5-5, for example, increases the loop counter by a user-selected step size. Instead of using i++ as the update expression, it uses the expression i = i + by, where *by* is the user-selected step size.

Listing 5-5 *bigstep.cpp*

```
// bigstep.cpp -- count as directed
#include <iostream.h>
int main(void)
{
        cout << "Enter an integer: ";
        int by;
        cin >> by;
        cout << "Counting by " << by << "s:\n";
        for (int i = 0; i < 100; i = i + by)
                cout << i << "\n";
        return 0;
}
```

Here is a sample run:

```
Enter an integer: 17
Counting by 17s:
0
17
34
51
68
85
```

Once i reaches the value *102,* the loop quits. The main point here is that the update expression can be any valid expression. For instance, if you wanted to square i and add 10 each cycle, you could use i = i * i + 10.

Inside Strings with the *for* Loop

The *for* loop provides a direct way to access each character in a string in turn. Listing 5-6, for example, lets you enter a string and then displays the string character-by-character in reverse order. The *strlen()* yields the number of characters in the string; the loop uses that value in its initializing expression to set i to the index of the last character in the string, not counting the null character. To count backwards, the program uses the *decrement* operator (--) to decrease the array subscript by 1 each loop. Also, Listing 5-6 uses the *greater than or equal to* relational operator (>=) to test whether the loop has reached the first element. We'll summarize all the relational operators soon.

Listing 5-6 *forstr1.cpp*

```
// forstr1.cpp -- using for with a string
#include <iostream.h>
#include <string.h>
const int ArSize = 20;
int main(void)
{
        cout << "Enter a word: ";
        char word[ArSize];
        cin >> word;

        // display letters in reverse order
        for (int i = strlen(word) - 1; i >= 0; i--)
                cout << word[i];
        cout << "\n";
        return 0;
}
```

Here is a sample run:

```
Enter a word: animal
lamina
```

Yes, the program succeeds in printing *animal* backwards; choosing *animal* as a test word more clearly illustrates the effect of this program than choosing, say, *redder* or *stats*.

The Increment (++) and Decrement (--) Operators

C++ features several operators that are frequently used in loops, so let's take a little time to examine them now. We've already used two: the increment operator (++), which inspired the name C++, and the decrement operator (--). These perform two exceedingly common loop operations: increasing or decreasing a loop counter by 1. However, there's more to their story than you've seen to date. Each operator comes in two varieties. The *prefix* version comes before the operand, as in ++x. The *postfix* version comes after the operand, as in x++. The two versions have the same effect upon the operand, but they differ in *when* they take place. It's like getting paid for mowing the lawn in advance or afterwards; both methods have the same final effect on your wallet, but they differ in when the money gets added. Listing 5-7 demonstrates this difference for the increment operator.

 Listing 5-7 *plus_one.cpp*

```
// plus_one.cpp -- the increment operator
#include <iostream.h>
int main(void)
```

```
{
      int a = 20;
      int b = 20;

      cout << "a   = " << a << ":    b = " << b << "\n";
      cout << "a++ = " << a++ << ": ++b = " << ++b << "\n";
      cout << "a   = " << a << ":    b = " << b << "\n";
      return 0;
}
```

Here is the output:

```
a      = 20:   b = 20
a++    = 20: ++b = 21
a      = 21:   b = 21
```

Roughly speaking, the notation a++ means "use the current value of a in evaluating an expression, then increment the value of a." Similarly, the notation ++b means "first increment the value of b, then use the new value in evaluating the expression." For example, we have the following relationships:

```
int x = 5;
int y = ++x;   // change x, then assign to y
               // y is 6, x is 6

int z = 5;
int y = z++;   // assign to y, then change z
               // y is 5, z is 6
```

The increment and decrement operators are a concise, convenient way to handle the common task of increasing or decreasing values by 1. You can use them with pointers as well as with basic variables. Recall that adding 1 to a pointer increases its value by the number of bytes in the type it points to. The same rule holds for incrementing and decrementing pointers.

 RULE

Incrementing and decrementing pointers follow pointer arithmetic rules. Thus if *pt* points to the first member of an array, then ++*pt* changes *pt* so that it points to the second member.

The increment and decrement operators are nifty little operators, but don't get carried away and increment or decrement the same value more than once in the same statement. The problem is that the use-then-change rule and change-then-use rule can become ambiguous. That is, a statement such as

```
x++ = 2 * x++ * (3 - ++x);   // don't do it
```

can produce quite different results on different systems. C++ does not define correct behavior for this sort of statement.

Combination Assignment Operators

Listing 5-5 uses the following expression to update a loop counter:

```
i = i + by
```

C++ has a combined addition and assignment operator that accomplishes the same result more concisely:

```
i += by
```

The += operator adds the values of its two operands together and assigns the result to the left-hand operand. This implies that the left-hand operand must be something you can assign to, such as a variable, an array element, a structure member, or data identified by dereferencing a pointer:

```
int k = 5;
k += 3;                     // ok, k set to 8
int *pa = new int[10];      // pa points to pa[0]
pa[4] = 12;
pa[4] += 6;                 // ok, pa[4] set to 18
*(pa + 4) += 7;            // ok, pa[4] set to 25
pa += 2;                    // ok, pa points to the former pa[2]
34 += 10;                   // quite wrong
```

Each arithmetic operator has a corresponding assignment operator, as summarized in Table 5-1. Each operator works analogously to +=. Thus the statement

```
k *= 10;
```

replaces the current value of *k* with a value ten times greater.

Operator	Effect (L=left operand, R=right operand)
+=	assigns L + R to L
−=	assigns L − R to L
*=	assigns L * R to L
/=	assigns L / R to L
%=	assigns L % R to L

Table 5-1 Combined assignment operators

Compound Statements, or Blocks

The format, or syntax, for writing a C++ *for* statement may seem restrictive to you because the body of the loop must be a single statement. That's awkward if you want the loop body to contain several statements. Fortunately, C++ provides a syntax loophole through which you may stuff as many statements as you like into a loop body.

The trick is to use paired braces to construct a *compound statement,* or *block.* The block consists of the braces and the enclosed statements and, for the purposes of syntax, counts as a *single* statement. For instance, the program in Listing 5-8 uses braces to combine three separate statements into a single block. This enables the body of the loop to prompt the user, read input, and do a calculation. The program calculates the running sum of the numbers you enter, and this provides a natural occasion for using the += operator.

Listing 5-8 *block.cpp*

```
// block.cpp -- use a block statement
#include <iostream.h>
int main(void)
{
        cout << "The Amazing Accounto will sum and average ";
        cout << "five numbers for you.\n";
        cout << "Please enter five values:\n";
        double number;
        double sum = 0.0;
        for (int i = 1; i <= 5; i++)
        {                                       // block starts here
            cout << "Value " << i << ": ";
            cin >> number;
            sum += number;
        }                                       // block ends here
        cout << "Five exquisite choices indeed! ";
        cout << "They sum to " << sum << "\n";
        cout << "and average to " << sum / 5 << ".\n";
        cout << "The Amazing Accounto bids you adieu!\n";
        return 0;
}
```

Here is a sample run:

```
The Amazing Accounto will sum and average five numbers for you.
Please enter five values:
Value 1: 1942
Value 2: 1948
Value 3: 1957
Value 4: 1974
Value 5: 1980
Five exquisite choices indeed! They sum to 9801
and average to 1960.2.
The Amazing Accounto bids you adieu!
```

Suppose you left in the indentation but omitted the braces:

```
for (int i = 1; i <= 5; i++)
        cout << "Value " << i << ": ";          // loop ends here
        cin >> number;                          // after the loop
        sum += number;
cout << "Five exquisite choices indeed! ";
```

The compiler ignores indentation, so only the first statement would be in the loop. Thus the loop would print the five prompts and do nothing more. After the loop completed, the program would move to the following lines, reading and summing just one number.

Compound statements have another interesting property. If you define a new variable inside a block, the variable persists only as long as the program is executing statements within the block. When execution leaves the block, the variable is deallocated. That means the variable is known only within the block:

```
#include  <iostream.h>
int main(void)
{
        int x = 20;
        {                                // block starts
                int y = 100;
                cout << x << "\n";       // ok
                cout << y << "\n";       // ok
        }                                // block ends
        cout << x << "\n";               // ok
        cout << y << "\n";               // invalid, won't compile
        return 0;
}
```

Note that a variable defined in an outer block is still defined in the inner block.

The Comma Operator (or More Syntax Tricks)

The block, as you saw, lets you sneak two statements into a place where C++ syntax allows just one statement. The comma operator does the same for expressions, letting you sneak two expressions into a place where C++ syntax allows only one expression. For instance, suppose you have a loop in which one variable increases by 1 each cycle and a second variable decreases by 1 each cycle. Doing both in the update part of a *for* loop control section would be convenient, but the loop syntax allows just one expression there. The solution is to use the comma operator to combine the two expressions into one:

```
j++, i--   // two expressions count as one for syntax purposes
```

The comma is not always a comma operator. For instance, the comma in the declaration

```
int i, j;  // comma is a separator here, not an operator
```

serves to separate adjacent names in a list of variables.

Listing 5-9 uses the comma operator twice in a program that reverses the contents of a character array. Note that Listing 5-6 displayed the contents of an array in reverse order, but Listing 5-9 actually moves characters around in the array. The program also uses a block to group several statements into one.

Listing 5-9 *forstr2.cpp*

```
// forstr2.cpp -- reversing an array
#include <iostream.h>
#include <string.h>
const int ArSize = 20;
int main(void)
{
        cout << "Enter a word: ";
        char word[ArSize];
        cin >> word;

        // physically modify array
        char temp;
        int i, j;
        for (j = 0, i = strlen(word) - 1; j < i; i--, j++)
        {                          // start block
             temp = word[i];
             word[i] = word[j];
             word[j] = temp;
        }                          // end block
        cout << word << "\n";
        return 0;
}
```

Here is a sample run:

```
Enter a word: parts
strap
```

Program Notes

Look at the *for* control section:

```
for (j = 0, i = strlen(word) - 1; j < i; i--, j++)
```

First, it uses the comma operator to squeeze two initializations into one expression for the first part of the control section. Then it uses the comma operator again to combine two updates into a single expression for the last part of the control section.

Next, look at the body. The program uses braces to combine several statements into a single unit. In the body, the program reverses the word by switching the first element of the array with the last element. Then it increments *j* and decrements *i* so that they now refer to the next-to-the-first element and to the next-to-the-last element. This accomplished, the program swaps those elements. Note that the test condition *j<i* makes the loop stop when it reaches the center of the array. If it were to continue past this point, it would begin swapping the switched elements back to their original positions. See Figure 5-2.

Another thing to note is the location for declaring the variables *temp, i,* and *j*. We declared *i* and *j* before the loop because you can't combine two declarations with a comma operator. That's because declarations already use the comma for another

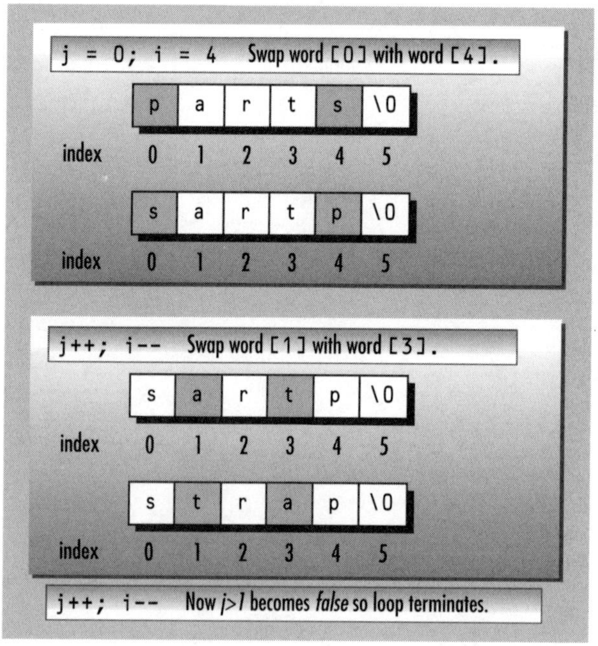

Figure 5-2 Reversing a string

purpose—separating items in a list. We could have used a single declaration-statement expression to create and initialize two variables, but it's a bit confusing visually:

```
int j = 0, i = strlen(word) - 1
```

In this case the comma is just a list separator, not the comma operator, so the expression declares and initializes both *j* and *i*. But it looks like it's just declaring *j*.

Comma Operator Tidbits

By far the most common use for the comma operator is to fit two or more expressions into a single *for* loop expression. But C++ does provide the operator with two additional properties. First, it guarantees that the first expression is evaluated before the second expression. So expressions such as the following are safe:

```
i = 20, j = 2 * i        // i set to 20, j set to 40
```

Second, C++ states that the value of a comma expression is the value of the second part. The value of the expression above, for instance, is *40*, since that is the value of *j* = *2 * i*.

The comma operator has the lowest precedence of any operator. For example, the statement

```
cat = 17,240;
```

gets read as

```
(cats = 17), 240;
```

That is, *cats* is set to *17,* and *240* does nothing.

Relational Expressions

Computers are more than relentless number crunchers. They have the gift of being able to compare values, and this ability is the foundation of computer decision making. In C++, *relational operators* embody this ability. C++ provides six relational operators for comparing numbers. Because characters are represented by their ASCII code, you can use these operators with characters, too. But they don't work with strings. Each relational expression reduces to the value *1* if the comparison is true and to *0* if the comparison is false, so they are well suited for use in a loop test expression. Table 5-2 summarizes these operators.

Operator	Meaning
<	is less than
<=	is less than or equal to
==	is equal to
>	is greater than
>=	is greater than or equal to
!=	is not equal to

Table 5-2 Relational operators

The six relational operators exhaust the comparisons C++ lets you make for numbers. If you want to compare two values to see which is the more beautiful or the luckier, you'll have to look elsewhere.

Here are some sample tests:

```
for (x = 20; x > 5; x--) // continue while x is greater than 5
for (x = 1; y != x; x++) // continue while y is not equal to x
for (cin.get(c); c == ' '; cin.get(c))     // continue while c
                                           //is a space
```

The relational operators have a lower precedence than the arithmetic operators. That means the expression

```
x + 3 > y - 2        // expression 1
```

corresponds to

```
(x + 3) > (y - 2)    // expression 2
```

and not the following:

```
x + (3 > y) - 2        // expression 3
```

Because the expression $(3 > y)$ is either *1* or *0*, expressions 2 and 3 both are valid. But most of us would want expression 1 to mean expression 2, and that is what C++ does.

ANSI/ISO C++ UPDATE

The ANSI/ISO C++ committee has accepted a proposal to define a new type called *bool* (Chapter 3). This type has two possible values, the literals *true* and *false*. Under the standard, relational expressions will evaluate to *true* and *false* instead of to *1* and *0*. However, this shouldn't affect code because *true* and *false* can be converted implicitly to *1* and *0* and vice versa. This edition of the book will continue to use *1* and *0* for the values of relational operators, but you can substitute *true* and *false* if your implementation supports the *bool* type.

The Mistake You'll Probably Make

Don't confuse testing the is-equal-to operator (==) with the assignment operator (=). The expression

```
musicians == 4     // comparison
```

asks the musical question, is *musicians* equal to *4?* The expression has the value *1* if the comparison is true and *0* if it is false. The expression

```
musicians = 4      // assignment
```

assigns the value *4* to *musicians*. The whole expression, in this case, has the value *4* because that's the value of the left-hand side.

The flexible design of the *for* loop creates an interesting opportunity for error. If you accidentally drop an equal sign (=) from the == operator and use an assignment expression instead of a relational expression for the test part of a *for* loop, you have still produced valid code. That's because you can use *any* valid C++ expression for a *for* loop test condition. Remember, the loop really checks to see if the expression is zero or nonzero, not if it is false or true. So an expression that assigns *4* to *musicians* has the value *4* and is treated as true. If you come from a language such as Pascal or BASIC that uses = to test for equality, you may be particularly prone to this slip.

Listing 5-10 shows a situation in which you could make this sort of error. The program attempts to examine an array of quiz scores and to stop when it reaches the first score that's not a *20*. We show a loop that correctly uses comparison and then one that mistakenly uses assignment in the test condition. The program also has another egregious design error that you'll see how to fix later. (You learn from your mistakes, and Listing 5-10 is happy to help in that respect.)

Listing 5-10 *equal.cpp*

```
// equal.cpp -- equality vs assignment
#include <iostream.h>
int main(void)
{
        int quizscores[10] =
                { 20, 20, 20, 20, 20, 19, 20, 18, 20, 20};

// NOTE: some implementations may need to use
//       static int quizscores[10] to enable initialization

        cout << "Doing it right:\n";
        for (int i = 0; quizscores[i] == 20; i++)
                cout << "quiz " << i << " is a 20\n";

        cout << "Doing it dangerously wrong:\n";
        for (i = 0; quizscores[i] = 20; i++)
                cout << "quiz " << i << " is a 20\n";

        return 0;
}
```

Since this program has a serious problem, you may prefer reading about it to actually running it. Here is some sample output:

```
Doing it right:
quiz 0 is a 20
quiz 1 is a 20
quiz 2 is a 20
quiz 3 is a 20
quiz 4 is a 20
Doing it dangerously wrong:
quiz 0 is a 20
quiz 1 is a 20
quiz 2 is a 20
quiz 3 is a 20
quiz 4 is a 20
quiz 5 is a 20
quiz 6 is a 20
quiz 7 is a 20
quiz 8 is a 20
quiz 9 is a 20
quiz 10 is a 20
quiz 11 is a 20
quiz 12 is a 20
quiz 13 is a 20
...
```

The first loop correctly halts after displaying the first five quiz scores. But the second starts by displaying the whole array. Worse than that, it says every value is *20*. Worse than that, it doesn't stop at the end of the array!

Where things go wrong, of course, is with the following test expression:

```
quizscores[i] = 20
```

First, simply because it assigns a nonzero value to the array element, the expression is always nonzero, hence always true. Second, because the expression assigns values to the array elements, it actually changes the data. Third, because the test expression remains true, the program continues changing data beyond the end of the array. It just keeps putting more and more *20*s into memory! This is not good. In our case, the computer eventually crashed.

Like C, C++ grants you more freedom than most languages in programming. This comes at the cost of requiring greater responsibility on your part. Nothing but your own good planning prevents a program from going beyond the bounds of a standard C++ array. However, with C++ classes, you can design a protected array type that prevents this sort of nonsense. Chapter 11 provides an example. In the meantime, you should build the protection into your programs when needed. For instance, our loop should have included a test that kept it from going past the last member. That's true even for the "good" loop. If all the scores had been *20*s, it, too, would have exceeded the array bounds. In short, the loop needed to test the value of the array *and* test the value of the array index. Chapter 6 will show you how to use logical operators to combine two such tests into a single condition.

Comparing Strings

Suppose you want to see if a string in a character array is the word *mate*. If *word* is the array name, the following test may not do what you think:

```
word == "mate"
```

Remember that the name of an array is a synonym for its address. Similarly, a quoted string constant is a synonym for its address. Thus the above relational expression doesn't test to see if the *strings* are the same—it checks to see if they are stored at the same *address*. And the answer to that is no, even if the two strings have the same characters.

Because C++ handles strings as addresses, you'll get little satisfaction trying to use the relational operators to compare strings. Instead, you can go to the C++ string library and use the *strcmp()* function to compare strings. This function takes two string addresses as arguments. That means the arguments can be pointers, string constants, or character array names. If the two strings are identical, the function returns the value zero. If the first string precedes the second alphabetically, *strcmp()* returns a negative value, and if the first string follows the second alphabetically, *strcmp()* returns a positive value. Actually, "in the system collating sequence" would be more accurate than "alphabetically." This means that characters are compared according to the system code for characters. For instance, in ASCII code, all uppercase letters have smaller codes than the lowercase letters, so uppercase precedes lowercase in the collating sequence. Therefore the string *"Zoo"* precedes the string *"aviary"*. The fact that comparisons are based on code values also means that uppercase and lowercase letters differ, so the string *"FOO"* is different from the *"foo"* string.

In some languages, such as BASIC and standard Pascal, strings stored in differently sized arrays are necessarily unequal to each other. But in C++ strings are defined by the terminating null character, not by the size of the containing array. That means that two strings can be identical even if contained in differently sized arrays:

```
char big[80] = "Daffy";            // 5 letters plus \0
char little[6] = "Daffy";          // 5 letters plus \0
```

By the way, although you can't use relational operators to compare strings, you can use them to compare characters because characters are really integer types. So

```
for (ch = 'a'; ch <= 'z'; ch++)
        cout << ch;
```

is valid code for displaying the characters of the alphabet.

Listing 5-11 uses *strcmp()* in the test condition of a *for* loop. The program displays a word, changes its first letter, displays the word again, and keeps going until *strcmp()* determines the word is the same as the string *"mate"*. Note that the listing includes the *string.h* file because it provides a function prototype for *strcmp()*.

Listing 5-11 *compstr.cpp*

```
// compstr.cpp -- comparing strings
#include <iostream.h>
#include <string.h>      // prototype for strcmp()
int main(void)
{
        char word[5] = "?ate";

// NOTE: some implementations may need to use
//      static char word[5] to enable initialization

        for (char ch = 'a'; strcmp(word, "mate"); ch++)
        {
                cout << word << "\n";
                word[0] = ch;
        }
        cout << "After loop ends, word is " << word << "\n";
        return 0;
}
```

Here is the output:

```
?ate
aate
bate
cate
date
eate
fate
```

continued on next page

continued from previous page

```
gate
hate
iate
jate
kate
late
After loop ends, word is mate
```

Program Notes

The program has some interesting points. One, of course, is the test. We want the loop to continue as long as *word* is not *mate*. That is, we want the test to continue as long as *strcmp()* says the two strings are not the same. The most obvious test for that is this:

```
strcmp(word, "mate") != 0    // strings are not the same
```

This statement has the value *1* (true) if the strings are unequal and the value *0* (false) if they are equal. But what about *strcmp(word, "mate")* by itself? It has a nonzero value (true) if the strings are unequal and the value *0* (false) if the strings are zero. In essence, the function returns true if the strings are different and false if they are the same. So you can use just the function instead of the whole relational expression. This produces the same behavior and involves less typing. Also, it's the way C and C++ programmers traditionally have used *strcmp()*.

Next, *compstr.cpp* uses the increment operator to march the variable *ch* through the alphabet:

```
ch++
```

You can use the increment and decrement operators with character variables because type *char* really is an integer type, so the operation actually changes the integer code stored in the variable. Also, note that using an array index makes it simple to change individual characters in a string:

```
word[0] = ch;
```

Finally, unlike most of the *for* loops to date, this loop isn't a counting loop. That is, it doesn't execute a block of statements a specified number of times. Instead, the loop watches for a particular circumstance (*word* being *"mate"*) to signal that it's time to stop. More typically, C++ programs use *while* loops for this second kind of test, so let's examine that form now.

The *while* Loop

The *while* loop is a *for* loop stripped of the initialization and update parts; it has just a test condition and a body:

```
while (test-condition)
       body
```

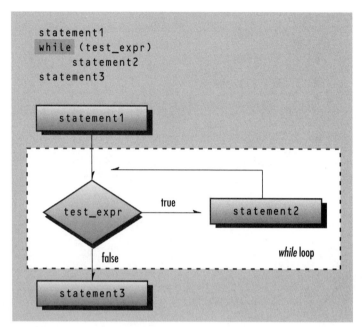

Figure 5-3 The *while* loop

First a program evaluates the *test-condition* expression. If the expression evaluates to a nonzero value (true), the program executes the statement(s) in the body. As with a *for* loop, the *body* consists of a single statement or of a block defined by paired braces. After finishing with the *body*, the program returns to the *test-condition* and reevaluates it. If the condition is nonzero, the program executes the *body* again. This cycle of testing and execution continues until the *test-condition* evaluates to *0* (false). See Figure 5-3. Clearly, if you want the loop to terminate eventually, something within the loop body must do something to affect the *test-condition* expression. For example, the loop could increment a variable used in the test condition or read a new value from keyboard input. Like the *for* loop, the *while* loop is an entry-condition loop. Thus if *test-condition* evaluates to *0* to begin with, the program never executes the body of the loop.

Listing 5-12 puts the *while* loop to work. The loop cycles through each character in a string and displays the character and its ASCII code. The loop quits when it reaches the null character. This technique of stepping through a string character-by-character until reaching the null characters is a standard C++ method for processing strings. Because a string contains its own termination marker, programs often don't need explicit information about how long a string is.

 **Listing 5-12** *while.cpp*

```
// while.cpp -- introducing the while loop
#include <iostream.h>
```

continued on next page

continued from previous page

```
const int ArSize = 20;
int main(void)
{
        char name[ArSize];

        cout << "Your first name, please: ";
        cin >> name;
        cout << "Here is your name, verticalized and ASCIIized:\n";
        int i = 0;                      // start at beginning of string
        while (name[i] != '\0')         // process to end of string
        {
                cout << name[i] << ": " << int(name[i]) << '\n';
                i++;                    // don't forget this step
        }
        return 0;
}
```

Here is a sample run:

```
Your first name, please: Muffy
Here is your name, verticalized and ASCIIized:
M: 77
u: 117
f: 102
f: 102
y: 121
```

(No, verticalized and ASCIIized are not real words or even good would-be words. But they do add a technoid tone to the output.)

Program Notes

The *while* condition looks like this:

```
while (name[i] != '\0')
```

It tests whether a particular character in the array is the null character. For this test to eventually succeed, the loop body needs to change the value of i. And it does so by incrementing i at the end of the loop body. Omitting this step would keep the loop stuck on the same array element, printing the character and its code until you managed to kill the program. Such an *infinite* loop is one of the most common problems with loops. Often it is caused by forgetting to update some value within the loop body.

You can rewrite the *while* line this way:

```
while (name[i])
```

With this change, the program will work just as it did before. That's because when *name[i]* is an ordinary character, its value is the character code, which is nonzero, or true. But when *name[i]* is the null character, its character-code value is 0, or false. This notation is more concise but less clear than what we used. Dumb compilers may produce faster code for the second version, but smart compilers will produce the same code for both.

To get the program to print the ASCII code for a character, we use a type cast to convert *name[i]* to an integer value. Then *cout* prints the value as an integer instead of interpreting it as a character code.

for vs. *while*

In C++ the *for* and *while* loops are essentially equivalent. For instance, the *for* loop

```
for (init-expression; test-expression; update-expression)
{
        statement(s)
}
```

could be rewritten this way:

```
init-expression;
while (test-expression)
{
        statement(s)
        update-expression;
}
```

Similarly, the *while* loop

```
while (test-expression)
        body
```

could be rewritten this way:

```
for ( ;test-expression;)
        body
```

The *for* loop requires three expressions, but they can be empty expressions. Only the two semicolons are mandatory. Incidentally, a missing test expression in a *for* loop is construed as being true, so the loop

```
for ( ; ; )
        body
```

runs forever.

Because the two loops are nearly equivalent, the one you use is a matter of style. (There is a slight difference if the body includes a *continue* statement, which is discussed in Chapter 6.) Typically, programmers use the *for* loop for counting loops because the *for* loop format lets you place all the relevant information—initial value, terminating value, and method of updating the counter—in one place. And the *while* loop most often is used when you don't know in advance precisely how many times the loop will execute.

BAD PUNCTUATION

Both the *for* loop and the *while* loop have bodies consisting of the *single* statement following the parenthesized expressions. As you've seen, that single statement can be a block, which can contain several statements. Keep in mind that braces, not indentation, define a block. Consider the following loop, for example:

```
i = 0;
while (name[i] != '\0')
        cout << name[i] << "\n";
        i++;
cout << "Done\n";
```

The indentation tells us the program author intended the *i++;* statement to be part of the loop body. The absence of braces, however, tells the compiler that the body consists solely of the first *cout* statement. Thus the loop keeps printing the first character of the array indefinitely. The program never reaches the *i++;* statement because it is outside the loop.

The next example shows another potential pitfall:

```
i = 0;
while (name[i] != '\0');      // problem semicolon
{
        cout << name[i] << "\n";
        i++;
}
cout << "Done\n";
```

This time we got the braces right, but we also inserted an extra semicolon. Remember, a semicolon terminates a statement, so this statement terminates the *while* loop. In other words, the body of the loop is a *null statement,* that is, nothing followed by a semicolon. All the material in braces now comes *after* the loop. It never gets reached. Instead, the loop cycles doing nothing forever. So beware the straggling semicolon.

Just a Moment

Sometimes it's useful to build a time delay into a program. For instance, you may have encountered programs that flash a message onscreen, then go on to something else before you can read it. You're left with the fear that you've missed irretrievable information of vital importance. It would be so much nicer if the program paused five seconds before moving on. The *while* loop is handy for producing this effect. One of the earlier techniques was to make the computer count for a while to use up time:

```
long wait = 0;
while (wait++ < 10000)
        ;                        // counting silently
```

The problem with this approach is that you have to change the counting limit when you change computer processor speed. Several games written for the original IBM PC, for instance, became unmanageably fast when run on its faster successors. A better approach is to let the system clock do the timing for you.

The ANSI C and the C++ libraries have a function to help you do this. The function is called *clock()*, and it returns the system time elapsed since a program started execution. There are a couple of complications. First, *clock()* doesn't necessarily return the time in seconds. Second, the function's return type might be *long* on some systems, *unsigned long* on others, or perhaps some other type.

But the *time.h* header file provides solutions to these problems. First, it defines a symbolic constant, *CLOCKS_PER_SEC* by name, that equals the number of system time units per second. So dividing the system time by this value yields seconds. Or you can multiply seconds by *CLOCKS_PER_SEC* to get time in the system units. Second, *time.h* establishes *clock_t* as an alias for the *clock()* return type. (See the note about Type Aliases.) This means you can declare a variable as type *clock_t* and the compiler will then convert that to *long* or *unsigned int* or whatever the proper type is for your system.

COMPATIBILITY NOTE

Some C++ implementations may have problems with *waiting.cpp* if the implementation's library component is not fully ANSI C compliant. That's because the *clock()* function is an ANSI addition to the traditional C library. Also, some premature implementations of ANSI C used *CLK_TCK* or *TCK_CLK* instead of the longer *CLOCKS_PER_SEC*. Version 2.0 of g++ doesn't recognize any of these defined constants. If you run this as a MVC++ 1.0 QuickWin program, the time delay works, but the beeps are suppressed, and the displaying of the *"starting\a\n"* string is delayed.

Listing 5-13 shows how to use *clock()* and the *time.h* header to create a time-delay loop.

Listing 5-13 *waiting.cpp*

```
// waiting.cpp -- using clock() in a time-delay loop
#include <iostream.h>
#include <time.h> // describes clock() function, clock_t type
int main(void)
{
        cout << "Enter the delay time, in seconds: ";
        float secs; cin >> secs;
        clock_t delay = secs * CLOCKS_PER_SEC;        // convert to clock ticks
        cout << "starting\a\n";
        clock_t start = clock();
        while (clock() - start < delay )     // wait until time elapses
            ;
```

continued on next page

continued from previous page

```
        cout << "done \a\n";
        return 0;
}
```

By calculating the delay time in system units instead of in seconds, the program avoids having to convert system time to seconds each loop cycle.

TYPE ALIASES

C++ has two ways to establish a new name as an alias for a type. One is to use the preprocessor:

```
#define BYTE char // preprocessor replaces BYTE with char
```

The preprocessor then replaces all occurrences of *BYTE* with *char* when you compile a program, thus making *BYTE* an alias for *char*.

The second method is to use the C++ (and C) keyword *typedef* to create an alias. For instance, to make *byte* an alias for *char*, do this:

```
typedef char byte;    // makes byte an alias for char
```

Here's the general form:

```
typedef type alias-name;
```

The *typedef* approach is the more powerful, for it can be used with more complex types, such as pointers:

```
typedef char * byte_pointer; // pointer to char type
```

You could try something similar with *#define,* but that won't work if you declare a list of variables. For instance, consider the following:

```
#define FLOAT_POINTER float *
FLOAT_POINTER pa, pb;
```

Preprocessor substitution converts the declaration to this:

```
float * pa, pb;   // pa a pointer to float, pb just a float
```

The *typedef* approach doesn't have that problem.

Notice that *typedef* doesn't create a new type. It just creates a new name for an old type. So if you make *word* an alias for *int,* cout will treat a type *word* value as the *int* it really is.

The *do while* Loop

You've now seen the *for* loop and the *while* loop. The third C++ loop is the *do while.* It's different from the other two because it's an *exit-condition* loop. That means this devil-may-care loop first executes the body of the loop, and only then evaluates the test expression to see if it should continue looping. If the condition evaluates to *0,* the loop terminates; otherwise, a new cycle of execution and testing begins. Such a loop always executes at least once because its program flow has to pass through the body of the loop before reaching the test. Here's the syntax:

```
do
        body
while (test-expression);
```

The *body* portion can be a single statement or a brace-delimited statement block. Figure 5-4 summarizes the program flow for the *do while* loop.

Usually, an entry-condition loop is a better choice than an exit-condition loop because the entry-condition loop checks before looping. For instance, suppose Listing 5-12 had used *do while* instead of *while*. Then the loop would have printed the null character and its code before finding it had already reached the end of the string. But sometimes a *do while* test does make sense. For instance, if you're requesting user input, the program has to obtain the input before testing it. Listing 5-14 shows how to use *do while* in that situation.

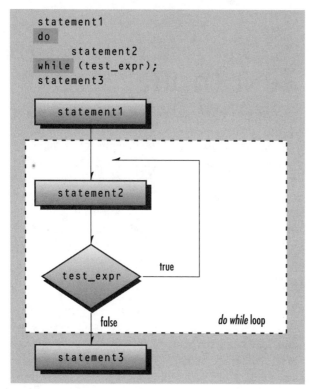

Figure 5-4 The *do while* loop

Listing 5-14 *dowhile.cpp*

```
// dowhile.cpp -- exit-condition loop
#include <iostream.h>
int main(void)
{
    int n;

    cout << "Enter numbers in the range 1-10 to find ";
    cout << "my favorite number\n";
    do
    {
        cin >> n;                   // execute body
    } while (n != 7);               // then test
    cout << "Yes, 7 is my favorite.\n" ;
    return 0;
}
```

Here's a sample run:

```
Enter numbers in the range 1-10 to find my favorite number
9
4
7
Yes, 7 is my favorite.
```

Loops and Text Input

Now that you've seen how loops work, let's look at one of the most common and important tasks assigned to loops: reading text character-by-character from a file or from the keyboard. For instance, you may wish to write a program that counts the number of characters, lines, and words in the input. Traditionally, C++, like C, uses the *while* loop for this sort of task. We'll investigate now how that is done. If you already know C, don't skim through this part too fast. Although the C++ *while* loop is the same as C's, C++'s I/O facilities are different. This can give the C++ loop a somewhat different look. In fact, the *cin* object supports three distinct modes of single-character input, each with a different user interface. So let's look at how to use these choices with *while* loops.

Using Unadorned *cin* for Input

If a program is going to use a loop to read input from the keyboard, it has to have some way of knowing when to stop. How can it know when to stop? One way is to choose some special character, sometimes called a sentinel character, to act as a stop sign. For instance, Listing 5-15 stops reading input when the program encounters a # character. The program counts the number of characters it reads and it *echoes* them. That is, it redisplays the characters that have been read. (Pressing a keyboard key doesn't automatically place a character on the screen; programs have to do that drudge work by echoing the input character.) When finished, it reports the total number of characters processed. Listing 5-15 shows the program.

Listing 5-15 *textin1.cpp*

```
// textin1.cpp -- reading chars with a while loop
#include <iostream.h>
int main(void)
{
        char ch;
        int count = 0;          // use basic input

        cin >> ch;              // get a character
        while (ch != '#')       // test the character
        {
                cout << ch;     // echo the character
                count++;        // count the character
                cin >> ch;      // get the next character
        }
        cout << "\n" << count << " characters read\n";
        return 0;
}
```

Here's a sample run:

see ken run#really fast
seekenrun
9 characters read

Apparently Ken runs so fast, he obliterates space itself—or at least the space characters in the input.

Program Notes

First, note the structure. The program reads the first input character *before* it reaches the loop. That way, the first character can be tested when the program reaches the loop statement. This is important, for the first character may be #. Because *textin1.cpp* uses an entry-condition loop, the program correctly skips the entire loop in that case. And because the variable *count* was set to zero previously, *count* has the correct value.

Suppose the first character read is not a #. Then the program enters the loop, displays the character, increments the count, and reads the next character. This last step is vital. Without it, the loop repeatedly processes the first input character forever. With it, the program advances to the next character.

This all sounds reasonable. So why does the program omit the spaces on output? Blame *cin*. When reading type *char* values, just as when reading other basic types, *cin* skips over spaces and newlines. So the spaces in the input did not get echoed and they did not get counted.

To further complicate things, the input to *cin* is buffered. That means the characters you type don't get sent to the program until you press (ENTER). This is why we were able to type characters after the #. Once we pressed (ENTER), the whole sequence of characters was sent to the program, but the program quit processing the input once it reached the # character.

cin.get() to the Rescue

Usually, programs that read input character-by-character need to examine every character, including spaces, tabs, and newlines. The *istream* class (defined in *iostream.h*), to which *cin* belongs, includes member functions that meet this need. In particular, the member function call *cin.get(ch)* reads the next character, even if it is a space, from the input and assigns it to the variable *ch*. By replacing *cin>>ch* with this function call, we can fix Listing 5-15. Listing 5-16 shows the result.

Listing 5-16 *textin2.cpp*

```
// textin2.cpp -- reading chars with a while loop
#include <iostream.h>
int main(void)
{
        char ch;
        int count = 0;

        cin.get(ch);                            // use the cin.get(ch) function
        while (ch != '#')
        {
                cout << ch;
                count++;
                cin.get(ch);                    // use it again
        }
        cout << "\n" << count << " characters read\n";
        return 0;
}
```

Here is a sample run:

Did you use a #2 pencil?
Did you use a
14 characters read

Now the program echoes and counts *every* character, including the spaces. Input is still buffered, so it's still possible to type more input than what eventually reaches the program.

If you are familiar with C, this program may strike you as being terribly wrong! The *cin.get(ch)* call places a value in the *ch* variable, which means it is altering the value of the variable. In C, you must pass the *address* of a variable to a function if you want to change the value of that variable. But the call to *cin.get()* in Listing 5-16 passes *ch*, not *&ch*. In C, code like this won't work. In C++ it can, providing the function declares the argument as a *reference*. This is a derived type new to C++. The *iostream.h* header file declares the argument to *cin.get(ch)* as a reference type, so this function can alter the value of its argument. We'll get to the details in Chapter 8. Meanwhile, the C mavens among you can relax—ordinarily, argument passing in C++ works just as it does in C. But for *cin.get(ch)* it doesn't.

Which *cin.get()*?

Chapter 4 used this code:

```
char name[ArSize];
...

cout << "Enter your name:\n";
cin.get(name, ArSize);
```

At that time *cin.get()* took two arguments: the array *name*, which is the address of the string (technically, type *char**), and *ArSize*, which is an integer of type *int*. (Recall that the name of an array is the address of its first element, so that makes the name of a character array type *char**.) But most recently, we've used *cin.get()* this way:

```
char ch;
cin.get(ch);
```

This time *cin.get()* has one argument, and it's type *char.*

Once again it is time for those of you familiar with C to get excited or confused. In C, if a function takes a pointer-to-*char* and an *int* as arguments, you can't successfully use the same function with a single argument of a different type. But you can do so in C++ because the language supports an OOP feature called *function overloading*. Function overloading allows you to create different functions having the same name providing they have different argument lists. If, for instance, you use *cin.get(name, ArSize)* in C++, the compiler will find the version of *cin.get()* that uses a *char** and an *int* as arguments. But if you use *cin.get(ch)*, the compiler fetches the version that uses a single type *char* argument. There is even another version of *cin.get()* that takes no arguments. Function overloading lets you use the same name for related functions that perform the same basic task in different ways or for different types. This is another topic awaiting you in Chapter 8. Meanwhile, you can get accustomed to function overloading by using the examples that come with the *istream* class. To distinguish between the different function versions, we'll include the argument list when referring to them. Thus *cin.get()* means the version that takes no arguments and *cin.get(ch)* means the version that takes one argument.

The End-of-File Condition

As Listing 5-16 showed, using a symbol such as # to signal the end of input is not satisfactory because such a symbol may be part of legitimate input. The same is true of other arbitrarily chosen symbols, such as @ or %. If the input comes from a file, you can employ a much more powerful technique—detecting the end-of-file (EOF). C++ input facilities cooperate with the operating system to detect when input reaches the end of a file and to report that information back to a program.

At first glance, reading information from files seems to have little to do with *cin* and keyboard input. But there are two connections. First, many operating systems, including UNIX and MS-DOS, support *redirection,* which lets you substitute a file for keyboard input. For instance, suppose in MS-DOS that you have an executable program called *gofish.exe* and a text file called *fishtale.* Then you can give this command line at the DOS prompt:

```
gofish <fishtale
```

This causes the program to take input from the *fishtale* file instead of from the keyboard. The < symbol is the redirection operator for both UNIX and DOS. Second, many operating systems let you simulate the end-of-file condition from the keyboard. In UNIX you do so by pressing (CTRL)-(D) at the beginning of a line. In DOS, you press (CTRL)-(Z), then (ENTER), anywhere on the line. Some implementations support similar behavior even though the underlying operating system doesn't. For instance, Symantec C++ for the Mac imitates UNIX and recognizes (CTRL)-(D) as a simulated EOF.

If your program can test for the end of a file, you can use it with redirected files and you can use it for keyboard input in which you simulate end-of-file. That sounds useful, so let's see how it's done.

The key is using the return value for the *cin.get(ch)* function call. The *cin.get(ch)* function does two things. First, it assigns a value to *ch;* this feature we've used. Second, and this is a new feature, the function returns a value to the calling program. That is, you can have a statement in the following form:

```
someobject = cin.get(ch);
```

Normally, the *cin.get(ch)* function returns an object of the *istream* class. The main point here is that the object is nonzero. But if the function determines that it has reached the end of the input file, it returns a value of zero instead and does not assign a value to *ch.* In other words, the return value is nonzero (true) if *cin.get(ch)* finds another character and zero (false) if the function finds the end-of-file. This means we can use the *cin.get(ch)* function as a test expression for a *while* loop. That way, the loop keeps reading characters until *cin.get(ch)* returns a zero value. This kind of loop is handy for reading character input, as shown in Listing 5-17.

COMPATIBILITY NOTE

Not all systems support simulated EOF from the keyboard.

Listing 5-17 *textin3.cpp*

```
// textin3.cpp -- reading chars to end of file
#include <iostream.h>
int main(void)
```

```
{
     char ch;
     int count = 0;

     while (cin.get(ch))          // cin.get(ch) is 0 on EOF
     {
           cout << ch;
           count++;
     }
     cout << count << " characters read\n";
     return 0;
}
```

Here is sample output. Because we ran the program on a DOS system, we pressed (CTRL)-(Z), (ENTER) to simulate the end-of-file condition. UNIX and Symantec C++ for the Mac users would press (CTRL)-(D) instead.

The green bird sings in the winter. (ENTER)
The green bird sings in the winter.
Yes, but the crow flies in the dawn. (ENTER)
Yes, but the crow flies in the dawn.
^Z (ENTER)
73 characters read

By using redirection, you can use this program to display a text file and report how many characters it has. This time we'll have a program read, echo, and count a two-line file on a UNIX system (the $ is a UNIX prompt):

$ textin3 < stuff
I am a UNIX file. I am proud
to be a UNIX file.
49 characters read
$

END-OF-FILE ENDS INPUT

When a *cin* method detects end-of-file, it sets a flag in the *cin* object indicating the end-of-file condition. When this flag is set, *cin* will not read any more input. For file input, this makes sense because you shouldn't read past the end of a file. For keyboard input, however, you might have used a simulated end-of-file to terminate a loop but then want to read more input later. The *cin.clear()* method clears the end-of-file flag and lets input proceed again. Chapter 15 discusses this further.

Yet Another *cin.get()*

The more nostalgic of the C users among you may yearn for C's character I/O functions, *getchar()* and *putchar()*. They are still available if you want them. Just use the *stdio.h* header file as you would in C. Or you can use member functions from the *istream* and *ostream* classes that work much the same way. We'll look at that approach now.

COMPATIBILITY NOTE

Some older implementations don't support the *cin.get()* member function (no arguments) discussed here.

The *cin.get()* member function with no arguments returns the next character from the input. That is, you use it in this way:

```
ch = cin.get();
```

(Recall that *cin.get(ch)* returns an object, not the character read.) This function works much the same as C's *getchar()*, returning the character code as a type *int* value. Similarly, you can use the *cout.put()* function (see Chapter 3) to display the character:

```
cout.put(ch);
```

It works much like C's *putchar()* except that its argument should be type *char* instead of type *int*.

COMPATIBILITY NOTE

Originally, the *put()* member had a single prototype of *put(char)*. You could pass it an *int* argument, which would then be type cast to *int*. The draft standard also calls for a single prototype. However, many current implementations provide three prototypes: *put(char)*, *put(signed char)*, and *put(unsigned char)*. Using *put()* with an *int* argument in these implementations generates an error message because there is more than one choice for coverting the *int*. An explicit type cast, such as *cin.put(char(c))* will work for *int* types.

To use *cin.get()* successfully, you need to know how it deals with the end-of-file condition. When the function reaches the end of a file, there are no more characters to be returned. Instead, *cin.get()* returns a special value represented by the symbolic constant *EOF.* This constant is defined in the *iostream.h* header file. The *EOF* value must be different from any valid character value so that the program won't confuse *EOF* with a regular character. Typically, *EOF* is defined as the value *-1* because no character has an ASCII code of -1. But you don't need to know the actual value. Just use *EOF* in the program. For instance, the heart of Listing 5-15 looked like this:

```
cin >> ch;
while (ch != '#')
{
        cout << ch;
        count++;
        cin >> ch;
}
```

We can replace *cin* with *cin.get()*, *cout* with *cout.put()*, and *'#'* with *EOF*:

```
ch = cin.get();
while (ch != EOF)
```

```
        {
            cout.put(ch); // cout.put(char(ch)) for some implementations
            count++;
            ch = cin.get();
        }
```

If *ch* is a character, the loop displays it. If *ch* is *EOF*, the loop terminates.

TIP

You should realize that *EOF* does not represent a character in the input. Rather, it's a signal that there are no more characters.

There's a subtle but important point about using *cin.get()* beyond the changes made so far. Because *EOF* represents a value outside of the valid character codes, it's possible that it may not be compatible with the *char* type. For instance, on some systems type *char* is unsigned, so a *char* variable could never have the usual *EOF* value of *-1*. For this reason, if you use *cin.get()* (no argument) and test for *EOF,* you need to assign the return value to type *int* instead of type *char.* Also, if you make *ch* type *int* instead of type *char,* you may have to do a type cast to *char* when displaying *ch.*

Listing 5-18 incorporates the *cin.get()* approach into a new version of Listing 5-15. It also condenses the code by combining character input with the *while* loop test.

Listing 5-18 *textin4.cpp*

```
// textin4.cpp -- reading chars with cin.get()
#include <iostream.h>
int main(void)
{
        int ch;                        // should be int, not char
        int count = 0;

        while ((ch = cin.get()) != EOF)       // test for end-of-file
        {
                cout << char(ch);      // typecast
                count++;
        }
        cout << count << " characters read\n";
        return 0;
}
```

Here's a sample run:

The sullen mackerel sulks in the shadowy shallows.
The sullen mackerel sulks in the shadowy shallows.
Yes, but the blue bird of happiness harbors secrets.
Yes, but the blue bird of happiness harbors secrets.
^Z
104 characters read

Let's analyze the loop condition:

```
while ((ch = cin.get()) != EOF)
```

The parentheses enclosing the subexpression *ch=cin.get()* cause the program to evaluate that expression first. To do the evaluation, the program first has to call the *cin.get()* function. Next it assigns the function return value to *ch*. Because the value of an assignment statement is the value of the left operand, the whole subexpression reduces to the value of *ch*. If this value is *EOF*, the loop terminates; otherwise, it continues. The test condition needs all the parentheses. Suppose we leave them out:

```
while (ch = cin.get() != EOF)
```

The *!=* operator has higher precedence than *=*, so first the program compares *cin.get()'s* return value to *EOF*. A comparison produces a *0* (false) or *1* (true) result, and that's the value that gets assigned to *ch*.

Using *cin.get(ch)* (with an argument) for input, on the other hand, doesn't create any type problems. The *cin.get(ch)* function, recall, doesn't assign a special value to *ch* on end-of-file. In fact it doesn't assign anything to *ch* in that case. So *ch* is never called upon to hold a non-*char* value. Table 5-3 summarizes the differences between *cin.get(ch)* and *cin.get()*.

So which should you use, *cin.get()* or *cin.get(ch)*? The form with the character argument is more fully integrated into the object approach since its return value is an object. This means, for example, that you can chain uses. For instance, the following code means read the next input character into *ch1* and the following input character into *ch2*:

```
cin.get(ch1).get(ch2);
```

This works because the function call *cin.get(ch1)* returns the *cin* object, which then acts as the object to which *get(ch2)* is attached.

Probably the main use for the *get()* form is to let you make quick-and-dirty conversions from the *getchar()* and *putchar()* functions of *<stdio.h>* to the *cin.get()* and *cout.put()* methods of *<iostream.h>*. Just replace one header file with the other and globally replace *getchar()* and *putchar()* with their act-alike method equivalents. (If the old code uses a type *int* variable for input, you will have to make further adjustments if your implementation has multiple prototypes for *put()*.)

Property	cin.get(ch)	ch=cin.get()
method for conveying input character	assign to argument *ch*	use function return value to assign to *ch*
function return value for character input	a class *istream* object	code for character as type *int* value
function return value at end-of-file	0	EOF

Table 5-3 *cin.get(ch)* versus *cin.get()*

Nested Loops and Two-Dimensional Arrays

Earlier you saw how the *for* loop is a natural tool for processing arrays. Let's go a step further and look at how a *for* loop within a *for* loop (*nested* loops) serves to handle two-dimensional arrays.

First, let's examine what a two-dimensional array is. The arrays used so far are termed one-dimensional arrays because you can visualize each array as a single row of data. You can visualize a two-dimensional array as being more like a table, having both rows and columns of data. You could use a two-dimensional array, for instance, to represent quarterly sales figures for six separate districts, with one row of data for each district. Or you could use a two-dimensional array to represent the position of RoboDork on a computerized game board.

C++ doesn't provide a special two-dimensional array type. Instead, you create an array for which each element is itself an array. For example, suppose you want to store maximum temperature data for five cities over a four-year period. In that case you can declare an array as follows:

```
int maxtemps[4][5];
```

This declaration means that *maxtemps* is an array with four elements. Each of these elements is an array of five integers. See Figure 5-5. You can think of the *maxtemps* array as representing four rows of five temperature values each.

The expression *maxtemps[0]* is the first element of the *maxtemps* array, hence *maxtemps[0]* is itself an array of five *int*s. The first element of the *maxtemps[0]* array is

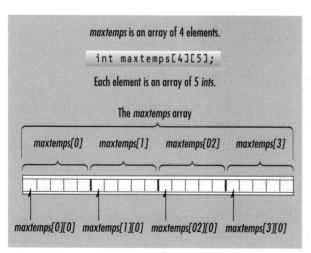

Figure 5-5 An array of arrays

```
int maxtemps[4][5];
```

The maxtemps array viewed as a table:

		0	1	2	3	4
maxtemps[0]	0	maxtemps[0][0]	maxtemps[0][1]	maxtemps[0][2]	maxtemps[0][3]	maxtemps[0][4]
maxtemps[1]	1	maxtemps[1][0]	maxtemps[1][1]	maxtemps[1][2]	maxtemps[1][3]	maxtemps[1][4]
maxtemps[2]	2	maxtemps[2][0]	maxtemps[2][1]	maxtemps[2][2]	maxtemps[2][3]	maxtemps[2][4]
maxtemps[3]	3	maxtemps[3][0]	maxtemps[3][1]	maxtemps[3][2]	maxtemps[3][3]	maxtemps[3][4]

Figure 5-6 Accessing array elements with subscripts

maxtemps[0][0], and this element is a single *int*. Thus you need to use two subscripts to access the *int* elements. You can think of the first subscript as representing the row and the second subscript as representing the column. See Figure 5-6.

Suppose you want to print all the array contents. Then you can use one *for* loop to change rows and a second, nested, *for* loop to change columns:

```
for (int row = 0; row < 4; row++)
{
        for (int col = 0; col < 5; col++)
                cout << maxtemps[row][col] << "\t";
        cout << "\n";
}
```

For each value of *row*, the inner *for* loop cycles through all the *col* values. This example prints a tab character (\t in C++ notation) after each value and a newline character after each complete row.

Initializing a Two-Dimensional Array

When you create a two-dimensional array, you have the option of initializing each element. The technique is based on that for initializing a one-dimensional array. That method, you remember, is to provide a comma-separated list of values enclosed in braces:

```
// initializing a one-dimensional array
int btus[5] = { 23, 26, 24, 31, 28};
```

For a two-dimensional array, each element is itself an array, so you can initialize each element using a form like that above. Thus the initialization consists of a comma-separated series of one-dimensional initializations all enclosed in a set of braces:

```
int maxtemps[4][5] =                    // 2-D array
{
```

```
    {94, 98, 87, 103, 101},          // values for maxtemps[0]
    {98, 99, 91, 107, 105},          // values for maxtemps[1]
    {93, 91, 90, 101, 104},          // values for maxtemps[2]
    {95, 100, 88, 105, 103}          // values for maxtemps[3]
};
```

The term *{94, 98, 87, 103, 101}* initializes the first row, represented by *maxtemps[0]*. As a matter of style, placing each row of data on its own line, if possible, makes the data easier to read.

Listing 5-19 incorporates an initialized two-dimensional array and a nested loop into a program. This time we reverse the order of the loops, placing the column loop (*city* index) on the outside and the row loop (*year* index) on the inside. Also, we use a common C++ practice of initializing an array of pointers to a set of string constants. That is, *cities* is declared as an array of pointers-to-*char*. That makes each element, such as *cities[0]*, a pointer-to-*char* that can be initialized to the address of a string. The program initializes *cities[0]* to the address of the *"Gribble City"* string, and so on. Thus this array of pointers essentially is an array of strings.

Listing 5-19 *nested.cpp*

```
// nested.cpp -- nested loops and 2-D array
#include <iostream.h>

const int Cities = 5;
const int Years = 4;
int main(void)
{
        char * cities[Cities] =          // array of pointers
        {                                // to 5 strings
                "Gribble City",
                "Gribbleton",
                "New Gribble",
                "San Gribble",
                "Gribble Vista"
        };

        int maxtemps[Years][Cities] =// 2-D array
        {
                {94, 98, 87, 103, 101},          // values for maxtemps[0]
                {98, 99, 91, 107, 105},          // values for maxtemps[1]
                {93, 91, 90, 101, 104},          // values for maxtemps[2]
                {95, 100, 88, 105, 103}          // values for maxtemps[3]
        };

        cout << "Maximum temperatures for 1990 - 1993\n\n";

        for (int city = 0; city < Cities; city++)
        {
                cout << cities[city] << ":\t";
                for (int year = 0; year < Years; year++)
```

continued on next page

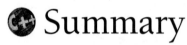

continued from previous page

```
                cout << maxtemps[year][city] << "\t";
                cout << "\n";
        }

        return 0;
}
```

Here is the program output:

```
Maximum temperatures for 1990 - 1993
Gribble City:  94     98     93     95
Gribbleton:    98     99     91     100
New Gribble:   87     91     90     88
San Gribble:   103    107    101    105
Gribble Vista: 101    105    104    103
```

Using tabs in the output spaced the data more regularly than using spaces would have. Chapter 15 presents more precise, but more complex, methods for formatting output.

Summary

C++ offers three varieties of loops: the *for* loop, the *while* loop, and the *do while* loop. A loop cycles through the same set of instructions repetitively as long as the loop test condition evaluates to nonzero, and the loop terminates execution when the test condition evaluates to zero. The *for* loop and the *while* loop are entry-condition loops, meaning they examine the test condition before executing the statements in the body of the loop. The *do while* loop is an exit-condition loop, meaning it examines the test condition after executing the statements in the body of the loop.

The syntax for each loop calls for the loop body to consist of a single statement. However, that statement can be a compound statement, or block, formed by enclosing several statements within paired curly braces.

Relational expressions, which compare two values, are often used as loop test conditions. Relational expressions are formed by using one of the six relational operators: <, <=, ==, >=, >, !=. Relational expressions evaluate to *1* if true and to *0* if false.

Many programs read text input or text files character-by-character. The *istream* class provides several ways to do this. If *ch* is a type *char* variable, the statement

```
cin >> ch;
```

reads the next input character into *ch*. However, it skips over spaces, newlines, and tabs. The member function call

```
cin.get(ch);
```

reads the next input character, regardless of its value, and places it in *ch*. The member function call *cin.get()* returns the next input character, including spaces, newlines, and tabs, so it can be used as follows:

```
ch = cin.get();
```

The *cin.get(char)* member function call reports encountering the end-of-file condition by returning the value *0*, while the *cin.get()* member function call reports end-of-file by returning the value *EOF*, which is defined in the *iostream.h* file.

A nested loop is a loop within a loop. Nested loops provide a natural way to process two-dimensional arrays.

Review Questions

1. What's the difference between an entry-condition loop and an exit-condition loop? Which kind is each of the C++ loops?

2. What would the following code fragment print if it were part of a valid program?

```
int i;
for (i = 0; i < 5; i++)
        cout << i;
        cout << "\n";
```

3. What would the following code fragment print if it were part of a valid program?

```
int j;
for (j = 0; j < 11; j += 3)
        cout << j;
cout << "\n" << j << "\n";
```

4. What would the following code fragment print if it were part of a valid program?

```
int j = 5;
while ( ++j < 9)
        cout << j++ << "\n";
```

5. What would the following code fragment print if it were part of a valid program?

```
int k = 8;
do
        cout <<" k = " << k << "\n";
while (k++ < 5);
```

6. Write a *for* loop that prints the values 1 2 4 8 16 32 64 by increasing the value of a counting variable by a factor of 2 each cycle.

7. How do you make a loop body include more than one statement?

8. Is the following statement valid? If not, why not? If so, what does it do?

```
int x = (1,024);
```

What about the following?

```
int y;
y = 1,024;
```

9. How does *cin>>ch* differ from *cin.get(ch)* and *ch=cin.get()* in how it views input?

Programming Exercises

1. Write a program that requests the user to enter two integers. The program then should calculate and report the sum of all the integers between and including the two integers. At this point, assume that the smaller integer is entered first. For instance, if the user enters **2** and **9**, the program would report that the sum of all the integers from 2 through 9 is 44.

2. Write a program that asks you to type in numbers. After each entry, the number reports the cumulative sum of the entries to date. The program terminates when you enter a zero.

3. Design a structure called *car* that holds the following information about an automobile: its make as a string in a character array and the year it was built as an integer. Write a program that asks the user how many cars to catalog. The program then should use *new* to create a dynamic array of that many *car* structures. Next, it should prompt the user to input the make and year information for each structure. Note that this requires some care, for it alternates reading strings with numeric data (Chapter 4). Finally, it should display the contents of each structure. A sample run should look something like the following:

```
How many cars do you wish to catalog? 2
Car #1:
Please enter the make: Hudson Hornet
Please enter the year made: 1952
Car #2:
Please enter the make: Kaiser
Please enter the year made: 1951
Here is your collection:
1952 Hudson Hornet
1951 Kaiser
```

CHAPTER 6

BRANCHING STATEMENTS AND LOGICAL OPERATORS

You will learn about the following in this chapter:

◇ The *if* statement

◇ The *if else* statement

◇ Logical operators: &&, ||, and !

◇ The *ctype.h* library of character functions

◇ The conditional operator: ?:

◇ The *switch* statement

◇ The *continue* and *break* statements

◇ Number-reading loops

One of the keys to designing intelligent programs is to give them the ability to make decisions. In Chapter 5 you saw one kind of decision making—looping—in which a program decides whether or not to continue looping. Now we'll investigate how C++ lets you use branching statements to decide among alternative actions. Which vampire-protection scheme (garlic or cross) should the program use? What menu choice has the user selected? Did the user enter a zero? C++ provides the *if* and *switch* statements for implementing decisions, and they are this chapter's main topics. We'll also look at the conditional operator, which provides another way to make a choice, and at the logical operators, which let you combine two tests into one.

The *if* Statement

When a C++ program must choose whether or not to take a particular action, you can use the *if* statement. The if comes in two forms: *if* and *if else*. We'll investigate the simple *if* first. It's modeled after ordinary English, as in "If you have a Captain Cookie

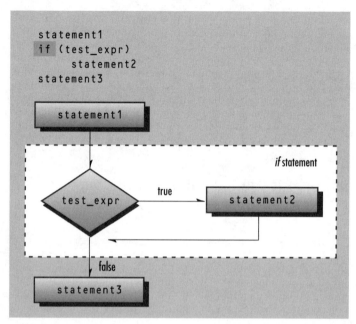

```
statement1
if (test_expr)
    statement2
statement3
```

Figure 6-1 The *if* statement

card, you get a free cookie." The *if* statement directs a program to execute a statement or statement block if a test condition is true and to skip that statement or block if the condition is false. The syntax is similar to the *while* syntax:

if (*test-condition*)
      statement

A nonzero *test-condition* (true) causes the program to execute *statement*, which can be a single statement or a block. A zero *test-condition* (false) causes the program to skip *statement.* See Figure 6-1. The entire *if* construction counts as a single statement.

Most often, *test-condition* will be a relational expression like those used to control loops. Suppose, for instance, you want a program that counts the spaces in the input as well as the total number of characters. You can use *cin.get(ch)* in a *while* loop to read the characters, then use an *if* statement to identify and count the space characters. Listing 6-1 does just that. (Remember that *cin.get(ch)* normally returns *cin,* which is nonzero, causing the loop to continue. But it returns zero when the program detects end-of-file, thus terminating the loop.)

COMPATIBILITY NOTE

This program, along with several others in the chapter, assume that your system allows you to simulate EOF from the keyboard. You can, of course, modify them so that they terminate when a particular character, such as a period or dollar sign, is read. For example, you can replace the *while* loop line with this:

```
while ((ch = cin.get()) != '$')
```

 ## Listing 6-1 *if.cpp*

```
// if.cpp -- using the if statement
#include <iostream.h>
int main(void)
{
        char ch;
        int spaces = 0;
        int total = 0;

        while (cin.get(ch))
        {
                if (ch == ' ') // check if ch is a space
                        spaces++;
                total++;                // done every time
        }
        cout << spaces << " spaces, " << total;
        cout << " characters total\n";
        return 0;
}
```

Here's some sample output:

```
The balloonist was an airhead. (ENTER)
(ENTER)
4 spaces, 31 characters total
```

As the comments indicate, the *spaces++;* statement gets executed only when *ch* is a space. Because it is outside the *if* statement, the *total++;* statement is executed every time. Note that the total count includes the newline character generated by pressing (ENTER).

The *if else* Statement

The *if* statement lets a program decide whether a particular statement or block is executed. The *if else* statement lets a program decide which of two statements or blocks is executed. It's an invaluable statement for creating alternative courses of action. The C++ *if else* is modeled after simple English, as in "If you have a Captain Cookie card, you get a Cookie Plus Plus, else you just get a Cookie d'Ordinaire." The *if else* statement has this general form:

```
if (test-condition)
        statement1
else
        statement2
```

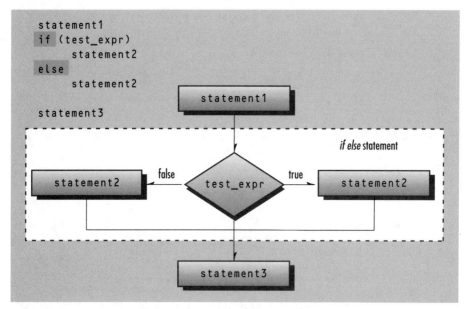

```
statement1
if (test_expr)
      statement2
else
      statement2

statement3
```

Figure 6-2 The *if else* statement

If *test-condition* is nonzero (true), the program executes *statement1* and skips over *statement2*. Otherwise, when *test-condition* is zero (false), the program skips *statement1* and executes *statement2* instead. So the code fragment

```
if (answer == 1492)
      cout << "That's right!\n";
else
      cout << "You'd better review Chapter 1 again.\n";
```

prints the first message if *answer* is *1492* and prints the second message otherwise. Each statement can be either a single statement or a statement block delimited by braces. See Figure 6-2. The entire *if else* construct counts syntactically as a single statement.

For instance, suppose you want to alter incoming text by scrambling the letters while keeping the newline character intact. That way, each line of input gets converted to an output line of equal length. This means you want the program to take one course of action for newline characters and a different course of action for all other characters. As Listing 6-2 shows, *if else* makes this task easy.

Listing 6-2 *ifelse.cpp*

```
// ifelse.cpp -- using the if else statement
#include <iostream.h>
int main(void)
{
      char ch;
```

```
        cout << "Type, and I shall repeat.\n";
        while (cin.get(ch))
        {
                if (ch == '\n')
                        cout << ch;        // done if newline
                else
                        cout << ++ch;      // done otherwise
        }
        // try ch + 1 instead of ++ch for interesting effect
        cout << "Please excuse the slight confusion.\n";
        return 0;
}
```

Here's some sample output:

```
Type, and I shall repeat.
I am extremely pleased to
J!bn!fyusfnfmz!qmfbtfe!up
use such a powerful computer!
vtf!tvdi!b!qpxfsgvm!dpnqvufs"
^Z
Please excuse the slight confusion.
```

Note that one of the program comments suggests that changing *++ch* to *ch+1* has an interesting effect. Can you deduce what it will be? If not, try it out, then see if you can explain what's happening. (Hint: Think about how *cout* handles different types.)

Formatting Your *if else* Statements

Keep in mind that the two *if else* alternatives must be single statements. If you need more than one statement, use braces to collect them into a single block statement. Unlike some languages, such as BASIC or FORTRAN, C++ does not automatically consider everything between *if* and *else* a block, so you have to use braces to make the statements a block. The following code, for instance, produces a compiler error. The compiler sees it as a simple *if* statement ending with the *zorro++;* statement. Then comes a *cout* statement. So far, so good. But then comes what the compiler perceives as an unattached *else*. And that gets flagged as a syntax error.

```
if (ch == 'Z')
        zorro++;                     // if ends here
        cout << "Another Zorro candidate\n";
else                     // wrong
        dull++;
        cout << "Not a Zorro candidate\n";
```

Adding the braces converts the code to what we want:

```
if (ch == 'Z')
{                                    // if true block
        zorro++;
        cout << "Another Zorro candidate\n";
}
```

continued on next page

continued from previous page

```
else
{                                    // if false block
       dull++;
       cout << "Not a Zorro candidate\n";
}
```

Because C++ is a free-form language, you can arrange the braces as you like as long as they enclose the statements. We've shown one popular format. Here's another:

```
if (ch == 'Z') {
       zorro++;
       cout << "Another Zorro candidate\n";
       }
else {
       dull++;
       cout << "Not a Zorro candidate\n";
       }
```

The first form emphasizes the block structure for the statements while the second form ties the blocks more closely to the keywords *if* and *else*. Either style should serve you well unless you encounter a passionate advocate for some particular style.

The *if else if else* Construction

Computer programs, like life, may present you with a choice from more than two selections. You can extend the C++ *if else* statement to meet that need. The *else*, you've seen, should be followed by a single statement, which can be a block. Because an *if else* statement itself is a single statement, it can follow an *else*:

```
if (ch == 'A')
       a_grade++;                    // alternative # 1
else
       if (ch == 'B')               // alternative # 2
              b_grade++;            // subalternative # 2a
       else
              soso++;               // subalternative # 2b
```

If *ch* is not *'A'*, then the program goes to the *else*. There, a second *if else* subdivides that alternative into two more choices. C++'s free formatting lets you arrange these elements into an easier-to-read format:

```
if (ch == 'A')
       a_grade++;                    // alternative # 1
else if (ch == 'B')
       b_grade++;                    // alternative # 2
else
       soso++;                       // alternative # 3
```

This looks like a new control structure—an *if else if else* structure. But it's really one *if else* contained within a second. This revised format is much cleaner looking, and it lets you skim through the code picking out the different alternatives. This entire construction still counts as one statement.

Listing 6-3 uses this preferred formatting to construct a modest quiz program.

Listing 6-3 *ifelseif.cpp*

```
// ifelseif.cpp -- using if else if else
#include <iostream.h>
const int Fave = 27;
int main(void)
{
        int n;

        cout << "Enter a number in the range 1-100 to find ";
        cout << "my favorite number: ";
        do
        {
                cin >> n;
                if (n < Fave)
                        cout << "Too low -- guess again: ";
                else if (n > Fave)
                        cout << "Too high -- guess again: ";
                else
                        cout << Fave << " is right!\n";
        } while (n != Fave);
        return 0;
}
```

Here's some sample output:

```
Enter a number in the range 1-100 to find my favorite number: 50
Too high -- guess again: 25
Too low -- guess again: 37
Too high -- guess again: 31
Too high -- guess again: 28
Too high -- guess again: 27
27 is right!
```

Logical Expressions

Many a time you will need to test for more than one condition. For instance, for a character to be a lowercase letter, its value must be greater than or equal to *a* and less than or equal to *z*. Or, if you ask a user to respond with a *y* or an *n*, you will want to accept uppercase (*Y* and *N*) as well as lowercase. To meet this kind of need, C++ provides three *logical* operators to combine or modify existing expressions. The operators are logical OR, written ||; logical AND, written &&, and logical NOT, written !. Let's examine them now.

The Logical *Or* Operator: ||

In English, we use the word *or* to indicate when one or another, or both, of two conditions satisfy a requirement. For instance, you can go to the MegaMicro company picnic if you *or* your spouse work for MegaMicro, Inc. The C++ equivalent is the logical OR operator, written ||. This operator combines two expressions into one. If either, or both, of the original expressions is nonzero (true), the resulting expression has the value 1 (true). Here are some examples:

```
5 ==5 || 5 == 9     // true because first expression is true
5 > 3 || 5 > 10     // true because first expression is true
5 > 8 || 5 < 10     // true because second expression is true
5 < 8 || 5 > 2      // true because both expressions are true
5 > 8 || 5 < 2      // false because both expressions are false
```

Because the || has a lower precedence than the relational operators, we don't need to use parentheses in these expressions. Table 6-1 summarizes how the || operator works.

C++ provides that the || operator is a sequence point. That is, any value changes indicated in the left-hand side take place before the right side is evaluated. For instance, consider the following expression:

```
i++ < 6 || i == j
```

Suppose *i* originally has the value 10. By the time the comparison with *j* takes place, *i* will have the value 11. Also, C++ won't bother evaluating the right-hand expression if the left-hand expression is true, for it only takes one true expression to make the whole logical expression true.

Listing 6-4 uses the || operator in an *if* statement to check for both uppercase and lowercase versions of a character. Also, it uses C++'s string concatenation feature (see Chapter 4) to spread a single string over three lines.

The Value of expr1 || expr2

	expr1 == true	expr1 == false
expr2 == true	1 (true)	1 (true)
expr2 == false	1 (true)	0 (false)

Table 6-1 The || operator

Listing 6-4 *or.cpp*

```
// or.cpp -- use logical OR operator
#include <iostream.h>
int main(void)
{
        cout << "This program may reformat your hard disk\n"
                "and destroy all your data.\n"
                "Do you wish to continue? <y/n> ";
```

```
        char ch;
        cin >> ch;
        if (ch == 'y' || ch == 'Y')                // y or Y
                cout << "You were warned!\a\a\n";
        else if (ch == 'n' || ch == 'N')
                cout << "A wise choice ... bye\n";
        else
                cout << "That wasn't a y or an n, so I guess I'll "
                             "trash your disk anyway.\n";
        return 0;
}
```

Here is a sample run:

```
This program may reformat your hard disk
and destroy all your data.
Do you wish to continue? <y/n> N
A wise choice ... bye
```

The program reads just one character, so only the first character in the response matters. That means the user could have replied NO! instead of N. The program would just read the N. But if the program tried to read more input later, it would start at the O.

The Logical AND Operator: &&

The logical AND operator, written &&, also combines two expressions into one. The resulting expression has the value 1 (true) only if both of the original expressions are true. Here are some examples:

```
5 == 5 && 4 == 4    // true because both expressions are true
5 == 3 && 4 == 4    // false because first expression is false
5 > 3 && 5 > 10     // false because second expression is false
5 > 8 && 5 < 10     // false because first expression is false
5 < 8 && 5 > 2      // true because both expressions are true
5 > 8 && 5 < 2      // false because both expressions are false
```

Because the && has a lower precedence than the relational operators, we don't need to use parentheses in these expressions. Like the || operator, the && operator acts as a sequence point, so the left-hand side is evaluated and any side effects carried out before the right side is evaluated. If the left side is false, the whole logical expression must be false, so C++ doesn't bother evaluating the right side in that case. Table 6-2 summarizes how the && operator works.

The Value of expr1 && expr2

	expr1 == true	expr1 == false
expr2 == true	1 (true)	0 (false)
expr2 == false	0 (false)	0 (false)

Table 6-2 The && operator

Listing 6-5 shows how to use && to cope with a common situation: terminating a *while* loop for two different reasons. In the listing, a *while* loop reads values into an array. One test (*i < ArSize*) terminates the loop when the array is full. The second test (*temp >= 0*) gives the user the option of quitting early by entering a negative number. The && operator lets you combine the two tests into a single condition. The program also uses two *if* statements, an *if else* statement, and a *for* loop, so it demonstrates several topics from this and the preceding chapter.

Listing 6-5 *and.cpp*

```
// and.cpp -- use logical AND operator
#include <iostream.h>
const int ArSize = 6;
int main(void)
{
        float iq[ArSize];
        cout << "Enter the IQs of your in-laws. Program term"
                "inates when you make\n" << ArSize << " entries ";
        cout << "or enter a negative value.\n";

        int i = 0;
        float temp;
        cin >> temp;
        while (i < ArSize && temp >= 0)         // 2 quitting criteria
        {
                iq[i++] = temp;
                if (i < ArSize)                 // room left in the array,
                        cin >> temp;            // so get next value
        }
        if (i == 0)
                cout << "No data--bye\n";
        else
        {
                cout << "Enter your IQ: ";
                float you;
                cin >> you;
                int count = 0;
                for (int j = 0; j < i; j++)
                        if (iq[j] > you)
                                count++;
                cout << count;
                cout << " of your in-laws are smarter than you.\n";
        }
        return 0;
}
```

Note that the program places input into a temporary variable *temp*. Only after verifying that the input is valid does the program assign the value to the array.

Here are a couple of sample runs. One terminates after six entries, and the second terminates after a negative value is entered:

```
Enter the IQs of your in-laws. Program terminates when you make
6 entries or enter a negative value.
120 140 115
85
123
100
Enter your IQ: 122
2 of your in-laws are smarter than you.

Enter the IQs of your in-laws. Program terminates when you make
6 entries or enter a negative value.
140
120
75
110
-3
Enter your IQ: 212.19
0 of your in-laws are smarter than you.
```

Program Notes

Let's look at the input part of the program:

```
cin >> temp;
while (i < ArSize && temp >= 0)              // 2 quitting criteria
{
        iq[i++] = temp;
        if (i < ArSize)                      // room left in the array,
                cin >> temp;                 // so read next value
}
```

The program begins by reading the first input value into a temporary variable called *temp*. Then the *while* test condition checks to see if there is still room left in the array (*i < ArSize*) and if the input value is nonnegative (*temp >= 0*). If so, it copies the *temp* value to the array and increases the array index by 1. At this point, since array numbering starts at 0, i equals the total number of entries to date. That is, if i starts out at 0, then the first cycle through the loop assigns a value to *iq[0]*, then sets i to 1.

The loop terminates when the array is filled or when the user enters a negative number. Note that the loop reads another value into *temp* only if i is less than *ArSize*, that is, only if there is still room left in the array.

After getting data, the program uses an *if else* statement to comment if no data were entered (that is, if the first entry was a negative number) and to process the data if any is present.

Setting Up Ranges with &&

The && operator also lets you set up a series of *if else if else* statements with each choice corresponding to a particular range of values. Listing 6-6 illustrates the approach. It also shows a useful technique for handling a series of messages. Just as a pointer-to-*char* variable can identify a string by pointing to its beginning, an array of pointers-to-*char* can identify a series of strings. Just assign the address of each string to a different array element. Listing 6-6 uses the *qualify* array to hold the addresses of four strings. For instance, *qualify[1]* holds the address of the string *"mud tug-of-war\n"*. The program can then use *qualify[1]* like any other pointer to a string, for example, with *cout* or with *strlen()* or *strcmp()*. Using the *const* qualifier protects these strings from accidental alterations.

Listing 6-6 *more_and.cpp*

```
// more_and.cpp -- use logical AND operator
#include <iostream.h>
const char * qualify[4] =        // an array of pointers
{                                // to strings
        "10,000-meter race.\n",
        "mud tug-of-war.\n",
        "masters canoe jousting.\n",
        "pie-throwing festival.\n"
};
int main(void)
{
        int age;
        cout << "Enter your age in years: ";
        cin >> age;
        int index;

        if (age > 17 && age < 35)
                index = 0;
        else if (age >= 35 && age < 50)
                index = 1;
        else if (age >= 50 && age < 65)
                index = 2;
        else
                index = 3;

        cout << "You qualify for the " << qualify[index];
        return 0;
}
```

COMPATIBILITY NOTE

You may recall that some C++ implementations require that you use the keyword *static* in an array declaration in order to make it possible to initialize that array. That restriction, as Chapter 8 will discuss, applies to arrays declared inside a function body. When an array is declared outside a function body, as is *qualify* in Listing 6-6, it's termed an *external* array and can be initialized even in pre-ANSI C implementations.

Here is a sample run:

```
Enter your age in years: 84
You qualify for the pie-throwing festival.
```

The entered age didn't match any of the test ranges, so the program set *index* to 3 and then printed the corresponding string.

Program Notes

The expression *age > 17 && age<35* tests for ages *between* the two values, that is, ages in the range 18–34. The expression *age>=35 && age<50* uses the <= operator to include 35 in its range, which is 35–49. If we had used *age>35 && age<50,* the value 35 would have been missed by all the tests. When you use range tests, you should check that the ranges don't have holes between them. Also, be sure to set up each range correctly; see the note on Range Tests.

The *if else* statement serves to select an array index, which, in turn, identifies a particular string.

RANGE TESTS

Note that each part of a range test should use the AND operator to join two complete relational expressions:

```
if (age > 17 && age < 35)    // OK
```

Don't borrow from mathematics and use the following notation:

```
if (17 < age < 35)           // Don't do this
```

If you make this error, the compiler won't catch it, for it is still valid C++ syntax. The < operator associates from left to right, so the previous expression means the following:

```
if ( (17 < age) < 35)
```

But *17<age* is either true, or 1, or else false, or 0. In either case, the expression *17<age* is less than *35,* so the entire test is always true!

The Logical NOT Operator: !

The ! operator negates, or reverses the truth value of, the expression following it. That is, if *expression* is true, then *!expression* is false, and vice versa. More precisely, if *expression* is nonzero, then *!expression* is zero. And if *expression* is zero, then *!expression* is 1. Incidentally, many people call the exclamation point *bang,* making *!x* bang-exe and *!!x* bang-bang-exe.

Usually you can express a relationship more clearly without using this operator:

```
if (!(x > 5))                  // if (x <= 5) is clearer
```

But the ! operator can be useful with functions that return true-false values. For instance, *strcmp(s1,s2)* returns a nonzero (true) value if the two strings *s1* and *s2* are different from each other and a zero value (false) if they are the same. This implies that *!strcmp(s1,s2)* is true if the two strings are equal.

Listing 6-7 uses this technique (applying the ! operator to a true-false function) to screen numeric input for suitability to be assigned to type *int*. The function *is_int()*, which we'll discuss further in a moment, returns true if its argument is within the range of values assignable to type *int*. The program then uses the test *while(!is_int(num))* to reject values that don't fit in the range.

Listing 6-7 *not.cpp*

```
// not.cpp -- using the not operator
#include <iostream.h>
#include <limits.h>
int is_int(double);
int main(void)
{
        double num;

        cout << "Yo, dude! Enter an integer value: ";
        cin >> num;
        while (!is_int(num))    // continue while num is not int-able
        {
                cout << "Out of range -- please try again: ";
                cin >> num;
        }
        int val = num;
        cout << "You've entered the integer " << val << "\n";
        return 0;
}

int is_int(double x)
{
        if (x <= INT_MAX && x >= INT_MIN)  // use limits.h values
                return 1;
        else
                return 0;
}
```

Here is a sample run on a system with a 2-byte *int:*

```
Yo, dude! Enter an integer value: 50000
Out of range -- please try again: -42000
Out of range -- please try again: 32767
You've entered the integer 32767
```

Program Notes

If you enter a too-large value to a program reading a type *int,* most implementations simply truncate the value to fit without informing you that data was lost. This program avoids that by first reading the potential *int* as a *double*. The *double* type has more than enough precision to hold a typical *int* value, and its range is much greater.

The *is_int()* function uses the two symbolic constants (*INT_MAX* and *INT_MIN*) defined in the *limits.h* file (discussed in Chapter 3) to determine whether its argument is within the proper limits. If so, the program returns a value of 1; otherwise, it returns 0.

The *main()* program uses a *while* loop to reject invalid input until the user gets it right. You could make the program friendlier by displaying the *int* limits when the input is out of range. Once the input has been validated, the program assigns it to an *int* variable.

Logical Operator Facts

As we mentioned, the C++ logical OR and logical AND operators have a lower precedence than relational operators. That means an expression such as

```
x > 5 && x < 10
```

is read this way:

```
(x > 5) && (x < 10)
```

The ! operator, on the other hand, has a higher precedence than any of the relational or arithmetic operators. Therefore, to negate an expression, you should enclose the expression in parentheses:

```
!(x > 5)     // is it false that x is greater than 5
!x > 5       // is !x greater than 5
```

The second expression, incidentally, is always false, for !x can only have the values 1 (true) or 0 (false).

The logical AND operator has a higher precedence than the logical OR operator. Thus the expression

```
age > 30 && age < 45 || weight > 300
```

means the following:

```
(age > 30 && age < 45) || weight > 300
```

That is, one condition is that *age* be in the range 31 to 44, and the second condition is that *weight* be greater than 300. The entire expression is true if one or the other or both of these conditions are true.

You can, of course, use parentheses to tell the program the interpretation you want. For instance, suppose you want to use && to combine the condition that *age* be greater than 50 or *weight* be greater than 300 with the condition that donation be greater than 1000. You have to enclose the OR part within parentheses:

```
(age > 50 || weight > 300) && donation > 1000
```

Otherwise, the compiler will combine the *weight* condition with the *donation* condition instead of with the *age* condition.

C++ guarantees that when a program evaluates a logical expression, it evaluates it from left to right and stops evaluation as soon as it knows what the answer is. Suppose, for instance, you have this condition:

```
x != 0  && 1.0 / x > 100.0
```

If the first condition is false, then the whole expression must be false. That's because for this expression to be true, each individual condition must be true. Knowing the first condition is false, the program doesn't bother evaluating the second condition. That's fortunate in this example, for evaluating the second condition would have resulted in dividing by 0, which is not in a computer's realm of possible actions.

The *ctype.h* Library of Character Functions

C++ has inherited from C a handy package of character-related functions, prototyped in the *ctype.h* header file, which simplify such tasks as determining whether a character is an uppercase letter or a digit or punctuation, and the like. For example, the *isalpha(ch)* function returns a true (nonzero) value if *ch* is a letter and a false value (zero) otherwise. Similarly, the *ispunct(ch)* returns a true value only if *ch* is a punctuation character, such as a comma or period. Using these functions is more convenient than using the AND and OR operators. For instance, here's how you might use AND and OR to test if a character *ch* is an alphabetic character:

```
if ((ch >= 'a' && ch <= 'z') || (ch >= 'A' && ch <= 'Z')
```

Compare that to using *isalpha()* :

```
if (isalpha(ch))
```

Not only is *isalpha()* easier to use, it is more general. The AND, OR form assumes that character codes for A through Z are in sequence, with no other characters having codes in that range. This assumption is true for the ASCII code, but it need not be true in general.

Listing 6-8 demonstrates some functions from this family. In particular, it uses *isalpha()*, which tests for alphabetic characters, *isdigits()*, which tests for digit characters, such as 3, *isspace()*, which tests for white-space characters, such as newlines, spaces, and tabs; and *ispunct()*, which tests for punctuation characters. The program also reviews the *if else if else* structure and using a *while* loop with *cin.get()*.

Listing 6-8 *ctypes.cpp*

```
// ctypes.cpp--use ctype.h library
#include <iostream.h>
#include <ctype.h>     // prototypes for character functions
```

```cpp
int main(void)
{
        cout << "Enter text for analysis, and simulate EOF"
                " to terminate input.\n";
                char ch;
        int whitespace = 0;
        int digits = 0;
        int chars = 0;
        int punct = 0;
        int others = 0;

        while (cin.get(ch))
        {
                if(isalpha(ch))         // is it an alphabetic character?
                        chars++;
                else if(isspace(ch))  // is it a whitespace character?
                        whitespace++;
                else if(isdigit(ch))  // is it a digit?
                        digits++;
                else if(ispunct(ch))  // is it punctuation?
                punct++;
                else
                        others++;
        }
        cout << chars << " letters, "
                << whitespace << " whitespace, "
                << digits << " digits, "
                << punct << " punctuations, "
                << others << " others.\n";
        return 0;
}
```

Here is a sample run; note that the white-space count includes newlines:

```
Enter text for analysis, and simulate EOF to terminate input.
Freddy "Fuzzball" Fribble had 143 career
home runs and 1237 career strikeouts.
^Z
57 letters, 12 whitespace, 7 digits, 3 punctuations, 0 others.
```

Table 6-3 summarizes the functions available in the *ctype.h* package. The list corresponds to the ANSI C definition, but some systems may lack some of these functions or have additional ones.

Function name	Return value
isalnum()	true if argument is alphanumeric, i.e., a letter or a digit
isalpha()	true if argument is alphabetic
iscntrl()	true if argument is a control character
isdigit()	true if argument is a decimal digit (0–9)

continued on next page

continued from previous page

Function name	Return value
isgraph()	true if argument is any printing character, other than a space
islower()	true if argument is a lowercase letter
isprint()	true if argument is any printing character, including a space
ispunct()	true if argument is a punctuation character
isspace()	true if argument is a standard white-space character, i.e., a space, formfeed, newline, carriage return, horizontal tab, or vertical tab
isupper()	true if argument is an uppercase letter
isxdigit()	true if argument is a hexadecimal digit character, i.e., 0–9, a–f, or A–F
tolower()	if the argument is an uppercase character, *tolower()* returns the lowercase version of that character; otherwise, it returns the argument unaltered
toupper()	if the argument is a lowercase character, *toupper()* returns the uppercase version of that character; otherwise, it returns the argument unaltered

Table 6-3 The *ctype.h* character functions

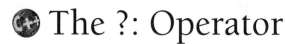 The ?: Operator

C++ has an operator that can often be used instead of the *if* statement. This operator is called the conditional operator, written ?:, and, for you trivia buffs, it is the only C++ operator that requires three operands. The general form looks like this:

expression1 ? *expression2* : *expression3*

If *expression1* is true, then the value of the whole conditional expression is the value of *expression2*. Otherwise, the value of the whole expression is the value of *expression3*. Here are two examples showing how the operator works:

```
5 > 3 ? 10 : 12  // 5 > 3 is true, so expression value is 10
3 == 9? 25 : 18  // 3 == 9 is false, so expression value is 18
```

We can paraphrase the first example this way: if 5 is greater than 3, the expression evaluates to 10; otherwise, it evaluates to 12. In real programming situations, of course, the expressions would involve variables.

Listing 6-9 uses the conditional operator to determine the larger of two values.

 Listing 6-9 *condit.cpp*

```
// condit.cpp -- using the conditional operator
#include <iostream.h>
```

```
int main(void)
{
        int a, b;
        cout << "Enter two numbers: ";
        cin >> a >> b;
        cout << "The larger of " << a << " and " << b;
        int c = a > b ? a : b;      // c = a if a > b, else c = b
        cout << " is " << c << "\n";
        return 0;
}
```

Here is a sample run:

```
Enter two numbers: 25 027              Note that 027 is octal
The larger of 25 and 23 is 25
```

The sample input should remind you that *cin,* like C++ in general, interprets integers beginning with the digit 0 as being written in octal. Thus 027 is interpreted to be the base 10 value 23.

The key part of the program is this statement:

```
int c = a > b ? a : b;
```

It produces the same result as the following statements:

```
int c;
if (a > b)
        c = a;
else
        c = b;
```

Compared to the *if else* sequence, the conditional operator is more concise but, at first, less obvious. One difference between the two approaches is that the conditional operator produces an expression and hence a single value that can be assigned or be incorporated into a larger expression, as we did in assigning the value of the conditional expression to the variable *c.* The conditional operator's concise form, unusual syntax, and overall weird appearance make it a great favorite among programmers who appreciate those qualities. One favorite trick for the reprehensible goal of concealing the purpose of code is to nest conditional expressions within one another, as the following mild example shows:

```
char x[2] [20] = {"Jason ","at your service\n"};
char * y = "Quillstone ";

for (int i = 0; i < 3; i++)
        cout << ((i < 2)? !i ? x [i] : y : x[1]);
```

This is merely an obscure (but, by no means, maximally obscure) way to print the three strings.

```
Jason Quillstone at your service
```

The *switch* Statement

Suppose you create a screen menu that asks the user to select one of five choices, for instance, Cheap, Moderate, Expensive, Extravagant, and Excessive. You can extend an *if else if else* sequence to handle five alternatives, but the C++ *switch* statement handles selecting a choice from an extended list more easily. Here's the general form for a *switch* statement:

```
switch (integer-expression)
{
        case label1 : statement(s)
        case label2 : statement(s)
    ...
        default     : statement(s)
}
```

A C++ *switch* statement acts as a routing device, telling the computer which line of code to execute next. On reaching a *switch,* the program jumps to the line labeled with the value corresponding to the value of *integer-expression.* For instance, if *integer-expression* has the value 4, the program will go to the line having a *case 4:* label. The value *integer-expression,* as the name suggests, must be an expression that reduces to an integer value. Also, each label must be an integer constant expression. Most often, labels are simple *int* or *char* constants such as *1* or *q* or enumerators. If *integer-expression* doesn't match any of the labels, the program jumps to the line labeled *default.* The *default* label is optional. If you omit it and there is no match, the program jumps to the next statement following the *switch.* See Figure 6-3.

The *switch* statement is different from similar statements in languages such as Pascal in a very important way. Each C++ *case* label functions only as a line label, not as a boundary between choices. That is, once a program jumps to a particular line in a

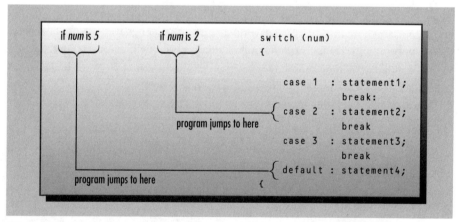

Figure 6-3 The *switch* statement

switch, it then sequentially executes all the statements following that line in the *switch* unless you explicitly direct it otherwise. Execution does NOT automatically stop at the next *case*. To make execution stop at the end of a particular group of statements, you must use the *break* statement. This causes execution to jump to the statement following the *switch*.

Listing 6-10 shows how to use *switch* and *break* together to implement a simple menu for executives. The program uses a *showmenu()* function to display a set of choices. A *switch* statement then selects an action based on the user's response.

COMPATIBILITY NOTE

Microsoft Visual C++ 1.0 treats the \a escape sequence as silent in QuickWin applications.

Listing 6-10 *switch.cpp*

```
// switch.cpp -- use the switch statement
#include <iostream.h>
void showmenu(void);    // function prototypes
void report(void);
void comfort(void);
int main(void)
{
        showmenu();
        int choice;
        cin >> choice;
        while (choice != 5)
        {
                switch(choice)
                {
                        case 1 : cout << "\a\n";
                                break;
                        case 2 : report();
                                break;
                        case 3 : cout << "The boss was in all day.\n";
                                break;
                        case 4 : comfort();
                                break;
                        default: cout << "That's not a choice.\n";
                }
                showmenu();
                cin >> choice;
        }
        cout << "Bye!\n";
        return 0;
}

void showmenu(void)
{
        cout << "Please enter 1, 2, 3, 4, or 5:\n"
```

continued on next page

continued from previous page

```
                              "1) alarm          2) report\n"
                              "3) alibi          4) comfort\n"
                              "5) quit\n";
}
void report(void)
{
        cout << "It's been an excellent week for business.\n"
                "Sales are up 120%. Expenses are down 35%.\n";
}
void comfort(void)
{
        cout << "Your employees think you are the finest CEO\n"
                "in the industry. The board of directors think\n"
                "you are the finest CEO in the industry.\n";
}
```

Here is a sample run of our executive menu program:

```
Please enter 1, 2, 3, 4, or 5:
1) alarm          2) report
3) alibi          4) comfort
5) quit
4
Your employees think you are the finest CEO
in the industry. The board of directors think
you are the finest CEO in the industry.
Please enter 1, 2, 3, 4, or 5:
1) alarm          2) report
3) alibi          4) comfort
5) quit
2
It's been an excellent week for business.
Sales are up 120%. Expenses are down 35%.
Please enter 1, 2, 3, 4, or 5:
1) alarm          2) report
3) alibi          4) comfort
5) quit
6
That's not a choice.
Please enter 1, 2, 3, 4, or 5:
1) alarm          2) report
3) alibi          4) comfort
5) quit
5
Bye!
```

The *while* loop terminates when the user enters a 5. Entering 1 through 4 activates the corresponding choice from the *switch* list, and entering 6 triggers the *default* statements.

As noted before, this program needs the *break* statements to confine execution to a particular portion of a *switch*. To see that this is so, you can remove the *breaks* from Listing 6-10 and see how it works afterwards. You'll find, for example, that entering 2 causes the program to execute all the statements associated with case labels *2, 3, 4,* and the *default*. C++ works this way because that sort of behavior can be useful. For one thing, it makes it simple to use multiple labels. For instance, suppose you rewrote Listing 6-10 using characters instead of integers as menu choices and *switch* labels. Then you could use both an uppercase and a lowercase label for the same statements:

```
char choice;
cin >> choice;
while (choice != 'Q' && choice != 'q')
{
        switch(choice)
        {
                case 'a':
                case 'A': cout << "\a\n";
                        break;
                case 'r':
                case 'R': report();
                        break;
                case 'l':
                case 'L': cout << "The boss was in all day.\n";
                        break;
                case 'c'
                case 'C': comfort();
                        break;
                default : cout << "That's not a choice.\n";
        }
        showmenu();
        cin >> choice;
}
```

Because there is no *break* immediately following *case 'a'* program execution passes on to the next line, which is the statement following *case 'A'*.

Using Enumerators As Labels

Listing 6-11 illustrates using *enum* to define a set of related constants and then using the constants in a *switch*. In general, *cin* doesn't recognize enumerated types (it can't know how you will define them), so the program reads the choice as an *int*. When the *switch* statement compares the *int* value to an enumerator case label, it promotes the enumerator to *int*. Also, the enumerators are promoted to type *int* in the *while* loop test condition.

Listing 6-11 *enum.cpp*

```
// enum.cpp -- use enum
#include <iostream.h>
// create named constants for 0 - 6
enum {red, orange, yellow, green, blue, purple, indigo};

int main(void)
{
        cout << "Enter color code: ";
        int code;
```

continued on next page

continued from previous page

```
        cin >> code;
        while (code >= red && code <= indigo)
        {
            switch (code)
            {
                case red      : cout << "Her lips were red.\n"; break;
                case orange   : cout << "Her hair was orange.\n"; break;
                case yellow   : cout << "Her shoes were yellow.\n"; break;
                case green    : cout << "Her nails were green.\n"; break;
                case blue     : cout << "Her sweatsuit was blue.\n"; break;
                case purple   : cout << "Her eyes were purple.\n"; break;
                case indigo   : cout << "Her mood was indigo.\n"; break;
            }
            cout << "Enter color code: ";
            cin >> code;
        }
        cout << "Bye\n";
        return 0;
}
```

Here's a sample output:

```
Enter color code: 3
Her nails were green.
Enter color code: 5
Her eyes were purple.
Enter color code: 2
Her shoes were yellow.
Enter color code: 8
Bye
```

switch and *if else*

Both the *switch* statement and the *if else* statement let a program select from a list of alternatives. The *if else* is the more versatile of the two. For instance, it can handle ranges, as in the following:

```
    if (age > 17 && age < 35)
            index = 0;
    else if (age >= 35 && age < 50)
            index = 1;
    else if (age >= 50 && age < 65)
            index = 2;
    else
            index = 3;
```

The *switch*, however, isn't designed to handle ranges. Each *switch* case label must be a single value. Also, that value must be an integer (which includes *char*), so a *switch* won't handle floating-point tests. And the *case* label value must be a constant. So if your alternatives involve ranges or floating-point tests or comparing two variables, use *if else*.

If, however, all the alternatives can be identified with integer constants, you can use a *switch* or an *if else* statement. Because that's precisely the situation that the *switch* statement is designed to process, the *switch* statement usually is the more efficient choice in terms of code size and execution speed, unless there are only a couple alternatives from which to choose.

TIP

If you can use either an *if else if* sequence or a *switch* statement, the usual rule is to use a *switch* if you have 3 or more alternatives.

The *break* and *continue* Statements

The *break* and *continue* statements enable a program to skip over parts of the code. The *break* statement can be used in a *switch* statement and in any of the loops. It causes program execution to pass to the next statement following the *switch* or the loop. The *continue* statement is used in loops and causes a program to skip the rest of the body of the loop. See Figure 6-4.

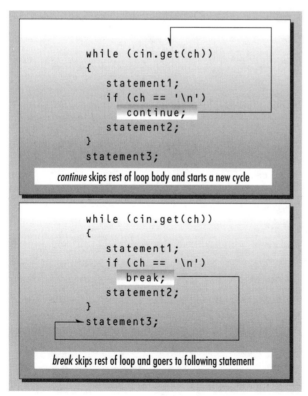

Figure 6-4 The *break* and *continue* statements

Listing 6-12 shows how the two statements work. The program lets you enter a line of text. The loop echoes each character and uses *break* to terminate the loop if the character is a period. This shows how you can use *break* to terminate a loop from within when some condition becomes true. Next the program counts spaces, but not other characters. The loop uses *continue* to skip over the counting part of the loop when the character isn't a space.

Listing 6-12 *jump.cpp*

```
// jump.cpp -- using continue and break
#include <iostream.h>
const int ArSize = 80;
int main(void)
{
        char line[ArSize];
        int spaces = 0;

        cout << "Enter a line of text:\n";
        cin.get(line, ArSize);
        for (int i = 0; line[i] != '\0'; i++)
        {
                cout << line[i];        // display character
                if (line[i] == '.')     // quit if it's a period
                        break;
                if (line[i] != ' ')     // skip rest of loop
                        continue;
                spaces++;
        }
        cout << "\n" << spaces << " spaces\n";
        return 0;
}
```

Here's a sample run:

```
Let's do lunch today. You can pay!
Let's do lunch today.
3 spaces
```

Program Notes

Note that while the *continue* statement causes the program to skip the rest of the loop body, it doesn't skip the loop update expression. In a *for* loop, the *continue* statement makes the program skip directly to the update expression, then to the test expression. For a *while* loop, however, *continue* makes the program go directly to the test expression. So any update expression in the loop body following the *continue* would be skipped. In some cases, that could be a problem.

This program didn't have to use *continue*. Instead, it could have used this code:

```
if (line[i] == ' ')
        spaces++;
```

However, the *continue* statement can make the program more readable when several statements follow the *continue*. That way, you don't need to make all those statements part of an *if* statement.

C++, like C, also has a *goto* statement. A statement like

```
goto paris
```

means to jump to the location bearing *paris:* as a label. That is, you can have code like this:

```
char ch;
cin >> ch;
if (ch == 'P')
        goto paris;
cout < ...
...
paris: cout << "You've just arrived at Paris.\n";
```

In most circumstances, using a *goto* is a bad hack, and you should use structured controls, such as *if else, switch, continue,* and the like, to control program flow.

Number-Reading Loops

You're preparing a program to read a series of numbers into an array. You would like to give the user the option to terminate input before filling the array. One way is make use of how *cin* behaves. Consider the following code:

```
int n;
cin >> n;
```

What happens if the user responds by entering a word instead of a number? Four things occur in such a mismatch:

- The value of *n* is left unchanged.

- The mismatched input is left in the input queue.

- An error flag is set in the *cin* object.

- The call to the *cin* method returns 0.

The fact that the method returns 0 means that you can use non-numeric input to terminate a number-reading loop. The fact that non-numeric input sets an error flag means that you have to reset the flag before the program can read more input. The *clear()* method, which also resets the end-of-file condition (Chapter 5), resets the bad input flag. (Either bad input or end-of-file can cause *cin* to return zero. Chapter 15 discusses how to distinguish between the two cases.) Let's look at a couple of examples illustrating these techniques.

You want to write a program to calculate the average weight of your day's catch of fish. There's a five-fish limit, so a five-element array can hold all the data, but it's possible that you could catch fewer fish. Listing 6-13 uses a loop that terminates if the array is full or if you enter non-numeric input.

Listing 6-13 *cinfish.cpp*

```
// cinfish.cpp -- non-numeric input terminates loop
#include <iostream.h>
const int Max = 5;
int main(void)
{
// get data
        double fish[Max];
        cout << "Please enter the weights of your fish.\n";
        cout << "You may enter up to " << Max
                    << " fish <q to terminate>.\n";
        cout << "fish #1: ";
        int i = 0;
        while (i < Max && cin >> fish[i]) {
                if (++i < Max)
                        cout << "fish #" << i+1 << ": ";
        }
// calculate average
        double total = 0.0;
        for (int j = 0; j < i; j++)
                total += fish[j];
// report results
        if (i == 0)
                cout << "No fish\n";
        else
                cout << total / i << " = average weight of "
                        << i << " fish\n";
        return 0;
}
```

The expression *cin >> fish[i]* really is a *cin* method function call, and the function returns *cin* if the input is a number and 0 otherwise. A 0 value for the expression terminates the loop. By the way, here's a sample run:

```
Please enter the weights of your fish.
You may enter up to 5 fish <q to terminate>.
fish #1: 30
fish #2: 35
fish #3: 25
fish #4: 40
fish #5: q
32.5 = average weight of 4 fish
```

Note the following line of code:

```
while (i < Max && cin >> fish[i]) {
```

Recall that C++ doesn't evaluate the right side of a logical AND expression if the left side is false. In this case, evaluating the right side means using *cin* to place input into the array. So if *i* does equal *Max,* the loop terminates without trying to read a value into a location past the end of the array.

The last example didn't attempt to read any input after non-numeric input. Let's look at a case that does. Suppose you are required to submit exactly five golf scores to a C++ program to establish your average. If a user enters non-numeric input, the program should object, insisting on numeric input. As you've seen, we can use the value of a *cin* input expression to test for non-numeric input. Suppose we find the user did enter the wrong stuff. We need to take three steps:

❧ Reset *cin* to accept new input.

❧ Get rid of the bad input.

❧ Prompt the user to try again.

Note that you have to reset *cin* before getting rid of the bad input. Listing 6-14 shows how these tasks can be accomplished.

Listing 6-14 *cingolf.cpp*

```cpp
// cingolf.cpp -- non-numeric input skipped
#include <iostream.h>
const int Max = 5;
int main(void)
{
// get data
    int golf[Max];
    cout << "Please enter your golf scores.\n";
    cout << "You must enter " << Max << " rounds.\n";
    for (int i = 0; i < Max; i++)
    {
        cout << "round #" << i+1 << ": ";
        while (!(cin >> golf[i])) {
            cin.clear();   // reset input
            while (cin.get() != '\n')
                continue;       // get rid of bad input
            cout << "Please enter a number: ";
        }
    }
// calculate average
    double total = 0.0;
    for (i = 0; i < Max; i++)
        total += golf[i];
// report results
    cout << total / Max << " = average score "
                << Max << " rounds\n";
    return 0;
}
```

Here is a sample run:

```
Please enter your golf scores.
You must enter 5 rounds.
round #1: 88
round #2: 87
round #3: must i?
Please enter a number: 103
round #4: 94
round #5: 86
91.6 = average score 5 rounds
```

Program Notes

The heart of the error-handling code is the following:

```
while (!(cin >> golf[i])) {
        cin.clear();           // reset input
        while (cin.get() != '\n')
                continue;      // get rid of bad input
        cout << "Please enter a number: ";
}
```

If the user enters **88**, the *cin* expression is true, a value is placed in the array, the expression *!(cin >> golf[i])* is false, and this inner loop terminates. But if the user enters **must i?**, the *cin* expression is false, nothing is placed into the array, the expression *!(cin >> golf[i])* is true, and the program enters a loop. The first statement in the loop uses the *clear()* method to reset input. If you omit this statement, the program refuses to read any more input. Next, the program uses *cin.get()* in a *while* loop to read the remaining input through the end of the line. This gets rid of the bad input along with anything else on the line. Another approach would be to read to the next white space, which would get rid of bad input one word at a time instead of one line at a time. Finally, the program tells the user to enter a number.

Summary

Programs and programming become more interesting when you introduce statements that guide the program through alternative actions. (Whether this also makes the programmer more interesting is a point we've not fully researched.) C++ provides the *if* statement, the *if else* statement, and the *switch* statements as means for managing choices. The C++ *if* statement lets a program execute a statement or statement block conditionally. That is, the program executes the statement or block if a particular condition is met. The C++ *if else* statement lets a program select from two choices which statement or statement block to execute. You can append additional *else if*s to the statement to present a series of choices. The C++ *switch* statement directs the program to a particular case in a list of choices.

C++ also provides operators to help in decision making. In Chapter 5 we discussed the relational expressions, which compare two values. The *if* and *if else* statements typically use relational expressions as test conditions. By using C++'s logical operators (&&, ||, and !), you can combine or modify relational expressions, constructing more elaborate tests. The conditional operator (?:) provides a compact way to choose from two values.

The *ctype.h* library of character functions provides a convenient and powerful set of tools for analyzing character input.

With C++'s loops and decision-making statements, you have the tools for writing interesting, intelligent, and powerful programs. But we've only begun to investigate the real powers of C++. Next, we'll look at functions.

Review Questions

1. Consider the following two code fragments for counting spaces and newlines:

```
// Version 1
while (cin.get(ch))
{
        if (ch == ' ')
                spaces++;
        if (ch == '\n')
                newlines++;
}
// Version 2
while (cin.get(ch))
{
        if (ch == ' ')
                spaces++;
        else if (ch == '\n')
                newlines++;
}
```

   What advantages, if any, does the second form have over the first?

2. In Listing 6-2, what is the effect of replacing ++*ch* with *ch+1*?

3. Consider carefully the following program:

```
#include <iostream.h>
int main(void)
{
        char ch;
        int ct1, ct2;

        ct1 = ct2 = 0;
        while ((ch = cin.get()) != '$')
        {
                cout << ch;
                ct1++;
                if (ch = '$')
                        ct2++;
                cout << ch;
```

continued on next page

continued from previous page

```
        }
        cout <<"ct1 = " << ct1 << ", ct2 = " << ct2 << "\n";
        return 0;
}
```

Suppose we provide the following input, where ↵ represents pressing (ENTER):

Hi!↵

Send $10 or $20 now!↵

What is the output? (Assume input is buffered.)

4. Construct logical expressions to represent the following conditions:

    a. *weight* is greater than or equal to 115 but less than 125.

    b. *ch* is q or Q.

    c. *x* is even, but is not 26.

    d. *donation* is in the range 1000–2000 or *guest* is 1.

    e. *ch* is a lowercase letter or an uppercase letter (assume the lowercase letters are coded sequentially and that the uppercase letters are coded sequentially but that there is a gap in the code between uppercase and lowercase).

5. In English the statement "I will not not speak" means the same as "I will speak." In C++, is *!!x* the same as *x?*

6. Construct a conditional expression that is equal to the absolute value of a variable. That is, if a variable *x* is positive, the value of the expression is just *x*, but if *x* is negative, the value of the expression is *-x*, which would be positive.

7. Rewrite the following fragment using *switch*:

```
if (ch == 'A')
        a_grade++;
else if (ch == 'B')
        b_grade++;
else if (ch == 'C')
        c_grade++;
else if (ch == 'D')
        d_grade++;
else
        f_grade++;
```

8. In Listing 6-10, what advantage would there be in using character labels, such as *a* and *c*, instead of numbers for the menu choices and *switch* cases? (Hint: Think about what happens if the user types **q** in either case and what happens if the user types **5** in either case.)

9. Consider the following code fragment:

```
        int line = 0;
char ch;
while (cin.get(ch))
{
        if (ch == 'Q')
```

```
            break;
    if (ch != '\n')
            continue;
    line++;
}
```

Rewrite this code without using *break* or *continue*.

Programming Exercises

1. Write a program that reads keyboard input to end-of-file and that echoes the input except for digits, converting each uppercase character to lowercase, and vice versa. (Don't forget the *ctype.h* family.)

2. Write a program that reads up to ten donation values into an array of *double*. The program should terminate input on non-numeric input. It should report the average of the numbers and also report how many numbers in the array are larger than the average.

3. Write a precursor to a menu-driven program. The program should display a menu offering four choices, each labeled with a letter. If the user responds with a letter other than one of the four valid choices, the program should prompt the user to enter a valid response until the user complies. Then the program should use a *switch* to select a simple action based on the user's selection. A program run could look something like this:

```
Please enter one of the following choices:
c) carnivore          p) pianist
t) tree               g) game
f
Please enter a c, p, t, or g: q
Please enter a c, p, t, or g: t
A maple is a tree.
```

4. When you join the Benelovent Order of Programmers, you can be known at BOP meetings by your real name, your job title, or by your secret BOP name. Write a program that can list members by real name, by job title, by secret name, or by a member's preference. Base the program on the following structure:

```
// Benevolent Order of Programmers name structure
struct bop {
        char fullname[strsize]; // real name
        char title[strsize];    // job title
        char bopname[strsize];  // secret BOP name
        int preference;         // 0 = fullname, 1 = title, 2 = bopname
};
```

In the program, create a small array of such structures and initialize it to suitable values. Have the program run a loop that lets the user select from different alternatives:

```
a. display by name      b. display by title
c. display by bopname   d. display by preference
q. quit
```

A sample run may look something like the following:

```
Benevolent Order of Programmers Report
a. display by name      b. display by title
c. display by bopname   d. display by preference
q. quit
Enter your choice: a
Wimp Macho
Raki Rhodes
Celia Laiter
Hoppy Hipman
Pat Hand
Next choice: d
Wimp Macho
Junior Programmer
MIPS
Analyst Trainee
LOOPY
Next choice: q
Bye!
```

CHAPTER 7

FUNCTIONS—C++'S PROGRAMMING MODULES

You will learn about the following in this chapter:

- ◇ Function basics (review)
- ◇ Function prototypes
- ◇ Passing function arguments by value
- ◇ Designing functions to process arrays
- ◇ Using *const* pointer arguments
- ◇ Designing functions to process text strings

- ◇ Designing functions to process structures
- ◇ Functions that call themselves (recursion)
- ◇ Pointers to functions

F un is where you find it. Look closely, and you'll find it in functions. C++ comes with a large library of useful functions (the standard ANSI C library plus some C++ classes), but real programming pleasure comes with writing your own. In this and the next chapter you'll examine how to define functions, how to convey information to them, and how to retrieve information from them. After reviewing how functions work, this chapter concentrates on how to use functions in conjunction with arrays, strings, and structures. Finally, it touches on recursion and on pointers to functions. If you've paid your C dues, you'll find much of this chapter familiar. But don't be lulled into a false sense of expertise. C++ has made several additions to what functions can do, and the next chapter deals primarily with them. Meanwhile, let's attend to the fundamentals.

Function Review

First, let's review what you've already seen about functions. To use a C++ function, you must do the following:

❧ Provide a function definition.

❧ Provide a function prototype.

❧ Call the function.

If you're using a library function, the function has already been defined and compiled for you. Also, you can use a standard library header file to provide the prototype. So all that's left to do is to call the function properly. The examples to date have done that several times. For example, the standard C++ library includes the *strlen()* function for finding the length of the string. The associated standard header file *string.h* contains the function prototype for *strlen()* and several other string-related functions. This advance work allows you to use the *strlen()* function in programs without further worries.

But when you create your own functions, you have to handle all three aspects—defining, prototyping, and calling—yourself. Listing 7-1 shows these steps in a short example.

Listing 7-1 *calling.cpp*

```cpp
// calling.cpp -- defining, prototyping, and calling a function
#include <iostream.h>

void simple(void);     // function prototype

int main(void)
{
        cout << "main() will call the simple() function:\n";
        simple();                // function call
        return 0;
}

// function definition
void simple(void)
{
        cout << "I'm just a simple country function.\n";
}
```

Here's the output:

```
main() will call the simple() function:
I'm just a simple country function.
```

Let's take a more detailed look at these steps now.

Defining a Function

Functions can be grouped into two categories: functions that don't have return values and functions that do have return values. Functions without return values are termed type *void* functions and have the following general form:

```
void functionname (argumentlist)
{
        statement(s)
        return;          // optional
}
```

Here *argumentlist* specifies the types and number of arguments that are passed to the function. We'll investigate this list more fully later. The optional *return* statement marks the end of the function. Otherwise the function terminates at the closing brace. Type *void* functions correspond to Pascal procedures, FORTRAN subroutines, and modern BASIC subprogram procedures. Typically, you use a *void* function to perform some sort of action. For instance, a function to print *Cheers!* a given number (*n*) of times could look like this:

```
void cheers(int n)          // no return value
{
        for (int i = 0; i < n; i++)
                cout << "Cheers! ";
        cout << "\n";
}
```

The *int n* argument list means that *cheers()* expects to be passed an *int* value as an argument when you call this function.

A function with a return value produces a value that it returns to the function that called it. In other words, if the function returns the square root of 9.0 (*sqrt(9.0)*), then the function call is replaced by the value *3.0*. Such a function is declared as having the same type as the value it returns. Here is the general form:

```
typename functionname (argumentlist)
{
        statements
        return value;    // value is of type typename
}
```

Functions with return values require that you use a *return* statement so that the value is returned to the calling statement. The value itself can be a constant, a variable, or a more general expression. The only requirement is that the expression reduce to a value having the *typename* type. The function then returns the final value to the function that called it. C++ does place a restriction on what types you can use for a return value: the return value cannot be an array. That leaves everything else possible—integers, floating-point numbers, pointers, even structures and objects! (Interestingly, even though a C++ function can't return an array directly, it can return an array that's part of a structure or object.)

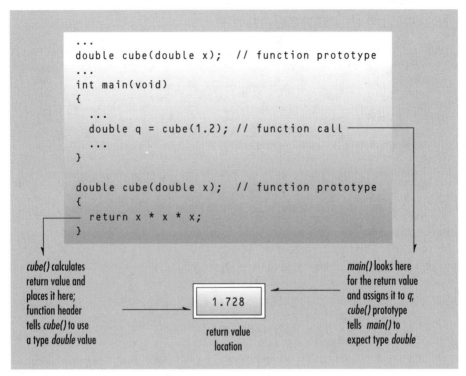

```
...
double cube(double x);  // function prototype
...
int main(void)
{
   ...
   double q = cube(1.2); // function call
   ...
}

double cube(double x);  // function prototype
{
      return x * x * x;
}
```

cube() calculates return value and places it here; function header tells cube() to use a type *double* value

1.728

return value location

main() looks here for the return value and assigns it to *q*; cube() prototype tells main() to expect type *double*

Figure 7-1 Typical return value mechanism

As a programmer, you don't need to know how a function returns a value, but knowing the method may make the concept clearer to you. (Also, it gives you something to talk about with your friends and family.) Typically, a function returns a value by copying the return value to a specified CPU register or memory location. Then the calling program examines that location. So both the returning function and the calling function have to agree on the type of data at that location. The function prototype tells the calling program what to expect, and the function definition tells the called program what to return. See Figure 7-1. Providing the same information in the prototype as in the definition may seem like extra work, but it does make good sense. Certainly, if you wanted a courier to pick up something from your desk at the office, you enhance the odds of the task being done right if you provide a description of what you want both to the courier and to someone at the office.

A function terminates after executing a *return* statement. If a function has more than one *return* statement—for example, as alternatives to different *if else* selections—the function terminates after executing the first *return* statement it reaches:

```
int bigger(int a, int b)
{
        if (a > b )
```

```
        return a;      // if a > b, function terminates here
    else
        return b;      // otherwise, function terminates here
}
```

Here the *else* isn't needed, but it does help the casual reader understand the intent.

Functions with return values are much like functions in Pascal, FORTRAN, and BASIC. They return a value to the calling program, which can then assign that value to a variable, or display the value, or otherwise use it. Here's a simple example that returns the cube of a type *double* value:

```
double cube(double x)       // x times x times x
{
        return x * x * x;   // a type double value
}
```

For instance, the function call *cube(1.2)* would return the value *1.728*. Note that this *return* statement uses an expression. The function computes the value of the expression (*1.728* in this case) and returns the value.

Function Prototyping and Function Calls

By now you are familiar with making function calls, but you may be less comfortable with function prototyping because that's often been hidden in the include files. So let's use the two functions we just defined in a program (Listing 7-2), paying notice to the function prototypes.

Listing 7-2 *protos.cpp*

```
// protos.cpp -- use prototypes and function calls
#include <iostream.h>
void cheers(int);                       // prototype: no return value
double cube(double x);                  // prototype: returns a double
int main(void)
{
        cheers(5);                      // function call
        cout << "Give me a number: ";
        double side;
        cin >> side;
        double volume = cube(side);     // function call
        cout << "A " << side <<"-foot cube has a volume of ";
        cout << volume << " cubic feet.\n";
        cheers(cube(2));                // prototype protection at work
        return 0;
}

void cheers(int n)
{
    for (int i = 0; i < n; i++)
```

continued on next page

continued from previous page

```
                cout << "Cheers! ";
    cout << "\n";
}

double cube(double x)
{
        return x * x * x;
}
```

Here's a sample run:

```
Cheers! Cheers! Cheers! Cheers! Cheers!
Give me a number: 5
A 5-foot cube has a volume of 125 cubic feet.
Cheers! Cheers! Cheers! Cheers! Cheers! Cheers! Cheers! Cheers!
```

Note that *main()* calls the type *void* function *cheers()* by using the function name and arguments followed by a semicolon: *cheers(s);*. That's an example of a function call statement. But because *cube()* has a return value, *main()* can use it as part of an assignment statement:

```
double volume = cube(side);
```

But we said you should concentrate on the prototypes. What should you know about prototypes? First, you should understand why C++ requires prototypes. Then, because C++ requires prototypes, you should know the proper syntax. Finally, you should appreciate what the prototype does for you. Let's look at these points in turn, using Listing 7-2 as a basis for discussion.

Why Prototypes?

The prototype describes the function interface to the compiler. That is, it tells the compiler what type of return value, if any, the function has, and it tells the compiler the number and the type of function arguments. Consider, for example, how a prototype affects this function call from Listing 7-2:

```
double volume = cube(side);
```

First, the prototype tells the compiler that *cube* should have one type *double* argument. If the program fails to provide one, prototyping allows the compiler to catch the error. Second, when the *cube()* function finishes its calculation, it places its return value at some specified location—perhaps in a CPU register, perhaps in memory. Then the calling function, *main()* in this case, retrieves the value from that location. Because the prototype states that *cube()* is type *double,* the compiler knows how many bytes to retrieve and how to interpret them. Without that information, the compiler could only guess.

Still, you may wonder, why does the compiler need a prototype? Can't it just look further in the file and see how the functions are defined? One problem with that approach is that it is less efficient. The compiler would have to put compiling *main()*

on hold while it searched the rest of the file. An even more serious problem is the fact that the function may not even be in the file. C++ allows you to spread a program over several files, which can be compiled independently, then combined later. If that's the case, then the compiler may not have access to the function code when it's compiling *main()*. The same is true if the function is part of a library. The only way to avoid using a function prototype is to place the function definition *above* its first use. That is not always possible. And the C++ programming style is to put *main()* first because it generally provides the structure for the whole program.

Prototype Syntax

A function prototype is a statement, so it must have a terminating semicolon. The simplest way to get a prototype is to copy the function heading from the function definition and add a semicolon. That's what we did for *cube()*:

```
double cube(double x); // add ; to heading to get prototype
```

However, the function prototype does not require that you provide names for the variables; a list of types is enough. So we prototyped *cheers()* just using the argument type:

```
void cheers(int); // okay to drop variable names in prototype
```

In general, you can either include or exclude variable names in the argument lists for prototypes. The variable names in the prototype just act as place holders, so if you do use names, they don't have to match the names in the function definition.

C++ VERSUS ANSI C PROTOTYPING

ANSI C borrowed prototyping from C++, but the two languages do have some differences. The most important is that ANSI C, to preserve compatibility with classic C, made prototyping optional, while C++ makes prototyping mandatory. For instance, consider the following function declaration:

```
void say_hi();
```

In C++, leaving the parentheses empty is the same as using the keyword *void* within the parentheses. It means the function has no arguments. In ANSI C, leaving the parentheses empty means that you decline to state what the arguments are. That is, it means you're foregoing prototyping the argument list.

What Prototypes Do for You

You've seen that prototypes help the compiler. But what do they do for you? They greatly reduce the chances for program errors. In particular, prototypes ensure the following:

¶ The compiler correctly handles the function return value.

> ◀ The compiler checks that you use the correct number of function arguments.

> ◀ The compiler checks that you use the correct type of arguments. If not, it converts the arguments to the correct type, if possible.

We've already discussed getting the return value handled correctly. Let's look now at what happens when you use the wrong number of arguments. For instance, suppose you made the following call:

```
double z = cube();
```

Without function prototyping, the compiler would let this go by. When the function was called, it would look where *cube()* should have placed a number and use whatever value happened to be there. This, for instance, is how C worked before ANSI C borrowed prototyping from C++. Since prototyping is optional for ANSI C, this is still how some C programs work. But in C++ prototyping is not optional, so you are guaranteed protection from that sort of error.

Next, suppose you use the correct number but the wrong type of argument. In C, this could create weird errors. For instance, if a function expected a type *int* value (assume that's 2 bytes) and you passed a *double* (assume that's 8 bytes), the function would look at just the first 2 bytes of the 8 and try to interpret them as an *int* value. C++, however, automatically converts the value you pass to the type specified in the prototype. For instance, Listing 7-2 manages to get two type mismatches in one statement:

```
cheers(cube(2));
```

First, the program passes the *int* value of 2 to *cube()*, which expects type *double*. The compiler, noting that the *cube()* prototype specifies a type *double* argument, converts 2 to 2.0, a type *double* value. Then *cube()* returns a type *double* value (8.0) to be used as an argument to *cheers()*. Again, the compiler checks the prototypes and notes that *cheers()* requires an *int*. So it converts the return value to the integer 8. In general, prototyping produces automatic type casts to the expected types. (Function overloading, discussed in Chapter 8, can create ambiguous situations, however, that prevent some automatic type casts.)

Automatic type conversion doesn't head off all possible errors. For instance, if you pass a value of 8.33E27 to a function that expects an *int,* such a large value cannot be converted correctly to a mere *int.* Some compilers will warn you of possible data loss when there is an automatic conversion from a larger type to a smaller.

Also, prototyping results in type conversion only when it makes sense. It won't, for example, convert an integer to a structure or to a pointer.

Prototyping takes place during compile time and is termed *static type checking*. Static type checking, as we've just seen, catches many errors that would be much more difficult to catch during run time.

Function Arguments and Passing by Value

It's time to take a closer look at function arguments. C++ normally passes arguments *by value*. That means the numerical value of the argument is passed to the function, where it is assigned to a new variable. For instance, Listing 7-2 has this function call:

```
double volume = cube(side);
```

Here *side* is a variable that, in the sample run, had the value 5. The function heading for *cube()*, recall, was this:

```
double cube(double x)
```

When this function is called, it creates a new type *double* variable called *x* and assigns the value 5 to it. This insulates data in *main()* from actions that take place in *cube()*, for *cube()* works with a copy of *side* instead of with the original data. You'll see an example of this protection soon. A variable that's used to receive passed values is called a *formal argument* or *parameter*. The value passed to the function is called the *actual argument*. Thus argument passing assigns the actual argument to the formal argument. See Figure 7-2.

Variables, including formal parameters, declared within a function are private to the function. When a function is called, the computer allocates the memory needed for these variables. When the function terminates, the computer frees the memory that

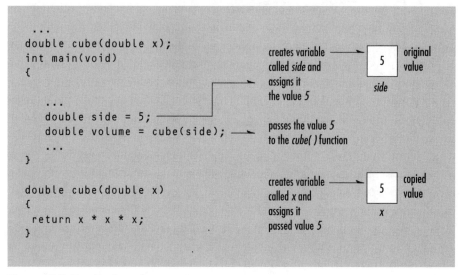

Figure 7-2 Passing by value

was used for those variables. (Some C++ literature refers to this allocation and freeing of memory as creating and destroying variables. That does make it sound much more exciting.) Such variables are called *local* variables because they are localized to the function. As we mentioned, this helps preserve data integrity. It also means that if you declare a variable called *x* in *main()* and another variable called *x* in some other function, that these are two distinct, unrelated variables much as the Albany in California is distinct from the Albany in New York. See Figure 7-3.

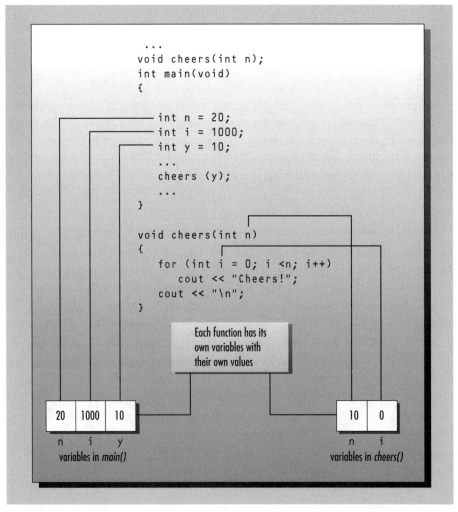

Figure 7-3 Local variables

Multiple Arguments

Functions can have more than one argument. In the function call, just separate the arguments with commas:

```
n_chars('R', 25);
```

This passes two arguments to the function *n_chars()*, soon to be defined.

Similarly, when you define the function, you use a comma-separated list of declarations in the function heading:

```
void n_chars(char c, int n)   // two arguments
```

This function heading states that the function *n_chars()* takes one type *char* argument and one type *int* argument. The variables *c* and *n* are assigned the values passed to the function. If a function takes two arguments of the same type, you have to give the type of each argument separately. You can't combine declarations the way you can when declaring regular variables:

```
void fifi(float a, float b)   // declare each variable separately
void fifi(float a, b)         // NOT acceptable
```

As with other functions, just add a semicolon to get a prototype:

```
void n_chars(char c, int n); // prototype, style 1
```

As with single arguments, you don't have to use the same variable names in the prototype as in the definition, and you can omit the variable names in the prototype:

```
void n_chars(char, int);     // prototype, style 2
```

However, providing variable names can make the prototype more understandable, particularly if two parameters are the same type. Then the names can remind you which argument is which:

```
double melon_density(double weight, double volume);
```

Listing 7-3 shows an example of a function with two arguments. It also illustrates how changing the value of a formal argument in a function has no effect on the data in the calling program.

 Listing 7-3 *twoarg.cpp*

```
// twoarg.cpp -- a function with 2 arguments
#include <iostream.h>
void n_chars(char, int);
int main(void)
{
        int times;
        char ch;
```

continued on next page

continued from previous page

```
        cout << "Enter a character: ";
        cin >> ch;
        while (ch != 'q')                // q to quit
        {
                cout << "Enter an integer: ";
                cin >> times;
                n_chars(ch, times);   // function with two arguments
                cout << "\nEnter another character or press the"
                                " q-key to quit: ";
                cin >> ch;
        }
        cout << "The value of times is " << times << ".\n";
        cout << "Bye\n";
        return 0;
}

void n_chars(char c, int n)   // displays c n times
{
        while (n-- > 0)                  // continue until n reaches 0
                cout << c;
}
```

Here is a sample run:

```
Enter a character: W
Enter an integer: 50
WWWWWWWWWWWWWWWWWWWWWWWWWWWWWWWWWWWWWWWWWWWWWWWWWWWW
Enter another character or press the q-key to quit: a
Enter an integer: 20
aaaaaaaaaaaaaaaaaaaa
Enter another character or press the q-key to quit: q
The value of times is 20.
Bye
```

Program Notes

The *main()* function uses a *while* loop to keep loops fresh in your mind. Note that it uses *cin >> ch* to read a character instead of *cin.get(ch)* or *cin = cin.get()*. There's a good reason for doing so. The *cin.get()* pair of functions, you recall, read *all* input characters, including spaces and newlines, while *cin* skips spaces and newlines. When you respond to the program prompt, you have to press (ENTER) at the end of each line, thus generating a newline character. The *cin >> ch* approach conveniently skips over these newlines, but the *cin.get()* siblings would read the newline following each number entered as the next character to display. You can program around this nuisance, but it's simpler to use *cin* as we did.

The *n_chars()* function takes two arguments: a character *c* and an integer *n*. It then uses a loop to display the character the number of times specified by the integer:

```
while (n-- > 0)              // continue until n reaches 0
        cout << c;
```

Notice that the program keeps count by decrementing the *n* variable, where *n* is the formal parameter from the argument list. This variable was assigned the value of the *times* variable in *main()*. The *while* loop then decreases *n* to zero, but, as the sample run demonstrates, changing the value of *n* has no effect on *times*.

Another Two-Argument Function

Let's create a more ambitious function, one that performs a nontrivial calculation. Also, the function will illustrate using local variables other than the function's formal arguments.

Many states in the United States now sponsor a lottery with some form of Lotto game. Lotto lets you pick a certain number of choices from a card. For instance, you might get to pick 6 numbers from a card having 49 numbers. Then the Lotto managers pick 6 numbers at random. If your choice exactly matches theirs, you win a few million dollars or so. Our function will calculate the probability that you have a winning pick. (Yes, a function that successfully predicts the winning picks themselves would be more useful, but C++, although powerful, has yet to implement psychic facilities.)

First, we need a formula. Suppose you have to pick 6 values out of 49. Then mathematics says you have one chance in R of winning, where R is given by the following formula:

$$R \quad = \quad \frac{49 \times 48 \times 47 \times 46 \times 45 \times 44}{6 \times 5 \times 4 \times 3 \times 2 \times 1}$$

For 6 choices the denominator is the product of the first 6 integers, or 6 factorial. The numerator also is the product of 6 consecutive numbers, this time starting with 49 and going down. More generally, if you pick *picks* values out of *numbers* numbers, the denominator is *picks* factorial and the numerator is the product of *picks* integers starting with the value *numbers* and working down. You can use a *for* loop to make that calculation:

```
long double result = 1.0;
for (n = numbers, p = picks; p > 0; n--, p--)
        result = result * n / p ;
```

Rather than multiplying all the numerator terms first, the loop begins by multiplying *1.0* by the first numerator term, then dividing by the first denominator term. Then, in the next cycle, the loop multiplies and divides by the second numerator and denominator terms. This keeps the running product smaller than if you did all the multiplication first. For instance, compare

```
(10 * 9) / (2 * 1)
```

with the following:

```
(10 / 2) * (9 / 1)
```

The first evaluates to 90 / 2, then to 45, while the second evaluates to 5 * 9, then to 45. Both give the same answer, but the first method produces a larger intermediate value (90) than does the second. The more factors you have, the bigger the difference gets. For large numbers, this strategy can keep the calculation from overflowing the maximum possible floating-point value.

Listing 7-4 incorporates this formula into an *odds()* function. Because the number of picks and the total number of choices should be positive values, the program uses the *unsigned int* type (*unsigned,* for short) for those quantities. Multiplying several integers together can produce pretty large results, so *lotto.cpp* uses the *long double* type for the function's return value. Also, terms such as 49 / 6 produce a truncation error for integer types.

COMPATIBILITY NOTE

Some C++ implementations don't support type *long double*. If your implementation falls into that category, try ordinary *double* instead.

Listing 7-4 *lotto.cpp*

```cpp
// lotto.cpp -- odds against winning
#include <iostream.h>
// Note: some implementations require double instead of long double
long double odds(unsigned numbers, unsigned picks);
int main(void)
{
        double total, choices;
        cout << "Enter total number of game card choices and\n"
                "number of picks allowed:\n";
        while ((cin >> total >> choices) && choices <= total)
        {
                cout << "You have one chance in ";
                cout << odds(total, choices);        // compute the odds
                cout << " of winning.\n";
                cout << "Next two numbers (q to quit): ";
        }
        cout << "bye\n";
        return 0;
}


// the following function calculates the odds of picking picks
// numbers correctly from numbers choices
long double odds(unsigned numbers, unsigned picks)
{
        long double result = 1.0;  // here come some local variables
        long double n;
        unsigned p;

        for (n = numbers, p = picks; p > 0; n--, p--)
                result = result * n / p ;
        return result;
}
```

Here's a sample run. Notice that increasing the number of choices on the game card greatly increases the odds against winning.

```
Enter total number of game card choices and
number of picks allowed:
49 6
You have one chance in 1.39838e+07 of winning.
Next two numbers (q to quit): 51 6
You have one chance in 1.80095e+07 of winning.
Next two numbers (q to quit): 38 6
You have one chance in 2.76068e+06 of winning.
Next two numbers (q to quit): q
bye
```

Program Notes

The *odds()* function illustrates two kinds of local variables you can have in a function. First, there are the formal parameters (*numbers* and *picks*), which are declared in the function heading before the opening brace. Then come the other local variables (*result*, *n*, and *p*). They are declared in between the braces bounding the function definition. The main difference between the formal parameters and the other local variables is that the formal parameters get their values from the function that calls *odds()*, while the other variables get values from within the function.

Functions and Arrays

So far the example functions have been simple, using only the basic types for arguments and return values. But functions can be the key to handling more involved types, such as arrays and structures. Let's take a look now at how arrays and functions get along with each other.

Suppose you've been using an array to keep track of how many cookies each person has eaten at the family picnic. (Each array index corresponds to a person, and the value of the element corresponds to the number of cookies that person ate.) Now you want the total. That's easy to do; just use a loop to add all the array elements. But adding array elements is such a common task that it makes sense to design a function to do the job. Then you won't have to write a new loop every time you have to sum an array.

Let's consider what the function interface involves. Since the function calculates a sum, it should return the answer. If we keep our cookies intact, we can use a function with a type *int* return value. So that the function knows what array to sum, we'll want to pass the array name as an argument. And to make the function general so that it is not restricted to an array of a particular size, we'll pass the size of the array. The only new ingredient here is that we have to declare that one of the formal arguments is an array name. Let's see what that and the rest of the function heading look like:

```
int sum_arr(int arr[], int n) // arr = array name, n = size
```

This looks plausible. The brackets seem to indicate that *arr* is an array, and the fact that the brackets are empty seems to indicate we can use the function with an array of any size. But things are not always what they seem: *arr* is not really an array; it's a pointer! The good news is that we can write the rest of the function just as if *arr* were an array. First, we'll see that this approach works, then we'll look into why it works.

Listing 7-5 illustrates using a pointer as if it were an array name. The program initializes the array to some values and uses the *sum_arr()* function to calculate the sum. You'll note that the *sum_arr()* function uses *arr* as if it were an array name.

Listing 7-5 *arrfun1.cpp*

```
// arrfun1.cpp -- functions with an array argument
#include <iostream.h>
const int ArSize = 8;
int sum_arr(int arr[], int n);                  // prototype
int main(void)
{
        int cookies[ArSize] = {1,2,4,8,16,32,64,128};
// some systems require preceding int with static to
// enable array initialization

        int sum = sum_arr(cookies, ArSize);
        cout << "Total cookies eaten: " << sum <<  "\n";
        return 0;
}

// return the sum of an integer array
int sum_arr(int arr[], int n)
{
        int total = 0;

        for (int i = 0; i < n; i++)
                total = total + arr[i];
        return total;
}
```

Here is the program output:

```
Total cookies eaten: 255
```

As you can see, the program works. Now let's look at why it works.

Arrays and Pointers (Again)

The key is that C++, like C, in most contexts treats the name of an array as if it were a pointer. Recall from Chapter 4 that C++ interprets an array name as the address of its first element:

```
cookies == &cookies[0]  // array name is address of first element
```

(There are two exceptions to this rule. First, the array declaration uses the array name to label the storage. Second, applying *sizeof* to an array name yields the size of the whole array, in bytes.)

Listing 7-5 makes the following function call:

```
int sum = sum_arr(cookies, ArSize);
```

Here *cookies* is the name of an array, hence, by C++ rules, the address of its first element. So the function passes an address. Because the array has type *int* elements, *cookies* must be type pointer-to-*int*, or *int* *. That suggests that the correct function heading should be this:

```
int sum_arr(int * arr, int n) // arr = array name, n = size
```

Here we've replaced *int arr[]* with *int *arr*. It turns out that both headings are correct, for in C++ the notations *int *arr* and *int arr[]* have the identical meaning when (and *only* when) used in a function heading or function prototype. Both mean that *arr* is a pointer-to-*int*. However, the array notation version (*int arr[]*) symbolically reminds us that *arr* not only points to an *int*, it points to the first *int* in an array of *ints*. So we'll use the array notation when the pointer is to the first element of an array, and we'll use the pointer notation when the pointer is to an isolated value. Don't forget that the notations *int *arr* and *int arr[]* are *not* synonymous in any other context. For instance, you can't use the notation *int tip[]* to declare a pointer in the *body* of a function.

Given that the variable *arr* is really a pointer, the rest of the function makes sense. As you may recall from the discussion of dynamic arrays in Chapter 4, you can use the bracket array notation equally well with array names or with pointers to access elements of an array. So whether *arr* is a pointer or an array name, the expression *arr[3]* means the fourth element of the array. And it probably will do no harm at this point to remind you of the following two identities:

```
arr[i] == *(ar + i)        // values in two notations
&arr[i] == ar + i          // addresses in two notations
```

Remember, adding 1 to a pointer, including an array name, actually adds a value equal to the size, in bytes, of the type the pointer points to. So pointer addition and array subscripting are two equivalent ways of counting elements from the beginning of an array.

Implications of Using Arrays As Arguments

Let's look at the implications of Listing 7-5. The function call *sum_arr(cookies, ArSize)* passes the address of the first element of the *cookies* array and the number of elements of the array to the *sum_arr()* function. The *sum_arr()* function assigns the *cookies* address to the pointer variable *arr* and assigns *ArSize* to the *int* variable *n*. This means Listing 7-5 doesn't really pass the array contents to the function. Instead, it tells the

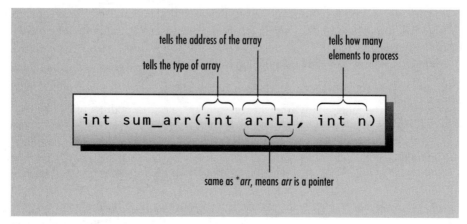

Figure 7-4 Telling a function about an array

function *where* the array is (the address), *what* kind of elements it has (the type), and *how many* elements it has (the *n* variable). See Figure 7-4. Armed with this information, the function then uses the *original* array. Pass an ordinary variable, and the function works with a copy. But pass an array, and the function works with the original. Actually, this difference doesn't violate C++'s pass-by-value approach. The *sum_arr()* function still passes a value that's assigned to a new variable. But that value is a single address, not the contents of an array.

Is the correspondence between array names and pointers a good thing? Indeed, it is. The design decision to use array addresses as arguments saves the time and memory needed to copy an entire array. The overhead for using copies can be prohibitive if you're working with large arrays. Not only would a program need more computer memory, but it would have to spend time copying large blocks of data. On the other hand, working with the original data raises the possibility of inadvertent data corruption. That's a real problem in classic C, but ANSI C and C++'s *const* modifier provides a remedy. We'll show an example soon. But first, let's alter Listing 7-5 to illustrate some points about how array functions operate. Listing 7-6 demonstrates that *cookies* and *arr* have the same value. It also shows how the pointer concept makes the *sum_arr* function more versatile than it may have appeared at first.

Listing 7-6 *arrfun2.cpp*

```
// arrfun2.cpp -- functions with an array argument
#include <iostream.h>
const int ArSize = 8;
int sum_arr(int arr[], int n);
int main(void)
{
    int cookies[ArSize] = {1,2,4,8,16,32,64,128};
//  some systems require preceding int with static to
```

```
//   enable array initialization

    cout << cookies << " = array address, ";
//   some systems require a type cast: unsigned (cookies)

    cout << sizeof cookies << " = sizeof cookies\n";
    int sum = sum_arr(cookies, ArSize);
    cout << "Total cookies eaten: " << sum <<  "\n";
    sum = sum_arr(cookies, 3);              // a lie
    cout << "First three eaters ate " << sum << " cookies.\n";
    sum = sum_arr(cookies + 4, 4);          // another lie
    cout << "Last four eaters ate " << sum << " cookies.\n";
    return 0;
}

// return the sum of an integer array
int sum_arr(int arr[], int n)
{
      int total = 0;
      cout << arr << " = arr, ";
// some systems require a type cast: unsigned (arr)

      cout << sizeof arr << " = sizeof arr\n";
      for (int i = 0; i < n; i++)
            total = total + arr[i];
      return total;
}
```

Here's the output (the address values and the array and integer sizes will vary from system to system):

```
0x8f8cffe6 = array address, 16 = sizeof cookies
0x8f8cffe6 = arr, 2 = sizeof arr
Total cookies eaten: 255
0x8f8cffe6 = arr, 2 = sizeof arr
First three eaters ate 7 cookies.
0x8f8cffee = arr, 2 = sizeof arr
Last four eaters ate 240 cookies.
```

Program Notes

Listing 7-6 illustrates some very interesting points about array functions. First, note that *cookies* and *arr* both evaluate to the same address, exactly as claimed. But *sizeof cookies* is *16,* while *sizeof arr* is only 2. That's because *sizeof cookies* is the size of the whole array, while *sizeof arr* is the size of the pointer variable. (Our system, remember, uses 2-byte addresses.) By the way, that's why we have to pass the size of the array explicitly instead of using *sizeof arr* in *sum_arr().*

Because the only way *sum_arr()* knows the number of elements in the array is through what we tell it with the second argument, we can lie to the function. For instance, the second time we use the function, we make this call:

```
sum = sum_arr(cookies, 3);
```

By telling the function that *cookies* has but three elements, we get the function to calculate the sum of the first three elements.

Why stop there? We also can lie about where the array starts:

```
sum = sum_arr(cookies + 4, 4);
```

Because *cookies* acts as the address of the first element, *cookies* + *4* acts as the address of the fifth element. So this statement sums the fifth, sixth, seventh, and eighth elements of the array. Note in the output how the third call to the function assigns a different address to *arr* than the first two calls did. And yes, you could use *&cookies[4]* instead of *cookies* + *4* as the argument; both mean the same thing.

More Array Functions

When you choose to use an array to represent data, you've made a design decision. But design decisions should go beyond how data is stored; they should also involve how the data is used. Often, you'll find it profitable to write specific functions to handle specific data operations. (The profits here are increased program reliability, ease of modification, and ease of debugging.) Also, when you start integrating storage properties with operations in your thinking about a program, you'll be taking an important step towards the OOP mind-set; that, too, may prove profitable in the future.

Let's examine a simple case. Suppose you want to use an array to keep track of the dollar values of your real estate. (If necessary, suppose you have real estate.) You'll have to decide on what type to use. Certainly, *double* is less restrictive in its range than *int* or *long,* and it provides enough significant digits to represent the values precisely. Next, you have to decide on the number of array elements. (With dynamic arrays created with *new,* you can put off that decision, but we'll keep things simple.) Let's say that you have no more than five properties, so you can use an array of five *doubles.*

Now consider the possible operations you might want to execute with the real estate array. Two very basic ones are reading values into the array and displaying the array contents. Let's add one more operation to the list: reassessing the value of the properties. For simplicity, assume that all your properties increase or decrease in value at the same rate. (Remember, this is a book on C++, not on real estate management.) Next, fit a function to each operation, then write the code accordingly. We'll go through these steps next.

Filling the Array

Because a function with an array name argument accesses the original array, not a copy, you can use a function call to assign values to array elements. So one argument to the function will be the name of the array to be filled. In general, a program might manage more than one person's investments, hence more than one array, so you won't want to build the array size into the function. Instead, pass the array size as a second argument, as in the previous example. Also, it's possible that you may wish to quit reading data before filling the array, so you'll want to build that feature into the function.

Because you may enter fewer than the maximum number of elements, it makes sense to have the function return the actual number of values entered. These considerations suggest the following function prototype:

```
int fill_array(double ar[], int limit);
```

The function takes an array name argument and an argument specifying the maximum number of items to be read, and the function returns the actual number of items read. For instance, if you use this function with an array of five elements, you would pass 5 as the second argument. And if you entered only three values, the function would return 3.

You can use a loop to read successive values into the array, but how can you terminate the loop early? One way is use a special value to indicate the end of input. Since no property should have a negative value, you can use a negative number to indicate the end of input. Given this, you can code the function as follows:

```
int fill_array(double ar[], int limit)
{
        double temp;
        for (int i = 0; i < limit; i++)
        {
                cout << "Enter value #" << i + 1 << ": ";
                cin >> temp;
                if (temp < 0)       // signal to terminate
                        break;
                ar[i] = temp;
        }
        return i;
}
```

Note that the code includes a prompt to the user in the program. If the user enters a non-negative value, the value is assigned to the array. Otherwise the loop terminates. If the user enters only valid values, the loop terminates after reading *limit* values. The last thing the loop does is increment *i*, so after the loop terminates, *i* is 1 greater than the last array index, hence it's equal to the number of filled elements. The function then returns that value.

Showing the Array and Protecting It with *const*

Building a function to display the array contents is simple. You pass the name of the array and the number of filled elements to the function, which then uses a loop to display each element. But there is another consideration—guaranteeing that the display function doesn't alter the original array. Unless the purpose of a function is to alter data, you should safeguard it from doing so. That protection comes automatically with ordinary arguments, since C++ passes them by value and the function works with a copy. But functions that use an array work with the original. After all, that's why the *fill_array()* function is able to do its job. To protect an array from being altered, you can use the keyword *const* (discussed in Chapter 3) when declaring the formal argument:

```
void show_array(const double ar[], int n);
```

The declaration states that the pointer *ar* points to constant data. This means that you can't use *ar* to change the data. That is, you can use a value such as *ar[0]*, but you can't change that value. Note that this doesn't mean that the original array need be constant; it just means that you can't use *ar* in the *show_array()* function to change the data. Suppose you accidentally violate this restriction by doing something like the following in the *show_array()* function:

```
ar[0] += 10;
```

Then the compiler will put a stop to your wrongful ways. Borland C++, for example, will give an error message like this (edited slightly):

```
Cannot modify a const object in function
        show_array(const double *,int)
```

The message reminds us that C++ interprets the declaration *const double ar[]* to mean *const double *ar*. Thus the declaration really says that *ar* points to a constant value. We'll discuss this in detail when we finish with the current example. Meanwhile, here is the code for the *show_array()* function:

```
void show_array(const double ar[], int n)
{
        for (int i = 0; i < n; i++)
        {
                cout << "Property #" << i + 1 << ": $";
                cout << ar[i] << "\n";
        }
}
```

Modifying the Array

The third operation for our array is multiplying each element by the same revaluation factor. You need to pass three arguments to the function: the factor, the array, and the number of elements. No return value is needed, so the function can look like this:

```
void reassess(double r, double ar[], int n)
{
        for (int i = 0; i < n; i++)
                ar[i] *= r;
}
```

Because this function is supposed to alter the array values, you don't use *const* to declare *ar*.

Putting the Pieces Together

Now that we've defined the data type in terms of how it's stored (an array) and how it's used (three functions), we can put together a program using the design. Because we've already built all the array-handling tools, we've greatly simplified programming *main()*. Most of the remaining programming work consists of having *main()* call the functions we've just developed. Listing 7-7 shows the result.

Listing 7-7 *arrfun3.cpp*

```
// arrfun3.cpp -- array functions and const
#include <iostream.h>
const int Max = 5;

// function prototypes
int fill_array(double ar[], int limit);
void show_array(const double ar[], int n);  // don't change data
void reassess(double r, double ar[], int n);

int main(void)
{
        double properties[Max];

        int size = fill_array(properties, Max);
        show_array(properties, size);
        cout << "Enter reassessment rate: ";
        double rate;
        cin >> rate;
        reassess(rate, properties, size);
        show_array(properties, size);
        return 0;
}

int fill_array(double ar[], int limit)
{
        double temp;
        for (int i = 0; i < limit; i++)
        {
                cout << "Enter value #" << i + 1 << ": ";
                cin >> temp;
                if (temp < 0)
                        break;
                ar[i] = temp;
        }
        return i;
}

// the following function can use, but not alter,
// the array whose address is ar
void show_array(const double ar[], int n)
{
        for (int i = 0; i < n; i++)
    {
                cout << "Property #" << i + 1 << ": $";
                cout << ar[i] << "\n";
        }
}

// multiplies each element of ar[] by r
void reassess(double r, double ar[], int n)
```

continued on next page

continued from previous page

```
{
        for (int i = 0; i < n; i++)
                ar[i] *= r;
}
```

Here are two sample runs. Recall that input should quit when the user enters five properties or enters a negative number, whichever comes first. The first example illustrates reaching the five-property limit, and the second example illustrates entering a negative value.

```
Enter value #1: 100000
Enter value #2: 80000
Enter value #3: 222000
Enter value #4: 240000
Enter value #5: 118000
Property #1: $100000
Property #2: $80000
Property #3: $222000
Property #4: $240000
Property #5: $118000
Enter reassessment rate: 1.10
Property #1: $110000
Property #2: $88000
Property #3: $244200
Property #4: $264000
Property #5: $129800

Enter value #1: 200000
Enter value #2: 84000
Enter value #3: 160000
Enter value #4: -2
Property #1: $200000
Property #2: $84000
Property #3: $160000
Enter reassessment rate: 1.20
Property #1: $240000
Property #2: $100800
Property #3: $192000
```

Program Notes

We've already discussed the important programming details, so let's reflect on the process. We began by thinking about the data type and designed appropriate functions to handle the data. Then we assembled these functions into a program. This sometimes is called *bottom-up* programming because the design process moves from the component parts to the whole. This approach is well suited to OOP, which concentrates on data representation and manipulation first. Traditional procedural programming, on the other hand, has leaned towards *top-down* programming, in which you develop a modular grand design first, then turn your attention to the details. Both methods are useful, and both lead to modular programs.

Pointers and *const*

Using *const* with pointers has some subtle aspects (pointers always seem to have subtle aspects), so let's take a closer look. You can use the *const* keyword two different ways with pointers. The first way is to make a pointer point to a constant object, and that prevents you from using the pointer to change the pointed-to value. The second way is to make the pointer itself constant, and that prevents you from changing where the pointer points. Now for the details.

First, let's declare a pointer *pt* that points to a constant:

```
int age = 39;
const int * pt = &age;
```

This declaration states that *pt* points to a *const int* (*39*, in this case). Therefore you can't use *pt* to change that value. In other words, the value **pt* is *const* and cannot be modified:

```
*pt += 1;          // INVALID because pt points to a const int
cin >> *pt;        // INVALID for the same reason
```

Now for a subtle point. Our declaration for *pt* doesn't necessarily mean that the value it points to is really a constant; it just means the value is a constant insofar as *pt* is concerned. For instance, *pt* points to *age*, and *age* is not *const*. So you can change the value of *age* directly by using the *age* variable, but you can't change the value indirectly via the *pt* pointer:

```
*pt = 20;          // INVALID because pt points to a const int
age = 20;          // VALID because age is not declared to be const
```

In the past, we've assigned the address of a regular variable to a regular pointer. Now we just assigned the address of a regular variable to a pointer-to-*const*. That leaves two other possibilities: assigning the address of a *const* variable to a pointer-to-*const* and assigning the address of a *const* to a regular pointer. Are they both possible? The first is, and the second isn't:

```
const float g_earth = 9.80;
const float * pe = &g_earth;  // VALID

const float g_moon = 1.63;
float * pm = &g_moon;         // INVALID
```

For the first case, you can use neither *g_earth* nor *pe* to change the value *9.80*. C++ doesn't allow the second case for a simple reason—if you could assign the address of *g_moon* to *pm*, then you could cheat and use *pm* to alter the value of *g_moon*. That would make a mockery of *g_moon*'s *const* status, so C++ prohibits assigning the address of a *const* to a non-*const* pointer.

Suppose you have an array of *const* data:

```
const int months[12] = {31,28,31,30,31,30, 31, 31,30,31,30,31};
```

The prohibition against assigning the address of a constant array means that you cannot pass the array name as an argument to a function using a non-constant formal argument:

```
int sum(int arr[], int n);   // should have been const int arr[]
...
int j = sum(months, 12);     // not allowed
```

The function call attempts to assign a *const* pointer (*months*) to a non-*const* pointer (*arr*), and the compiler disallows the function call.

USE *const* WHEN YOU CAN

There are two strong reasons to declare pointer arguments as pointers to constant data:

√ Using *const* protects you against programming errors that inadvertently alter data.

√ Using *const* allows a function to process both *const* and non-*const* actual arguments, while a function omitting *const* in the prototype can only accept non-*const* data.

So you should declare formal pointer arguments as pointers to *const* whenever it's appropriate to do so.

Now another subtle point: the declaration

```
int age = 39;
const int * pt = &age;
```

only prevents you from changing the value *pt* points to, which is *39*. It doesn't prevent you from changing the value of *pt* itself. That is, you can assign a new address to *pt*:

```
int sage = 80;
pt = &sage;                   // okay to point to another location
```

But you still can't use *pt* to change the value it points to (now *80*).

The second way to use *const* makes it impossible to change the value of the pointer itself:

```
int sloth = 3;
const int * ps = &sloth;       // a pointer to const int
int * const finger = &sloth;  // a const pointer to int
```

Note that the last declaration has repositioned the keyword *const*. This form of declaration constrains *finger* to point only to *sloth*. However, it does allow you to use *finger* to alter the value of *sloth*. The middle declaration does not allow you to use *ps* to alter the value of *sloth*, but it does permit you to have *ps* point to another location. In short, *finger* and **ps* are both *const*, and **finger* and *ps* are not *const*. See Figure 7-5.

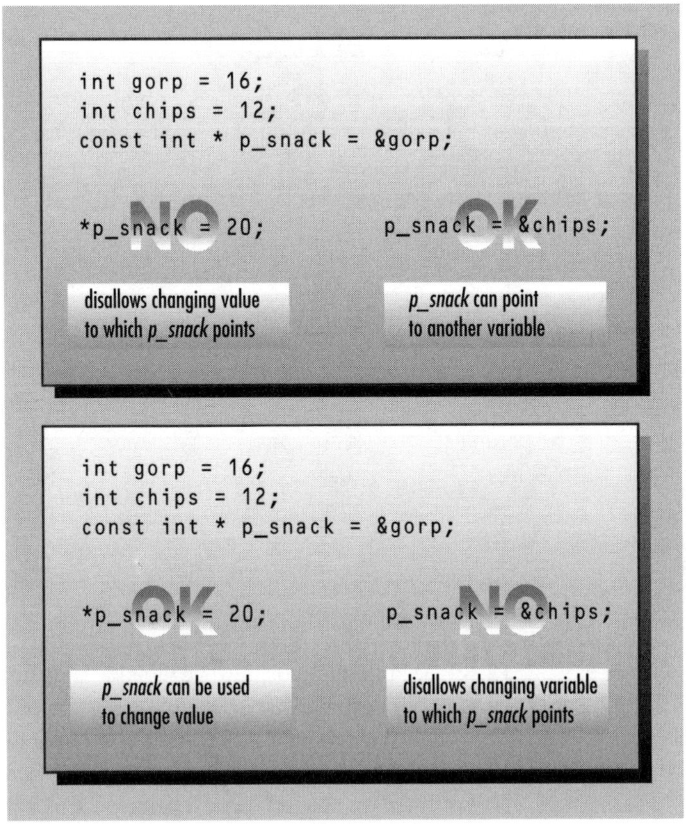

Figure 7-5 Pointers-to-*const* and *const* pointers

If you like, you can declare a *const* pointer to a *const* object:

```
double trouble = 2.0E30;
const double * const stick = &trouble;
```

Here *stick* can point only to *trouble,* and *stick* cannot be used to change the value of *trouble.* In short, both *stick* and **stick* are *const.*

Most often we'll be using the pointer-to-*const* form to protect data when we pass pointers as function arguments. For example, recall the *show_array()* prototype from Listing 7-5:

```
void show_array(const double ar[], int n);
```

Using *const* in that declaration means that *show_array()* cannot alter the values in any array passed to it.

255

Functions and Strings

A string, you'll recall, consists of a series of characters terminated by the null character. Much of what you've learned about designing array functions applies to string functions, too. But there are a few special twists to strings that we'll unravel now.

Suppose you wish to pass a string as an argument to a function. You have three choices for representing a string:

❧ An array of *char*

❧ A quoted string constant (also called a string literal)

❧ A pointer-to-*char* set to the address of a string

All three choices, however, are type pointer-to-*char* (more concisely, type *char **), so all three can be used as arguments to string-processing functions:

```
char ghost[15] = "galloping";
char * str = "galumphing";
int n1 = strlen(ghost);          // ghost is &ghost[0]
int n2 = strlen(str);            // pointer to char
int n3 = strlen("gamboling");    // address of string
```

Informally, we may say we're passing a string as an argument, but we're really passing the address of the first character in the string. This implies that a string function prototype should use type *char ** as the type for the formal parameter representing a string.

One important difference between a string and a regular array is that the string has a built-in terminating character. (Recall that a *char* array containing characters but no null character is just an array and not a string.) That means you don't have to pass the size of the string as an argument. Instead, the function can use a loop to examine each character in the string in turn until the loop reaches the terminating null character. Listing 7-8 illustrates that approach with a function that counts the number of times a given character appears in a string.

 Listing 7-8 *strgfun.cpp*

```
// strgfun.cpp -- functions with a string argument
#include <iostream.h>
int c_in_str(const char * str, char ch);
int main(void)
{
    char mmm[15] = "minimum"; // string in an array
// some systems require preceding char with static to
// enable array initialization

        char *wail = "ululate";        // wail points to string

        int ms = c_in_str(mmm, 'm');
```

```
            int us = c_in_str(wail, 'u');
            cout << ms << " m characters in " << mmm << "\n";
            cout << us << " u characters in " << wail << "\n";
            return 0;
}

// this function counts the number of ch characters
// in the string str
int c_in_str(const char * str, char ch)
{
            int count = 0;

            while (*str)            // quit when *str is '\0'
            {
                    if (*str == ch)
                            count++;
                    str++;          // move pointer to next char
            }
            return count;
}
```

Here's the output:

```
3 m characters in minimum
2 u characters in ululate
```

Program Notes

Because the *c_int_str()* function shouldn't alter the original string, it uses the *const* modifier when declaring the formal parameter *str*. Then, if you mistakenly let the function alter part of the string, the compiler will catch your error. Of course, you can use array notation instead for declaring *str* in the function heading:

```
int c_in_str(const char str[], char ch) // also okay
```

However, using pointer notation reminds us that the argument doesn't have to be the name of an array but can be some other form of pointer.

The function itself demonstrates a standard way to process the characters in a string:

```
while (*str)
{
        statements
        str++;
}
```

Initially, *str* points to the first character in the string, so **str* represents the first character itself. For instance, immediately after the first function call, **str* has the value *m*, the first character in *minimum*. As long as the character is not the null character (\0), **str* is nonzero, so the loop continues. At the end of each loop the expression *str++* increments the pointer by 1 byte so it points to the next character in the string.

Eventually, *str* points to the terminating null character, making **str* equal to *0*, which is the numeric code for the null character. That condition terminates the loop.

Functions That Return Strings

Now suppose you want to write a function that returns a string. Well, a function can't do that. But it can return the address of a string, and that's even better. Listing 7-9 for instance, defines a function called *buildstr()* that returns a pointer. This function takes two arguments: a character and a number. Using *new*, the function creates a string whose length equals the number, and then it initializes each element to the character. Then it returns a pointer to the new string.

Listing 7-9 *strgback.cpp*

```
// strgback.cpp -- a function returning a pointer to char
#include <iostream.h>
char * buildstr(char c, int n);                    // prototype
int main(void)
{
        int times;
        char ch;

        cout << "Enter a character: ";
        cin >> ch;
        cout << "Enter an integer: ";
        cin >> times;
        char *ps = buildstr(ch, times);
        cout << ps << "\n";
        delete [] ps;                              // free memory
        ps = buildstr('+', 20);                    // reuse pointer
        cout << ps << "-DONE-" << ps << "\n";
        delete [] ps;
        return 0;
}

// builds string made of n c characters
char * buildstr(char c, int n)
{
        char * pstr = new char[n + 1];
        pstr[n] = '\0';                            // terminate string
        while (n-- > 0)
                pstr[n] = c;                       // fill rest of string
        return pstr;
}
```

Here's a sample run:

```
Enter a character: V
Enter an integer: 46
VVVVVVVVVVVVVVVVVVVVVVVVVVVVVVVVVVVVVVVVVVVVVVVV
++++++++++++++++++++-DONE-++++++++++++++++++++
```

Program Notes

To create a string of *n* visible characters, you need storage for *n* + *1* characters in order to have space for the null character. So the function asks for *n* + *1* bytes to hold the string. Next, it sets the final byte to the null character. Then it fills in the rest of the array from back to front. The loop

```
while (n-- > 0)
      pstr[n] = c;
```

cycles *n* times as *n* decreases to zero, filling *n* elements. At the start of the final cycle, *n* has the value *1*. Because *n*-- means use the value, then decrement it, the *while* loop test condition compares *1* to *0*, finds the test to be true, and continues. But after making the test, the function decrements *n* to *0*, so *pstr[0]* is the last element set to *c*. The reason for filling the string from back to front instead of front to back is to avoid using an additional variable. Using the other order would involve something like this:

```
int i = 0;
while (i < n)
      pstr[i++] = c;
```

Note that the variable *pstr* is local to the *buildstr* function, so when that function terminates, the memory used for *pstr* is freed. But because the function returns the value of *pstr,* the program is able to access the new string through the *ps* pointer in *main()*.

Just to keep in practice, we used *delete* to free memory used for the string after the string was no longer needed. We then reused *ps* to point to the new block of memory obtained for the next string.

Functions and Structures

Let's move from arrays to structures. It's easier to write functions for structures than for arrays. Although structure variables resemble arrays in that both can hold several data items, structure variables behave like basic, single-valued variables when it comes to functions. You can pass structures by value, just as you do with ordinary variables. In that case, the function works with a copy of the original structure. And a function can return a structure. There's no funny business like the name of an array being the address of its first element. The name of a structure is simply the name of the structure, and if you want its address, you have to use the & address operator.

The most direct way to program using structures is to treat them as you would treat the basic types; that is, pass them as arguments and use them, if necessary, as return values. However, there is one disadvantage to passing structures by value. If the structure is large, the space and effort involved in making a copy of a structure can increase memory requirements and slow the system down. For those reasons (and because, at first, C didn't allow passing structures by value), many C programmers prefer passing the address of a structure, then using a pointer to access the structure contents. C++ provides a third alternative, called passing by reference, that we'll discuss in Chapter 8. We'll examine the other two choices now, beginning with passing and returning entire structures.

Passing and Returning Structures

Passing structures by value makes the most sense when the structure is relatively compact, so let's develop a couple of examples along those lines. The first example deals with travel time (not to be confused with time travel). Some maps will tell you that it is 3 hours, 50 minutes, from Thunder Falls to Bingo City and 1 hour, 25 minutes, from Bingo City to Grotesquo. We can use a structure to represent such times, using one member for the hour value and a second member for the minute value. Adding two times is a little tricky because you may have to transfer some of the minutes to the hours part. For instance, the two times above sum to 4 hours, 75 minutes, which should be converted to 5 hours, 15 minutes. Let's develop a structure to represent a time value, then develop a function that takes two such structures as arguments and returns a structure representing their sum.

Defining the structure is simple:

```
struct travel_time
{
        int hours;
        int mins;
};
```

Next, consider the prototype for a *sum()* function that returns the sum of two such structures. The return value should be type *travel_time,* and so should the two arguments. Thus the prototype should look like this:

```
travel_time sum(travel_time t1, travel_time t2);
```

To add two times, first add the minute members. Integer division by 60 yields the number of hours to carry over, and the modulus operator (%) yields the number of minutes left. Listing 7-10 incorporates this approach into the *sum()* function and adds a *show_time()* function to display the contents of a *travel_time* structure.

Listing 7-10 *travel.cpp*

```
// travel.cpp -- using structures with functions
#include <iostream.h>
struct travel_time
{
        int hours;
        int mins;
};
const int Mins_per_hr = 60;
```

```
travel_time sum(travel_time t1, travel_time t2);
void show_time(travel_time t);

int main(void)
{
        travel_time day1 = {5, 45};             // 5 hrs, 45 min
        travel_time day2 = {4, 55};             // 4 hrs, 55 min
// Some implementations require using static travel_time
// to allow structure initialization

        travel_time trip = sum(day1, day2);
        cout << "Two-day total: ";
        show_time(trip);

        travel_time day3= {4, 32};
        cout << "Three-day total: ";
        show_time(sum(trip, day3));

        return 0;
}

travel_time sum(travel_time t1, travel_time t2)
{
        travel_time total;

        total.mins = (t1.mins + t2.mins) % Mins_per_hr;
        total.hours = t1.hours + t2.hours +
                                (t1.mins + t2.mins) / Mins_per_hr;
        return total;
}

void show_time(travel_time t)
{
        cout << t.hours << " hours, "
             << t.mins << " minutes\n";
}
```

Here *travel_time* acts just like a standard type name; you can use it to declare variables, function return types, and function argument types. Because variables like *total* and *t1* are *travel_time* structures, you can apply the dot membership operator to them. Note that because the *sum()* function returns a *travel_time* structure, it can be used as an argument for the *show_time()* function. Because C++ functions, by default, pass arguments by value, the *show_time(sum(trip, day3))* function call first evaluates the *sum(trip, day3)* function call in order to find its return value. The *show_time()* call then passes *sum()*'s return value, not the function itself, to *show_time()*. Here's the program output:

```
Two-day total: 10 hours, 40 minutes
Three-day total: 15 hours, 12 minutes
```

Another Example

Much of what you learn about functions and C++ structures will carry over to C++ classes, so it's worth looking at a second example. This time we'll deal with space instead of time. In particular, we'll define two structures representing two different ways of describing positions, then develop functions to convert one form to the other and to show the result. This example is a bit more mathematical than the last, but you don't have to follow the mathematics to follow the C++.

Suppose you want to describe the position of a point on the screen or a location on a map relative to some origin. One way is to state the horizontal offset and the vertical offset of the point from the origin. Traditionally, mathematicians use the symbol x to represent the horizontal offset and y to represent the vertical offset. See Figure 7-6. Together, x and y constitute *rectangular coordinates*. We can define a structure consisting of two coordinates to represent a position:

```
struct rect
{
        double x;          // horizontal distance from origin
        double y;          // vertical distance from origin
};
```

A second way to describe the position of a point is to state how far it is from the origin and in what direction it is (for example, 40 degrees north of east). Traditionally,

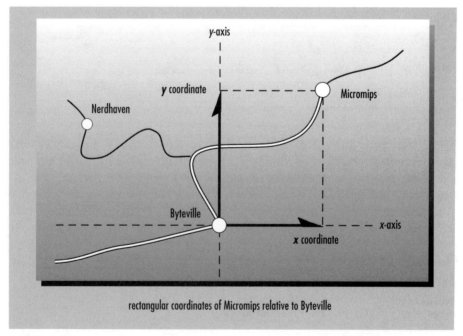

rectangular coordinates of Micromips relative to Byteville

Figure 7-6 Rectangular coordinates

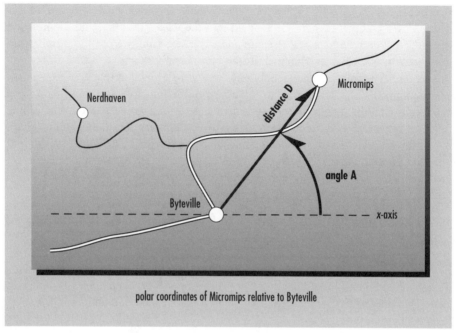

polar coordinates of Micromips relative to Byteville

Figure 7-7 Polar coordinates

mathematicians measure the angle counterclockwise from the positive horizontal axis. See Figure 7-7. The distance and angle together constitute *polar coordinates*. We can define a second structure to represent this view of a position:

```
struct polar
{
      double distance;      // distance from origin
      double angle;         // direction from origin
};
```

Let's construct a function that displays the contents of a type *polar* structure. The math functions in the C++ library assume angles are in radians, so we'll measure angles in that unit. But for display purposes, we'll convert radian measure to degrees. That means multiplying by $180/\pi$, which is approximately 57.29577951. Here's the function:

```
// show polar coordinates, converting angle to degrees
void show_polar (polar dapos)
{
      const double Rad_to_deg = 57.29577951;

      cout << "distance = " << dapos.distance;
      cout << ", angle = " << dapos.angle * Rad_to_deg;
      cout << " degrees\n";
}
```

Notice that the formal variable is type *polar.* When you pass a *polar* structure to this function, the structure contents are copied into the *dapos* structure, and the function then uses that copy in its work. Because *dapos* is a structure, we use the membership (dot) operator (see Chapter 4) to identify structure members.

Next, let's try something more ambitious and write a function that converts rectangular coordinates to polar coordinates. We'll write the function so that we pass a *rect* structure to the function and have the function return a *polar* structure to the calling program. This involves using functions from the math library, so the program will have to include the *math.h* header file. Also, on some systems you'll have to tell the compiler to load the math library (see Chapter 1). We can use the Pythagorean theorem to get the distance from the horizontal and vertical components:

```
distance = sqrt( x * x + y * y)
```

The *atan2()* function from the math library calculates the angle from the *x* and *y* values:

```
angle = atan2(y, x)
```

(There's also an *atan()* function, but it doesn't distinguish between angles 180 degrees apart. That uncertainty is no more desirable in a math function than it is in a wilderness guide.)

Given these formulas, we can write the function as follows:

```
// convert rectangular to polar coordinates
polar rect_to_polar(rect xypos)        // type polar
{
        polar answer;

        answer.distance =
                sqrt( xypos.x * xypos.x + xypos.y * xypos.y);
        answer.angle = atan2(xypos.y, xypos.x);
        return answer;        // returns a polar structure
}
```

The main new point to notice is that in order to return a type *polar* structure, you have to declare the function to be type *polar.*

Now that we have the functions ready, we can write the rest of the program. Listing 7-11 presents the result.

Listing 7-11 *strctfun.cpp*

```
// strctfun.cpp -- functions with a structure argument
#include <iostream.h>
#include <math.h>

// structure templates
struct polar
{
        double distance;        // distance from origin
        double angle;           // direction from origin
```

```
};
struct rect
{
        double x;             // horizontal distance from origin
        double y;             // vertical distance from origin
};

// prototypes
polar rect_to_polar(rect xypos);
void show_polar(polar dapos);

int main(void)
{
        rect rplace;
        polar pplace;

        cout << "Enter the x and y values: ";
        while (cin >> rplace.x >> rplace.y)  // slick use of cin
        {
                pplace = rect_to_polar(rplace);
                show_polar(pplace);
                cout << "Next two numbers (q to quit): ";
        }
        return 0;
}

// convert rectangular to polar coordinates
polar rect_to_polar(rect xypos)
{
        polar answer;

        answer.distance =
                sqrt( xypos.x * xypos.x + xypos.y * xypos.y);
        answer.angle = atan2(xypos.y, xypos.x);
        return answer;        // returns a polar structure
}

// show polar coordinates, converting angle to degrees
void show_polar (polar dapos)
{
        const double Rad_to_deg = 57.29577951;

        cout << "distance = " << dapos.distance;
        cout << ", angle = " << dapos.angle * Rad_to_deg;
        cout << " degrees\n";
}
```

Here is a sample run:

```
Enter the x and y values: 30 40
distance = 50, angle = 53.1301 degrees
Next two numbers (q to quit): -100 100
distance = 141.421, angle = 135 degrees
Next two numbers (q to quit): q
```

Program Notes

We've already discussed the two functions, so let's review how the program uses *cin* to control a *while* loop:

```
while (cin >> rplace.x >> rplace.y)
```

Recall that *cin* is an object of the *istream* class. The extraction operator (>>) is designed in such a way that *cin >> rplace.x* also is an object of that type. As you'll see in Chapter 10, class operators are implemented with functions. What really happens when you use *cin >> rplace.x* is that the program calls a function that returns a type *istream* value. Apply the extraction operator to the *cin >> rplace.x* object *(cin >> rplace.x >> rplace.y)*, and you again get an object of the *istream* class. Thus the *while* loop test expression is an *istream* object, which normally is nonzero, hence true. If, however, the input data does not match *cin's* expectations, the returned value is *0*, or false. (Actually, the *iostream* methods use a trick to replace the actual return value, which is an object, with *0* if the expression is being evaluated in a test condition.) In this loop, for example, *cin* expects the user to enter two numbers. If, instead, you enter **q**, as we did, *cin >>* recognizes that *q* is not a number. So it leaves the *q* in the input queue and returns a *0* value, terminating the loop.

Compare this approach for reading numbers to the one in Listing 7-7:

```
for (int i = 0; i < limit; i++)
    {
            cout << "Enter value #" << i + 1 << ": ";
            cin >> temp;
            if (temp < 0)
                    break;
            ar[i] = temp;
    }
```

To terminate that loop early, you enter a negative number. That restricts input to non-negative values. That restriction fits the needs of that program, but more typically you would want a means of terminating a loop that didn't exclude certain numeric values. Using *cin >>* as the test condition eliminates such restrictions, for it accepts all valid numeric input. So keep this trick in mind when you need an input loop for numbers. Also keep in mind that non-numeric input will set an error condition that prevents reading any more input. So if your program needs input subsequent to the input loop, you must use *cin.clear()* to reset input, as described in Chapters 6 and 15.

Passing Structure Addresses

Suppose you want to save time and space by passing the address of a structure instead of passing the entire structure. This requires rewriting the functions so that they use pointers to structures. First, let's see how to rewrite the *show_polar()* function. You need to make three changes:

◀ When calling the function, pass it the address of the structure *(&pplace)* instead of the structure itself *(pplace)*.

◀ Declare the formal parameter to be a pointer to *polar,* that is, type *polar *.* Because the function shouldn't modify the structure, use the *const* modifier.

◀ Because the formal parameter is a pointer instead of a structure, use the indirect membership operator (->) instead of the membership operator (dot).

After the changes, the function looks like this:

```
// show polar coordinates, converting angle to degrees
void show_polar (const polar * pda)
{
        const double Rad_to_deg = 57.29577951;

        cout << "distance = " << pda->distance;
        cout << ", angle = " << pda->angle * Rad_to_deg;
        cout << " degrees\n";
}
```

Next, let's alter *rect_to_polar.* This is more complicated because the original *rect_to_polar* function returns a structure. To take full advantage of pointer efficiency, you should use a pointer instead of a return value. The way to do this is to pass *two* pointers to the function. The first will point to the structure to be converted, and the second will point to the structure that's to hold the conversion. So instead of returning a new structure, the function will modify an existing structure in the calling function. Otherwise, apply the same principles used to convert *show_polar()* to pointer arguments. Listing 7-12 shows the reworked program.

Listing 7-12 *strctptr.cpp*

```
// strctptr.cpp -- functions with pointer to structure arguments
#include <iostream.h>
#include <math.h>

// structure templates
struct polar
{
        double distance;        // distance from origin
        double angle;           // direction from origin
};
struct rect
{
        double x;               // horizontal distance from origin
        double y;               // vertical distance from origin
};

// prototypes
```

continued on next page

continued from previous page

```cpp
void rect_to_polar(const rect * pxy, polar * pda);
void show_polar (const polar * pda);

int main(void)
{
        rect rplace;
        polar pplace;

        cout << "Enter the x and y values: ";
        while (cin >> rplace.x >> rplace.y)
        {
                rect_to_polar(&rplace, &pplace);     // pass addresses
                show_polar(&pplace);                 // pass address
                cout << "Next two numbers (q to quit): ";
        }
        return 0;
}

// convert rectangular to polar coordinates
void rect_to_polar(const rect * pxy, polar * pda)
{
        pda->distance =
                sqrt(pxy->x * pxy->x + pxy->y * pxy->y);
        pda->angle = atan2(pxy->y, pxy->x);
}

// show polar coordinates, converting angle to degrees
void show_polar (const polar * pda)
{
        const double Rad_to_deg = 57.29577951;

        cout << "distance = " << pda->distance;
        cout << ", angle = " << pda->angle * Rad_to_deg;
        cout << " degrees\n";
}
```

From the user's standpoint, the program in Listing 7-12 behaves like that in Listing 7-11. The hidden difference is that 7-11 works with copies of structures, while 7-12 uses pointers to the original structures.

Recursion

And now for something completely different. A C++ function has the interesting characteristic that it can call itself. (Unlike C, however, C++ does not let *main()* call itself.) This ability is termed *recursion*. Recursion is an important tool in certain types of programming, such as artificial intelligence, but we'll just take a superficial look (artificial shallowness) at how it works.

If a recursive function calls itself, then the newly called function calls itself, and so on ad infinitum unless the code includes something to terminate the chain of calls.

The usual method is to make the recursive call part of an *if* statement. For instance, a type *void* recursive function called *recurs()* could have a form like this:

```
void recurs(argumentlist)
{
        statements1
        if (test)
                recurs(arguments)
        statements2
}
```

With luck or foresight, *test* eventually becomes false, and the chain of calls is broken.

Recursive calls produce an intriguing chain of events. As long as the *if* statement remains true, each call to *recurs()* executes *statements1,* then invokes a new incarnation of *recurs()* without reaching *statements2*. When the *if* statement becomes false, the current call then proceeds to *statements2*. Then, when the current call terminates, program control returns to the previous version of *recurs()* that called it. Then that version of *recurs()* completes executing its *statements2* section and terminates, returning control to the prior call, and so on. Thus if *recurs()* undergoes five recursive calls, first the *statements1* section is executed five times in the order in which the functions were called, then the *statements2* section is executed five times in the opposite order in which the functions were called. After going in five levels of recursion, the program then has to back out through the same five levels. Listing 7-13 illustrates this behavior.

Listing 7-13 *recur.cpp*

```
// recur.cpp -- use recursion
#include <iostream.h>
void countdown(int n);

int main(void)
{
        countdown(4);                      // call the recursive function
        return 0;
}

void countdown(int n)
{
        cout << "Counting down ... " << n << "\n";
        if (n > 0)
                countdown(n-1);        // function calls itself
        cout << n << ": Kaboom!\n";
}
```

Here's the output:

```
Counting down ... 4   ← level 1—beginning to add levels of recursion
Counting down ... 3   ← level 2
Counting down ... 2   ← level 3
Counting down ... 1   ← level 4
```

continued on next page

continued from previous page

```
Counting down ... 0        ← level 5
0: Kaboom!                 ← level 5—beginning to back out through the series of calls
1: Kaboom!                 ← level 4
2: Kaboom!                 ← level 3
3: Kaboom!                 ← level 2
4: Kaboom!                 ← level 1
```

Note that each recursive call creates its own set of variables, so by the time the program reaches the fifth call, it has five separate variables called *n*, each with a different value.

Recursion is particularly useful for situations that call for repeatedly subdividing a task into two smaller, similar tasks. For instance, consider this approach to drawing a ruler. Mark the two ends, locate the midpoint and mark it. Then apply this same procedure to the left half of the ruler, then to the right half. If you want more subdivisions, apply the same procedure to each of the current subdivisions. This recursive approach sometimes is called the *divide-and-conquer* strategy. Listing 7-14 illustrates this approach with the recursive function *subdivide()*. It uses a string initially filled with spaces except for a | character at each end. The main program uses a loop to call the *subdivide()* function six times, each time increasing the number of recursion levels, and each time printing the resulting string. Thus each line of output represents an additional level of recursion.

Listing 7-14 *ruler.cpp*

```cpp
// ruler.cpp - use recursion to subdivide a ruler
#include <iostream.h>
const int Len = 66;
const int Divs = 6;
void subdivide(char ar[], int low, int high, int level);
int main(void)
{
        char ruler[Len];
        for (int i = 1; i < Len - 2; i++)
                ruler[i] = ' ';
        ruler[Len - 1] = '\0';
        int max = Len - 2;
        int min = 0;
        ruler[min] = ruler[max] = '|';
        cout << ruler << "\n";
        for (i = 1; i <= Divs; i++)
        {
                subdivide(ruler,min,max, i);
                cout << ruler << "\n";
                for (int i = 1; i < Len - 2; i++)
                        ruler[i] = ' ';  // reset to blank ruler
        }

        return 0;
}
void subdivide(char ar[], int low, int high, int level)
{
```

```
      if (level == 0)
            return;
      int mid = (high + low) / 2;
      ar[mid] = '|';
      subdivide(ar, low, mid, level - 1);
      subdivide(ar, mid, high, level - 1);
}
```

Here is the program's output:

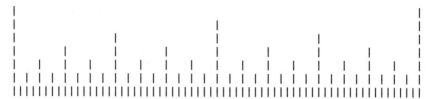

Program Notes

The *subdivide()* function uses a variable called *level* to control the recursion level. When the function calls itself, it reduces *level* by 1, and the function with a *level* of 0 terminates. Note that *subdivide()* calls itself twice, once for the left subdivision and once for the right subdivision. The original midpoint becomes the right end for one call and the left end for the other call. Notice that the number of calls grows geometrically. That is, one call generates two, which generate four calls, which generate eight, and so on. That's why the level 6 call is able to fill in 64 elements ($2^6 = 64$).

Pointers to Functions

No discussion of C or C++ functions would be complete without mention of pointers to functions. We'll take a quick look at this topic, leaving the full exposition of the possibilities to more advanced texts.

Functions, like data items, have addresses. A function's address is the memory address at which the stored machine language code for the function begins. Normally, it's neither important nor useful for us or the user to know that address. But it can be useful to a program. For example, it's possible to write a function that takes the address of another function as an argument. That enables the first function to find the second function and run it. This approach is more awkward than simply having the first function call the second one directly, but it leaves open the possibility of passing different function addresses at different times. And that means the first function can use different functions at different times.

Function Pointer Basics

Let's clarify this process with an example. Suppose you want to design an *estimate()* function that estimates the amount of time needed to write a given number of lines of code, and you want different programmers to use the function. Part of the code for *estimate()* will be the same for all users, but the function will allow each programmer to provide his or her own algorithm for estimating time. The mechanism for that will be to pass to *estimate()* the address of the particular algorithm function the programmer wishes to use. To implement this plan, you need to be able to do the following:

❧ Take the address of a function

❧ Declare a pointer to a function

❧ Use a pointer to a function to invoke the function

Obtaining the Address of a Function

Taking the address of a function is simple: just use the function name without trailing parentheses. That is, if *think()* is a function, then *think* is the address of the function. So to pass a function as an argument, pass the function name. Be sure you distinguish between passing the *address* of a function and passing the *return value* of a function:

```
process(think);      // passes address of think() to process()
thought(think());    // passes return value of think() to thought()
```

The *process()* call enables the *process()* function to invoke the *think()* function from within *process()*. The *thought()* call first invokes the *think()* function, then passes the return value of *think()* to the *thought()* function.

Declaring a Pointer to a Function

When we've declared pointers to data types, the declaration has had to specify exactly what type to which the pointer points. Similarly, a pointer to a function has to specify the type of function the pointer points to. This means the declaration should identify the function's return type and the function's signature (its argument list). For instance, suppose Pam LeCoder has written a time-estimating function with the following prototype:

```
double pam(int);    // prototype
```

Here's what a declaration of an appropriate pointer type looks like:

```
double (*pf)(int);    // pf points to a function that takes
                      // one int argument and that
                      // returns type double
```

Note that this looks just like the *pam()* declaration, with (*pf) playing the part of *pam*. Since *pam* is a function, so is (*pf). And if (*pf) is a function, then *pf* is a pointer to a function.

TIP

In general, to declare a pointer to a particular kind of function, you can first write a prototype for a regular function of the desired kind, then replace the function name by an expression in the form of *(*pf)*. That will make *pf* a pointer to a function of that type.

The declaration requires the parentheses around *(*pf)* to provide the proper operator precedence. Parentheses have a higher precedence than the * operator, so *pf()* means *pf()* is a function that returns a pointer, while *(*pf)(int)* means *pf* is a pointer to a function:

```
double (*pf)(int);    // pf points to a function
double *pf(int);      // pf() a function that returns a pointer
```

Once you've declared *pf* properly, you can assign it the address of a matching function:

```
double pam(int);
double (*pf)(int);
pf = pam;             // pf now points to the pam() function
```

Note that *pam()* has to match *pf* in both signature and return type. The compiler rejects nonmatching assignments:

```
double ned(double);
int ted(int);
double (*pf)(int);
pf = ned;             // invalid -- mismatched signature
pf = ted;             // invalid -- mismatched return types
```

Let's return to the *estimate()* function we mentioned earlier. Suppose you want to pass it the number of lines of code to be written and the address of an estimating algorithm, such as the *pam()* function. Then it could have the following prototype:

```
void estimate(int lines, double (*pf)(int));
```

This declaration says the second argument is a pointer to a function having an *int* argument and a *double* return value. To have *estimate()* use the *pam()* function, we pass it *pam()*'s address:

```
estimate(50, pam);
```

Clearly, the tricky part about using pointers to functions is writing the prototypes, while passing the address is very simple.

Using a Pointer to Invoke a Function

Now we get to the final part of the technique, which is using a pointer to call the pointed-to function. The clue comes in the pointer declaration. There, recall, *(*pf)* played the same role as a function name. Thus all we have to do is use *(*pf)* as if it were a function name:

```
double pam(int);
double (*pf)(int);
pf = pam;             // pf now points to the pam() function
double x = pam(4);    // call pam() using the function name
double y = (*pf)(5);  // call pam() using the pointer pf
```

Actually, C++ also allows you to use *pf* as if it were a function name:

```
double y = pf(5);      // also call pam() using the pointer pf
```

We'll use the first form. It is uglier, but it provides a strong visual reminder that the code is using a function pointer.

HISTORY VERSUS LOGIC

Holy syntax! How can *pf* and *(*pf)* be equivalent? Historically, one school of thought maintained that since *pf* is a pointer to a function, then **pf* is a function; hence you should use *(*pf)()* as a function call. A second school maintained that since the name of a function is a pointer to that function, then a pointer to that function should act like the name of a function; hence you should use *pf()* as a function call. C++ takes the compromise view that both forms are correct, or at least allowable, even though they are logically inconsistent with each other. Before you judge that compromise too harshly, reflect that the ability to hold views that are not logically self-consistent is a hallmark of the human mental process.

Listing 7-15 demonstrates using function pointers in a program. It calls the *estimate()* function twice, once passing the *betsy()* function address, and once passing the *pam()* function address. In the first case, *estimate()* uses *betsy()* to calculate the number of hours needed, and in the second case, *estimate()* uses *pam()* for the calculation. This design facilitates future program development. When Ralph develops his own algorithm for estimating time, he doesn't have to rewrite *estimate()*. Instead, he merely needs to supply his own *ralph()* function, making sure it has the correct signature and return type. Of course, rewriting *estimate()* isn't a difficult task, but the same principle applies to more complex code. Also, the function pointer method allows Ralph to modify the output of *estimate()* even if he doesn't have access to the source code for *estimate()*.

Listing 7-15 *fun_ptr.cpp*

```
// fun_ptr.cpp -- pointers to functions
#include <iostream.h>
double betsy(int);
double pam(int);

// second argument is pointer to a type double function that
// takes a type int argument
void estimate(int lines, double (*pf)(int));

int main(void)
{
        int code;

        cout << "How many lines of code do you need? ";
        cin >> code;
```

```
        cout << "Here's Betsy's estimate:\n";
        estimate(code, betsy);
        cout << "Here's Pam's estimate:\n";
        estimate(code, pam);
        return 0;
}

double betsy(int lns)
{
        return 0.05 * lns;
}

double pam(int lns)
{
        return 0.03 * lns + 0.0004 * lns * lns;
}

void estimate(int lines, double (*pf)(int))
{
        cout << lines << " lines will take ";
        cout << (*pf)(lines) << " hour(s)\n";
}
```

Here are two sample runs:

```
How many lines of code do you need? 30
Here's Betsy's estimate:
30 lines will take 1.5 hour(s)
Here's Pam's estimate:
30 lines will take 1.26 hour(s)

How many lines of code do you need? 100
Here's Betsy's estimate:
100 lines will take 5 hour(s)
Here's Pam's estimate:
100 lines will take 7 hour(s)
```

Summary

Functions are the C++ programming modules. To use a function, you need to provide a definition and a prototype, and you have to use a function call. The function definition is the code that implements what the function does. The function prototype describes the function interface: how many and what kinds of values to pass to the function and what sort of return type, if any, to get from it. The function call causes the program to pass the function arguments to the function and to transfer program execution to the function code.

By default, C++ functions pass arguments by value. This means that the formal parameters in the function definition are new variables that are initialized to the values provided by the function call. Thus C++ functions protect the integrity of the original data by working with copies.

C++ treats an array name argument as the address of the first element of the array. Technically, this is still passing by value, for the pointer is a copy of the original address. But the function uses the pointer to access the contents of the original array. When declaring formal parameters for a function (and *only* then), the following two declarations are equivalent:

typename `arr[];`
typename `* arr;`

Both mean *arr* is a pointer to *typename*. When writing the function code, however, you can use *arr* as if it were an array name in order to access elements: *arr[i]*. Even when passing pointers, you can preserve the integrity of the original data by declaring the formal argument to be a pointer to a *const* type. Because passing the address of an array conveys no information about the size of the array, you normally would pass the array size as a separate argument.

C++ provides three ways to represent strings: a character array, a string constant, and a pointer to a string. All are type *char** (pointer-to-*char*), so they are passed to a function as a type *char** argument. C++ uses the null character (\0) to terminate strings, and string functions use that fact to determine the end of any string they are processing.

C++ treats structures the same as basic types, meaning that you can pass them by value and use them as function return types. However, if the structure is large, it may be more efficient to pass a pointer to the structure and let the function work with the original data.

A C++ function can be recursive; that is, the code for a particular function can include a call of itself.

The name of a C++ function acts as the address of the function. By using a function argument that is a pointer to a function, you can pass to a function the name of a second function that you wish the first function to evoke.

Review Questions

1. What are the three steps in using a function?

2. Construct function prototypes that match the following descriptions:

  a. *igor()* takes no arguments and has no return value.

  b. *tofu()* takes an *int* argument and returns a *float*.

  c. *mpg()* takes two type *double* arguments and returns a *double*.

  d. *summation()* takes the name of a *long* array and an array size as values and returns a *long* value.

  e. *doctor()* takes a string argument (the string is not to be modified) and returns a *double* value.

f. *ofcourse()* takes a *boss* structure as an argument and returns nothing.

g. *plot()* takes a pointer to a *map* structure as an argument and returns a string.

3. Write a function that takes three arguments: the name of an *int* array, the array size, and an *int* value. Have the function set each element of the array to the *int* value.

4. Write a function that takes a *double* array name and an array size as arguments and that returns the largest value in that array. Note that this function shouldn't alter the contents of the array.

5. Why don't we use the *const* qualifier for function arguments that are one of the fundamental types?

6. Listing 7-7 uses a negative property value to terminate the input loop. Suppose, instead, that it used non-numeric input to terminate the input loop. Rewrite *fill_array()* to meet this new design goal.

7. What are the three forms a string can take in a C++ program?

8. Write a function having this prototype:

```
int replace(char * str, char c1, char c2);
```

Have the function replace every occurrence of *c1* in the string *str* with *c2*, and have the function return the number of replacements it makes.

9. What does the expression **"pizza"* mean? What about *"taco"[2]*?

10. C++ lets you pass a structure by value and it lets you pass the address of a structure. If *glitz* is a structure variable, how would you pass it by value? How would you pass its address? What are the trade-offs of the two approaches?

11. The function *judge()* has a type *int* return value. As an argument, it takes the address of a function that takes a pointer to a *const char* as an argument and which also returns an *int*. Write the function prototype.

Programming Exercises

1. Write a program that repeatedly asks you to enter pairs of numbers until at least one of the pair is zero. For each pair, the program should use a function to calculate the harmonic mean of the numbers. The function should return the answer to *main()*, which reports the result. The harmonic mean of the numbers is the inverse of the average of the inverses and can be calculated as follows:

harmonic mean = 2.0 * x * y / (x + y)

2. Write a program that asks you to enter up to ten golf scores. You should provide a means for the user to terminate input prior to entering ten scores. The program should

display all the scores on one line and report the average score. Handle input, display, and the average calculation with three separate functions.

3. Here is a structure template:

```
struct box
{
        char maker[40];
        float height;
        float width;
        float length;
        float volume;
};
```

   a. Write a function that passes a *box* structure by value and that displays the value of each member.

   b. Write a function that passes the address of a *box* structure and that sets the *volume* member to the product of the other three dimensions.

   c. Write a simple program using these two functions.

4. Define a recursive function that takes an integer argument and returns the factorial of that argument. Recall that 3 factorial, written 3!, equals 3 x 2!, and so on, with 0! defined as 1. In general, n! = n * (n - 1)!. Test it in a program that uses a loop to allow the user to enter various values for which the program reports the factorial.

5. This exercise provides practice in writing functions dealing with arrays and structures. Below is a program skeleton. Complete it by providing the described functions.

```
#include <iostream.h>

const int SLEN = 30;
struct student {
        char fullname[SLEN];
        char hobby[SLEN];
        int ooplevel;
};
// getinfo() has two arguments: a pointer to the first element of
// an array of student structures and an int representing the
// number of elements of the array. The function solicits and
// stores data about students. It terminates input upon filling
// the array or upon encountering a blank line for the student
// name. The function returns the actual number of array elements
// filled.
int getinfo(student pa[], int n);

// display1() takes a student structure as an argument
// and displays its contents
void display1(student st);

// display2() takes the address of student structure as an
// argument and displays the structure's contents
void display2(const student * ps);
```

```
// display3() takes the address of the first element of an array
// of student structures and the number of array elements as
// arguments and displays the contents of the structures
void display3( const student pa[], int n);

int main(void)
{
        cout << "Enter class size: ";
        int class_size;
        cin >> class_size;
        while (cin.get() != '\n')
                continue;

        student * ptr_stu = new student[class_size];
        int entered = getinfo(ptr_stu, class_size);
        for (int i = 0; i < entered; i++)
        {
                display1(ptr_stu[i]);
                display2(&ptr_stu[i]);
        }
        display3(ptr_stu, entered);
        cout << "Done\n";
        return 0;
}
```

6. Design a function *calculate()* that takes two type *double* values and a pointer to a function that takes two *double* arguments and returns a *double*. The *calculate()* function also should be type *double,* and it should return the value that the pointed-to function calculates using the *double* arguments to *calculate()*. For example, suppose we have this definition for the *add()* function:

```
double add(double x, double y)
{
        return x + y;
}
```

Then the function call in

```
double q = calculate(2.5, 10.4, add);
```

would cause *calculate()* to pass the values *2.5* and *10.4* to the *add()* function and then to return the *add()* return value *(12.9)*.

Use these functions and at least one additional function in the *add()* mold in a program. The program should use a loop allowing the user to enter pairs of numbers. For each pair, use *calculate()* to invoke *add()* and at least one other function. If you are feeling adventurous, try creating an array of pointers to *add()*-style functions and use a loop to successively apply *calculate()* to a series of functions by using these pointers. Hint: Here's how to declare such an array:

```
double (*pf[3])(double, double);
```

You can initialize such an array using the usual array initialization syntax and using function names as addresses.

CHAPTER 8

ADVENTURES IN FUNCTIONS

You will learn about the following in this chapter:

- ◇ Inline functions
- ◇ Reference variables
- ◇ Passing function arguments by reference
- ◇ Default arguments
- ◇ Function overloading
- ◇ Function templates
- ◇ Template specializations
- ◇ Separate compilation
- ◇ Storage classes, scope, and linkage

With the last chapter under your belt, you now know a lot about C++ functions, but there's much more to come. C++ provides many new function features that separate C++ from its C heritage. The new features include inline functions, passing variables by reference, default argument values, function overloading (polymorphism), and template functions. This chapter discusses these C++ enhancements to functions. Also, it examines multifile programs, and C++'s varieties of storage classes. This chapter, more than any other you've read so far, explores features found in C++ but not C, so it marks our first major foray into plus-plussedness.

Inline Functions

Let's begin by examining *inline* functions, a C++ enhancement designed to speed up programs. The primary distinction between normal functions and inline functions is not in how you code them but in how the C++ compiler incorporates them into a program. To understand the distinction between inline functions and normal functions, you need to peer more deeply into a program's innards than we have so far. Let's do that now.

The final product of the compilation process is an executable program, which consists of a set of machine language instructions. When you start a program, the operating system loads these instructions into the computer's memory, so each instruction has a particular memory address. The computer then goes through these instructions step-by-step. Sometimes, as when you have a loop or a branching statement, program execution will skip over instructions, jumping back or forward to a particular address. Normal function calls also involve having a program jump to another address (the function's address), then jumping back when the function terminates. Let's look at a typical implementation of that process in a little more detail. When the program reaches the function call instruction, the program stores the memory address of the instruction immediately following the function call, copies arguments to the stack (a block of memory reserved for that purpose), jumps to the memory location that marks the beginning of the function, executes the function code, perhaps placing a return value in a register, then jumps back to the instruction whose address it saved.[1] Jumping back and forth and keeping track of where to jump means that there is an overhead in elapsed time to using functions.

The C++ inline function provides an alternative. This is a function whose compiled code is "in line" with the other code in the program. That is, the compiler replaces the function call with the corresponding function code. With inline code, the program doesn't have to jump to another location to execute the code, then jump back. Inline functions thus run a little faster than regular functions. But there is a memory penalty. If a program calls an inline function ten times, then the program winds up with ten copies of the function inserted into the code. See Figure 8-1.

You should be selective about using inline functions. The speed gain is usually minimal unless the function itself is so short that the time needed to execute the function is comparable to the time spent jumping to and from the function. In that case, the function is already fast, so about the only time you would get much of a benefit is if the function were the main time-consumer in a crucial loop.

To use this feature, you have to do two things:

◀ Preface the function definition with the keyword *inline*.

◀ Place the function definition above all functions that call it.

Note that you have to place the entire definition (meaning the function header and all the function code), not just the prototype, above the other functions.

The compiler does not have to honor your request to make a function inline. It may decide the function is too large or notice that it calls itself (recursion is not allowed for inline functions), or the feature may not be implemented for your particular compiler.

---

[1] It's a bit like having to leave off reading some text to find out what a footnote says, then, upon finishing the footnote, returning to where you were reading in the text.

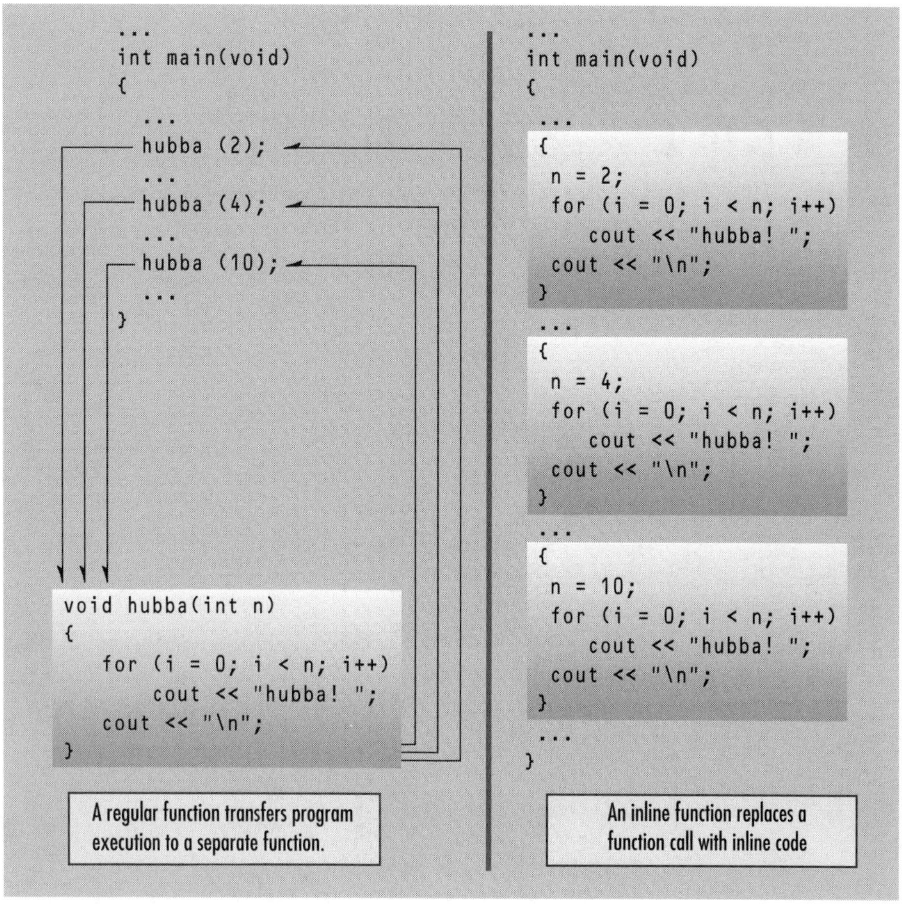

Figure 8-1 Inline functions vs. regular functions

Listing 8-1 illustrates the inline method with an inline *square()* function that squares its argument. Note that we've placed the entire definition on one line. That's not required, but if the definition doesn't fit on one line, the function probably is a poor candidate for being an inline function.

Listing 8-1 *inline.cpp*

```
// inline.cpp -- use an inline function
#include <iostream.h>

// an inline function must be defined before first use
inline double square(double x) { return x * x; }

int main(void)
{
```

continued on next page

continued from previous page

```
    double a, b;
    double c = 13.0;

    a = square(5.0);
    b = square(4.5 + 7.5);   // can pass expressions
    cout << "a = " << a << ", b = " << b << "\n";
    cout << "c = " << c;
    cout << ", c squared = " << square(c++) << "\n";
    cout << "Now c = " << c << "\n";
    return 0;
}
```

Here's the output:

```
a = 25, b = 144
c = 13, c squared = 169
Now c = 14
```

The output illustrates that inline functions pass arguments by value just like regular functions do. If the argument is an expression such as *4.5 + 7.5*, the function passes the value of the expression, *12* in this case. This makes C++'s inline facility far superior to C's macro definitions. See the note below on Inline Versus Macros.

Even though we didn't provide a separate prototype, C++'s prototyping features are still in play. That's because the entire definition, coming before the function's first use, serves as a prototype. This means you can use *square()* with an *int* argument or a *long* argument, and the program will automatically type cast the value to type *double* before passing it to the function.

INLINE VERSUS MACROS

The *inline* facility is a C++ addition. C uses the preprocessor *#define* statement to provide *macros*, a crude implementation of inline code. For instance, here's a macro for squaring a number:

```
#define SQUARE(X) X*X
```

This works not by passing arguments but by text substitution, with the *X* acting as a symbolic label for the "argument":

```
a = SQUARE(5.0); is replaced by a = 5.0*5.0;
b = SQUARE(4.5 + 7.5); is replaced by b = 4.5 + 7.5 * 4.5 + 7.5;
d = SQUARE(c++); is replaced by d = c++*c++;
```

Only the first example works properly. You can improve matters with a liberal application of parentheses:

```
#define SQUARE(X) ((X)*(X))
```

Still, the problem remains that macros don't pass by value. Even with this new definition, *SQUARE(c++)* increments *c* twice. But our inline *square()* function in Listing 8-1 evaluates *c*, passes that value to be squared, then increments *c* once.

The intent here is not to show you how to write C macros. Rather, it is to suggest that if you have been using C macros to perform function-like services, consider converting them to C++ inline functions.

Reference Variables

C++ adds a new derived type to the language—the *reference* variable. A reference is a name that acts as a name, or alternative name, for a previously defined variable. For instance, if you make *twain* a reference to the *clemens* variable, you can use *twain* and *clemens* interchangeably to represent that variable. Of what use is such an alias? Is it to help people who are embarrassed by their choice of variable names? Maybe, but the main use for a reference is as a formal argument to a function. By using a reference as an argument, the function works with the original data instead of with a copy. References provide a convenient alternative to pointers for processing large structures with a function, and they are essential to designing classes. Before seeing how to use references with functions, however, let's examine the basics of defining and using a reference.

Creating a Reference Variable

You may recall that C and C++ use the *&* symbol to indicate the address of a variable. C++ assigns an additional meaning to the *&* symbol and presses it into service for declaring references. For example, to make *rodents* an alternative name for the variable *rats,* do the following:

```
int rats;
int & rodents = rats;    // makes rodents an alias for rats
```

In this context, *&* is *not* the address operator. Instead, it serves as part of the type identifier. Just as *char ** in a declaration means pointer-to-*char, int &* means reference-to-an-*int.* The reference declaration allows you to use *rats* and *rodents* interchangeably; both refer to the same value and the same memory location. Listing 8-2 illustrates the truth of this claim.

Listing 8-2 *firstref.cpp*

```
// firstref.cpp -- defining and using a reference
#include <iostream.h>
int main(void)
{
        int rats = 101;
        int & rodents = rats;    // rodents is a reference

        cout << "rats = " << rats;
        cout << ", rodents = " << rodents << "\n";
        rodents++;
        cout << "rats = " << rats;
```

continued on next page

continued from previous page

```
        cout << ", rodents = " << rodents << "\n";

// some implementations require type casting the following
// addresses to type unsigned
        cout << "rats address = " << &rats;
        cout << ", rodents address = " << &rodents << "\n";
        return 0;
}
```

Note that the & operator in the statement

```
int & rodents = rats;
```

is not the address operator, but declares that *rodents* is of type *int &,* that is, a reference to an *int* variable. But the & operator in the statement

```
cout<<", rodents address ="<< &rodents << "\n";
```

is the address operator, with &*rodents* representing the address of the variable to which *rodents* refers. Here is the program's output:

```
rats = 101, rodents = 101
rats = 102, rodents = 102
rats address = 0x8fa2fff4, rodents address = 0x8fa2fff4
```

As you can see, both *rats* and *rodents* have the same value and the same address. And incrementing *rodents* by 1 affects both variables. More precisely, the *rodents++* operation increments a single variable for which we have two names. (Keep in mind that while this example shows you how a reference works, it doesn't represent the typical use for a reference, which is as a function parameter, particularly for structure and object arguments. We'll look into these uses pretty soon.)

References tend to be a bit confusing to C veterans coming to C++ because they are tantalizingly reminiscent of pointers, yet somehow different. For instance, you can create both a reference and a pointer to refer to *rats:*

```
int rats = 101;
int & rodents = rats; // rodents a reference
int * prats = &rats;  // prats a pointer
```

Then you could use the expressions *rodents* and **prats* interchangeably with *rats* and use the expressions &*rodents* and *prats* interchangeably with &*rats.* From this standpoint, a reference looks a lot like a pointer in disguised notation in which the * dereferencing operator is understood implicitly. And, in fact, that's more or less what a reference is. But there are differences besides those of notation. For one, in our example it was necessary to initialize the reference when declaring it; you can't declare the reference, then assign it a value later, the way you can with a pointer:

```
int rat;
int & rodent;
rodent = rat;   // No, you can't do this.
```

RULE

You should initialize a reference variable when you declare it.

Also, a reference is more like a *const* pointer; once a reference pledges its allegiance to a particular variable, it sticks to its pledge. Listing 8-3 shows what happens if you try to make a reference change allegiance from a *rats* variable to a *bunnies* variable.

Listing 8-3 *secref.cpp*

```
// secref.cpp -- defining and using a reference
#include <iostream.h>
int main(void)
{
        int rats = 101;
        int & rodents = rats;    // rodents is a reference

        cout << "rats = " << rats;
        cout << ", rodents = " << rodents << "\n";

// some implementations require type casting the following
// addresses to type unsigned
        cout << "rats address = " << &rats;
        cout << ", rodents address = " << &rodents << "\n";

        int bunnies = 50;
        rodents = bunnies;        // can we change the reference?
        cout << "bunnies = " << bunnies;
        cout << ", rats = " << rats;
        cout << ", rodents = " << rodents << "\n";

// some implementations require type casting the following
// addresses to type unsigned
        cout << "bunnies address = " << &bunnies;
        cout << ", rodents address = " << &rodents << "\n";
        return 0;
}
```

Here's the output:

```
rats = 101, rodents = 101
rats address = 0x8f87fff4, rodents address = 0x8f87fff4
bunnies = 50, rats = 50, rodents = 50
bunnies address = 0x8f87fff2, rodents address = 0x8f87fff4
```

Initially, *rodents* refers to *rats*, but then the program attempts to make *rodents* a reference to *bunnies:*

```
rodents = bunnies;
```

For a moment, it looks as if this attempt has succeeded, for the value of *rodents* changes from *101* to *50*. But closer inspection reveals that *rats* also has changed to *50* and that *rats* and *rodents* still share the same address, which differs from the *bunnies* address. Because we made *rodents* an alias for *rats*, our assignment statement really means the same as the following:

```
rats = bunnies;
```

That is, it means "assign the value of the *bunnies* variable to the *rat* variable." In short, you can set a reference by an initializing declaration, not by assignment.

Suppose you tried the following:

```
int rats = 101;
int * pi = &rats;
int & rodents = *pi;
int bunnies = 50;
pi = &rodents;
```

Initializing *rodents* to **pi* makes *rodents* refer to *rats*. Subsequently altering *pi* to point to *bunnies* does not alter the fact that *rodents* refers to *rats*.

References As Function Parameters

Most often, references are used as function parameters, making a variable name in the function an alias for a variable in the calling program. This method of passing arguments is called *passing by reference*. Passing by reference allows a called function to access variables in the calling function. C++'s addition of the feature is a break from C, which only passes by value. Passing by value, recall, results in the called function working with copies of values from the calling program. See Figure 8-2. Of course, C lets you get around the passing by value limitation by using pointers.

Let's compare using references and using pointers in a common computer problem, swapping the values of two variables. A swapping function has to be able to alter values of variables in the calling program. That means the usual approach of passing variables by value won't work, since the function will end up swapping the contents of copies of the original variables instead of the variables themselves. If you pass references, however, the function can work with the original data. Or you can pass pointers in order to access the original data. Listing 8-4 shows all three methods, including the one that doesn't work, so that you can compare them.

Listing 8-4 *swaps.cpp*

```
// swaps.cpp -- swapping with references and with pointers
#include <iostream.h>
void swapr(int & a, int & b); // a, b are aliases for ints
void swapp(int * p, int * q); // p, q are addresses of ints
void swapv(int a, int b);     // a, b are new variables
int main(void)
{
```

```
        int wallet1 = 300;
        int wallet2 = 350;

        cout << "wallet1 = $" << wallet1;
        cout << " wallet2 = $" << wallet2 << "\n";

        cout << "Using references to swap contents:\n";
        swapr(wallet1, wallet2);    // pass variables
        cout << "wallet1 = $" << wallet1;
        cout << " wallet2 = $" << wallet2 << "\n";

        cout << "Using pointers to swap contents:\n";
        swapp(&wallet1, &wallet2); // pass addresses of variables
        cout << "wallet1 = $" << wallet1;
        cout << " wallet2 = $" << wallet2 << "\n";

        cout << "Trying to use passing by value:\n";
        swapv(wallet1, wallet2);    // pass values of variables
        cout << "wallet1 = $" << wallet1;
        cout << " wallet2 = $" << wallet2 << "\n";
        return 0;
}

void swapr(int & a, int & b) // use references
{
        int temp;

        temp = a;       // use a, b for values of variables
        a = b;
        b = temp;
}

void swapp(int * p, int * q) // use pointers
{
        int temp;

        temp = *p;      // use *p, *q for values of variables
        *p = *q;
        *q = temp;
}

void swapv(int a, int b)              // try using values
{
        int temp;

        temp = a;       // use a, b for values of variables
        a = b;
        b = temp;
}
```

Here's the output:

```
wallet1 = $300 wallet2 = $350                    ← original values
Using references to swap contents:
```

continued on next page

continued from previous page

```
wallet1 = $350 wallet2 = $300          ← values swapped
Using pointers to swap contents:
wallet1 = $300 wallet2 = $350          ← values swapped again
Trying to use passing by value:
wallet1 = $300 wallet2 = $350          ← swap failed
```

As we expected, the reference method and pointer method successfully swapped the contents of the two wallets, while the passing by value method failed.

Program Notes

First, note how each function is called:

```
swapr(wallet1, wallet2);          // pass variables
swapp(&wallet1, &wallet2);        // pass addresses of variables
swapv(wallet1, wallet2);          // pass values of variables
```

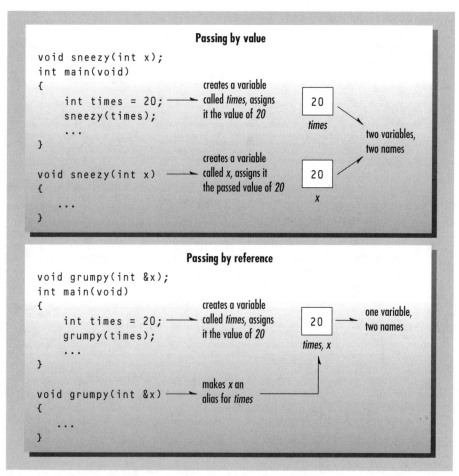

Figure 8-2 Passing by value and passing by reference

Passing by reference *(swapr(wallet1, wallet2))* and passing by value *(swapv(wallet1, wallet2))* look identical. The only way you can tell that *swapr()* passes by reference is by looking at the prototype or at the function definition. However, the presence of the address operator (&) makes it obvious when a function passes by address *((swapp(&wallet1, &wallet2))*. (Recall that the type declaration *int *p* means that *p* is a pointer to an *int* and therefore the argument corresponding to *p* should be an address, like *&wallet1*.)

Next, compare the code for the two functions *swapr()* (passing by reference) and *swapv()* (passing by value). The only outward difference between the two is how the function parameters are declared:

```
void swapr(int & a, int & b)
void swapv(int a, int b)
```

The internal difference, of course, is that in *swapr()*, the variables *a* and *b* serve as aliases for *wallet1* and *wallet2*, so swapping *a* and *b* swaps *wallet1* and *wallet2*. But in *swapv()*, the variables *a* and *b* are new variables that copy the values of *wallet1* and *wallet2*, so swapping *a* and *b* has no effect on *wallet1* and *wallet2*.

Finally, compare the functions *swapr()* (passing a reference) and *swapp()* (passing a pointer). The first difference is in how the function parameters are declared:

```
void swapr(int & a, int & b)
void swapp(int * p, int * q)
```

The second difference is that the pointer version requires using the * dereferencing operator throughout when the function uses *p* and *q*.

Earlier, we said you should initialize a reference variable when you define it. You can consider reference function arguments as being initialized to the argument passed by the function call. That is, the function call

```
swapr(wallet1, wallet2);
```

initializes the formal parameter *a* to *wallet1* and *b* to *wallet2*.

Reference Properties and Oddities

Using reference arguments has several twists you'll need to know about. First, consider Listing 8-5. It uses two functions to cube an argument. One takes a type *double* argument, while the other takes a reference to *double*. The actual code for cubing is a bit odd to illustrate a point.

 Listing 8-5 *cubes.cpp*

```
// cubes.cpp -- regular and reference arguments
#include <iostream.h>
double cube(double a);
double refcube(double &ra);
int main (void)
```

continued on next page

continued from previous page

```
{
        double x = 3.0;

        cout << cube(x);
        cout << " = cube of " << x << "\n";
        cout << refcube(x);
        cout << " = cube of " << x << "\n";
        return 0;
}

double cube(double a)
{
        a *= a * a;
        return a;
}

double refcube(double &ra)
{
        ra *= ra * ra;
        return ra;
}
```

Here is the output:

```
27 = cube of 3
27 = cube of 27
```

Note that the *refcube()* function modified the value of *x* in *main()* while *cube()* didn't, reminding us why passing by value is the norm. The variable *a* is local to *cube()*. It was initialized to the value of *x*, but changing *a* has no effect on *x*. But because *refcube()* uses a reference argument, the changes it makes to *ra* actually are made to *x*. If your intent is that a function use the information passed to it without modifying the information and if you're using a reference, you should use a constant reference. Here, for example, we should have used *const* in the function prototype and function heading:

```
double refcube(const double &ra);
```

Had we done this, the compiler would have generated an error message when it found code altering the value of *ra*.

Incidentally, if you need to write a function along the lines of this example, use passing by value rather than the more exotic passing by reference. Reference arguments become useful with larger data units, such as structures and classes, as you'll see soon.

Functions that pass by value, such as the *cube()* function in Listing 8-5, can use many kinds of actual arguments. For instance, all the following calls are valid:

```
double z = cube(x + 2.0);      // evaluate x + 2.0, pass value
z = cube(8.0);                 // pass the value 8.0
int k = 10;
z = cube(k);             // convert value of k to double, pass value
double yo[3] = { 2.2, 3.3, 4.4};
z = cube (yo[2]);                // pass the value 4.4
```

Suppose you try similar arguments for a function with a reference parameter. It would seem that passing a reference should be more restrictive. After all, if *ra* is the alternative name for a variable, then the actual argument should *be* that variable. Something like

```
double z = refcube(x + 3.0); // may not compile
```

doesn't appear to make sense because the expression *x + 3.0* is not a variable. For instance, you can't assign a value to such an expression:

```
x + 3.0 = 5.0; // nonsensical
```

What happens if you try a function call like *refcube(x + 3.0)?* According to the ARM, that's an error, and some compilers will tell you so. Others will give you a warning along the following lines:

```
Warning: Temporary used for parameter 'ra' in call to refcube(double &)
```

The reason for this milder response is that C++, in its early years, did allow you to pass expressions to a reference variable. In some cases, it still does. What happens is this: because *x + 3.0* is not a type *double* variable, the program creates a temporary, nameless variable, initializing it to the value of the expression *x + 3.0*. Then *ra* becomes a reference to that temporary variable. Let's take a closer look at temporary variables and see when they are and are not created.

Temporary Variables, Reference Arguments, and *const*

C++ can generate a temporary variable if the actual argument doesn't match a reference argument. Currently, C++ permits this only if the argument is a *const* reference, but this is a new restriction. Let's look at the cases in which C++ does generate temporary variables and see why the restriction to a *const* reference makes sense.

First, when is a temporary variable created? Providing the reference parameter is a *const,* the compiler generates a temporary variable in two kinds of situations:

❧ The actual argument is the correct type, but isn't an Lvalue

❧ The actual argument is of the wrong type, but of a type that can be converted to the correct type

An argument that's an Lvalue is a data object that can be referenced. For instance, a variable, an array element, a structure member, a reference, and a dereferenced pointer are Lvalues. Non-Lvalues include literal constants and expressions with multiple terms. For example, suppose we redefine *refcube()* so that it has a constant reference argument:

```
double refcube(const double &ra)
{
    return ra * ra * ra;
}
```

Now consider the following code:

```
double side = 3.0;
double * pd = &side;
double & rd = side;
long edge = 5L;
double lens[4] = { 2.0, 5.0, 10.0, 12.0};
double c1 = refcube(side);          // ra is side
double c2 = refcube(lens[2]);       // ra is lens[2]
double c3 = refcube(rd);            // ra is rd is side
double c4 = refcube(*pd)            // ra is *pd is side
double c4 = refcube(edge);          // ra is temporary variable
double c5 = refcube(7.0);           // ra is temporary variable
double c6 = refcube(side + 10.0);   // ra is temporary variable
```

The arguments *side, lens[2], rd,* and **pd* are type *double* data objects with names, so it is possible to generate a reference for them, and no temporary variables are needed. (Recall that an element of an array behaves like a variable of the same type as the element.) But *edge,* although a variable, is of the wrong type. A reference to a *double* can't refer to a *long.* The arguments *7.0* and *side + 10.0,* on the other hand, are the right type, but are not named data objects. In each of these cases, the compiler generates a temporary, anonymous variable and makes *ra* refer to it. These temporary variables last for the duration of the function call, but then the compiler is free to dump them.

So why is this behavior okay for constant references but not otherwise? Recall the *swapr()* function of Listing 8-4:

```
void swapr(int & a, int & b)  // use references
{
        int temp;

        temp = a;       // use a, b for values of variables
        a = b;
        b = temp;
}
```

What would happen if we did the following under the freer rules of early C++?

```
long a = 3, b = 5;
swapr(a, b);
```

Here there is a type mismatch, so the compiler would create two temporary *int* variables, initializing them to 3 and 5, then swap the contents of the temporary variables, leaving *a* and *b* unaltered.

In short, if the intent of a function with reference arguments is to *modify* variables passed as arguments, situations that create temporary variables thwart that purpose. The solution is to prohibit creating temporary variables in these situations, and that is what C++ now does.

Now think about the *refcube()* function. Its intent is merely to use passed values, not to modify them, so temporary variables cause no harm and they make the function more general in the sorts of arguments that it can handle. Therefore, if the declaration states that a reference is *const*, C++ generates temporary variables when necessary. In essence, a C++ function with a *const* reference argument and a nonmatching real argument mimics the traditional passing by value behavior, guaranteeing that the original data is unaltered and using a temporary variable to hold the value.

RULE

If a function call argument isn't an Lvalue or does not match the type of the corresponding *const* reference parameter, C++ creates an anonymous variable of the correct type, assigns the value of the function call argument to the anonymous variable, and has the parameter refer to that variable.

USE *const* WHEN YOU CAN

There are three strong reasons to declare reference arguments as references to constant data:

❶ Using *const* protects you against programming errors that inadvertently alter data.

❶ Using *const* allows a function to process both *const* and non-*const* actual arguments, while a function omitting *const* in the prototype can only accept non-*const* data.

❶ Using a *const* reference allows the function to generate and use a temporary variable appropriately.

So you should declare formal reference arguments as *const* whenever it's appropriate to do so.

Using References with a Structure

References work wonderfully with structures and classes, C++'s user-defined types. Indeed references were introduced primarily for use with these types, not for use with the basic built-in types.

The method for using a reference to a structure is the same as the method for using a reference to a basic variable; just use the & reference operator when declaring a structure parameter. The program in Listing 8-6 does exactly that. It also adds an interesting twist by having a function return a reference. This makes it possible to use a function invocation as an argument to a function. Well, that's true of any function with a return value. But it also makes it possible to assign a value to a function invocation, and that's possible only with a reference return type. We'll explain these points after showing the program's output. The program has a *use()* function that displays two members of a structure and increments a third member. Thus the third member can keep track of how many times a particular structure has been handled by the *use()* function.

Listing 8-6 *strtref.cpp*

```cpp
// strtref.cpp -- using structure references
#include <iostream.h>
struct sysop
{
        char name[26];
        char quote[64];
        int used;
};

sysop & use(sysop & sysopref);          // function with a reference return type

int main(void)
{
// NOTE: some implementations require using the keyword static
// in the two structure declarations to enable initialization
        sysop looper =
        {
                "Rick \"Fortran\" Looper",
                "I'm a goto kind of guy.",
                0
        };

        use(looper);                    // looper is type sysop
        cout << looper.used << " use(s)\n";

        use (use(looper));              // use(looper) is type sysop
        cout << looper.used << " use(s)\n";

        sysop morf =
        {
                "Polly Morf",
                "Polly's not a hacker.",
                0
        };
        use(looper) = morf;                     // can assign to function!
        cout << looper.name << " says:\n" << looper.quote << '\n';
        return 0;
}

// use() returns the reference passed to it
sysop & use(sysop & sysopref)
{
        cout << sysopref.name << " says:\n";
        cout << sysopref.quote << "\n";
        sysopref.used++;
        return sysopref;
}
```

Here's the output:

```
Rick "Fortran" Looper says:
```

```
I'm a goto kind of guy.
1 use(s)
Rick "Fortran" Looper says:
I'm a goto kind of guy.
Rick "Fortran" Looper says:
I'm a goto kind of guy.
3 use(s)
Rick "Fortran" Looper says:
I'm a goto kind of guy.
Polly Morf says:
Polly's not a hacker.
```

Program Notes

The program ventures into three new areas. The first is using a reference to a structure, illustrated by the first function call:

```
use(looper);
```

It passes the structure *looper* by reference to the *use()* function, making *sysopref* a synonym for *looper*. So when the *use()* function displays the *name* and *quote* members of *sysopref* it really displays the members of *looper*. Also, when the function increments *sysopref.used* to 1, it really increments *looper.used,* as the program output shows:

```
Rick "Fortran" Looper says:
I'm a goto kind of guy.
1 use(s)
```

The second new area is using a reference as a return value. Because *use()* returns a type *sysop* reference, it can be used as an argument to any function expecting type *sysop* reference arguments, such as *use()* itself. Thus the next function call in Listing 8-6 is really two function calls, with one function serving as the argument for the second:

```
use(use(looper));
```

The inner function call prints the *name* and *quote* members and increments the *used* member to 2. The function returns *sysopref,* reducing what's left to the following:

```
use(sysopref) :
```

Because *sysopref* is a reference to *looper,* this function call is equivalent to the following:

```
use(looper) :
```

So *use()* displays the two string members again, and it increments the *used* member to 3.

 RULE

A function that returns a reference is actually an alias for the referred-to variable.

The fact that a function returning a reference can be used as an argument to another function turns out to be useful for aspects of C++ class design. For instance, recall

297

that the *ostream* class defines the << operator so that you can concatenate expressions as follows:

```
cout << looper.used <<  " use(s)\n";
```

The C++ mechanism for defining (overloading) operators is to write a function describing how the operator works. Concatenating the operator, as above, turns out to be equivalent to having nested function calls, such as *use(use(looper))*, in which the argument and return values are references to the same type. We'll return to this topic in Chapter 10.

The third new area the program explores is that you can assign a value to a function if that function has a reference type return value:

```
use(looper) = morf;
```

For nonreference return values, this assignment would be a syntax error, but it's okay for *use()*. This is the order of events. First, the *use()* function is evaluated. That means *looper* is passed by reference to *use()*. As usual, the function displays two members and increments the *used* member to 4. Then the function returns the reference. Because the return value refers to *looper*, this makes the final step equivalent to the following:

```
looper = morf;
```

C++ allows you to assign one structure to another, so this copies the contents of the *morf* structure into *looper*, as is shown when displaying *looper.name* produces Morf's name and not Looper's. In short, the statement

```
use(looper) = morf;
```

is equivalent to the following:

```
use(looper);
looper = morf;
```

RULE

You can assign a value (including a structure or a class object) to a C++ function only if the function returns a reference to a variable or, more generally, to a data object. In that case, the value is assigned to the referred-to variable or data object.

This is another property that enables certain forms of operator redefinition. Chapter 11 will use it, for instance, to redefine the array subscript operator [] for a class that defines a more powerful version of the array.

Considerations When Returning a Reference or a Pointer

When a function returns a reference or a pointer to a data object, that object had better continue to exist once the function terminates. The simplest way to do that is to have the function return a reference or pointer that was passed to it as an argument.

That way, the reference or pointer already refers to something in the calling program. The *use()* function in Listing 8-6 uses this technique.

A second method is to use *new* to create new storage. We've already seen examples in which *new* creates space for a string and the function returns a pointer to that space. Here's how you could do something similar with a reference:

```
sysop & clone(sysop & sysopref)
{
        sysop * psysop = new sysop;
        *psysop = sysopref;    // copy info
        return *psysop;        // return reference to copy
}
```

The first statement creates a nameless *sysop* structure. The pointer *psysop* points to the structure, so **psysop* is the structure. The code appears to return the structure, but the function declaration indicates the function really returns a reference to this structure. You then could use the function this way:

```
sysop & jolly = clone(looper);
```

This would make *jolly* a reference to the new structure. There is a problem with this approach, which is that you should use *delete* to free memory allocated by *new* when the memory is no longer needed. A call to *clone()* hides the call to *new*, making it simpler to forget to use *delete* later.

What you want to avoid is code along these lines:

```
sysop & clone2(sysop & sysopref)
{
        sysop newguy;         // big error
        newguy = sysopref;    // copy info
        return newguy;        // return reference to copy
}
```

This has the unfortunate effect of returning a reference to a temporary variable (*newguy*) that passes from existence as soon as the function terminates. (This chapter discusses the persistence of various kinds of variables, later, in the section on storage classes.) Similarly, you should avoid returning pointers to such temporary variables.

When to Use Reference Arguments

There are two main reasons for using reference arguments:

❧ To allow you to alter a data object in the calling function

❧ To speed up a program by passing a reference instead of an entire data object

The second reason is most important for larger data objects such as structures and class objects. These two reasons are the same reasons one might have for using a pointer argument. This makes sense, for reference arguments are really just a different interface for pointer-based code. So when should you use a reference? a pointer? pass by value? Here are some guidelines.

A function uses passed data without modifying it:

◀ If the data object is small, such as a built-in data type or a small structure, pass it by value.

◀ If the data object is an array, use a pointer because that's your only choice. Make the pointer a pointer to *const*.

◀ If the data object is a good-sized structure, use a *const* pointer or a *const* reference to increase program efficiency. You save the time and space needed to copy a structure or a class design. Make the pointer or reference *const*.

◀ If the data object is a class object, use a *const* reference. The semantics of class design often require using a reference, which is the main reason why C++ added this feature. Thus the standard way to pass class object arguments is by reference.

A function modifies data in the calling function:

◀ If the data object is a built-in data type, use a pointer. If you spot code like *fixit(&x)*, where *x* is an *int*, it's pretty clear that this function intends to modify *x*.

◀ If the data object is an array, use your only choice, a pointer.

◀ If the data object is a structure, use a reference or a pointer.

◀ If the data object is a class object, use a reference.

Of course, these are just guidelines, and there may be reasons for making different choices. For instance, *cin* uses references for basic types so that you can use *cin >> n* instead of *cin >> &n*.

Default Arguments

Let's look at another topic from C++'s bag of new tricks—the *default argument*. A default argument is a value that's used automatically if you omit the corresponding actual argument from a function call. For example, if you set up *void wow(int n)* so that *n* has a default value of *1*, then the function call *wow()* is the same as *wow(1)*. This gives you greater flexibility in how you use a function. Suppose you have a function called *left()* that returns the first *n* characters of a string, with the string and *n* being arguments. More precisely, the function will return a pointer to a new string consisting of the selected portion of the original string. For instance, the call *left("theory", 3)* would construct a new string *"the"* and return a pointer to it. Now suppose you establish a default value of *1* for the second argument. The call *left("theory", 3)* would work as before, with your choice of 3 overriding the default. But the call *left("theory")*, instead of being an error, would assume a second argument of *1* and return a pointer to the string *"t"*. This kind of default is helpful if your program often needs to extract a one-character string but occasionally needs to extract longer strings.

How do you establish a default value? You must use the function prototype. Because the compiler looks at the prototype to see how many arguments a function uses, the function prototype *also* has to alert the program to the possibility of default arguments. The method is to assign a value to the argument in the prototype. For instance, here's the prototype fitting this description of *left()*:

```
char * left(const char * str, int n = 1);
```

We want the function to return a new string, so its type is *char**, or pointer-to-*char*. We want to leave the original string unaltered, so we use the *const* qualifier for the first argument. We want *n* to have a default value of *1*, so we assign that value to *n*. A default argument value is an initialization value. Thus the prototype above initializes *n* to the value *1*. So if you leave *n* alone, it has the value *1*, but if you pass an argument, the new value overwrites the *1*.

When you use a function with an argument list, you must add defaults from right to left. That is, you can't provide a default value for a particular argument unless you also provide defaults for all the arguments to its right:

```
int harpo(int n, int m = 4, int j = 5);          // VALID
int chico(int n, int m = 6, int j);              // INVALID
int groucho(int n = 1, int m = 2, int n = 3);    // VALID
```

The *harpo()* prototype, for example, permits calls with one, two, or three arguments:

```
beeps = harpo(2);           // same as harpo(2,4,5)
beeps = harpo(1,8);         // same as harpo(1,8,5)
beeps = harpo (8,7,6);      // no default arguments used
```

The actual arguments are assigned to the corresponding formal arguments from left to right; you can't skip over arguments. Thus the following isn't allowed:

```
beeps = harpo(3, ,8); // invalid, doesn't set m to 4
```

Listing 8-7 puts default arguments to use. Note that *only* the prototype indicates the default. The function definition is the same as it would have been without default arguments.

Listing 8-7 *left.cpp*

```
// left.cpp -- string function with a default argument
#include <iostream.h>
const int ArSize = 80;
char * left(const char * str, int n = 1);
int main(void)
{
        char sample[ArSize];
        cout << "Enter a string:\n";
        cin.get(sample,ArSize);
        char *ps = left(sample, 4);
```

continued on next page

continued from previous page

```
            cout << ps << "\n";
            delete [] ps;          // free old string
            ps = left(sample);
            cout << ps << "\n";
            delete [] ps;          // free new string
            return 0;
}


// This function returns a pointer to a new string
// consisting of the first n characters in the str string.
char * left(const char * str, int n)
{
        if(n < 0)
                n = 0;
        char * p = new char[n+1];
        for (int i = 0; i < n && str[i]; i++)
                p[i] = str[i];         // copy characters
        while (i <= n)
                p[i++] = '\0';         // set rest of string to '\0'
        return p;
}
```

Here's a sample run:

```
Enter a string:
bestir
best
b
```

Program Notes

The program uses *new* to create a new string for holding the selected characters. One awkward possibility is that an uncooperative user requests a negative number of characters. In that case, the function sets the character count to 0 and eventually returns the null string. Another awkward possibility is that an irresponsible user requests more characters than the string contains. The function protects against this by using a combined test:

```
i < n && str[i]
```

The *i* < *n* test stops the loop after *n* characters have been copied. The second part of the test, the expression *str[i]*, is the code for the character about to be copied. If the loop reaches the null character, the code is zero, and the loop terminates. The final *while* loop terminates the string with the null character, then sets the rest of the allocated space, if any, to null characters.

Another approach for setting the size of the new string would be to set *n* to the smaller of the passed value and the string length:

```
int len = strlen(str);
n = (n < len) ? n : len;      // the lesser of n and len
char * p = new char[n+1];
```

This ensures that *new* doesn't allocate more space than what's needed to hold the string. That can be useful if you make a call like *left("Hi!", 32767)*. Our first approach copies the *"Hi!"* into an array of 32767 characters, setting all but the first three characters to the null character. The second approach copies *"Hi!"* into an array of 4 characters. But, by adding another function call *(strlen())*, it increases the program size, slows the process, and requires that you remember to include the *string.h* header file. C programmers have tended to opt for faster running, more compact code and leaving a greater burden on the programmer to use functions correctly. The C++ tradition, however, places greater weight on reliability. After all, a slower program working correctly is better than a fast program that works incorrectly. If the time taken to call *strlen()* turns out to be a problem, you can let *left()* determine the lesser of *n* and the string length directly. For instance, the following loop quits when *m* reaches *n* or the end of the string, whichever comes first:

```
int m = 0;
while ( m <= n && str[m] != '\0')
        m++;
char * p = new char[m+1]:
// use m instead of n in rest of code
```

Function Polymorphism (Function Overloading)

Function polymorphism is a neat C++ addition to C's capabilities. While default arguments let you call the same function using varying numbers of arguments, function polymorphism, also called *function overloading*, lets you use multiple functions sharing the same name. The expression "polymorphism" means having many forms, so function polymorphism lets a function have many forms. Similarly, the expression "function overloading" means you can attach more than one function to the same name, thus overloading the name. Both expressions boil down to the same thing, but we'll usually use the expression function overloading—it sounds harder working. You can use function overloading to design a family of functions that do essentially the same thing, but using different argument lists.

Overloaded functions are analogous to verbs having more than one meaning. For instance, Miss Piggy can root at the ball park for the home team, and pigs can root in the soil for potatoes. The context (one hopes) tells you which meaning of *root* is intended in each case. Similarly, C++ uses the context to decide which version of an overloaded function is intended.

The key to function overloading is a function's argument list, also called the function *signature*. If two functions use the same number and types of arguments in the same order, they have the same signature; the variable names don't matter. C++ lets you define two functions by the *same* name providing the functions have *different* signatures. The signature can differ in the number of arguments or in the type of arguments, or both. For instance, you could define a set of *print()* functions with the following prototypes:

```
void print(const char * str, int width);    // #1
void print(double d, int width);             // #2
void print(long l, int width);               // #3
void print(int i, int width);                // #4
void print(const char *str);                 // #5
```

When you then use a *print()* function, the compiler matches your use to the prototype having the same signature:

```
print("Pancakes", 15);                   // use #1
print("Syrup");                          // use #5
print(1995.0, 10);                       // use #2
print(1995, 12);                         // use #4
print(1995L, 15);                        // use #3
```

For instance, *print("Pancakes", 15)* uses a string and an integer as arguments, and that matches prototype #1.

When using overloaded functions, be sure you use the proper argument types in the function call. For instance, consider the following statements:

```
unsigned int year = 3210;
print(year, 6);                // ambiguous call
```

Which prototype does the *print()* call match here? It doesn't match any of them. A lack of a matching prototype doesn't automatically rule out using one of the functions, for C++ will try to use standard type conversions to force a match. If, say, the only *print()* prototype were #2, the function call *print(year, 6)* would convert the *year* value to type *double*. But in the code above, there are *three* prototypes that take a number as the first argument, providing three different choices for converting *year*. Faced with this ambiguous situation, C++ will reject the function call as an error.

Some signatures that appear different from each other can't coexist. For instance, consider these two prototypes:

```
double cube(double x);
double cube(double & x);
```

You might think this is a place we could use function overloading, for the function signatures appear to be different. But consider things from the compiler's standpoint. Suppose you have code like this:

```
cout << cube(x);
```

The *x* argument matches both the *double x* prototype and the *double &x* prototype. Thus, the compiler has no way of knowing which function to use. Therefore, to avoid such confusion, when checking function signatures, the compiler considers a reference to a type and the type itself to be the same signature.

The function matching process does discriminate between *const* and non-*const* variables. Consider the following prototypes:

```
void dribble(char * bits);
void dribble (const char *cbits);
void dabble(char * bits);
void drivel(const char * bits);
```

Here's what various function calls would match:

```
const char * p1 = "How's the weather?";
char * p2 = "How's business?";
dribble(p1);    // dribble(const char *);
dribble(p2);    // dribble(char *);
dabble(p1);     // no match
dabble(p2);     // dabble(char *);
drivel(p1);     // drivel(char *);
drivel(p2);     // drivel(char *);
```

The *dribble()* function has two prototypes, one for *const* pointers, one for regular pointers, and the compiler selects one or the other depending on whether or not the actual argument is *const*. The *dabble()* function only matches a call with a non-*const* argument, but the *drivel()* function matches calls with either *const* or non-*const* arguments. The reason for this difference in behavior between *drivel()* and *dabble()* is that it's valid to assign a non-*const* value to a *const* variable, but not vice versa.

Keep in mind that it's the signature, not the function type, that enables function overloading. For instance, the following two declarations are incompatible:

```
long gronk(int n, float m);       // same signatures,
double gronk(int n, float m);     // hence not allowed
```

Therefore C++ won't permit you to overload *gronk()* in this fashion. You can have different return types, but only if the signatures also are different:

```
long gronk(int n, float m);       // different signatures,
double gronk(float n, float m);   // hence allowed
```

After discussing templates later in this chapter, we'll discuss function matching further.

An Overloading Example

We've already developed a *left()* function that returns a pointer to the first *n* characters in a string. Let's add a second *left()* function, one that returns the first *n* digits in an integer. You could use it, for example, to examine the first three digits of a U.S. postal zip code stored as an integer, a useful act if you wish to sort for urban areas.

The integer function is a bit more difficult to program than the string version because we don't have the benefit of each digit stored in its own array element. One approach is to first compute the number of digits in the number. Dividing a number by 10 lops off one digit, so you can use division to count digits. More precisely, you can do so with a loop like this:

```
unsigned digits = 1;
while (n /= 10)
      digits++;
```

This loop counts how many times you can remove a digit from *n* until none are left. Recall that *n* /= 10 is short for *n* = *n* / 10. If *n* is 8, for example, the test condition assigns to *n* the value 8 / 10, or 0, since it's integer division. That terminates the loop, and *digits* remains at 1. But if *n* is 238, the first loop test sets *n* to 238 / 10, or 23. That's nonzero, so the loop increases *digits* to 2. The next cycle sets *n* to 23 / 10, or 2. Again, that's nonzero, so *digits* grows to 3. The next cycle sets *n* to 2 / 10, or 0, and the loop quits, leaving *digits* set to the correct value, 3.

Now suppose you know the number has five digits and you want to return the first three digits. You can get that value by dividing the number by 10, then dividing the answer by 10 again. Each division by 10 lops one more digit off the right end. We can calculate the number of digits to lop—just subtract the number of digits to be shown from the total number of digits. For instance, to show four digits of a nine-digit number, lop off the last five digits. You can code this approach as follows:

```
ct = digits - ct;
while (ct--)
        num /= 10;
return num;
```

Listing 8-8 incorporates this code into a new *left()* function. The function includes some additional code to handle special cases, such as asking for zero digits or asking for more digits than the number possesses. Because the signature of the new *left()* differs from that of the old *left()*, we can, and do, use both functions in the same program.

 Listing 8-8 *leftover.cpp*

```
// leftover.cpp -- overloading the left() function
#include <iostream.h>
unsigned long left(unsigned long num, unsigned ct);
char * left(const char * str, int n = 1);

int main(void)
{
        char * trip = "Hawaii!!";              // test value
        unsigned long n = 12345678;            // test value
        int i;
        char * temp;                           // point to temporary storage
        for (i = 1; i < 10; i++)
        {
                cout << left(n, i) << "\n";
                temp = left(trip,i);
                cout << temp << "\n";
                delete [] temp
        }
        return 0;

}

// This function returns the first ct digits of the number num.
```

```
unsigned long left(unsigned long num, unsigned ct)
{
        unsigned digits = 1;
        unsigned long n = num;

        if (ct == 0 || num == 0)
        return 0;                       // return 0 if no digits
        while (n /= 10)
           digits++;
        if (digits > ct)
        {
           ct = digits - ct;
           while (ct--)
               num /= 10;
           return num;          // return left ct digits
        }
        else                    // if ct >= number of digits
           return num;          // return the whole number
}

// This function returns a pointer to a new string
// consisting of the first n characters in the str string.
char * left(const char * str, int n)
{
        if(n < 0)
                n = 0;
        char * p = new char[n+1];
        for (int i = 0; i < n && str[i]; i++)
                p[i] = str[i]; // copy characters
        while (i <= n)
                p[i++] = '\0'; // set rest of string to '\0'
        return p;
}
```

Here's the output:

```
1
H
12
Ha
123
Haw
1234
Hawa
12345
Hawai
123456
Hawaii
1234567
Hawaii!
12345678
Hawaii!!
12345678
Hawaii!!
```

When to Use Function Overloading

You may find function overloading fascinating, but don't overuse the facility. You should reserve function overloading for functions that perform basically the same task but with different forms of data. Also, you may want to check whether you can accomplish the same end with default arguments. For example, you can replace the single, string-oriented *left()* function with two overloaded functions:

```
char * left(const char * str, unsigned n);   // two arguments
char * left(const char * str);               // one argument
```

But using the single function with a default argument is simpler. There's just one function to write, instead of two, and the program will require memory for just one function instead of two. If you decide to modify the function, there's only one you have to edit. However, if you require different types of arguments, default arguments are of no avail, so then you should use function overloading.

 # Function Templates

Many C++ compilers now implement one of the newest C++ additions, *function templates*. Function templates are a generic function description. By passing a type as a parameter to a template, you cause the compiler to generate a function for that particular type. Let's see why such a feature is useful and how it works.

Earlier we defined a function that swapped two *int* values. Suppose you want to swap two *double* values instead. One approach is to duplicate the original code, but replace each *int* with *double*. If you needed to swap two *char* values, you could use the same technique again. Still, it's wasteful of your valuable time to have to make these petty changes, and there's always the possibility of making an error. If you make the changes by hand, you might overlook an *int*. If you do a global search-and-replace, you may do something such as converting

```
int integer;
```

to the following:

```
double doubleeger;
```

C++'s function template capability automates the process, saving you time and providing greater reliability.

Function templates let you define a function in terms of some arbitrary type. For instance, we can set up a swapping template like this:

```
template <class Any>
void swap(Any &a, Any &b)
{
        Any temp;
        temp = a;
```

```
        a = b;
        b = temp;
};
```

The first line specifies that we are setting up a template and that we're naming the arbitrary type *Any*. The keywords *template* and *class* are obligatory, as are the angle brackets. The type name is your choice, as long as you follow the usual C++ naming rules; many programmers use simple names like *T*. The rest of the code describes the algorithm for swapping two values of type *Any*. The template does not create any functions. Instead, it provides the compiler with directions about how to define a function. If you want a function to swap *ints*, then the compiler will create a function following the template pattern, substituting *int* for *Any*. Similarly, if you need a function to swap *doubles*, the compiler will follow the template, substituting the *double* type for *Any*.

TIP

Use templates if you need functions that apply the same algorithm to a variety of types.

To let the compiler know that you need a particular form of swap function, just use a function called *swap()* in your program. The compiler will check the argument types you use, then generate the corresponding function. Listing 8-9 shows how this works. The program layout follows the usual pattern for ordinary functions with a template function prototype near the top of the file and the template function definition following *main()*.

COMPATIBILITY NOTE

Many C++ compilers don't yet support templates at the time of this writing. Also, until the final version of the ANSI/ISO C++ standard comes out, template details are subject to change.

Listing 8-9 *funtemp.cpp*

```cpp
// funtemp.cpp -- using a function template
#include <iostream.h>
// function template prototype
template <class Any>
void swap(Any &a, Any &b);

int main(void)
{
        int i = 10, j = 20;
        cout << "i, j = " << i << ", " << j << ".\n";
        cout << "Using compiler-generated int swapper:\n";
        swap(i,j);     // generates void swap(int &, int &)
        cout << "Now i, j = " << i << ", " << j << ".\n";
```

continued on next page

continued from previous page

```
        double x = 24.5, y = 81.7;
        cout << "x, y = " << x << ", " << y << ".\n";
        cout << "Using compiler-generated double swapper:\n";
        swap(x,y);      // generates void swap(double &, double &)
        cout << "Now x, y = " << x << ", " << y << ".\n";

        return 0;
}

// function prototype definition
template <class Any>
void swap(Any &a, Any &b)
{
        Any temp;
        temp = a;
        a = b;
        b = temp;
};
```

The first *swap()* function has two *int* arguments, so the compiler generates an *int* version of the function. That is, it produces a definition that looks like this:

```
void swap(int &a, int &b)
{
        int temp;
        temp = a;
        a = b;
        b = temp;
};
```

You don't see this code, but the compiler does. The second *swap()* function has two *double* arguments, so the compiler generates a *double* version. Here's the program output; you can see the process has worked:

```
i, j = 10, 20.
Using compiler-generated int swapper:
Now i, j = 20, 10.
x, y = 24.5, 81.7.
Using compiler-generated double swapper:
Now x, y = 81.7, 24.5.
```

Note that function templates don't make your executable programs any shorter. In Listing 8-9, you still wind up with two separate function definitions, just as if you had defined each function manually. And the final code doesn't contain any templates; it just contains the actual functions generated for your program. The benefits of templates are that they make generating multiple function definitions simpler and more reliable.

Overloaded Templates

You use templates when you need functions that apply the same algorithm to a variety of types, as in Listing 8-8. It may be, however, that not all types would use the same algorithm. To meet this possibility, you can overload template definitions, just as you overload regular function definitions. As with ordinary overloading, overloaded templates need distinct function signatures. For instance, Listing 8-10 adds a new swapping template, one for swapping elements of two arrays. The original template has the signature *(Any &, Any &)*, while the new template has the signature *(Any [], Any [], int)*. Note that one of its arguments is a specific type *(int)* rather than a generic type. When the compiler encounters the first use of *swap()*, it notices that it has two *int* arguments and matches it to the original template. The second use, however, has two *int* arrays and an *int* value as arguments, and this matches the new template.

Listing 8-10 *twotemps.cpp*

```
// twotemps.cpp -- using overloaded template functions
#include <iostream.h>
template <class Any>            // original template
void swap(Any &a, Any &b);

template <class Any>            // new template
void swap(Any *a, Any *b, int n);

void show(int a[]);
const int Lim = 8;
int main(void)
{
        int i = 10, j = 20;
        cout << "i, j = " << i << ", " << j << ".\n";
        cout << "Using compiler-generated int swapper:\n";
        swap(i,j);               // matches original template
        cout << "Now i, j = " << i << ", " << j << ".\n";

        int d1[Lim] = {0,7,0,4,1,7,7,6};
        int d2[Lim] = {0,7,2,0,1,9,6,9};
        cout << "Original arrays:\n";
        show(d1);
        show(d2);
        swap(d1,d2,int(Lim)); // matches new template
        cout << "Swapped arrays:\n";
        show(d1);
        show(d2);

        return 0;
}

template <class Any>
void swap(Any &a, Any &b)
{
        Any temp;
        temp = a;
        a = b;
        b = temp;
};

template <class Any>
```

continued on next page

continued from previous page

```
void swap(Any a[], Any b[], int n)
{
        Any temp;
        for (int i = 0; i < n; i++)
        {
                temp = a[i];
                a[i] = b[i];
                b[i] = temp;
        }
};

void show(int a[])
{
        cout << a[0] << a[1] << "/";
        cout << a[2] << a[3] << "/";
        for (int i = 4; i < Lim; i++)
                cout << a[i];
        cout << "\n";
}
```

Here is the program's output:

```
i, j = 10, 20.
Using compiler-generated int swapper:
Now i, j = 20, 10.
Original arrays:
07/04/1776
07/20/1969
Swapped arrays:
07/20/1969
07/04/1776
```

You may have noticed that we used *int(Lim)* rather than *Lim* as the final argument to the second *swap()*. The reason is that template matching is a bit picky. Because *Lim* is a *const int*, the compiler looks for a template having a *const int* as its third argument and doesn't find one. But the type cast expression *int(Lim)* is just type *int*, so it matches the template in the listing. This bit of code raises two points:

- It's possible to convert a *const* type to a non-*const* type by *casting away const*. C++ intends the *const* qualifier as a safety precaution, not an absolute prohibition.

- This pickiness about not matching *const int* to *int* is an example of the sort of detail that may change by the time the final C++ standard emerges.

Specializations

Suppose you define a structure like the following:

```
struct job
{
        char name[40];
```

```
        double salary;
        int floor;
};
```

Also suppose you want to be able to swap the contents of two such structures. The original template uses the following code to effect a swap:

```
temp = a;
a = b;
b = temp;
```

Because C++ allows you to assign one structure to another, this works fine, even if type *Any* is *job*. But suppose you only wanted to swap the *salary* and *floor* members. This would require different code. But the arguments to *swap()* would be the same as for the first case (references to two *jobs*), so we can't use template overloading to supply the alternative code.

However, we can supply a specialized definition, called a *specialization,* with the required code. If the compiler finds a specialized definition exactly matching a function call, it uses that definition without looking for templates.

The specialization mechanism has changed with the evolution of the ANSI/ISO C++ standard. We'll look at the original form, which is what several compilers support at the time of this writing, and at the proposed change.

Old Form

Originally, a regular function declaration that exactly matched a function call overrode a template definition. For instance, consider the following code fragments:

```
template <class Any>
void swap(Any &a, Any &b);    // template prototype
void swap(int & n, int & m);  // regular prototype
int main(void)
{
        double u, v;
        ...
        swap(u,v);     // use template
        int a, b;
        ...
        swap(a,b);     // use void swap(int &, int &)
```

When the compiler reaches the *swap(a,b);* function call, it has the choice of generating a function definition using the template or of using the nontemplate *swap(int &, int &)* function. The original template facility called for the compiler to use the nontemplate version, treating it as a specialization of the template.

New Form

Currently, the draft ANSI/ISO C++ standard calls for different treatment. In the case of the code above, the draft requires the compiler to use the template and ignore the regular function prototype and definition. The reason is that the old form could lead to unexpected results. For instance, you might include a header file that, unknown to you, had a regular function prototype that had the same name as a template you had devised. Your program might then wind up using the regular function even though you intended that it use a template.

Making this change, however, didn't remove the need for specializations. Therefore, the draft standard provides a new syntax for declaring and defining specializations. The idea is to follow the function name with angle brackets containing the specialized type. For instance, a specialized prototype of *swap()* for *ints* would look like this:

```
void swap<int>(int &a, int & b);
```

This prototype has to appear before the first function call with matching arguments:

```
template <class Any>
void swap(Any &a, Any &b);          // template prototype
void swap<int>(int & n, int & m);   // specialization prototype
int main(void)
{
        double u, v;
        ...
        swap(u,v);      // use template
        int a, b;
        ...
        swap(a,b);      // use void swap<int>(int &, int &)
```

Note that the *<int>* appears in the prototype, not in the function call. It also should appear in the function definition.

An Example

Listing 8-11 illustrates how specialization works. It's set up to work in the old manner, for that's the form in use at the time of this writing. The first call to *swap()* uses the template to generate the required code, but the second call to *swap()* uses the *void swap(job &, job &)* function defined in the program.

To convert to the new form, add *<job>* to the specialized prototype and function definition.

Listing 8-11 *twoswap.cpp*

```
// twoswap.cpp -- function overrides a template
#include <iostream.h>
template <class Any>
void swap(Any &a, Any &b);    // template prototype

struct job
{
        char name[40];
        double salary;
        int floor;
```

```
};
void swap(job &j1, job &j2); // specialization
// void swap<job>(job &j1, job &j2); // new form

void show(job &j);

int main(void)
{
        cout.precision(2);
        cout.setf(ios::fixed, ios::floatfield);
        int i = 10, j = 20;
        cout << "i, j = " << i << ", " << j << ".\n";
        cout << "Using compiler-generated int swapper:\n";
        swap(i,j);     // generates void swap(int &, int &)
        cout << "Now i, j = " << i << ", " << j << ".\n";

        job sue = {"Susan Yaffee", 56235.99, 5};
        job sunny = {"Sunny Yazzi", 58309.54, 7};
        cout << "Before job swapping:\n";
        show(sue);
        show(sunny);
        swap(sue, sunny);       // uses void swap(job &, job &)
        cout << "After job swapping:\n";
        show(sue);
        show(sunny);

        return 0;
}

template <class Any>
void swap(Any &a, Any &b)       // general version
{
        Any temp;
        temp = a;
        a = b;
        b = temp;
};

void swap(job &j1, job &j2)   // specialized version
// void swap<job>(job &j1, job &j2)  // new form
// swaps just the salary and floor fields of a job structure
{
        double t1;
        int t2;
        t1 = j1.salary;
        j1.salary = j2.salary;
        j2.salary = t1;
        t2 = j1.floor;
        j1.floor = j2.floor;
        j2.floor = t2;
}

void show(job &j)
```

continued on next page

continued from previous page

```
{
        cout << j.name << ": $" << j.salary
                << " on floor " << j.floor << "\n";
}
```

Here's the program output:

```
i, j = 10, 20.
Using compiler-generated int swapper:
Now i, j = 20, 10.
Before job swapping:
Susan Yaffee: $56235.99 on floor 5
Sunny Yazzi: $58309.54 on floor 7
After job swapping:
Susan Yaffee: $58309.54 on floor 7
Sunny Yazzi: $56235.99 on floor 5
```

Which Function?

What with function overloading, function templates, and function template overloading, C++ needs a well-defined strategy for deciding which function definitions to use. Here is the original strategy, which applied before the changed rules on template function specializations:

> ❧ Phase 1: Look for an exact match between actual arguments and a function prototype. If precisely one match is found, the search is over. If more than one is found, the compiler reports an ambiguity error.

> ❧ Phase 2: If phase one fails, look for a function template from which an exact match can be generated. Again, if precisely one match is found, the search is over. If more than one is found, the compiler reports an ambiguity error.

> ❧ Phase 3: If a match has not yet been found, see if any of the ordinary functions in scope can be made to match via type conversions.

The new specialization rules flip Phases 1 and 2. Each of these phases has additional ramifications. Indeed, the ARM (Section 13.2) devotes 15 pages to how C++ matches arguments for regular (nontemplate) function overloading. Meanwhile, the ANSI/ISO C++ standards committee has been discussing the rules and making changes. We'll take a less detailed overview.

In the first phase, C++ allows some "trivial conversions" when making an exact match. Table 8-1 lists them, with *Type* standing for some arbitrary type. Note that *Type* can be something like *int &*, so these rules include converting *int &* to *const int &*. The *Type (argument-list)* entry means that a function name as an actual argument matches a function pointer as a formal argument as long as both have the same return type and argument list. (We'll discuss the *volatile* keyword later in this chapter.)

From an actual argument	To a formal argument
Type	Type &
Type &	Type
Type []	* Type
Type (argument-list)	Type (*)(argument-list)
Type	const Type
Type	volatile Type
Type *	const Type *
Type *	volatile Type *

Table 8-1 Trivial conversions allowed for an exact match

In the second phase, C++ doesn't allow even trivial conversions when matching function call arguments to template arguments. (This rule may wind up being relaxed somewhat.) However, keep in mind that *Type* isn't limited to the built-in types. For instance, consider the following template prototype:

```
template <class Type>
void recycle (Type t);
```

Suppose the program containing this template also contained the following code:

```
struct blot {int a; char b[10]};
blot ink = {25, "spots"};
...
recycle (&ink);        // address of a structure
```

The *recycle(&ink)* call would match the template with *Type* being interpreted as *blot **. Now suppose the program also contained this template:

```
template <class Type>
void recycle (Type * t);
```

Since this also matches the *recycle(&ink)* function call, the compiler will generate an ambiguity error.

The third phase is the most involved. Having failed to find an exact match, the compiler looks to see if the actual argument can be converted to the type of the formal argument. It does so in successive steps.

First, look for a match by promotion. This means promoting *char* and *short* to *int*, *unsigned short* to *int* or *unsigned int* (depending on the relative size of *short* versus *int*), or *float* to *double*. A match of this sort is better than any of the following matches.

Next, try for standard conversions other than promotion. This includes conversions of *int* to *long*, *long* to *int*, floating-point to integral, integral to floating-point, and for class objects, conversions from derived classes to base classes.

Next, try for user-defined conversions. (These are user-defined conversions for user-defined classes.)

Where matters get really involved is when a function call with multiple arguments is being matched to prototypes with multiple arguments. The compiler must establish for each argument a set consisting of the prototypes that best match that particular argument. It follows the steps listed above, with an exact match being better than a match by integer promotion being better than a match by some other standard conversion, and so on. Then it looks at the intersection of those sets to see if there is exactly one function that is in all the sets. If so, that function is awarded "best-matching function" status. If not, there is no match. But even the best-matching function may not make the grade, for it has to pass one more test. It is compared to each other prototype, and it must have at least one argument that it matches better than the other prototype. If it passes this test against all the competitors, it becomes the matching prototype.

This book does not intend to challenge the matching process with complex examples, particularly since the rules are still evolving.

Separate Compilation

C++, like C, allows you, even encourages you, to locate the component functions to a program in separate files. As Chapter 1 described, you can compile the files separately, then link them into the final executable program. (A C++ compiler typically compiles programs and also manages the linker program.) If you modify just one file, you can recompile just that one file, then link it to the previously compiled versions of the other files. This facility makes it easier to manage large programs. Furthermore, most C++ environments provide additional facilities to help with the management. UNIX systems, for example, have the *make* program; it keeps track of which files a program depends upon and when they were last modified. If you run *make* and it detects you've changed one or more source files since the last compilation, *make* remembers the proper steps needed to reconstitute the program. The Symantec C++, Turbo C++, Borland C++, Microsoft Visual C++, and Metrowerks CodeWarrior environments provide similar facilities with their Project menus.

Let's look at a simple example. Instead of looking at compilation details, which will depend on the implementation, let's concentrate on more general aspects, such as design.

Suppose, for example, you decide to break up the program in Listing 7-11 by placing the functions in a separate file. That listing, recall, converted rectangular coordinates to polar coordinates, then displayed the result. You can't simply cut the original file on a dotted line after the end of *main()*. The problem is that *main()* and the other two functions all use the same structure templates, so you need to put the templates in both files. Simply typing them in is an invitation to err. Even if you copy the templates correctly, you have to remember to modify both sets of templates if you make changes later. In short, spreading a program over multiple files creates new problems.

Who wants more problems? The developers of C and C++ didn't, so they've provided the *#include* facility to deal with this sort of situation. Instead of placing the structure declarations in each file, you can place them in a header file, then include that header file in each source code file. That way, if you modify the structure declaration, you can do so just once, in the header file. Also, you can place the function prototypes in the header file. Thus you can divide the original program into three parts:

❧ A header file that contains the structure declarations and prototypes for functions using those structures

❧ A source code file that contains the code for the structure-related functions

❧ A source code file that contains the code that calls upon those functions

This is a useful strategy for organizing a program. If, for instance, you write another program that uses those same functions, just include the header file and add the function file to the project or *make* list. Also, this organization reflects the OOP approach. One file, the header file, contains the definition of the user-defined types. A second file contains the function code for manipulating the user-defined types. Together, they form a package you can use for a variety of programs.

Listings 8-12, 8-13, and 8-14 show the result of dividing Listing 7-11 into separate parts. Note that we use *"coordin.h"* instead of *<coordin.h>* when including the header file. If the file name is enclosed in brackets, the C++ compiler looks at the part of the host system's file system that holds the standard header files. But if the file name is enclosed in double quotation marks, the compiler first looks at the current working directory (or equivalent). If it doesn't find the header file there, it then looks in the standard location.

Figure 8-3 outlines the steps for putting this program together on a UNIX system. Note that you just give the *CC* compile command and the other steps follow automatically. Symantec C++, Borland C++, Turbo C++, Metrowerks CodeWarrior, and Microsoft Visual C++ go through essentially the same steps, but, as outlined in Chapter 1, you initiate the process differently, using menus that let you create a project and associate source code files with it. Note that you only add source code files, not header files to projects. That's because the *#include* directive manages the header files.

Listing 8-12 *coordin.h*

```
// coordin.h -- structure templates and function prototypes
// structure templates
struct polar
{
        double distance;     // distance from origin
        double angle;        // direction from origin
};
struct rect
{
```

continued on next page

continued from previous page

```
        double x;              // horizontal distance from origin
        double y;              // vertical distance from origin
};

// prototypes
polar rect_to_polar(rect xypos);
void show_polar(polar dapos);
```

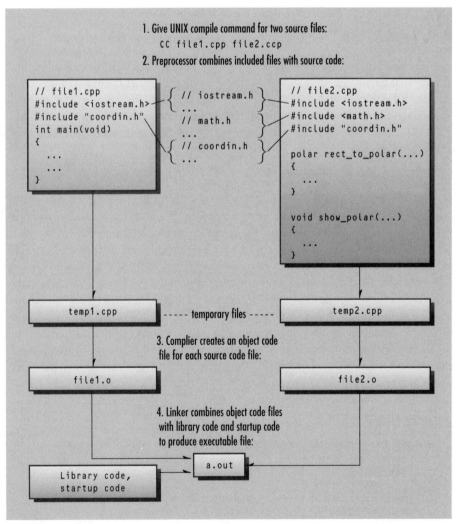

Figure 8-3 Compiling a multifile C++ program on a UNIX system

Listing 8-13 *file1.cpp*

```cpp
// file1.cpp -- example of a two-file program
#include <iostream.h>
#include "coordin.h" // structure templates, function prototypes
int main(void)
{
        rect rplace;
        polar pplace;

        cout << "Enter the x and y values: ";
        while (cin >> rplace.x >> rplace.y)  // slick use of cin
        {
                pplace = rect_to_polar(rplace);
                show_polar(pplace);
                cout << "Next two numbers (q to quit): ";
        }
        return 0;
}
```

Listing 8-14 *file2.cpp*

```cpp
// file2.cpp -- contains functions called in file1.cpp
#include <iostream.h>
#include <math.h>
#include "coordin.h" // structure templates, function prototypes

// convert rectangular to polar coordinates
polar rect_to_polar(rect xypos)
{
        polar answer;

        answer.distance =
                sqrt( xypos.x * xypos.x + xypos.y * xypos.y);
        answer.angle = atan2(xypos.y, xypos.x);
        return answer;        // returns a polar structure
}

// show polar coordinates, converting angle to degrees
void show_polar (polar dapos)
{
        const double Rad_to_deg = 57.29577951;

        cout << "distance = " << dapos.distance;
        cout << ", angle = " << dapos.angle * Rad_to_deg;
        cout << " degrees\n";
}
```

Storage Classes, Scope, and Linkage

Now that you've seen a multifile program, it's a good time to extend the discussion of storage classes in Chapter 4, for storage classes affect how information can be shared across files. It may have been awhile since you last read Chapter 4, so let's review what it said about storage classes. C++ uses three separate schemes for storing data, and the schemes differ in how long they preserve data in memory.

- Automatic variables are those declared inside a function definition; that includes function parameters. They are created when program execution enters the function or block in which they are defined, and the memory used for them is freed when execution leaves the function or block.

- Static variables are those defined outside of a function definition or else using the keyword *static*. They persist for the entire time a program is running.

- Dynamic storage allocated by the *new* operator persists until freed with the *delete* operator or until the program ends, whichever comes first.

We'll fill you in on the rest of the story now, including fascinating details about when variables of different types are *in scope*, or *visible* (usable by the program), and about *linkage*, which determines what information is shared across files.

Scope and Linkage

Scope describes how widely visible a name is in a program. A C++ variable can have one of two scopes. A variable having *block scope* is known only within the block in which it is defined. A block, you remember, is a series of statements enclosed in braces. A function body, for example, is a block, but you can have other blocks nested within the function body. A variable having *file scope* is known throughout the file after the point where it is defined. Automatic variables have block scope, and a static variable can have either scope, depending on how it is defined. C++ functions (other than class member functions, which we'll discuss in later chapters) have file scope.

Linkage determines which names refer to variables or functions in one file only and which can be used in several files to refer to the same variable or function. A variable or function with *internal linkage* is known only to the file containing its definition. A variable or function with *external linkage* can be shared among different files.

Let's look in more detail at the scope and linkage properties of C++'s various storage classes.

Automatic Variables

Function parameters and variables declared inside a function belong, by default, to the automatic storage class. These variables have *local* visibility, or scope. That is, if you declare a variable called *texas* in *main()* and declare another variable with the same name in a function called *oil()*, you've created two independent variables, each known only in the function in which it's defined. Anything you do to the *texas* in *oil()* has no effect on the *texas* in *main()*, and vice versa. Also, each variable is allocated when its function begins execution, and each fades from existence when its function terminates.

If you define a variable inside of a block, the variable's persistence and scope is confined to that block. Suppose, for instance, you define a variable called *teledeli* at the beginning of *main()*. Now suppose you start a new block within *main()* and define a new variable, also called *teledeli,* in that block. The program interprets the *teledeli* name to mean the local block variable while the program executes statements within the block. We say the new definition *hides* the prior definition. The new definition is *in scope,* and the old definition temporarily is *out of scope.* When the program leaves the block, the original definition comes back into scope. See Figure 8-4.

Listing 8-15 illustrates how automatic variables are localized to the function or block that contains them.

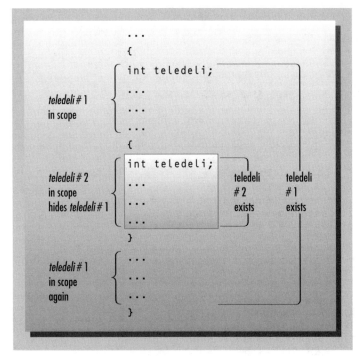

Figure 8-4 Blocks and scope

Listing 8-15 *auto.cpp*

```
// auto.cpp -- illustrating scope of automatic variables
#include <iostream.h>
void oil(int x);
int main(void)
{
// NOTE: some implementations require that you type cast the
// addresses in this program to type unsigned

        int texas = 31;
        int year = 1992;
        cout << "In main(), texas = " << texas << ", &texas =";
        cout << &texas << "\n";
        cout << "In main(), year = " << year << ", &year =";
        cout << &year << "\n";
        oil(texas);
        cout << "In main(), texas = " << texas << ", &texas =";
        cout << &texas << "\n";
        cout << "In main(), year = " << year << ", &year =";
        cout << &year << "\n";
        return 0;
}

void oil(int x)
{
        int texas = 5;

        cout << "In oil(), texas = " << texas << ", &texas =";
        cout << &texas << "\n";
        cout << "In oil(), x = " << x << ", &x =";
        cout << &x << "\n";
        {                                       // start a block
                int texas = 113;
                cout << "In block, texas = " << texas;
                cout << ", &texas = " << &texas << "\n";
                        cout << "In block, x = " << x << ", &x =";
                cout << &x << "\n";
        }                                       // end a block
        cout << "Post-block texas = " << texas;
        cout << ", &texas = " << &texas << "\n";
}
```

Here is the output:

```
In main(), texas = 31, &texas =0x8f95fff4
In main(), year = 1992, &year =0x8f95fff2
In oil(), texas = 5, &texas =0x8f95ffea
In oil(), x = 31, &x =0x8f95fff0
In block, texas = 113, &texas = 0x8f95ffe8
In block, x = 31, &x =0x8f95fff0
Post-block texas = 5, &texas = 0x8f95ffea
```

```
In main(), texas = 31, &texas =0x8f95fff4
In main(), year = 1992, &year =0x8f95fff2
```

Notice how each of the three *texas* variables has its own distinct address and how the program uses only the particular variable in scope at the moment, so assigning the value *113* to the *texas* in the inner block in *oil()* has no effect on the other variables of the same name.

Let's summarize the sequence of events. When *main()* starts, the program allocates space for *texas* and *year,* and these variables come into scope. When the program calls *oil()*, these variables remain in memory but pass out of scope. Two new variables, *x* and *texas,* are allocated and come into scope. When program execution reaches the inner block in *oil()*, the new *texas* passes out of scope as it is superseded by an even newer definition. The variable *x,* however, stays in scope because the block doesn't define a new *x.* When execution exits the block, the memory for the newest *texas* is freed, and *texas* number 2 comes back into scope. When the *oil()* function terminates, that *texas* and *x* expire, and the original *texas* and *year* come back into scope.

Incidentally, you can use the C++ (and C) keyword *auto* to indicate the storage class explicitly:

```
int froob(int n)
{
        auto float ford;
            ...
}
```

Because you can use the *auto* keyword only with variables that already are automatic by default, programmers rarely bother using it. Occasionally, it's used to clarify code to the reader. For example, you can use it to indicate that you purposely are creating an automatic variable that overrides a global definition, such as those we'll be discussing shortly.

Automatic Variables and the Stack

You may gain a better understanding of automatic variables by seeing how a typical C++ compiler implements them. Because the number of automatic variables grows and shrinks as functions start and terminate, the program has to manage automatic variables as it runs. The usual means is to set aside a section of memory and treat it as a *stack* for managing the flow and ebb of variables. It's called a stack because new data figuratively is stacked atop old data, then removed from the stack when a program is finished with it. The default size of the stack depends on the implementation, but·a compiler generally provides the option of changing the size. The program keeps track of the stack by using two pointers. One points to the base of the stack, where the memory set aside for the stack begins, and one points to the top of the stack, which is the next free memory location. When a function is called, its automatic variables are added to the stack, and the pointer to the top points to the next available free space following the variables. When the function terminates, the top pointer is reset to the value it had before the function was called, effectively freeing the memory that had been used for the new variables.

A stack is a LIFO (last in-first out) design, meaning the last variables added to the stack are the first to go. The design simplifies argument passing. The function call places the values of its arguments on top of the stack and resets the top pointer. The called function uses the description of its formal arguments to determine the addresses of each argument. Figure 8-5, for example, shows a *fib()* function that, when called,

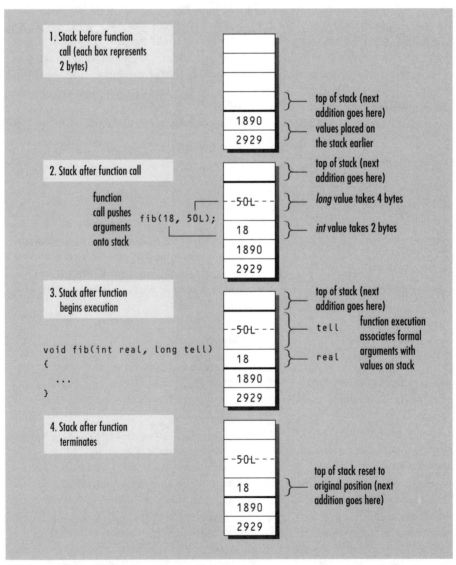

Figure 8-5 Passing arguments with a stack

passes a 2-byte *int* and a 4-byte *long*. These values go on the stack. When *fib()* begins execution, it associates the names *real* and *tell* with the two values. When *fib()* terminates, the top-of-stack pointer is relocated to its former position. The new values aren't erased, but they no longer are labeled, and the space they occupy will be used by the next process that places values on the stack. (The figure is somewhat simplified, for function calls may pass additional information, such as a return address.)

You may have noticed that addresses in Listing 8-15 decreased rather than increased as new variables were added. That's because this particular C++ compiler implements the stack upside down. This changes the direction the stack grows, but it retains the basic concept.

Type *register* Variables

C++, like C, supports the *register* keyword for declaring automatic variables. This keyword is a hint to the compiler that you would like it to use a CPU register instead of the stack to handle a particular variable. The idea is that the CPU can access a value in one of its registers more rapidly than it can access memory in the stack. To declare a *register* variable, preface the type with the keyword:

```
register int count_fast;  // request for a register variable
```

You've probably noticed the qualifying words "hint" and "request." The compiler doesn't have to honor the request. For example, the registers may already be occupied, or you might request a type that doesn't fit in a register. Current feeling is that modern compilers are often smart enough not to need the hint. If you write a *for* loop, for example, the compiler may take it upon itself to use a register for the loop index.

The Static Storage Class

Variables that belong to the static storage class last for the duration of the program; they are less ephemeral than automatic variables. Because the number of static variables doesn't change as the program runs, the program doesn't need a special device like a stack to manage them. Instead, the compiler allocates a fixed block of memory to hold all the static variables, and those variables stay present as long as the program executes. Also, if you don't explicitly initialize a static variable, the compiler sets it to zero. Static arrays and structures have each element or member set to zero by default.

COMPATIBILITY NOTE

Classic K&R C did not allow you to initialize automatic arrays and structures, but it did allow you to initialize static arrays and structures. ANSI C and C++ 2.0 allow you to initialize both kinds. But some C++ 2.0 translators use C compilers that are not fully ANSI C compliant. If you are using such an implementation, you may need to use one of the three varieties of static storage classes for initializing arrays and structures.

C++, like C, provides three varieties of static variables: external, static, and external static. If that looks a little confusing to you, you're right. Unfortunately, C++ uses the word static in two different senses. One is that of a variable that persists for the duration of the program. In that sense, all three varieties are static. The second sense limits how widely known the variable is; it affects the scope and linkage. The external variable is available to all files of a program (file scope, external linkage); the external static variable is available to all the functions in a single file (file scope, internal linkage); and the static variable is confined to a single function (block scope, internal linkage). Table 8-2 summarizes the storage class features; you've seen some of this information already, but we'll take a closer look now.

External Variables

External variables are called external because they are defined outside of, hence external to, any function. For example, they could be declared above the *main()* function. You can use an external variable in any function that follows the external variable's definition in the file. Thus external variables are often termed *global* variables in contrast to automatic variables, which are *local* variables. However, if you define an automatic variable having the same name as an external variable, the automatic variable is the one in scope when the program executes that particular function. Listing 8-16 illustrates these points. It also shows how you can use the keyword *extern* to redeclare an external variable defined earlier and how you can use C++'s scope resolution operator to access an otherwise hidden external variable.

Storage Class	How Created	Scope	Linkage	Duration
automatic	default for function parameters and variables declared inside a function	block	internal	while defining block is being executed
external	default for variables declared outside of any function	file	external	while program is running
static	by applying the *static* keyword to a variable declared inside a function	block	internal	while program is running
extern static	by applying the *static* keyword to a variable declared outside any function	file	internal	while program is running

Table 8-2 Storage classes

Listing 8-16 *external.cpp*

```cpp
// external.cpp -- external variables
#include <iostream.h>
// external variable
double warming = 0.3;

// function prototypes
void update(double dt);
void local(void);

int main(void)                       // uses global variable
{
      cout << "Global warming is " << warming << " degrees.\n";
      update(0.1);                   // call function to change warming
      cout << "Global warming is " << warming << " degrees.\n";
      local();                       // call function with local warming
      cout << "Global warming is " << warming << " degrees.\n";
      return 0;
}

void update(double dt)               // modifies global variable
{
      extern double warming;         // optional redeclaration
      warming += dt;
      cout << "Updating global warming to " << warming;
      cout << " degrees.\n";
}

void local(void)                     // uses local variable
{
      double warming = 0.8;          // new variable hides external one

      cout << "Local warming = " << warming << " degrees.\n";
            // Access global variable with the
            // scope resolution operator
      cout << "But global warming = " << ::warming;
      cout << " degrees.\n";
}
```

Here is the output:

```
Global warming is 0.3 degrees.
Updating global warming to 0.4 degrees.
Global warming is 0.4 degrees.
Local warming = 0.8 degrees.
But global warming = 0.4 degrees.
Global warming is 0.4 degrees.
```

Program Notes

The program output illustrates that both *main()* and *update()* can access the external variable *warming*. Note that the change that *update()* makes to *warming* shows up in subsequent uses of the variable.

The *update()* function redeclares the *warming* variable using the keyword *extern*. This keyword means "use the variable by this name previously defined externally." Since that is what *update()* would do anyway if you omitted the entire declaration, this declaration is optional. It serves to document that the function is designed to use the external variable. The original declaration

```
double warming = 0.3;
```

is called a *defining declaration,* or, simply, a *definition.* It causes storage for the variable to be allocated. The redeclaration

```
extern double warming;
```

is called a *referencing declaration,* or, simply, a *declaration.* It does not cause storage to be allocated, for it refers to an existing variable. You can use the *extern* keyword *only* in declarations referring to previously defined variables (or functions—more on that later). Also, you cannot initialize a variable in a referencing declaration:

```
extern double warming = 0.5;   // INVALID
```

You can initialize a variable in a declaration only if the declaration allocates the variable, that is, only in a defining declaration. After all, the term initialization means assigning a value to a memory location when that location is allocated.

The *local()* function demonstrates that when you define a local variable having the same name as a global variable, the local version hides the global version. The *local()* function, for example, uses the local definition of *warming* when displaying *warming*'s value.

C++ takes a step beyond C by offering the scope resolution operator (::). When prefixed to the name of a variable, this operator means to use the global version of that variable. Thus *local()* displays *warming* as *0.8,* but it displays *::warming* as *0.4.* You'll encounter this operator again in a different context when we discuss classes.

GLOBAL OR LOCAL?

Now that you have a choice of using global or local variables, which should you use? At first, global variables have a seductive appeal—because all functions have access to a global variable, you don't have to bother passing arguments. But this easy access has a heavy price—unreliable programs. Computing experience has shown that the better job your program does of isolating data from unnecessary access, the better job the program does in preserving the integrity of the data. So most often, you should use local variables and pass data to functions on a need-to-know basis rather than making data available indiscriminately with global variables. As you will see, OOP takes this data isolation a step further.

Global variables do have their uses, however. For example, you may have a block of data that's to be used by several functions, such as an array of month names or of the atomic weights of the elements. The external storage class is particularly suited to representing constant data, for then you can use the keyword *const* to protect the data from change.

```cpp
const char * const months[12] =
{
        "January", "February", "March", "April", "May",
        "June", "July", "August", "September", "October",
        "November", "December"
};
```

The first *const* protects the strings from change, and the second *const* makes sure that each pointer in the array remains pointing to the same string it pointed to initially.

The *static* Modifier (Local Variables)

The *static* modifier can be used either with a local variable or with a global variable. We'll look at the local case now. When used inside a function, *static* makes a local variable have the static storage class. That means that even though the variable is known only to that function, it exists even while the function is inactive. Thus a static local variable can preserve its value between function calls. (Static variables would be useful for reincarnation—you could use them to pass bank deposit information to your next appearance.) Also, if you initialize a static local variable, the program initializes the variable once, when the program starts up. Subsequent calls to the function don't reinitialize the variable, the way they do for automatic variables. Listing 8-17 illustrates these points.

Listing 8-17 *static.cpp*

```cpp
// static.cpp -- using a static local variable
#include <iostream.h>
// constants
const int ArSize = 80;

// function prototype
void strcount(char *str);

int main(void)
{
        char input[ArSize];

        cout << "Enter a line:\n";
// NOTE: if your implementation doesn't support getline(), you'll
```

continued on next page

continued from previous page

```
// have to rewrite the program using get(char *, int) and
// get(char)

        cin.getline(input, ArSize);
        while (input[0] != '\0')
        {
                strcount(input);
                cout << "Enter next line (empty line to quit):\n";
                cin.getline(input, ArSize);
        }
        cout << "Bye\n";
        return 0;
}

void strcount(char * str)
{
        static int total = 0;        // static local variable
        int count = 0;               // automatic local variable

        while (*str++)               // go to end of string
                count++;
        total += count;
        cout << count << " characters in this string\n";
        cout << total << " characters total\n";
}
```

Here is the program's output:

```
Enter a line:
Say, haven't we met somewhere before?
37 characters in this string
37 characters total
Enter next line (empty line to quit):
There's really something quite special about you!
49 characters in this string
86 characters total
Enter next line (empty line to quit):

Bye
```

Note that the automatic variable *count* is reset to 0 each time the function is called. However, the static variable *total* is set to 0 once, at the beginning. After that, *total* retains its value between function calls, so it's able to maintain a running total.

Linkage and External Variables

Applying the *static* modifier to an external variable becomes meaningful in multifile programs. In that context, a *static* external variable is local to the file containing it. It has *internal linkage*. But a regular external variable has *external linkage,* meaning it can be used in different files. For external linkage, one and only one file can contain the external definition for the variable. Other files wishing to use that variable must use the keyword *extern* in a reference declaration. See Figure 8-6.

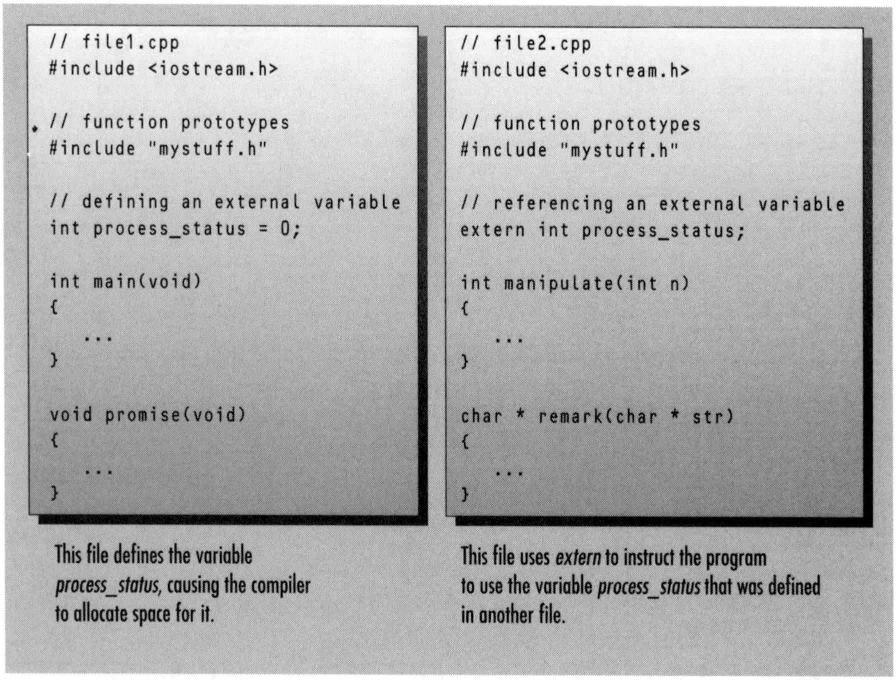

```
// file1.cpp                          // file2.cpp
#include <iostream.h>                 #include <iostream.h>

// function prototypes                // function prototypes
#include "mystuff.h"                  #include "mystuff.h"

// defining an external variable      // referencing an external variable
int process_status = 0;              extern int process_status;

int main(void)                        int manipulate(int n)
{                                     {
    ...                                   ...
}                                     }

void promise(void)                    char * remark(char * str)
{                                     {
    ...                                   ...
}                                     }
```

This file defines the variable *process_status*, causing the compiler to allocate space for it.

This file uses *extern* to instruct the program to use the variable *process_status* that was defined in another file.

Figure 8-6 Defining declaration and referencing declaration

If a file doesn't provide the *extern* declaration of a variable, it can't use an external variable defined elsewhere:

```
// file1
int errors = 20;              // external declaration
...
------------------------------------------------
// file 2
...                           // missing an extern int errors declaration
void froobish()
{
    cout << errors;           // doomed attempt to use errors
..
```

If a file attempts to define a second external variable by the same name, that's an error:

```
// file1
int errors = 20;              // external declaration
...
------------------------------------------------
// file 2
int errors;                   // invalid declaration
void froobish()
{
    cout << errors;           // doomed attempt to use errors
..
```

The correct approach is to use the keyword *extern* in the second file:

```
// file1
int errors = 20;              // external declaration
...
------------------------------------------------
// file 2
extern int errors;           // refers to errors from file1
void froobish()
{
      cout << errors;        // uses errors defined in file1
..
```

But if a file declares a *static* external variable having the same name as an ordinary external variable declared in another file, the *static* version is the one in scope for that file:

```
// file1
int errors = 20;              // external declaration
...
------------------------------------------------
// file2
static int errors = 5;       // known to file2 only
void froobish()
{
      cout << errors;        // uses errors defined in file2
      ...
```

RULE

In a multifile program, you can define an external variable in one and only one file. All other files using that variable have to declare that variable with the *extern* keyword.

Use a regular external variable to share data among different parts of a multifile program. Use a *static* external variable to share data among functions found in just one file. Also, if you make an external variable static, you needn't worry about its name conflicting with external variables found in other files.

Listings 8-18 and 8-19 show how C++ handles external and static external variables. Listing 8-18 *(twofile1.cpp)* defines the external variables *tom* and *dick* and the static external variable *harry*. The *main()* function in that file displays the addresses of the three variables, then calls the *remote_access()* function, which is defined in a second file. Listing 8-19 *(twofile2.cpp)* shows that file. In addition to defining *remote_access()*, the file uses the *extern* keyword to share *tom* with the first file. Next, the file defines a static variable called *dick*. The *static* modifier makes this variable local to the file and overrides the global definition. Then the file defines an external variable called *harry*. It can do so without conflicting with the *harry* of the first file because the first *harry* is local to *twofile1.cpp*. Then the *remote_access()* function displays the addresses of these three variables so that you can compare them with the addresses of the corresponding variables in the first file. Remember to compile both files and to link them together to get the complete program.

Listing 8-18 *twofile1.cpp*

```
// twofile1.cpp -- external and static external variables
#include <iostream.h>          // to be compiled with twofile2.cpp
int tom = 3;                   // external variable definition
int dick = 30;                 // external variable definition
static int harry = 300;        // static external variable definition

// function prototype
void remote_access(void);

int main(void)
{
// NOTE: some implementations require that you type cast
// the addresses to type unsigned

        cout << "main() reports the following addresses:\n";
        cout << &tom << " = &tom, " << &dick << " = &dick, ";
        cout << &harry << " = &harry\n";
        remote_access();
        return 0;
}
```

Listing 8-19 *twofile2.cpp*

```
// twofile2.cpp -- external and static external variables
#include <iostream.h>
extern int tom;                // tom defined elsewhere
static int dick = 10;          // overrides external dick
int harry = 200;               // external variable definition,
                               // no conflict with twofile1 harry

void remote_access(void)
{
// NOTE: some implementations require that you type cast
// the addresses to type unsigned

        cout << "remote_access() reports the following addresses:\n";
        cout << &tom << " = &tom, " << &dick << " = &dick, ";
        cout << &harry << " = &harry\n";
}
```

Here is the output:

```
main() reports the following addresses:
0x8fa000a8 = &tom, 0x8fa000aa = &dick, 0x8fa000ac = &harry
remote_access() reports the following addresses:
0x8fa000a8 = &tom, 0x8fa000f8 = &dick, 0x8fa000fa = &harry
```

As you can see, both files use the same *tom* variable, but different *dick* and *harry* variables.

Storage Class Qualifiers: *const, volatile,* and *mutable*

Certain C++ keywords, called qualifiers, provide additional information about storage. The most commonly used is *const,* and you've already seen its purpose. It indicates that memory, once initialized, should not be altered by a program. We'll come back to *const* in a moment.

The *volatile* keyword indicates that the value in a memory location may be altered even though nothing in the program code modifies the contents. This is less mysterious than it sounds. For example, you could have a pointer to a hardware location that contains the time or information from a serial port. Here the hardware, not the program, would change the contents. The intent of this keyword is to improve the optimization abilities of compilers. For instance, suppose the compiler notices that a program uses the value of a particular variable twice within a few statements. Rather than have the program look up the value twice, the compiler might cache the value in a register. This optimization assumes that the value of the variable doesn't change between the two uses. If you don't declare a variable to be *volatile,* then the compiler can feel free to make this optimization. If you do declare the variable to be *volatile,* you're telling the compiler not to make that sort of optimization.

The ANSI/ISO C++ draft standard adds a new qualifier: *mutable.* It can be used to indicate that a particular member of a structure (or class) can be altered even if a particular structure (or class) variable is a *const.* For example, consider the following code:

```
struct data
{
        char name[30];
        mutable int accesses;
        ...
};
const data veep = {"Claybourne Clodde", 0, ... };
strcpy(veep.name, "Joye Joux");      // not allowed
veep.accesses++;                     // allowed
```

The *const* qualifier to *veep* prevents a program from changing *veep*'s members, but the *mutable* qualifier to the *accesses* member shields *accesses* from that restriction.

This book won't be using *volatile* or *mutable,* but there is more to learn about *const.*

More About *const*

In C++ (but not C), the *const* modifier alters the default storage classes slightly. While an external variable has *external* linkage by default, a *const* external variable has *internal* linkage by default. That is, C++ treats an external *const* definition like a *static* external definition. You can think of the keyword *const,* when used in an external definition, as being preceded by an implicit *static* keyword.

```
const int fingers = 10;      // same as static const int fingers;
```

```
int main(void)
{
    ...
```

C++ bent the rules for constant types to make life easier for you. Suppose, for instance, you have a set of constants that you'd like to place in a header file and that you use this header file in several files in the same program. After the preprocessor includes the header file contents in each source file, each source file will contain definitions like this:

```
const int fingers = 10;
const char * warning = "Wak!";
```

If external *const* declarations had external linkage like regular variables, this would be an error, for you can define an external variable in one file only. That is, only one file could contain the above declaration, while the other files would have to use the *extern* keyword. Moreover, only the declarations without the *extern* keyword could initialize values:

```
// extern would be required if const had external linkage
extern const int fingers;        // can't be initialized
extern const char * warning;
```

So you would need one set of definitions for one file and a different set of declarations for the other files. But, because externally defined *const* data have internal linkage, you can use the same declarations in all files.

Internal linkage also means that each file gets its own set of constants rather than sharing them. Each definition is private to the file containing it.

If, for some reason, you want to make a constant have external linkage, you can use the *extern* keyword to override the default internal linkage:

```
extern const states = 50;    // external linkage
```

You must use the *extern* keyword to declare the constant in *all* files using the constant. This differs from regular external variables, in which you don't use the keyword *extern* when defining a variable, but use *extern* in other files using that variable. Also, unlike regular variables, you can initialize an *extern const* value. Indeed, you have to, for *const* data requires initialization.

When you declare a *const* within a function or block, it has block scope, meaning the constant is usable only when the program is executing code within the block. This means that you can create constants within a function or block and not have to worry about the name conflicting with constants defined elsewhere.

Storage Classes and Functions

Functions, too, have storage classes, although the selection is more limited than for variables. C++, like C, does *not* allow you to define one function inside another, so all functions automatically have a static storage class, meaning they are all present as long as the program is running. By default, functions are external, meaning they have external linkage and can be shared across files. You can, in fact, use the keyword *extern* in a function prototype to indicate the function is defined in another file, but that is optional. (For the program to find the function in another file, that file must be one of the files being compiled as part of the program or a library file searched by the linker.) You can also use the keyword *static* to give a function file scope. You would apply this keyword to the prototype and to the function definition:

```
static int private(double x);
...
static int private(double x)
{
    ...
}
```

That means the function will be known only in that file. It also means you can use the same name for another function in a different file. As with variables, a static function overrides an external definition for the file containing the static declaration. So if you defined your own *strlen()* function in one file of a multifile program and declared the function *static*, that one file would use your definition of *strlen()*, while the other files would use the library version. If you defined your own *strlen()* function and did not declare it as *static*, then the compiler would use your version in all the files of your program. See the note on Where C++ Finds Functions.

Inline functions behave differently from regular functions. By default, they have internal linkage and hence are local to the file containing them.

WHERE C++ FINDS FUNCTIONS

Suppose you call a function in a particular file in a program. Where does C++ look for the function definition? If the function prototype in that file indicates that function is static, the compiler will look only in that file for the function. Otherwise, the compiler (and we use the word to include the linker, too) looks in all the program files. If it finds two definitions, the compiler sends you an error message, for you can have only one definition for an external function. If it fails to find any definition in your files, the function then searches the libraries. This implies that if you define a function having the same name as a library function, the compiler will use your version rather than the library version. (However, there will be problems if you use a header file declaring the library function and if that prototype doesn't match your version.)

Storage Classes and Dynamic Allocation

Storage classes describe memory allocated for variables (including arrays and structures) and functions. They don't apply to memory allocated by using the C++ *new* operator (or by the older C *malloc()* function). We'll call that kind of memory *dynamic* memory. As you saw in Chapter 4, dynamic memory is controlled by the *new* and *delete* operators, not by scope and linkage rules. Thus dynamic memory can be allocated from one function and freed from another function. Unlike automatic memory, dynamic memory is not LIFO; the order of allocation and freeing depends upon when and how *new* and *delete* are used. Typically, the compiler will use three separate memory chunks: one for static variables (this chunk may be subdivided), one for automatic variables, and one for dynamic storage.

Although storage class concepts don't apply to dynamic memory, they do apply to the pointer variables used to keep track of dynamic memory. For instance, suppose we have the following statement inside a function:

```
float * p_fees = new float [20];
```

The 80 bytes (assuming a *float* is 4 bytes) of memory allocated by *new* remains in memory until the *delete* operator frees it. But the *p_fees* pointer passes from existence when the function containing this declaration terminates. So if you wish to have the 80 bytes of allocated memory available to another function, you need to pass or return its address to that function. On the other hand, if you make the same declaration externally, then the *p_fees* pointer will be available to all the functions following that declaration in the file. And by using

```
extern float * p_fees;
```

in a second file, you make that same pointer available in the second file.

COMPATIBILITY NOTE

Memory allocated by *delete* typically is freed when the program terminates. However, this is not always true. Under DOS, for example, a request for a large block of memory may result in a block that is not deleted automatically when the program terminates.

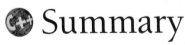 Summary

C++ has expanded C function capabilities. By using the *inline* keyword with function definition and by placing that definition ahead of the first call to that function, you suggest to the C++ compiler that it make the function inline. That is, instead of having the program jump to a separate section of code to execute the function, the compiler replaces the function call with the corresponding code inline. An inline facility should be used only when the function is short.

A reference variable is a kind of disguised pointer that lets you create an alias (a second name) for a variable. Reference variables primarily are used as arguments to functions processing structures and class objects.

C++ prototypes let you define default values for arguments. If a function call omits the corresponding argument, the program uses the default value. If the function includes an argument value, the program uses that value instead of the default. Default arguments can be provided only from right to left in the argument list. Thus if you provide a default value for a particular argument, you must also provide default values for all arguments to the right of that argument.

A function's signature is its argument list. You can define two functions having the same name providing they have different signatures. This is called function polymorphism, or function overloading. Typically, you would overload functions to provide essentially the same service to different data types.

Function templates automate the process of overloading functions. You define a function using a generic type and a particular algorithm, and the compiler generates appropriate function definitions for the particular argument types you use in a program.

C++ encourages you to use multiple files in developing programs. An effective organizational strategy is to use a header file to define user types and provide function prototypes for functions to manipulate the user types. Use a separate source code file for the function definitions. Together, the header file and the source file define and implement the user-defined type and how it can be used. Then *main()* and other functions using those functions can go into a third file.

C++'s storage classes determine how long variables remain in memory and what parts of a program have access to them (scope and linkage). Automatic variables are those defined within a block, such as a function body or a block within the body. They exist and are known only while the program executes statements in the block containing the definition.

Static variables exist for the duration of the program. A variable defined outside of any function has external storage class. It's known to all functions in the file following its definition (file scope) and is made available to other files in the program (external linkage). For another file to use such a variable, it must declare it using the *extern* keyword. A variable defined outside any function but qualified with the keyword *static* has file scope but is not made available to other files (internal linkage). A variable defined inside a block but qualified with the keyword *static* is local to that block but retains its value for the duration of the program.

C++ functions, by default, have external storage class, so they can be shared across files. But inline functions and functions qualified with the keyword *static* have internal linkage and are confined to the defining file.

Review Questions

1. What kinds of functions are good candidates for *inline* status?

2. Suppose the *song()* function has this prototype:

```
void song(char * name, int times);
```

    a. How would you modify the prototype so that the default value for *times* is 1?

    b. What changes would you make in the function definition?

     c. Can you provide a default value of *"O, My Papa"* for *name?*

3. Write overloaded versions of *iquote()*, a function that displays its argument enclosed in double quotation marks. Write three versions: one for an *int* argument, one for a *double* argument, and one for a string argument.

4. Here is a structure template:

```
struct box
{
        char maker[40];
        float height;
        float width;
        float length;
        float volume;
};
```

     a. Write a function that passes a *box* structure by reference and that displays the value of each member.

     b. Write a function that passes a *box* structure by reference and sets the *volume* member to the product of the other three dimensions.

5. Here are some desired effects. Indicate whether each can be accomplished with default arguments, with function overloading, with both, or with neither. Provide appropriate prototypes.

     a. *mass(density, volume)* returns the mass of an object having a density of *density* and a volume of *volume*, while *mass(density)* returns the mass having a density of *density* and a volume of 1.0 cubic meters. All quantities are type *double*.

     b. *repeat(10, "I'm OK")* displays the indicated string ten times, while *repeat("But you're kind of stupid")* displays the indicated string five times.

     c. *average(3,6)* returns the *int* average of two *int* arguments, while *average(3.0, 6.0)* returns the *double* average of two *double* values.

     d. *mangle("I'm glad to meet you")* returns the character *I* or a pointer to the string *"I'm mad to gleet you"* depending on whether you assign the return value to a *char* variable or to a *char** variable.

     e. *average(3,6)* returns an *int* average of the two *int* arguments when called in one file, and it returns a *double* average of the two *int* arguments when called in a second file in the same program.

6. Write a function template that returns the larger of its two arguments.

7. What storage class would you use for the following situations?

     a. *homer* is a formal argument (parameter) to a function.

     b. The *secret* variable is to be shared by two files.

     c. The *topsecret* variable is to be shared by the functions in one file but hidden from other files.

d. *beencalled* keeps track of how many times the function containing it has been called.

Programming Exercises

1. Write a function that normally takes one argument, the address of a string, and prints that string once. However, if a second, type *int* argument is provided and is nonzero, the function prints the string a number of times equal to the number of times that function has been called to that point. (Yes, this is a silly function, but it makes you use some of the techniques discussed in this chapter.) Use the function in a simple program that demonstrates how the function works.

2. Below is a program skeleton. Complete it by providing the described functions and prototypes. Note that there should be two *show()* functions, each using default arguments. Use *const* arguments when appropriate. Note that *set()* should use *new* to allocate sufficient space to hold the designated string. The techniques used here are similar to those used in designing and implementing classes.

```
#include <iostream.h>
#include <string.h>    // for strlen(), strcpy()
struct stringy {
        char * str;      // points to a string
        int ct;          // length of string (not counting '\0')
        };

// prototypes for set(), show(), and show() go here
int main(void)
{
        stringy beany;
        char testing[] = "Reality isn't what it used to be.";

        set(beany, testing);  // first argument is a reference,
                      // allocates space to hold copy of testing,
                      // sets str member of beany to point to the
                      // new block, copies testing to new block,
                      // and sets ct member of beany
        show(beany);          // prints member string once
        show(beany, 2);       // prints member string twice
        testing[0] = 'D';
        testing[1] = 'u';
        show(testing);        // prints testing string once
        show(testing, 3);     // prints testing string thrice
        show("Done!");
        return 0;
}
```

3. Here is the header file:

```
// golf.h -- for pe8-3.cpp

const int Len = 40;
```

```
struct golf
{
        char fullname[Len];
        int handicap;
};

// function solicits name and handicap from user
// returns 1 if name is entered, 0 if name is empty string
int setgolf(golf & g);

// function sets golf structure to provided name, handicap
void setgolf(golf & g, const char * name, int hc);

// function resets handicap to new value
void handicap(golf & g, int hc);

// function displays contents of golf structure
void showgolf(const golf & g);
```

Put together a multifile program based on this header. One file, named *golf.cpp*, should provide suitable function definitions to match the prototypes in the header file. A second file should contain *main()* and should demonstrate all the features of the prototyped functions. For example, a loop should solicit input for an array of *golf* structures and terminate when the array is full or when the user enters an empty string for the golfer's name. The program should use only the prototyped functions to access the *golf* structures.

CHAPTER 9

OBJECTS AND CLASSES

You will learn about the following in this chapter:

- ◇ Procedural and object-oriented programming
- ◇ The class concept
- ◇ How to define and implement a class
- ◇ Public and private class access
- ◇ Class data members
- ◇ Class methods (class function members)
- ◇ Creating and using class objects

- ◇ Class constructors and destructors
- ◇ *const* member functions
- ◇ The *this* pointer
- ◇ Creating arrays of objects
- ◇ Class scope
- ◇ Abstract data types (ADTs)

Object-oriented programming (OOP) is a particular conceptual approach to designing programs, and C++ has enhanced C with features that ease the way to applying that approach. The most important OOP features are these:

❖ Abstraction

❖ Encapsulation and data hiding

❖ Polymorphism

❖ Inheritance

❖ Reusable code

The class is the single most important C++ enhancement for implementing these features and tying them together. This chapter begins our examination of classes, explaining abstraction, encapsulation, and data hiding, and showing how classes implement these features. It discusses how to define a class, how to provide a class with public and

345

private sections, and how to create member functions that work with the class data. Also, the chapter acquaints you with *constructors* and *destructors,* special member functions for creating and disposing of objects belonging to a class. Finally, you'll meet the *this* pointer, an important component of some class programming. The following chapters will extend the discussion to operator overloading (another variety of polymorphism) and inheritance, the basis for reusing code.

Procedural and Object-Oriented Programming

Although we have explored the OOP perspective on programming every so often, we've usually stuck pretty close to the standard procedural approach of languages such as C, Pascal, and BASIC. Let's look at an example that clarifies how the OOP outlook differs from that of procedural programming.

As the newest member of the Genre Giants softball team, you've been asked to keep the team statistics. Naturally, you turn to your computer for help. If you were a procedural programmer, you might think along these lines:

> Let's see, I want to enter the name, times at bat, number of hits, batting averages (For those who don't follow baseball or softball, the batting average is the number of hits divided by the player's official number of times at bat. An at bat terminates when a player gets on base or makes an out, but certain events, such as getting a walk, don't count as official times at bat.), and all those other great basic statistics for each player. Wait, the computer is supposed to make life easier for me, so let's have it figure out some of that stuff, like the batting average. And I want the program to report the results. How should I organize this? I guess I should do things right and use functions. Yeah, I'll make *main()* call a function to get the input, then call a function to make the calculations, and then call a function to report the results. Hmmm, what happens when I get data from the next game? I don't want to start from scratch again. Okay, I can add a function to update the statistics. Golly, maybe I'll need a menu in *main()* to select between entering, calculating, updating, and showing the data. Hmmm—how am I going to represent the data? I could use an array of strings to hold the players' names, another array to hold the at bats for each player, another array to hold the hits, and so on. No, that's dumb. I can design a structure to hold all the information for a single player, then use an array of those structures to represent the whole team.

In short, you would first concentrate upon the procedures you would follow, then think about how to represent the data. (Note: So that you don't have to keep the program running the whole season, you'll probably also want to be able to save data to a file and read data from a file. But as we haven't covered files yet, we'll ignore that complication for now.)

Now let's see how your perspective changes when you don your OOP hat (an attractive polymorphic design). You would start by thinking about the data. Furthermore, you would think about the data not only in terms of how to represent it, but in terms of how it's to be used:

> Let's see—what am I keeping track of? A ball player, of course. So I want an object that represents the whole player, not just her batting average or times at bat. Yeah, that'll be my fundamental data unit, an object representing the name and statistics for a player. I'll need some methods to handle this object. Hmmm, I guess I need a method to get basic information into this unit. The computer should calculate some of the stuff, like the batting averages—I can add methods to do calculations. And the program should do those calculations automatically, without the user having to remember to ask to have them done. Also, I'll need methods for updating the information and displaying it. So the user gets three ways to interact with the data: initialization, updating, and reporting. That's the user interface.

In short, you would concentrate upon the object as the user perceives it, thinking about the data needed to describe the object and about the operations that will describe the user's interaction with the data. After developing a description of that interface, you'd move on to deciding how to implement the interface and data storage. Finally, you'd put together a program to use your new design.

Abstraction and Classes

Life is full of complexities, and one way we cope with complexity is to frame simplifying abstractions. You are a collection of over an octillion atoms. Some students of the mind would say your mind is a collection of semiautonomous agents. But it's much simpler to think of yourself as a single entity. In computing, *abstraction* is the crucial step of representing information in terms of its interface with the user. That is, you abstract the essential operational features of a problem and express a solution in those terms. In the softball statistics example, the interface describes how the user initializes, updates, and displays the data. From abstraction, it is a short step to the *user-defined type*, which in C++ is a class design that implements that interface.

What's a Type?

Let's think a little more about what constitutes a type. For example, what is a nerd? If you subscribe to the popular stereotype, you may think of a nerd in visual terms—

thick, black-rimmed glasses, pocket protector full of pens, and so on. After a little reflection, you may conclude that a nerd is better defined operationally, for example, in how he or she responds to an awkward social situation. We have a similar situation, if you don't mind stretched analogies, with a procedural language like C. At first, you tend to think of a data type in terms of its appearance—how it is stored in memory. A *char*, for example, typically is 1 byte of memory, and a *double* is often 8 bytes of memory. But a little reflection leads us to conclude that a data type is also defined in terms of the operations that can be performed upon it. For instance, the *int* type can use all the arithmetic operations. You can add, subtract, multiply, and divide integers. You can also use the modulus operator (%) with them. On the other hand, consider pointers. A pointer may very well require the same amount of memory as an *int*. It may even be represented internally as an integer. But a pointer doesn't allow the same operations that an integer does. You can't, for example, multiply two pointers times each other. The concept makes no sense, so C++ doesn't implement it. Thus when you declare a variable as an *int* or as a pointer-to-*float*, you're not just allocating memory—you are also establishing which operations can be performed with the variable. In short, specifying a basic type does two things:

- It determines how much memory will be needed for a data object.

- It determines what operations, or methods, can be performed using the data object.

For built-in types, this information is built into the compiler. But when you define a user-defined type in C++, you have to provide the same kind of information yourself. In exchange for this extra work, you gain the power and flexibility to custom fit new data types to match real-world requirements.

The Class

The *class* is the C++ vehicle for translating an abstraction to a user-defined type. It combines data representation and methods for manipulating that data into one neat package. Let's look at a class representing, say, stocks.

First, we have to think a bit about how to represent stocks. We could take one share of stock as the basic unit and define a class to represent a share. However, that implies that you would need 100 objects to represent 100 shares, and that's not practical. Instead, let's represent a person's current holdings in a particular stock as a basic unit. The number of shares owned would be part of the data representation. A realistic approach would have to maintain records of such things as initial purchase price and date of purchase, for tax purposes. Also, it would have to manage events such as stock splits. That seems a bit ambitious for our first effort at defining a class, so let's take an idealized, simplified view of matters. In particular, let's limit the operations we can perform to the following:

- Acquire stock in a company
- Buy more shares of the same stock
- Sell stock
- Update the per-share value of a stock
- Display information about our holdings

We'll use this list to define the public interface for our stock class, leaving additional features as exercises for the interested. To support this interface, we'll need to store some information. Again, we'll use a simplified approach. For example, we won't worry about the standard U.S. practice of evaluating stocks in multiples of eighths of a dollar. We will store the following information:

- Name of company
- Number of stocks owned
- Value of each share
- Total value of all shares

Next, let's define the class. Roughly speaking, the class declaration provides a class overview, while the method definitions supply the details. Generally, a class specification has two parts:

- A class declaration, which describes the data component, in terms of data members, and the public interface, in terms of member functions
- The class method definitions, which describe how certain class member functions are implemented

Listing 9-1 presents a tentative class declaration for a *Stock* class. (To help identify classes, we'll follow a common, but not universal, convention of capitalizing class names.) You'll notice it looks like a structure declaration with a few additional wrinkles, such as member functions and *public* and *private* sections. We'll improve on this declaration shortly, but first let's see how this definition works.

 Listing 9-1 *stocks.cpp*

```
// beginning of stocks.cpp file
class Stock            // class declaration
{
private:
        char company[30];
        int shares;
        double share_val;
```

continued on next page

continued from previous page

```
        double total_val;
        void set_tot() { total_val = shares * share_val; }
public:
        void acquire(const char * co, int n, double pr);
        void buy(int num, double price);
        void sell(int num, double price);
        void update(double price);
        void show();
};
```

You'll get a closer look at the class details later, but first let's examine the more general features. To begin, the C++ keyword *class* identifies this code as defining the design of a class. The syntax identifies *Stock* as being the type name for this new class. This declaration enables us to declare variables, called *objects,* or *instances,* of the *Stock* type. Each individual object would represent a single holding. For example, the declarations

```
Stock sally;
Stock solly;
```

would create two *Stock* objects called *sally* and *solly.* The *sally* object, for example, could represent Sally's stock holdings in a particular company.

Next, notice that the information we decided to store appears in the form of class data members, such as *company* and *shares.* The *company* member of *sally,* for example, would hold the name of the company, the *share* member would hold the number of shares Sally owns, the *share_val* member would hold the value of each share, and the *total_val* member would hold the total value of all the shares. Similarly, the operations we desired appear as class function members, such as *sell()* and *update().* Class member functions are also termed *class methods.* A member function can be defined in place, like *set_tot(),* or it can be represented by a prototype, like the other member functions in this class. The full definitions for the other member functions will come later, but the prototypes suffice to describe the function interfaces. The binding of data and methods into a single unit is the most striking feature of the class. Because of this design, creating a *Stock* object automatically establishes the rules governing how that object can be used.

We've talked about how the *istream* and *ostream* classes have member functions, such as *get()* and *getline().* The function prototypes in the *Stock* class declaration demonstrate how member functions are established. The *iostream.h* header file, for example, has a *getline()* prototype in the *istream* class declaration.

Also new are the keywords *private* and *public.* These labels describe *access control* for class members. Any program using an object of a particular class can access the public portions directly. But a program can access the private members of an object *only* by using the public member functions (or, as you'll see in Chapter 10, via a friend function). For instance, the only way to alter the *shares* member of the *Stock* class is to use one of the *Stock* member functions. Thus the public member functions act as go-betweens between a program and an object's private members; they provide the interface between object and program. This insulation of data from direct access by a program is called *data hiding*. (C++ provides a third visibility keyword, *protected*, which we'll discuss when we cover class inheritance in Chapter 12.) See Figure 9-1. While data hiding may be an unscrupulous act in, say, a stock fund prospectus, it's a good practice in computing because it preserves the integrity of the data.

A class design attempts to separate the public interface from the specifics of the implementation. The public interface represents the abstraction component of the design. Gathering the implementation details together and separating them from the abstraction is called *encapsulation*. Data hiding (putting data into the private section of a class) is an example of encapsulation, and so is hiding functional details of an implementation in the private section, as the *Stock* class does with *set_tot()*. Another example of encapsulation is the usual practice of placing class function definitions in a separate file from the class declaration.

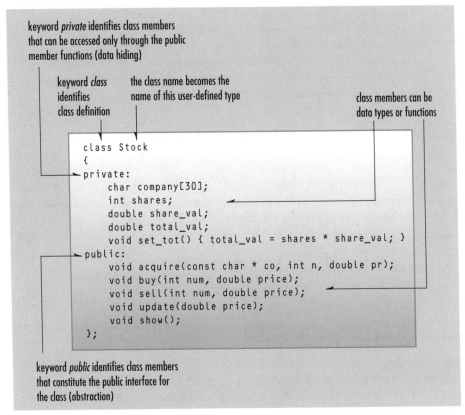

Figure 9-1 The *Stock* class

OOP AND C++

Object-oriented programming is a programming style that you can use with any language. Certainly, you can incorporate many OOP ideas into ordinary C programs. For instance, Chapter 8 provided an example (Listings 8-12, 13, 14) in which a header file contained a structure prototype along with the prototypes for functions to manipulate that structure. Thus the *main()* function simply defined variables of that structure type and used the associated functions to handle those variables; *main()* did not directly access structure members. In essence, that example defined an abstract type that placed the storage format and the function prototypes in a header file, hiding the actual data representation from *main()*. C++, however, includes features specifically intended to implement the OOP approach, so it lets you take the process a few steps further than you can with C. First, placing the data representation and the function prototypes into a single class declaration instead of into a file unifies the description by placing everything in one class declaration. Second, making the data representation *private* enforces the structure that data be accessed by authorized functions only. If, in the C example, *main()* directly accessed a structure member, it would be violating the spirit of OOP, but it wouldn't be breaking any C language rules. But trying to access, say, the *shares* member of a *Stock* object directly does break a C++ language rule, and the compiler will catch it.

Note that data hiding not only prevents you from accessing the data directly, but it also absolves you from needing to know how the data is represented. For example, the *show()* member will display, among other things, the total value of a holding. This value could be stored as part of an object, as our code does, or it could be calculated when needed. From the standpoint of the user, it makes no difference which approach was used. What you do need to know is what the different member functions accomplish; that is, you need to know what kinds of arguments a member function takes and what kind of return value it has. The principle is to separate the details of the implementation from the design of the interface. If you later find a better way to implement the data representation or the details of the member functions, you can change those details without changing the program interface, and that makes programs much easier to maintain.

Public or Private?

Class members, whether they are data items or member functions, can be declared either in the public section or the private section of a class. But because one of the main OOP precepts is to hide the data, data items normally go into the private section. The member functions that constitute the class interface go into the public section; otherwise, you couldn't call those functions from a program. As our sample declaration shows, you can also put member functions in the private section. You can't call such functions directly from a program, but the public methods can use them. Typically, you would use private member functions to handle implementation details that don't form part of the public interface.

You don't have to use the keyword *private* in class declarations, for that is the default visibility for class objects:

```
class World
{
        float mass;                    // private by default
        char name[20];                 // private by default
public:
        void tellall(void);
        ...
}
```

However, we'll use the *private* label explicitly in order to emphasize the concept of data hiding.

CLASSES AND STRUCTURES

Class descriptions look much like structure declarations with the addition of member functions and the *public* and *private* visibility labels. In fact, C++ has extended to structures the same features classes have. The only difference is that the default visibility type for a structure is *public,* while the default type for the class is *private.* But C++ programmers commonly use classes to implement class descriptions while restricting structures to represent pure data objects.

Implementing Class Member Functions

We still have the second part of the class specification to do: providing code for those member functions represented by a prototype in the class declaration. Let's look at that next. Member function definitions are much like regular function definitions. They have a function heading and a function body. They can have return types and arguments. But they also have two special characteristics:

❧ When defining a member function, you use the scope operator (::) to identify the class to which the function belongs.

❧ Class methods can access the *private* components of the class.

Let's look at these points now.

First, the function heading for a member function uses the scope operator (::) to indicate to which class the function belongs. For example, the heading for the *update()* member function looks like this:

```
void Stock::update(double price)
```

This notation means we are defining the *update()* function that is a member of the *Stock* class. Not only does this identify *update()* as a member function, it means we can use the same name for a member function for a different class. For instance, an *update()* function for a *Buffoon* class would have this function heading:

```
void Buffoon::update()
```

Thus the scope resolution operator resolves the question of which class a method definition applies to. We say that the identifier *update()* has *class scope*. Other member functions of the *Stock* class can, if necessary, use the *update()* method without using the scope resolution operator. That's because they belong to the same class, making *update()* in scope. Using *update()* outside of the class declaration and method definitions, however, will require special measures, which we'll get to soon.

One way of looking at method names is that the complete name of a class method includes the class name. We say that *Stock::update()* is the *qualified name* of the function. A simple *update()*, on the other hand, is an abbreviation for the full name, one that can be used just in class scope.

The second special characteristic for methods is that the function can access the *private* members of a class. For instance, the *show()* method can use code like this:

```
cout << "Company: " << company
     << "  Shares: " << shares << '\n'
     << "  Share Price: $" << share_val
     << "  Total Worth: $" << total_val << '\n';
```

Here *Company, shares,* and so on, are private data members of the *Stock* class. If you try to use a nonmember function to access these data members, the compiler will stop you cold in your tracks. (However, friend functions, discussed in Chapter 10, provide an exception.)

With these two points in mind, we can implement the class methods as shown in Listing 9-2. These method definitions can go in a separate file or in the same file with the class declaration. Since we are starting simple, we'll assume that these definitions follow the class declaration in the same file. This is the easiest, although not the best, way to make the class declaration available to the method definitions. (The best way, which we'll apply later, is to use a header file for the class declaration and a source code file for the class member function definitions.)

Listing 9-2 *stocks.cpp*

```
//more stocks.cpp -- implementing the class member functions
#include <iostream.h>
#include <stdlib.h>   // for exit()
#include <string.h>   // for strcpy()
void Stock::acquire(const char * co, int n, double pr)
{
        strcpy(company, co);
        shares = n;
        share_val = pr;
```

```
                set_tot();
}

void Stock::buy(int num, double price)
{
        shares += num;
        share_val = price;
        set_tot();
}

void Stock::sell(int num, double price)
{
        if (num > shares)
        {
                cerr << "You can't sell more than you have!\n";
                exit(1);
        }
        shares -= num;
        share_val = price;
        set_tot();
}

void Stock::update(double price)
{
        share_val = price;
        set_tot();
}

void Stock::show()
{
        cout << "Company: " << company
                << "  Shares: " << shares << '\n'
                << "  Share Price: $" << share_val
                << "  Total Worth: $" << total_val << '\n';
}
```

Member Function Notes

The *acquire()* function manages the first acquisition of stock for a given company, while *buy()* and *sell()* manage adding to or subtracting from an existing holding. If the user attempts to sell more shares than he or she has, the *sell()* function calls the *exit()* function, which terminates the program. (Exceptions, discussed in Chapter 14, allow a more flexible response.) Four of the member functions set or reset the *total_val* member value. Instead of writing this calculation four times, we had each function call the *set_tot()* function. Because this function is merely the means of implementing the code and not part of the public interface, we made *set_tot()* a private member function. If the calculation were lengthy, this could save some typing and code space. Here, however, the main value is that by using a function call instead of retyping the calculation each time, we insure that the exact same calculation gets done. Also, if we have to revise the calculation (not likely in this particular case), we'll have to revise it in just one location.

CERR AND EXIT()

The *cerr* object, like *cout,* is an *ostream* object. The difference is that operating system redirection affects *cout* but not *cerr*. The *cerr* object is used for error messages. Thus, if you redirect program output to a file and there is an error, you'll still get the error message onscreen. The *exit()* function terminates a program. Commonly, nonzero arguments are used to indicate that the program terminated abnormally, and a zero argument is used to indicate normal termination. However, for maximum ANSI portability, you can use EXIT_SUCCESS and EXIT_FAILURE as return values. Calling *exit()* from *main()* has the same effect of calling *return* from *main()*, but, unlike *return*, *exit()* terminates a program regardless of the function from which it's called. The *stdlib.h* header file provides the function prototype and defines the portable return values.

Inline Methods

Any function defined in the class declaration automatically becomes an inline function. Thus, *Stock::set_tot()* is an inline function. Class declarations often use inline functions for short member functions, and *set_tot()* qualifies on that account.

You can, if you like, define a member function outside the class declaration and still make it inline. To do so, just use the *inline* qualifier when defining the function in the class implementation section:

```
class Stock
{
private:
     ...
     void set_tot();        // definition kept separate
public:
     ...
};

inline void Stock::set_tot() // use inline in definition
{
     total_val = shares * share_val;
}
```

Because inline functions have internal linkage, they are known only to the file in which they are declared. The easiest way to make sure that inline definitions are available to all files in a multifile program is to include the inline definition in the same header file in which the corresponding class is defined. (Some development systems may have *smart linkers* that allow the inline definitions to go into a separate implementation file.)

Incidentally, according to the *rewrite* rule, defining a method in a class declaration is equivalent to replacing the method definition with a prototype and then rewriting the definition as an inline function immediately after the class declaration. That is, our original definition of *set_tot()* is equivalent to the one just shown above.

Which Object?

Now we've come to one of the most important aspects of using objects: how you apply a class method to an object. Code such as

```
shares += num;;
```

uses the *shares* member of an object. But which object? That's an excellent question! To answer it, first consider how you create an object. The simplest way is to declare class variables:

```
Stock kate, joe;
```

This creates two objects of the *Stock* class, one named *kate* and one named *joe*.

Next, consider how to use a member function with one of these objects. The answer, as with structures and structure members, is to use the membership operator:

```
kate.show();    // the kate object calls the member function
joe.show();     // the joe object calls the member function
```

The first call invokes *show()* as a member of the *kate* object. This means the method will interpret *shares* as *kate.shares* and *share_val* as *kate.share_val*. Similarly, the call *joe.show()* makes the *show()* method interpret *shares* and *share_val* as *joe.shares* and *joe.share_val*.

RULE

When you call a member function, it uses the data members of the particular object used to invoke the member function.

Similarly, the function call *kate.sell()* invokes the *set_tot()* function as if it were *kate.set_tot()*, causing that function to get its data from the *kate* object.

Each new object you create contains storage for its own internal variables, the class members. But all objects of the same class share the same set of class methods. Suppose, for instance, that *kate* and *joe* are *Stock* objects. Then *kate.shares* occupies one chunk of memory and *joe.shares* occupies a second chunk of memory. But *kate.show()* and *joe.show()* both invoke the same method, that is, both execute the same block of code. They just apply the code to different data. Calling a member function is what some OOP languages term sending a message. Thus sending the same message to two different objects invokes the same method but applies it to two different objects. See Figure 9-2.

Using a Class

Now you've seen how to define a class and its class methods. The next step is to produce a program that creates and uses objects of a class. The C++ goal is to make using classes as similar as possible to using the basic, built-in types, such as *int* and *char*. So you can create a class object by declaring a class variable or using *new* to allocate an

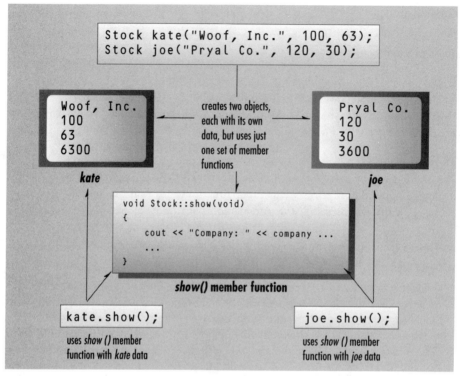

Figure 9-2 Objects, data, and member functions

object of a class type. You can pass objects as arguments, return them as function return values, and assign one object to another. C++ provides facilities for initializing objects, for teaching *cin* and *cout* to recognize objects, and even for providing automatic type conversions between objects of similar classes. It will be a while before you can do all these things, but let's start now with the simpler properties. Indeed, you've already seen how to declare a class object and to call a member function. Listing 9-3 combines those techniques with the class declaration and the member function definitions to form a complete program. It creates a *Stock* object named *stock1*. The program is simple, but it does test the features we built into the class.

Listing 9-3 *stocks.cpp*

```
// stocks.cpp
#include <iostream.h>
#include <stdlib.h>   // for exit()
#include <string.h> // for strcpy()

class Stock
{
```

```
private:
        char company[30];
        int shares;
        double share_val;
        double total_val;
        void set_tot() { total_val = shares * share_val; }
public:
        void acquire(const char * co, int n, double pr);
        void buy(int num, double price);
        void sell(int num, double price);
        void update(double price);
        void show();
};


void Stock::acquire(const char * co, int n, double pr)
{
        strcpy(company, co);
        shares = n;
        share_val = pr;
        set_tot();
}

void Stock::buy(int num, double price)
{
        shares += num;
        share_val = price;
        set_tot();
}

void Stock::sell(int num, double price)
{
        if (num > shares)
        {
                cerr << "You can't sell more than you have!\n";
                exit(1);
        }
        shares -= num;
        share_val = price;
        set_tot();
}

void Stock::update(double price)
{
        share_val = price;
        set_tot();
}

void Stock::show()
{
        cout << "Company: " << company
                << "  Shares: " << shares << '\n'
                << "  Share Price: $" << share_val
```

continued on next page

continued from previous page

```
                      << "  Total Worth: $" << total_val << '\n';
}

int main(void)
{
        Stock stock1;

        stock1.acquire("NanoSmart", 20, 12.50);
        cout.precision(2);                        // #.## format
        cout.setf(ios::fixed, ios::floatfield);        // #.## format
        cout.setf(ios::showpoint);     // #.## format
        stock1.show();
        stock1.buy(15, 18.25);
        stock1.show();
        return 0;
}
```

The program uses three formatting commands. The net effect is to display two digits to the right of the decimal, including trailing zeros. Actually, only the first two are needed according to the draft standard, and older implementations just need the first and third. Using all three produces the same output for both implementations. See Chapter 15 for the details. Meanwhile, here is the program output:

```
Company: NanoSmart  Shares: 20
  Share Price: $12.50  Total Worth: $250.00
Company: NanoSmart  Shares: 35
  Share Price: $18.25  Total Worth: $638.75
```

Note that *main()* is just a vehicle for testing the design of the *Stock* class. Given that the class works as we like, we can now use the *Stock* class as a user-defined type in other programs. The critical point in using the new type is understanding what the member functions do; you shouldn't have to think about the implementation details. See the note on The Client-Server Model.

THE CLIENT-SERVER MODEL

OOP programmers often discuss program design in terms of a client-server model. In this conceptualization, the client is a program that uses the class. The class declaration, including the class methods, constitute the server, which is a resource available to the programs that need it. The client uses the server through the publicly defined interface only. This means the client's only responsibility, and, by extension, the client's programmer's only responsibility, is to know that interface. The server's responsibility, and, by extension, the server's designer's responsibility, is to see that the server reliably and accurately performs according to that interface. Any changes the server designer makes to the class design should be to details of implementation, not to the interface. This allows programmers to improve the client and the server independently of each other, without changes in the server having unforeseen repercussions in the client's behavior.

Our Story to Date

The first step in specifying a class design is providing a class declaration. The class declaration is modeled after a structure declaration and can include data members and function members. The declaration has a *private* section, and members declared in that section can be accessed only through the member functions. The declaration also has a *public* section, and members declared there can be accessed directly by a program using class objects. Typically, data members go into the *private* section and member functions go into the *public* section, so a typical class declaration has this form:

```
class classname
{
private:
data member declarations
public:
member function prototypes
};
```

The contents of the *public* section constitute the abstract part of the design, the public interface. Encapsulating data in the private section protects the integrity of the data and is called data hiding. Thus the class is the C++ way of making it easy to implement the OOP goals of abstraction, data hiding, and encapsulation.

The second step in specifying the class design is to implement the class member functions. You can use a complete function definition instead of a function prototype in the class declaration, but the usual practice, except for very brief functions, is to provide the function definitions separately. In that case, you need to use the scope operator to indicate to which class a member function belongs. For instance, suppose the *bozo* class has a member function called *retort()* that returns a pointer to a *char*. Then the function heading would look like this:

```
char * bozo::retort()
```

In other words, *retort()* is not just a type *char* * function; it is a type *char* * function that belongs to the *bozo* class. The full, or qualified, name of the function is *bozo::retort()*. The name *retort()*, on the other hand, is an abbreviation of the qualified name, and it can be used only in certain circumstances, such as in class method code.

To create an object, which is a particular instance, or example, of a class, use the class name as if it were a type name:

```
bozo bozetta;
```

This works because a class is a user-defined type.

A class member function, or method, can be invoked only by a class object. You can do so by using the dot membership operator:

```
cout << bozetta.retort();
```

This invokes the *retort()* member function, and whenever the code for that function refers to a particular data member, the function will use the value that member has in the *bozetta* object.

Class Constructors and Destructors

Meanwhile, there's more to be done with the *Stock* class. There are certain standard functions, called ~~constructors~~ and ~~destructors~~, you usually should provide for a class. Let's see why they are needed and how to write them.

One of C++'s aims is to make using class objects similar to using standard types. However, you can't yet initialize a *Stock* object the way you can an ordinary *int* or *struct:*

```
int year = 2001;                                   // okay
struct thing
{
        char * pn;
        int m;
};
thing amabob = {"widget", -23};                    //okay
Stock hot = {"Suzie's Autos, Inc.", 200, 50.25};   // NO!
```

The reason you can't initialize a *Stock* object this way is because the data parts have *private* visibility, which means a program cannot access the data members directly. As you've seen, the only way a program can access the data members is through a member function. Therefore, we need to devise an appropriate member function if we're to succeed in initializing an object. (You could initialize a class object as shown above *if* you made the data members public instead of private, but making the data public goes against one of the main justifications for classes, that is, data hiding.)

In general, it's best that all objects be initialized when they are created. For example, consider the following code:

```
Stock gift;
gift.buy(10, 24.75);
```

With our current implementation, the *gift* object has no value for the company member. The class design assumes that the user calls *acquire ()* before calling any other member functions, but there is no way to enforce that assumption. One way around this difficulty is to have objects initialized automatically when they are created. To accomplish this, C++ provides for special member functions, called *class constructors,* especially for constructing new objects and assigning values to their data members. More precisely, C++ provides a name for these member functions and a syntax for using them, and you provide the method definition. The name is the same as the class name. For instance, a possible constructor for the *Stock* class is a member function called *Stock ()*. The constructor prototype and heading have an interesting property— although the constructor has no return value, it's not declared type *void*. In fact, a constructor has no declared type.

Declaring and Defining Constructors

Let's build a *Stock* constructor. Because a *Stock* object has three values to be provided from the outside world, we'll give the constructor three arguments. (The fourth value, the *total_val* member, is calculated from *shares* and *share_val,* so we don't have to provide it to the constructor.) Possibly, we'll just want to set the company member and set the other values to zero, so we'll provide default arguments (see Chapter 8). Thus the prototype would look like this:

```
// constructor prototype with some default arguments
Stock(const char * co, int n = 0, double pr = 0.0);
```

The first argument is a pointer to the string that will be used to initialize the *company* character array class members. The *n* and *pr* arguments provide values for the *shares* and *share_val* members. Note that there is no return type. The prototype goes in the public section of the class declaration.

Next, here's one possible definition for the constructor:

```
// constructor definition
Stock::Stock(const char * co, int n, double pr)
{
        strcpy(company, co);
        shares = n;
        share_val = pr;
        set_tot();
}
```

This is the same code that we used for the *acquire()* function. The difference is that a program invokes the constructor automatically when it declares an object.

Incidentally, the definition doesn't check to see if the initialization string fits into the target array. If this bothers you, you can use the *strncpy()* function instead. The call *strncpy(s2, s1, n)* copies *s1* to *s2* or else up to *n* characters from *s1* to *s2,* whichever comes first. If *s1* contains fewer characters than *n,* the *strncpy()* function pads *s2* with null characters. That is, *strncpy(firstname,"Tim", 6)* would copy the characters *T, i,* and *m* to *firstname,* then add 3 null characters to bring the total to 6 characters. But if *s1* is longer than *n,* no null characters are appended. That is, *strncpy(firstname, "Priscilla", 4)* just copies the characters *P, r, i,* and *s* to *firstname,* making it a character array, but, since it lacks a terminating null character, not a string. So to make sure the constructor creates a true string, you could use code like this:

```
// constructor definition
Stock:: Stock(const char * co, int n, double pr)
{
        strncpy(co, fn, 29);        // use first 29 elements
        firstname[29] = '\0'; // set 30th element to '\0'
        ...
}
```

We'll continue, however, to assume benign input that doesn't require such special treatment.

Using a Constructor

C++ provides two ways to initialize an object using the constructor. The first is to call the constructor explicitly:

```
Stock food = Stock("World Cabbage", 250, 1.25);
```

This sets the *company* member of the *food* object to the string *"World Cabbage"*, the *shares* member to *250*, and so on.

The second way is to call the constructor implicitly:

```
Stock garment("Furry Mason", 50, 2.5);
```

This more compact form is equivalent to the following explicit call:

```
Stock garment = Stock("Furry Mason", 50, 2.5));
```

If you provide a class constructor, C++ uses it whenever you create an object of that class, even when you use *new* for dynamic memory allocation. Here's how to use the constructor with *new*:

```
Stock *pstock = new Stock("Electroshock Games", 18, 19.0);
```

This statement creates a *Stock* object, initializes it to the values provided by the arguments, and assigns the address of the object to the *pstock* pointer. In this case, the object doesn't have a name, but you can use the pointer to manage the object. We'll put off further discussion of pointers to objects until Chapter 10.

The Default Constructor

Once you define a constructor, a program *must* use it when creating an object. Because our first *Stock()* constructor requires at least one argument, you now always have to explicitly initialize a *Stock* object when creating one. That is, you no longer can create uninitialized objects as in Listing 9-3:

```
Stock stock1; // not possible with current constructor
```

Yet this is something you might want to do.

The key to creating objects without explicit initialization is to define a *default constructor*. This is a constructor that takes no arguments. You can define a default constructor two ways. One is to provide default values for all the arguments to the existing constructor:

```
Stock(const char * co = "Error", int n = 0, double pr = 0.0);
```

The second is to use function overloading to define a second constructor that has no arguments:

```
Stock();
```

(With early versions of C++, you could use only the second method for creating a default constructor.)

Actually, objects usually should be initialized in order to insure that all members begin with known, reasonable values. Thus the default constructor typically provides implicit initialization for all member values. Here, for example, is how you might define one for the *Stock* class:

```
Stock::Stock()
{
    strcpy(company, "no name");
    shares = 0;
    share_val = 0.0;
    total_val = 0.0;
}
```

One more reason for providing a default constructor is that one is required if you wish to create an array of objects and explicitly initialize each element.

TIP

When designing a class, you usually should provide a default constructor that implicitly initializes all class members.

Once you've used either method to create the default constructor, you can declare object variables without initializing them explicitly:

```
Stock first;              // calls default constructor implicitly
Stock first = Stock();    // calls it explicitly
Stock *prelief = new Stock; // calls it implicitly
```

However, don't be misled by the implicit form of the nondefault constructor:

```
Stock first("Concrete Conglomerate");     // calls constructor
Stock second();                           // declares a function
Stock third;                    // calls default constructor
```

The first declaration calls the nondefault constructor, that is, the one that takes arguments. The second declaration states that *second()* is a function that returns a *Stock* object. So when calling the default constructor implicitly, don't use parentheses.

The Implicit Default Constructor

C++ always calls a constructor when creating an object. Therefore, if you fail to define any constructors, as we did in Listing 9-3, the compiler provides its own version of a default constructor, one that does nothing. For instance, the compiler generated the following constructor for the original *Stock* class:

```
Stock() {}     // implicit default constructor
```

It was this constructor that enabled us to declare objects:

```
Stock stock1; // called implicit default constructor
```

However, if you define any kind of constructor (default or otherwise), the compiler no longer generates a default constructor. In that case you should provide an explicit default constructor.

Destructors

When you use a constructor to create an object, the program undertakes the responsibility of tracking that object until it expires. At that time, the program automatically calls a special member function bearing the formidable title of *destructor*. The destructor should clean up any debris, so it actually serves a constructive purpose. For instance, if your constructor uses *new* to allocate memory, the destructor should use *delete* to free that memory. Our constructor doesn't do anything fancy like using *new*, so it doesn't really need a destructor. But it's a good idea to provide one anyway in case a future class revision needs one.

Like a constructor, the destructor has a special name: the class name preceded by a tilde (~). Thus the destructor for the *Stock* class would be called ~*Stock*(). Also, like a constructor, a destructor can have no return value and has no declared type. Unlike the constructor, the destructor can have no arguments. Thus the prototype for a *Stock* destructor must be this:

```
~Stock();
```

Because a *Stock* destructor has no vital duties, we can code it as a do-nothing function:

```
Stock::~Stock()
{
}
```

However, just so that we can see when the destructor is called, we'll code it this way:

```
Stock::~Stock()                 // class destructor
{
        cout << "Bye, " << company << "!\n";
}
```

And when should a destructor be called? If you create a static storage class object, its destructor is called when the program terminates. If you create an automatic storage class object, as we have been doing, its destructor is called when the program exits the block of code in which the object was defined. If the object was created using *new*, it resides in heap memory, or the free store, and its destructor is called when you use *delete* to free the memory. Finally, a program may create temporary objects to carry out certain operations; in that case the program calls the destructor for the object when it has finished using it.

Improving the *Stock* Class

The next step is to incorporate the constructors and the destructor into the class and method definitions. This time we'll follow the usual C++ practice and organize the program into separate files. We'll place the class declaration in a header file called *stock1.h*. (As the name suggests, we have future revisions in mind.) The class methods go into a file called *stock1.cpp*. In general, the header file containing the class declaration and the source code file containing the methods definitions should have the same base name so that you can keep track of which files belong together. Using separate files for the class declaration and the member functions separates the abstract definition of the interface (the class declaration) from the details of implementation (the member functions). You could, for example, distribute the class declaration as a text header file but distribute the function definitions as compiled code. Finally, we'll place the program using these resources in a third file, which we'll call *usestok1.cpp*.

Listing 9-4 shows the header file. It adds prototypes for the constructor and destructor functions to the original class declaration. Also, it dispenses with the *acquire()* function, which no longer is needed.

Listing 9-4 *stock1.h*

```
// stock1.h
#ifndef _STOCK1_H_
#define _STOCK1_H_

class Stock
{
private:
      char company[30];
      int shares;
      double share_val;
      double total_val;
      void set_tot() { total_val = shares * share_val; }
public:
      Stock();              // default constructor
      Stock(const char * co, int n = 0, double pr = 0.0);
      ~Stock();             // verbose destructor
      void buy(int num, double price);
      void sell(int num, double price);
      void update(double price);
      void show();
};

#endif
```

HEADER FILE MANAGEMENT

You should include a header file just once in a file. That might seem to be an easy thing to remember, but it's possible to include a header file several times without knowing you do so. For instance, you may use a header file that includes another header file. There's a standard C/C++ technique for avoiding multiple inclusions. It's based on the preprocessor *#ifndef* (for *if not defined*) directive. A code segment like

```
#ifndef _STOCK1_H_
...
#endif
```

means process the statements between the *#ifndef* and *#endif* only if the name *_STOCK1_H_* has not been defined previously by the preprocessor *#define* directive.

Normally, you use the *#define* statement to create symbolic constants, as in the following:

```
#define MAXIMUM 4096
```

But simply using *#define* with a name is enough to establish that a name is defined, as in the following:

```
#define _STOCK1_H_
```

The technique, which Listing 9-4 uses, is to wrap the file contents in an *#ifndef*:

```
#ifndef _STOCK1_H_
#define _STOCK1_H_
// place include file contents here
#endif
```

The first time the compiler encounters the file, the name *_STOCK1_H_* should be undefined. (We chose a name based on the include file name with a few underscore characters tossed in so as to create a name unlikely to be defined elsewhere.) That being the case, the compiler looks at the material between the *#ifndef* and the *#endif,* which is what we want. In the process of looking at the material, the compiler reads the line defining *_STOCK1_H_*. If it should then encounter a second inclusion of *stock1.h* in the same file, the compiler will note that *_STOCK1_H_* is defined and skip to the line following the *#endif*. Note that this method doesn't keep the compiler from including a file twice. Instead, it makes it ignore the contents of all but the first inclusion. Most of the standard C and C++ header files use this scheme.

Listing 9-5 provides the method definitions. It includes the *stock1.h* file in order to provide the class declaration. (Recall that enclosing the file name in double quotation marks instead of in brackets means the compiler searches for it at the same location your source files are found.) Also, the listing includes the system *iostream.h* and *string.h* files because the methods use *cin, cout,* and *strcpy().* This file adds the constructor and destructor method definitions to the prior methods.

Listing 9-5 *stock1.cpp*

```
// stock1.cpp -- Stock class methods
#include <iostream.h>
#include <stdlib.h>    // for exit()
```

```
#include <string.h> // for strcpy()
#include "stock1.h"

// constructors
Stock::Stock()          // default constructor
{
        strcpy(company, "no name");
        shares = 0;
        share_val = 0.0;
        total_val = 0.0;
}

Stock::Stock(const char * co, int n, double pr)
{
        strcpy(company, co);
        shares = n;
        share_val = pr;
        set_tot();
}

// class destructor
Stock::~Stock()                  // class destructor
{
        cout << "Bye, " << company << "!\n";
}

// other methods
void Stock::buy(int num, double price)
{
        shares += num;
        share_val = price;
        set_tot();
}

void Stock::sell(int num, double price)
{
        if (num > shares)
        {
                cerr << "You can't sell more than you have!\n";
                exit(1);
        }
        shares -= num;
        share_val = price;
        set_tot();
}

void Stock::update(double price)
{
        share_val = price;
        set_tot();
}

void Stock::show()
```

continued on next page

continued from previous page

```
{
        cout << "Company: " << company
             << "  Shares: " << shares << '\n'
             << "  Share Price: $" << share_val
             << "  Total Worth: $" << total_val << '\n';
}
```

Listing 9-6 provides a short program for testing the new methods. Like *stock1.cpp*, it includes the *stock1.h* file to provide the class declaration. The program demonstrates constructors and destructors. It also uses the same formatting commands invoked by Listing 9-3. To compile the complete program, use the techniques for multifile programs described in Chapters 1 and 8.

Listing 9-6 *usestok1.cpp*

```
// usestok1.cpp -- use the Stock class
#include <iostream.h>
#include "stock1.h"

int main(void)
{
// using constructors to create new objects
        Stock stock1("NanoSmart", 12, 20.0);            // syntax 1
        Stock stock2 = Stock ("Boffo Objects", 2, 2.0); // syntax 2

        cout.precision(2);                         // #.## format
        cout.setf(ios::fixed, ios::floatfield);    // #.## format
        cout.setf(ios::showpoint);                 // #.## format

        stock1.show();
        stock2.show();
        stock2 = stock1;                           // object assignment

// using a constructor to reset an object
        stock1 = Stock("Nifty Foods", 10, 50.0);   // temp object

        cout << "After stock reshuffle:\n";
        stock1.show();
        stock2.show();
        return 0;
}
```

Here's the program output:

```
Company: NanoSmart  Shares: 12
  Share Price: $20.00  Total Worth: $240.00
Company: Boffo Objects  Shares: 2
  Share Price: $2.00  Total Worth: $4.00
Bye, Nifty Foods!
After stock reshuffle:
Company: Nifty Foods  Shares: 10
  Share Price: $50.00  Total Worth: $500.00
```

```
Company: NanoSmart  Shares: 12
   Share Price: $20.00  Total Worth: $240.00
Bye, NanoSmart!
Bye, Nifty Foods!
```

Program Notes

The statement

```
Stock stock1("NanoSmart", 12, 20.0);
```

creates a *Stock* object called *stock1* and initializes its data members to the indicated values. The statement

```
Stock stock2 = Stock ("Boffo Objects", 2, 2.0);
```

uses the second variety of syntax to create and initialize an object called *stock2*.

You can use the constructor for more than initializing a new object. For instance, the program has this statement in *main()*:

```
stock1 = Stock("Nifty Foods", 10, 50.0);
```

The *stock1* object already exists. Thus instead of initializing *stock1*, this statement assigns new values to the object.

The statement

```
stock2 = stock1;                        // object assignment
```

illustrates that you can assign one object to another of the same type. As with structure assignment, class object assignment, by default, copies the members of one object to the other. In this case, the original contents of *stock2* get overwritten.

RULE

When you assign one object to another of the same class, C++, by default, copies the contents of each data member of the source object to the corresponding data member of the target object.

Note that output shows the program saying *Bye, Nifty Foods!* before it displays the new *stock1* contents. Later, at the end, the program says *Bye, NanoSmart!* and *Bye, Nifty Foods!*. Where do these farewells come from? Recall that we inserted an output statement to this effect in the destructor definition so that we could see when the destructor was invoked. The final two farewells happen when the *main()* terminates and the two local objects we created (*stock1* and *stock2*) pass from our plane of existence. Because such automatic variables go on the stack, the last object created is the first deleted, and the first created is the last deleted. (Note that *"NanoSmart"* originally was in *stock1* but later was transferred to *stock2*.)

But what about the first farewell to Nifty Foods? When we used the constructor to reassign the Nifty Food values to the *stock1* object, the program first created a temporary, nameless object having the provided values. Then those values were copied to the *stock1* object. Finally, when the temporary object expired, the program called the destructor function for it. So, the first Nifty Foods deleted is the temporary object, and the second Nifty Foods deleted is the *stock1* object. Incidentally, C++ doesn't really specify when a temporary object is disposed. This implementation (Borland C++ 3.1) deleted it as soon as it was no longer needed, while Turbo C++ 2.0 deleted the temporary object when the function terminated.

This little episode points out that there is a fundamental difference between the following two statements:

```
Stock stock2 = Stock ("Boffo Objects", 2, 2.0);
stock1 = Stock("Nifty Foods", 10, 50.0);    // temp object
```

The first statement is initialization; it creates an object with the indicated value. The second statement is assignment. It creates a temporary object, then copies it to an existing object. This clearly is less efficient than initialization.

TIP

If you can set object values either by initialization or by assignment, choose initialization. It is more efficient.

The *show()* output near the end of the program demonstrates that both object assignment and object resetting worked.

const Member Functions

Consider the following code snippets:

```
const Stock land = Stock("Kludgehorn Properties");
land.show();
```

With current C++, the compiler should object to the second line. Why? Because the code for *show()* fails to guarantee that it won't modify the invoking object. We've solved this kind of problem before by declaring a function's argument to be a *const* reference or a pointer to *const*. But here we have a syntax problem: the *show()* method doesn't have any arguments. Instead, the object it uses is provided implicitly by the method invocation. What's needed is a new syntax, one that says a function promises not to modify the invoking object. The C++ solution is to place the *const* keyword *after* the function parentheses. That is, the *show()* declaration should look like this:

```
void show() const;    // promises not to change invoking object
```

Similarly, the beginning of the function definition should look like this:

```
void stock::show() const    // promises not to change invoking object
```

Class functions declared and defined this way are called *const member functions*. Just as you should use *const* references and pointers as formal function arguments whenever appropriate, you should make class methods *const* whenever they don't modify the invoking object. We'll follow this rule from here on out.

Constructors and Destructors in Review

Now that we've gone through a few examples of constructors and destructors, you may wish to pause and assimilate what has passed. To help you, here is a summary of these methods.

A constructor is a special class member function that's called whenever an object of that class is created. A class constructor has the same name as its class, but, through the miracle of function overloading, you can have more than one constructor with the same name, providing each has its own signature, or argument list. Also, a constructor has no declared type. Usually, the constructor is used to initialize members of a class object. Your initialization should match the constructor's argument list. For instance, suppose the *Bozo* class has the following prototype for a class constructor:

```
Bozo(char * fname, char * lname);    // constructor prototype
```

Then you would use it to initialize new objects as follows:

```
Bozo bozetta = bozo("Bozetta", "Biggens");   // primary form
Bozo fufu("Fufu", "O'Dweeb");                // short form
Bozo *pc = new Bozo("Popo", "Le Peu");       // dynamic object
```

If a constructor has just one argument, that constructor is invoked if you initialize an object to a value having the same type as the constructor argument. For instance, suppose you have this constructor prototype:

```
Bozo(int age);
```

Then you can use any of the following forms to initialize an object:

```
Bozo dribble = bozo(44);     // primary form
Bozo roon(66);               // secondary form
Bozo tubby = 32;             // special form for one-argument constructors
```

Actually, the third example is a new point, not a review point, but it seemed like a nice time to tell you about it.

RULE

A constructor that can be used with a single argument allows you to use assignment syntax to initialize an object to a value:

Classname object = *value*;

The default constructor has no arguments, and it is used if you create an object without explicitly initializing it. If you fail to provide any constructors, the compiler defines a default constructor for you. Otherwise, you have to supply your own default constructor. It can have no arguments or else have default values for all arguments:

```
Bozo();                 // default constructor prototype
Bistro(const char * s = "Chez Zero");       // default for Bistro class
```

The program uses the default constructor for uninitialized objects:

```
Bozo bubi;         // use default
Bozo *pb = new Bozo;   // use default
```

Just as a program invokes a constructor when an object is created, it invokes a destructor when an object is destroyed. You can have only one destructor per class. It has no return type, not even *void;* it has no arguments; and its name is the class name preceded with a tilde. The *Bozo* class destructor, for example, has the following prototype:

```
~Bozo();              // class destructor
```

Class destructors become necessary when class constructors use *new.*

Knowing Your Objects: The *this* Pointer

There's still more to be done with the *Stock* class. So far each class member function has dealt with but a single object, which has been the object that invokes it. Sometimes, however, a method may need to deal with two objects, and doing so may involve a curious C++ pointer called *this.* Let's see how this need may unfold.

Although our class declaration displays data, it's deficient in analytic power. For instance, by looking at the *show()* output, you can tell which of your holdings has the greatest value, but the program can't tell because it can't access *total_val* directly. The most direct way of letting a program know about stored data is to provide methods to return values. Typically, you would use inline code for this:

```
class Stock
{
private:
      ...
      double total_val;
      ...
public:
      double total() { return total_val; }
      ...
};
```

This definition, in effect, makes *total_val* read-only memory as far as a direct program access is concerned.

By adding this function to the class declaration, we could let a program investigate a series of stocks to find the one with the greatest value. However, we'll take a different approach, mainly so you can learn about the *this* pointer. The approach is to define a member function that looks at two *Stock* objects and returns a reference to the larger of the two. Attempting to implement this approach raises some interesting questions, and we'll look into them now.

First, how do you provide the member function with two objects to compare? Suppose, for example, you decide to name the method *topval()*. Then the function call *stock1.topval()* accesses the data of the *stock1* object, while the message *stock2.topval()* accesses the data of the *stock2* object. If you want the method to compare *two* objects, you have to pass the second object as an argument. For efficiency, pass the argument by reference. That is, have the *topval()* method use a type *const Stock &* argument.

Second, how do you communicate the method's answer back to the calling program? The most direct way is to have the method return a reference to the object having the larger total value. Thus the comparison method should have the following prototype:

```
const Stock & topval(const Stock & s) const;
```

This function accesses one object implicitly, one object explicitly, and it returns a reference to one of those two objects. The *const* in the parentheses states that the function won't modify the explicitly accessed object, and the *const* following the parentheses states that the function won't modify the implicitly accessed object. Because the function will return one of the two *const* objects, the return type also has to be a *const* reference.

Suppose, then, that you want to compare *Stock* objects *stock1* and *stock2* and assign the one with the greater total value to the object *top*. You can use either of the following statements:

```
top = stock1.topval(stock2);
top = stock2.topval(stock1);
```

The first form accesses *stock1* implicitly and *stock2* explicitly, while the second accesses *stock1* explicitly and *stock2* implicitly. See Figure 9-3. Either way, the method compares the two objects and returns a reference to the one with the higher total value.

Actually, this notation is a bit confusing. It would be clearer if we could somehow use the relational operator > to compare the two objects. And you can do so with operator overloading, which we'll discuss in Chapter 10.

Meanwhile, there's still the implementation of *topval()* to attend to. And that raises a slight problem. Here's a partial implementation that highlights the problem:

```
const Stock & Stock::topval(const Stock & s) const
{
        if (s.total_val > total_val)
                return s;                // argument object
        else
                return ?????;            // invoking object
}
```

Here *s.total_val* is the total value for the object passed as an argument, and *total_val* is the total value for the object to which the message is sent. If *s.total_val* is greater than *total_val*, the function returns *s*. Otherwise, it returns the object used to evoke the

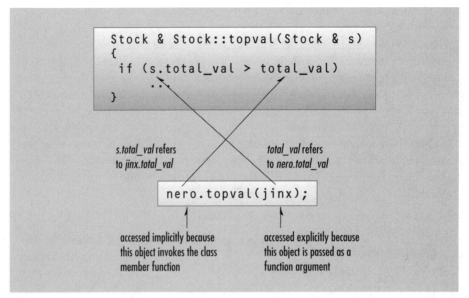

```
Stock & Stock::topval(Stock & s)
{
  if (s.total_val > total_val)
    ...
}
```

s.total_val refers
to jinx.total_val

total_val refers
to nero.total_val

```
nero.topval(jinx);
```

accessed implicitly because
this object invokes the class
member function

accessed explicitly because
this object is passed as a
function argument

Figure 9-3 Accessing two objects with a member function

method. (In OOP talk, that would be the object to which the *topval* message is sent.) The problem is, what do you call that object? If you make the call *stock1.topval(stock2)*, then *s* is a reference for *stock2* (that is, an alias for *stock2*), but there is no alias for *stock1*.

The C++ solution to this problem is a special pointer called *this*. The *this* pointer points to the object used to invoke a member function. Thus the function call *stock1.topval(stock2)* sets *this* to the address of the *stock1* object and makes that pointer available to the *topval()* method. Similarly, the function call *stock2.topval(stock1)* sets *this* to the address of the *stock2* object. In general, all class methods have a *this* pointer set to the address of the object invoking the method. Indeed, *total_val* in *topval()* is just shorthand notation for *this->total_val*. (Recall from Chapter 4 that you use the -> operator to access structure members via a pointer. The same is true for class members.) See Figure 9-4.

THE *this* POINTER

Each member function, including constructors and destructors, has a *this* pointer. The special property of the *this* pointer is that it points to the invoking object. If you use the *const* qualifier after the function argument parentheses, then you can't use *this* to change the object's value. Also, it is a *const* pointer, so you cannot make it point to some other object. (Early versions of C++, however, did allow you to assign another object to *this*.)

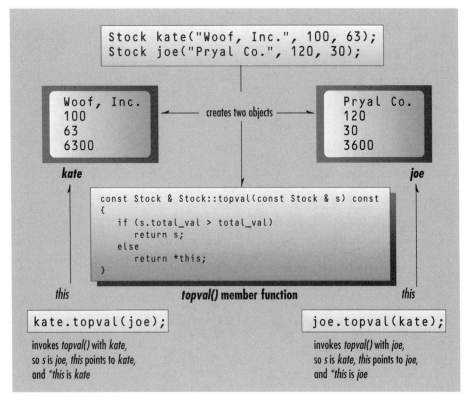

```
Stock kate("Woof, Inc.", 100, 63);
Stock joe("Pryal Co.", 120, 30);
```

Woof, Inc.
100
63
6300

◄— creates two objects —►

Pryal Co.
120
30
3600

kate

joe

```
const Stock & Stock::topval(const Stock & s) const
{
    if (s.total_val > total_val)
        return s;
    else
        return *this;
}
```

this

topval() member function

this

```
kate.topval(joe);
```

invokes *topval()* with *kate*,
so *s* is *joe*, *this* points to *kate*,
and **this* is *kate*

```
joe.topval(kate);
```

invokes *topval()* with *joe*,
so *s* is *kate*, *this* points to *joe*,
and **this* is *joe*

Figure 9-4 *this* points to the invoking object

What we want to return, however, is not *this*, because *this* is the address of the object. We want to return the object itself, and that is symbolized by **this*. (Recall that applying the dereferencing operator * to a pointer yields the value to which the pointer points.) Now we can complete the method definition by using **this* as an alias for the invoking object.

```
const Stock & Stock::topval(const Stock & s) const
{
    if (s.total_val > total_val)
        return s;              // argument object
    else
        return *this;          // invoking object
}
```

The fact that the return type is a reference means the returned object is the invoking object itself rather than a copy passed by the *return* mechanism. Listing 9-7 shows the new header file.

Listing 9-7 *stock2.h*

```
// stock2.h
#ifndef _STOCK2_H_
#define _STOCK2_H_

class Stock
{
private:
        char company[30];
        int shares;
        double share_val;
        double total_val;
        void set_tot() { total_val = shares * share_val; }
public:
        Stock();                    // default constructor
        Stock(const char * co, int n, double pr);
        ~Stock() {}                 // do-nothing destructor
        void buy(int num, double price);
        void sell(int num, double price);
        void update(double price);
        void show() const;
        const Stock & topval(const Stock & s) const;
};

#endif
```

Listing 9-8 presents the revised class methods file. It includes the new *topval()* method. Also, now that we've seen how the destructor method works, we'll replace it with a silent version.

Listing 9-8 *stock2.cpp*

```
// stock2.cpp  // Stock class methods
#include <iostream.h>
#include <stdlib.h>    // for exit()
#include <string.h> // for strcpy()
#include "stock2.h"

// constructors
Stock::Stock()
{
        strcpy(company, "no name");
        shares = 0;
        share_val = 0.0;
        total_val = 0.0;
}

Stock::Stock(const char * co, int n, double pr)
```

```
{
        strcpy(company, co);
        shares = n;
        share_val = pr;
        set_tot();
}

void Stock::buy(int num, double price)
{
        shares += num;
        share_val = price;
        set_tot();
}

void Stock::sell(int num, double price)
{
        if (num > shares)
        {
                cerr << "You can't sell more than you have!\n";
                exit(1);
        }
        shares -= num;
        share_val = price;
        set_tot();
}

void Stock::update(double price)
{
        share_val = price;
        set_tot();
}

void Stock::show() const
{
        cout << "Company: " << company
                << "  Shares: " << shares << '\n'
                << "  Share Price: $" << share_val
                << "  Total Worth: $" << total_val << '\n';
}

const Stock & Stock::topval(const Stock & s) const
{
        if (s.total_val > total_val)
                return s;
        else
                return *this;
}
```

Of course, we want to see if the *this* pointer works, and a natural place to use our new method is in a program with an array of objects, which leads us to the next topic.

An Array of Objects

Often, as with the *Stock* examples so far, you'll want to create several objects of the same class. You can create separate object variables, as we have done so far, but it may make more sense to create an array of objects. That may sound like a major leap into the unknown, but, in fact, you declare an array of objects the same way you would an array of any of the standard types:

```
Stock mystuff[4]; // creates an array of 4 Stock objects
```

Recall that a program always calls the default class constructor when creating class objects that aren't explicitly initialized. So this declaration requires either that we have no constructor defined, in which case the implicit do-nothing default constructor is used, or, as in our case, that we have an explicit default constructor defined. Each element—*mystuff[0], mystuff[1],* and so on—is a *Stock* object and thus can be used with the *Stock* methods:

```
mystuff[0].update();        // apply update() to 1st element
mystuff[3].show();          // apply show() to 4th element
Stock tops = mystuff[2].topval(mystuff[1]);
                            // compare 3rd and 2nd elements
```

You can use a constructor to initialize the array elements. In that case, you have to call the constructor for each individual element:

```
const int STKS = 4;
Stock stocks[STKS] = {
      Stock("NanoSmart", 12.5, 20),
      Stock("Boffo Objects", 200, 2.0),
      Stock("Monolithic Obelisks", 130, 3.25),
      Stock("Fleep Enterprises", 60, 6.5)
      };
```

Here we've used the standard form for initializing an array: a comma-separated list of values enclosed in braces. In this case, each value is represented by a call to the constructor method.

Listing 9-9 applies these principles to a short program that initializes four array elements, displays their contents, and tests the elements to find the one with the highest total value. Because *topval()* examines just two objects at a time, we use a *for* loop to examine the whole array. Use the header file and methods file shown in Listings 9-7 and 9-8.

Listing 9-9 *usestok2.cpp*

```
// usestok2.cpp -- use the Stock class
#include <iostream.h>
#include "stock2.h"

const int STKS = 4;
```

```
int main(void)
{
// create an array of initialized objects
        Stock stocks[STKS] = {
                Stock("NanoSmart", 12, 20.0),
                Stock("Boffo Objects", 200, 2.0),
                Stock("Monolithic Obelisks", 130, 3.25),
                Stock("Fleep Enterprises", 60, 6.5)
                };

        cout.precision(2);                          // #.## format
        cout.setf(ios::fixed, ios::floatfield);     // #.## format
        cout.setf(ios::showpoint);                  // #.## format

        cout << "Stock holdings:\n";
        for (int st = 0; st < STKS; st++)
                stocks[st].show();

        Stock top = stocks[0];
        for (st = 1; st < STKS; st++)
                top = top.topval(stocks[st]);
        cout << "\nMost valuable holding:\n";
        top.show();

        return 0;
}
```

Here is the output:

```
Stock holdings:
Company: NanoSmart  Shares: 12
  Share Price: $20.00  Total Worth: $240.00
Company: Boffo Objects  Shares: 200
  Share Price: $2.00  Total Worth: $400.00
Company: Monolithic Obelisks  Shares: 130
  Share Price: $3.25  Total Worth: $422.50
Company: Fleep Enterprises  Shares: 60
  Share Price: $6.50  Total Worth: $390.00

Most valuable holding:
Company: Monolithic Obelisks  Shares: 130
  Share Price: $3.25  Total Worth: $422.50
```

One thing to note is how most of the work has gone into designing the class. Once that's been done, writing the program itself is rather simple.

Incidentally, knowing about the *this* pointer makes it easier to see how C++ works under the skin. For instance the C++ front end *cfront* converts C++ programs to C programs. To handle method definitions, all it has to do is convert a method definition like

```
void Stock::show() const
{
```

continued on next page

continued from previous page

```
        cout << "Company: " << company
            << "  Shares: " << shares << '\n'
            << "  Share Price: $" << share_val
            << "  Total Worth: $" << total_val << '\n';
}
```

to the following:

```
void show(const Stock * const this)
{
        cout << "Company: " << this->company
            << "  Shares: " << this->shares << '\n'
            << "  Share Price: $" << this->share_val
            << "  Total Worth: $" << this->total_val << '\n';
}
```

That is, it converts a *Stock::* qualifier to a function argument that is a pointer to *Stock*, then uses the pointer to access class members.

Similarly, the front end would convert function calls like

```
top.show();
```

to:

```
show(&top);
```

In this fashion, the *this* pointer winds up being assigned the address of the invoking object. (The actual details may be more involved.)

Class Scope

Chapter 8 discussed file scope and block scope. A variable with file scope, recall, can be used anywhere in the file containing its definition, while a variable with block scope is local to the block containing its definition. Function names, too, can have file scope, but they never have block scope. C++ classes introduce a new kind of scope: *class scope*. Class scope applies to names defined in a class, such as the names of class data members and of class member functions. Items having class scope are known within the class but not outside the class. Thus you can use the same class member names in different classes without conflict: the *shares* member of the *Stock* class would be a distinct variable from the *shares* member of a *JobRide* class. Also, class scope means you can't access members of a class directly from the outside world. This is true even for *public* function members. That is, to invoke a public member function, you have to use an object:

```
Stock sleeper("Exclusive Ore", 100. 0.25;   // create object
sleeper.show();        // use object to invoke a member function
show();                // invalid -- can't call method directly
```

Similarly, we had to use the scope resolution operator when defining member functions:

```
void Stock::update(double price)
{
        ...
}
```

In short, within a class declaration or within a member function definition you can use an unadorned member name, as when *sell()* calls the *set_tot()* member function. Otherwise, you must use the direct membership operator (.) or the indirect membership operator (->) or the scope resolution operator (::), depending on the context, when using a class member name.

Sometimes it would be nice to have symbolic constants of class scope. For instance, the *Stock* class declaration used a literal 30 to specify the array size for *classname*. You might think the following would be a solution:

```
class Stock
{
private:
        const int Len = 30;    // won't work
        char company[Len];
        ...
```

However, as the comment indicates, this won't work. That's because declaring a class doesn't create storage for the data. Only creating objects causes memory to be allocated. A class declaration can't initialize member variables because such variables don't even exist until later, when an object is created.

You could declare *Len* this way:

```
const int Len;
```

Then each object would contain a *Len* member that would have to be initialized when the object was created. But the compiler needs to know the array size at compile time, so that won't work, either.

In many cases, enumerations (Chapter 4) can help. An enumeration given in a class declaration has class scope, so you can use enumerations to provide class scope symbolic names for integer constants. That is, you can start off the *Stock* declaration this way:

```
class Stock
{
private:
        enum {Len = 30};       // class-specific constant
        char company[Len];
        ...
```

Because we are using the enumeration merely to create a symbolic constant and don't contemplate creating variables of the enumeration type, we needn't provide an enumeration tag.

The ANSI/ISO C++ standards committee recently has introduced a namespace facility to help deal more generally with creating names of restricted scope. Chapter 14 discusses this facility.

An Abstract Data Type

The *Stock* class is pretty specific. Often, however, programmers define classes to represent more general concepts. For instance, classes are a good way to implement what computer scientists describe as *abstract data types,* or ADTs, for short. As the name suggests, an ADT describes a data type in a general fashion, without bringing in implementation details. Consider, for example, the *stack.* The stack is a way of storing data in which data is always added to or deleted from the top of the stack. C++ programs, for example, use a stack to manage automatic variables. As new automatic variables are generated, they are added to the top of the stack. When they expire, they are removed from a stack.

Let's describe the properties of a stack in a general, abstract way. First, a stack holds a number of items. It's a particular case of even a more general abstraction, the container. Next, a stack is characterized by the operations you can perform on one.

- You can create an empty stack.

- You can add an item to the top of a stack (*push* an item).

- You can remove an item from the top (*pop* an item).

- You can check to see if the stack is full.

- You can check to see if the stack is empty.

We can match this description with a class declaration in which the public member functions provide an interface representing the stack operations. The private data members will take care of storing the stack data.

The private section will have to commit itself to how to hold the data. For instance, we could use an ordinary array or a dynamically allocated array or some more advanced data structure, such as a linked list. The public interface, however, should hide the exact representation. Instead, it should be expressed in general terms such as creating a stack, pushing an item, and so on. Listing 9-10 shows one approach. It assumes that we've defined a *booly.h* file, as shown in Listing 9-11. The ANSI/ISO C++ committee has adopted a *bool* type (Chapter 3) that will make this unnecessary.

Listing 9-10 *stack.h*

```
// stack.h -- class declaration for the stack ADT
#ifndef _STACK_H_
#define _STACK_H_
#include "booly.h" // define Bool, False, True
typedef unsigned long Item;

class Stack
{
private:
```

```
      enum {MAX = 10};       // constant specific to class
      Item items[MAX];       // holds stack items
      int top;               // index for top stack item
public:
      Stack();
      Bool isempty() const;
      Bool isfull() const;
      // push() returns False if stack already is full, True otherwise
      Bool push(const Item & item); // add item to stack
      // pop() returns False if stack already is empty, True otherwise
      Bool pop(Item & item);        // pop top into item
};
#endif
```

COMPATIBILITY NOTE

Many implementations have defined some form of Boolean types for convenience, and it's possible the *booly.h* file could conflict with such a definition. If you experience a problem, use the built-in type or else try varying the spelling. For instance, you could change *Bool* to *BooL*.

Listing 9-11 *booly.h*

```
// booly.h -- Boolean definitions
// eventually to be replaced by new C++ bool type
#ifndef _BOOLY_H_
#define _BOOLY_H_
enum Bool {False, True}; // False = 0, True = 1
#endif
```

In this example, the private section shows that the stack is implemented using an array, but the public section doesn't reveal that fact. Thus, you can replace the array with, say, a dynamic array without changing the class interface. That means changing the stack implementation doesn't require that you recode programs using the stack. You would just recompile the stack code and link it with existing program code.

The interface is slightly redundant in that *pop()* and *push()* return information about the stack status (full or empty) instead of being type *void*. This provides the programmer a couple of options as to how to handle exceeding the stack limit or emptying the stack. He or she can use *isempty()* and *isfull()* to check before attempting to modify the stack, or else use the return value of *push()* and *pop()* to determine if the operation was successful.

Rather than define the stack in terms of some particular type, the class describes it in terms of a general *Item* type. In this case, the header file uses *typedef* to make *Item* the same as *unsigned long*. If you want, say, a stack of *double* or of a structure type, you can change the *typedef* and leave the class declaration and method definitions unaltered. Class templates (Chapter 13) provide a more powerful method for isolating the type of data stored from the class design.

Next, let's implement the class methods. Listing 9-12 shows one possibility.

Listing 9-12 *stack.cpp*

```cpp
// stack.cpp -- Stack member functions
#include "stack.h"
Stack::Stack() // create an empty stack
{
        top = 0;
}

Bool Stack::isempty() const
{
        return top == 0 ? True: False;
}

Bool Stack::isfull() const
{
        return top == MAX ? True: False;
}

Bool Stack::push(const Item & item)
{
        if (top < MAX)
        {
                items[top++] = item;
                return True;
        }
        else
                return False;
}

Bool Stack::pop(Item & item)
{
        if (top > 0)
        {
                item = items[--top];
                return True;
        }
        else
                return False;
}
```

The default constructor guarantees that all stacks are created empty. The code for *pop()* and *push()* guarantees that the top of the stack is kept track of properly. Guarantees like this are one of the things that make object-oriented programming more reliable. Suppose, instead, we created a separate array to represent the stack and an independent variable to represent the index of the top. Then it would be our responsibility to get the code right each time we created a new stack. And without the protection that private data offers, there's always the possibility of making some program blunder that alters data unintentionally.

Let's test this stack. Listing 9-13 models the life of a clerk who processes purchase orders from the top of his in-basket, using the LIFO (last in-first out) approach of a stack.

Listing 9-13 *stacker.cpp*

```
// stacker.cpp -- test Stack class
#include <iostream.h>
#include <ctype.h>
#include "stack.h"
int main(void)
{
        Stack st;        // create an empty stack
        char c;
        unsigned long po;
        cout << "Please enter A to add a purchase order,\n"
                << "P to process a PO, or Q to quit.\n";
        while (cin >> c && toupper(c) != 'Q')
        {
                while (cin.get() != '\n')
                        continue;                // get rid of rest of line
                if (!isalpha(c))
                {
                    cout << '\a';
                    continue;
                }
                switch(c)
                {
                        case 'A':
                        case 'a':        cout << "Enter a PO number to add: ";
                                         cin >> po;
                                         if (st.isfull())
                                                 cout << "stack already full\n";
                                         else
                                                 st.push(po);
                                         break;
                        case 'P':
                        case 'p':        if (st.isempty())
                                                 cout << "stack already empty\n";
                                         else {
                                                 st.pop(po);
                                                 cout << "PO #" << po << " popped\n";
                                                 break;
                                         }
                }
                cout << "Please enter A to add a purchase order,\n"
                        << "P to process a PO, or Q to quit.\n";
        }
        cout << "Bye\n";
        return 0;
}
```

The little *while* loop that gets rid of the rest of the line isn't needed here, but it will come in handy in a modification of this program in Chapter 13. Here's a sample run:

```
Please enter A to add a purchase order,
P to process a PO, or Q to quit.
A
Enter a PO number to add: 17885
Please enter A to add a purchase order,
P to process a PO, or Q to quit.
P
PO #17885 popped
Please enter A to add a purchase order,
P to process a PO, or Q to quit.
A
Enter a PO number to add: 17965
Please enter A to add a purchase order,
P to process a PO, or Q to quit.
A
Enter a PO number to add: 18002
Please enter A to add a purchase order,
P to process a PO, or Q to quit.
P
PO #18002 popped
Please enter A to add a purchase order,
P to process a PO, or Q to quit.
P
PO #17965 popped
Please enter A to add a purchase order,
P to process a PO, or Q to quit.
P
stack already empty
Please enter A to add a purchase order,
P to process a PO, or Q to quit.
Q
Bye
```

 # Summary

Object-oriented programming emphasizes how a program represents data. The first step to solving a programming problem using the OOP approach is to describe the data in terms of its interface with the program, specifying how the data is used. Next, design a class that implements the interface. Typically, private data members store the information, while public member functions, also called methods, provide the only access to the data. The class combines data and methods into one unit, and the private aspect accomplishes data hiding.

Usually, you separate the class declaration into two parts, typically kept in separate files. The class declaration proper goes into a header file, with the methods being represented by function prototypes. The source code that defines the member functions goes into a methods file. This approach separates the description of the interface from the details of the implementation. In principle, you need know only the public class interface to use the class. Of course, you can look at the implementation (unless it's been supplied to you in compiled form only), but your program shouldn't rely upon details of the implementation, such as knowing a particular value is stored as an *int*. As long as a program and a class communicate only through methods defining the interface, you are free to improve either part separately without worrying about unforeseen interactions.

A class is a user-defined type, and an object is an instance of a class. That means an object is a variable of that type or the equivalent of a variable, such as memory allocated by *new* according to the class specification. C++ tries to make user-defined types as similar as possible to standard types, so you can declare objects, pointers to objects, and arrays of objects. You can pass objects as arguments, return them as function return values, and assign one object to another of the same type. If you provide a constructor method, you can initialize objects when they are created. If you provide a destructor method, the program will execute that method when the object expires.

Each object holds its own copies of the data portion of a class declaration, but they share the class methods. If *mr_object* is the name of a particular object and *try_me()* is a member function, you invoke the member function by using the dot membership operator: *mr_object.try_me()*. OOP terminology describes this function call as sending a *try_me* message to the *mr_object* object. Any reference to class data members in the *try_me()* method will then apply to the data members of the *mr_object* object. Similarly, the function call *i_object.try_me()* would access the data members of the *i_object* object.

If you want a member function to act upon more than one object, you can pass additional objects to the method as arguments. If a method needs to refer explicitly to the object that evoked it, it can use the *this* pointer. The *this* pointer is set to the address of the evoking object, so **this* is an alias for the object itself.

Classes are well matched to describing abstract data types (ADTs). The public member function interface provides the services described by an ADT, and the class's private section and the code for the class methods provide an implementation hidden from clients of the class.

Review Questions

1. What is a class?

2. How does a class accomplish abstraction, encapsulation, and data hiding?

3. What is the relationship between an object and a class?

4. In what way, aside from being functions, are class function members different from class data members?

5. Define a class to represent a bank account. Data members should include the depositor's name, the account number (use a string), and the balance. Member functions should allow the following:

  ❧ Assigning starting values to the data members

  ❧ Displaying the depositor's name, account number, and balance

  ❧ Depositing an amount of money given by an argument

  ❧ Withdrawing an amount of money given by an argument

6. When are class constructors called? When are class destructors called?

7. Provide a constructor for the bank account class of question 5.

8. What is a default constructor and what's the advantage of having one?

9. Modify the *Stock* class so that it has member functions that return the values of the individual data members. Note: A member that returns the company name should not provide a weapon for altering the array. That is, it can't simply return a *char **. It could return a *const* pointer, or it could return a pointer to a copy of the array, manufactured by using *new*.

10. What are *this* and **this?*

Programming Exercises

1. Write a short program illustrating all the features of the class described in review question 5.

2. Do programming exercise 3 from Chapter 8, but replace the code shown there with an appropriate *golf* class declaration.

3. Consider the following structure declaration:
```
struct customer {
        char fullname[35];
        double payment;
};
```
Write a program that adds and removes *customer* structures from a stack, represented by a class declaration. Each time a customer is removed, his payment is added to a running total and the running total is reported.

4. Here's a class declaration:
```
class Move
{
private:
        double x;
        double y;
```

```
public:
        Move(double a = 0, double b = 0); // sets x, y to a, b
        showmove() const;       // shows current x, y values
        Move add(const Move & m) const;
// this function adds x of m to x of invoking object to get new x,
// adds y of m to y of invoking object to get new y, creates a new
// move object initialized to new x, y values and returns it
        reset(double a = 0, double b = 0); // resets x,y to a, b
};
```

Supply member function definitions and a program that exercises the class.

5. We can describe a *simple* list as follows:

   ❧ A simple list can hold zero or more items of some particular type.

   ❧ You can create an empty list.

   ❧ You can add items to a list.

   ❧ You can determine if the list is empty.

   ❧ You can determine if the list is full.

   ❧ You can visit each item in a list and perform some action upon it.

As you can see, this list really is simple, not allowing insertion or deletion, for example. The main use of such a list is to provide a simplified programming project. In this case, create a class matching this description. You can implement the list as an array or, if you're familiar with the data type, as a linked list. But the public interface should not depend on your choice. That is, the public interface should not have array indices, pointers to nodes, and so on. It should be expressed in the general concepts of creating a list, adding an item to the list, and so on. The usual way to handle visiting each item and performing an action is to use a function that takes a function pointer as an argument:

```
void visit(void (*pf)(Item &));
```

Here *pf* points to a function that takes a reference to *Item* argument, where *Item* is the type for items in the list. The *visit()* function would apply this function to each item in the list.

You also should provide a short program utilizing your design.

CHAPTER 10

WORKING WITH CLASSES

You will learn about the following in this chapter:

- ◇ Operator overloading
- ◇ Friend functions
- ◇ Overloading the << operator for output
- ◇ State members
- ◇ Using *rand()* to generate random values
- ◇ Automatic conversions and type casts for classes
- ◇ Class conversion functions

C++ classes are feature-rich, complex, and powerful. In Chapter 9 you began a journey toward object-oriented programming by learning to define and use a simple class. You saw how a class defines a data type by defining the type of data to be used to represent an object and by also defining, through member functions, the operations that can be performed with that data. And you learned about two special member functions, the constructor and the destructor, that manage creating and discarding objects made to a class specification. This chapter will take you a few steps further in the exploration of class properties. It concentrates on class design techniques rather than on general principles. You'll probably find some of the features covered here straightforward, some a bit more subtle. To best understand these new features, you should try the examples and experiment with them. What happens if I use a regular argument instead of a reference argument for this function? What happens if I leave something out of a destructor? Don't be afraid to make mistakes, for usually you can learn more from unraveling an error than by doing something correctly, but by rote. (On the other hand, don't assume that a maelstrom of mistakes inevitably leads to incredible insight.) In the end, you'll be rewarded with a fuller understanding of how C++ works and of what C++ can do for you.

This chapter starts with operator overloading, which lets you use standard C++ operators such as = and + with class objects. Then it examines *friends,* the C++ mechanism for letting nonmember functions access private data. Finally, it looks at how you can instruct C++ to perform automatic type conversions with classes. As you go through this and the next chapter, you'll gain a greater appreciation for the roles class constructors and class destructors play. Also, you'll see some of the stages you may go through as you develop and improve a class design.

One difficulty with learning C++, at least by the time you've gotten this far into the subject, is that there is an awful lot to remember. And it's unreasonable to expect to remember it all until you've logged enough experience on which to hang your memories. Learning C++, in this respect, is like learning a feature-laden word processor or spreadsheet program. No one feature is that daunting, but, in practice, most people really know well only those features they use regularly, such as searching for text or italicizing. You may recall having read somewhere how to generate alternative characters or create a table of contents, but those skills probably won't be part of your daily repertoire until you find yourself in a situation in which you need them frequently. Probably the best approach to absorbing the wealth of material in this chapter is to begin incorporating just some of these new features into your own C++ programming. As your experiences enhance your understanding and appreciation of these features, begin adding other C++ features. As Bjarne Stroustrup, the creator of C++, suggested at a C++ conference for professional programmers: "Ease yourself into the language. Don't feel you have to use all of the features, and don't try to use them all on the first day."

Operator Overloading

Let's look at a technique for giving object operations a prettier look. *Operator overloading* is another example of C++ polymorphism. In Chapter 8 you saw how C++ enables you to define several functions having the same name as long as they have different signatures (argument lists). That was function overloading, or functional polymorphism. Its purpose is to let you use the same function name for the same basic operation even though you are applying the operation to different data types. (Imagine how awkward English would be if you had to use a different verb form for each different type of object—lift_lft your left foot, but lift_sp your spoon.) Operator overloading extends the overloading concept to operators, letting you assign multiple meanings to C++ operators. Actually, many C++ (and C) operators already are overloaded. For instance, the * operator, when applied to an address, yields the value stored at that address. But applying * to two numbers yields the product of the values. C++ uses the number and type of operands to decide which action to take.

C++ lets you extend operator overloading to user-defined types, permitting you, say, to use the + symbol to add two objects. Again, the compiler will use the number and type of operands to determine which definition of addition to use. Overloaded operators often can make code look more natural. For instance, a common computing task is adding two arrays. Usually this winds up looking like the following *for* loop:

```
for (int i = 0; i < 20; i++)
        evening[i] = sam[i] + janet[i];        // add element by element
```

But in C++ you can define a class that represents arrays and that overloads the + operator so that you can do this:

```
evening = sam + janet;                          // add two array objects
```

We'll do just that in Chapter 12. (Why not now? Because you also have to overload the [] operator, and that's a bit more involved than overloading the + operator.) This simple addition notation conceals the mechanics and emphasizes what is essential, and that is another OOP goal.

To overload an operator, you use a special function form called an *operator function*. An operator function has the form,

operator*op*(*argument-list*)

where *op* is the symbol for the operator being overloaded. The *op* has to be a valid C++ operator; you can't just make up a new symbol. For instance, you can't have an *operator@*() function because C++ has no @ operator. But the *operator+*() function would overload the + operator. Suppose, for example, that you have a *salesperson* class for which you define an *operator+*() member function to overload the + operator so that it adds sales figures of one *salesperson* object to another. Then, if *district2, sid,* and *sara* are objects of the *salesperson* class, you would be able to write this equation:

```
district2 = sid + sara;
```

The compiler, recognizing the operands as belonging to the *salesperson* class, will replace the operator with the corresponding operator function:

```
district2 = sid.operator+(sara);
```

The function will then use the *sid* object implicitly (because it invoked the method) and the *sara* object explicitly (because it's passed as an argument) to calculate the sum, which it then returns. Of course, the nice part is that you can use the nifty + operator notation instead of the clunky function notation.

C++ imposes some restrictions on operator overloading, but they're easier to understand after you've seen how overloading works. So let's develop a few examples first to clarify the process, then discuss the limitations.

A Vector Class with Operator Overloading

To show how overloading is useful in real applications, we'll develop an example based on vectors. Not only will the example present operator overloading, it will also illustrate further aspects of class design, such as incorporating two different ways of describing the same thing into an object. Even if you don't care for vectors, you'll be able to use many of the new techniques in other contexts. A vector, as the term is used in engineering and physics, is a quantity having both a magnitude (size) and a direction. For instance, if you push something, the effect depends on how hard you push (the magnitude) and in what direction you push. A push in one direction could save a tottering vase, while a push in the opposite direction could hasten its rush to doom. To fully describe the motion of your car, you should give both the speed (the magnitude) and the direction; arguing with the highway patrol that you were driving under the speed limit carries little weight if you were traveling in the wrong direction. (Immunologists and computer scientists may use the term vector differently; ignore them.) The note on Vectors will tell you more about vectors, but understanding them completely isn't necessary for following the C++ aspects of the examples.

VECTORS

You're a worker bee that's discovered a marvelous nectar cache. You rush back to the hive and announce you've found nectar 120 yards away. "Not enough information," buzz the other bees. "You have to tell us the direction, too!" You answer, "It's 30 degrees north of the sun direction." Knowing both the distance (magnitude) and the direction, the other bees rush to the sweet site. Bees know vectors.

Many quantities involve both a magnitude and a direction. The effect of a push, for instance, depends on both its strength and direction. Moving an object on a computer screen involves a distance and a direction. You can describe such things using vectors. For instance, you can describe moving (displacing) an object on the screen with a vector, which you can visualize as an arrow drawn from the starting position to the final position. The length of the vector is its magnitude, and that describes how far the point has been displaced. The orientation of the arrow describes the direction. See Figure 10-1. A vector representing such a change in position is called a *displacement vector*.

Now you're Lhanappa, the great mammoth hunter. Scouts report a mammoth herd 14.1 kilometers to the northwest. But, because of a southeast wind, you don't want to approach from the southeast. So you go 10 kilometers west, then 10 kilometers north, approaching the herd from the south. You know these two displacement vectors bring you to the same location as the single 14.1-kilometer vector pointing northwest. Lhanappa, the great mammoth hunter, also knows how to add vectors.

Adding two vectors has a simple geometric interpretation. First, draw one vector. Then draw the second vector starting from the arrow-end of the first vector. Finally, draw a vector from the starting point of the first vector to the end point of the second vector. This third vector represents the sum of the first two. See Figure 10-2. Note that the length of the sum can be less than the sum of the individual lengths.

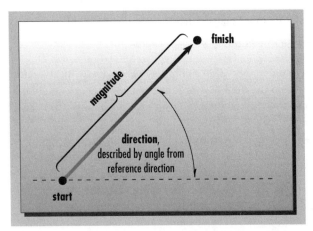

Figure 10-1 Describing a displacement with a vector

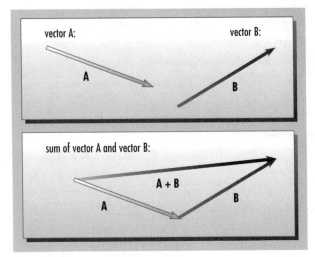

Figure 10-2 Adding two vectors

Vectors make a natural choice for operator overloading. First, you can't represent a vector with a single number, so it makes sense to create a class to represent vectors. Second, vectors have analogs to ordinary arithmetic operations such as addition and subtraction. This parallel suggests overloading the corresponding operators so you can use them with vectors.

To keep things simple, we'll implement a two-dimensional vector, such as a screen displacement, instead of a three-dimensional vector, such as might represent movement of a helicopter or a gymnast. You need just two numbers to describe a two-dimensional vector, but you have a choice of what set of two numbers:

❧ You can describe a vector by its magnitude (length) and direction (an angle).

❧ You can represent the vector by its *x* and *y* components.

The components are a horizontal vector (the *x* component) and a vertical vector (the *y* component), which add up to the final vector. For instance, you can describe a motion as moving a point 30 units to the right and 40 units up. See Figure 10-3. That motion puts the point at the same spot as moving 50 units at an angle of 53.1° from the horizontal. Therefore a vector with a magnitude of 50 and an angle of 53.1° is equivalent to a vector having a horizontal component of 30 and a vertical component of 40. What counts with displacement vectors is where you start and where you end up, not the exact route taken to get there. This choice of representation is basically the same thing we covered with the Chapter 7 program that converted between rectangular and polar coordinates.

Sometimes one form is more convenient, sometimes the other, so we'll incorporate both representations into the class description. See the note on Multiple Representations and Classes coming up shortly. Also, we'll design the class so that if you alter one representation of a vector, the object automatically updates the other representation. The ability to build such intelligence into an object is another C++ class virtue. Listing 10-1 presents a preliminary class declaration that doesn't yet include operator overloading.

Listing 10-1 *vector0.h*

```
// vector0.h -- vector class before operator overloading
#ifndef _VECTOR0_H_
#define _VECTOR0_H_
class Vector
{
private:
        double x;                         // horizontal value
        double y;                         // vertical value
        double mag;                       // length of vector
        double ang;                       // direction of vector
        void set_mag(void);
        void set_ang(void);
public:
        Vector(void);
        Vector(double h, double v);       // set x, y values
        ~Vector(void);
        void set_by_polar(double m, double a);
        double xval() const {return x;}   // report x value
        double yval() const {return y;}   // report y value
        double magval() const {return mag;} // report magnitude
        double angval() const {return ang;} // report angle
        void show_polar(void) const; // show polar values
        void show_vector(void) const ;    // show rectangular values
};
#endif
```

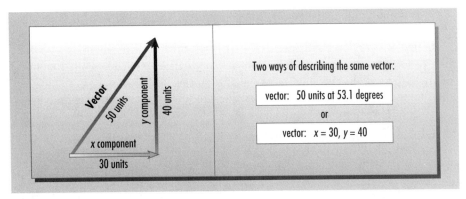

Figure 10-3 *x* and *y* components of a vector

Notice that the four functions that report component values are defined in the class declaration. This automatically makes them inline functions. The fact that these functions are so short makes them excellent candidates for inlining. None of them should alter object data, so they are declared using the *const* modifier. As you may recall from Chapter 9, this is the syntax for declaring a function that doesn't modify the object it implicitly accesses.

MULTIPLE REPRESENTATIONS AND CLASSES

Quantities having different, but equivalent, representations are common. For example, you can measure gasoline consumption in miles per gallon, as they do in the United States, or in liters per 100 kilometers, as they do in Europe. You can represent a number in string form or numeric form, and you can represent intelligence as an IQ or in kiloturkeys. Classes lend themselves nicely to encompassing different aspects and representations of an entity in a single object. First, you can store multiple representations in one object. Second, you can write the class functions so that assigning values for one representation automatically assigns values for the other representation(s). For instance, the *set_by_polar()* method for the *Vector* class sets the magnitude and angle members to the function arguments, but it also sets the *x* and *y* members. By handling conversions internally, a class can help you think of a quantity in terms of its essential nature rather than in terms of its representation.

This particular class declaration emphasizes the rectangular coordinate approach, with a class constructor that takes arguments representing the horizontal and vertical values. The constructor implementation will call the private functions *set_mag()* and *set_ang()* to set the corresponding magnitude and angle values. However, if you want to specify a vector by its polar coordinates (magnitude and angle), you can use the *set_by_polar()* method. Provide the method with magnitude and angle arguments, and it sets the *x* and *y* horizontal values. Also, the declaration provides methods for displaying both vector representations.

You may have wondered why we didn't provide a third constructor, one that initializes a vector using the magnitude and angle values. The problem is that magnitude and angle require the same function signature *(double, double)* as *x* and *y*, but C++ requires distinct function signatures for overloading. So we have a choice of providing a constructor for one or the other representation, but not both. Later, we'll refine this example and show a way around that problem.

Note that it is the public interface, not the private data representation, that shows the class deals with both representations. It isn't really necessary to simultaneously store both representations in the private section. Instead, for instance, the private section of the class could store just the rectangular representation. In that case, functions like *show_polar()* would calculate the polar values instead of just looking them up. This would slow up the *show_polar()* function, but it would speed up the constructor, for it would just have to construct the rectangular coordinates. Also, this approach would make a *Vector* object smaller, since it would hold less data. Which approach is better depends on what a program does. If it has to make frequent conversions from polar to rectangular representations and vice versa, then storing both forms most likely is the better choice. If a program needs polar forms only rarely, then storing just the rectangular coordinates makes more sense. As long as you kept the same public interface, you could use different implementations with different programs, matching the implementation to a program's needs.

Overloading the + Operator

Meanwhile, let's add operator overloading. Adding two vectors is simple in rectangular coordinates. Just add the two *x* components together to get the new *x* component and add the two *y* components together to get the new *y* component. Here is a sample prototype for a class operator overloading method (it goes into the class declaration) and its implementation (it goes into the class member function file):

```
Vector operator+(const Vector & b) const;          // prototype
Vector Vector::operator+(const Vector & b) const    // definition
{
        double sx, sy;
        sx = x + b.x;                   // x component of sum
        sy = y + b.y;                   // y component of sum
        Vector sum = Vector(sx, sy);
        return sum;
}
```

The prototype defines a function named *operator+()*. The function returns a *Vector* and it takes a *Vector* argument. To save time and memory, we pass the vector by reference (type *Vector &*), making *b* an alias for the vector passed to the function. Because the function should not alter the value of the vectors it is adding, we declare the argument as a *const* type and declare the function a *const* method. Because *operator+()* is a class method, it uses the invoking object implicitly. For instance, suppose *move1* and *move2* are two vectors and that we use the *operator+()* function to add them:

```
Vector q = move1.operator+(move2);
```

The *operator+()* function definition contains the following statement:

```
sx = x + b.x;                    // x component of sum
```

In this statement, the term *b.x* refers to the object passed as an argument (*move2*, in this case), and *x* refers to the object invoking the member function (*move1*, in this case), making the statement equivalent to the following:

```
sx = move1.x + move2.x;              // x component of sum
```

After calculating the *x* and *y* components of the sum, the method uses the *Vector(sx,sy)* constructor to initialize the vector *sum* to the proper values:

```
Vector sum = Vector(sx, sy);
```

As you'll see soon, this constructor also sets the *mag* and *ang* members. Thus *sum* is a *Vector* object having both its rectangular representation and its polar representation set to the correct values. Then the *operator+()* function returns the *sum* vector to the calling program.

You may wonder why the function uses reference arguments but doesn't return a reference. After all, if reference arguments save time and memory, shouldn't a reference return value do the same? The answer is yes, returning a reference can save time and memory. However, there is a more important consideration. The object *sum* is a local variable, so it expires when the function terminates. Thus a returned reference would be a reference to an object that no longer exists. Returning *sum* instead of a reference to *sum* means the value of *sum* gets copied and saved, which is much more useful.

TIP

Don't return a reference to a local variable or other temporary object.

So far, *operator+()* looks like a regular class member function with a funny name. Here's where C++ gets cute. As we indicated earlier, C++ offers an alternative syntax for the function call that makes it look as if you were using an operator. The alternative syntax for

```
Vector q = move1.operator+(move2);   // function call syntax
```

is this:

```
Vector q = move1 + move2;            // alternative syntax
```

Both mean the same thing, but the second form is easier on the eyes and on the mind, and it is the one we'll use.

Let's take one more look at the planning steps in overloading the + operator for the *Vector* class:

❧ Create a member function named *operator+()*.

❧ Addition requires two operands. Invoking the function with an object provides one operand, so use an argument to provide the second operand. This operand can be type *Vector,* or, in the interests of efficiency, type *const Vector &*.

❧ The sum of two *Vector* objects is also a *Vector* object, so give the function a *Vector* return type. (Don't use a reference in this case.)

❧ Put the following prototype in the class declaration:

```
Vector operator+(const Vector & b) const;            // prototype
```

❧ Use the following function heading in the methods definition file:

```
Vector Vector::operator+(const Vector & b) const     // definition
```

❧ Write code to handle the intended operation.

At this point, if you're programming a Bobo the Space Barbarian game, you can write code like the following:

```
#include <iostream.h>
#include "vector.h"                         // class declaration
int main (void)
{
    ...
    Vector movebobo1(20,30);
    Vector movebobo2(50, 10);
    Vector bobo = movebobo1 + movebobo2;    // add 2 vectors
    bobo.showpolar();                       // display result
    ...
}
```

But, having gone this far, it's worth the extra effort to add a few more features to the class declaration. In particular, we'll investigate how to overload an overloaded operator and when friends are useful for overloading.

More Refinement: Overloading an Overloaded Operator

Let's start by overloading the - operator. In ordinary C++, this operator already has two meanings. First, when used with two operands, it's the subtraction operator. The subtraction operator is termed a *binary* operator because it has exactly two operands. Second, when used with one operand, as in -*x*, it's a minus sign. This form is termed a *unary* operator, meaning it has exactly one operand. Both operations—subtraction and sign reversal—make sense for vectors, too, so we'll extend them to the *Vector* class, beginning with subtraction. To subtract vector B from vector A, you just subtract components, so the definition for overloading subtraction is quite similar to the one for addition:

```
Vector operator-(const Vector & b) const;          // prototype
Vector Vector::operator-(const Vector & b) const    // definition
{
        double dx, dy;
        dx = x - b.x;
        dy = y - b.y;
        Vector diff = Vector(dx, dy);
        return diff;
}
```

Next, let's overload the unary minus operator, which takes just one operand. Applying this operator to a regular number, as in -*x*, changes the sign of the value. We'll want to define it so that applying it to a vector reverses the sign of each component. More precisely, we'll have the function return a new vector that is the reverse of the original. (In polar terms, negation leaves the magnitude unchanged, but reverses the direction. Many politicians with little or no mathematical training nonetheless have an intuitive mastery of this operation.) Here are the prototype and definition for overloading negation:

```
Vector operator-() const;
Vector Vector::operator-() const
{
        double nx, ny;
        nx = -x;
        ny = -y;
        Vector neg = Vector(nx, ny);
        return neg;
}
```

Note that now there are two separate definitions for *operator-()*. That's fine, for the two definitions have different signatures. You can define both binary and unary versions of the - operator because C++ provides both binary and unary versions of that operator to begin with. An operator having only a binary form, such as division (/), can only be overloaded as a binary operator.

RULE

Because operator overloading is implemented with functions, you can overload the same operator many times, as long as each operator function has a distinct signature and as long as each operator function has the same number of operands as the corresponding built-in C++ operator.

As with overloading functions, you should use sensible restraint in overloading operators. For instance, don't overload the * operator so that it swaps the components of a *Vector* object. Nothing in the notation would suggest what the operator did, so it would be better to define a class method with an explanatory name like *swap()*.

Friends and Operator Overloading

As you've seen, C++ controls access to the private portions of a class object. Usually public class methods serve as the only access, but this restriction sometimes is too rigid to fit particular programming problems. In such cases C++ provides another form of access, the friend. Friends come in three varieties:

- Friend functions
- Friend classes
- Friend member functions

By making a function a friend to a class, you allow the function the same access privileges that a member function of the class has. We'll look into friend functions now, leaving the other two varieties to Chapter 14.

Before seeing how to make friends, let's look into why they might be needed. Often overloading a binary operator (one with two arguments) for a class generates a need for friends. Multiplying a vector by a real number provides just such a situation, so let's study that case.

In visual terms, multiplying a vector by a number makes the vector longer or shorter by that factor. So multiplying a vector by 3 produces a vector with three times the length, but still pointed in the same direction. It's easy to translate that image into how the class represents a vector. In polar terms, multiply the magnitude and leave the angle alone. In rectangular terms, you multiply a vector by a number by multiplying its x and y components separately by the number. That is, if a vector has components of 5 and 12, multiplying by 3 makes the components 15 and 36. Here are the prototype (goes in the class declaration) and the implementation (goes in the methods file) for multiplication:

```
Vector operator*(double n) const;         // prototype
// multiplies invoking vector by n
Vector Vector::operator*(double n) const  // definition
{
        double mx, my;
        mx = n * x;
        my = n * y;
        Vector mult = Vector(mx, my);
        return mult;
}
```

This code works fine for multiplying a vector times a number, but it fails for multiplying a number times a vector! To see this, first consider multiplying a vector times a number:

```
Vector borge = piano * 2.0;               // valid code
```

This translates to the following function call:

```
Vector borge = piano.operator*(2.0);
```

That statement requires that *operator*()* be a member function of the *Vector* class, for it is invoked by a *Vector* object. It also requires that the function take a type *double* argument. These two requirements match the function just defined, so the program automatically uses that definition.

But suppose you reverse the order of the operands while writing a program:

```
Vector borge = 2.0 * piano;                   // not supported
```

That would correspond to a meaningless function call:

```
Vector borge = 2.0.operator*(piano); // nonsense
```

That is, this demands a function that is a member of the *double* class (which doesn't even exist) and that takes a type *Vector* argument. But our definition of multiplication requires that a *Vector* object (piano, in this case) be the *first* operand and the *double* value (2.0) be the second operand.

One way around this difficulty is to tell everyone (and to remember yourself) that you can only write *piano * 2.0* but never write *2.0 * piano*. This is a programmer-friendly, user-beware solution, and that's not what OOP is about.

Can you write a second member function to handle this reverse-order problem? No, you can't, because the invoking object is always the *first* operand; the *piano* object *must* come before the *2.0* if you use a member function. What you need is a *nonmember* function like the following:

```
Vector operator*(double n, const Vector & a);
```

Because it is an ordinary, nonmember function, you don't need an object to invoke it. For nonmember functions, C++ interprets the first argument to an *operator+()* function as the left operand of the + operator and the second argument as the right operand. That means the expression

```
2.0 * piano
```

becomes the following function call:

```
operator+(2.0, piano);
```

This appears to be just what we need, but there is a big problem: nonmember functions don't access the private data of an object. Here's where friend functions come into play.

Making Friends

A *friend function* is a nonmember function that is allowed access to an object's private section. To indicate that a function is a friend, declare the function in the class declaration using the keyword *friend*. In this particular case, place the following prototype in the *Vector* declaration:

```
friend Vector operator*(double n, const Vector & a);      //nonmember friend
```

Note that a friend function has to supply an object explicitly, by an argument. You use the *friend* keyword only in the prototype found in the class declaration. You don't use it in the function definition.

The simplest way to implement this particular friend function is to have it reverse the order of its arguments and then call the original function:

```
Vector operator*(double n, const Vector & a)
{
        return a * n;          // calls original operator function
}
```

Thus the friend function translates

```
Vector borge = 2.0 * piano;          // now supported
```

to the following:

```
Vector borge = piano * 2.0;
```

Using a friend function to reverse the operand order is a common and useful technique for overloading an operator that takes two different types of operands.

TIP

If you want to overload an operator for a class and you want to use the operator with a nonclass term as the first operand, you have to use a friend function to reverse the operand order.

By the way, we didn't have this kind of problem when defining the *operator+()* member function because, in that case, *both* arguments were type *Vector,* so either could come first.

Friends vs. Class Member Functions

Incidentally, you can define all the operator functions as friend functions. In that case, each binary operator function would require two *Vector* arguments, and the unary *operator-()* function would take a single *Vector* argument. (A friend function always requires one more argument than the equivalent member function; the extra argument explicitly represents the object that a member function uses implicitly.)

For instance, you can define subtraction this way:

```
// prototype
friend Vector operator-(const Vector & a, const Vector & b);
// definition
Vector operator-(const Vector & a, const Vector & b)
{
        double dx, dy;
        dx = a.x - b.x;
        dy = a.y - b.y;
        Vector diff = Vector(dx, dy);
        return diff;
}
```

Calling this version would look different from calling the first version if you used function notation:

```
a = b.operator-(c);    // - defined as class method
a = operator-(b, c);   // - defined as friend function
```

But either definition would let you use the same operator notation:

```
a = b - c;                     // permitted by either definition
```

There is an advantage to using the friend method if conversions to the *Vector* class are available. We'll return to this point later in the chapter when we discuss type conversions.

ARE FRIENDS UNFAITHFUL TO OOP?

At first glance it may seem that friends violate the OOP principle of data hiding, for the friend mechanism allows nonmember functions to access private data. However, that's an overly narrow view. Instead, think of friend functions as part of an extended interface for a class. For instance, from a conceptual point of view, multiplying a *double* times a *Vector* is pretty much the same as multiplying a *Vector* times a *double*. That the first requires a friend function while the second can be done with a member function is the result of C++ syntax, not of a deep conceptual difference. By using both a friend function and a class method, we can express either operation with the same user interface. Also, keep in mind that only a class declaration can decide which functions are friends, so the class declaration still controls which functions access private data. In short, class methods and friends are just two different mechanisms for expressing a class interface.

Defining the *Vector* Class: Nearly the Final Version

Now that we have the operator functions ready, we can put together a full *Vector* class declaration. Listing 10-2 presents the complete declaration for the *Vector* class.

Listing 10-2 *vector1.h*

```
// vector1.h -- Vector class, introduce operator overloading
#ifndef _VECTOR1_H_
#define _VECTOR1_H_
class Vector
{
private:
        double x;                      // horizontal value
        double y;                      // vertical value
        double mag;                    // length of vector
        double ang;                    // direction of vector
        void set_mag(void);
```

continued on next page

continued from previous page

```
            void set_ang(void);
public:
        Vector(void);
        Vector(double h, double v);
    ~Vector(void);
        double xval() const {return x;}       // report x value
        double yval() const {return y;}       // report y value
        double magval() const {return mag;}   // report magnitude
        double angval() const {return ang;}   // report angle
        void set_by_polar(double m, double a);
        void show_polar(void);                // show polar values
        void show_vector(void);               // show rectilinear values
// operator overloading
        Vector operator+(const Vector & b) const;
        Vector operator-(const Vector & b) const;
        Vector operator-() const;
        Vector operator*(double n) const;
// friend function
        friend Vector operator*(double n, const Vector & a);
};
#endif
```

Listing 10-3 defines the class member functions declared in Listing 10-2. Note how the constructor functions and the *set_by_polar()* function each set both the rectangular and the polar representations of the vector. Thus either set of values is available immediately without further calculation should you need them. Also, as mentioned in Chapters 4 and 7, C++'s built-in math functions use angles in radians, so we've built conversion to and from degrees into the methods. The implementation hides such things as converting from polar coordinates to rectangular coordinates or converting radians to degrees from the user. All the user needs to know is that the class uses angles in degrees and that it makes a vector available in two equivalent representations.

These design decisions follow the OOP tradition of having the class interface concentrate on the essentials (the abstract model) while hiding the details. Thus when you use the *Vector* class, you can think about a vector's general features, such as that they can represent displacements and that you can add two vectors. Whether you express a vector in component notation or in magnitude, direction notation becomes secondary, for you can set a vector's values and display them in whichever format is most convenient at the time.

By the way, these definitions use math functions, and some C++ systems don't automatically search the math library. For instance, some UNIX systems require that you do the following:

```
$ CC source_file(s) -lm
```

The *-lm* option instructs the linker to search the math library. So, when you eventually compile programs using the *Vector* class, if you get a message about undefined externals, try the *-lm* option or check to see if your system requires something similar.

Listing 10-3 *vector1.cpp*

```cpp
// vector1.cpp -- methods for Vector class
#include <iostream.h>
#include <math.h>
#include "vector1.h"
const double Rad_to_deg = 57.2957795130823;

// private methods
// calculates magnitude from x and y
void Vector::set_mag(void)
{
        mag = sqrt(x * x + y * y);
}

// calculates angle from x and y
void Vector::set_ang(void)
{
        if (x == 0.0 && y == 0.0)
                ang = 0.0;
        else
                ang = atan2(y, x);
}

// public methods
Vector::Vector(void)  // default constructor
{
        x = y = mag = ang = 0.0;
}

// constructs a Vector from rectangular coordinates
Vector::Vector(double h, double v)
{
        x = h;
        y = v;
        set_mag();
        set_ang();
}

Vector::~Vector(void) // destructor
{
}

// sets Vector members from polar coordinates
void Vector::set_by_polar(double m, double a)
{
        mag = m;
        ang = a / Rad_to_deg;
        x = m * cos (a);
        y = m * sin (a);
}
```

continued on next page

continued from previous page

```cpp
// shows magnitude and direction of vector
void Vector::show_polar(void)
{
        cout << "(" << mag << ", ";
        cout << ang * Rad_to_deg << ")\n";
}

// shows x and y components of vector
void Vector::show_vector(void)
{
        cout << "(" << x << ", " << y << ")\n";
}

// operator overloading
// add two Vectors
Vector Vector::operator+(const Vector & b) const
{
        double sx, sy;
        sx = x + b.x;
        sy = y + b.y;
        Vector sum = Vector(sx, sy);
        return sum;
}

// subtract Vector b from a
Vector Vector::operator-(const Vector & b) const
{
        double dx, dy;
        dx = x - b.x;
        dy = y - b.y;
        Vector diff = Vector(dx, dy);
        return diff;
}

// reverse sign of Vector
Vector Vector::operator-() const
{
        double nx, ny;
        nx = -x;
        ny = -y;
        Vector neg = Vector(nx, ny);
        return neg;
}

// multiply vector by n
Vector Vector::operator*(double n) const
{
        double mx, my;
        mx = n * x;
        my = n * y;
        Vector mult = Vector(mx, my);
        return mult;
}
```

```
// friend method
// multiply n by Vector a
Vector operator*(double n, const Vector & a)
{
        return a * n;
}
```

The next step, of course, is to use these definitions in a program. Listing 10-4 does that using vectors representing movements. It demonstrates using both the rectangular and polar representations, and it shows addition and multiplication. All in all, it is pretty dull, but the test program for the next refinement will investigate the fabulous random walk problem. Remember to compile Listing 10-3 along with Listing 10-4.

Listing 10-4 *use_vect.cpp*

```
// use_vect.cpp -- use the Vector class
// compile with vector1.cpp
#include <iostream.h>
#include "vector1.h"
int main(void)
{
        Vector first_move(120, 50);
        Vector second_move(50, 120);
        Vector result;

        cout.precision(3);                       // format output
        cout.setf(ios::fixed, ios::floatfield);
        cout.setf(ios::showpoint);
        result = first_move + second_move;   // adding objects!
        cout << "First move: ";
        first_move.show_vector();                // display first_move
        cout << "Magnitude, angle = ";
        first_move.show_polar();
        cout << "Second move: ";
        second_move.show_vector();
        cout << "Magnitude, angle = ";
        second_move.show_polar();
        cout << "Result: ";
        result.show_vector();
        cout << "Magnitude, angle = ";
        result.show_polar();

        Vector twotimes = result * 2.0;       // member function
        cout << "Doubled result: ";
        twotimes.show_vector();

        result = 0.5 * result;                // friend function
        cout << "Halved result: ";
        result.show_vector();

        return 0;
}
```

Here is the program's output:

```
First move: (120.000, 50.000)
Magnitude, angle = (130.000, 22.620)
Second move: (50.000, 120.000)
Magnitude, angle = (130.000, 67.380)
Result: (170.000, 170.000)
Magnitude, angle = (240.416, 45.000)
Doubled result: (340.000, 340.000)
Halved result: (85.000, 85.000)
```

Program Notes

The *first_move* vector represents moving 120 units to the right and 50 units up. The net result is the same as moving 130 units in a direction 22.62 degrees counterclockwise from the *x*-axis. The first two output lines display these two descriptions of the *first_move* vector. Similarly, the second move of 50 units to the right and 120 units up is the same as a move of 130 units in a direction 67.38 degrees from the *x*-axis. The combined effect of the two moves is moving 170 units to the right (120 + 50) and 170 units up, just as the output for the result vector shows. And that is equivalent to moving 240.42 units at an angle of 45 degrees from the *x*-axis, as the sixth line of output shows. Note that you can't simply add the magnitudes of two vectors to get the magnitude of the sum. That's why we used rectangular coordinates rather than polar coordinates to calculate the sum. Finally, the program illustrates that both overloadings of the * function work.

Overloading Restrictions

C++ does impose some limits on user-defined operator overloading as follows:

1. The overloaded operator must have at least one operand that is a user-defined type. This prevents you from overloading operators for the standard types. Thus you can't redefine the minus operator (-) so that it yields the sum of two *double* values instead of their difference. This restriction preserves program sanity, although it may hinder creative accounting.

2. You can't use an operator in a manner that violates the syntax rules for the original operator. For instance, you can't overload the modulus operator (%) so that it can be used with a single operand:

    ```
    int x;
    Vector shiva;
    % x;            // invalid for modulus operator
    % shiva;        // invalid for overloaded operator
    ```

    Similarly, you can't alter operator precedence. So if you overload the addition operator to let you add two classes, the new operator has the same precedence as ordinary addition.

3. You can't create new operator symbols. For instance, you can't use the combination ** to denote exponentiation.

4. You cannot overload the following five operators:

sizeof	the *sizeof* operator
.	membership operator
.*	pointer-to-member operator
::	scope resolution operator
?:	conditional operator

This still leaves all the operators in Table 10-1 available for overloading.

5. Most of the operators in Table 10-1 can be overloaded by using either member or nonmember functions. However, you can use *only* member functions to overload the following operators:

=	assignment operator
()	function call operator
[]	subscripting operator
->	class member access by pointer operator

Note: We have not covered, nor will we cover, every operator mentioned in the list of restrictions or in Table 10-1. However, Appendix E does summarize those operators not covered in the main body of this text.

+	-	*	/	%	^	&	|
~!	!	=	<	>	+=	-=	*=
/=	%=	^=	&=	|=	<<	>>	>>=
<<=	==	!=	<=	>=	&&	||	++
--	,	->*	->	()	[]	*new*	*delete*

Table 10-1 Operators that can be overloaded

Overloading the << Operator

One of the more useful features of classes is that you can overload the << operator so that you can use it with *cout* to display an object's contents. In some ways, this overloading is a bit trickier than the earlier examples, so we'll develop it in two steps instead of in one.

Suppose *hector* is a *Vector* object. To display *Vector* values, we've been using *show_vector()* and *show_polar()*. Wouldn't it be nice, however, if you could do the following?

```
cout << hector;        // make cout recognize Vector class?
```

You can, because << is one of the C++ operators that can be overloaded. In fact, it already is heavily overloaded. In its most basic incarnation, the << operator is one of C and C++'s bit manipulation operators; it shifts bits left in a value (see Appendix E). But the *ostream* class overloads the operator, converting it into an output tool. Recall that *cout* is an *ostream* object and that it is smart enough to recognize all the basic C++ types. That's because the *ostream* class declaration includes an overloaded *operator<<()* definition for each of the basic types. That is, one definition uses an *int* argument, one uses a *double* argument, and so on. So one way to teach *cout* to recognize a *Vector* object is to add a new function operator definition to the *ostream* class declaration. But it's not a good idea to alter the *iostream.h* file and mess around with a standard interface. It's better to use the *Vector* class declaration to teach the *Vector* class how to use *cout*.

First Version of Overloading <<

To teach the *Vector* class to use *cout*, you'll have to use a friend function. Why? Because a statement like

```
cout << hector;
```

uses two objects, with the *ostream* class object (*cout*) first. If you use a *Vector* member function to overload <<, the *Vector* object would come first, as it did when we overloaded the * operator with a member function. That means you would have to use the << operator this way:

```
hector << cout;    // if operator<<() were a member function
```

That would be confusing. But by using a friend function, you can overload the operator this way:

```
void operator<<(ostream & os, const Vector & v)
{
      os << "(x,y) = (" << v.x << "," << v.y <<")";
}
```

This lets you use

```
cout << hector;
```

to print data in the following format:

```
(x,y) = (120,50)
```

Note that the new *operator* << () definition uses an *ostream* reference *os* as its first argument. Normally, *os* will refer to the *cout* object, as it does in the expression *cout* <<

hector. But you could use the operator with other *ostream* objects, in which case *os* would refer to those objects. (What? You don't know of any other *ostream* objects? In Chapter 15, you'll learn how to create new objects to manage output to files, and these objects will be able to use *ostream* methods. You then will be able to use our *operator<<()* definition to write to files as well as to the screen.) Furthermore, the call *cout << hector* should use the *cout* object, not a copy, so the function passes the object as a reference instead of by value. Thus the expression *cout << hector* causes *os* to be an alias for *cout.* The *Vector* object can be passed by value or by reference, since either form makes the object values available to the function. Again, passing by reference uses less memory and time than passing by value.

Second Version of Overloading <<

The implementation we just presented has a problem. Statements such as

```
cout << hector;
```

work fine, but the implementation doesn't allow you to combine the redefined << operator with the ones *cout* normally uses:

```
cout << "hector value: " << hector << "\n"; // can't do
```

To understand why this doesn't work and what must be done to make it work, you first need to know a bit more about how *cout* operates. Consider the following statements:

```
int x = 5;
int y = 8;
cout << x << y;
```

C++ reads the output statement from left to right, meaning it is equivalent to the following:

```
(cout << x) << y;
```

The << operator, as defined in *iostream.h,* takes an *ostream* object to its left. Clearly, the expression *cout << x* satisfies that requirement because *cout* is an *ostream* object. But the output statement also requires that the whole expression *(cout << x)* be a type *ostream* object, because that expression is to the left of *<< y.* Therefore, the *ostream* class implements the *operator<<()* function so that it returns an *ostream* object. In particular, it returns the invoking object, *cout* in this case. Thus the expression *(cout << x)* is itself an *ostream* object, and it can be used to the left of the << operator.

You can take the same approach with the friend function. Just revise the *operator<<()* function so that it returns a reference to an *ostream* object:

```
ostream & operator<<(ostream & os, const Vector & v)
{
        os << "(x,y) = (", << v.x << "," << v.y <<")";
        return os;
}
```

Note that the return type is *ostream &*. That means, recall, that the function returns a reference to an *ostream* object. Because a program passes an object reference to the function to begin with, the net effect is that the function's return value is just the object passed to it. That is, the statement

```
cout << hector;
```

becomes the following function call:

```
operator<<(cout, hector);
```

And that call returns the *cout* object. So now the following statement does work:

```
cout << "hector value: " << hector << "\n"; // can do
```

Let's break this into separate steps to see how it works. First,

```
cout << "hector value: "
```

invokes the particular *ostream* definition of << that displays a string and returns the *cout* object, so the expression *cout << "hector value: "* displays the string, then is replaced by its return value, *cout*. This reduces the original statement to the following one:

```
cout << hector << "\n";
```

Next, the program uses the *Vector* declaration of << to display the *hector* values and to return the *cout* object again. This reduces the statement to the following:

```
cout << "\n";
```

The program now finishes up by using the *ostream* definition of << for strings to display the final string.

TIP

In general, to overload the << operator to display an object of class c_name, use a friend function with a definition of this form:

```
ostream & operator<<(ostream & os, const c_name & obj)
{
        os << ... ;   // display object contents
        return os;
}
```

A Friendless Approach

If a class has member functions that access class contents, you can use *cout* without using a friend function. For example, we can do the following for the *Vector* class:

```
void operator<<(ostream & os, const Vector & v)
{
        os << "(x,y) = (" << v.xval() << "," << v.yval() <<")";
}
```

Because this version doesn't directly access an object's data, it need not be a friend function. This would be the better choice, for it's more in accord with the need-to-know policy. However, if a class doesn't provide member function access to needed information, then a friend function is your only choice.

Improving the Class by Adding a State Member

Once you start playing with class declarations, it can be hard to stop, so let's add one more improvement! Our definition of the << operator displays just the rectangular representation of a vector. Can you overload the definition so that the operator can also display the polar representation? No. Separate definitions require separate function signatures. The operator takes two operands, so the friend operator function takes two arguments, and they have to be an *ostream* object and a *Vector* object. So you have no freedom to select another function signature.

But you can change the class declaration. The idea is to add a *state member*. This is a variable that affects how the object behaves, sort of like a switch on a printer that lets you set which printer emulation to use. For instance, you can add a type *char* member that can be set to 'p' or 'r'. The object will display in polar mode if the state member is 'p' and in rectangular mode if the state member is 'r'. (The *ostream* class, incidentally, uses the same state member technique to control the various formatting options discussed in Chapter 15.) Suppose that you call this state member *mode*. Then you can rewrite *operator<<()* this way:

```
ostream & operator<<(ostream & os, const Vector & v)
{
        if (v.mode == 'r')
                os << "(x,y) = (" << v.x << ", " << v.y << ")";
        else if (v.mode == 'p')
        {
                os << "(m,a) = (" << v.mag << ", "
                    << v.ang * Rad_to_deg << ")";
        }
        else
                os << "Vector object mode is invalid";
        return os;
}
```

The program labels its output with (x,y) or (m,a) so that you can readily see if the output is in x- and y-coordinates or in magnitude and angle values. That way, you don't have to check the program code in order to interpret the program output. (Keep that output user-friendly!)

To use this approach, you need to alter the *Vector* class declarations and rewrite several member functions. First, of course, you have to add the *mode* member to the private part of the class. Then you have to add methods to set the mode to the desired value. Also, you should make it impossible to set an invalid mode. True, the *operator<<()* definition prints an error message if the mode isn't a 'p' or an 'r', but that's more a debugging tool. If a program generates that error message, you know you should work more on the class design. The most direct way to prevent invalid modes is to modify the constructors so that they always initialize a new object to a correct mode. For instance, you can define the default constructor this way:

```
Vector::Vector()                        // default constructor
{
        x = y = mag = ang = 0.0;
        mode = 'r';                     // default mode
}
```

Yet Another Trick

Remember how the other constructor is biased towards the *x-y* view of vectors? The prohibition on duplicate signatures prevented us from making a constructor using the magnitude-angle view. But now you can use the new mode member to rewrite the other constructor so that it can initialize a vector either to *x-y* values or to magnitude-angle values. The trick is to add the mode as the third argument to the constructor:

```
Vector::Vector(double n1, double n2, char form)
{
        mode = form;            // set mode member to form argument
        if (form == 'r')
        {
                x = n1;
                y = n2;
                set_mag();
                set_ang();
        }
        else if (form == 'p')
        {
                mag = n1;
                ang = n2 / Rad_to_deg;
                set_x();        // add to class declaration
                set_y();        // add to class declaration
        }
        else
        {
                cout << "Incorrect 3rd argument to Vector() -- ";
                cout << "vector set to 0\n";
                x = y = mag = ang = 0.0;
                mode = 'r';
        }
}
```

Further, you can use 'r' as the default value for the third argument. This lets you continue to use the two-argument form to initialize vectors in the *x-y* mode.

Listing 10-5 shows the revised class declaration. It adds a *mode* member and private functions for setting the *x* and *y* values from the polar values. It provides a new prototype for one of the constructors. Note that the prototype provides a default value of 'r' for *mode*. Because the new constructor can set either polar or rectangular values, we drop the old *set_to_polar()* function. Next, the *operator<<()* method replaces the old *show_vector()* and *show_polar()* methods.

Listing 10-5 *vector2.h*

```
// vector2.h -- Vector class with <<, mode state
#ifndef _VECTOR2_H_
#define _VECTOR2_H_
class Vector
{
private:
        double x;           // horizontal value
        double y;           // vertical value
        double mag;         // length of vector
        double ang;         // direction of vector
        char mode;          // 'r' = rectangular, 'p' = polar
        void set_mag(void);
        void set_ang(void);
        void set_x(void);
        void set_y(void);
public:
        Vector(void);
        Vector(double n1, double n2, char form = 'r');
        void set(double n1, double n2, char form = 'r');
        ~Vector(void);
        double xval() const {return x;}     // report x value
        double yval() const {return y;}     // report y value
        double magval() const {return mag;} // report magnitude
        double angval() const {return ang;} // report angle
        void polar_mode();
        void rect_mode();
// operator overloading
        Vector operator+(const Vector & b) const;
        Vector operator-(const Vector & b) const;
        Vector operator-() const;
        Vector operator*(double n) const;
// friends
        friend Vector operator*(double n, Vector & a);
        friend ostream& operator<<(ostream& os, const Vector & v);
};
#endif
```

FRIEND OR NO FRIEND?

The new *Vector* class declaration makes the *operator<<()* function a friend function to the *Vector* class. But this function, although not inimical to the *ostream* class, is not a friend to it. The *operator<<()* function takes an *ostream* argument and a *Vector* argument, so it might seem this function has to be friends to both classes. If you look at the code for the function, however, you'll notice that the function accesses individual members of the *Vector* object but only uses the *ostream* object as a whole. Because *operator<<()* accesses *private Vector* object members directly, it has to be a friend to the *private Vector* class. But because it does not directly access *private ostream* object members, the function does not have to be a friend to the *ostream* class. That's nice, for it means you don't have to tinker with the *ostream* definition.

Listing 10-6 lists the revised methods for the *Vector* class. We've already discussed most of these changes individually. Keep in mind that default values appear just in the prototypes in Listing 10-5, not in the methods file.

Listing 10-6 *vector2.cpp*

```
// vector2.cpp -- methods for Vector class
#include <iostream.h>
#include <math.h>
#include "vector2.h"
const double Rad_to_deg = 57.2957795130823;

// private methods
// calculates magnitude from x and y
void Vector::set_mag(void)
{
        mag = sqrt(x * x + y * y);
}

void Vector::set_ang(void)
{
        if (x == 0.0 && y == 0.0)
                ang = 0.0;
        else
                ang = atan2(y, x);
}
// set x from polar coordinate
void Vector::set_x(void)
{
        x = mag * cos(ang);
}

// set y from polar coordinate
void Vector::set_y(void)
{
        y = mag * sin(ang);
}

// public methods
Vector::Vector(void)            // default constructor
{
        x = y = mag = ang = 0.0;
        mode = 'r';
}
```

```
// construct vector from rectangular coordinates if form is r
// or else from polar coordinates if form is p
Vector::Vector(double n1, double n2, char form)
{
        mode = form;
        if (form == 'r')
        {
                x = n1;
                y = n2;
                set_mag();
                set_ang();
        }
        else if (form == 'p')
        {
                mag = n1;
                ang = n2 / Rad_to_deg;
                set_x();
                set_y();
        }
        else
        {
                cout << "Incorrect 3rd argument to Vector() -- ";
                cout << "vector set to 0\n";
                x = y = mag = ang = 0.0;
                mode = 'r';
        }
}

// set vector from rectangular coordinates if form is r
// or else from polar coordinates if form is p
void Vector:: set(double n1, double n2, char form)
{
        mode = form;
        if (form == 'r')
        {
                x = n1;
                y = n2;
                set_mag();
                set_ang();
        }
        else if (form == 'p')
        {
                mag = n1;
                ang = n2 / Rad_to_deg;
                set_x();
                set_y();
        }
        else
        {
                cout << "Incorrect 3rd argument to Vector() -- ";
                cout << "vector set to 0\n";
                x = y = mag = ang = 0.0;
                mode = 'r';
```

continued on next page

continued from previous page

```
        }
}

Vector::~Vector(void) // destructor
{
}

void Vector::polar_mode()      // set to polar mode
{
        mode = 'p';
}

void Vector::rect_mode()               // set to rectangular mode
{
        mode = 'r';
}

// operator overloading
// add two Vectors
Vector Vector::operator+(const Vector & b) const
{
        double sx, sy;
        sx = x + b.x;
        sy = y + b.y;
        Vector sum = Vector(sx, sy);
        return sum;
}

// substract two Vectors
Vector Vector::operator-(const Vector & b) const
{
        double dx, dy;
        dx = x - b.x;
        dy = y - b.y;
        Vector diff = Vector(dx, dy);
        return diff;
}

// change sign of Vector
Vector Vector::operator-() const
{
        double nx, ny;
        nx = -x;
        ny = -y;
        Vector neg = Vector(nx, ny);
        return neg;
}

// multiply Vector by n
Vector Vector::operator*(double n) const
{
        double mx, my;
        mx = n * x;
```

```
        my = n * y;
        Vector mult = Vector(mx, my);
        return mult;
}

// friend methods
// multiply n by Vector a
Vector operator*(double n, const Vector & a)
{
        return a * n;
}

// display rectangular coordinates if mode is r,
// else display polar coordinates if mode is p
ostream& operator<<(ostream & os, const Vector & v)
{
        if (v.mode == 'r')
                os << "(x,y) = (" << v.x << ", " << v.y << ")";
        else if (v.mode == 'p')
        {
                os << "(m,a) = (" << v.mag << ", "
                        << v.ang * Rad_to_deg << ")";
        }
        else
                os << "Vector object mode is invalid";
        return os;
}
```

Listing 10-7 provides a short program using the revised class. It simulates the famous Drunkard's Walk problem. Actually, now that the drunk is recognized as someone with a serious health problem rather than as a source of amusement, it's usually called the Random Walk problem. The idea is that you place someone at a lamp post. The subject begins walking, but the direction of each step varies randomly from the preceding step. One way of phrasing the problem is, how many steps does it take the random walker to travel, say, 50 feet way from the post. In terms of vectors, this amounts to adding a bunch of randomly oriented vectors until the sum exceeds 50 feet.

Listing 10-7 lets you select the target distance to be traveled and the length of the wanderer's step. It maintains a running total representing the position after each step (represented as a vector), and reports the number of steps needed to reach the target distance along with the walker's location (in both formats). As you'll see, the walker's progress is quite inefficient. A journey of a thousand steps, each two feet long, may carry the walker only 50 feet from the starting point. The program divides the net distance traveled (50 feet in this case) by the number of steps to provide a measure of the walker's inefficiency. All the random direction changes make this average much smaller than the length of a single step. To select directions randomly, the program uses the standard library functions *rand()*, *srand()*, and *time()*, described in the Program Notes. Remember to compile Listing 10-6 along with Listing 10-7.

Listing 10-7 *randwalk.cpp*

```cpp
// randwalk.cpp -- use the revised Vector class
// compile with the vector2.cpp file
#include <iostream.h>
#include <stdlib.h>    // rand(), srand() prototypes
#include <time.h>                  // time() prototype
#include "vector2.h"
int main(void)
{
        srand(time(0));                 // seed random-number generator
        double direction;
        Vector step;
        Vector result(0.0, 0.0);
        unsigned long steps = 0;
        double target;
        double dstep;
        cout << "Enter target distance (q to quit): ";
        while (cin >> target)
        {
                cout << "Enter step length: ";
                if (!(cin >> dstep))
                        break;

                while (result.magval() < target)
                {
                        direction = rand() % 360;
                        step.set(dstep, direction, 'p');
                        result = result + step;
                        steps++;
                }
                cout << "After " << steps << " steps, the subject "
                        "has the following location:\n";
                cout << result << "\n";
                result.polar_mode();
                cout << " or\n" << result << "\n";
                cout << "Average outward distance per step = "
                        << result.magval()/steps << "\n";
                steps = 0;
                result.set(0.0, 0.0);
                cout << "Enter target distance (q to quit): ";
        }
        cout << "Bye!\n";

        return 0;
}
```

Here is a sample run:

```
Enter target distance (q to quit): 50
Enter step length: 2
After 253 steps, the subject has the following location:
(x,y) = (46.1512, 20.4902)
  or
```

```
(m,a) = (50.495, 23.9402)
Average outward distance per step = 0.199587
Enter target distance (q to quit): 50
Enter step length: 2
After 951 steps, the subject has the following location:
(x,y) = (-21.9577, 45.3019)
 or
(m,a) = (50.3429, 115.8593)
Average outward distance per step = 0.0529362
Enter target distance (q to quit): 50
Enter step length: 1
After 1716 steps, the subject has the following location:
(x,y) = (40.0164, 31.1244)
 or
(m,a) = (50.6956, 37.8755)
Average outward distance per step = 0.0295429
Enter target distance (q to quit): q
```

The random nature of the process produces considerable variation from trial to trial, even if the initial conditions are the same. On the average, however, halving the step size quadruples the number of steps needed to cover a given distance. Probability theory suggests that, on the average, the number of steps (N) of length s needed to reach a net distance of D is given by the following equation:

$$N = (D/s)^2$$

This is just an average, but there will be considerable variations from trial to trial. For example, a hundred trials of attempting to travel 50 feet in 2-foot steps yielded an average of 665 steps (close to the theoretical value of 625) to travel that far, but the range was from 103 to 3393. Similarly, traveling 50 feet in 1-foot steps averaged 2655 steps (close to the theoretical value of 2500) with a range of 556 to 11690. So if you find yourself walking randomly, be confident and take long steps. You still won't have any control over the direction you wind up going, but at least you'll get farther.

Program Notes

First, let's talk about random numbers. The standard ANSI C/C++ library includes a *rand()* function that returns a random integer in the range from 0 to some implementation-dependent value. Our program uses the modulus operator to get an angle value in the range 0–359. The *rand()* function works by applying an algorithm to an initial seed value to get a random value. That value is used as the seed for the next function call, and so on. The numbers are really pseudorandom, for ten consecutive calls normally produce the same ten random numbers. (The exact values will depend on the implementation.) However, the *srand()* function lets you override the default seed value and initiate a different sequence of random numbers. This program uses the return value of *time(0)* to set the seed. The *time(0)* function returns the current calendar time, often implemented as the number of seconds since some specific date. (More generally, *time()* takes the address of a type *time_t* variable and puts the time into that variable and also returns it. Using a 0 address argument obviates the need for an otherwise unneeded *time_t* variable.) Thus, the statement

```
srand(time(0));
```

sets a different seed each time you run the program, making the random output appear even more random. The *stdlib.h* header file contains the prototypes for *srand()* and *rand()*, while *time.h* contains the *time()* prototype.

The program uses the *result* vector to keep track of the walker's progress. Each cycle of the inner loop, the program sets the *step* vector to a new direction and adds it to the current *result* vector. When the magnitude of *result* exceeds the target distance, the loop terminates.

By setting the vector mode, the program displays the final position in rectangular terms and in polar terms.

Incidentally, the statement

```
result = result + step;
```

has the effect of placing *result* in the 'r' mode regardless of the initial modes of *result* and *step*. Here's why. First, the addition operator function creates and returns a new vector holding the sum of the two arguments. The function creates that vector using the default constructor, which creates vectors in the 'r' mode. Thus the vector being assigned to *result* is in the 'r' mode. By default, assignment assigns each member variable individually, so 'r' is assigned to *result.mode*. If you would prefer some other behavior, such as *result* retaining its original mode, you can override default assignment by defining an assignment operator for the class. The next chapter shows examples of this.

We've used the *Vector* class to illustrate operator overloading with member functions and with friend functions. We've used it to illustrate overloading the << operator to display *Vector* values, and we've used it to illustrate how a state variable can add flexibility to a design. This entire sequence of examples shows how a class declaration can grow in flexibility and power as you work with it. When developing a new class, it's usually a good idea to proceed as these examples did, starting with a basic implementation, getting it to work, then expanding the class. By now, however, the *Vector* class is getting too involved to add new features without risking the new ideas being buried in the clutter. So we'll retire the *Vector* class and return to simpler classes as we explore still more class concepts and techniques. Before proceeding to new material, you may wish to pause to take a deep, relaxing breath and reward yourself with a treat, perhaps a cookie, perhaps a good movie, perhaps a short trip to Tahiti.

Automatic Conversions and Type Casts for Classes

The next topic on the class menu is type conversion. We'll look into how C++ handles conversions to and from user-defined types. To set the stage, let's first review how C++

handles conversions for its built-in types. When you make a statement assigning a value of one standard type to a variable of another standard type, C++ automatically will convert the value to the same type as the receiving variable, providing the two types are compatible. For instance, the following statements all generate numeric type conversions:

```
long count = 8;       // int value 8 converted to type long
double time = 11;     // int value 11 converted to type double
int side = 3.33;      // double value 3.33 converted to type int 3
```

These assignments work because C++ recognizes that the diverse numeric types all represent the same basic thing, a number, and because C++ incorporates built-in rules for making the conversions. Recall, however (from your reading of Chapter 3), that you can lose some precision in these conversions. For instance, assigning 3.33 to the *int* variable *side* results in *side* getting the value 3, losing the 0.33 part.

The C++ language does not automatically convert types that are not compatible. For instance, the statement

```
int * p = 10;  // type clash
```

fails because the left-hand side is a pointer-type, while the right-hand side is a number. And even though a computer may represent an address internally with an integer, integers and pointers conceptually are quite different. For instance, you wouldn't square a pointer. However, when automatic conversions fail, you may be able to use a type cast:

```
int * p = (int *) 10; // ok, p and (int *) 10 both pointers
```

This sets a pointer to the address *10* by type casting *10* to type pointer-to-*int* (that is, type *int **).

You may define a class sufficiently related to a basic type or to another class that it makes sense to convert from one form to another. In that case, you can instruct C++ how to make such conversions automatically or, perhaps, via a type cast. To show how that works, let's recast the pounds-to-stone program from Chapter 3 into class form. First, design an appropriate type. Fundamentally, we're representing one thing (a weight) two ways (pounds and stone). A class provides an excellent way to incorporate two representations of one concept into a single entity. Therefore, it makes sense to place both representations of weight into the same class and then to provide class methods for expressing the weight in different forms. Listing 10-8 provides the class header.

 Listing 10-8 *stonewt.h*

```
// stonewt.h -- declaration for Stonewt class
#ifndef _STONEWT_H_
#define _STONEWT_H_
class Stonewt
{
```

continued on next page

continued from previous page

```
private:
        enum {Lbs_per_stn = 14};       // pounds per stone
        int stone;      // whole stones
        double pds_left;       // fractional pounds
        double pounds; // entire weight in pounds
public:
        Stonewt(double lbs);  // constructor for double pounds
        Stonewt(int stn, double lbs);// constructor for stone, lbs
        Stonewt();      // default constructor
        ~Stonewt();
        void show_lbs() const;       // show weight in pounds format
        void show_stn() const;       // show weight in stone format
};
#endif
```

Note that the class has three constructors. They allow you to initialize a *Stonewt* object to a floating-point number of pounds, or to a stone and pound combination. Or you can create a *Stonewt* object without initializing it.

Also, the class provides two display functions. One displays the weight in pounds, and the other displays the weight in stone and pounds. Listing 10-9 shows the class methods implementation. Note that each constructor assigns values to all three private members. Thus, creating a *Stonewt* object automatically sets both representations of weight.

As first mentioned in Chapter 9, *enum* provides a convenient way to define class-specific constants, providing that they are integers.

Listing 10-9 *stonewt.cpp*

```
// stonewt.cpp -- Stonewt class methods
#include <iostream.h>
#include "stonewt.h"

// construct Stonewt object from double value
Stonewt::Stonewt(double lbs)
{
        stone = int (lbs) / Lbs_per_stn;       // integer division
        pds_left = int (lbs) % Lbs_per_stn + lbs - int(lbs);
        pounds = lbs;
}

// construct Stonewt object from stone, double values
Stonewt::Stonewt(int stn, double lbs)
{
        stone = stn;
        pds_left = lbs;
        pounds =  stn * Lbs_per_stn +lbs;
}

Stonewt::Stonewt()      // default constructor, wt = 0
{
```

```
                stone = pounds = pds_left = 0;
}

Stonewt::~Stonewt()    // destructor
{
}

// show weight in stones
void Stonewt::show_stn() const
{
        cout << stone << " stone, " << pds_left << " pounds\n";
}

// show weight in pounds
void Stonewt::show_lbs() const
{
        cout << pounds << " pounds\n";
}
```

Because a *Stonewt* object represents a single weight, it makes sense to provide ways to convert an integer or a floating-point value to a *Stonewt* object. And we have already done so! In C++, any constructor taking a *single* argument acts as a blueprint for converting a value of that argument type to the class type. Thus the constructor

```
Stonewt(double lbs);  // template for double-to-Stonewt conversion
```

serves as instructions for converting type *double* values to a type *Stonewt* value. However, the constructor

```
Stonewt(int stn, double lbs);
```

has two arguments, so it cannot be used to convert types.

RULE

A C++ constructor containing one argument defines a type conversion from the argument type to the class type.

When will the compiler use the *Stonewt(double)* function? It will use it in the following circumstances:

- When you initialize a *Stonewt* object to a type *double* value

- When you assign a type *double* value to a *Stonewt* object

- When you pass a type *double* value to a function expecting a *Stonewt* argument

- When a function that's declared to return a *Stonewt* value tries to return a *double* value

- When any of the situations above uses a built-in type that unambiguously can be converted to type *double*

Let's look at the last point in more detail. The argument-matching process provided by function prototyping will let the *Stonewt(double)* constructor act as conversions for other numerical types. That is, both of the following statements work by first converting *int* to *double*, then using the *Stonewt(double)* constructor.

```
Stonewt Jumbo(7000);    // uses Stonewt(double), converting int to double
Jumbo = 7300;           // uses Stonewt(double), converting int to double
```

However, this two-step conversion process works only if there is an unambiguous choice. That is, if the class also defined a *Stonewt(long)* constructor, the compiler would reject these statements, probably pointing out that an *int* can be converted to either a *long* or a *double*, so the call is ambiguous.

Listing 10-10 uses the class constructors to initialize some *Stonewt* objects and to handle type conversions. Remember to compile Listing 10-9 along with Listing 10-10.

Listing 10-10 *stone.cpp*

```
// stone.cpp -- user-defined conversions
// compile with stonewt.cpp
#include <iostream.h>
#include "stonewt.h"
void display(const Stonewt & st, int n);
int main(void)
{
        Stonewt pavarotti = 260;       // uses constructor to initialize
        Stonewt wolfe((double)285.7);// same as Stonewt wolfe = 285.7;
        Stonewt taft(21, 8);

        cout << "The tenor weighed ";
        pavarotti.show_stn();
        cout << "The detective weighed ";
        wolfe.show_stn();
        cout << "The President weighed ";
        taft.show_lbs();
        pavarotti = double(265.8);    // uses constructor for conversion
        taft = 325;                   // same as taft = Stonewt(325);
        cout << "After dinner, the tenor weighed ";
        pavarotti.show_stn();
        cout << "After dinner, the President weighed ";
        taft.show_lbs();
        display(taft, 2);      // Stonewt argument
        cout << "The wrestler weighed even more.\n";
        display(422, 2);       // convert 422 to double, then to Stonewt
        cout << "No stone left unearned\n";
        return 0;
}

void display(const Stonewt & st, int n)
{
        for (int i = 0; i < n; i++)
        {
```

```
                cout << "Wow! ";
                st.show_stn();
        }
}
```

Here is the output:

```
The tenor weighed 18 stone, 8 pounds
The detective weighed 20 stone, 5.7 pounds
The President weighed 302 pounds
After dinner, the tenor weighed 18 stone, 13.8 pounds
After dinner, the President weighed 325 pounds
Wow! 23 stone, 3 pounds
Wow! 23 stone, 3 pounds
The wrestler weighed even more.
Wow! 30 stone, 2 pounds
Wow! 30 stone, 2 pounds
No stone left unearned
```

Program Notes

First, note that when a constructor has a single argument, you can use the following form when initializing a class object:

```
// a syntax for initializing a class object when
// using a constructor with one argument
Stonewt pavarotti = 260;
```

This is equivalent to the other two forms we've used:

```
// standard syntax forms for initializing class objects
Stonewt pavarotti(260);
Stonewt pavarotti = Stonewt(260);
```

However, the last two forms can also be used with constructors having multiple arguments.

Next, note the following two assignments from Listing 10-10:

```
pavarotti = 265.8;
taft = 325;
```

The first assignment uses the constructor with a type *double* argument to convert *265.8* to a type *Stonewt* value. This sets the *pounds* member of *pavarotti* to *265.8*. Because it uses the constructor, this assignment also sets the *stone* and *pds_left* members of the class. Similarly, the second assignment converts a type *int* value to type *double,* then uses *Stonewt(double)* to set all three member values in the process.

Finally, note the following function call:

```
display(422, 2);      // convert 422 to double, then to Stonewt
```

The prototype for *display()* indicates that its first argument should be the *Stonewt* object. Confronted with an *int* argument, the compiler looks for a *Stonewt(int)* constructor to convert the *int* to the desired *Stonewt* type. Failing to find that constructor, the compiler looks for a constructor with some other built-in type to which an *int* can be converted. The *Stonewt(double)* constructor fits the bill. So the compiler converts *int* to *double*, then uses *Stonewt(double)* to convert the result to a *Stonewt* object.

Conversion Functions

Listing 10-10 converts a number to a *Stonewt* object. Can you do the reverse? That is, can you convert a *Stonewt* object to a *double* value, as in the following?

```
Stonewt wolfe(285.7);
double host = wolfe;  // ?? possible ??
```

The answer is that you can do this, but not by using constructors. Constructors only provide for converting another type *to* the class type. To do the reverse, you have to use a special form of C++ operator function called a *conversion function*.

Conversion functions resemble user-defined type casts, and you can use them the way you would use a type cast. For instance, if you define a *Stonewt*-to-*double* conversion function, you can use the following conversions:

```
Stonewt wolfe(285.7);
double host = double (wolfe);      // syntax #1
double thinker = (double) wolfe;   // syntax #2
```

Or you can let the compiler figure out what to do:

```
Stonewt wells(20, 3);
double star = wells;  // implicit use of conversion function
```

The computer, noting that the right-hand side is type *Stonewt* and the left-hand side is type *double,* looks to see if you've defined a conversion function matching that description.

So how do you create a conversion function? To convert to type *typename,* use a conversion function of this form:

```
operator typename ();
```

Note the following points:

- The conversion function must be a class method.

- The conversion function must *not* specify a return type.

- The conversion function must have *no* arguments.

For instance, a function to convert to type *double* would have this prototype:

```
operator double();
```

The *typename* part tells the conversion the type to which to convert, so no return type is needed. The fact that the function is a class method means it has to be invoked by a particular class object, and that tells the function which value to convert. Thus the function doesn't need arguments.

To add functions converting *stone_wt* objects to type *int* and to type *double,* then, requires adding the following prototypes to the class declaration:

```
operator int();
operator double();
```

Listing 10-11 shows the modified class declaration.

Listing 10-11 *stonewt1.h*

```
// stonewt1.h -- revised declaration for Stonewt class
#ifndef _STONEWT1_H_
#define _STONEWT1_H_
class Stonewt
{
private:
        enum {Lbs_per_stn = 14};       // pounds per stone
        int stone;      // whole stones
        double pds_left;      // fractional pounds
        double pounds; // entire weight in pounds
public:
        Stonewt(double lbs);  // construct from double pounds
        Stonewt(int stn, double lbs);  // construct from stone, lbs
        Stonewt();      // default constructor
        ~Stonewt();
        void show_lbs() const;       // show weight in pounds format
        void show_stn() const;       // show weight in stone format
        // conversion functions
        operator int() const;
        operator double() const;
};
#endif
```

Next, Listing 10-12 shows the definitions for these two conversion functions; these definitions should be added to the class member function file. Note that each function does return the desired value even though there is no declared return type. Also note the *int* conversion definition rounds to the nearest integer rather than truncating.

Listing 10-12 *stonewt1.cpp*

```
// stonewt1.cpp -- Stonewt class methods + conversion functions
#include <iostream.h>
#include "stonewt1.h"

// previous definitions go here

// conversion functions
Stonewt::operator int() const
{
        if (pounds - (int) pounds < 0.5)
                return pounds;
        else
```

continued on next page

continued from previous page

```
                    return pounds + 1;
}

Stonewt::operator double()const
{
        return pounds;
}
```

Listing 10-13 tests the new conversion functions. The assignment statement in the program uses an implicit conversion, while the final *cout* statement uses an explicit type cast. Remember to compile Listing 10-12 along with Listing 10-13.

Listing 10-13 *stone1.cpp*

```
// stone1.cpp -- user-defined conversion functions
// compile with stonewt1.cpp
#include <iostream.h>
#include "stonewt1.h"

int main(void)
{
        Stonewt poppins(9,2.8);              // 9 stone, 2.8 pounds
        double p_wt = poppins;               // implicit conversion
        cout << "Convert to double => ";
        cout << "Poppins: " << p_wt << " pounds.\n";
        cout << "Convert to int => ";
        cout << "Poppins: " << int (poppins) << " pounds.\n";
        return 0;
}
```

Here's the program output; it shows the result of converting the type *Stonewt* object to type *double* and to type *int*:

```
Convert to double => Poppins: 128.8 pounds.
Convert to int => Poppins: 129 pounds.
```

Applying Type Conversions Automatically

The last example used *int (poppins)* with *cout*. Suppose, instead, it omitted the explicit type cast:

```
cout << "Poppins: " << poppins << " pounds.\n";
```

Would the program use an implicit conversion, as it did in the following statement?

```
double p_wt = poppins;
```

The answer is no. In the *p_wt* example, the context indicates that *poppins* should be converted to type *double*. But in the *cout* example, nothing indicates whether the conversion should be to *int* or to *double*. Facing this lack of information, the compiler would complain that you were using an ambiguous conversion. Nothing in the statement indicates what type to use.

Interestingly, if the class had defined only the *double* conversion function, the compiler would accept our statement. That's because with only one conversion possible, there is no ambiguity.

You can have a similar situation with assignment. With the current class declarations, the compiler rejects the following statement as ambiguous.

```
long gone = poppins;   // ambiguous
```

In C++ you can assign both *int* and *double* values to a *long* variable, so the compiler legitimately could use either conversion function. The compiler doesn't want the responsibility of choosing which. But if you eliminate one of the two conversion functions, the compiler accepts the statement. For example, suppose you omit the *double* definition. Then the compiler will use the *int* conversion to convert *poppins* to a type *int* value. Then it converts the *int* value to type *long* when assigning it to *gone*.

When the class defines two or more conversions, you can still use an explicit type cast to indicate which conversion function to use. You can use either type cast notation:

```
long gone = (double) poppins; // use double conversion
long gone = int (poppins);    // use int conversion
```

The first statement converts *poppins* weight to a *double* value, then assignment converts the *double* value to type *long*. Similarly, the second statement converts *poppins* first to type *int*, then to *long*.

In summary, then, C++ provides the following type conversions for classes:

❧ A class constructor that has but a single argument serves as an instruction for converting a value of the argument type to the class type. For example, the *Stonewt* class constructor with a type *int* argument is invoked automatically when you assign a type *int* value to a *Stonewt* object.

❧ A special class member operator function called a conversion function serves as an instruction for converting a class object to some other type. The conversion function is a class member, has no declared return type, has no arguments, and is called *operator typename()*, where *typename* is the type to which the object is to be converted. This conversion function is invoked automatically when you assign a class object to a variable of that type or use the type cast operator to that type.

Conversions and Friends

Let's bring addition to the *Stonewt* class. As we mentioned when discussing the *Vector* class, we can use either a member function or a friend function to overload addition. We can implement addition with the following member function:

```
Stonewt Stonewt::operator+(const Stonewt & st) const
{
        double pds = pounds + st.pounds;
        Stonewt sum(pds);
```

continued on next page

continued from previous page

```
        return sum;
}
```

Or we can implement addition as a friend function this way:

```
Stonewt operator+(const Stonewt & st1, const Stonewt & st2)

{
        double pds = st1.pounds + st2.pounds;
        Stonewt sum(pds);
        return sum;
}
```

Either form lets us do the following:

```
Stonewt jenny(9, 12);
Stonewt benny(12, 8);
Stonewt total;
total = jenny + benny;
```

Also, given the *Stonewt(double)* constructor, each form lets us do the following:

```
Stonewt jenny(9, 12);
double kenny = 176.0;
Stonewt total;
total = jenny + kenny;
```

But only the friend function lets us do this:

```
Stonewt jenny(9, 12);
double penny = 146.0;
Stonewt total;
total = penny + jenny;
```

To see why, translate each addition into the corresponding function calls. First,

```
total = jenny + benny;
```

becomes

```
total = jenny.operator+(benny);             // member function
```

or else

```
total = operator+(jenny, benny);     // friend function
```

In either case, the actual argument types match the formal arguments. Also, the member function is invoked, as required, by a *Stonewt* object.

Next,

```
total = jenny + kenny;
```

becomes

```
total = jenny.operator+(kenny);             // member function
```

or else

```
total = operator+(jenny, kenny);     // friend function
```

Again, the member function is invoked, as required, by a *Stonewt* object. This time, in each case, one argument is type *double,* which invokes the *Stonewt(double)* constructor to convert the argument to a *Stonewt* object.

Finally,

```
total = penny + jenny;
```

becomes

```
total = operator+(jenny, kenny);     // friend function
```

Here, both arguments are type *double,* which invokes the *Stonewt(double)* constructor to convert them to *Stonewt* objects. The member function cannot be invoked, however.

```
total = penny.operator+(jenny);           // not meaningful
```

The reason is that only a class object can invoke a member function. C++ will not attempt to convert *penny* to a *Stonewt* object. Conversion takes place for member function arguments, not for member function invokers.

The lesson here is that by defining addition as a friend, we make it easier for a program to accommodate automatic type conversions. The reason is that both operands become function arguments, so function prototyping comes into play for both operands.

A Choice

Given that you want to be able to add *double* quantities to *Stonewt* quantities, you have a couple of choices. The first, which we just outlined, is to define *operator+(const Stonewt &, const Stonewt &)* as a friend function and have the *Stonewt(double)* constructor handle conversions of type *double* arguments to type *Stonewt* arguments.

The second choice is to further overload the addition operator with functions that explicitly use one type *double* argument:

```
Stonewt operator+(double x); // member function
friend Stonewt operator+(double x, Stonewt & s);
```

That way, the statement

```
total = jenny + kenny;        // Stonewt + double
```

exactly matches the *operator+(double x)* member function, and the statement

```
total = penny + jenny;        // double + Stonewt
```

exactly matches the *operator+(double x, Stonewt &s)* friend function. Earlier, we did something similar for *Vector* multiplication.

Each choice has its advantages. The first choice results in a shorter program because you define fewer functions. That also implies less work for you and fewer chances to mess up. The disadvantage is the added overhead in time and memory needed to invoke the conversion constructor whenever a conversion is needed. The second choice, on the other hand, is the mirror image. It makes for a longer program and more work on your part, but it runs a bit faster.

If your program makes intensive use of adding *double* values to *Stonewt* objects, it may pay to overload addition to handle such cases directly. If the program just uses such addition occasionally, it's simpler to rely on automatic conversions.

Summary

This chapter covers many important aspects of defining and using classes. Some of the material in this chapter may seem vague to you until your own experiences enrich your understanding. Meanwhile, let's summarize the chapter.

Normally, the only way you can access private class members is by using a class method. C++ alleviates that restriction with friend functions. To make a function a friend function, declare the function in the class declaration and preface the declaration with the keyword *friend*.

C++ extends overloading to operators by letting you define special operator functions that describe how particular operators relate to a particular class. An operator function can be a class member function or a friend function. C++ lets you invoke an operator function either by calling the function or by using the overloaded operator with its usual syntax. An operator function for the operator *op* has this form:

operator*op* (*argument-list*)

The *argument-list* represents operands for the operator. If the operator function is a class member function, then the first operand is the invoking object and isn't part of the *argument-list*. For instance, we overloaded addition by defining an *operator+()* member function for the *Vector* class. If *up, right,* and *result* are three vectors, you can use either of the following statements to invoke vector addition:

```
result = up.operator+(right);
result = up + right;
```

For the second version, the fact that the operands *up* and *right* are type *Vector* tell C++ to use the *Vector* definition of addition.

When an operator function is a member function, the first operand is the object invoking the function. In the statements above, for example, the *up* object is the invoking object. If you want to define an operator function so that the first operand is not a class object, you must use a friend function. Then you can pass the operands to the function definition in whichever order you want.

One of the most common tasks for operator overloading is defining the << operator so that it can be used in conjunction with the *cout* object to display an object's contents. To allow an *ostream* object to be the first operand, define the operator function as a friend. To allow the redefined operator to be concatenated with itself, make the return type *ostream &.* Here's a general form satisfying those requirements:

```
ostream & operator<<(ostream & os, const c_name & obj)
{
        os << ... ;  // display object contents
        return os;
}
```

If, however, the class has methods that return values for the data members you wish to display, you can use those methods instead of direct access in *operator<<()*. In that case, the function needn't (and shouldn't) be a friend.

C++ lets you establish conversions to and from class types. First, any class constructor taking a single argument acts as a conversion function, converting values of the argument type to the class type. C++ invokes the constructor automatically if you assign a value of the argument type to an object. For instance, suppose you have a *string* class with a constructor that takes *char* * value as its sole argument. Then, if bean is a *string* object, you can use the following statement:

```
bean = "pinto";   // converts type char * to type string
```

To convert from a class to another type, you must define a conversion function providing instruction about how to make the conversion. A conversion function must be a member function. If it is to convert to type *typename,* it should have the following prototype:

```
operator typename();
```

Note that it must have no declared return type, must have no arguments, and must (despite having no declared return type) return the converted value. For instance, a function to convert type *Vector* to type *double* would have this function form:

```
vector::operator double()
{
        ...
        return a_double_value;
}
```

As you may have noticed, classes require much more care and attention to detail than do simple C-style structures. In return, they do much more for you.

📖 Review Questions

1. Use a member function to overload the multiplication operator for the *Stonewt* class; have the operator multiply the data members by a type *double* value. Note that this will require carryover for the stone-pound representation. That is, twice 10 stone 8 pounds is 21 stone 2 pounds.

2. What are the differences between a friend function and a member function?

3. Does a nonmember function have to be a friend to access a class's members?

4. Use a friend function to overload the multiplication operator for the *Stonewt* class; have the operator multiply the *double* value by the *Stone* value.

5. Which operators cannot be overloaded?

6. What restriction applies to overloading the following operators? = () [] ->

7. Define a conversion function for the *vector* class that converts a vector to a type *double* value representing the vector's magnitude.

 # Programming Exercises

1. Modify Listing 10-7 so that instead of reporting the results of a single trial for a particular target-step combination, it reports the highest, lowest, and average number of steps for N trials, where N is an integer entered by the user.

2. Rewrite the *Stonewt* class so that it has a state member governing whether the object is interpreted in stone form, integer pounds form, or floating-point pounds form. Overload the << operator to replace the *show_stn()* and *show_lbs()* methods. Overload the addition, subtraction, and multiplication operators so that one can add, subtract, and multiply *Stonewt* values. Test your class with a short program.

3. A complex number has two parts: a real part and an imaginary part. One way to write an imaginary number is this: (3.0, 4.0i). Here 3.0 is the real part and 4.0 is the imaginary part. Suppose a = (A,Bi) and c = (C,Di). Here are some complex operations:

   ❧ Addition: a + c = (A + C, (B + D)i)

   ❧ Subtraction: a – c = (A – C, (B – D)i)

   ❧ Multiplication: a * c = (A * C – B*D, (A*D + B*C)i)

   ❧ Multiplication: (x a real number): x * c = (x*C,x*Di)

   ❧ Conjugation: ~a = (A, – Bi)

   Define a complex class so that the following program can use it with correct results. Note that you have to overload the << and >> operators. Many systems already have complex support in a *complex.h* header file, so use *complex0.h* to avoid conflicts. Use *const* whenever warranted.

```
#include <iostream.h>
#include "complex0.h" // to avoid confusion with complex.h
int main(void)
{
        complex a(3.0, 4.0);  // initialize to (3,4i)
        complex c;
        cout << "Enter a complex number (q to quit):\n";
        while (cin >> c)
```

```
    {
            cout << "c is " << c << '\n';
            cout << "complex conjugate is " << ~c << '\n';
            cout << "a + c is " << a + c << '\n';
            cout << "a * c is " << a * c << '\n';
            cout << "2 * c is " << 2 * c << '\n';
            cout << "Enter a complex number (q to quit):\n";
    }
    cout << "Done!\n";
    return 0;
}
```

Here is a sample run. Note that *cin >> c*, through overloading, now prompts for real and imaginary parts

```
Enter a complex number (q to quit):
real: 10
imaginary: 12
c is (10,12i)
complex conjugate is (10,-12i)
a + c is (13,16i)
a * c is (-18,76i)
2 * c is (20,24i)
Enter a complex number (q to quit):
real: q
Done!
```

CHAPTER 11

CLASSES AND DYNAMIC MEMORY ALLOCATION

You will learn about the following in this chapter:

- ◇ Using dynamic memory allocation for class members
- ◇ Implicit and explicit copy constructors
- ◇ Implicit and explicit overloaded assignment operators
- ◇ What you must do if you use *new* in a constructor
- ◇ Using pointers to objects

- ◇ Implementing a queue ADT

This chapter looks at how to use *new* and *delete* with classes and how to deal with some of the subtle problems that using dynamic memory can cause. This may sound like a short list of topics, but these topics affect constructor design, destructor design, and operator overloading.

Let's look at a specific example of how C++ can add to your memory load. Suppose you want to create a class with a member representing someone's last name. The simplest way is to use a character array member to hold the name. But this has some drawbacks. You might use a 14-character array, then run into Bartholomew Smeadsbury-Crafthovingham. Or, to be safer, you may use a 40-character array. But, if you then create an array of 2000 such objects, you'll be wasting a lot of memory with character arrays that are only partly filled. (At this point we're adding to the computer's memory load.) There is an alternative.

Often it is much better to decide many matters, such as how much storage to use, when a program runs than when it's compiled. The usual C++ approach to storing a name in an object is to use the *new* operator in a class constructor to allocate the correct amount of memory while the program is running. But introducing *new* to a class constructor raises several new problems unless you remember to take a series of additional steps, such as expanding the class destructor, bringing all constructors into harmony with the new destructor, and writing additional class methods to facilitate correct initialization and assignment! (This chapter, of course, will explain all these steps.) If you're just learning C++, you may be better off sticking initially to the simple, if inferior, character array approach. Then, when a class design works well, you can return to your OOP workbench and enhance the class declaration by using *new*. In short, grow gradually into C++.

Dynamic Memory and Classes

What would you like for breakfast, lunch, and dinner for the next month? How many ounces of milk for dinner on the 3rd day? How many raisins in your cereal for breakfast on the 15th day? If you're like most people, you'd rather postpone some of those decisions until the actual mealtimes. Part of C++ strategy is to take the same attitude towards memory allocation, letting the program decide about memory during run time rather than during compile time. That way, memory use can depend on the needs of a program instead of upon a rigid set of storage-class rules. To gain dynamic control of memory, you remember, C++ utilizes the *new* and *delete* operators. Unhappily, using these operators with classes can pose some new programming problems. As you'll see, destructors can become necessary instead of merely ornamental. And sometimes you have to overload the assignment operator to get programs to behave properly. We'll look into these matters now.

Review Example and *static* Class Members

We haven't used *new* and *delete* for a while, so let's review them with a short program. While we're at it, we'll introduce a new storage class: the *static* class member. The vehicle will be a *String* class. The class will hold a pointer to a string and a value representing the string length. We'll use the *String* class primarily to give an inside look at how *new, delete,* and *static* class members operate. For that reason, the constructors and destructors will display messages when called so that you can follow the action. Also, we'll omit several useful member and friend functions, such as overloaded ++ *and* >> operators and a conversion function, in order to simplify the class interface. (But rejoice! The review questions for this chapter give you the opportunity to add those useful support functions.) Listing 11-1 shows the class declaration. We've called the file *strng1.h* instead of *string.h* to avoid conflicting with the standard library file *string.h*. (The draft ANSI/ISO C++ standard will add a standard *string* class to the language definition; our simpler version will give you some idea of what's involved.)

Listing 11-1 *strng1.h*

```
// strng1.h -- string class declaration
#ifndef _STRNG1_H_
#define _STRNG1_H_
#include <iostream.h>
class String
{
private:
        char * str;                     // pointer to string
        int len;                        // length of string
        static int num_strings;         // number of objects
public:
        String(const char * s);         // constructor
        String();                       // default constructor
        ~String();                      // destructor
// friend function
        friend ostream & operator<<(ostream & os, const String & st);
};
#endif
```

You should note two points about this declaration. First, it uses a pointer-to-*char* instead of a *char* array to represent a name. This means that the class declaration does not allocate storage space for the string itself. Instead, it will use *new* in the constructors to allocate space for the string. This arrangement avoids straitjacketing the class declaration with a predefined limit to the string size.

Second, the definition declares the *num_strings* member as belonging to the *static* storage class. A static class member has a special property—a program creates only one copy of a static class variable regardless of the number of objects created. That is, a static member is *shared* among all objects of that class, much as a phone number might be shared among all members of a family. If, say, you create ten *String* objects, there would be ten *str* members and ten *len* members, but just one shared *num_strings* member. See Figure 11-1. This is convenient for data that should be private to a class but that should have the same value for all class objects. The *num_strings* member, for example, is intended to keep track of the number of objects created.

By the way, we've used the *num_strings* member as a convenient means of illustrating static data members. In general, a *String* class doesn't need such a member. If you did need such a facility, a better approach would be to define a more general *String* class, then use class inheritance (Chapter 12) to add this feature to a derived class.

Let's look at the implementation of the class methods in Listing 11-2. There you'll see how these two points (using a pointer and using a static member) are handled.

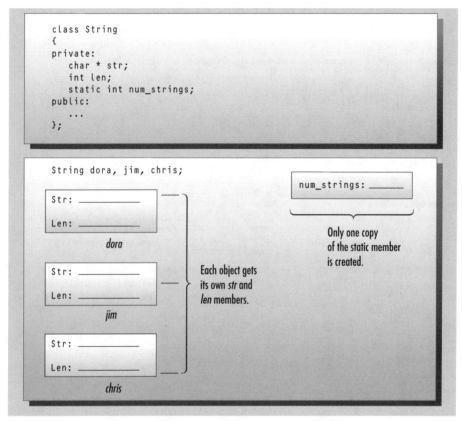

```
class String
{
private:
    char * str;
    int len;
    static int num_strings;
public:
    ...
};
```

```
String dora, jim, chris;
```

num_strings: _____

Only one copy
of the static member
is created.

Str: _____
Len: _____

dora

Str: _____
Len: _____

jim

Each object gets
its own *str* and
len members.

Str: _____
Len: _____

chris

Figure 11-1 The static data member

Listing 11-2 *strngs1.cpp*

```
// strngs1.cpp -- String class methods
#include <iostream.h>
#include <string.h>
#include "strng1.h"

// initializing static class member
int String::num_strings = 0;

// class methods
String::String(const char * s)                 // construct String from C string
{
        len = strlen(s);           // set size
        str = new char[len + 1];   // allot storage
```

```
        strcpy(str, s);              // initialize pointer
        num_strings++;               // set object count
        cout << num_strings << ": \"" << str
             << "\" object created\n";    // For Your Information
}

String::String()                          // default constructor
{
        static const char * s = "C++";
        len = strlen(s);
        str = new char[len + 1];
        strcpy(str, s);                   // default string
        num_strings++;
        cout << num_strings << ": \"" << str
             << "\" object created\n";    // FYI
}

String::~String()                         // necessary destructor
{
        cout << "\"" << str << "\" object deleted, ";    // FYI
        --num_strings; // required
        cout << num_strings << " left\n";           // FYI
        delete [] str;                    // required
}

ostream & operator<<(ostream & os, const String & st)
{
        os << st.str;
        return os;
}
```

First, notice the following statement from Listing 11-2:

```
int String::num_strings = 0;
```

This statement initializes the static *num_strings* member to zero. Note that you cannot
initialize a static member variable inside the class declaration. That's because the declaration is a description of how memory is to be allocated, but it doesn't allocate memory. You allocate and initialize memory by creating an object using that format. In the
case of a static class member, you initialize the static member independently with a
separate statement outside the class declaration. That's because the static class member
is stored separately rather than as part of an object. Note that the initialization statement gives the type and uses the scope operator.

```
int String::num_strings = 0;
```

This initialization goes in the methods file, not in the class declaration file. That's
because the class declaration is in a header file, and a program may include a header
file in several other files. That would result in multiple copies of the initialization statement, which is an error.

RULE

A static data member is declared in the class declaration and is initialized in the file containing the class methods. The scope operator is used in the initialization to indicate to which class the static member belongs.

Next, notice that each constructor contains the expression *num_strings++*. This ensures that each time a program creates a new object, the shared variable *num_strings* increases by one, keeping track of the total number of *String* objects. Also, the destructor contains the expression *--num_strings*. Thus the *String* class also keeps track of deleted objects, keeping the value of the *num_strings* member current.

Now look at the first constructor, which initializes a *String* object with a regular C string:

```
String::String(const char * s)
{
        len = strlen(str);           // set size
        str = new char[len + 1];     // allot storage
        strcpy(str, s);              // initialize pointer
        num_strings++;               // set object count
        cout << num_strings << ": \"" << str
                << "\" object created\n";      // For Your Information
}
```

The class *str* member, recall, is just a pointer, so the constructor has to provide the memory for holding a string. You can pass a string pointer to the constructor when you initialize an object:

```
String boston("Boston");
```

First, the function initializes the *len* member, using the *strlen()* function to compute the length of the string. Next, it uses *new* to allocate sufficient space to hold the string, then assigns the address of the new memory to the *str* member. (Recall that *strlen()* returns the length of a string not counting the terminating null character, so the constructor adds 1 to *len* to allow space for the string including the null character.)

Next, the constructor uses *strcpy()* to copy the passed string into the new memory. Then it updates the object count. Finally, to help us monitor what's going on, the constructor displays the current number of objects and the string stored in the object. This feature will come in handy later, when we deliberately lead the *String* class into trouble.

The default constructor behaves similarly, except that it provides a default string of C++. The constructor uses a static local variable initialized to this string. Because the variable is static, it's initialized just once, not every time the constructor is called.

The destructor contains the example's most important addition to our handling of classes:

```
String::~String()
{
```

```
        cout << "\"" << str << "\" object deleted, ";      // FYI
        --num_strings;                  // required
        cout << num_strings << " left\n";    // FYI
        delete [] str;                  // required
}
```

The destructor begins by announcing when the destructor gets called. This part is informative, but not essential. The *delete* statement, however, is vital. Recall that the *str* member points to memory allocated with *new*. When a *String* object expires, the *str* pointer expires. But the memory *str* pointed to remains allocated unless we use *delete* to free it. Freeing memory *occupied* by an object's members does not automatically free memory *pointed to* by an object's members. By placing the *delete* statement in the destructor, we ensure that the memory allocated with *new* is freed when the object expires.

TIP

Whenever you use *new* in a constructor to allocate memory, you should use *delete* in the corresponding destructor to free that memory. If you use *new* with brackets, then you should use *delete* with brackets.

Listing 11-3, taken from a program under development at *The Daily Vegetable*, illustrates when and how the *String* constructors and destructor work. Remember to compile Listing 11-2 along with Listing 11-3.

Listing 11-3 *vegnews.cpp*

```
// vegnews.cpp -- using new and delete with classes
// compile with strngs1.cpp
#include <iostream.h>
#include "strng1.h"

String sports("Spinach Leaves Bowl for Dollars");
                                // sports is an external object
void callme1(void);            // creates local object
String * callme2(void);            // creates dynamic object

int main(void)
{
        cout << "Top of main()\n";
        String headlines[2] = // local object array
        {
                String("Celery Stalks at Midnight"),
                String("Lettuce Prey")
        };
        cout << headlines[0] << "\n";
        cout << headlines[1] << "\n";
        callme1();
        cout << "Middle of main()\n";
```

continued on next page

continued from previous page

```
        String *pr = callme2();        // set pointer to object
        cout << sports << "\n";
        cout << *pr << "\n";           // invoke class method
        delete pr;                     // delete object
        cout << "End of main()\n";
        return 0;
}

void callme1(void)
{
        cout << "Top of callme1()\n";
        String grub;                   // local object
        cout << grub << "\n";
        cout << "End of callme1()\n";
}

String * callme2(void)
{
        cout << "Top of callme2()\n";
        String *pveg = new String("Cabbage Heads Home");
                    // dynamic object uses constructor
        cout << *pveg << "\n";
        cout << "End of callme2()\n";
        return pveg;                   // pveg expires, object lives
}
```

COMPATIBILITY NOTE

This first draft of a design for *String* has some deliberate flaws, which, for many compilers, don't show up at this stage. However, the class flaws do affect some compilers, and they won't reproduce the output below. The subsequent section about revising the *String* class discusses and remedies the class problems.

Here is the output:

```
1: "Spinach Leaves Bowl for Dollars" object created
Top of main()
2: "Celery Stalks at Midnight" object created
3: "Lettuce Prey" object created
Celery Stalks at Midnight
Lettuce Prey
Top of callme1()
4: "C++" object created
C++
End of callme1()
"C++" object deleted, 3 left
Middle of main()
Top of callme2()
4: "Cabbage Heads Home" object created
Cabbage Heads Home
End of callme2()
```

```
Spinach Leaves Bowl for Dollars
Cabbage Heads Home
"Cabbage Heads Home" object deleted, 3 left
End of main()
"Lettuce Prey" object deleted, 2 left
"Celery Stalks at Midnight" object deleted, 1 left
"Spinach Leaves Bowl for Dollars" object deleted, 0 left
```

Program Notes

You should make sure you understand the sequence of events in this example program, so let's run through them now. The *sports* object is an external variable, so it's created before *main()* begins execution. The next objects created are the two elements of the *headlines* array. The program calls the constructor twice, once to initialize each array element. Each element is a class object, so the calls

```
cout << headlines[0] << "\n";
cout << headlines[1] << "\n";
```

evoke the friend method *operator<<()* for the two objects *headlines[0]* and *headlines[1]*.

Next, the program calls the *callme1()* function. This function uses the default constructor to create a local object called *grub*. The default constructor initializes the *str* member to *"C++"*. This object expires when the *callme1()* function finishes execution, as is shown by the following output lines:

```
Top of callme1()
4: "C++" object created
C++
End of callme1()
"C++" object deleted, 3 left
```

In addition to printing its farewell message, the destructor also frees the memory that held the string *"C++"*.

Now we come to the thorniest part of the example. The program calls *callme2()*, and this function uses *new* to create and initialize a *String* object:

```
String *pveg = new String("Cabbage Heads Home");
```

The function assigns the address of this new object to the *pveg* pointer. Because we provide *new String* with a string argument, the program calls the corresponding constructor to initialize the object. Figure 11-2 summarizes the statement.

Note that because *pveg* is a pointer to an object, **pveg* is an object. That means we can use **pveg* in the same way that we use a declared object:

```
cout << *pveg << "\n";
```

This causes the function to display the *"Cabbage Heads Home"* string.

Then the function terminates, automatically freeing the memory used by its variables. This means the memory used to hold the pointer *pveg* is freed. But because *callme2()* doesn't use *delete pveg*, the memory holding the object to which *pveg* pointed

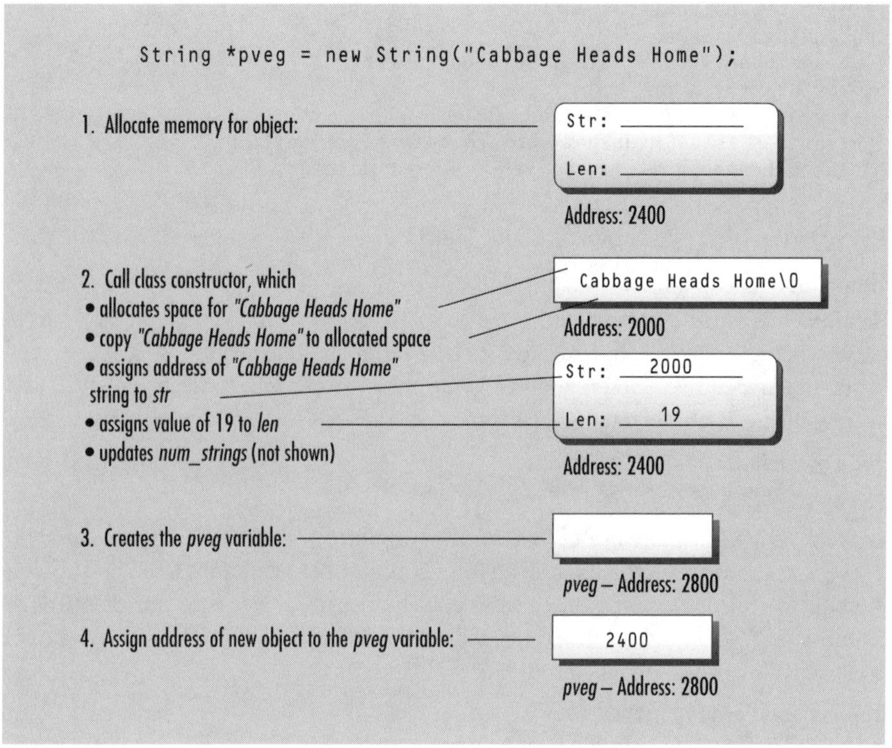

```
String *pveg = new String("Cabbage Heads Home");
```

1. Allocate memory for object: ——————

   Str: _____
   Len: _____
   Address: 2400

2. Call class constructor, which
   • allocates space for *"Cabbage Heads Home"*
   • copy *"Cabbage Heads Home"* to allocated space
   • assigns address of *"Cabbage Heads Home"* string to *str*
   • assigns value of 19 to *len*
   • updates *num_strings* (not shown)

   Cabbage Heads Home\0
   Address: 2000

   Str: ____2000____
   Len: ____19____
   Address: 2400

3. Creates the *pveg* variable: ——————

   pveg — Address: 2800

4. Assign address of new object to the *pveg* variable: ———

   2400

   pveg — Address: 2800

Figure 11-2 Creating an object with *new*

is still allocated. Note that there is no destructor message when *callme2()* terminates; that shows the object still is present—the string *"Cabbage Heads Home"* lives on! But because *pveg* has expired, the program no longer can access that object with *pveg*. However, the program passes the value of *pveg* back to the calling program and assigns it to the pointer *pr*. In short, at first *pveg* pointed to the *String* object. Then *pveg* expired, but meanwhile the program set *pr* to point to the *String* object. Thus the program now can use *pr* to access the dynamic object. And it does so after first displaying the *sports* object:

```
Top of callme2()
4: "Cabbage Heads Home" object created
Cabbage Heads Home                    ← uses pveg pointer in callme2()
End of callme2()
Spinach Leaves Bowl for Dollars
Cabbage Heads Home                    ← uses pr pointer in main()
```

Now the program moves to the sad tasks of deleting the remaining objects. Because it created the cabbage object with *new*, it can remove it with *delete*:

```
delete pr;
```

Recall that this frees the memory that *pr* points to and not *pr* itself. In short, this statement deleted the object. Deleting the object, in turn, activates the class destructor, which then deletes the memory occupied by the *"Cabbage Heads Home"* string:

```
"Cabbage Heads Home" object deleted, 3 left
```

Scoping rules control the existence of the remaining objects. The two array elements are automatic variables, so they expire when execution leaves the block in which they are defined. In this case, the block is the body of the *main()* function, so these two objects are freed when *main()* terminates. Last of all, the external object expires when the program terminates:

```
End of main()
"Celery Stalks at Midnight" object deleted, 2 left
"Lettuce Prey" object deleted, 1 left
"Spinach Leaves Bowl for Dollars" object deleted, 0 left
```

Looking Again at *new* and *delete*

Note that the program uses *new* and *delete* on two levels. First, it uses *new* to allocate storage space for the name strings for each object that is created. This happens in the constructor functions, so the destructor function uses *delete* to free that memory. Because each string is an array of characters, the destructor uses *delete* with brackets. Thus, memory used to store the string contents is freed automatically when an object is destroyed. Second, the program uses *new* to allocate an entire object in the *callme2()* function. This allocates space not for the name string but for the object, that is, for the *str* pointer that holds the address of the string and for the *len* member. (It does not allocate space for the *num_strings* member because that is a static member stored separately from the objects.) Creating the object, in turn, calls the constructor, which allocates space for storing the string and assigns the string's address to *str.* The program then used *delete* to delete this object when it was finished with it. The object is a single object, so the program uses *delete* without brackets. Again, this frees only the space used to hold the *str* pointer and the *len* member. It doesn't free the memory used to hold the string *str* points to, but the destructor takes care of that final task.

Let's emphasize again when destructors get called. (Also see Figure 11-3.)

1. If an object is an automatic variable, the object's destructor is called when the program exits the block in which the object is defined. Thus, the destructor is called for *headlines[0]* and *headlines[1]* when the program exits *main()*, and the destructor for *grub* is called when the program exits *callme1()*.

2. If an object is a static variable (external, static, or static external), its destructor is called when the program terminates. This is what happened for the *sports* object.

3. If an object is created by *new,* its destructor is called only when you explicitly delete the object, as is the case for the object created in *callme2()* and deleted in *main()*.

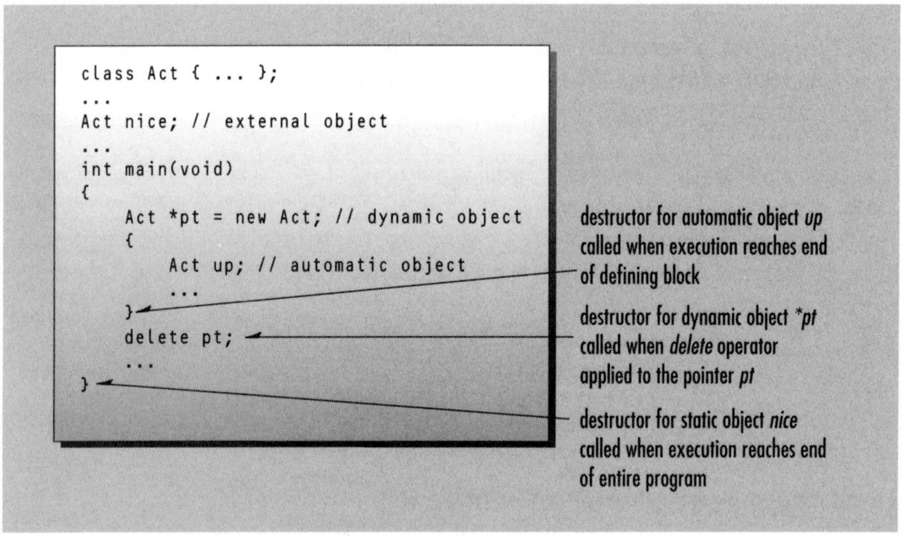

Figure 11-3 When destructors are called

The way this example uses *new* to create an object in one function and deletes the object in another function is a potential problem source, for it relies upon the programmer to remember to delete the object. For instance, consider the following hideous variation:

```
String * ps;
for (int i = 0; i < 100; i++)
{
        ps = callme2();
        cout << *ps << "\n";
}
delete ps;
```

This code creates 100 distinct objects. Each loop cycle sets *ps* to point to the most recent object, losing track of the location of the preceding object. Finally, the code deletes only the last object created. The other 99 wind up occupying memory to which the program has no access. This sort of programming bumbling is called a *memory leak*. Properly designed destructors prevent internal memory leaks in an object once an object is destroyed, but you still have to explicitly delete objects you explicitly create by using *new*.

Trouble in String City

Our definition of a *String* class is incomplete. Of course, for brevity's sake, it fails to implement many useful methods, such as overloading the < , ==, and > operators to facilitate string comparisons. But the class flaws are more fundamental than that. As proof, consider this simple program (Listing 11-4), using the current *String* implementation:

Listing 11-4 *problem1.cpp*

```
// problem1.cpp -- uses a function with a String argument
// compile with strng1.cpp
#include <iostream.h>
#include "strng1.h"

void showit(String s, int n);
int main(void)
{
        String motto("Home Sweet Home");
        showit(motto, 3);
        return 0;
}

void showit(String s, int n)           // show String s n times
{
        for (int i = 0; i < n; i++)
                cout << s << "\n";
}
```

COMPATIBILITY NOTE

Because this and the next two programs demonstrate a design flaw, the output will vary from compiler to compiler. The samples shown here are from Borland C++ 3.1.

The example passes a *String* object to the *showit()* function, which then displays the string the indicated number of times. Here is the output for one system:

```
1: "Home Sweet Home" object created
Home Sweet Home
Home Sweet Home
Home Sweet Home
"Home Sweet Home" object deleted, 0 left
"Home Sweet Home" object deleted, -1 left
Null pointer assignment
```

You'll note a couple of peculiar features. First, the program shows just one object being created but two objects being destroyed, leaving a total of -1 objects in memory! Then there is the cryptic message about a null pointer assignment. (Whether you get this message or some other message or no message at all depends upon your compiler, but regardless of the message, there is an underlying problem.)

Here's another simple program (Listing 11-5) that falters:

Listing 11-5 *problem2.cpp*

```
// problem2.cpp -- initializes one string to another
// compile with strng1.cpp
```

continued on next page

continued from previous page

```
#include <iostream.h>
#include "strng1.h"

int main(void)
{
        String motto("Home Sweet Home");
        String ditto(motto);  // initialize ditto to motto

        cout << motto << "\n";
        cout << ditto << "\n";
        return 0;
}
```

It attempts to do something that the class declaration apparently doesn't handle: using one *String* object to initialize another. However, as the following output shows, it succeeds in doing so. The program also exhibits the same weird behavior that the preceding example did:

```
1: "Home Sweet Home" object created
Home Sweet Home
Home Sweet Home
"Home Sweet Home" object deleted, 0 left
"Home Sweet Home" object deleted, -1 left
Null pointer assignment
```

Implicit Member Functions

What these two examples have in common is that they invoke implicit member functions that are defined automatically and whose behavior is inappropriate to the class design. In particular, C++ automatically provides the following member functions:

- A default constructor if you define no constructors
- A copy constructor if you don't define one
- An assignment operator if you don't define one
- An address operator if you don't define one

The implicit address operator returns the address of the invoking object (that is, the value of the *this* pointer). That's fine for our purposes, and we won't discuss this member function further. But the others do warrant more discussion.

The Default Constructor

If you fail to provide any constructors at all, C++ provides you with a default constructor. For instance, suppose you define a *Klunk* class and omit any constructors. Then the compiler will supply the following default:

```
Klunk::Klunk() { }    // implicit default constructor
```

That is, it supplies a constructor that takes no arguments and that does nothing. It's needed because creating an object always invokes a constructor:

```
Klunk lunk;    // invokes default constructor
```

The default constructor makes *lunk* like an ordinary automatic variable; that is, its value at initialization is unknown.

Once you define any constructor, C++ doesn't bother to define a default constructor. If you want to create objects that aren't initialized explicitly, or if you want to create an array of objects, you then have to define a default constructor explicitly. It's the constructor with no arguments, but you can use it to set particular values:

```
Klunk::Klunk() // explicit default constructor
{
        klunk_ct = 0;
        ...
}
```

A constructor with arguments still can be a default constructor if all its arguments have default values. For instance, the *Klunk* class could have the following inline constructor:

```
Klunk(int n = 0) { klunk_ct = n; }
```

However, you can have only one default constructor. That is, you can't do this:

```
Klunk() { klunk_ct = 0 }
Klunk(int n = 0) { klunk_ct = n; }    // ambiguous
```

The Copy Constructor

The copy constructor is used to copy an object to a newly created object. That is, it's used during initialization, not during ordinary assignment. The copy constructor for a class has this prototype:

Class_name(const *Class_name* &);

Note that it takes a constant reference to a class object as its argument. For instance, the copy constructor for the *String* class would have this prototype:

```
String(const String &);
```

You need to know two things about the copy constructor: when it's used and what it does.

When the Copy Constructor Is Used

The copy constructor is invoked whenever a new object is created and initialized to an existing object of the same kind. This happens in several situations. The most obvious situation is when you explicitly initialize a new object to an existing object. For instance, given that *motto* is a *String* object, the following four defining declarations invoke the copy constructor:

```
String ditto(motto);  // calls String(const String &)
String metoo = motto; // calls String(const String &)
String also = String(motto); // calls String(const String &)
String * pstring = new String(motto);       // calls String(const String &)
```

Depending upon the implementation, the middle two declarations may use the copy constructor directly to create *metoo* and *also*, or they may use the copy constructor to generate temporary objects whose contents are then assigned to *metoo* and *also*. The last example initializes an anonymous object to *motto* and assigns the address of the new object to the *pstring* pointer.

Less obviously, the compiler uses the copy constructor whenever a program generates copies of an object. In particular, it's used when a function passes an object by value or when it returns an object. Remember, passing by value means creating a copy of the original variable. The compiler also uses the copy constructor whenever it generates temporary objects. For instance, a compiler might generate a temporary *Vector* object to hold an intermediate result when adding three *Vector* objects. Compilers will vary as to when they generate temporary objects, but all will invoke the copy constructor when passing objects by value and when returning them. In particular, the function call in Listing 11-4 invoked the copy constructor:

```
showit(motto, 3);    // creates and passes copy of motto object
```

The program uses the copy constructor to initialize *st*, the formal *String*-type parameter for the *showit()* function.

By the way, the fact that passing an object by value involves invoking a copy constructor is a good reason for passing a reference instead. That saves the time of invoking the constructor and the space for storing the new object.

What the Copy Constructor Does

The default copy constructor performs a member-by-member copy of the nonstatic members (*memberwise copying*). Each member is copied by value. In Listing 11-5 this amounts to the following:

```
ditto.str = motto.str;
ditto.len = motto.len;
```

If a member is itself a class object, the copy constructor for that class is used to copy one member object to another. Static members, such as *num_strings,* are unaffected, for they belong to the class as a whole instead of to individual objects. Figure 11-4 illustrates the action of the implicit copy constructor.

Where We Went Wrong

We are now in a position to understand the threefold weirdness of Listings 11-4 and 11-5. The first weirdness is that the program output showed one object constructed but two destroyed. The explanation is that each program did create two objects, with the second object being created by the copy constructor. The default copy constructor

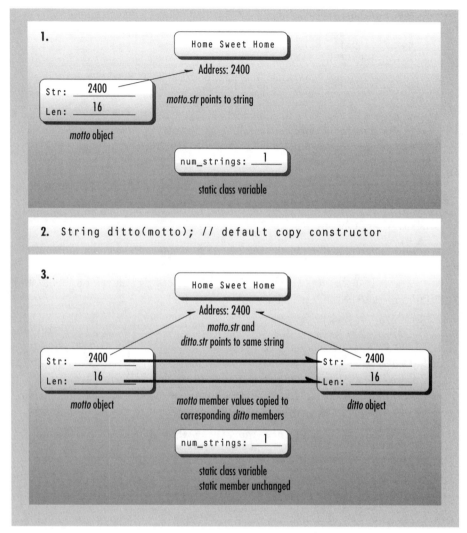

1.

Home Sweet Home

Address: 2400

Str: ___2400___

Len: ___16___

motto object

motto.str points to string

num_strings: ___1___

static class variable

2. String ditto(motto); // default copy constructor

3.

Home Sweet Home

Address: 2400

motto.str and
ditto.str points to same string

Str: ___2400___

Len: ___16___

motto object

Str: ___2400___

Len: ___16___

ditto object

motto member values copied to
corresponding *ditto* members

num_strings: ___1___

static class variable
static member unchanged

Figure 11-4 Memberwise copying

doesn't vocalize its activities, so it didn't announce its creations. This weirdness is merely cosmetic in nature and doesn't affect the reliability of the program.

The second weirdness is that each program reported that -1 objects were left. The explanation for this is that the default constructor doesn't affect static members. Thus, the copy constructor didn't update the *num_strings* count. The destructor, however, does update the count, and it's invoked upon the demise of all objects, regardless of how they were constructed. This weirdness is a problem, for it means the program doesn't keep an accurate object count. The solution is to provide an explicit copy constructor that does update the count:

```
String::String(const String & s)
{
        num_strings++;
        ...// important stuff to go here
}
```

TIP

If your class has a static data member whose value changes when new objects are created, provide an explicit copy constructor that handles the accounting.

The third weirdness is the most subtle and dangerous of the bunch. The symptom, on our system, was the following message, which appeared after the program terminated:

```
Null pointer assignment
```

Other systems might provide different messages or even no message, but the same evil lurks within the programs.

The cause is that the implicit copy constructor copies by value. Consider Listing 11-5, for example. The effect, recall, is this:

```
ditto.str = motto.str;
```

This does *not* copy the string; it copies the pointer to a string. That is, after *ditto* is initialized to *motto*, we wind up with *two* pointers to the *same* string. That's not a problem when the *operator<<()* function uses the pointer to display the string. It is a problem when the destructor is called. The *String* destructor, recall, frees the memory pointed to by the *str* pointer. The effect of destroying *ditto* is this:

```
delete [] ditto.str;  // delete the string that ditto.str points to
```

This frees the memory occupied by the string *"Home Sweet Home"*. Next, the effect of destroying *motto* is this:

```
delete [] motto.str;  // effect is undefined
```

Here, *motto.str* points to a memory location that has already been freed, and this results in undefined, possibly harmful, behavior. In our case, the program produced the null pointer warning, which usually is a sign of memory mismanagement.

The cure is to make a *deep copy*. That is, rather than just copying the address of the string, the copy constructor should duplicate the string and assign the address of the duplicate to the *str* member. That way, each object gets its own string rather than referring to another object's string. And each call of the destructor frees a different string rather than having duplicate attempts at freeing the same string. Here's how we can code the *String* copy constructor:

```
String::String(const String & st)
{
        num_strings++; // handle static member update
```

```
    len = st.len;              // same length
    str = new char [len + 1];     // allot space
    strcpy(str, st.str);   // copy string to new location
    cout << num_strings << ": \"" << str
          << "\" object created\n";       // For Your Information
}
```

What makes defining the copy constructor necessary is the fact that some class members were *new*-initialized pointers to data rather than the data themselves. Figure 11-5 illustrates deep copying.

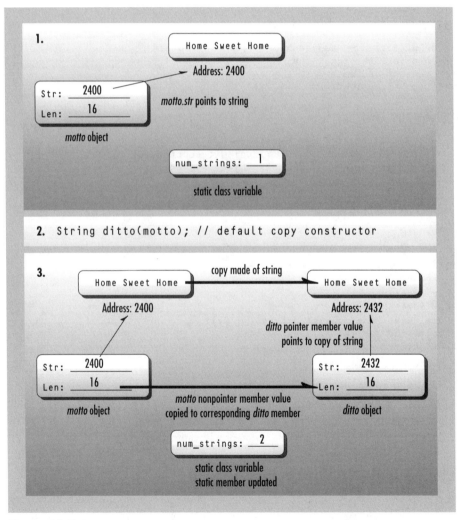

Figure 11-5 Deep copying

TIP

If a class contains members that are pointers initialized by *new*, then you should define a copy constructor that copies the pointed-to data instead of copying the pointers themselves. This is termed deep copying.

We'll test the new copy constructor soon, but first, let's look at yet another problem, one demonstrated by the short but flawed program of Listing 11-6. It assigns one object to another.

Listing 11-6 *problem3.cpp*

```cpp
// problem3.cpp -- assigns one object to another
// compile with strng1.cpp
#include <iostream.h>
#include "strng1.h"

int main(void)
{
        String motto("Home Sweet Home");
        String ditto;           // default constructor
        ditto = motto;          // object assignment
        cout << motto << "\n";
        cout << ditto << "\n";
        return 0;
}
```

Here's what happens when we run it (the exact consequences are compiler-dependent):

```
1: "Home Sweet Home" object created
2: "C++" object created
Home Sweet Home
Home Sweet Home
"Home Sweet Home" object deleted, 1 left
 Sweet Home" object deleted, 0 left
Null pointer assignment
```

Here at least the destructions balance the creations. However, one destruction seems to have messed up the string in the other object, for it reports a different string when it's destroyed. And once more the null pointer message disturbs our peace of mind. Again, the details of the output depend upon the compiler, but even if your output winds up looking correct, there still is a hidden, potentially dangerous problem.

The Assignment Operator

Just as ANSI C allows structure assignment, C++ allows class object assignment. It does so by automatically overloading the assignment operator for a class. It has the following prototype:

```
Class_name & Class_name::operator=(const Class_name &);
```

That is, it takes and returns a reference to an object of the class. For example, here's the prototype for the *String* class:

```
String & String::operator=(const String &);
```

When the Asignment Operator Is Used

The overloaded assignment operator is used when you assign one object to another existing object:

```
string motto("Home Sweet Home");
string ditto;
ditto = motto; // use overloaded assignment operator
```

It is *not* necessarily used when initializing an object:

```
string metoo = ditto; // use copy constructor
```

Here *metoo* is a newly-created object being initialized to *ditto*'s values; hence the copy constructor is used. However, as mentioned before, implementations have the option of handling this statement in two steps: using the copy constructor to create a temporary object, then using assignment to copy the values to the new object. That is, initialization always invokes the copy constructor, and forms using the = operator may also invoke the assignment operator.

What the Asignment Operator Does

Like the copy constructor, the implicit implementation of the assignment operator performs a member-to-member copy. If a member is itself an object of some class, the program uses the assignment operator defined for that class to do the copying for that particular member. Static data members are unaffected.

Where We Went Wrong

Listing 11-6 showed two oddities. First, the second call to the destructor displayed a string that had been altered mysteriously. Second, upon terminating, the program generated a null pointer assignment message. Both are indications of memory misman-agement. The problem is the same one we saw for the copy constructor: member-by-member copying copies the values of pointers instead of the pointed-to data. Thus, when the destructor is called for *ditto,* it deletes the string *"Home Sweet Home"*, and when it's called for *motto,* it attempts to delete the previously deleted string. As mentioned earlier, the effect of attempting to delete previously deleted data is undefined. Also, the effect of deleting memory *may* change the memory contents. In Listings 11-4 and 11-5, the first *delete* actually left the string unchanged, for the second call to the destructor displayed the string correctly. In Listing 11-6, however, the initial deletion modified the string. As some like to point out, if the effect of a particular operation is undefined, your compiler can do anything it wants, including displaying the *Declaration of Independence* or freeing your hard disk of unsightly files.

Fixing Assignment

The solution for the problems created by an inappropriate default assignment operator is to provide your own assignment operator definition, one that makes a deep copy. The implementation is similar to that of the copy constructor, but there are some differences.

1. Because the target object may already refer to previously allocated data, the function should use *delete* to free former obligations.

2. The function should protect against assigning an object to itself; otherwise, the freeing of memory described above could erase the object's contents before they are reassigned.

3. The function returns a reference to the invoking object.

By returning an object, the function can emulate the way ordinary assignment for built-in types can be chained. That is, if *A, B,* and *C* are *String* objects, you can write the following:

```
A = B = C;
```

In function notation, this becomes the following:

```
A.operator=(B.operator=(C));
```

Thus, the return value of *B.operator=(C)* becomes the argument of the *A.operator=()* function. Since the return value is a reference to a *String* object, it is the correct argument type.

Here's how we could write an assignment operator for the *String* class:

```
String & String::operator=(const String & s)
{
        if (this == &s)          // object assigned to itself
              return *this;  // all done
        delete [] str; // free old string
        len = s.len;
        str = new char [len + 1];     // get space for new string
        strcpy(str, s);        // copy the string
        return *this;          // return reference to invoking object
}
```

First, the code checks for self-assignment. It does so by seeing if the address of the right-hand side of the assignment (*&s*) is the same as the address of the receiving object *(this)*. If so, the program returns **this* and terminates. You may recall from Chapter 10 that the assignment operator is one of the operators that can be overloaded *only* by a class member function.

Otherwise, the function proceeds to free the memory that *str* pointed to. The reason for this is that shortly thereafter *str* will be assigned the address of a new string. If we didn't first apply the *delete* operator, the previous string would remain in memory. Since the program no longer has a pointer to the old string, that memory would be wasted.

Next, the program proceeds like the copy constructor, allocating enough space for the new string, then copying the string from the right-hand object to the new location.

Once finished, the program returns **this* and terminates.

Assignment does not create a new object, so we don't have to adjust the value of the static data member *num_strings*.

The New, Improved *String* Class

Now that we are a bit wiser, let's revise the *String* class. First, we'll add the copy constructor and the assignment operator we just discussed so that the class correctly manages the memory used by class objects. Next, now that we've seen when objects are constructed and destroyed, we can mute the class constructors and destructors so that they no longer announce each time they are used. Also, now that we're no longer watching the constructors at work, let's simplify the default constructor so that it constructs an empty string instead of *"C++"*. And now that we've seen how a static data member works, we can remove the object-counting feature.

Next, let's add a few capabilities to the class. A useful *String* class would incorporate all the functionality of the standard *string.h* library of string functions, but we'll add just enough to show the way. (Keep in mind that our *String* class is just an illustrative example and that the draft ANSI/ISO C++ standard describes a much more extensive *string* class.) In particular, we'll add the following methods:

```
int length () { return len; }
friend Bool operator>(const String &st1, const String &st2);
friend Bool operator<(const String &st, const String &st2);
friend Bool operator==(const String &st, const String &st2);
friend operator>>(istream & is, String & st);
```

As in Chapter 9, we'll use an enumeration in a *booly.h* header file to define *Bool, True,* and *False*. The first new method returns the length of the stored string, and the next three allow you to compare strings. The *operator>()* function, for example, returns *True* if the first string comes after the second string alphabetically (or, more precisely, in the machine collating sequence). The simplest way to implement the string comparison functions is to use the standard *strcmp()* function, which returns a negative value if its first argument precedes the second alphabetically, zero if the strings are the same, and a positive value if the first follows the second alphabetically. So we can use *strcmp()* like this:

```
Bool operator>(const String &st1, const String &st2)
{
        if (strcmp(st1.str, st2.str) > 0)
                return True;
        else
                return False;
}
```

Making the comparison functions friends facilitates comparisions between *String* objects and regular C strings. For instance, suppose *answer* is a *String* object and that we have the following code:

```
if ("love" == answer)
```

This gets translated to the following:

```
if (operator==("love", answer))
```

The compiler then uses one of the constructors to convert the code, in effect, to this:

```
if (operator==(String("love"), answer))
```

And this matches the prototype.

The new default constructor merits notice. It will look like this:

```
String::String()
{
    len = 0;
    str = new char[1];
    str[0] = '\0';                  // default string
}
```

You may wonder why the code does this:

```
str = new char[1];
```

and not this:

```
str = new char;
```

Both forms allocate the same amount of memory. The difference is that the first form is compatible with the class destructor and the second is not. The destructor, recall, contains this code:

```
delete [] str;
```

Using *delete* with brackets is compatible with pointers initialized by using *new* with brackets and with the null pointer. Its effect is undefined for pointers initialized any other way.

 COMPATIBILITY NOTE

As mentioned before, the draft ANSI/ISO C++ standard calls for a new *bool* type with *true* and *false* values, and these can be used in place of *Bool*, *True*, and *False* here. Some current implementations have preempted the use of the terms, *Bool*, *True*, and *False*, so you may have to use alternative terms, such as *BooL*.

Before looking at the new listings, let's consider another matter. Suppose you want to copy an ordinary string to a *String* object. For instance, suppose you use *getline()* to read a string and you want to place it in a *String* object. The class methods already allow us to do the following:

```
String name;
char temp[40];
cin.getline(temp, 40);
name = temp;   // use constructor to convert type
```

However, this may not be a satisfactory solution if you have to do it often. To see why, let's review how the final statement works:

1. The program uses the *String(const char *)* constructor to construct a temporary *String* object containing a copy of the string stored in *temp*. Remember (Chapter 10) that a constructor with a single argument serves as a conversion function.

2. The program uses the *String & String::operator=(const String &)* function to copy information from the temporary object to the *name* object.

3. The program calls the *~String()* destructor to delete the temporary object.

The simplest way to make the process more efficient is to overload the assignment operator so that it works directly with ordinary strings. This removes the extra steps of creating and destroying a temporary object. Here's one possible implementation:

```
String & String::operator=(const char * s)

{
        delete [] str;
        len = strlen(s);
        str = new char[len + 1];
        strcpy(str, s);
        return *this;
}
```

As usual, we need to deallocate memory formerly managed by *str* and allocate enough memory for the new string.

Listing 11-7 shows the revised class declaration.

Listing 11-7 *strng2.h*

```
// strng2.h -- String class declaration
#ifndef _STRNG2_H_
#define _STRNG2_H_
#include <iostream.h>
#include "booly.h"  // our definitions of Bool, False, and True
class String
{
private:
        char * str;                     // pointer to string
        int len;                        // length of string
public:
        String(const char * s);         // constructor
        String();                       // default constructor
        String(const String & st);
```
continued on next page

continued from previous page

```
        ~String();                            // destructor
        int length () { return len; }
// overloaded operators
        String & operator=(const String & st); // Assignment operator
        String & operator=(const char * s); // Assignment operator #2
// friend functions
        friend Bool operator>(const String &st1, const String &st2);
        friend Bool operator<(const String &st, const String &st2);
        friend Bool operator==(const String &st, const String &st2);
        friend ostream & operator<<(ostream & os, const String & st);
        friend istream & operator>>(istream & is, String & st);
};
#endif
```

Next, Listing 11-8 presents the revised method definitions.

Listing 11-8 *strng2.cpp*

```
// strng2.cpp -- String class methods
#include <iostream.h>
#include <string.h>
#include "strng2.h"

// class methods

String::String(const char * s)      // make String from C string
{
        len = strlen(s);
        str = new char[len + 1];    // allot storage
        strcpy(str, s);             // initialize pointer
}

String::String()                    // default constructor
{
        len = 0;
        str = new char[1];
        str[0] = '\0';              // default string
}

String::String(const String & st)   // copy constructor
{
        len = st.len;
        str = new char[len + 1];
        strcpy(str, st.str);
}

String::~String()                   // destructor
{
        delete [] str;              // required
}

        // assign a String to a String
String & String::operator=(const String & st)
{
```

468

```
        if (this == &st)
                return *this;
        delete [] str;
        len = st.len;
        str = new char[len + 1];
        strcpy(str, st.str);
        return *this;
}


        // assign a C string to a String
String & String::operator=(const char * s)
{
        delete [] str;
        len = strlen(s);
        str = new char[len + 1];
        strcpy(str, s);
        return *this;
}


        // true if st1 follows st2 in collating sequence
Bool operator>(const String &st1, const String &st2)
{
        if (strcmp(st1.str, st2.str) > 0)
                return True;
        else
                return False;
}


        // true if st1 precedes st2 in collating sequence
Bool operator<(const String &st1, const String &st2)
{
        if (strcmp(st1.str, st2.str) < 0)
                return True;
        else
                return False;
}


        // true if st1 is the same as st2
Bool operator==(const String &st1, const String &st2)
{
        if (strcmp(st1.str, st2.str) == 0)
                return True;
        else
                return False;
}


        // display string
ostream & operator<<(ostream & os, const String & st)
{
        os << st.str;
        return os;
}


        // quick and dirty String input
```

continued on next page

continued from previous page

```
istream & operator>>(istream & is, String & st)
{
        char temp[80];
        is.getline(temp, 80);
        if (is)
                st = temp;
        return is;
}
```

The overloaded >> operator provides a simple way to read a line of keyboard input into a *String* object. However, it's not foolproof, for it assumes an input line of 79 characters or fewer. Keep in mind that the value of an *istream* object in an *if* condition evaluates to zero if input fails for some reason, such as encountering an end-of-file condition.

Let's exercise the class with a short program that lets you enter a few strings. The program has the user enter sayings, puts the strings into *String* objects, displays them, and reports which string is the shortest and which comes first alphabetically. Listing 11-9 shows the program.

Listing 11-9 *sayings1.cpp*

```
// sayings1.cpp -- uses expanded String class
// compile with strng2.cpp
#include <iostream.h>
#include "strng2.h"
const ArSize = 10;
const MaxLen = 81;
int main(void)
{
        String name;
        cout <<"Hi, what's your name?\n>> ";
        cin >> name;

        cout << name << ", please enter up to " << ArSize
                << " short sayings <empty line to quit>:\n";
        String sayings[ArSize];      // array of objects
        char temp[MaxLen];           // temporary string storage
        for (int i = 0; i < ArSize; i++)
        {
                cout << i+1 << ": ";
                cin.getline(temp, MaxLen);
                if (temp[0] == '\0')  // empty line?
                        break;        // i not incremented
                else
                        sayings[i] = temp;    // overloaded assignment
        }
        int total = i;                        // total # of lines read

        cout << "Here are your sayings:\n";
        for (i = 0; i < total; i++)
                cout << sayings[i] << "\n";
```

```
        int shortest = 0;
        int first = 0;
        for (i = 1; i < total; i++)
        {
                if (sayings[i].length() < sayings[shortest].length())
                        shortest = i;
                if (sayings[i] < sayings[first])
                        first = i;
        }
        cout << "Shortest saying:\n" << sayings[shortest] << "\n";
        cout << "First alphabetically:\n" << sayings[first] << "\n";
        return 0;
}
```

The program asks the user to enter up to ten sayings. Each saying is read into a temporary character array, then copied to a *String* object. If the user enters a blank line, a *break* statement terminates the input loop. After echoing the input, the program uses the *length()* and *operator<()* member functions to locate the shortest string and the alphabetically earliest string. Here's a sample run:

```
Hi, what's your name?
>> Misty Gutz
Misty Gutz, please enter up to 10 short sayings <empty line to quit>:
1: a fool and his money are soon parted
2: penny wise, pound foolish
3: the love of money is the root of much evil
4: out of sight, out of mind
5: absence makes the heart grow fonder
6: absinthe makes the hart grow fonder
7:
Here are your sayings:
a fool and his money are soon parted
penny wise, pound foolish
the love of money is the root of much evil
out of sight, out of mind
absence makes the heart grow fonder
absinthe makes the hart grow fonder
Shortest saying:
penny wise, pound foolish
First alphabetically:
a fool and his money are soon parted
```

When Using *new* in Constructors...

By now you've noticed that you must take special care when using *new* to initialize pointer members of an object. In particular, you should do the following:

> If you use *new* to initialize a pointer member in a constructor, you should use *delete* in the destructor.

> The uses of *new* and *delete* should be compatible. If a constructor uses *new* with brackets, then the destructor should use *delete* with brackets. If a

constructor uses *new* without brackets, the destructor should use *delete* without brackets.

❧ If there are multiple constructors, all should use *new* the same way, either all with brackets or all without brackets. There's only one destructor, so all constructors have to be compatible to that destructor. It is, however, permissible to initialize a pointer with *new* in one constructor and with the null pointer (*NULL* or *0*) in another constructor because it's okay to apply the *delete* operation (with or without brackets) to the null pointer.

❧ You should define a copy constructor that initializes one object to another by doing deep copying. Typically, the constructor would emulate the following example:

```
String::String(const String & s)
{
        num_strings++; // handle static member update
        len = str.len; // same length
        str = new char [len + 1];     // allot space
        strcpy(str, s);        // copy string to new location
}
```

In particular, the copy constructor should allocate space to hold the copied data, and it should copy the data, not just the address of the data. Also, it should update any static class members whose value would be affected by the process.

❧ You should define an assignment operator that copies one object to another by doing deep copying. Typically, the class method would emulate the following example:

```
String & String::operator=(const String & s)
{
        if (this == &s)        // object assigned to itself
                return *this; // all done
        delete [] str; // free old string
        len = s.len;
        str = new char [len + 1];     // get space for new string
        strcpy(str, s);        // copy the string
        return *this;          // return reference to invoking object
}
```

In particular, the method should check for self-assignment; it should free memory formerly pointed to by the member pointer; it should copy the data, not just the address of the data; and it should return a reference to the invoking object.

The following excerpt contains two examples of what *not* to do and one example of a good constructor:

```
String::String()
{
   str = "default string";    // oops, no new []
   len = strlen(str);
}

String::String(const char * s)
{
   len = strlen(s);
   str = new char;            // oops, no []
   strcpy(str, s);            // oops, no room
}

String::String(const String & st)
{
      len = st.len;
      str = new char[len + 1];       // good, allocate space
      strcpy(str, st.str);           // good, copy value
}
```

The first constructor fails to use *new* to initialize *str*. The destructor, when called for a default object, will apply *delete* to *str*. The result of applying *delete* to a pointer not initialized by *new* is undefined, but probably bad. Any of the following would be okay:

```
String::String()
{
   len = 0;
   str = new char[1]; // uses new with []
   str[0] = '\0';
}

String::String()
{
   len = 0;
   str = NULL;
}

String::String()
{
      static const char * s = "C++";        // initialized just once
      len = strlen(s);
      str = new char[len + 1];      // uses new with []
      strcpy(str, s);
   }
```

The second constructor in the original excerpt applies *new*, but it fails to request the correct amount of memory; hence *new* will return a block containing space for but one character. Attempting to copy a longer string to that location is asking for memory problems. Also, the use of *new* without brackets is inconsistent with the correct form of the other constructors.

The third constructor is fine.

Finally, here's a destructor that won't work correctly with the above constructors.

```
String::~String()
{
    delete str;                     // oops, should be delete [] str;
}
```

The destructor uses *delete* incorrectly. Because the constructors request arrays of characters, the destructor should *delete* an array.

Using Pointers to Objects

C++ programs often use pointers to objects, so let's get in a bit of practice. Listing 11-9 used array index values to keep track of the shortest string and of the first string alphabetically. Another approach is to use pointers to point to the current leaders in these categories. Listing 11-10 implements this approach, using two pointers to *String*. Initially the *shortest* pointer points to the first object in the array. Each time the program finds an object with a shorter string, it resets *shortest* to point to that object. Similarly, a *first* pointer tracks the alphabetically earliest string. Note that these two pointers do not create new objects; they merely point to existing objects.

For variety, the program uses a pointer that does keep track of a new object:

```
String * favorite = new String(sayings[choice]);
```

Here the pointer *favorite* provides our only access to the nameless object created by *new*. This particular syntax means to initialize the new *String* object by using the object *sayings[choice]*. That invokes the copy constructor because the argument type for the copy constructor *(const String &)* matches the initialization value *(sayings[choice])*. The program uses *srand()*, *rand()*, and *time()* to select a value for *choice* at random.

OBJECT INITIALIZATION WITH *new*

In general, if *Class_name* is a class and if *value* is of type *Type_name*, the statement

```
Class_name * pclass = new Class_name(value);
```

invokes the

```
Class_name(Type_name);
```

constructor. There may be trivial conversions, such as to:

```
Class_name(const Type_name &);
```

Also, the usual conversions invoked by prototype matching, such as from *int* to *double*, will take place as long as there is no ambiguity. An initialization of the form

```
Class_name * ptr = new Class_name;
```

invokes the default constructor.

Listing 11-10 *sayings2.cpp*

```
// sayings2.cpp -- uses pointers to objects
// compile with strng2.cpp
#include <iostream.h>
#include <stdlib.h>             // for rand(), srand()
#include <time.h>               // for time()
#include "strng2.h"
const ArSize = 10;
const MaxLen = 81;
int main(void)
{
        String name;
        cout <<"Hi, what's your name?\n>> ";
        cin >> name;

        cout << name << ", please enter up to " << ArSize
                << " short sayings <empty line to quit>:\n";
        String sayings[ArSize];
        char temp[MaxLen];              // temporary string storage
        for (int i = 0; i < ArSize; i++)
        {
                cout << i+1 << ": ";
                cin.getline(temp, MaxLen);
                if (temp[0] == '\0')  // empty line?
                        break;                  // i not incremented
                else
                        sayings[i] = temp;      // overloaded assignment
        }
        int total = i;                          // total # of lines read

        cout << "Here are your sayings:\n";
        for (i = 0; i < total; i++)
                cout << sayings[i] << "\n";

// use pointers to keep track of shortest, first strings
        String * shortest = &sayings[0];  // initialize to first object
        String * first = &sayings[0];
        for (i = 1; i < total; i++)
        {
                if (sayings[i].length() < shortest->length())
                        shortest = &sayings[i];
                if (sayings[i] < *first)        // compare values
                        first = &sayings[i];  // assign address
        }
        cout << "Shortest saying:\n" << * shortest << "\n";
        cout << "First alphabetically:\n" << * first << "\n";

        srand(time(0));
        int choice = rand() % total; // pick index at random
// use new to create, initialize new String object
```

continued on next page

continued from previous page

```
    String * favorite = new String(sayings[choice]);
    cout << "My favorite saying:\n" << *favorite << "\n";
    delete favorite;
    return 0;
}
```

Here's a sample run:

```
Hi, what's your name?
>> Kirt Rood
Kirt Rood, please enter up to 10 short sayings <empty line to quit>:
1: a friend in need is a friend indeed
2: neither a borrower nor a lender be
3: a stitch in time saves nine
4: a niche in time saves stine
5: it takes a crook to catch a crook
6: cold hands, warm heart
7:
Here are your sayings:
a friend in need is a friend indeed
neither a borrower nor a lender be
a stitch in time saves nine
a niche in time saves stine
it takes a crook to catch a crook
cold hands, warm heart
Shortest saying:
cold hands, warm heart
First alphabetically:
a friend in need is a friend indeed
My favorite saying:
a stitch in time saves nine
```

You should note several points about using pointers to objects. (Also see Figure 11-6.)

❧ You declare a pointer to an object using the usual notation:

```
String * glamour;
```

❧ You can initialize a pointer to point to an existing object:

```
String * first = &sayings[0];
```

❧ You can initialize a pointer using *new*; this creates a new object:

```
String * favorite = new String(sayings[choice]);
```

❧ Using *new* with a class invokes the appropriate class constructor to initialize the newly created object:

```
// invokes default constructor
String * gleep = new String;

// invokes the String(const char *) constructor
```

```
String * glop  new String("my my my");

// invokes the String(const String &) constructor
String * favorite = new String(sayings[choice]);
```

❧ You use the -> operator to access a class method via a pointer:

```
if (sayings[i].length() < shortest->length())
```

❧ You apply the dereferencing operator (*) to a pointer to an object to obtain an object:

```
if (sayings[i] < *first)     // compare object values
        first = &sayings[i]; // assign object address
```

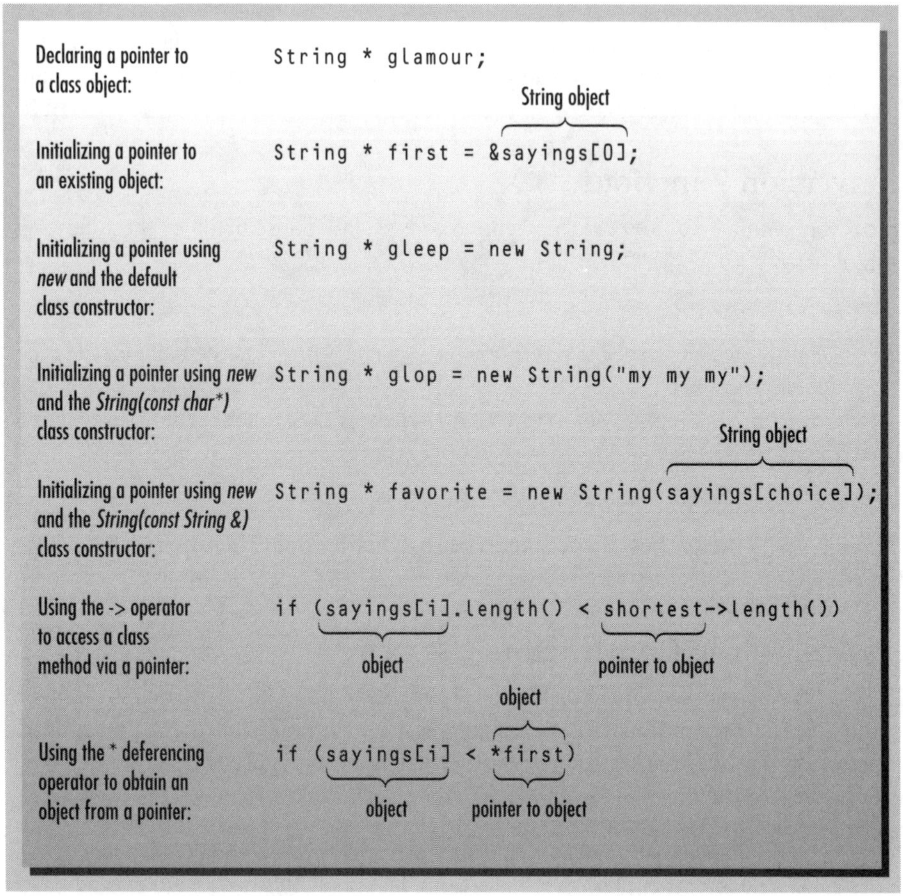

Declaring a pointer to a class object:	`String * glamour;`
Initializing a pointer to an existing object:	`String * first = &sayings[0];`
Initializing a pointer using *new* and the default class constructor:	`String * gleep = new String;`
Initializing a pointer using *new* and the *String(const char*)* class constructor:	`String * glop = new String("my my my");`
Initializing a pointer using *new* and the *String(const String &)* class constructor:	`String * favorite = new String(sayings[choice]);`
Using the -> operator to access a class method via a pointer:	`if (sayings[i].length() < shortest->length())`
Using the * dereferencing operator to obtain an object from a pointer:	`if (sayings[i] < *first)`

Figure 11-6 Pointers and Objects

Reviewing Techniques

By now you've encountered several programming techniques for dealing with various class-related problems, and you may be having trouble keeping track of all of them. So let's summarize several techniques and when they are used.

Overloading the << Operator

To redefine the << operator so that you use it with *cout* to display an object's contents, define a friend operator function of the following form:

```
ostream & operator<<(ostream & os, const c_name & obj)
{
        os << ... ;  // display object contents
        return os;
}
```

Here *c_name* represents the name of the class. If the class provides public methods that return the required contents, you can use those methods in the operator function and dispense with the friend status.

Conversion Functions

To convert a single value to a class type, create a class constructor of the following form of prototype:

c_name (*type_name value*) ;

Here *c_name* represents the class name, and *type_name* represents the name of the type that you wish to convert.

To convert a class type to some other type, create a class member function having the following prototype:

```
operator type_name();
```

Although the function has no declared return type, it should return a value of the desired type.

Classes Whose Constructors Use *new*

Classes that use the *new* operator to allocate memory pointed to by a class member require several precautions in the design. (Yes, we summarized these precautions recently, but the rules are very important to remember, particularly because the compiler does not know them and thus won't catch your mistakes.)

1. Any class member pointing to memory allocated by *new* should have the *delete* operator applied to it in the class destructor. This frees the allocated memory.

2. If a destructor frees memory by applying *delete* to a pointer that is a class member, then every constructor for that class should initialize that pointer either by using *new* or by setting the pointer to the *null* pointer.

3. Constructors should settle on using either *new* with brackets or *new* without brackets, but not a mixture of both. The destructor should use *delete* with brackets if the constructors use *new* with brackets, and it should use *delete* without brackets if the constructors use *new* without brackets.

4. You should define a copy constructor that allocates new memory rather than copying a pointer to existing memory. This enables a program to initialize one class object to another. The constructor should have the following form of prototype:

```
classname(const classname &)
```

5. You should define a class member function overloading the assignment operator and having the following form of function definition (here *c_pointer* is a member of the *c_name* class and has the type pointer-to-*type_name*):

```
c_name & c_name::operator=(const c_name & cn)
{
        delete c_pointer;
        c_pointer = new type_name[size];
        // then copy data pointed to by cn.c_pointer to
        // location pointed to by c_pointer
        ...
        return *this;
}
```

🔵 A Queue Simulation

Let's apply our improved understanding of classes to a programming problem. The Bank of Heather wishes to open an automatic teller in the Food Heap supermarket. The Food Heap management is concerned about lines at the automatic teller interfering with traffic flow in the market and may wish to impose a limit on the number of people allowed to line up at the teller machine. The Bank of Heather people want estimates of how long customers will have to wait in line. Our task is to prepare a program to simulate the situation so that management can see what the effect of the automatic teller might be.

A rather natural way of representing the problem is to use a queue of customers. A *queue* is an abstract data type (ADT) that holds an ordered sequence of items. New items are added to the rear of the queue, and items can be removed from the front. A queue is a bit like a stack, except that a stack has additions and removals at the same end. This makes a stack a LIFO (last in-first out) structure, while the queue is a FIFO (first in-first out) structure. Conceptually, a queue is like a line at a checkout stand or automatic teller, so it's ideally suited to the task. So one part of our project will be to define a *Queue* class.

The items in our queue will be customers. A Bank of Heather representative tells us that, on the average, a third of the customers will take one minute to be processed, a third will take two minutes, and a third will take three minutes. Furthermore, customers arrive at random intervals, but the average number of customers per hour is fairly constant. Two more parts of our project will be to design a class representing customers and to put together a program simulating the interactions between customers and the queue. See Figure 11-7.

A Queue Class

The first order of business is designing a queue class. First, let's list the attributes of the kind of queue we'll need:

- A queue holds an ordered sequence of items.
- A queue has a limit to the number of items it can hold.
- We should be able to create an empty queue.
- We should be able to check if a queue is empty.

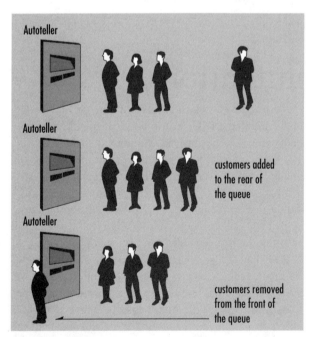

Figure 11-7 A queue

❥ We should be able to check if a queue is full.

❥ We should be able to add an item to the end of a queue.

❥ We should be able to remove an item from the front of the queue.

❥ We should be able to determine the number of items in the queue.

As usual when designing a class, we'll need to develop a public interface and a private implementation.

The Interface

The queue attributes suggest the following public interface for a queue class:

```
#include "booly.h"  // our definitions of Bool, False, and True

class Queue
{
        enum {Q_SIZE = 10};
private:
// private representation to be developed later
public:
        Queue(int qs = Q_SIZE);         // create an empty queue with a qs limit
        ~Queue();
        Bool isempty() const;
        Bool isfull() const;
        int queuecount() const;
        Bool enqueue(const Item &item);         // add item to end
        Bool dequeue(Item &item);               // remove item from front
};
```

The constructor creates an empty queue. By default, the queue can hold up to ten items, but that can be overridden with an explicit initialization argument:

```
Queue line1;                // queue with 10-item limit
Queue line2(20);            // queue with 20-item limit
```

When using the queue, we can use a *typedef* to define *Item*. (In Chapter 13 you'll learn how to use class templates instead.)

The Implementation

Next, let's implement the interface. First, we have to decide how to represent the queue data. One approach is to use *new* to dynamically allocate an array with the required number of elements. However, arrays aren't a good match to queue operations. For instance, removing an item from the front of the array should be followed up by shifting every remaining element one unit closer to the front. Or else you'll need to do something more elaborate, such as treating the array as circular. The *linked list*, on the other hand, is a good fit to the requirements of a queue. A linked list consists of a sequence of *nodes*. Each node contains the information to be held in the list plus a

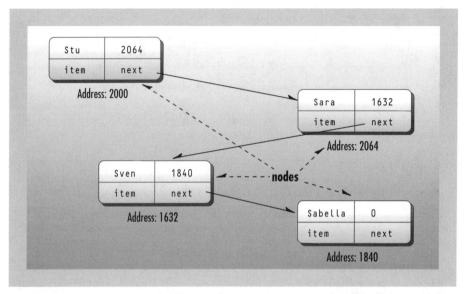

Figure 11-8 A linked list

pointer to the next node in the list. For our queue, each data part will be a type *Item* value, and we can use a structure to represent a node:

```
struct Node
{
    Item item;            // data stored in the node
    struct Node * next;   // pointer to next node
};
```

Figure 11-8 illustrates a linked list. This particular form of linked list is called a singly linked list because each node has a single link, or pointer, to another node. If you have the address of the first node, you can follow the pointers to each subsequent list. Commonly the pointer in the last node in the list is set to *NULL* to indicate that there are no further nodes. To keep track of a linked list, we need to know the address of the first node. We can use a data member of the *Queue* class to point to the beginning of the list. In principle, that's all the information we need, for we can trace down the chain of nodes to find any other node. However, because a queue always adds a new item to the end of the queue, it will be convenient to have a data member pointing to the last node, too. See Figure 11-9. In addition, we can use data members to keep track of the maximum number of items allowed in the queue and of the current number of items. Thus, the private part of the class declaration can look like this:

```
class Queue
{
// class scope definition
    // Node is a nested structure definition local to this class
```

```
        struct Node { Item item; struct Node * next;};
private:
        Node * front;          // pointer to front of Queue
        Node * rear;           // pointer to rear of Queue
        int items;             // current number of items in Queue
        const int qsize;       // maximum number of items in Queue
public:
//
};
```

The declaration uses a new C++ feature: the ability to nest a structure or class declaration inside a class. By placing the *Node* declaration inside the *Queue* class, we give it class scope. That is, *Node* is a type that we can use to declare class members and as a type in class methods, but the type is restricted to the class. That way we don't have to worry about this declaration of *Node* conflicting with some global declaration or with a *Node* declared inside some other class. Not all compilers currently support nested structures and classes. If yours doesn't, then you'll have to define a *Node* structure globally, giving it file scope.

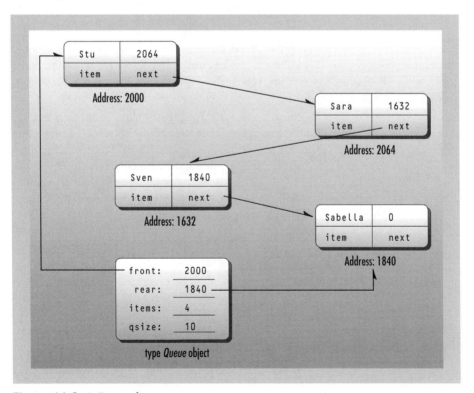

Figure 11-9 A *Queue* object

NESTED STRUCTURES AND CLASSES

A structure, class, or enumeration declared within a class declaration is said to be nested in the class. It has class scope. Such a declaration doesn't create a data object. Rather, it specifies a type that can be used internally within the class.

Once we've settled upon a data representation, the next step is to code the class methods.

The Class Methods

The class constructor should provide values for the class members. Because we begin with an empty queue, we should set the *front* and *rear* pointers to NULL and *items* to 0. Also, we should set the maximum queue size *qsize* to the constructor argument *qs*. Here's an implementation that does not work:

```
Queue::Queue(int qs)
{
        front = rear = NULL;
        items = 0;
        qsize = qs;    // not acceptable
}
```

The problem is that *qsize* is a *const,* so it can be initialized to a value, but it can't be assigned a value. Conceptually, calling a constructor creates an object *before* the code within the brackets is executed. Thus, calling the *Queue(int qs)* constructor causes the program to first allocate space for the four member variables. Then program flow enters the brackets and uses ordinary assignment to place values into the allocated space. Therefore, if we wish to initialize a *const* data member, we have do so *before* the brackets. C++ provides a special syntax for doing just that. It's called an *initializer list.* The initializer list consists of a comma-separated list of initializers preceded by a colon. It's placed after the closing parenthesis of the argument list and before the opening bracket of the function body. If a data member is named *mdata* and if it's to be initialized to value *val,* the initializer has the form *mdata(val).* Using this notation, we can write the *Queue* constructor like this:

```
Queue::Queue(int qs) : qsize(qs)       // initialize qsize to qs
{
        front = rear = NULL;
        items = 0;
}
```

In general, the initial value can involve constants and arguments from the constructor's argument list. We also could write the *Queue* constructor like this:

```
Queue::Queue(int qs) : qsize(qs), front(NULL), rear(NULL), items(0)

{
}
```

Only constructors can use this initializer-list syntax. As you've seen, you have to use this syntax for *const* class members. You also have to use it for class members that are declared as references:

```
class Agency {...};
class Agent
{

private:
        Agency & belong;        // must use initializer list to initialize
        ...
};
Agent::Agent(Agency & a) : belong(a) {...}
```

That's because references, like *const* data, can be initialized only when created. For simple data members, like *front* and *items*, it doesn't make much difference whether you use an initializer list or use assignment in the function body. As you'll see in Chapter 13, however, it's more efficient to use the initializer list for members that are themselves class objects.

 ## THE INITIALIZER LIST SYNTAX

If *Classy* is a class and if *mem1, mem2,* and *mem3* are class data members, a class constructor can use the following syntax to initialize the data members:

```
Classy::Classy(int n, int m) :mem1(n), mem2(0), mem3(n*m + 2)
{
//
}
```

This initializes *mem1* to *n, mem2* to *0,* and *mem3* to *n*m + 2.* Conceptually, these initializations take place when the object is created and before any code within the brackets is executed. Note the following:

⚓ This form can be used only with constructors.

⚓ You must use this form to initialize a nonstatic *const* data member.

⚓ You must use this form to initialize a reference data member.

Data members get initialized in the order in which they appear in the class declaration, not in the order in which initializers are listed.

Incidentally, the initializer form used in the initializer list can be used elsewhere. That is, if you like, you can replace code like

```
int games = 162;
double  talk = 2.71828;
```

with

```
int games(162);
double  talk(2.71828);
```

This lets initializing built-in types look like initializing class objects.

The code for *isempty()*, *isfull()*, and *queuecount()* is simple. If *items* is 0, the queue is empty. If *items* is *qsize*, the queue is full. Returning the value of *items* answers the question of how many items are in the queue. We'll show the code in a header file later.

Adding an item to the rear of the queue (*enqueuing*) is more involved. Here is one approach:

```
Bool Queue::enqueue(const Item & item)
{
        if (isfull())
                return False;
        Node * add = new Node;          // create node
        if (add == NULL)
                return False;           // quit if none available
        add->item = item;           // set node pointers
        add->next = NULL;
        items++;
        if (front == NULL)              // if queue is empty,
                front = add;            // place item at front
        else
                rear->next = add;       // else place at rear
        rear = add;                     // have rear point to new node
        return True;
}
```

In brief, the method goes through the following phases (also see Figure 11-10):

1. Terminate if the queue is already full.

2. Create a new node, terminating if it can't do so—for example, if the request for more memory fails.

3. Place proper values into the node. In this case, the code copies an *Item* value into the data part of the node and sets the node's *next* pointer to *NULL*. This prepares the node to be the last item in the queue.

4. Increase the item count (*items*) by one.

5. Attach the node to the rear of the queue. There are two parts to this process. The first is linking the node to the other nodes in the list. This is done by having the *next* pointer of the currently rear node point to the new rear node. The second part is to set the *Queue* member pointer, *rear*, to point to the new node so that the queue can access the last node directly. If the queue is empty, we also need to set the *front* pointer to point to the new node. (If there's just one node, it's both the front and the rear node.)

Removing an item from the front of the queue (*dequeuing*) also has several steps.

```
Bool Queue::dequeue(Item & item)
{
        if (front == NULL)
                return False;
        item = front->item;                 // set item to first item in queue
```

```
      items--;
      Node * temp = front;    // save location of first item
      front = front->next;    // reset front to next item
      delete temp;                    // delete former first item
      if (items == 0)
            rear = NULL;
      return True;
}
```

In brief, the method goes through the following phases (also see Figure 11-11):

1. Terminate if the queue is already empty.

2. Provide the first item in the queue to the calling function. This is accomplished by copying the data portion of the current front node into the reference variable passed to the method.

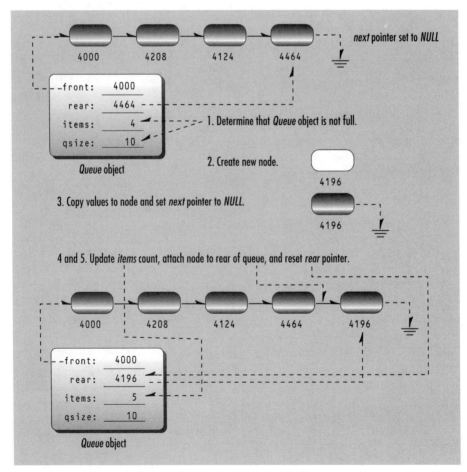

Figure 11-10 Enqueuing an item

3. Decrease the item count *(items)* by one.

4. Save the location of the front node for later deletion.

5. Take the node off the queue. This is accomplished by setting the *Queue* member pointer *front* to point to the next node, whose address is provided by *front->next*.

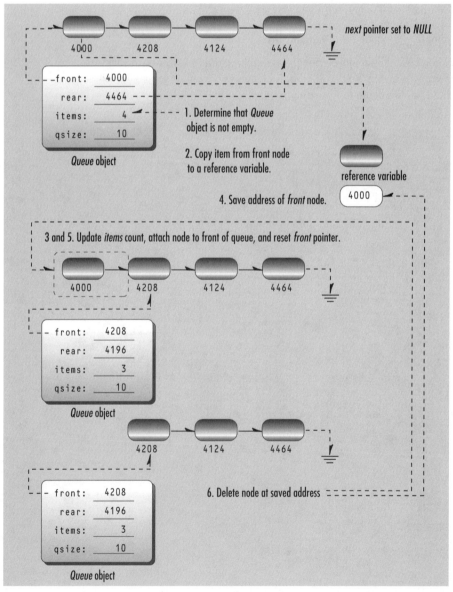

Figure 11-11 Dequeuing an item

6. To conserve memory, delete the former first node.

7. If the list is now empty, set *rear* to *NULL*. (The *front* pointer already would be NULL in this case after being set to *front->next*.)

The reason step 4 is necessary is that step 5 erases the queue's memory of where the former first node is.

Other Class Methods?

Do we need any more methods? The class constructor doesn't use *new*, so at first glance it may appear we don't have to worry about the special requirements of classes that do use *new* in the constructors. Of course, that first glance is misleading, for adding objects to a queue does invoke *new* to create new nodes. It's true that the *dequeue()* method cleans up by deleting nodes, but there's no guarantee that a queue will be empty when it expires. Therefore, the class does require an explicit destructor, one that deletes all remaining nodes. Here's an implementation:

```
Queue::~Queue()
{
        Node * temp;
        while (front != NULL) // while queue is not yet empty
        {
                temp = front;        // save address of front item
                front = front->next; // reset pointer to next item
                delete temp;         // delete former front
        }
}
```

It starts at the front of the list and deletes each node in turn.

Hmmm. We've seen that classes using *new* usually require explicit copy constructors and assignment operators that do deep copying. Is that the case here? The first question to answer is, does the default memberwise copying do the right thing? The answer is no. Memberwise copying of a *Queue* object would produce a new object that pointed to the front and rear of the same linked list as the original. Thus adding an item to the copy *Queue* object changes the shared linked list. That's bad enough. What's worse is that only the copy's *rear* pointer gets updated, essentially corrupting the list from the standpoint of the original object. Clearly, then, cloning or copying queues requires providing a copy constructor and an assignment constructor that do deep copying.

Of course, that raises the question of why would we want to copy a queue? Well, perhaps one would want to save snapshots of a queue during different stages of a simulation. Or one would like to provide identical input to two different strategies. Actually, it might be useful to have operations that split a queue, the way supermarkets sometimes do when opening an additional checkout stand. Similarly, one might wish to combine two queues into one or truncate a queue.

But we don't want to do *any* of these things in our simulation. Can't we simply ignore those concerns and use the methods we already have? Of course we can.

However, at some time in the future, we may need to use a queue again, this time with copying. And we might forget that we failed to provide proper code for copying. Our programs will compile and run, but will generate puzzling results and crashes. So maybe we'd better provide a copy constructor and an assignment operator, even though we don't need them now.

Fortunately, there is a sneaky way to avoid doing this extra work while still protecting ourselves from future program crashes. The idea is to define the required methods as dummy private methods:

```
class Queue
{
private:
        Queue(const Queue & q) : qsize(0) { }         // preemptive definition
        Queue & operator=(const Queue & q) { return *this;}
//
};
```

This has two effects. First, it overrides the implicit method definitions. Second, because these methods are private, they can't be used by the world at large. That is, if *nip* and *tuck* are *Queue* objects, the compiler won't allow the following:

```
Queue snick(nip);     // not allowed
tuck = nip;           // not allowed
```

Thus, instead of being faced with mysterious runtime malfunctions in the future, you'll get an easier-to-trace compiler error stating that these methods aren't accessible. Also, this trick is useful when you define a class whose objects should not be copied.

Are there any other effects to note? Yes. Recall that the copy constructor is invoked when objects are passed (or returned) by value. However, this is no problem if you follow the preferred practice of passing objects as references. Also, the copy constructor is used to create other temporary objects. But the *Queue* definition lacks operations that lead to temporary objects, such as overloading the addition operator.

The Customer Class

Next, we need to design a customer class. In general, a teller machine customer has many properties, such as a name, account numbers, and account balances. However, the only properties we need for the simulation are when a customer joins the queue and the time required for the customer's transaction. When the simulation produces a new customer, the program will create a new customer object, storing in it the customer's time of arrival and a randomly generated value for the transaction time. When the customer reaches the front of the queue, the program will note the time and subtract the queue-joining time to get the customer's waiting time. Here's how we can define and implement the *Customer* class:

```
class Customer
{
private:
```

```
        long arrive;           // arrival time for customer
        int processtime;       // processing time for customer
public:
        Customer() { arrive = processtime = 0; }
        void set(long when);
        long when() const { return arrive; }
        int ptime() const { return processtime; }
};
void Customer::set(long when)
{
        processtime = rand() % 3 + 1;
        arrive = when;
}
```

The default constructor creates a null customer. The *set()* member function sets the arrival time to its argument and randomly picks a value from *1* through *3* for the processing time.

Listing 11-11 gathers together the *Queue* and *Customer* class declarations, and Listing 11-12 provides the methods.

Listing 11-11 *queue.h*

```
// queue.h -- interface for a queue
#ifndef _QUEUE_H_
#define _QUEUE_H_
#include "booly.h"  // our definitions of Bool, False, and True
// This queue will contain Customer items
class Customer
{
private:
        long arrive;           // arrival time for customer
        int processtime;       // processing time for customer
public:
        Customer() { arrive = processtime = 0; }
        void set(long when);
        long when() const { return arrive; }
        int ptime() const { return processtime; }
};

typedef Customer Item;

class Queue
{
// class scope definitions
        // Node is a nested structure definition local to this class
        struct Node { Item item; struct Node * next;};
        enum {Q_SIZE = 10};
private:
        Node * front;           // pointer to front of Queue
        Node * rear;            // pointer to rear of Queue
        int items;              // current number of items in Queue
```
continued on next page

continued from previous page

```
        const int qsize;        // maximum number of items in Queue
        Queue(const Queue & q) : qsize(0) { }         // preemptive definition
        Queue & operator=(const Queue & q) { return *this;}
public:
        Queue(int qs = Q_SIZE);       // create queue with a qs limit
        ~Queue();
        Bool isempty() const;
        Bool isfull() const;
        int queuecount() const;
        Bool enqueue(const Item &item);       // add item to end
        Bool dequeue(Item &item);             // remove item from front
};
#endif
```

Listing 11-12 *queue.cpp*

```
// queue.cpp -- Queue and Customer methods
#include "queue.h"
#include <stdlib.h>            // for rand()

// Queue methods
Queue::Queue(int qs) : qsize(qs)
{
        front = rear = NULL;
        items = 0;
}

Queue::~Queue()
{
        Node * temp;
        while (front != NULL) // while queue is not yet empty
        {
                temp = front;          // save address of front item
                front = front->next;// reset pointer to next item
                delete temp;           // delete former front
        }
}

Bool Queue::isempty() const
{
        return items == 0 ? True : False;
}

Bool Queue::isfull() const
{
        return items == qsize ? True : False;
}

int Queue::queuecount() const
{
        return items;
}
```

```
// Add item to queue
Bool Queue::enqueue(const Item & item)
{
        if (isfull())
                return False;
        Node * add = new Node;          // create node
        if (add == NULL)
                return False;           // quit if none available
        add->item = item;               // set node pointers
        add->next = NULL;
        items++;
        if (front == NULL)              // if queue is empty,
                front = add;            // place item at front
        else
                rear->next = add;       // else place at rear
        rear = add;                     // have rear point to new node
        return True;
}

// Place front item into item variable and remove from queue
Bool Queue::dequeue(Item & item)
{
        if (front == NULL)
                return False;
        item = front->item;             // set item to first item in queue
        items--;
        Node * temp = front;            // save location of first item
        front = front->next;            // reset front to next item
        delete temp;                    // delete former first item
        if (items == 0)
                rear = NULL;
        return True;
}

// customer method

// when is the time at which the customer arrives
// the arrival time is set to when and the processing
// time set to a random value in the range 1 - 3
void Customer::set(long when)
{
        processtime = rand() % 3 + 1;
        arrive = when;
}
```

The Simulation

We now have the tools needed for the automatic teller simulation. Our program will allow the user to enter three quantities: the maximum queue size, the number of hours the program will simulate, and the average number of customers per hour. The program will use a loop in which each cycle represents one minute. During each minute cycle the program will do the following:

1. Determine if a new customer has arrived. If so, add the customer to the queue if there is room, otherwise turn the customer away.

2. If no one is being processed, take the first person from the queue. Determine how long the person has been waiting, and set a *wait_time* counter to the processing time that the new customer will need.

3. If a customer is being processed, decrement the *wait_time* counter one minute.

4. Track various quantities, such as the number of customers served, customers turned away, cumulative time spent waiting in line, and cumulative queue length.

Once the simulation cycle is finished, the program will report various statistical findings.

An interesting matter is how the program determines if a new customer has arrived. Suppose, on the average, 10 customers arrive an hour. That, on the average, amounts to a customer every 6 minutes. The program computes and stores that value in the variable *min_per_cust*. However, having a customer show up exactly every 6 minutes is unrealistic. What we really want (at least most of the time) is a more random process that *averages* to a customer every 6 minutes. Our program will use this function to determine if a customer shows up during a cycle:

```
Bool newcustomer(double x)
{
        if (rand() * x / RAND_MAX < 1)
                return True;
        else
                return False;
}
```

Here's how it works. The value *RAND_MAX* is defined in the *stdlib.h* file and represents the largest value the *rand()* function can return (*0* is the lowest value). Suppose that *x*, the average time between customers, is *6*. Then the value of *rand() * x / RAND_MAX* will be somewhere between *0* and *6*. In particular, it will be less than *1* a sixth of the time, on the average. However, it's possible that this function might yield two customers spaced 1 minute apart one time, or 20 minutes apart another time. This behavior leads to the clumpiness that often distinguishes real processes from the clocklike regularity of exactly one customer every 6 minutes. This particular method breaks down if the average time between arrivals drops below 1 minute, but the simulation is not intended to handle that scenario. If you did need to deal with such a case, you'd use a finer time resolution, perhaps letting each cycle represent 10 seconds.

COMPATIBILITY NOTE

Some compilers don't define *RAND_MAX*. If you face that situation, you can define a value for *RAND_MAX* yourself by using *#define* or else a *const int.* If you can't find the correct value documented, try using the largest possible *int* value, given by *INT_MAX* in the *limits.h* header file.

Listing 11-13 presents the details of the simulation. Running the simulation for a long time period provides insight into long-term averages, and running it for short times provides insight into short-term variations.

Listing 11-13 *bank.cpp*

```
// bank.cpp -- use the Queue interface
#include <iostream.h>
#include <stdlib.h>    // for rand() and srand()
#include <time.h>      // for time()
#include "queue.h"
const long MIN_PER_HR = 60;

Bool newcustomer(double x);           // is there a new customer?

int main(void)
{
// setting things up
        srand(time(0));                       //  random initializing of rand()

        cout << "Case Study: Bank of Heather Automatic Teller\n";
        cout << "Enter maximum size of queue: ";
        int qs;
        cin >> qs;
        Queue line(qs);                       // line queue holds up to qs people

        cout << "Enter the number of simulation hours: ";
        int hours;                            //  hours of simulation
        cin >> hours;
    // simulation will run 1 cycle per minute
        long cyclelimit = MIN_PER_HR * hours; // # of cycles

        cout << "Enter the average number of customers per hour: ";
        double perhour;          //  average # of arrival per hour
        cin >> perhour;
        double min_per_cust;  //  average time between arrivals
        min_per_cust = MIN_PER_HR / perhour;

        Item temp;                // new customer data
        long turnaways = 0;       // turned away by full queue
        long customers = 0;       // joined the queue
        long served = 0;          // served during the simulation
        long sum_line = 0;        // cumulative line length
        int wait_time = 0;        // time until autoteller is free
        long line_wait = 0;       // cumulative time in line


// running the simulation
        for (long cycle = 0; cycle < cyclelimit; cycle++)
```

continued on next page

continued from previous page

```
        {
                if (newcustomer(min_per_cust))         // have newcomer
                {
                        if (line.isfull())
                                turnaways++;
                        else
                        {
                                customers++;
                                temp.set(cycle);        // cycle = time of arrival
                                line.enqueue(temp);    // add newcomer to line
                        }
                }
                if (wait_time <= 0 && !line.isempty())
                {
                        line.dequeue (temp);     // attend next customer
                        wait_time = temp.ptime(); // for wait_time minutes
                        line_wait += cycle - temp.when();
                        served++;
                }
                if (wait_time > 0)
                        wait_time--;
                sum_line += line.queuecount();
        }

// reporting results
        if (customers > 0)
        {
                cout << "customers accepted: " << customers << '\n';
                cout << "  customers served: " << served << '\n';
                cout << "          turnaways: " << turnaways << '\n';
                cout << "average queue size: ";
                cout.precision(2);              // #.## format
                cout.setf(ios::fixed, ios::floatfield);
                cout.setf(ios::showpoint);
                cout << (double) sum_line / cyclelimit << '\n';
                cout << " average wait time: "
                        << (double) line_wait / served << " minutes\n";
        }
        else
                cout << "No customers!\n";

        return 0;
}

//   x = average time, in minutes, between customers
//   return value is True if customer shows up this minute
Bool newcustomer(double x)
{
        if (rand() * x / RAND_MAX < 1)
                return True;
        else
                return False;
}
```

Here are a few sample runs for a longer time period:

```
Case Study: Bank of Heather Automatic Teller
Enter maximum size of queue: 10
Enter the number of simulation hours: 100
Enter the average number of customers per hour: 15
customers accepted: 1485
  customers served: 1485
         turnaways: 0
average queue size: 0.15
 average wait time: 0.63 minutes

Case Study: Bank of Heather Automatic Teller
Enter maximum size of queue: 10
Enter the number of simulation hours: 100
Enter the average number of customers per hour: 30
customers accepted: 2896
  customers served: 2888
         turnaways: 101
average queue size: 4.64
 average wait time: 9.63 minutes

Case Study: Bank of Heather Automatic Teller
Enter maximum size of queue: 20
Enter the number of simulation hours: 100
Enter the average number of customers per hour: 30
customers accepted: 2943
  customers served: 2943
         turnaways: 93
average queue size: 13.06
 average wait time: 26.63 minutes
```

Note that going from 15 customers an hour to 30 customers an hour doesn't double the average wait time, it increases it by about a factor of 15. Allowing a longer queue just makes matters worse. However, the simulation doesn't allow for the fact that many customers, frustrated with a long wait, would simply leave the queue.

Here are a few more sample runs. These illustrate the short-term variations one might see, even though the average number of customers per hour is kept constant.

```
Case Study: Bank of Heather Automatic Teller
Enter maximum size of queue: 10
Enter the number of simulation hours: 4
Enter the average number of customers per hour: 30
customers accepted: 114
  customers served: 110
         turnaways: 0
average queue size: 2.15
 average wait time: 4.52 minutes

Case Study: Bank of Heather Automatic Teller
Enter maximum size of queue: 10
Enter the number of simulation hours: 4
Enter the average number of customers per hour: 30
```

continued on next page

continued from previous page

```
customers accepted: 121
  customers served: 116
        turnaways: 5
average queue size: 5.28
 average wait time: 10.72 minutes

Case Study: Bank of Heather Automatic Teller
Enter maximum size of queue: 10
Enter the number of simulation hours: 4
Enter the average number of customers per hour: 30
customers accepted: 112
  customers served: 109
        turnaways: 0
average queue size: 2.41
 average wait time: 5.16 minutes
```

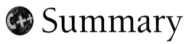 Summary

This chapter covers many important aspects of defining and using classes. Several of these aspects are subtle, even difficult, concepts. If some of them seem obscure or unusually complex to you, don't feel bad—they affect most newcomers to C++ that way. Often, the way you come to really appreciate concepts like copy constructors is through getting into trouble by ignoring them. So some of the material in this chapter may seem vague to you until your own experiences enrich your understanding. Meanwhile, let's summarize the chapter.

You can use *new* in a class constructor to allocate memory for data and then assign the address of the memory to a class member. This enables a class, for example, to handle strings of various sizes without committing the class design in advance to a fixed array size. Using *new* in class constructors also raises potential problems when an object expires. If an object has member pointers pointing to memory allocated by *new*, freeing the memory used to hold the object does not automatically free the memory pointed to by the object member pointers. Therefore, if you use *new* in a class constructor to allocate memory, you should use *delete* in the class constructor to free that memory. That way, the demise of an object automatically triggers the deletion of pointed-to memory.

Objects having members pointing to memory allocated by *new* also have problems with initializing one object to another or assigning one object to another. By default, C++ uses memberwise initialization and assignment, which means that the initialized or the assigned-to object winds up with exact copies of the original object's members. If an original member points to a block of data, the copy member points to the same block. When the program eventually deletes the two objects, the class destructor will attempt to delete the same block of memory twice, which is an error. The solution is to define a special copy constructor that redefines initialization and to overload the assignment operator. In each case, the new definition should create duplicates of any pointed-to data and have the new object point to the copies. That way, both the old and the new object refer to separate, but identical, data with no overlap. The same reasoning applies to defining an assignment operator. In each case, the goal is making a deep copy, that is, copying the real data and not just pointers to them.

C++ allows you to place structure, class, and enumeration definitions inside a class. Such nested types have class scope, meaning that they are local to the class and don't conflict with structures, classes, and enumerations of the same name defined elsewhere.

C++ provides a special syntax for class constructors that can be used to initialize data members. This syntax consists of a colon followed by a comma-separated list of initializers. This is placed after the closing parenthesis of the constructor arguments and before the opening brace of the function body. Each initializer consists of the name of the member being initialized followed by parentheses containing the initialization value. Conceptually, these initializations take place when the object is created and before any statements in the function body are executed. The syntax looks like this:

```
queue(int qs) : qsize(qs), items(0), front(NULL), rear(NULL) { }
```

This form is obligatory if the data member is a nonstatic *const* member or a reference.

As you may have noticed, classes require much more care and attention to detail than do simple C-style structures. In return, they do much more for you.

Review Questions

1. Suppose a *String* class has the following private members:

```
class String
{
private:
        char * str;     // points to string
        int len;        // holds length of string
    //
};
```

a. What's wrong with this default constructor?

```
String::String() {}
```

b. What's wrong with this constructor?

```
String::String(const char * s)
{
    str = s;
    len = strlen(s);
}
```

c. What's wrong with this constructor?

```
String::String(const char * s)
{
    strcpy(str, s);
```

continued on next page

continued from previous page

```
            len = strlen(s);
     }
```

2. Name three problems that may arise if you define a class in which a pointer member is initialized using *new* and indicate how they can be remedied.

3. What class methods does the compiler generate automatically if you don't provide them explicitly? Describe how these implicitly generated functions behave.

4. Identify and correct errors in the following class declaration:

```
class nifty
{
// data
        char personality[];
        int talents;
// methods
        nifty();
        nifty(char * s);
        ostream & operator<<(ostream & os, nifty & n);
}

nifty:nifty()
{
        personality = NULL;
        talents = 0;
}

nifty:nifty(char * s)
{
        personality = new char [strlen(s)];
        personality = s;
        talents = 0;
}

ostream & nifty:operator<<(ostream & os, nifty & n)
{
        os << n;
}
```

5. Consider the following class declaration:

```
class Golfer
{
private:
        char * fullname;      // points to string containing golfer's name
        int games;            // holds number of golf games played
        int * scores;  // points to first element of array of golf scores
public:
        Golfer();
        Golfer(const char * name, int g= 0);
                // creates empty dynamic array of g elements if g > 0
        Golfer(const Golfer & g);
        ~Golfer();
};
```

a. What class methods would be invoked by each of the following statements?

```
Golfer nancy;                         // #1
Golfer lulu("Little Lulu");           // #2
Golfer roy("Roy Hobbs", 12);          // #3
Golfer * par = new Golfer;            // #4
Golfer next = lulu;                   // #5
Golfer hazzard = "Weed Thwacker";     // #6
*par = nancy;                         // #7
nancy = "Nancy Putter";               // #8
```

b. Clearly, the class requires several more methods to make it useful, but what additional method does it require to protect against data corruption?

Programming Exercises

1. Enhance the *String* class declaration (the *strng2.h* version) by doing the following:

   a. Overload the + operator to allow you to join two strings into one.

   b. Provide a *stringlow()* member function that converts all alphabetic characters in a string to lowercase.

   c. Provide a *stringup()* member function that converts all alphabetic characters in a string to uppercase.

   d. Provide a member function that takes a *char* argument and returns the number of times that character appears in the string.

Test your work in the following program:

```
// pe11_1.cpp
#include <iostream.h>
#include "strng2.h"
int main(void)
{
        String s1(" and I am a C++ student.");
        String s2 = "Please enter your name: ";
        String s3;
        cout << s2;                         // overloaded << operator
        cin >> s3;                          // overloaded >> operator
        s2 = "My name is " + s3             // overloaded =, + operators
        cout << s2 << ".\n";
        s2 = s2 + s1;                       // + concatenates strings
        s2.stringup();                      // converts string to uppercase
        cout << "The string\n" << s2 << "\ncontains " << s2.has('A')
                << " 'A' characters in it.\n";
        s1 = "red";
        String rgb[3] = {String(s1), String("green"), String("blue")};
        cout << "Enter the name of a primary color for mixing light: ";
        String ans;
        int success = 0;
```

continued on next page

continued from previous page

```
        while (cin >> ans)
        {
                ans.stringlow();                // converts string to lowercase
                for (int i = 0; i < 3; i++)
                {
                        if (ans == rgb[i])    // overloaded == operator
                        {
                                cout << "That's right!\n";
                                success = 1;
                                break;
                        }
                }
                if (success == 1)
                        break;
                else
                        cout << "Try again!\n";
        }
        cout << "Bye\n";
        return 0;
}
```

Your output should look like this sample run:

```
Please enter your name: Fretta Farbo
My name is Fretta Farbo.
The string
MY NAME IS FRETTA FARBO AND I AM A C++ STUDENT.
contains 6 'A' characters in it.
Enter the name of a primary color for mixing light: yellow
Try again!
BLUE
That's right!
Bye
```

2. Rewrite the *Stock* class, as described in Listings 9-7 and 9-8, so that it uses dynamically allocated memory instead of fixed arrays to hold the stock names. Also, replace the *show()* member function with an overloaded *operator<<()* definition. Test the new definition program in Listing 9-9.

3. Consider the following variation of the *Stack* class defined in Listing 9-10.

```
// stack.h -- class declaration for the stack ADT
typedef unsigned long Item;

enum Bool {False, True}; // False = 0, True = 1

class Stack
{
private:
        enum {MAX = 10};        // constant specific to class
        Item  * pitems;         // holds stack items
        int size;               // number of elements in stack
        int top;                // index for top stack item
```

```
public:
        Stack(int n = 10);      // creates stack with n elements
        ~Stack();
        Bool isempty() const;
        Bool isfull() const;
        // push() returns False if stack already is full, True otherwise
        Bool push(const Item & item); // add item to stack
        // pop() returns False if stack already is empty, True otherwise
        Bool pop(Item & item);        // pop top into item
};
```

As the private members suggest, this class uses a dynamically allocated array to hold the stack items. Rewrite the methods to fit this new representation, and write a program that demonstrates all the methods.

4. The Bank of Heather has performed a study showing that autoteller customers won't wait more than one minute in line. Using the simulation of Listing 11-13, find a value for number of customers per hour that leads to an average wait time of one minute. (Use at least a 100-hour trial period.)

The Bank of Heather would like to know what would happen if they added a second automatic teller. Modify the simulation so that it has two queues. Assume a customer will join the first queue if it has fewer people in it than the second queue and that he or she will join the second queue otherwise. Again, find a value for number of customers per hour that leads to an average wait time of one minute. (Note: This is a nonlinear problem in that doubling the number of machines doesn't double the number of customers that can be handled per hour with a one-minute wait maximum.)

CHAPTER 12

CLASS INHERITANCE

You will learn about the following in this chapter:

- ◇ How to define an array class
- ◇ Inheritance as an *is-a* relationship
- ◇ How to publicly derive one class from another
- ◇ Protected access
- ◇ Constructor initialization lists
- ◇ Upcasting and downcasting
- ◇ Virtual member functions

- ◇ Early (static) binding and late (dynamic) binding
- ◇ Pure virtual functions
- ◇ When and how to use public inheritance

One of the main goals of object-oriented programming is providing reusable code. When you develop a new project, particularly if the project is large, it's nice to be able to reuse proven code rather than to reinvent it. Employing old code saves time and, because it has already been used and tested, can help suppress the introduction of bugs into a program. Also, the less you have to concern yourself with details, the better you can concentrate upon overall program strategy.

Traditional C function libraries provide reusability through predefined, precompiled functions, such as *strlen()*, that you can use in your programs. Many vendors furnish specialized C libraries providing functions beyond those of the standard C library. For example, you can purchase libraries of database management functions and of screen control functions. However, function libraries have a limitation. Unless the vendor supplies the source code for its library functions (and often it doesn't), you can't extend or modify the functions to meet your particular needs. Instead, you have to shape your program to meet the workings of the library. Even if the vendor does supply the source code, you run the risk of unintentionally modifying how part of a function works or of altering the relationships among library functions as you add your changes.

C++ classes bring you a higher level of reusability. Many vendors now offer class libraries, which consist of class declarations and implementations. Because a class combines data representation with class methods, it provides a more integrated package than does a function library. A single class, for example, may provide all the resources for managing a dialog box. Often, class libraries are available in source code, meaning that you can modify them to meet your needs. But C++ has a better method than code modification for extending and modifying classes. This method, called *class inheritance,* lets you derive new classes from old ones, with the derived class inheriting the properties, including the methods, of the old class, called a base class. Just as inheriting a fortune usually is easier than earning one from scratch, deriving a class through inheritance usually is easier than designing a new one. Here are some things you can do with inheritance:

- You can add functionality to an existing class. For instance, given a basic queue class, you could derive a class that adds the capability to view all members of the queue.

- You can add to the data that a class represents. For instance, given a basic string class, you could derive a class that adds a data member representing a color to be used when displaying the string.

- You can modify how a class method behaves. For instance, given a *Passenger* class that represents the services provided to an airline passenger, you can derive an *Upgrade* class that provides a higher level of services.

Of course, you could accomplish the same aims by duplicating the original class code and modifying it, but the inheritance mechanism allows you to proceed by just providing the new features. You don't even need access to the source code to derive a class. Thus, if you purchase a class library that provides only the header files and the compiled code for class methods, you still can derive new classes based upon the library classes. Conversely, you can distribute your own classes to others, keeping parts of your implementation secret, yet still giving your clients the option of adding features to your classes.

Inheritance is a splendid concept, and its basic implementation is quite simple. But managing inheritance so that it works properly in all situations requires some adjustments. This chapter looks at both the simple and the subtle aspects of inheritance.

An Array Base Class

When one class inherits from another, the original class is called a *base* class and the inheriting class is called a *derived* class. So, to illustrate inheritance, we need to begin with a base class. We'll use an array class for that purpose. Perhaps you're wondering what the point is to creating an array class when C++ already has arrays. One way to answer that is to look at a few shortcomings of the built-in array.

Shortcoming #1: C++ arrays have no bounds checking. That is, suppose you have this array definition:

```
double binwits[4] = { 1.27, 1.98, 1.63, 1.85 };
```

Nothing, other than your customary vigilance, keeps you from making statements like the following:

```
binwits[23185] = 2.45;
binwits[-28] = -42.34;
```

These would write data to memory locations calculated with the usual pointer arithmetic, ignoring the fact that the resulting locations are far removed from being in the array. True, not checking for array bounds helps make C and C++ programs lean and, if error-free, efficient, but sometimes it would be nice to have a safety net.

Shortcoming #2: In some contexts, you can't really distinguish between an array and a pointer to a single element. For instance, consider the following function prototype:

```
void up(double * x, int n);
```

This might represent a function whose first argument is an array of *double* and whose second argument is the number of elements in the array. Or it might represent a function that performs some operation upon a particular *double* value whose address is passed. The fact that the name of an array is a pointer to its first element often is convenient, but it obscures the difference between an array (a collection of values) and a pointer (an address).

Shortcoming #3: Once you pass an array name as an argument to a function, the function has no way of knowing the array size unless you tell it so explicitly.

Shortcoming #4: Often, you can't treat an array as an entity. For instance, you can't initialize one array to another or assign one array to another:

```
double binwits[4] = { 1.27, 1.98, 1.63, 1.85 };
double binwits2[4] = binwits; // you can't do this
double pleegs[4];
pleegs = binwits;      // you can't do this
```

By defining an array class, you can fix these shortcomings, adding features missing from standard C++ arrays. In fact, you could add many other features, such as array arithmetic and giving the arrays the option of starting indexing with values other than zero. But don't get carried away. It's a poor idea to define some humongous class that implements every conceivable array enhancement. Such a definition would be weighed down with features that were rarely, if ever, used. Not being part of a committee or of a government agency, we can use a better strategy. And that is to define a simple base class, then use class inheritance to add features as needed. (For pedagogical reasons, we'll provide one feature—bounds checking—that might be better treated as a derived feature.)

Class Declaration

Let's begin with a base class modeled after a type *double* array. The first point to decide is how to represent the data. The obvious choice of using a standard type *double* array as a class member works poorly because C++ requires that the number of elements in an array be a compile-time constant. That is, the class would have to use an array with a predetermined number of elements, as in the following:

```
class dumbarray
{
private:
        double arr[20];       // array element has fixed size
...
};
```

To represent arrays of two different sizes, you'd need two different classes, making this a poor design choice. A better idea is to incorporate a dynamic array allocated with *new*. Recall that you can use the *new* operator to return the address of the first element of a dynamic array. One class member can store that address, while a second class member stores the number of elements. That way a single class can represent any valid size of array:

```
class smartarray
{
private:
        double * arr;        // address of first element
        unsigned int size;   // variable number of array elements
...
};
```

As you saw in Chapter 11, using *new* to initialize a member pointer entails providing a copy constructor, assignment operator, and destructor. Listing 12-1 shows a class declaration based on this approach. The class name *ArrayDb* is short for *Array of Double*. (Incidentally, the idea of a dynamic array is sufficiently useful that the draft ANSI/ISO C++ standard library includes a template class for creating fancier versions of what's described here.)

Listing 12-1 *arraydb.h*

```
// arraydb.h -- define array class
#ifndef _ARRAYDB_H_
#define _ARRAYDB_H_
#include <iostream.h>

class ArrayDb
{
private:
        unsigned int size;            // number of array elements
```

```
protected:
        double * arr;                           // address of first element
public:
        ArrayDb();                              // default constructor
        // create an ArrayDb of n elements, set each to val
        ArrayDb(unsigned int n, double val = 0.0);
        // create an ArrayDb of n elements, initialize to array pn
        ArrayDb(const double * pn, unsigned int n);
        ArrayDb(const ArrayDb & a);             // copy constructor
        ~ArrayDb();                             // destructor
        unsigned int arsize() const {return size;}  // returns array size
// overloaded operators
        double & operator[](int i);                 // array indexing
        const double & operator[](int i) const;     // array indexing (no =)
        ArrayDb & operator=(const ArrayDb & a);
        friend ostream & operator<<(ostream & os, const ArrayDb & a);
};
```

```
#endif
```

As usual, the class declaration wraps data and methods into a single package. The *public* section of the class declaration provides prototypes for the various class member functions, including operator functions, and for a friend function overloading the << operator. And the *private* and *protected* sections provide the data members—an *arr* member to hold the address of the array of data and a *size* member to indicate the number of elements. See Figure 12-1.

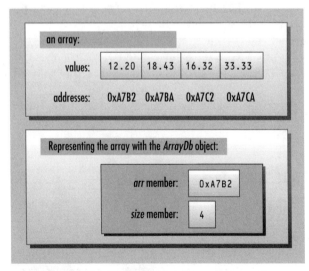

Figure 12-1 The *ArrayDb* class data representation

Protected and Private

Wait a moment—where did that *protected* come from? Up to now the examples have used *private* to hide data. But classes intended to serve as base classes often use *protected* instead of *private*. The *protected* keyword is like *private* in that the outside world can access class members in a protected section only by using class members. The difference between *private* and *protected* comes into play only within classes derived from the base class. Members of a derived class can access protected members of a base class directly, but they cannot directly access private members of the base class. Let's see what that means. Suppose you derive a class from *ArrayDb*. Then the new class will inherit the *arr* and *size* members along with class member functions like *arsize()*. Because *arr* is protected, any member functions added to the derived class will be able to access *arr* by name. These same member functions, however, cannot access *size* by name. But they can use the public interface for *ArrayDb*. This means a derived class can use the *arsize()* function to determine the size of an array.

RULE

Protected class members are private to the world at large, but public to a derived class.

If you intend to make a class into a base class, you'll need to decide whether to make data members private or protected. Clearly, protected data members make it simpler for derived classes to access base class information. But it does make data less secure. For instance, a derived class can define a public method to alter a base class data member, even though the base class had no such method. To ensure that a base class data member can be altered only by the base class methods, make the data member private. If restricting access is not of paramount importance, consider using protected data members for convenience and efficiency.

Our main reason for making *arr* protected and *size* private is to provide an example of each kind. However, there is at least some justification for this choice from a design standpoint. As you'll see shortly, the class methods provide public access to array elements, so there is no strong reason to prohibit derived classes from accessing them. On the other hand, the base class interface does not provide methods for altering *size*, so making *size* private maintains that interface.

The Class Methods

The class declaration follows the data elements with several constructors, a destructor, a method that returns the array size, and some overloaded operators. Note that the first operator function overloads [], the index operator. Remember, the data is protected, so you can access it only through class member functions, not by using regular array notation. But overloading the [] operator makes using that operator function to access elements inside an *ArrayDb* object look just like using the usual array notation.

We'll discuss this point more fully in a moment or two, along with why there are two versions of the *operator[]()* function. Listing 12-2 shows the code for these methods.

 Listing 12-2 *arraydb.cpp*

```
// arraydb.cpp -- ArrayDb class methods
#include <iostream.h>
#include <stdlib.h>    // exit() prototype
#include "arraydb.h"

// default constructor -- no arguments
ArrayDb::ArrayDb()
{
        arr = NULL;
        size = 0;
}

// constructs array of n elements, each set to val
ArrayDb::ArrayDb(unsigned int n, double val)
{
        arr = new double[n];
        size = n;
        for (int i = 0; i < size; i++)
                arr[i] = val;
}

// initialize ArrayDb object to a nonclass array
ArrayDb::ArrayDb(const double *pn, unsigned int n)
{
        arr = new double[n];
        size = n;
        for (int i = 0; i < size; i++)
                arr[i] = pn[i];
}

// initialize ArrayDb object to another ArrayDb object
ArrayDb::ArrayDb(const ArrayDb & a)
{
        size = a.size;
        arr = new double[size];
        for (int i = 0; i < size; i++)
                arr[i] = a.arr[i];
}

ArrayDb::~ArrayDb()
{
        delete [] arr;
}

// let user access elements by index (assignment allowed)
double & ArrayDb::operator[](int i)
{
```

continued on next page

511

continued from previous page

```
            // check index before continuing
            if (i < 0 || i >= size)
            {
                    cerr << "Error in array limits: "
                            << i << " is a bad index\n";
                    exit(1);
            }
            return arr[i];
    }


    // let user access elements by index (assignment disallowed)
    const double & ArrayDb::operator[](int i) const
    {
            // check index before continuing
            if (i < 0 || i >= size)
            {
                    cerr << "Error in array limits: "
                            << i << " is a bad index\n";
                    exit(1);
            }
            return arr[i];
    }


    // define class assignment
    ArrayDb & ArrayDb::operator=(const ArrayDb & a)
    {
            if (this == &a)                  // if object assigned to self,
                    return *this;  // don't change anything
            delete arr;
            size = a.size;
            arr = new double[size];
            for (int i = 0; i < size; i++)
                    arr[i] = a.arr[i];
            return *this;
    }


    // quick output, 5 values to a line
    ostream & operator<<(ostream & os, const ArrayDb & a)
    {
            for (int i = 0; i < a.size; i++)
            {
                    os << a.arr[i] << " ";
                    if (i % 5 == 4)
                            os << "\n";
            }
            if (i % 5 != 0)
                    os << "\n";
            return os;
    }
```

Let's take a quick look at the class methods to see what they do. Not only will this acquaint you with the class, it will review some of the class properties you've been studying in the preceding three chapters.

First, notice that the class constructors (except for the default constructor) use *new* to allocate memory for the array. That, after all, is the basic idea that gives this class the ability to accommodate different array sizes. But, as Chapter 11 illustrated, when you use *new* in a class constructor, you have to support that use with several other design features. It's the old story of how power brings with it the responsibility to use it correctly. In this case, using *new* requires the following features:

1. The class destructor should free memory allocated by *new* in the constructors.

2. If any one constructor uses *new* to assign an address to a class member, all constructors should assign a valid address to that member, either by using *new* or by assigning the *null* pointer. These are the only kinds of addresses that can be used correctly with *delete;* it's okay to apply *delete* to the *null* pointer but not to an uninitialized pointer.

3. There should be a special constructor for initializing an object to an object of the same class.

4. There should be an operator function for assigning one object to another. Both the copy constructor and the assignment operator should copy data instead of merely copying addresses.

Fortunately, Chapter 11 showed how to do these very tasks. Now let's look at the methods individually.

Constructors and Destructor

The default constructor initializes the *arr* pointer to *NULL* so that the destructor will work correctly:

```
ArrayDb::ArrayDb()
{
        arr = NULL;
        size = 0;
}
```

This, recall, is the constructor used if you declare an *ArrayDb* object without explicitly initializing it.

The second constructor lets you initialize an *ArrayDb* object to a particular number of elements and initialize each element to a particular value:

```
// constructs array of n elements, each set to val
ArrayDb::ArrayDb(unsigned int n, double val)
{
        arr = new double[n];
        size = n;
        for (int i = 0; i < size; i++)
                arr[i] = val;
}
```

For instance, the declaration

```
ArrayDb ofsun(365, 1.0);
```

creates an *ArrayDb* object called *ofsun* having *365* elements and sets each element to *1.0*. The class prototype provides a default value of *0.0* for the second argument, so you can call the constructor using a single argument:

```
ArrayDb snits(40);     // 40 elements, each set to 0.0
```

Don't forget that you can use a pointer as if it were an array name. Of course, you can ignore that fact and use *(arr + i)* instead of *arr[i]*.

The third constructor lets you initialize an *ArrayDb* object to a regular array:

```
// initialize to a nonclass array
ArrayDb::ArrayDb(const double *pn, unsigned int n)
{
        arr = new double[n];
        size = n;
        for (int i = 0; i < size; i++)
                arr[i] = pn[i];
}
```

This is useful, for if other parts of a program use a regular C++ array, you can use this constructor to create an *ArrayDb* object equivalent. To use this constructor, pass it the name of an array (more generally, the address of an array element) and the number of elements. The constructor creates an *ArrayDb* object with the same number of elements, then copies the original array into the object.

Here's a sample use:

```
double gas_costs[4] = {11.84, 12.43, 18.39, 22.74};
ArrayDb gas_bills(gas_costs, 4);
```

The first declaration creates an ordinary array of four elements and initializes them to the values in the brackets. The second declaration creates an *ArrayDb* object containing a copy of this array.

Incidentally, this example shows a second important use for this constructor. The *ArrayDb* class does not have a mechanism for initializing an *ArrayDb* object to a set of values enclosed in braces. That is, you can't do the following:

```
ArrayDb beads(4) = { 1.2, 2.3, 3.4, 4.5};   // won't work
```

But you can initialize an *ArrayDb* object to a set of numbers in two steps, as the *gas_bill* example shows: create and initialize a regular array, then create an *ArrayDb* object and initialize it to the array.

The final constructor is the special copy constructor used to initialize one *ArrayDb* object to another:

```
// initialize to a class array
ArrayDb::ArrayDb(const ArrayDb & a)
{
        size = a.size;
```

```
        arr = new double[size];
        for (int i = 0; i < size; i++)
                arr[i] = a.arr[i];
}
```

As you may recall, a program calls a copy constructor in four circumstances:

❧ When you initialize one *ArrayDb* object to another

❧ When you pass an *ArrayDb* object by value to a function

❧ When a function returns an *ArrayDb* object

❧ When the compiler needs to construct a temporary object

If you omit a copy constructor, C++ uses memberwise copying in these four situations. If the object contains a pointer, this default method copies the pointer, not the data, and that leads to the memory management problems detailed in Chapter 11. However, this wonderful copy constructor overrides the default initialization, provides a copy of the data, and thus sidesteps those troublesome memory problems.

The last three constructors allocate memory with *new*, so the destructor must free that memory by using *delete:*

```
ArrayDb::~ArrayDb()
{
        delete [] arr;
}
```

Other Methods of the *ArrayDb* Class

The class member functions do more than let you create and destroy arrays, enjoyable though that may be in itself. The other methods, which include operator functions and a friend function, return the array size, provide a means to access individual elements of an *ArrayDb* object, define object assignment, and provide an output function. Let's look at each now.

The *arsize()* member, defined inline, returns the number of elements in the array:

```
unsigned int arsize() const {return size;}
```

This brings us to the overloaded operators. The first lets you access *ArrayDb* elements using array notation:

```
// let user access elements by index (assignment allowed)
double & ArrayDb::operator[](int i)
{
        return arr[i];
}
```

Let's investigate why this function is necessary and how it works. First, why is it necessary? Suppose *funds* is an *ArrayDb* object. Then *funds.arr* is the member pointer to the array storage, and *funds.arr[i]* is the element with index i. But *arr* is a *protected* member, so a client program cannot access the data directly with this notation. Making the data completely inaccessible takes data hiding a bit too far. Of course, member functions and friend functions can access the data, so to access an individual element, you must define a member function that does that job. The most direct way is to have the member function take an array element index as an argument and to return the corresponding element value:

```
// let user access elements by index-- the direct way, but
//                              not good enough for us
double ArrayDb::value(int i)
{
        return arr[i];
}
```

Then, say, *funds.value(3)* would represent the value of the fourth element of the array represented by the *funds* object. (Element numbering starts at 0, remember.) But this approach lacks style; for one thing, *funds.value(3)* doesn't look like an array element. Wouldn't you rather write *funds[3]* than *funds.value(3)*?

There's an elegant way to satisfy this wish. First, note that the *[]* in *funds[3]* really constitutes an operator. This operator takes two operands, *funds* and *3,* and returns the value stored at the address *funds+3.* Since *[]* is an operator, you can overload it with an operator function that returns the element value. That's what the *operator[]()* definition does. It also checks to see if the index is valid for the array:

```
// let user access elements by index (assignment allowed)
double & ArrayDb::operator[](int i)
{
        // check index before continuing
        if (i < 0 || i >= size)
        {
                cerr << "Error in array limits: "
                        << i << " is a bad index\n";
                exit(1);
        }
        return arr[i];
}
```

Suppose, then, you use the *funds* object in the following statement:

```
double abscond = funds[3];
```

The compiler will replace this with the corresponding operator function:

```
double abscond = funds.operator[](3);
```

Because the *funds* object invokes the method with an argument of 3, the method's return statement

```
return arr[i];
```

is interpreted as follows:

```
return funds.arr[3];
```

In short, operator overloading makes the expression *funds[3]* represent an element in the *funds* object.

Note that the operator function is of type *double &,* that is, it's a reference. This is vital because you can assign a value to a function that returns a reference. The effect, as you may recall from Chapter 8, is assigning to the referred-to variable. This feature lets you use statements like the following:

```
funds[2] = 3432.23;
```

This looks reasonable in form, but remember that this statement really means the following:

```
funds.operator[](2) = 3432.23;
```

And that syntax is possible only when a function returns a reference. Because this operator can alter the array contents, it is not declared as a *const* member function.

The *cerr* object, recall from Chapter 9, is commonly used for error messages, and the *exit()* function (Chapter 9) terminates program execution.

The *operator[]()* function only defines element access through array notation. Redefining the [] operator does not redefine pointer addition and the dereferencing operator (*):

```
double whammy[5];
//  whammy[2] is the same as *(whammy + 2)
ArrayDb grammy[5];
// *(grammy + 2) is not even defined
```

So if you are the sort of programmer that enjoys replacing expressions like *whiffle[10]* with *(whiffle + 10)*, you can't do so with an *ArrayDb* object.

As defined, the *operator[]()* function has one problem: it can't be used with *const* objects. For instance, consider the following (nonmember) function definition:

```
void show(const ArrayDb & ar)
{
        unsigned int size = ar.arsize();
        for (int i = 0; i < size; i++)
                cout << (i+1) << ": " << ar[i] << "\n";
}
```

This definition won't compile. The reason is that the prototype promises that *show()* won't change the value of the *ar* object, but the *operator[]()* definition, which is used in the function, doesn't conform to that promise.

Fortunately, it's possible to overload the *operator[]()* function with a version that can be used with *const* objects:

```
// let user access elements by index (assignment disallowed)
const double & ArrayDb::operator[](int i) const
{
        // check index before continuing
        if (i < 0 || i >= size)
        {
```

continued on next page

continued from previous page

```
                    cerr << "Error in array limits: "
                            << i << " is a bad index\n";
                    exit(1);
            }
            return arr[i];
    }
```

Recall that changing a function's return value isn't enough to overload the argument. However, the *const* at the right end of the function header does enable overloading. Remember that every member function has a hidden argument, the *this* pointer, which points to the invoking object. The terminating *const* applies to *this,* so it really does alter the function signature. See Figure 12-2. Because the return type is a reference to an element of a *const* array, it, too, should be *const.*

The *operator[]()* members are the crucial part of the *ArrayDb* interface, but we still have two more functions to cover. The first overloads the assignment operator so that it copies the pointed-to data rather than the pointers themselves:

```
// define class assignment
ArrayDb & ArrayDb::operator=(const ArrayDb & a)
{
        delete arr;
        size = a.size;
        arr = new double[size];
        for (int i = 0; i < size; i++)
                arr[i] = a.arr[i];
        return *this;
}
```

```
    ArrayDb bugs(5);                         hidden variable declaration:
    bugs[2] = 4.4;                               ArrayDb * const this;

1. Invokes this version of operator[]()        ⟶ double & ArrayDb::operator[](int i)
2. The this pointer set to &bugs and i set to 2    {
3. ar[i] is this ->ar[2] is bugs.ar[2]                  ...
4. Return value of bugs.ar[2] is set to 4.4           return ar[i];
                                                   }

                        The object member is nits.ar[2]                      The object nits is
                           is not to be changed                             not to be changed

    const ArrayDb nits(5);                      hidden variable declaration:
    double val = nits[2];                           const ArrayDb * const this;

1. Invokes this version of operator[]()        ⟶ const double & ArrayDb::operator[](int i) const
2. The this pointer set to &nits and i set to 2    {
3. ar[i] is this ->ar[2] is nits.ar[2]                  ...
4. val set to return value of nits.ar[2]              return ar[i];
                                                   }
```

Figure 12-2 The overloaded *operator[]()* function

The definition follows the pattern developed in Chapter 11 for overloading assignment for classes containing pointers:

❧ The function argument is an object passed by reference (type *ArrayDb &*).

❧ The function returns a reference to a new object, which is a copy of the one passed as an argument.

❧ The function uses *delete* to free the memory to which *arr* points. This clears the old data, preparing *arr* to point to new data.

❧ The function allocates space for the data being copied, assigns the address to *arr*, then copies the data from the old array to the new.

In case you've forgotten why the assignment operator returns a reference to a value, it's to make it resemble ordinary assignment. Recall that an assignment expression such as

```
x = y
```

has the value of the left-hand side if *x* is a standard type such as *int*. But if *x* and *y* are *ArrayDb* objects, then that expression becomes the following function call:

```
x.operator=(y)
```

The definition above causes the operator function to return a reference to *x*, so this expression, too, has the value of the left-hand side of the original expression *x = y*.

The final method displays the array contents:

```
// quick display, 5 values to a line
ostream & operator<<(ostream & os, const ArrayDb & a)
{
        for (int i = 0; i < a.size; i++)
        {
                os << a.arr[i] << " ";
                if (i % 5 == 4)
                    os << "\n";
        }
        if (i % 5 != 0)
                os << "\n";
        return os;
}
```

The method uses the modulus operator to display five values per line. The *if* statement at the end adds a newline if there are fewer than five items on the final line. If you want to organize the information differently, you can use the index operator function to access the elements individually. But if you just want to see what's in the array, use this method.

Using the Class

Let's be prudent and test this class in a program before trying to derive other classes from it. Listing 12-3 provides a short program for that purpose. The program follows the usual C++ pattern for organization: a header file containing the class declaration (Listing 12-1), a methods file containing the member and friend function definitions (Listing 12-2), and a program that uses the class (Listing 12-3). Therefore you should use whatever technique your implementation requires for a multifile program. Chapters 1 and 8 provided some general guidelines.

Listing 12-3 uses the statement

```
cout.width(5);
```

to set the field width for displaying data to five characters. As Chapter 15 discusses, the setting affects only the very next output statement, so the listing places the request inside the printing loop in order to set the width for each output item.

Listing 12-3 *tinsel.cpp*

```
// tinsel.cpp -- use the ArrayDb class
// compile with arraydb.cpp
#include <iostream.h>
#include "arraydb.h"
void display(ArrayDb & ar);
int main(void)
{
        cout << "Enter number of regions: ";
        unsigned int regions;  // read number of regions
        cin >> regions;

        ArrayDb tons(regions);  // create an "array" of that size
        cout << "Enter the regional tinsel sales in tons:\n";
        for (int i = 0; i < regions; i++)
        {
                cout << "Region " << (i+ 1) << ": ";
                cin >> tons[i];          // use array notation
        }

        ArrayDb dup;   // default object
        dup = tons;    // array assignment
        cout << "Here's the original data:\n" << tons;
        cout << "Here's the copy:\n";
        display(dup);  // pass array without passing size

        double wts[5] = {155.2, 189.6, 174.3, 256.9, 203.5};
        ArrayDb bod(wts, 5);  // initialize an ArrayDb to an array
        cout << "Here are the weights of the Board of Directors:\n"
                << bod;

        // try to exceed array limit
        cout << "Index: value\n";
        for (i = 0; i <= regions; i++)
        {
                cout.width(5);
                cout << i << ": " << tons[i] << "\n";
        }
```

```
        return 0;
}

void display(ArrayDb & ar)
{
        cout << "copy!\n";
        cout << ar;
        cout << "copy!\n";
}
```

Here's a sample run:

```
Enter number of regions: 3
Enter the regional tinsel sales in tons:
Region 1: 5147
Region 2: 4872
Region 3: 5027
Here's the original data:
5147 4872 5027
Here's the copy:
copy!
5147 4872 5027
copy!
Here are the weights of the Board of Directors:
155.2 189.6 174.3 256.9 203.5
Index: value
    0: 5147
    1: 4872
    2: 5027
Error in array limits: 3 is a bad index
```

Notes on Using the *ArrayDb* Class

Let's look at some of the main points about using the *ArrayDb* class. Because it's possible to establish the number of elements in an *ArrayDb* object at run time, you can enter the number of elements from the keyboard and then create an *ArrayDb*-style array of that size:

```
cin >> regions;
ArrayDb tons(regions);
```

Thus you get the flexibility of dynamic memory combined with the ease of use of an ordinary array; the details about using *new* are hidden from the user.

The next nice touch is that the *operator[]()* function lets you use array notation to access individual elements:

```
cin >> tons[i];
```

This makes using the *ArrayDb* object as simple as using an ordinary array.

The statements

```
ArrayDb dup;
dup = tons;    // array assignment
```

illustrate default initialization and array assignment. Incidentally, we did this to check that assignment worked. It would be more efficient to initialize the *dup* object directly:

```
ArrayDb dup(tons);
```

That way, we call just one function (the copy constructor) instead of two (the default constructor and the assignment operator function).

The statement

```
display(dup);
```

shows that we can pass an array as an entity without having to pass size information. Because the *display()* function takes a reference argument, it uses the *dup* object itself instead of passing an object by value and using the copy constructor to create a new object.

Next, the program demonstrates its ability to initialize an *ArrayDb* object using an ordinary array. Finally, the program deliberately exceeds the bounds of an array in order to demonstrate bounds checking.

Inheritance—An *Is-a* Relationship

Now that *ArrayDb* has joined the ranks of the working class, we can derive a new class from it. Before doing so, however, let's examine the underlying model for C++ inheritance. Actually, C++ has three varieties of inheritance: public, protected, and private. Public inheritance is the most common form, and it models an *is-a* relationship. This is shorthand for saying that an object of a derived class should also be an object of the base class. Anything you do with a base object, you should be able to do with a derived object. Suppose, for instance, we have a *Fruit* class. It could store, say, the weight and caloric content of a fruit. Because a banana is a particular kind of fruit, we could derive a *Banana* class from the *Fruit* class. The new class would inherit all the data members of the original class, so a *Banana* object would have members representing the weight and caloric content of a banana. The new *Banana* class also might add members that apply particularly to bananas and not to fruit in general, such as the Banana Institute Peel Index. Since the derived class can add features, it's probably more accurate to describe the relationship as an *is-a-kind-of* relationship, but *is-a* is the usual term.

To clarify the *is-a* relationship, let's look at some examples that don't match that model. Public inheritance doesn't model a *has-a* relationship. A lunch, for instance, might contain a fruit. But a lunch, in general, is not a fruit. Therefore, we should not derive a *Lunch* class from the *Fruit* class in an attempt to place fruit in a lunch. The correct way to handle putting fruit into a lunch is to consider the matter as a *has-a* relationship: a lunch has a fruit. As we'll see in Chapter 13, that's most easily modeled by including a *Fruit* object as a data member of a *Lunch* class. See Figure 12-3.

FRUIT ONLY

A banana *is a* fruit,
but
a lunch *has a* banana.

Figure 12-3 *Is-a* and *has-a* relationships

Public inheritance doesn't model an *is-like-a* relationship, that is, it doesn't do similes. It's often pointed out that lawyers are like sharks. But it is not literally true that a lawyer is a shark. For instance, sharks can live underwater. Therefore, you shouldn't derive a *Lawyer* class from a *Shark* class. Inheritance can add properties to a base class; it doesn't remove properties from a base class. In some cases, shared characteristics can be handled by designing a class encompassing those characteristics, then using that class, either in an *is-a* or *has-a* relationship, to define the related classes.

Public inheritance doesn't model an *is-implemented-as-a* relationship. For instance, we could implement a stack using an array. However, it wouldn't be proper to derive a *Stack* class from an *ArrayDb* class. A stack is not an array. For example, array indexing is not a stack property. Also, a stack could be implemented in some other way, such as by using a linked list. A proper approach would be to hide the array implementation by giving the stack a private *ArrayDb* object member.

Public inheritance doesn't model a *uses-a* relationship. For example, a computer can use a laser printer, but it doesn't make sense to derive a *Printer* class from a *Computer* class or vice versa. One might, however, devise friend functions or classes to handle communication between *Printer* objects and *Computer* objects.

Nothing in the C++ language prevents you from using public inheritance to model *has-a, is-implemented-as-a,* or *uses-a* relationships. However, doing so usually leads to programming problems. So let's stick to the *is-a* relationships. For example, suppose you find you're working on a project that does a lot of arithmetic with arrays—adding two arrays (combining inventories), subtracting an array from another (subtracting commissions), dividing the elements of one array by the elements of another (getting advertising costs per item), multiplying every value in an array by the same number (across the board price increase), and so on. You'd like to use the *ArrayDb* class, but it doesn't support these operations. What you can do is define a new class that inherits all the properties of the *ArrayDb* class and that additionally has all the new arithmetic methods you need. By basing the new class on *ArrayDb* instead of starting from scratch, you take advantage of the work that already has gone into developing *ArrayDb,* and you take advantage of the fact that *ArrayDb* has already been tested. In other words, you reuse proven code. The net result is less work and, perhaps, a better product.

Does the new class (call it *ArithArr*) meet the *is-a* test? Sure. Everything that is true of an *ArrayDb* object will be true for an *ArithArr* object. That is, it makes sense to use the [] operator to access individual members and to use an *arsize()* function to report the number of elements. Note that the *is-a* relationship is not, in general, reversible. A fruit, in general, is not a banana. An *ArrayDb* object won't have all the capabilities of an *ArithArr* object.

Declaring a Derived Class

A derived class has to identify the class from which it is derived. The C++ way is to include the base class name in the derived class declaration. If we derive an *ArithArr* class from the *ArrayDb* class, we would begin the class declaration like this:

```
class ArithArr : public ArrayDb
{
```

The colon indicates the *ArithArr* class is based upon the *ArrayDb* class. This particular heading indicates that *ArrayDb* is a public base class; this is termed *public derivation.* An object of a derived class incorporates a base class object. With public derivation, the public members of the base class become public members of the derived class, and the protected members of the base class become protected members of the derived class. The private portions of a base class become part of the derived class, but they can be accessed only through the protected and public methods of the base class. Thus they aren't public, protected, or private.

For instance, the *ArrayDb operator[]()* function becomes a public function of the *ArithArr* class, too, while the *arr* member of the *ArrayDb* class becomes a protected member of the *ArithArr* class. The *size* member of *ArrayDb* becomes part of an *ArithArr* object, but it can be accessed only through *ArrayDb* methods, such as *arsize()* and the *ArrayDb* constructors. In short, the *ArithArr* class inherits public and protected members from the base class along with access to them. You don't have to redefine them for the new class. A derived class contains the private members of a base class, but can't access them except by using the public and protected base class methods. See Figure 12-4.

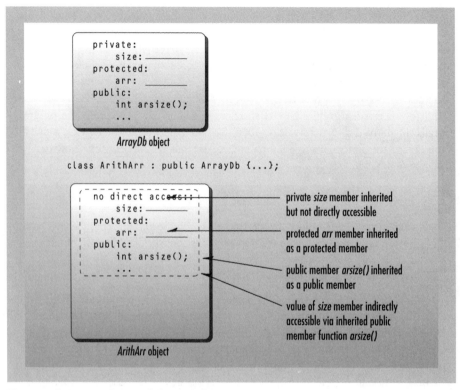

```
    private:
        size: _____
    protected:
        arr: _____
    public:
        int arsize();
        ...
```
ArrayDb object

```
class ArithArr : public ArrayDb {...};
```

```
    no direct access:
        size: _____
    protected:
        arr: _____
    public:
        int arsize();
        ...
```
private *size* member inherited
but not directly accessible

protected *arr* member inherited
as a protected member

public member *arsize()* inherited
as a public member

value of *size* member indirectly
accessible via inherited public
member function *arsize()*

ArithArr object

Figure 12-4 Base class and derived class objects

C++ also supports *protected derivations* and *private derivations:*

```
class informer : protected witness
{
class gradeschool : private school
{
```

We'll discuss these forms in Chapter 13.

Once you derive a class, you can add new members to it. In fact, you *must* provide new constructors. That's because the name of a constructor matches the name of the class:

```
ArrayDb hifi;      // needs ArrayDb() constructor
ArithArr bonuses;  // needs ArithArr() constructor
```

When you create an object of a derived class, the program first calls the constructor for the base class, then the constructor for the derived class. This makes sense because the constructor for the derived class may build upon data members from the base class; hence the base class object has to be constructed first. It's a bit like building the first floor of a building before adding the second story. Thus when you define the new constructors, they shouldn't duplicate the work of the base constructors. Instead, they should handle just the additional details that the derived class requires. For example, the constructor could initialize new data members. In general, a derived class constructor also has to pass information to a base class constructor; we'll look at the technique for doing so shortly.

You don't have to add a new destructor unless the new class requires cleanup work beyond that performed by the base destructor. When an object expires, the program first calls the derived destructor, if any, then the base destructor. The new class doesn't need a destructor, but we'll provide one anyway so that we can examine how derived classes handle destructors.

RULE

When creating an object of a derived class, a program first calls the base class constructor, then the derived class constructor. When an object of a derived class expires, the program first calls the derived class destructor, if any, then the base class destructor.

In general, a derived class inherits the member functions of the base class. If the base class member functions are public or protected, then objects of the derived class can invoke them. The constructors and destructor are exceptions, but derived class constructors and destructors can use base class constructors and destructors, as the examples will show. The other noninherited member function is the assignment operator. It merits special discussion, which we'll provide when the time comes. Note that friends are not member functions, so they are not inherited.

You know how to start the declaration of a derived class:

```
class ArithArr : public ArrayDb
{
```

Now let's add some new class methods. Listing 12-4 shows the class declaration. It only adds public member functions and no new data members. However, in general, you can add both methods and data members, and each can be public, protected, or private. Note that you don't have to do a thing to the base class to derive a class. All the derivation takes place in defining the new class and its methods. Thus you can derive a class even if you don't have access to the source code for the base class.

Listing 12-4 *aritharr.h*

```
// aritharr.h -- derived array class with more arithmetic
#ifndef _ARITHARR_H_
#define _ARITHARR_H_

#include "arraydb.h"

class ArithArr : public ArrayDb  // derived from ArrayDb class
{
```

```
private:
        // no new data members
public:
// base class constructors not inherited,
// need ArithArr constructors
    ArithArr(){}
    ArithArr(unsigned int n, double val = 0.0)
                        : ArrayDb(n, val) {}
    ArithArr(const double *pn, unsigned int n)
                        : ArrayDb(pn, n) {}
    ArithArr(const ArithArr & aa) : ArrayDb(aa) {}
    ArithArr(const ArrayDb & ad) : ArrayDb(ad) {}

// destructor ArrrayDb part is inherited, but you can define a new one
        ~ArithArr() {}

// new methods
        double sum() const;
        double average() const;
// overloaded operators
        ArithArr operator+(const ArithArr & a) const;
        ArithArr operator-(const ArithArr & a) const;
        ArithArr operator-() const;
        ArithArr operator*(const ArithArr & a) const;
        ArithArr operator*(double d) const;
        friend ArithArr operator*(double d, const ArithArr & a);
};
```

```
#endif
```

The constructors have been implemented as inline functions, and we'll examine them next.

Implementing the Derived Class

Let's examine how to implement the derived class and look at the rationale for some of the methods, beginning with the constructors. First, let's think about the construction process. The program can't construct an *ArithArr* object until it first constructs an *ArrayDb* object. So the base constructor has to be called *before* the program enters the code for the derived constructor. On the other hand, the base constructor can't be called until *after* the derived constructor is called because calling the derived constructor is what tells the program it needs the base constructor. Consider the following inline default *ArithArr* constructor:

```
ArithArr() {}
```

(Remember, C++ uses a free-form format, so the function braces can be placed on the same line with the function heading.) In particular, look at the space between the () and the {}. Somewhere in there (after the function call, before the function body) is when the base constructor must be called. And that's what C++ does. Unless instructed to do otherwise, the program will call the default base constructor. Thus, when the program enters the *ArithArr()* function body, it can assume that the base class data members (the *arr* pointer and the *size* member) of the new *ArithArr* object have been set already. It is then the duty of the derived class constructor to initialize new members added by the derived class. In this case, there are no more data members, so the function body doesn't have to do anything. Since the function does nothing, does it have to exist? Yes, because if you omit it, the *ArrayDb* default constructor doesn't get called either.

RULE

The derived class constructors are responsible for initializing any data members added to those inherited from the base class. The base class constructors are responsible for initializing the inherited data members.

The next constructor, if we hadn't inlined it, would have had this prototype:

```
ArithArr(unsigned int n, double val = 0.0);
```

The intent is that this constructor creates a dynamic array with *n* elements and initializes each element to *val*. That is, the statement

```
ArithArr lear(3, 2.0);
```

should create an *ArithArr* object with three array elements, each set to the value *2.0*, just like the equivalent *ArrayDb* constructor did for *ArrayDb* objects. But there is a problem here. Suppose we did something like this:

```
ArithArr::ArithArr(unsigned int n, double val)
{
...
}
```

As with the previous constructor, this would call the default *ArrayDb* constructor, creating an array with zero elements. However, what we would like to call is the *ArrayDb(unsigned int n, double val)* constructor so that the base component gets constructed correctly. Also, we'd like to transfer the size and value information from *ArithArr(unsigned int n, double val)* to *ArrayDb(unsigned int n, double val)* so that it has the correct values with which to work. C++ provides a special syntax for doing this. It looks like this:

```
ArithArr::ArithArr(unsigned int n, double val) : ArrayDb(n, val)
{
}
```

This syntax means pass the *ArithArr()* arguments *n* and *val* to the *ArrayDb()* constructor. That constructor will then initialize the *ArrayDb* portion of the *ArithArr* object. The program will pass the arguments and execute the *ArrayDb()* function *before* executing any statements in the body of the *ArithArr()* function. Thus the derived

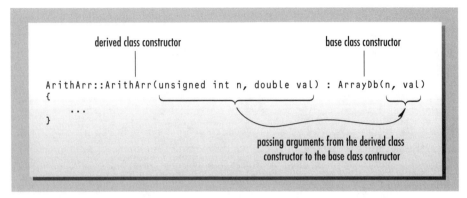

Figure 12-5 Passing arguments through to a base class constructor

constructor can assume that the base constructor has completed its work before the derived constructor begins. See Figure 12-5. Because an *ArithArr* object has no additional data members, we have no further objects to initialize. Again, this makes the function a good candidate for automatic inlining. In that case, we can combine providing default arguments, normally a prototype duty, with the function definition:

```
ArithArr(unsigned int n, double val = 0.0) : ArrayDb(n, val) {}
```

 ## INITIALIZATION LISTS

A constructor for a derived class can use the initialization list mechanism to pass values along to a base class constructor.

```
derived::derived(type1 x, type2 y) : base(x,y) // initialization list
{
       ...
}
```

Here, *derived* is the derived class, *base* is the base class, and *x* and *y* are variables used by the base class constructor. If, say, the *derived* constructor receives the arguments 10 and 12, this mechanism then passes 10 and 12 on to the *base* constructor defined as taking arguments of these types. Except for the case of virtual base classes (Chapter 14), a class can pass values back only to its immediate base class. However, that class can use the same mechanism to pass back information to its immediate base class, and so on. If you don't supply a base class constructor in an initialization list, the program will use the default base class constructor. The initialization list can be used only with constructors.

You can use the same technique for the remaining constructors. Just pass the constructor arguments to the corresponding base class constructor. That's what we did in the class declaration.

In Chapter 11 you encountered a syntax for initializing specific class members. For instance, the constructor

```
Queue::Queue(int qs) : qsize(qs)      // initialize qsize to qs
{
        front = rear = NULL;
        items = 0;
}
```

initializes the *qsize* member of a *Queue* object to *qs*. The syntax we've used here is a variant of this earlier form. The difference is that you use the name of a class *member* to initialize a particular member of an object, but you use the name of a base *class* to initialize the base class component of an object.

Initializing Objects to Objects

Two of the constructors let you initialize one object to another, and they merit further attention. First, consider the following inline definition:

```
ArithArr(const ArrayDb & aa) : ArrayDb(aa) {}
```

It lets you initialize an *ArithArr* object to an *ArrayDb* object. Because both classes have the same data representation, this makes sense. It is also useful. First, by initializing an *ArithArr* object to an *ArrayDb* object, you make it possible to apply the *ArithArr* methods to data previously placed in an *ArrayDb* object. Second, recall that any constructor with exactly one argument defines a type conversion from the argument type to the class type. Thus the *ArithArr(const ArrayDb & aa)* function defines *ArrayDb* to *ArithArr* conversion.

This means that you can do the following:

```
ArrayDb motels(10);
ArithArr inns;
inns = motels;        // inns is an ArithArr version of motels
```

The last line uses the constructor to create a temporary and anonymous *ArithArr* object initialized to the *motels* value. Then the contents of that temporary object are copied into *inns*.

The last example may make you wonder if you have to redefine assignment for the *ArithArr* class. No, you don't have to. Recall that if you don't define an assignment operator, the compiler will do so for you. For regular members, the default is member-wise copying. For inherited members, however, the default assignment operator uses the base class assignment operator to handle assignment for the base class portion of a derived class. Thus the expression *inns = hotels* will use the *ArrayDb* assignment operator to handle *arr* and *size* even if *inns* and *hotels* are type *ArithArr*—another bonus from inheritance. We'll talk more about assignment operators later.

What about the constructor that initializes one *ArithArr* object to another?

```
ArithArr(const ArithArr & ad) : ArrayDb(ad) {}
```

As usual, we allow a base class constructor to construct the base class component of the new object. But what argument do we pass to the base constructor? After all, no *ArrayDb* constructor had an *ArithArr &* argument. The answer lies in the fact that a reference to a derived class object automatically is converted to a reference to a base class object when used as an argument to a function whose formal argument is a base class reference. So the type *ArithArr &* argument becomes an *ArrayDb &* argument for an *ArrayDb* constructor, meaning the *ArrayDb(const ArrayDb & a)* constructor is called.

Do we really need to define the copy constructor explicitly? The answer, in this particular case, is no. The implicitly generated copy constructor uses memberwise copying. However, like the assignment operator, it uses any copy constructors defined for member objects or inherited subobjects. In this case, the default copy constructor automatically uses the *ArrayDb* copy constructor for the *ArrayDb* subobject. The *ArithArr* class doesn't add any new data members, so no special steps are needed. However, our explicit copy constructor does illustrate how to pass information to a base class constructor, so we provided one for that purpose.

RULE

A reference or pointer to a derived class object is converted to a reference or pointer to a base class object when used as an argument to a function defined as accepting a reference or a pointer to a base class object.

Next, you don't have to define an *ArithArr* destructor because the base destructor already frees the memory to which *arr* points. But it does no harm to define an empty destructor:

```
~ArithArr() {}
```

Other Member Functions

Defining the *sum()* and *average()* methods for the derived class points out the difference between private and protected members of a base class. Here, for example, is code implementing the *sum()* function:

```
double ArithArr::sum() const
{
        unsigned int size = arsize();          // access base via method
        double total = 0.0;
        for (int i = 0; i < size; i++)
                total += arr[i];               // access base directly
        return total;
}
```

Because *size* is a private member of the base class, an *ArithArr* method can't access *size* directly. But it can use *arsize()*, part of the *ArrayDb* public interface, to obtain the value.

531

The *arr* member, on the other hand, is a protected member of the base class, so an *ArithArr* method can use *arr* directly, without going through the overloaded [] operator.

Suppose *arr* had been a private member. We still could have accessed array elements by using the overloaded [] operator. Instead of using *arr[i]*, we could write this:

```
total += (*this)[i];
```

Here, *this is an *ArithArr* object. Because the *ArithArr* object is derived from the *ArrayDb* class, it can use the *ArrayDb* public interface. In particular, it can use the overloaded [] operator.

For the operations involving two arrays, such as addition and multiplication, we need to decide what to do if the arrays have different lengths. We've taken the easy road and have made such attempts an error. C++ exceptions, discussed in Chapter 13, provide a more flexible treatment.

Listing 12-5 shows the definitions for all the new methods. (The constructors and destructor, recall, are inline functions in the class declaration, so they don't appear here.)

Listing 12-5 *aritharr.cpp*

```
// aritharr.cpp -- ArithArr class methods
#include <iostream.h>
#include <stdlib.h>                    // exit() prototype
#include "aritharr.h"


// new methods
double ArithArr::sum() const
{
        unsigned int size = arsize();        // access base via method
        double total = 0.0;
        for (int i = 0; i < size; i++)
                total += arr[i];             // access base directly
        return total;
}

double ArithArr::average() const
{
        unsigned int size = arsize();
        if (size < 1)
        {
                cout << "Computing an average requires at least "
                                "one array element -- bye.\n";
                exit(1);
        }
        return sum() / size;
}

// overloaded operators
ArithArr ArithArr::operator+(const ArithArr & a) const
```

```
{
        unsigned int size = arsize();
        unsigned int asize = a.arsize();
        if (size != asize)
        {
                cerr << "+ not defined for arrays of unequal size\n";
                exit(1);
        }
        ArithArr total(size);
        for (int i = 0; i < size; i++)
                total[i] = arr[i] + a.arr[i];
        return total;
}

ArithArr ArithArr::operator-(const ArithArr & a) const
{
        unsigned int size = arsize();
        unsigned int asize = a.arsize();
        if (size != asize)
        {
                cerr << "- not defined for arrays of unequal size\n";
                exit(1);
        }
        ArithArr diff(size);
        for (int i = 0; i < size; i++)
                diff[i] = arr[i] - a.arr[i];
        return diff;
}

ArithArr ArithArr::operator-() const
{
        unsigned int size = arsize();
        ArithArr neg(size);
        for (int i = 0; i < size; i++)
                neg[i] = -arr[i];
                return neg;
}


ArithArr ArithArr::operator*(const ArithArr & a) const
{
        unsigned int size = arsize();
        unsigned int asize = a.arsize();
        if (size != asize)
        {
                cout << "Array multiplication error: arrays must "
                                        "be of same size. Bye.\n";
                exit(1);
        }
        ArithArr product(size);
        for (int i = 0; i < size; i++)
                product[i] = arr[i] * a.arr[i];
        return product;
```

continued on next page

continued from previous page

```
}

ArithArr ArithArr::operator*(double d) const
{
        unsigned int size = arsize();
        ArithArr temp(size);
        for (int i = 0; i < size; i++)
                temp[i] = arr[i]*d;
        return temp;
}


ArithArr operator*(double d, const ArithArr & a)
{
        return a*d;
}
```

Using the Derived Class

Listing 12-6 tests the new class. It uses a couple of formatting features that we've used before:

```
cout.precision(2);              // 2 places to right of decimal
cout.setf(ios::showpoint);      // show trailing 0s
cout.setf(ios::fixed, ios::floatfield); // fixed point
```

Chapter 15 discusses these options in more detail.

Listing 12-6 *derived.cpp*

```
// derived.cpp -- use a derived class
// compile with aritharr.cpp and arraydb.cpp
#include <iostream.h>
#include <stdlib.h>                     // exit() prototype
#include "aritharr.h"

void show(const ArrayDb & ar, int index);

const int things = 4;
double price[things] = { 9.95, 28.55, 8.99, 1.50 };
int main(void)
{
        ArithArr prices1(price, things);
        ArithArr prices2(prices1);
        prices2 = 1.05 * prices1;  // multiplication, assignment
        ArithArr sales1(things);
        ArithArr sales2(things);
        cout << "Enter sales for first half:\n"
                << "disks    mitts    tapes    cards\n";
        for (int i = 0; i < things; i++)
                cin >> sales1[i];
        cout << "Enter sales for second half:\n"
```

```
                << "disks   mitts  tapes    cards\n";
        for (i = 0; i < things; i++)
            cin >> sales2[i];
        ArithArr allsales = sales1 + sales2;
        cout << "Total sales:\n" << allsales;
        ArithArr gross = sales1 * prices1 + sales2 * prices2;
        cout.precision(2);    // 2 places to right of decimal
        cout.setf(ios::showpoint);   // show trailing 0s
        cout.setf(ios::fixed, ios::floatfield); // fixed point
        cout << "Gross take in dollars per item:\n" << gross;
        cout << "Let's see that with a $:\n";
        for (i = 0; i < things; i++)
            show(gross, i);                   // ArrayDb reference
        cout << "Total gross: $" << gross.sum() << "\n";

        return 0;
}

void show(const ArrayDb & ar, int index)
{
        cout << index << ": $" << ar[index] << "\n";
}
```

Here's a sample run:

```
Enter sales for first half:
disks   mitts  tapes    cards
225     196    169      289
Enter sales for second half:
disks   mitts  tapes    cards
251     201    277      301
Total sales:
476 397 446 590
Gross take in dollars per item:
4861.07 11621.28 4134.05 907.58
Let's see that with a $:
0: $4861.07
1: $11621.28
2: $4134.05
3: $907.58
Total gross: $21523.98
```

Program Notes

Let's examine parts of the program more closely. First, the statements

```
ArithArr prices1(price, things);
ArithArr prices2(prices1);
```

invoke two of the constructors to create two *ArithArr* objects.

Next, the statement

```
prices2 = 1.05 * prices1;  // multiplication, assignment
```

invokes the friend function *operator*(double, const ArithArr&)*, which, in turn, invokes the member function *operator*(double)*. The copy constructor handles the function return values, producing a temporary *ArithArr* object that is assigned to *prices2* using the default *ArithArr* assignment operator, which uses the base class *ArrayDb* assignment operator. Then *ArithArr* and *ArrayDb* destructors are called to eliminate the temporary object. C++ notation can hide quite a few function calls!

Skipping ahead a bit, the loop

```
for (int i = 0; i < things; i++)
    cin >> sales1[i];
```

illustrates how a derived class object *(sales1)* can use a base class method *(ArrayDb::operator[] ())*.

Also notice the following loop:

```
for (int i = 0; i < things; i++)
    show(gross, i);              // ArrayDb reference
```

Note that the *show()* function definition indicates that it takes an *ArrayDb &* argument. Public inheritance means, among other things, that a reference to a derived class can be converted to a reference to a base class, so the *show()* function accepts an *ArithArr* reference as an argument.

The *Is-a* Relationship, References, and Pointers

One way public inheritance models the *is-a* relationship is in how it handles pointers and references to objects. Normally, C++ does not allow you to assign an address of one type to a pointer of another type. Nor does it let a reference to one type refer to another type:

```
double x = 2.5;
int * pi = &x; // invalid assignment, mismatched pointer types
long & rl = x; // invalid assignment, mismatched reference type
```

However, as we've mentioned a couple of times, a reference or a pointer to a base class *can* refer to a derived class object without using an explicit type cast. The *show()* example we just discussed, for example, allows the *ar* variable in *show()* (a reference to *ArrayDb*) to refer to the *ArithArr* object *gross*. Similarly, code like the following is valid:

```
ArithArr styles(10);
ArrayDb * pa = &styles;
```

Converting a derived class reference or pointer to a base class reference or pointer is called *upcasting*, and it is always allowed for public inheritance without the need for an explicit type cast. This rule is part of expressing the *is-a* relationship. An *ArithArr* object is an *ArrayDb* object in that it inherits all the data members of an *ArrayDb* object. Therefore, anything that you can do to an *ArrayDb* object, you can do to an *ArithArr* object. So a function designed to handle an *ArrayDb* reference can, without fear of creating problems, perform the same acts upon an *ArithArr* object. The same idea applies if you pass a pointer to an object as a function argument.

The opposite process, converting a base class pointer or reference to a derived class pointer or reference, is called *downcasting,* and it is not allowed without an explicit type cast. The reason for this restriction is that the *is-a* relationship is not, in general, reversible. A derived class could add new data members, and the class member functions that used these data members wouldn't apply to the base class. For example, suppose we derive a *Singer* class from an *Employee* class, adding a data member representing a singer's vocal range and a member function, called *range(),* that reports the value for the vocal range. It wouldn't make sense to apply the *range()* method to an *Employee* object. But if implicit downcasting were allowed, you could accidentally set a pointer-to-*Singer* to the address of an *Employee* object and use the pointer to invoke the *range()* method. See Figure 12-6.

```
class Employee
{
private:
    char name[40];
    ...
public:
    void show_name();
    ...
};
class Singer : public Employee
{
    ...
public:
    void range();
    ...
};
...
Employee veep;
Singer trala;
...
Employee * pe = &trala;          ─── upcast—implicit type cast allowed
Singer * ps = (Singer *) &veep;  ─── downcast—explicit type cast required
...
pe->show_name();    ─── Upcasting leads to a safe operation because
ps->range();             a Singer is an Employee (every Singer
                         inherits name).

                    ─── Downcasting can lead to an unsafe operation
                         because an Employee isn't a Singer (an
                         Employee need not have a range() method).
```

Figure 12-6 Upcasting and downcasting

Deriving Another Class

Inheritance can add methods, add data members, and modify methods. The last example just added methods, so let's investigate another example, one that adds data members and modifies methods. The first version will have a slight flaw, one designed to lead to a new topic.

Our new undertaking will be to derive an array class for which the initial index needn't be 0. For instance, if you wanted an array to represent rainfall for the years 1986–1995, you could use an array whose index values ranged from 1986 through 1995 instead of from 0 through 9. In short, we want definable array-index bounds. Since a derived class can serve as a base class, we could derive the new class from the *ArithArr* class, but to keep things simple, we'll use *ArrayDb* as the base class once again, and we'll name the new class *LimitArr*.

One way to achieve the goal of definable array-index bounds is to add a new member to hold the desired lower bound and to modify the *operator[] ()* function so that it handles the new index range. This leads to the class declaration shown in Listing 12-7.

Listing 12-7 *limarr.h*

```
// limarr.h -- LimitArr class

#ifndef _LIMARR_H_
#define _LIMARR_H_

#include "arraydb.h"

class LimitArr : public ArrayDb
{
protected:
        unsigned int low_bnd;        // new data member
        void ok(int i) const;        // handle bounds checking
public:
// constructors
        LimitArr();
        LimitArr(unsigned int n, double val = 0.0);
        LimitArr(unsigned int n, int lb, double val = 0.0);
        LimitArr(const double * pn, unsigned int n);
        LimitArr(const LimitArr & a);
        LimitArr(const ArrayDb & a);
// new methods
        void new_lb(int lb) {low_bnd = lb; }  // reset lower bound
        int lbound() const {return low_bnd;}     // return lower bound
        int ubound() const {return low_bnd + arsize() -1;} // return upper bound
// redefined operators
        double & operator[](int i);
        const double & operator[](int i) const;
};

#endif
```

The new member *low_bnd* will hold the index value for the first element of the array. The *lbound()* method returns that value, and the *ubound()* member returns the index of the last array element. The class could store this value, but it's a simple matter to calculate it from the lower bound and the array size. The *new_lb()* function lets you reset the lower bound. These three methods are short enough to be inline. The *ok()* function, as you'll soon see, provides bounds-checking code shared by the two over-loaded *operator[]()* functions.

Because each new class needs its own constructors, we've provided *LimitArr* with a fair sampling of them.

The Implementation

Listing 12-8 presents the implementation for the new class.

Listing 12-8 *limarr.cpp*

```
// limarr.cpp -- LimitArr methods
#include "limarr.h"
#include <iostream.h>
#include <stdlib.h>

// private method
        // lower bound for array index is now low_bnd, and
        // upper bound is now low_bnd + size - 1
void LimitArr::ok(int i) const  // variable lower bound
{
        unsigned long size = arsize();
        if (i < low_bnd)
        {
                cout << "Error in array limits:\n"
                                << "index " << i << " less than "
                                << low_bnd <<  "\n";
                exit(2);
        }
        else if (i >= size + low_bnd)
        {
                cout << "Error in array limits:\n"
                                << "index " << i << " greater than "
                                << size + low_bnd - 1 << "\n";
                exit(3);
        }
}

// constructors -- initialize the new data member
LimitArr::LimitArr() : ArrayDb()
{
        low_bnd = 0;   // default sets starting subscript to 0
}

LimitArr::LimitArr(unsigned int n, double val) : ArrayDb(n, val)
```

continued on next page

continued from previous page

```
{
        low_bnd = 0;   // default value
}

LimitArr::LimitArr(unsigned int n, int lb, double val)
        : ArrayDb(n, val)
{
        low_bnd = lb;  // set starting subscript explicitly
}

LimitArr::LimitArr(const double * pn, unsigned int n)
        : ArrayDb(pn, n)
{
        low_bnd = 0;
}

LimitArr::LimitArr(const LimitArr & a) : ArrayDb(a)
{
        low_bnd = a.low_bnd;
}

LimitArr::LimitArr(const ArrayDb & a) : ArrayDb(a)
{
        low_bnd = 0;
}

// redefined operators
double & LimitArr::operator[](int i)
{
        ok(i);
        return arr[i - low_bnd];
}

const double & LimitArr::operator[](int i) const
{
        ok(i);
        return arr[i - low_bnd];
}
```

As with the previous example, the constructors call upon base class constructors to create the *ArrayDb* portion of a *LimitArr* object. Note that automatic upcasting and the *is-a* relationship make it permissible to pass a *LimitArr &* argument to the *ArrayDb* copy constructor. After calling upon a base class constructor, the derived class constructor has a new responsibility, initializing the new *low_bnd* data member.

In its heart of hearts, C++ has to use an index of 0 for the first element of an array because it uses the index to calculate address offsets from the beginning of an array. However, we can use the new *operator[] ()* functions to act as translators between a program's view of array indices, say 1986–1995, and the internal representation of 0–9. In fact, all that the functions have to do is subtract the lower bound from the index value to get the internal value. For instance, an index of 1988 would correspond to an internal index of 1988 - 1986, or 2. The *operator[] ()* functions also call upon an *ok()* function that checks for a valid index and reports if there is a problem.

Using the New Class

The next step is to try out the new class. Listing 12-9 does so with a program that creates an array with index values ranging from 1977–1981. It checks to see if assignment works, even though we haven't defined an assignment operator, and it demonstrates what happens when we pass a *LimitArr* argument to a function expecting a reference to an *ArrayDb* object.

Listing 12-9 *use_lim.cpp*

```cpp
// use_lim.cpp -- use the LimitArr class
// Compile with limarr.cpp and arraydb.cpp
#include <iostream.h>
#include "limarr.h"

void show(const ArrayDb & ar, int index);
const int YEAR = 1977;
const int YEARS = 5;
int main(void)
{
        LimitArr vintages(YEARS, YEAR);
        cout << "Enter bids for the following vintages of "
                        "Chateau Spiff:\n";
        for (int year = YEAR; year < YEAR + YEARS; year++)
        {
                cout << "Year " << year << ": $";
                cin >> vintages[year];
        }
        cout.precision(2);
        cout.setf(ios::showpoint);
        cout.setf(ios::fixed, ios::floatfield);
        cout << "Recapitulating, here are the bids in dollars:\n";
        cout << vintages;
        cout << vintages[1978] << "\n";
        cout << "The following bids were accepted:\n";
        LimitArr copy;
        copy = vintages;
        int bid1 = 1978;
        int bid2 = 1980;
        cout << bid1 << ": $" << copy[bid1] << "\n";
        show(copy, bid2);
        return 0;
}

void show(const ArrayDb & ar, int index)
{
        cout << index << ": $" << ar[index] << "\n";
}
```

Here is a sample run:

```
Enter bids for the following vintages of Chateau Spiff:
Year 1977: $26.50
Year 1978: $35
Year 1979: $29.99
Year 1980: $1.65
Year 1981: $14.60
Recapitulating, here are the bids in dollars:
26.50 35.00 29.99 1.65 14.60
35.00
The following bids were accepted:
1978: $35.00
Error in array limits: 1980 is a bad index
```

As you can see, everything works fine at first. The *LimitArr* object *vintages* successfully uses an index range of 1977–1981. (But Cousin Creeble's bid to run the winery in 1980 was a bust.) The expression *copy[bid1]*, where *bid1* is 1978, evaluated correctly. But then the program passes *copy* and *bid2* (1980) as arguments to *show()*, and suddenly 1980 is a bad index! The problem is that, in *show()*, the variable *ar* is a reference to a type *ArrayDb* object, and this causes *ar[index]* to invoke the *ArrayDb* version of *operator[]()*. The *LimitArr* class declaration has strained the *is-a* relationship to the point that some of the *ArrayDb* class methods no longer perform correctly when applied to the objects of the derived class. The situation, however, is fixable, as the next section will reveal.

Virtual Member Functions

When you derive one class from another, you may have to redefine how certain methods work. For instance, the *LimitArr* class required a new version of the *operator[]()* function. When you use an object to invoke a method, the program uses the object type to figure out which version of the method to use:

```
ArrayDb thelma(5);
LimitArr thea(6,100);
thelma[2] = 99.98;      // use ArrayDb::operator[]()
thea[102] = 86.64;      // use LimitArr::operator[]()
```

There's a problem, however, if you use a reference or pointer to invoke a method:

```
// default behavior (static binding)
ArrayDb & ra = thea;          // thea a LimitArr object
ArrayDb * pa = &thea;
ra[102] = 86.64;              // use ArrayDb::operator[]()
(*pa)[102] = 86.64;          // use ArrayDb::operator[]()
pa->[102] = 86.64;           // use ArrayDb::operator[]()
```

The C++ default behavior uses the type of the pointer or reference to decide which function to use, ignoring the type of the object referred to or pointed to. There's a good reason for this behavior—often the compiler doesn't know the type. For instance, consider the *show()* function in the last example. It has a reference argument, and it could be used in a different file from the one containing its definition. When the compiler compiles the source code file containing the function definition, it has no way of knowing what type of object will be passed to it as an argument in some other file. The only choice the compiler can make at compile time is to match class methods to the type of reference or pointer. This strategy is called *early binding,* or *static binding.* The term *binding* refers to attaching a function call to a particular function definition. (In C, you have only one function per name, so the choice is obvious. But C++, with function overloading and redefined member functions, can have more than one function matching a given name.)

C++ offers a second strategy, called *late binding,* or *dynamic binding.* With this strategy, the compiler doesn't make the decision of which class method to use. Instead, it passes responsibility to the program, which then makes a runtime decision whenever it actually executes a method function call. If we use this strategy, we can have a program choose a method based on the type of object to which a reference or pointer refers:

```
// dynamic binding
LimitArr thea(6,100);
ArrayDb & ra = thea;          // thea a LimitArr object
ArrayDb * pa = &thea;
ra[102] = 86.64;              // use LimitArr::operator[]()
(*pa)[102] = 86.64;          // use LimitArr::operator[]()
pa->[102] = 86.64;           // use LimitArr::operator[]()
```

Dynamic binding is a good thing. With it, Listing 12-9 will work correctly. The *ArrayDb* reference argument in *show()* will refer to a *LimitArr* object and thus invoke the *LimitArr* version of the [] operator.

This discussion should raise some questions in your mind:

❧ How do you activate dynamic binding?

❧ Why have two kinds of binding?

❧ If dynamic binding is so good, why isn't it the default?

❧ How does it work?

We'll look at answers to these questions next.

Activating Dynamic Binding

You can turn on dynamic binding only for member functions. To do so, precede the function prototype with the keyword *virtual* in the base class declaration. We then call the method a *virtual method.* If you then redefine the function in a derived class, a program will use dynamic binding to determine which definition to use. Once you've made a method virtual, it remains virtual for all classes derived from the base class, along with any classes derived from the derived classes, and so on. For a given method, you only have to use the keyword *virtual* once, in the base class.

> ## RULE
>
> Virtual member functions are created by preceding the prototype with the keyword *virtual*. C++ programs use dynamic, or late, binding for virtual methods, and static, or early, binding for nonvirtual methods. For virtual functions, the type of object referred to or pointed to determines which method a pointer or reference invokes.

Let's fix the last example program so that *show()* will use the correct method. The only file we need to change is *arraydb.h*, and the only change we need to make is to add the keyword *virtual* to the prototypes for the two *operator[]()* functions. Actually, we also should make the destructor virtual for reasons we'll discuss soon. Listing 12-10 shows the revised header file.

Listing 12-10 *arraydb.h*

```
// arraydb.h -- revised array class, making [] virtual
#ifndef _ARRAYDB_H_
#define _ARRAYDB_H_
#include <iostream.h>

class ArrayDb
{
private:
        unsigned int size;                  // number of array elements
protected:
        double * arr;                       // address of first element
public:
        ArrayDb();                          // default constructor
        // create an ArrayDb of n elements, set each to val
        ArrayDb(unsigned int n, double val = 0.0);
        // create an ArrayDb of n elements, initialize to array pn
        ArrayDb(const double * pn, unsigned int n);
        ArrayDb(const ArrayDb & a);         // copy constructor
        virtual ~ArrayDb();                 // destructor
        unsigned int arsize() const {return size;} // returns array size
// overloaded operators -- note use of keyword virtual
        virtual double & operator[](int i);        // array indexing
        virtual const double & operator[](int i) const; // array indexing (no =)
        ArrayDb & operator=(const ArrayDb & a);
        friend ostream & operator<<(ostream & os, const ArrayDb & a);
};

#endif
```

Make these changes to *arraydb.h* and recompile the program consisting of Listing 12-2 (*arraydb.cpp*), Listing 12-8 (*limarr.cpp*), and Listing 12-9 (*use_lim.cpp*). You now should have a version that uses dynamic linking. Here is some sample output:

```
Enter bids for the following vintages of Chateau Spiff:
Year 1977: $26.50
Year 1978: $35
```

```
Year 1979: $29.99
Year 1980: $1.65
Year 1981: $14.60
Recapitulating, here are the bids in dollars:
26.50 35.00 29.99 1.65 14.60
35.00
The following bids were accepted:
1978: $35.00
1980: $1.65
```

Now the statement *show(copy,bid2)* works correctly, with the *ArrayDb &* formal argument invoking the *LimitArr* version of *[]*.

Why Two Kinds of Binding?

Since dynamic binding allows you to redefine class methods while static binding makes a partial botch of it, why have static binding at all? There are two reasons: efficiency and a conceptual model.

First, consider efficiency. For a program to be able to make a runtime decision, it has to have some way to keep track of what sort of object a base class pointer or reference refers to, and that entails some extra processing overhead. (We'll describe one method of dynamic binding later.) If, for example, you design a class that won't be used as a base class for inheritance, you don't need the dynamic binding feature. In that case, it makes more sense to use static binding and gain a little efficiency. The fact that static binding is more efficient is why it is the default choice for C++. Stroustrup says one of the guiding principles of C++ is that.you shouldn't have to pay (in memory usage or processing time) for those features you don't use. Go to virtual functions only if your program design needs them.

Next, consider the conceptual model. When you design a class, you may have member functions that you don't want redefined in derived classes. For instance, the *ArrayDb arsize()* function, which returns the number of elements in the array, seems like a function that shouldn't be redefined. By making this function nonvirtual, we accomplish two things. First, we make it more efficient. Second, we announce that it is our intention that this function not be redefined. That suggests the following rule of thumb.

TIP

If a method in a base class will be redefined in a derived class, make it virtual. If the method should not be redefined, make it nonvirtual.

Of course, when you design a class, it's not always obvious into which category a method falls. Like many aspects of real life, class design is not a linear process.

How Virtual Functions Work

C++ specifies how virtual functions should work, but it leaves the implementation up to the compiler writer. You don't need to know the implementation method to use virtual functions, but seeing how it is done may help you understand the concepts better, so let's take a look.

The usual way compilers handle virtual functions is to add a hidden member to each object. The hidden member holds a pointer to an array of function addresses. Such an array usually is termed a *table*. The table holds the addresses of the virtual functions declared for objects of that class. For instance, an object of a base class will contain a pointer to a table of addresses of all the virtual functions for that class. An object of a derived class will contain a pointer to a separate table of addresses. If the derived class provides a new definition of a virtual function, the table holds the address of the new function. If the derived class doesn't redefine the virtual function, the table holds the address of the original version of the function. If the derived class defines a new function and makes it virtual, its address is added to the table. See Figure 12-7. Note that whether you define one or ten virtual functions for a class, you add just one address member to an object.

When you call a virtual function, the program looks at the table address stored in an object and goes to the corresponding table of function addresses. If you use the first virtual function defined in the class declaration, the program will use the first function address in the array and execute the function having that address. If you use the third virtual function in the class declaration, the program will use the function whose address is in the third element of the array.

In short, using virtual functions has the following modest costs in memory and execution speed:

- Each object has its size increased by the amount needed to hold an address.

- For each class, the compiler creates a table (an array) of addresses of virtual functions.

- For each function call, there's an extra step of going to a table to look up an address.

Keep in mind that although nonvirtual functions are slightly more efficient than virtual functions, they don't provide dynamic binding.

Virtual Things to Know

We've already discussed the main points about virtual functions:

- Beginning a class method definition with the keyword *virtual* in a base class makes the function virtual for the base class and all classes derived from the base class, including classes derived from the derived classes, and so on.

- If a virtual method is invoked by using a reference to an object or by a pointer to an object, the program will use the method defined for the object type rather than the method defined for the reference or pointer type. This is called dynamic, or late, binding. This behavior is important, for it's always valid for a base class pointer or reference to refer to an object of a derived type.

If you're defining a class that will be used as a base class for inheritance, declare as virtual functions those class methods that may have to be redefined in derived classes.

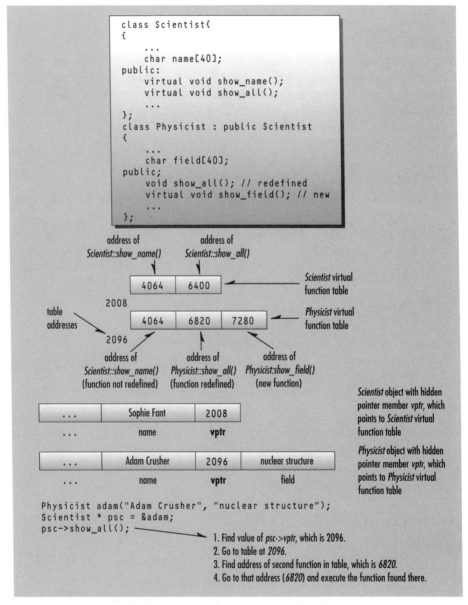

```
class Scientist{
{
    ...
    char name[40];
public:
    virtual void show_name();
    virtual void show_all();
    ...
};
class Physicist : public Scientist
{
    ...
    char field[40];
public:
    void show_all(); // redefined
    virtual void show_field(); // new
    ...
};
```

address of
Scientist::show_name()

address of
Scientist::show_all()

| 4064 | 6400 |

Scientist virtual
function table

2008

table addresses

| 4064 | 6820 | 7280 |

Physicist virtual
function table

2096

address of
Scientist::show_name()
(function not redefined)

address of
Physicist::show_all()
(function redefined)

address of
Physicist:show_field()
(new function)

| ... | Sophie Fant | 2008 |
| ... | name | **vptr** |

Scientist object with hidden pointer member *vptr*, which points to *Scientist* virtual function table

| ... | Adam Crusher | 2096 | nuclear structure |
| ... | name | **vptr** | field |

Physicist object with hidden pointer member *vptr*, which points to *Physicist* virtual function table

```
Physicist adam("Adam Crusher", "nuclear structure");
Scientist * psc = &adam;
psc->show_all();
```

1. Find value of *psc->vptr*, which is 2096.
2. Go to table at *2096*.
3. Find address of second function in table, which is *6820*.
4. Go to that address (*6820*) and execute the function found there.

Figure 12-7 A virtual function mechanism

There are several other things you may need to know about virtual functions, some of which we've mentioned in passing already. Let's look at them next.

Constructors

Constructors can't be virtual. A derived class doesn't inherit the base class constructors, so usually there's not much point to making them virtual, anyway.

Destructors

Destructors should be virtual unless a class isn't to be used as a base class. For instance, suppose *Employee* is a base class and *Singer* is a derived class that adds a *char* * member that points to memory allocated by *new*. Then, when a *Singer* object expires, it's vital that the *~Singer()* destructor be called to free that memory.

Now consider the following code:

```
Employee * pe = new Singer; // legal because Employee is base for Singer

delete pe;          // ~Employee() or ~Singer()?
```

If the default static binding applies, the *delete* statement will invoke the *~Employee()* destructor. This will free memory pointed to by the *Employee* components of the *Singer* object but not memory pointed to by the new class members. However, if the destructors are virtual, the same code invokes the *~Singer()* destructor, which frees memory pointed to by the *Singer* component, then calls the *~Employee()* destructor to free memory pointed to by the *Employee* component.

Friends

Friends can't be virtual functions because friends are not class members, and only members can be virtual functions. If this poses a problem for a design, you may be able to sidestep it by having the friend function use virtual member functions internally.

No Redefinition

If a derived class fails to redefine a virtual function, the class will use the base class version of the function. If a derived class is part of a long chain of derivations, it will use the most recently defined version of the virtual function. The exception is if the base versions are hidden, as described next.

Redefinition Hides Methods

Suppose you create something like the following:

```
class Dwelling
{
public:
      virtual void showperks(int a) const;
...
```

```
};
class Hovel : public Dwelling
{
{
public:
        void showperks();
...
};
```

You should get a compiler warning similar to the following:

```
Warning: Hovel::showperks(int) hides Dwelling::showperks(int)
```

This has the following implications:

```
Hovel trump;
trump.showperks();      // valid
trump.showperks(5);     // invalid
```

The new definition defines a *showperks()* that takes no arguments. This definition hides the base class version that takes an *int* argument. In short, redefining inherited methods is not a variation of overloading. If you redefine a function in a derived class, it doesn't just override the base class declaration with the same function signature. Instead, it hides *all* base class methods of the same name, regardless of the argument signatures.

This fact of life leads to a couple of rules of thumb. First, if you redefine an inherited method, make sure you match the original prototype exactly. One exception is that a return type that is a reference or pointer to a base class can be replaced by a reference or pointer to the derived class. (This exception is new, and not all compilers recognize it yet. Also, note that this exception applies only to return values, not to arguments.) Second, if the base class declaration is overloaded, redefine all the base class versions in the derived class:

```
class Dwelling
{
public:
// three overloaded showperks()
        virtual void showperks(int a) const;
        virtual void showperks(double x) const;
        virtual void showperks() const;
        ...
};
class Hovel : public Dwelling
{
public:
// three redefined showperks()
        void showperks(int a) const;
        void showperks(double x) const;
        void showperks() const;
        ...
};
```

If you redefine just one version, the other two become hidden and cannot be used by objects of the derived class.

Pure Virtual Functions and ABCs

C++ has a variation of the virtual function called a *pure virtual function*. It's a virtual function with a prototype but no definition. There's a special syntax for such functions — you place = 0 before the closing semicolon of the prototype:

```
class Shape
{
public:
        virtual void draw() const = 0;      // pure virtual function
        virtual double area() const = 0;    // another one
        ...
};
```

When a class declaration contains a pure virtual function, you can't create an object of that class. The idea is that classes with pure virtual functions exist solely to serve as base classes. Generally, such a class defines, in the abstract, general properties that will apply to several derived classes. For this reason, such a class is called an *abstract base class,* or ABC, for short. Here, for example, the *Shape* class can serve as a base for a *Circle* class, a *Hexagon* class, a *Rectangle* class, a *Triangle* class, and so on. All these classes will share certain abstract properties, such as they can be drawn and their areas computed, but the implementation will depend on the specific object. So *Circle::area()* will use a different calculation than *Triangle::area()* does. The *Shape* class, however, is too abstract to allow us to define a *Shape::area()* function. Thus, it makes sense to provide it with a pure virtual function; then let derived classes provide their own non-pure versions.

In short, an ABC describes an interface in terms of pure virtual functions, and a class derived from an ABC uses regular virtual functions to implement the interface in terms of the properties of the particular derived class.

Class Design Review

C++ can be applied to a wide variety of programming problems, and you can't reduce class design to some paint-by-the-numbers routine. However, there are some guidelines that often apply, and this is as good a time as any to go over them, by reviewing and amplifying earlier discussions.

Member Functions That the Compiler Generates for You

As first discussed in Chapter 11, the compiler automatically generates certain public member functions. The fact that it does suggests that these member functions are particularly important. Let's look again at some of them now.

The Default Constructor

A default constructor is one with no arguments, or else one for which all the arguments have default arguments. If you don't define any constructors, the compiler defines a default constructor for you. It doesn't do anything, but it must exist for you to do certain things. For instance, suppose *Star* is a class. You need a default constructor to do the following:

```
Star rigel;            // create an object without explicit initialization
Star pleiades[6];      // create an array of non-explicitly initialized objects
```

Also, if you write a derived class constructor without explicitly invoking a base class constructor in the initialization list, the compiler will use the base class default constructor to construct the base class portion of the new object.

If you do define a constructor of any kind, the compiler will not define a default constructor for you. In that case, it's up to you to provide a default constructor.

Note that one of the motivations for having constructors is to insure that objects always are properly initialized. Also, if your class has any pointer members, they certainly should be initialized. Thus, it's a good idea to supply an explicit default constructor that initializes all class data members to reasonable values.

The Copy Constructor

The copy constructor is a constructor that takes a constant reference to the class type as its argument. For instance, the copy constructor for a *Star* class would have this prototype:

```
Star(const Star &);
```

The class copy constructor is used in the following situations:

❧ When a new object is initialized to an object of the same class

❧ When an object is passed to a function by value

❧ When an object returns an object by value

❧ When the compiler generates a temporary object

If your program doesn't need a copy constructor, the compiler provides a prototype, but not a function definition. Otherwise, the program defines a copy constructor that performs memberwise initialization. That is, each member of the new object is initialized to the value of the corresponding member of the original object.

In some cases, memberwise initialization is undesirable. For example, member pointers initialized with *new* generally require that you institute deep copying, as with the *ArrayDb* class. Or a class may have a static variable that needs to be modified. In such cases, you need to define your own copy constructor.

The Assignment Operator

The default assignment operator handles assigning one object to another of the same class. Don't confuse assignment with initialization. If the statement creates a new object, it's using initialization, and if it alters the value of an existing object, it's assignment:

```
Star sirius;
Star alpha = sirius;        // initialization (one notation)
Star dogstar;
dogstar = sirius;           // assignment
```

If you need to define the copy constructor explicitly, you also need, for the same reasons, to define the assignment operator explicitly. The prototype for a *Star* class assignment operator is this:

```
Star & Star(const Star &);
```

Note that the assignment operator function returns a reference to a *Star* object. The *ArrayDb* class shows a typical example of an explicit assignment operator function.

The compiler doesn't generate assignment operators for assigning one type to another. Suppose you want to be able to assign a string to a *Star* object. One approach is to define such an operator explicitly:

```
Star & Star::operator=(const char *) {...}
```

A second approach is to rely upon a conversion function (see "Conversions" in the next section) to convert a string to a *Star* object and use the *Star*-to-*Star* assignment function. The first approach runs more quickly, but requires more code.

Other Class Method Considerations

There are several other points to keep in mind as you define a class. Here are some.

Constructors

Constructors are different from other class methods in that they create new objects, while other methods are invoked by existing methods.

Destructors

Remember to define an explicit destructor that deletes any memory allocated by *new* in the class constructors and takes care of any other special bookkeeping that destroying a class object requires.

Conversions

Any constructor that can be invoked with exactly one argument defines conversion from the argument type to the class type. For instance, consider the following constructor prototypes for a *Star* class:

```
Star(const char *);                    // converts const char * to Star
Star(const Spectral, int members = 1); // converts const Spectral to Star
```

Conversion constructors get used, for example, when a convertible type is passed to a function defined as taking a class argument. For example, suppose we have the following:

```
Star north;
north = "polaris";
```

The second statement would invoke the *Star::operator=(const Star &)* function, using *Star::Star(const char *)* to generate a *Star* object to be used as an argument for the assignment operator function. This assumes that you haven't defined a *(char *)-to-Star* assignment operator.

To convert from a class object to some other type, define a conversion function (Chapter 10). A conversion function is a class member function with no arguments, no declared return type, and having the name of the type to be converted to. Despite having no declared return type, the function should return the desired conversion value. Here are some samples:

```
Star::Star double() {...}         // converts star to double
Star: Star const char * () {...}  // converts to const char
```

You should be judicious with such functions, only using them if they make good sense. Also, with some class designs, having conversion functions increases the likelihood of writing ambiguous code. For instance, suppose we had defined a *double* conversion for the *vector* type of Chapter 10, and suppose we had the following code:

```
vector ius(6.0, 0.0);
vector lux = ius + 20.2;    // ambiguous
```

The compiler could convert *ius* to *double* and use *double* addition, or else convert 20.2 to *vector* (using one of the constructors) and use *vector* addition. Instead, it would do neither and inform you of an ambiguous construction.

Passing an Object by Value vs. Passing a Reference

In general, if you write a function using an object argument, you should pass the object by reference rather than by value. One reason is efficiency. Passing an object by value involves generating a temporary copy, which means calling the copy constructor, then later calling the destructor. Calling these functions takes time, and copying a large object can be quite a bit slower than passing a reference. If the function doesn't modify the object, declare the argument as a *const* reference.

Another reason for passing objects by reference is that, in the case of inheritance using virtual functions, a function defined as accepting a base class reference argument can also be used successfully with derived classes, as we saw earlier in this chapter. Also see the discussion of virtual methods later this chapter.

Returning an Object vs. Returning a Reference

Some class methods have return objects. You've probably noticed that some of these members return objects directly while others return references. Sometimes a method *must* return an object, but if it isn't necessary, you should use a reference instead. Let's look at this more closely.

First, the only coding difference between returning an object directly and returning a reference is in the function prototype and header:

```
Star nova(const Star &);      // returns a Star object
Star & nova(const Star &);    // returns a reference to a Star
```

Next, the reason that you should return a reference rather than an object is that returning an object involves generating a temporary copy of the returned object. It's the copy that's made available to the calling program. Thus, returning an object involves the time cost of calling a copy constructor to generate the copy and of calling the destructor to get rid of the copy. Returning a reference saves time and memory use. Returning an object directly is analogous to passing an object by value: both processes generate temporary copies. Similarly, returning a reference is analogous to passing an object by reference: both the calling and the called function operate upon the same object.

However, it's not always possible to return a reference. A function shouldn't return a reference to a temporary object created in the function, for the reference becomes invalid when the function terminates and the object disappears. In this case, the code should return an object in order to generate a copy that will be available to the calling program.

As a rule of thumb, if a function returns a temporary object created in the function, don't use a reference. For example, the following method creates a new object *(neg)*, which it returns.

```
ArithArr ArithArr::operator-() const
{
        unsigned int size = arsize();
        ArithArr neg(size);
        for (int i = 0; i < size; i++)
                neg[i] = -arr[i];
                return neg;
}
```

If a function returns an object that was passed to it via a reference or pointer, return the object by reference. For example, the following code returns, by reference, the object that invokes the function:

```
ArrayDb & ArrayDb::operator=(const ArrayDb & a)
{
        delete arr;
        size = a.size;
        arr = new double[size];
        for (int i = 0; i < size; i++)
```

```
                arr[i] = a.arr[i];
        return *this;
}
```

Using *const*

Be alert to opportunities to use *const*. You can use it to guarantee that a method doesn't modify an argument:

```
Star::Star(const char * s) {...} // won't change the string to which s points
```

You can use *const* to guarantee that a method won't modify the object that invokes it:

```
void Star::show() const {...} // won't change invoking object
```

Here *const* means *const Star * const this,* where *this* points to the invoking object.

You can use *const* to insure that a reference or pointer return value can't be used to modify data in an object:

```
const double & LimitArr::operator[](int i) const
{
        ok(i);
        return arr[i - low_bnd];
}
```

Here the method returns a reference to an element in the array. Note that if a method promises not to change the invoking object and if it returns a reference or pointer to that object or part of that object, then you must declare the return value to be *const*. Otherwise, you could use the return value to modify the object. Fortunately, the compiler won't let you omit the *const* in this situation.

Note that if a function declares an argument as a reference or pointer to a *const*, then it cannot pass along that argument to another function unless that function also guarantees not to change the argument.

Public Inheritance Considerations

Naturally, adding inheritance to a program brings in more things to keep in mind. Let's look at a few.

The *Is-a* Relationship

Be guided by the *is-a* relationship. If your proposed derived class is not a particular kind of the base class, don't use public derivation. For instance, don't derive a *Brain* class from a *Programmer* class. If you want to represent the belief that a programmer has a brain, use a *Brain* class object as a member of the *Programmer* class.

Remember that one expression of the *is-a* relationship is that a base class pointer can point to a derived class object and that a base class reference can refer to a derived class object without an explicit type cast. Also remember that the reverse is not true; thus, you cannot have a derived class pointer or reference refer to a base class object without an explicit type cast. Depending upon the class declarations, such an explicit type cast (a downcast) may or may not make sense.

What's Not Inherited

Constructors are not inherited. However, derived class constructors typically use the initialization list syntax to call upon base class constructors to construct the base class portion of a derived object. If the derived class constructor doesn't explicitly call a base constructor in using the initialization list syntax, it will use the base class's default constructor. In an inheritance chain, each class can use an initialization list to pass back information to its immediate base class.

Destructors are not inherited. When an object is destroyed, the program first calls the derived constructor, then the base constructor. If there is a default base class constructor, the compiler generates a default derived class destructor. Generally speaking, if a class serves as a base class, its destructor should be virtual.

The assignment operator is not inherited. It does have some interesting properties that we'll look at next.

The Assignment Operator

The compiler automatically supplies every class with an assignment operator for assigning one object to another of the same class. The default version of this operator uses memberwise assignment, with each member of the target object being assigned the value of the corresponding member of the source object. However, if the object belongs to a derived class, the compiler uses the base class assignment operator to handle assignment for the base class portion of the derived object. If you've explicitly provided an assignment operator for the base class, that operator is used. Similarly, if a class contains a member that is an object of another class, the assignment operator for that class is used for that member.

As you've seen several times, you need to provide an explicit assignment operator if class constructors use *new* to initialize pointers. Because C++ uses the base class assignment operator for the base part of derived objects, you don't need to redefine the assignment operator for a derived class unless it adds data members that require special care. For example, the *ArrayDb* class defined assignment explicitly, but the derived *ArithArr* and *LimitAr* classes use the default assignment operators generated for those classes.

Suppose, however, that a derived class does use *new*, and you have to provide an explicit assignment operator. The operator must provide for *every* member of the class, not just the new members. For instance, suppose your boss wants a friendly array class in which each array object contains a string holding a name for the array. You could do something like this:

```
class Folksy : public ArrayDb
{
private:
```

```
char * arname; // to be initialized using new
...
};
```

The presence of the *arname* pointer requires that you provide an assignment operator, and this operator must also insure that assignment is handled for the base class members *size* and *ar*. You can handle the base class assignment by using the base name qualifier to invoke the base class assignment operator:

```
Folksy & Folksy::operator=(const Folksy & fo)
{
        if (this == *fo)
                return *this;
        ArrayDb::operator=(fo);        // base-portion assignment
        delete [] arname;
        arname = new char [strlen(fo.arname) + 1];
        strcpy(arname, fo.arname);
        return *this;
}
```

The *ArrayDb::* qualifier means the program uses the *ArrayDb* version of assignment. That operator, recall, has an argument type of *const ArrayDb &*, while *fo* is of type *const Folksy &*. But the *is-a* relationship means that the *ArrayDb* reference can refer to a *Folksy* object. Because the *ArrayDb* assignment operator deals with just the *size* and *ar* members, applying this operator to a *Folksy* object handles only those members. Then the rest of the code in the *Folksy* assignment operator handles the added *arname* member.

What about assigning a derived object to a base object? (Note: This is not the same as initializing a base class reference to a derived object.)

```
ArrayDb blips;             // base class
LimitAr snips(10, 1.44);   // derived class
blips = snips;             // assign derived object to base object
```

Which assignment operator is used? Remember that the assignment statement is translated into a method invoked by the left-hand object:

```
blips.operator=(snips);
```

Here the left-hand object is an *ArrayDb* object, so it invokes the *ArrayDb::operator=(const ArrayDb &)* function. The *is-a* relationship allows the *ArrayDb* reference to refer to a derived class object, such as *snips*. The assignment operator only deals with base class members, so the *lwr_bnd* member of *snips* is ignored in the assignment. In short, you can assign a derived object to a base object, and only the base class members are involved.

What about the reverse? Can you assign a base class object to a derived object?

```
LimitAr snips;           // derived class
ArrayDb blips(5, 1.96);  // base class
snips = blips;           // allowed?
```

Here the assignment statement would be translated as follows:

```
snips.operator=(blips);
```

The left-hand object is a *LimitArr* object, so it invokes the *LimitArr::operator=(const LimitArr &)* function. However, a derived class reference cannot automatically refer to a base object, so this code won't run unless there also is a conversion constructor:

```
LimitArr(const ArrayDb Y);
```

In that case, the program will use this constructor to create a temporary *LimitArr* object from *blips,* which will then be used as an argument to the assignment operator.

Alternatively, you could define an assignment operator for assigning a base class to a derived class:

```
LimitArr & LimitArr::operator=(const ArrayDb &) {...}
```

Here the types match the assignment statement exactly, and no type conversions are needed.

Private vs. Protected

Remember that protected members act like public members as far as a derived class is concerned, but like private members for the world at large. A derived class can access protected members of a base class directly, but can access private members only via base class member functions. Thus, making base class members private offers more security, while making them protected makes coding simpler and speeds up access. Stroustrup feels that it's better to use private data members than protected data members, but that protected methods are useful. (Bjarne Stroustrup,*The Design and Evolution of C++*. Reading, MA: Addison-Wesley Publishing Company, 1994.)

Let's see how protected members can pose a problem. Suppose we change the definition of the *ArrayDb* class to look like this:

```
class ArrayDb
{
protected:
        unsigned int size;
        double * ar;
        ...
};
```

As before, we can use the *arsize()* member function to find the value of *size,* but, as is proper, we can modify *size* only by using the constructors or the explicit assignment operator. This insures that *size* can't accidentally be set to the wrong value.

Now suppose we want to create a resizable array. One way is to use a base class constructor to create a new array of the desired size, copy data to the new array, and delete the old array. This can be done without accessing *size* directly. Another, quite wrong, approach is this:

```
class ReSzAr : public ArrayDb
{
public:
        resize(unsigned int nsize) { size = resize; } // don't do this
```

```
        ...
};
```

It's wrong because it pays no attention to memory management. It also violates the original *ArrayDb* interface by providing a public way to alter a protected member of *ArrayDb*. This loophole is blocked by the original *ArrayDb* definition, which made *size* a private member.

On the other hand, if a base class provides a member function that allows you to directly modify a data member and if altering that member doesn't involve any other changes, such as updating a state variable, there's usually no strong reason to make such a member private instead of protected.

Virtual Methods

When you design a base class, you have to decide whether to make class methods virtual or not. If you want a derived class to be able to redefine a method, define the method as virtual in the base class. This enables late, or dynamic, binding. If you don't want the method redefined, don't make it virtual. This doesn't prevent someone from redefining the method, but it should be interpreted as meaning that you don't want it redefined.

Note that inappropriate code can circumvent dynamic binding. Consider, for example, the following two functions:

```
void show(const ArrayDb & ar, int index)
{
        cout << index << ": $" << ar[index] << "\n";
}

void sloppy(ArrayDb ar, int index)
{
        cout << index << ": $" << ar[index] << "\n";
}
```

The first passes an object by reference, and the second passes an object by value.

Now suppose you use each with a derived class argument:

```
LimitAr income(10, 1983, 33450.99);
show(income, 1991);
sloppy(income, 1991);
```

The *show()* function call results in the *ar* argument being a reference to the *LimitAr* object income, so *ar[index]* is interpreted as the *LimitAr* version of the [] operator, as it should be. But in the *sloppy()* function, which passes an object by value, *ar* is an *ArrayDb* object constructed by the *ArrayDb(const ArrayDb &)* constructor. (Automatic upcasting allows the constructor argument to refer to a *LimitAr* object.) Thus, in *sloppy()*, *ar[i]* is an *ArrayDb* object using the [] operator, so the *ArrayDb* version of [] gets called, producing an index out-of-bounds error.

Destructors

As mentioned before, a base class constructor should be virtual. That way, when you delete a derived object via a base class pointer or reference to the object, the program uses the derived class destructor followed by the base class constructor rather than using only the base class constructor.

Class Function Summary

C++ class functions come in many variations. Some can be inherited, some can't. Some operator functions can be either member functions or friends, while others can only be member functions. Table 12-1, based on a similar table from the ARM, summarizes these properties. In it, the notation *op=* stands for assignment operators of the form +=, *=, and so on. Note that the properties for the *op=* operators are no different from those of the "other operators" category. The reason for listing *op=* separately is to point out that these operators don't behave like the = operator.

Function	Inherited	Member or friend	Generated by default	Can be virtual	Can have a return type
constructor	no	member	yes	no	no
destructor	no	member	yes	yes	no
=	no	member	yes	yes	yes
&	yes	either	yes	yes	yes
conversion	yes	member	no	yes	no
()	yes	member	no	yes	yes
[]	yes	member	no	yes	yes
->	yes	member	no	yes	yes
op=	yes	either	no	yes	yes
new	yes	static member	no	no	void *
delete	yes	static member	no	no	void
other operators	yes	either	no	yes	yes
other members	yes	member	no	yes	yes
friends	no	friend	no	no	yes

Table 12-1 Member function properties

Summary

Inheritance enables you to adapt programming code to your particular needs by defining a new class (a derived class) from an existing class (the base class). Public inheritance models an *is-a* relationship, meaning a derived class object also should be a kind of base class object. As part of the *is-a* model, a derived class inherits the data members and most methods of the base class. However, a derived class doesn't inherit the base class constructors, destructor, and assignment operator. A derived class can access the public and protected members of the base class directly and the private base class members via the public and protected base class methods. You then can add new data members and methods to the class, and you can use the derived class as a base class for further development. Each derived class requires its own constructors. When a program creates a derived class object, it first calls a base class constructor, then the derived class constructor. When a program deletes an object, it first calls the derived class destructor, then the base class destructor.

If a class is meant to be a base class, you may choose to use protected members instead of private members so that derived classes can access those members directly. However, using private members will, in general, reduce the scope for programming bugs. If you intend that a derived class can redefine a base class method, make it a virtual function by declaring it with the keyword *virtual*. This enables objects accessed by pointers or references to be handled on the basis of the object type rather than on the basis of the reference type or pointer type. In particular, the destructor for a base class normally should be virtual.

You may want to define an ABC (abstract base class) that defines an interface without getting into implementation matters. For instance, the usual example is that of a *Shape* class from which particular shape classes, such as *Circle* and *Square,* will be derived. You can define pure virtual methods that are set to *0*:

```
virtual double area() const = 0;
```

You don't define pure virtual methods, and you can't create an object of a class containing pure virtual members. Instead, they serve to define a common interface to be used by derived classes.

Review Questions

1. What does a derived class inherit from a base class?

2. What doesn't a derived class inherit from a base class?

3. Suppose the return type for the *ArrayDb::operator[]()* function were defined as *ArrayDb* instead of *ArrayDb &*. What effect, if any, would that have?

4. In what order are class constructors and class destructors called when a derived class object is created and deleted?

5. If a derived class doesn't add any data members to the base class, does the derived class require constructors?

6. Suppose a base class and a derived class both define a method of the same name and a derived class object invokes the method. What method is called?

7. Why doesn't the *LimitArr* class define an assignment operator?

8. Can you assign the address of an object of a derived class to a pointer to the base class? Can you assign the address of an object of a base class to a pointer to the derived class?

9. Can you assign an object of a derived class to an object of the base class? Can you assign an object of a base class to an object of the derived class?

10. Suppose we define a function that takes a reference to a base class object as an argument. Why can this function also use a derived class object as an argument?

11. Suppose we define a function that takes a base class object as an argument (that is, the function passes a base class object by value). Why can this function also use a derived class object as an argument?

12. Why is it usually better to pass objects by reference than by value?

13. Suppose *corporation* is a base class and *department* is a derived class. Also suppose that each class defines a *head()* member function, that *ph* is a pointer to the *corporation* type, and that *ph* is assigned the address of a *department* object. How is *ph->head()* interpreted if the base class defines *head()* as a

    a. Regular function

    b. Virtual function

14. What's wrong, if anything, with the following code?

```
class Kitchen
{
private:
        double kit_sq_ft;
public:
        Kitchen() {kit_sq_ft = 0.0; }
        virtual double area() { return kit_sq_ft * kit_sq_ft; }
};
class House : public Kitchen
{
private:
        double all_sq_ft;
public:
        House() {all_sq_ft += kit_sq_ft;}
        double area(const char *s) { cout << s; return all_sq_ft; }
};
```

Programming Exercises

1. Start with the following class declaration:

```
// base class
class Cd {        // represents a CD disk
protected:
        char * performers;
        char * label;
        int selections;        // number of selections
        double playtime;       // playing time in minutes
public:
        Cd(char * s1, char * s2, int n, double x);
        Cd(const Cd & d);
        Cd();
        ~Cd();
        void report() const;  // reports all CD data
        Cd & operator=(const Cd & d);
};
```

Derive a *Classic* class that adds a *char ** member that will point to a string identifying the primary work on the CD. If the base class requires that any functions be virtual, modify the base class declaration to make it so. Test your product with the following program:

```
#include <iostream.h>
#include "Cd.h"
void bravo(Cd & disk);
int main(void)
{
        Cd c1("Beatles", "Capitol", 14, 35.5);
        Classic c2 = classic("Piano Sonata in B flat, Fantasia in C",
                             "Alfred Brendel", "Philips", 2, 57.17);
        Cd *pcd = &c1;

        cout << "Using object directly:\n";
        c1.report();    // use Cd method
        c2.report();    // use Classic method

        cout << "Using type cd * pointer to objects:\n";
        pcd->report();  // use Cd method for cd object
        pcd = &c2;
        pcd->report();  // use Classic method for classic object

        bravo(c1);
        bravo(c2);

        return 0;
}

void bravo(Cd & disk)
{
        disk.report();
}
```

2. Your boss feels the *ArrayDb* class is too impersonal, and he wants you to derive a new class, one that provides each array object with a pointer to a string holding a name for the array. So derive a class *NameAr* from the *ArrayDb* class. The new class will have a new data member, *name,* which is a pointer to type *char.* It will point to memory holding a name for the array. Your boss decrees that the default name will be "Smiley". Define constructors for the new class that ensure data is properly initialized. Include a copy constructor (why?), an assignment operator (why?), a constructor with an *ArrayDb* & argument, and a destructor (why?). Overload the << operator so that it displays the name stored in a *NameAr* object.

Test your class with the following program:

```
// use_nam.cpp -- test the NameAr class
#include <iostream.h>
#include "namear.h"
const int SZ = 5;
int main(void)
{
        double it[SZ] = {19.0, 20.0, 18.0, 16.0, 18.5};
        ArrayDb ita(it,SZ);
        cout << "Displaying an ArrayDb object:\n";
        cout << ita;
        NameAr itna(ita);       // default name
        cout << "Displaying a NameAr object:\n";
        cout << itna;
        NameAr aldo("Aldo", 2 * SZ, 13.2);
        for (int i = 0; i < 2* SZ; i++)      // check [] operator
                aldo[i] = aldo[i] + i/2.0;
        cout << aldo;
        itna = aldo;   // check assignment
        cout << itna;
                return 0;
}
```

CHAPTER 13

REUSING CODE IN C++

You will learn about the following in this chapter:

◇ *Has-a* relationships

◇ Classes with member objects (containment)

◇ Private and protected inheritance

◇ Creating class templates

◇ Using class templates

◇ Template specializations

◇ Multiple inheritance

◇ Virtual base classes

O ne of the main goals of C++ is to facilitate the reuse of code. Public inheritance is one mechanism for achieving this goal, but not the only one. This chapter will investigate other choices. One technique is using class members that are themselves objects of another class. This is referred to as *containment* or *composition* or *layering*. Another option is using private or protected inheritance. Containment, private inheritance, and protected inheritance typically are used to implement *has-a* relationships, that is, relationships for which the new class has an object of another class. For instance, a *Stereo* class might have a *CdPlayer* object. *Multiple inheritance* lets you create classes that inherit from two or more base classes, combining their functionality.

Chapter 9 introduced function templates. Now we'll look at class templates, which provide another way of reusing code. Class templates let you define a class in generic terms. Then you can use the template to create specific classes defined for specific types. For instance, you could define a general stack template and then use the template to create one class representing a stack of *int* values and another class representing a stack of *double* values. You could even generate a class representing a stack of stacks.

Classes with Object Members

Let's begin with classes that include class objects as members. Some classes, such as the *String* class of Chapter 11 or the array classes of Chapter 12, offer convenient ways of representing components of a more extensive class. We'll look at a particular example now.

What is a student? Someone enrolled in a school? Someone engaged in thoughtful investigation? A refugee from the harsh exigencies of the real world? Someone with an identifying name and a set of quiz scores? Clearly, the last definition is a totally inadequate characterization of a person, but it is well-suited for a simple computer representation. So let's develop a *Student* class based on that definition.

Simplifying a student to a name and a set of quiz scores suggests using a *String* class object (Chapter 11) to hold the name and an *ArithArr* class object (Chapter 12) to hold the scores. You might be tempted to publicly derive a *Student* class from these two classes. That would be an example of multiple inheritance, which C++ allows, but it would be inappropriate here. The reason is that these classes don't fit the *is-a* model. A student is not a name. A student is not an array of quiz scores. What we have here is a *has-a* relationship. A student has a name, and a student has an array of quiz scores. The usual C++ technique for modeling *has-a* relationships is to use composition or containment; that is, to create a class composed of, or containing, members that are objects of another class. For instance, we can begin a *Student* class declaration like this:

```
class Student
{
private:
        String name;        // use a String object for name
        ArithArr scores;    // use an ArithArr object for scores
        ...
};
```

As usual, we make the data members private. This implies that the *Student* class member functions can use the public interfaces of the *String* and *ArithArr* classes to access and modify the *name* and *scores* objects, but that the outside world cannot do so. The only access the outside world will have to *name* and *scores* is through the public interface defined for the *Student* class. See Figure 13-1. A common way of describing this is saying that the *Student* class acquires the *implementation* of its member objects, but doesn't inherit the *interface*. For instance a *Student* object uses the *String* implementation rather than, say, a *char * name* or a *char name[26]* implementation for holding the name. But a *Student* object does not innately have the ability to use the *String operator==()* function. Similarly, the *Student* class implements storing scores with an *ArithArr* object rather than with an ordinary array, but a *Student* object can't invoke the *ArithArr average()* function directly.

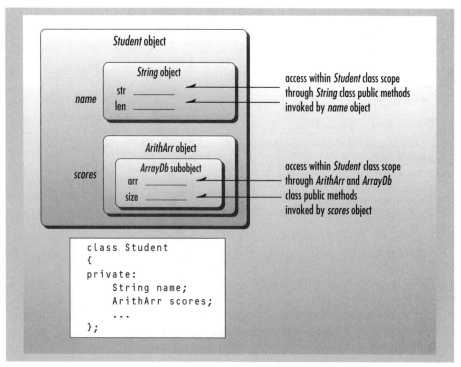

Figure 13-1 Containment

INTERFACES AND IMPLEMENTATIONS

With public inheritance, a class inherits an interface, and, perhaps, an implementation. (Pure virtual functions in a base class provide an interface without an implementation.) Acquiring the interface is part of the *is-a* relationship. With composition, on the other hand, a class acquires the implementation without the interface. Not inheriting the interface is part of the *has-a* relationship.

The fact that a class object doesn't automatically acquire the interface of a contained object is a good thing for a *has-a* relationship. For instance, the *ArithArr* class defines an addition operator, but, conceptually, it doesn't make sense to add two *Student* objects. That's one reason not to use public inheritance in this case. On the other hand, parts of the interface for the contained class may make sense for the new class. For instance, you might want to use the *average()* method from the *ArithArr* interface to compute the average of a student's scores. You can do so by defining a *Student::average()* member function that, internally, uses the *ArithArr::average()* function. Let's move on to class declaration details.

The *Student* Class Example

First, let's provide the *Student* class declaration. It should, of course, include constructors and at least a few functions to provide an interface for the *Student* class. Listing 13-1 does this, defining all the constructors inline.

Listing 13-1 *studentc.h*

```
// studentc.h -- defining a Student class using containment
#ifndef _STUDENTC_H_
#define _STUDENTC_H_

#include <iostream.h>
#include "aritharr.h"  // from Chapter 12
#include "strng2.h"    // from Chapter 11

class Student
{
private:
        String name;
        ArithArr scores;
public:
        Student() : name("Null Student"), scores() {}
        Student(const String & s)
                : name(s), scores() {}
        Student(int n) : name("Nully"), scores(n) {}
        Student(const String & s, int n)
                : name(s), scores(n) {}
        Student(const String & s, const ArithArr & a)
                : name(s), scores(a) {}
        Student(const char * str, const double * pd, int n)
                : name(str), scores(pd, n) {}
        ~Student() {}
        double & operator[](int i);
        const double & operator[](int i) const;
        double average() const;

// friends
        friend ostream & operator<<(ostream & os, const Student & stu);
        friend istream & operator>>(istream & os, Student & su);
};

#endif
```

Initializing Contained Objects

Note that constructors all use the initialization-list syntax to initialize the *name* and *scores* member objects. We've used this syntax before. In some cases we used it to initialize members that were built-in types:

```
Queue::Queue(int qs) : qsize(qs)      // initialize qsize to qs
```

This code uses the name of the data member *(qsize)* in the initialization list. Also, we've used the initialization list to initialize the base class portion of a derived object:

```
ArithArr(const ArrayDb & aa) : ArrayDb(aa) {}
```

For inherited objects, we used the class name in the initialization list to invoke a specific base class constructor.

Now look at the last constructor in the listing:

```
Student(const char * str, const double * pd, int n)
     : name(str), scores(pd, n) {}
```

Because we are initializing member objects, not inherited objects, we use the member names, not the class names, in the initialization list. Each item in this initialization list invokes the matching constructor. That is, *name(str)* invokes the *String(const char *)* constructor, and *scores(pd, n)* invokes the *ArithArr(const double *, int)* constructor.

What happens if you don't use the initialization-list syntax? As with inherited components, C++ requires that all member objects be constructed before the rest of an object is constructed. So if you omit the initialization list, C++ will use the default constructors defined for the member objects' classes.

Using an Interface for a Contained Object

The interface for a contained object isn't public, but it can be used within the class methods. For instance, here is how we can define a function that returns the average of a student's scores:

```
double Student::average() const
{
     return scores.average();
}
```

This defines a function that can be invoked by a *Student* object. Internally, it uses the *ArithArr::average()* function. That's because *scores* is an *ArithArr* object, so it can invoke the member functions of the *ArithArr* class.

Similarly, we can define a friend function that uses *String* and *ArrayDb* versions of the << operator:

```
ostream & operator<<(ostream & os, const Student & stu)
{
     os << "Scores for " << stu.name << ":\n";
     os << stu.scores;
     return os;
}
```

Because *stu.name* is a *String* object, it invokes the *operator<<(ostream &, const String &)* function. Similarly, the *ArithArr* object *stu.scores* invokes the *operator<<(ostream &, const ArrayDb &)* function. Recall that a base class reference argument matches a derived class object. Note that the new function has to be a friend to the *Student* class so that it can access the *name* and *scores* member of a *Student* object.

Listing 13-2 shows the class methods file for the *Student* class. It includes methods that allow you to use the [] operator to access individual scores in a *Student* object.

Listing 13-2 *studentc.cpp*

```cpp
#include "studentc.h"
double Student::average() const
{
        return scores.average();
}

double & Student::operator[](int i)
{
        return scores[i];
}

const double & Student::operator[](int i) const
{
        return scores[i];
}

// friends
ostream & operator<<(ostream & os, const Student & stu)
{
        os << "Scores for " << stu.name << ":\n";
        os << stu.scores;
        return os;
}

istream & operator>>(istream & is, Student & stu)
{
        is >> stu.name;
        return is;
}
```

We haven't had to write much new code. By using containment, we take advantage of the code we've already written.

Using the New Class

Let's put together a small program to test the new class. To keep things simple, we'll use an array of just three *Student* objects, each holding five quiz scores. And we'll use an unsophisticated input cycle that doesn't verify input and that doesn't let you cut the input process short. Listing 13-3 presents the test program. Compile it along with *studentc.cpp, strng2.cpp, arraydb.cpp,* and *aritharr.cpp.*

Listing 13-3 *use_stuc.cpp*

```cpp
// use_stuc.cpp -- use a composite class
// compile with studentc.cpp, strng2.cpp, arraydb.cpp, and aritharr.cpp
#include <iostream.h>
```

```
#include "studentc.h"

void set(Student & sa, int n);

const int pupils = 3;
const int quizzes = 5;

int main(void)
{
        Student ada[pupils] = {quizzes, quizzes, quizzes};

        for (int i = 0; i < pupils; i++)
                set(ada[i], quizzes);
        for (i = 0; i < pupils; i++)
        {
                cout << "\n" << ada[i];
                cout << "average: " << ada[i].average() << "\n";
        }
        return 0;
}

void set(Student & sa, int n)
{
        cout << "Please enter the student's name: ";
        cin >> sa;
        cout << "Please enter " << n << " quiz scores:\n";
        for (int i = 0; i < n; i++)
                cin >> sa[i];
        while (cin.get() != '\n')
                continue;
}
```

Here is a sample run:

```
Please enter the student's name: Gil Bayts
Please enter 5 quiz scores:
92 94 96 93 95
Please enter the student's name: Pat Roone
Please enter 5 quiz scores:
83 89 72 78 95
Please enter the student's name: Fleur O'Day
Please enter 5 quiz scores:
92 89 96 78 64

Scores for Gil Bayts:
92 94 96 93 95
average: 94

Scores for Pat Roone:
83 89 72 78 95
average: 83.4

Scores for Fleur O'Day:
92 89 96 78 64
average: 83.8
```

Private Inheritance

C++ has a second means of implementing the *has-a* relationship—private inheritance. With private inheritance, public and protected members of the base class become private members of the derived class. This means the methods of the base class do not become part of the public interface of the derived object. They can be used, however, inside the member functions of the derived class.

Let's look at the interface topic more closely. With public inheritance, the public methods of the base class become public methods of the derived class. In short, the derived class inherits the base class interface. This is part of the *is-a* relationship. With private inheritance, the public methods of the base class become private methods of the derived class. In short, the derived class does not inherit the base class interface. As we saw with contained objects, this lack of inheritance is part of the *has-a* relationship.

With private inheritance, you do inherit the implementation. That is, if we base a *Student* class on a *String* class, the *Student* class winds up with an inherited *String* class component that can be used to store a string. Furthermore, the *Student* methods can use the *String* methods internally to access the *String* component.

Containment adds an object to a class as a named member object, while private inheritance adds an object to a class as an unnamed inherited object. We'll use the term *subobject* to denote an object added by inheritance rather than by containment.

Private inheritance, then, provides the same features as containment: acquire the implementation, don't acquire the interface. Therefore it, too, can be used to implement a *has-a* relationship. Let's see how we can use private inheritance to redesign the *Student* class.

The *Student* Class Example (New Version)

To get private inheritance, use the keyword *private* instead of *public* when defining the class. (Actually, *private* is the default, so omitting an access qualifier also leads to private inheritance.) In the case of the *Student* class, we'll want to inherit from two classes, so we'll list both:

```
class Student : private String, private ArithArr
{
public:
    ...
};
```

Having more than one base class is called multiple inheritance, or MI. In general, multiple inheritance, particularly public multiple inheritance, leads to several problems that have to be resolved with additional syntax rules. We'll talk about such matters later in this chapter. But in this particular case, MI causes no problems.

Note that the new class won't need a private section. That's because the two inherited base classes already provide all the needed data members. With containment, we had two explicitly named objects as members. With private inheritance, we have two nameless subobjects as inherited members.

Initializing Base Class Components

Having implicitly inherited components instead of member objects will affect the coding, for we no longer can use *name* and *scores* to describe the objects. Instead, we have to go back to the techniques we used for public inheritance. For instance, consider constructors. Before, we had this constructor:

```
Student(const char * str, const double * pd, int n)
        : name(str), scores(pd, n) {}
```

For our new version, we'll use the initialization syntax for inherited classes, which uses the class name instead of a member name to identify constructors:

```
Student(const char * str, const double * pd, int n)
        : String(str), ArithArr(pd, n) {}
```

Listing 13-4 shows the new class declaration. The only changes we've made to the method declarations is to modify the inline constructors to use class names instead of member names.

Listing 13-4 *studenti.h*

```
// studenti.h -- defining a Student class using private inheritance
#ifndef _STUDENTI_H_
#define _STUDENTI_H_

#include <iostream.h>
#include "aritharr.h"
#include "strng2.h"

class Student : private String, private ArithArr
{
public:
        Student() : String("Null Student"), ArithArr() {}
        Student(const String & s)
                : String(s), ArithArr() {}
        Student(int n) : String("Nully"), ArithArr(n) {}
        Student(const String & s, int n)
                : String(s), ArithArr(n) {}
        Student(const String & s, const ArithArr & a)
                : String(s), ArithArr(a) {}
        Student(const char * str, const double * pd, int n)
                : String(str), ArithArr(pd, n) {}
        ~Student() {}
        double & operator[](int i);
        const double & operator[](int i) const;
        double average() const;
// friends
```

continued on next page

continued from previous page

```
        friend ostream & operator<<(ostream & os, const Student & stu);
        friend istream & operator>>(istream & os, Student & su);
};

#endif
```

Using Base Class Methods

Private inheritance limits the use of base class methods to within derived class methods. Sometimes, however, you might like to make a base class facility available publicly. For instance, the class declaration suggests we'll be able to use an *average()* function. As with containment, the technique for doing this is to use the private *ArithArr::average()* function within a public *Student::average()* function (see Figure 13-2). Here, for example, is how we can implement the *average()* member function:

```
double Student::average() const
{
        return ArithArr::average();
}
```

Omitting the *ArithArr::* qualifier would have caused the compiler to interpret the *average()* function call as *Student::average()*, leading to a highly undesirable recursive function definition.

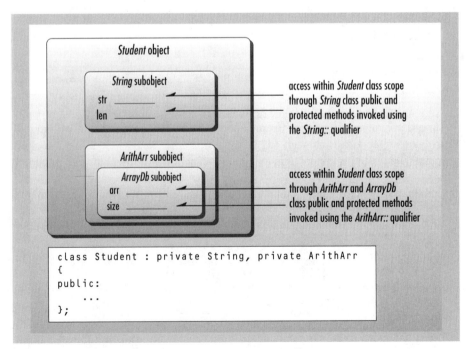

Figure 13-2 Private inheritance

This technique of explicitly qualifying a function name with its class name doesn't work for friend functions because they don't belong to a class. However, we can use an explicit type cast to the base class to invoke the correct functions. For example, consider the following friend function definition:

```
ostream & operator<<(ostream & os, const Student & stu)
{
        os << "Scores for " << (const String &) stu << ":\n";
        os << (const ArithArr &) stu;
        return os;
}
```

If *plato* is a *Student* object, then the statement

```
cout << plato;
```

will invoke this function, with *stu* being a reference to *plato* and *os* being a reference to *cout*. Within the code, the type cast in

```
os << "Scores for " << (const String &) stu << ":\n";
```

explicitly converts *stu* to a reference to a type *String* object, and that matches the *operator<<(ostream &, String &)* function. Similarly, the type cast in

```
os << (const ArithArr &) stu;
```

invokes the *operator<<(ostream &, ArrayDb &)* function, with the automatic implicit conversion of a derived reference to a base class reference.

The reference *stu* doesn't get converted automatically to a *String* or *ArithArr* reference. The fundamental reason is this:

> With private inheritance, a reference or pointer to a base class cannot be assigned a reference or pointer to a derived class without an explicit type cast.

However, even if our example had used public inheritance, it would have had to use explicit type casts. One reason is that without a type cast, code like

```
os << stu;
```

would match the friend function prototype, leading to a recursive call. A second reason is that because we've used multiple inheritance, the compiler couldn't tell which base class to convert to in this case, for both possible conversions match existing *operator<<()* functions.

Listing 13-5 shows all the class methods, other than those defined inline in the class declaration.

COMPATIBILITY NOTE

The version of g++ available to the author (2.0) didn't accept the explicit type cast of a derived object reference to a private base class.

Listing 13-5 *studenti.cpp*

```
#include "studenti.h"
double Student::average() const
{
        return ArithArr::average();
}

double & Student::operator[](int i)
{
        return  ArithArr::operator[](i);
}

const double & Student::operator[](int i) const
{
        return ArithArr::operator[](i);
}

// friends
ostream & operator<<(ostream & os, const Student & stu)
{
        os << "Scores for " << (const String &) stu << ":\n";
        os << (const ArithArr &) stu;
        return os;
}

istream & operator>>(istream & is, Student & stu)
{
        is >> (String &) stu;
        return is;
}
```

Using the New (Revised)Class

Once again it's time to test a new class. Note that our two versions of the *Student* class
have exactly the same public interface, so we can test it with exactly the same program. The only difference is that we have to include *studenti.h* instead of *studentc.h*,
and we have to link the program with *studenti.cpp* instead of with *studentc.cpp*. Listing
13-6 shows the program. Compile it along with *studenti.cpp*, *strng2.cpp*, *arraydb.cpp*,
and *aritharr.cpp*.

Listing 13-6 *use_stui.cpp*

```
// use_stui.cpp -- use a class with private derivation
// compile with studenti.cpp, strng2.cpp, arraydb.cpp, and aritharr.cpp
#include <iostream.h>
#include "studenti.h"

void set(Student & sa, int n);
```

```
const int pupils = 3;
const int quizzes = 5;

int main(void)
{
        Student ada[pupils] = {quizzes, quizzes, quizzes};

        for (int i = 0; i < pupils; i++)
                set(ada[i], quizzes);
        for (i = 0; i < pupils; i++)
        {
                cout << "\n" << ada[i];
                cout << "average: " << ada[i].average() << "\n";
        }
        return 0;
}

void set(Student & sa, int n)
{
        cout << "Please enter the student's name: ";
        cin >> sa;
        cout << "Please enter " << n << " quiz scores:\n";
        for (int i = 0; i < n; i++)
                cin >> sa[i];
        while (cin.get() != '\n')
                continue;
}
```

Here is a sample run:

```
Please enter the student's name: Gil Bayts
Please enter 5 quiz scores:
92 94 96 93 95
Please enter the student's name: Pat Roone
Please enter 5 quiz scores:
83 89 72 78 95
Please enter the student's name: Fleur O'Day
Please enter 5 quiz scores:
92 89 96 78 64

Scores for Gil Bayts:
92 94 96 93 95
average: 94

Scores for Pat Roone:
83 89 72 78 95
average: 83.4

Scores for Fleur O'Day
92 89 96 78 64
average: 83.8
```

The same input as before leads to the same output as before.

Containment or Private Inheritance?

Given that you can model a *has-a* relationship either with containment or with private inheritance, which should you use? Most C++ programmers prefer containment. First, it's easier to follow. When you look at the class declaration, you see explicitly named objects representing the contained classes, and your code can refer to these objects by name. Using inheritance makes the relationship appear more abstract. Second, inheritance can raise problems, particularly if a class inherits from more than one base class. You may have to deal with issues such as separate base classes having methods of the same name or of separate base classes sharing a common ancestor. All in all, you're less likely to run into trouble using containment.

However, private inheritance does offer features beyond those provided by containment. Suppose, for example, that a class has protected members, which could either be data members or member functions. Such members are available to derived classes, but not to the world at large. If you include such a class in another class using composition, the new class is part of the world at large, not a derived class. Hence it can't access protected members. But using inheritance makes the new class a derived class, so it can access protected members.

Another situation that calls for using private inheritance is if you wish to redefine virtual functions. Again, this is a privilege accorded to a derived class but not to a containing class. With private inheritance, the redefined functions would be usable just within the class, not publicly.

TIP

In general, use containment to model a *has-a* relationship. Use private inheritance if the new class needs to access protected members in the original class or if it needs to redefine virtual functions.

Protected Inheritance

Protected inheritance is a variation on private inheritance. It uses the keyword *protected* when listing a base class:

```
class Student : protected String, protected ArithArr {...};
```

With protected inheritance, public and protected members of a base class become protected members of the derived class. As with private inheritance, the interface for the base class is available to the derived class, but not to the outside world. The main difference between public and protected inheritance comes if you derive another class from the derived class. With private inheritance, this third-generation class doesn't get the internal use of the base class interface. That's because the public base class methods become private in the derived class, and private members and methods can't be directly accessed by the next level of derivation. With protected inheritance, public base methods become protected in the second generation and so are available internally to the next level of derivation.

Table 13-1 summarizes public, private, and protected inheritance. The term *implicit upcasting* means that you can have a base class pointer or reference refer to a derived class object without using an explicit type cast.

Property	Public inheritance	Protected inheritance	Private inheritance
public members become	public members of the derived class	protected members of the derived class	private members of the derived class
protected members become	protected members of the derived class	protected members of the derived class	private members of the derived class
private members become	accessible only through the base class interface	accessible only through the base class interface	accessible only through the base class interface
implicit upcasting	yes	yes (but only within the derived class)	no

Table 13-1 Varieties of inheritance

Redefining Access

Public members of a base class become protected or private when you use protected or private derivation. Sometimes you might want one or more of these inherited members to be public instead. You can use an *access declaration* to do so. For example, *studenti.h* (Listing 13-4) redefined [] operators that called upon the *ArithArr* base class versions of those operators. Another choice would have been to make these base class operators *public* in the *Student* class, too. Here's how that would be done:

```
class Student : private String, private ArithArr
{
public:
        ArithArr::operator[];  // redeclare as public, just use name
 ...

};
```

In the *public* section, you redeclare the name of the member (which can be a data member or a member function), preceding it with the appropriate class qualifier. Here, the *ArithArr::operator[];* declaration makes the *operator[]()* functions (both overloaded versions) available as public members instead of private members. Thus, they can be invoked by *Student* class objects. Note that when redeclaring methods, you don't provide function parentheses or return types. If you make this change to *studenti.h,* you can remove the *Student* versions of the *operator[]()* functions from the *studenti.h* and *studenti.cpp* files, and the program in Listing 13-6 will work as before. However, this time it will use the base class versions of *operator[] ()* directly.

Class Templates

Inheritance (public, private, or protected) and containment aren't always the answer to a desire to reuse code. Consider, for instance, the *Stack* class (Chapter 9), the *Queue* class (Chapter 11), and the *ArrayDb* class (Chapter 12). These are all examples of *container* classes, which are classes designed to hold other objects or data types. Our *Stack* class, for example, stored *unsigned long* values. We could just as easily define a stack class for storing *double* values or *String* objects. The code would be identical other than for the type of object stored. However, rather than writing new class declarations, it would be nice if we could define a stack in a generic (that is, type-independent) fashion and then provide a specific type as a parameter to the class. Then we could use the same generic code to produce stacks of different kinds of values. In Chapter 9, we used *typedef* as a first pass at dealing with this desire. However, that approach has a couple of drawbacks. First, you have to edit the header file each time you change the type. Second, you can use the technique to generate just one kind of stack per program. That is, you can't have a *typedef* represent two different types simultaneously, so you can't use the method to define a stack of *ints* and a stack of *Strings* in the same program.

C++'s class templates provide a better way to generate generic class declarations. At the time of this writing, not all C++ compilers support templates, but they are part of the ARM and of the ANSI/ISO working document for standard C++. Templates provide *parameterized types,* that is, the capability of passing a type name as an argument to an algorithm for building a class or a function. By feeding the type name *int* to a queue template, for example, you can get the compiler to construct a queue class for queuing *ints*.

Defining a Class Template

Let's use the *Stack* class from Chapter 9 as the basis from which to build a template. Here's the original class declaration:

```
#include "booly.h" // define Bool, False, True
typedef unsigned long Item;

class Stack
{
private:
        enum {MAX = 10};        // constant specific to class
        Item items[MAX];        // holds stack items
        int top;                // index for top stack item
public:
        Stack();
```

```
    Bool isempty() const;
    Bool isfull() const;
    // push() returns False if stack already is full, True otherwise
    Bool push(const Item & item);// add item to stack
    // pop() returns False if stack already is empty, True otherwise
    Bool pop(Item & item);       // pop top into item
};
```

The template approach will replace the *Stack* definition with a template definition and the *Stack* member functions with template member functions. As with template functions, we preface a template class with code of the following form:

```
template <class Type>
```

The keyword *template* informs the compiler that we're about to define a template. The part in angle brackets is analogous to an argument list to a function. You can think of the keyword *class* as serving as a type name for a variable that accepts a type as a value, and of *Type* representing a name for this variable. (Using *class* here doesn't mean that *Type* must be a class; it just means that *Type* serves as a generic type specifier for which a real type will be substituted when the template is used.) You can use your choice of generic type name in the *Type* position. Popular choices include *T* and *Type;* we'll use the latter. When a template is invoked, *Type* will be replaced with a specific type value, such as *int* or *String*. Within the template definition, use the generic type name to identify the type to be stored in the stack. For our case, that would mean using *Type* wherever we formerly used the *typedef* identifier *Item*. For instance,

```
Item items[MAX];      // holds stack items
```

becomes the following:

```
Type items[MAX];      // holds stack items
```

Similarly, we'll replace the class methods of the original class with template member functions. Each function heading will be prefaced with the same template announcement:

```
template <class Type>
```

Again, we'll replace the *typedef* identifier *Item* with the generic type name *Type*. One more change is that we need to change the class qualifier from *Stack::* to *Stack<Type>::*. For instance,

```
Bool Stack::push(const Item & item)
{
...
}
```

becomes the following:

```
template <class Type>
Bool Stack<Type>::push(const Type & item)
{
...
}
```

If you define a method within the class declaration (an inline definition), you can omit the template preface and the class qualifier.

Listing 13-7 shows the combined class and member function templates. It's important to realize that these are not class and member function definitions. Rather, they are instructions to the C++ compiler about how to generate class and member functions. A particular actualization of a template, such as a stack class for handling *String* objects, is called an *instantiation*. Unless you have a very clever compiler, placing the template member functions in a separate implementation file won't work. Because the templates aren't functions, they can't be compiled separately. Templates have to be used in conjunction with requests for particular instantiations of templates. The simplest way to make this work is to place all the template information in a header file and to include the header file in the file that will use the templates.

Listing 13-7 *stacktp.h*

```
// stacktp.h
#include "booly.h"

template <class Type>
class Stack
{
private:
        enum {MAX = 10};        // constant specific to class
        Type items[MAX];        // holds stack items
        int top;                // index for top stack item
public:
        Stack();
        Bool isempty();
        Bool isfull();
        Bool push(const Type & item); // add item to stack
        Bool pop(Type & item);        // pop top into item
};

template <class Type>
Stack<Type>::Stack()
{
        top = 0;
}

template <class Type>
Bool Stack<Type>::isempty()
{
        return top == 0? True: False;
}

template <class Type>
Bool Stack<Type>::isfull()
{
        return top == MAX? True :False;
```

```
}

template <class Type>
Bool Stack<Type>::push(const Type & item)
{
        if (top < MAX)
        {
                items[top++] = item;
                return True;
        }
        else
                return False;
}

template <class Type>
Bool Stack<Type>::pop(Type & item)
{
        if (top > 0)
        {
                item = items[--top];
                return True;
        }
        else
                return False;
}
```

Using a Template Class

Merely including a template in a program doesn't generate a template class. You have to ask for an instantiation. To do so, declare an object of the template class type, replacing the generic type name with the particular type you want. For instance, here's how you would create two stacks, one for stacking *ints* and one for stacking *String* objects:

```
Stack<int> kernels;          // create a stack of ints
Stack<String> colonels;      // create a stack of String objects
```

Seeing these two declarations, the compiler will follow the *Stack<Type>* template to generate two separate class declarations and two separate sets of class methods. The *Stack<int>* class declaration will replace *Type* throughout with *int,* while the *Stack<String>* class declaration will replace *Type* throughout with *String.* Of course, the algorithms you use have to be consistent with the types. The stack class, for example, assumes that you can assign one item to another. This assumption is true for basic types, structures, and classes (unless you make the assignment operator private), but not for arrays.

Generic type identifiers like *Type* in the example above are called *type parameters,* meaning that they act something like a variable, but instead of assigning a numeric value to them, you assign a type to them. So in the *kernel* declaration above, the type parameter *Type* has the value *int.*

Notice that you have to provide the desired type explicitly. This is different from ordinary function templates, for which the compiler used the argument types to a function to figure out what kind of function to generate:

```
Template <class T>
void simple(T t) { cout << t << '\n';}
...
simple(2);      // generate void simple(int)
simple("two")   // generate void simple(char *)
```

Listing 13-8 modifies the original stack-testing program (Listing 9-13) to use string purchase order IDs instead of *unsigned long* values. Since it uses our *String* class, compile it with *strng2.cpp*.

Listing 13-8 *stacktem.cpp*

```
// stacktem.cpp -- test template stack class
// compiler with strng2.cpp
#include <iostream.h>
#include <ctype.h>
#include "stacktp.h"
#include "strng2.h"
int main(void)
{
        Stack<String> st;      // create an empty stack for Strings
        char c;
        String po;
        cout << "Please enter A to add a purchase order,\n"
                << "P to process a PO, or Q to quit.\n";
        while (cin >> c && toupper(c) != 'Q')
        {
            while (cin.get() != '\n')
                    continue;
            if (!isalpha(c))
            {
                    cout << '\a';
                    continue;
            }
            switch(c)
            {
                    case 'A':
                    case 'a':   cout << "Enter a PO number to add: ";
                                cin >> po;
                                if (st.isfull())
                                        cout << "stack already full\n";
                                else
                                        st.push(po);
                                break;
                    case 'P':
                    case 'p':   if (st.isempty())
                                        cout << "stack already empty\n";
                                else {
```

```
                            st.pop(po);
                            cout << "PO #" << po << " popped\n";
                            break;
                        }
                }
                cout << "Please enter A to add a purchase order,\n"
                        << "P to process a PO, or Q to quit.\n";
        }
        cout << "Bye\n";
        return 0;
}
```

Here's a sample run:

```
Please enter A to add a purchase order,
P to process a PO, or Q to quit.
A
Enter a PO number to add: red911porsche
Please enter A to add a purchase order,
P to process a PO, or Q to quit.
A
Enter a PO number to add: green325bmw
Please enter A to add a purchase order,
P to process a PO, or Q to quit.
A
Enter a PO number to add: silver747boing
Please enter A to add a purchase order,
P to process a PO, or Q to quit.
P
PO #silver747boing popped
Please enter A to add a purchase order,
P to process a PO, or Q to quit.
P
PO #green325bmw popped
Please enter A to add a purchase order,
P to process a PO, or Q to quit.
P
PO #red911porsche popped
Please enter A to add a purchase order,
P to process a PO, or Q to quit.
P
stack already empty
Please enter A to add a purchase order,
P to process a PO, or Q to quit.
Q
Bye
```

A Closer Look at the Template Class

We can use a built-in type or a class object as the type for our *Stack<Type>* class template. What about a pointer? For example, can we use a pointer to a *char* instead of a *String* object in Listing 13-8? After all, such pointers are the built-in way for handling

C++ strings. The answer is that we can create a stack of pointers, but it wouldn't work very well without major modifications in the program. The compiler can create the class, but it's your task to see that it's used sensibly. Let's see why such a stack doesn't work very well with Listing 13-8, then let's look at an example where a stack of pointers is useful.

Using a Stack of Pointers Incorrectly

We'll quickly look at three simple, but flawed, attempts to adapt Listing 13-8 to use a stack of pointers. These attempts illustrate the lesson that you should keep the design of a template in mind and not just use it blindly. All three begin with this perfectly valid invocation of the *Stack<Type>* template:

```
Stack<char *> st; // create a stack for pointers-to-char
```

Version 1 then replaces

```
String po;
```

with:

```
char * po;
```

The idea is to use a *char* pointer instead of a *String* object to receive the keyboard input. This approach fails immediately because merely creating a pointer doesn't create space to hold the input strings.

Version 2 replaces

```
String po;
```

with:

```
char po[40];
```

This allocates space for an input string. Furthermore, *po* is of type *char **, so it can be placed on the stack. But an array is fundamentally at odds with the assumptions made for the *pop()* method:

```
template <class Type>
Bool Stack<Type>::pop(Type & item)
{
        if (top > 0)
        {
                item = items[--top];
                return True;
        }
        else
                return False;
}
```

First, the reference variable *item* has to refer to an Lvalue of some sort, not to an array name. Second, the code assumes that you can assign to *item*. Even if *item* could refer to an array, you can't assign to an array name. So this approach fails, too.

Version 3 replaces

```
String po;
```

with:

```
char * po = new char[40];
```

This allocates space for an input string. Furthermore, *po* is a variable and hence compatible with the code for *pop()*. Here, however, we come up against the most fundamental problem. There is only one *po* variable, and it always points to the same location memory. True, the contents of the memory change each time a new string is read, but every push operation puts exactly the same address onto the stack. So when you pop the stack, you always get the same address back, and it always refers to the last string read into memory. In particular, the stack is not storing each new string as it comes in, and it serves no useful purpose.

Using a Stack of Pointers Correctly

One way to use a stack of pointers is to have the calling program provide an array of pointers, with each pointer pointing to a different string. Putting these pointers on a stack then makes sense, for each pointer will refer to a different string.

For example, suppose we have to simulate the following situation. Someone has delivered a cart of folders to Plodson. If Plodson's in-basket is empty, he removes the top folder from the cart and places it in his in-basket. If his in-basket is full, Plodson removes the top file from the basket, processes it, and places it in his out-basket. If the in-basket is neither empty nor full, Plodson may process the top file in the in-basket, or he may take the next file from the cart and put it into his in-basket. In what he secretly regards as a bit of madcap self-expression, he flips a coin to decide which of these actions to take. We'd like to investigate the effects of his method on the original file order.

We can model this with an array of pointers to strings representing the files on the cart. Each string will contain the name of the person described by the file. We can use a stack to represent the in-basket, and we can use a second array of pointers to represent the out-basket. Adding a file to the in-basket is represented by pushing a pointer from the input array onto the stack and processing a file is represented by popping an item from the stack, and adding it to the out-basket.

Given the importance of examining all aspects of this problem, it would be useful to be able to try different stack sizes. Listing 13-9 redefines the *Stack<Type>* class slightly so that the *Stack* constructor accepts an optional size argument. This involves using a dynamic array internally, so the class now needs a destructor. Also, the definition shortens the code by making several of the methods inline.

COMPATIBILITY NOTE

The noncurrent version of g++ (2.0) available to the author doesn't compile the following unless the destructor is omitted.

Listing 13-9 *stcktp1.h*

```
// stcktp1.h
#include "booly.h"

template <class Type>
class Stack
{
private:
        enum {MAX = 10};        // constant specific to class
        int stacksize;
        Type * items;           // holds stack items
        int top;                // index for top stack item
public:
        Stack(int ss = MAX);
        ~Stack() { delete [] items; }
        Bool isempty() { return top == 0? True: False; }
        Bool isfull() { return top == stacksize? True :False; }
        Bool push(const Type & item); // add item to stack
        Bool pop(Type & item);                      // pop top into item
};

template <class Type>
Stack<Type>::Stack(int ss) : stacksize(ss), top(0)
{
        items = new Type [stacksize];
}

template <class Type>
Bool Stack<Type>::push(const Type & item)
{
        if (top < stacksize)
        {
                items[top++] = item;
                return True;
        }
        else
                return False;
}

template <class Type>
Bool Stack<Type>::pop(Type & item)
{
        if (top > 0)
        {
                item = items[--top];
                return True;
        }
        else
                return False;
}
```

The program in Listing 13-10 uses the new stack template to implement the Plodson simulation. It uses *rand()*, *srand()*, and *time()* in the same way previous simulations have to generate random numbers. Here, randomly generating a 0 or a 1 simulates the coin toss.

Listing 13-10 *stkoptr1.cpp*

```
// stkoptr1.cpp -- test stack of pointers
#include <iostream.h>
#include <stdlib.h>          // for rand(), srand()
#include <time.h>            // for time()
#include "stcktp1.h"
const int Stacksize = 4;
const int Num = 10;
int main(void)
{
        srand(time(0));        // randomize rand()
        cout << "Please enter stack size: ";
        int stacksize;
        cin >> stacksize;
        Stack<char *> st(stacksize); // create an empty stack with 4 slots

        char * in[Num] = {
                    " 1: Hank Gilgamesh", " 2: Kiki Ishtar",
                    " 3: Betty Rocker", " 4: Ian Flagranti",
                    " 5: Wolfgang Kibble", " 6: Portia Koop",
                    " 7: Joy Almondo", " 8: Xaverie Paprika",
                    " 9: Juan Moore", "10: Misha Mache"
                    };
        char * out[Num];

        int processed = 0;
        int nextin = 0;
        while (processed < Num)
        {
                if (st.isempty())
                        st.push(in[nextin++]);
                else if (st.isfull())
                        st.pop(out[processed++]);
                else if (rand() % 2  && nextin < Num)        // 50-50 chance
                        st.push(in[nextin++]);
                else
                        st.pop(out[processed++]);
        }
        for (int i = 0; i < Num; i++)
                cout << out[i] << "\n";

        cout << "Bye\n";
        return 0;
}
```

Two sample runs follow. Note that the final file ordering can differ quite a bit from one trial to the next, even when the stack size is kept unaltered.

```
Please enter stack size: 5
 2: Kiki Ishtar
 1: Hank Gilgamesh
 3: Betty Rocker
 5: Wolfgang Kibble
 4: Ian Flagranti
 7: Joy Almondo
 9: Juan Moore
 8: Xaverie Paprika
 6: Portia Koop
10: Misha Mache
Bye

Please enter stack size: 5
 3: Betty Rocker
 5: Wolfgang Kibble
 6: Portia Koop
 4: Ian Flagranti
 8: Xaverie Paprika
 9: Juan Moore
10: Misha Mache
 7: Joy Almondo
 2: Kiki Ishtar
 1: Hank Gilgamesh
Bye
```

Program Notes

The strings themselves never move. Pushing a string onto the stack really creates a new pointer to an existing string. That is, it creates a pointer whose value is the address of an existing string. And popping a string off the stack copies that address value into the *out* array.

What effect does the stack destructor have upon the strings? None. The class constructor uses *new* to create an array for holding pointers. The class destructor eliminates that array, not the strings to which the array elements pointed.

An Array Template Example

Templates are most frequently used for container classes, for the idea of type parameters matches well with the need to apply a common storage plan to a variety of types. Indeed, the desire to provide reusable code for container classes was the main motivation for introducing templates, so let's look at another example, exploring a few more facets of template design and use. In particular, we'll look at *expression arguments* and at using an array to handle an inheritance family.

Let's begin with a simple array template that lets us specify an array size. One technique, which we used for the *Stack* template, is using a dynamic array within the class and a constructor argument to provide the number of elements. Another approach, which we'll try now, is using a template argument to provide the size for a regular array. Listing 13-11 shows how this can be done.

Listing 13-11 *arraytp.h*

```
//arraytp.h  -- Array Template

template <class T, int n>
class ArrayTP
{
private:
      T ar[n];
public:
      ArrayTP();
      ArrayTP(const T & v);
      virtual T & operator[](int i) { return ar[i]; }
      virtual const T & operator[](int i) const { return ar[i]; }
};

template <class T, int n>
ArrayTP<T,n>::ArrayTP()
{
      for (int i = 0; i < n; i++)
            ar[i] = 0;
};

template <class T, int n>
ArrayTP<T,n>::ArrayTP(const T & v)
{
      for (int i = 0; i < n; i++)
            ar[i] = v;
};
```

Note the template heading:

```
template <class T, int n>
```

The keyword *class* identifies *T* as a type parameter, or type argument. The *int* identifies *n* as being an *int* type. This second kind of parameter, one which specifies a particular type instead of acting as a generic name for a type, is called an *expression argument.* Suppose we have the following declaration:

```
ArrayTP<double, 12> eggweights;
```

This causes the compiler to define a class called *ArrayTP<double,12>* and to create an *eggweights* object of that class. When defining the class, the compiler replaces *T* with *double* and *n* with *12*.

This approach for sizing an array has one advantage over the constructor approach. The constructor approach uses heap memory managed by *new* and *delete,* while the expression argument approach uses the memory stack maintained for automatic variables. This provides faster execution time, particularly if you have a lot of small arrays.

The main drawback to the expression argument approach is that each array size generates its own template. That is, the declarations

```
ArrayTP<double, 12> eggweights;
ArrayTP(double, 13> donuts;
```

generate two separate class declarations. But the declarations

```
Stack<int> eggs(12);
Stack<int> dunkers(13);
```

generate just one class declaration, and the size information is passed to the constructor for that class.

Another difference is that the constructor approach is more versatile because the array size is stored as a class member rather than being hard-coded into the definition. This makes it possible, for example, to define assignment from an array of one size to an array of another size or to build a class that allows resizable arrays.

Using the Template with a Family of Classes

Suppose we have a family of classes. In particular, suppose we have a base class, a class derived from the base, and a class derived from the derived class. Now suppose we have several objects of these classes that we'd like to store in an array. One problem is that all elements of an array should be of the same type, but an object of a derived class is a different type from the base class. It may not even be the same size as an object of the base class, so lying about its type won't work. In short, we have a tool suited for *homogeneous* elements (elements all of the same kind), but we have a *heterogeneous* collection of objects (objects of various kinds). It's in situations like this where the *is-a* relationship and virtual functions come in handy. The idea is to create an array of base class pointers. Public inheritance means you can assign the address of any derived class object to a base class pointer, so such an array can hold addresses of a variety of types. The sizes of the types may differ, but the pointers are all the same size. Furthermore, if we use these pointers to invoke class methods, virtual functions ensure that a base class pointer to a derived object will invoke the derived object's class methods.

Let's try this out. First, we need a family of classes. For illustrative purposes, let's keep the classes simple. Listing 13-12 defines a *Worker* class, a *Waiter* class, and a *SingingWaiter* class. A *Worker* class provides a name and an identification number. The *Waiter* class, derived from *Worker,* adds a panache rating. And the *SingingWaiter* class, derived from *Waiter,* adds a vocal range descriptor.

Listing 13-12 *worker.h*

```
// worker.h  -- working classes
#include "strng2.h"

class Worker
{
private:
        String fullname;
        long id;
protected:
        virtual void data() const;
public:
        Worker() : fullname("no one"), id(0L) {}
        Worker(const String & s, long n)
                        : fullname(s), id(n) {}
        virtual void set();
        virtual void show() const;
};

class Waiter : public Worker
{
private:
        int panache;
protected:
        void data() const;
public:
        Waiter() : Worker(), panache(0) {}
        Waiter(const String & s, long n, int p = 0)
                        : Worker(s, n), panache(p) {}
        Waiter(const Worker & wk, int p = 0)
                        : Worker(wk), panache(p) {}
        void set();
        void show() const;
};

class SingingWaiter : public Waiter
{
protected:
        enum {other, alto, contralto, soprano,
                                bass, baritone, tenor};
        enum {Vtypes = 7};
        void data() const;
private:
        static char *pv[Vtypes];        // string equivs of voice types
        int voice;
public:
        SingingWaiter() : Waiter(), voice(other) {}
        SingingWaiter(const String & s, long n, int p = 0, int v = other)
                        : Waiter(s, n, p), voice(v) {}
        SingingWaiter(const Worker & wk, int p = 0, int v = other)
```

continued on next page

continued from previous page

```
                            : Waiter(wk,p), voice(v) {}
            SingingWaiter(const Waiter & wt, int v = other)
                            : Waiter(wt), voice(v) {}
            void set();
            void show() const;
};
```

Note that *SingingWaiter* constructors use the initialization list to pass information to the constructors for the immediate base class, *Waiter.* The *Waiter* constructors, in turn, pass information to the constructors for its base class, *Worker.* In particular, note that the *SingingWaiter* constructor with a *Worker* argument passes it on to a *Waiter* class constructor, not to a *Worker* constructor. That's because (as discussed in Chapter 11) for ordinary inheritance, a constructor can pass information only to constructors of its immediate base. This poses no problem, for the invoked *Waiter* constructor passes the *Worker* information on to a *Worker* constructor.

Another point to note is that one of the *Waiter* constructors calls upon the *Worker(const Worker &)* constructor even though we didn't define one. Recall, however, that the compiler generates this constructor (the copy constructor) if we don't. The default constructor is fine for this particular description.

Next, we need to define those functions that don't already have inline definitions. Listing 13-13 provides that information. It also initializes a class-scope array of pointers to data used by the *SingingWaiter* class. In service of brevity, the example doesn't make a serious effort to check the validity of all input.

COMPATIBILITY NOTE

The version of g++ available to the author (2.0) required replacing

```
char * SingingWaiter::pv[] = {"other", "alto", "contralto",
            "soprano", "bass", "baritone", "tenor"};
```

in Listing 13-13 with the following:

```
char * SingingWaiter::pv[SingingWaiter::Vtypes] = {"other", "alto", ←
"contralto", "soprano", "bass", "baritone", "tenor"};
```

It also required making *Vtypes* a *public enum* in the *SingingWaiter* class instead of *protected*. Metrowerks CodeWarrior required the form used in the listing. The other compilers tested accepted either form.

Listing 13-13 *worker.cpp*

```
// worker.cpp -- working class methods
#include "worker.h"
#include <iostream.h>
// Worker methods
void Worker::set()
{
        cout << "Enter worker's name: ";
```

```
            cin >> fullname;
            cout << "Enter worker's ID: ";
            cin >> id;
            while (cin.get() != '\n')
                    continue;
}

void Worker::show() const
{
            cout << "Category: worker\n";
            data();
}

// protected method
void Worker::data() const
{
            cout << "Name: " << fullname << "\n";
            cout << "Employee ID: " << id << "\n";
}

// Waiter methods
void Waiter::set()
{
            Worker::set();
            cout << "Enter waiter's panache rating: ";
            cin >> panache;
            while (cin.get() != '\n')
                    continue;
}

void Waiter::show()  const
{
            cout << "Category: waiter\n";
            data();
}

// protected method
void Waiter::data() const
{
            Worker::data();
            cout << "Panache rating: " << panache << "\n";
}

// SingingWaiter methods

char * SingingWaiter::pv[] = {"other", "alto", "contralto",
                        "soprano", "bass", "baritone", "tenor"};

void SingingWaiter::set()
{
            Waiter::set();
            cout << "Enter number for singer's vocal range:\n";
            for (int i = 0; i < Vtypes; i++)
```

continued on next page

continued from previous page

```
        {
                cout << i << ": " << pv[i] << "    ";
                if ( i % 4 == 3)
                        cout << '\n';
        }
        if (i % 4 != 0)
                cout << '\n';
        cin >>  voice;
        while (cin.get() != '\n')
                continue;
}

void SingingWaiter::show() const
{
        cout << "Category: singing waiter\n";
        data();
}

// protected method
void SingingWaiter::data() const
{
        Waiter::data();
        cout << "Vocal range: " << pv[voice] << "\n";
}
```

You'll note that the *show()* functions call upon *data()* functions to display part of the output. The idea is that the *data()* functions display information that derived classes also display, while the *show()* functions explicitly display information relevant only to their own classes. That is, *show()* displays information like *Category: worker,* which makes sense just for *Worker* objects. But *data()* displays information like a worker's name, which would be displayed by derived classes, too. With this organization, a *show()* function for a derived class can display its own category message, then call upon the base class *data()* to display name and ID information.

The *data()* functions are protected. This means they can be used by derived classes but not by the world at large. The reason for this choice is that the *data()* functions are part of the internal implementation of the *show()* functions, and, as such, should be private to the class. However, the derived classes need access to the base class versions, which means that they can't be private. It's precisely for this situation that the *protected* access class was provided.

 TIP

Use protected access for internal implementation member functions that need to be inherited by derived classes.

Finally, we need a program to test the scheme of using an array of base class pointers to manage a family of classes. Listing 13-14 meets that need. In it, the Cafe Lola hires its first employees.

COMPATIBILITY NOTE

If your system doesn't support templates, you can use an ordinary array
of pointers to *Worker* instead. See the instructions in the listing.

Listing 13-14 *workarr.cpp*

```
// workarr.cpp -- array of workers
// compile with worker.cpp
#include <iostream.h>
#include <string.h>
#include "worker.h"
#include "arraytp.h"   // omit if templates not implemented
const int SIZE = 5;
int main(void)
{
        ArrayTP<Worker *, (int) SIZE> lolas;
        // if no templates, omit the above line and use the one below
        // Worker * lolas[SIZE];

        for (int ct = 0; ct < SIZE; ct++)
        {
                char choice;
                cout << "Enter the employee category:\n"
                        << "e: worker  w: waiter  s: singing waiter  "
                        << "q: quit\n";
                cin >> choice;
                while (strchr("ewsq", choice) == NULL)
                {
                        cout << "Please enter an e, w, s, or q: ";
                        cin >> choice;
                }
                if (choice == 'q')
                        break;
                switch(choice)
                {
                        case 'e':     lolas[ct] = new Worker;
                                        break;
                        case 'w':     lolas[ct] = new Waiter;
                                        break;
                        case 's':     lolas[ct] = new SingingWaiter;
                                        break;
                }
                cin.get();
                lolas[ct]->set();
        }

        cout << "\nHere is your staff:\n";
        for (int i = 0; i < ct; i++)
        {
```

continued on next page

continued from previous page

```
                cout << '\n';
                lolas[i]->show();
        }
        for (i = 0; i < ct; i++)
                delete lolas[i];
        return 0;
}
```

Here is a sample run:

```
Enter the employee category:
e: worker  w: waiter  s: singing waiter   q: quit
e
Enter worker's name: Glitter Pigspeed
Enter worker's ID: 2001
Enter the employee category:
e: worker  w: waiter  s: singing waiter   q: quit
w
Enter worker's name: Ursula Major
Enter worker's ID: 2002
Enter waiter's panache rating: 7
Enter the employee category:
e: worker  w: waiter  s: singing waiter   q: quit
s
Enter worker's name: Dirk Decibello
Enter worker's ID: 2003
Enter waiter's panache rating: 8
Enter number for singer's vocal range:
0: other    1: alto    2: contralto   3: soprano
4: bass     5: baritone   6: tenor
6
Enter the employee category:
e: worker  w: waiter  s: singing waiter   q: quit
q

Here is your staff:

Category: worker
Name: Glitter Pigspeed
Employee ID: 2001

Category: waiter
Name: Ursula Major
Employee ID: 2002
Panache rating: 7

Category: singing waiter
Name: Dirk Decibello
Employee ID: 2003
Panache rating: 8
Vocal range: tenor
```

Program Notes

The declaration

```
ArrayTP<Worker *, (int) SIZE> lolas;
```

causes the compiler to generate a class declaration for an array class of 5 (*SIZE*) elements, each of which is a pointer to a *Worker* object. The variable *lolas* then represents an object of this new class. The code type casts *SIZE* to type *int*. The reason is that *SIZE* is of type *const int*, which is not an exact match to the *int* type specified in the template. At the time of this writing, not even trivial conversions (Chapter 8) are allowed in matching expression arguments in a template, but this restriction may be relaxed in the final ANSI/ISO standard.

The ANSI C standard function *strchr(const char * str, char ch)* searches for the character *ch* in the string *str.* It returns the address of the first occurrence of *ch* if it finds it; otherwise, the function returns the null pointer. Thus the code

```
while (strchr("ewsq", choice) == NULL)
```

provides a convenient way to see that the entered character is a valid choice.

The *switch* statement assigns the address of a new object to one of the pointer-to-*Worker* elements of the array:

```
switch(choice)
{
        case 'e':       lolas[ct] = new Worker;
                        break;
        case 'w':       lolas[ct] = new Waiter;
                        break;
        case 's':       lolas[ct] = new SingingWaiter;
                        break;
}
```

Depending upon the user's input, the pointer may point to a *Worker* object, a *Waiter* object, or a *SingingWaiter* object. Because a base pointer may point to an object of any descendant class, no type casts are needed.

Because *set()* and *show()* are defined as virtual functions, invoking these functions with a pointer-to-*Worker* invokes the function appropriate to the pointed-to class:

```
lolas[ct]->set();
...
lolas[i]->show();
```

Thus we can use a homogeneous collection of pointers to manage a heterogeneous collection of objects. This is an example of polymorphism at work: one function call can activate different functions, depending upon the context.

Note the following code:

```
for (i = 0; i < ct; i++)
        delete lolas[i];
```

Memory allocated by *new* should be freed using *delete*. It's not the job of the *ArrayTP* class to do this, for the *lolas* object neither creates nor destroys the *Worker*-family objects. It merely stores the addresses of the objects.

Template Versatility

You can apply the same techniques to template classes as you do to regular classes. Template classes can serve as base classes, and they can be component classes. They can themselves be type arguments to other templates. For example, you can implement a stack template using an array template. Or you can have an array template used to construct an array whose elements are stacks based on a stack template. That is, you can have code along the following lines:

```
template <class T>
class Array
{
private:
        T entry;
...
};

template <class Type>
class GrowArray : public Array<Type> {...};  // inheritance

template <class Tp>
class Stack
{
        Array<Tp> ar;  // use an Array<> as a component
        ...
};
...
Array < Stack<int> > asi;    // an array of stacks of int
```

In the last statement, you must separate the two > symbols by at least one white-space character in order to avoid confusion with the >> operator.

Another example of template versatility is that you can use templates recursively. For instance, given our earlier definition of an array template, you can use it as follows:

```
ArrayTP< ArrayTP<int,20>, 10> twodee;
```

This makes *twodee* an array of *10* elements, each of which is an array of *20 ints*.

You can have templates with more than one type parameter. For instance, suppose you want a class that holds two kinds of values. You can create and use a *Pair* template class for holding two disparate values. The short program in Listing 13-15 shows an example.

Listing 13-15 *pairs.cpp*

```
// pairs.cpp -- define and use a Pair template
#include <iostream.h>
```

```
template <class T1, class T2>
class Pair
{
private:
        T1 a;
        T2 b;
public:
        T1 & first(const T1 & f);
        T2 & second(const T2 & s);
        T1 first() const { return a; }
        T2 second() const { return b; }
        Pair(const T1 & f, const T2 & s) : a(f), b(s) { }
};

template<class T1, class T2>
T1 & Pair<T1,T2>::first(const T1 & f)
{
        a = f;
        return a;
}
template<class T1, class T2>
T2 & Pair<T1,T2>::second(const T2 & s)
{
        b = s;
        return b;
}

int main(void)
{
Pair<char *, int> ratings[4] =
        {    Pair<char *, int>("The Purple Duke", 5),
             Pair<char *, int>("Jake's Frisco Cafe", 4),
             Pair<char *, int>("Mont Souffle", 5),
             Pair<char *, int>("Gertie's Eats", 3)
        };

        int joints = sizeof(ratings) / sizeof (Pair<char *, int>);
        cout << "Rating:\t Eatery\n";
        for (int i = 0; i < joints; i++)
            cout << ratings[i].second() << ":\t " <<
                            ratings[i].first() << "\n";

        ratings[3].second(6);
        cout << "Oops! Revised rating:\n";
        cout << ratings[3].second() << ":\t " << ratings[3].first() << "\n";

        return 0;
}
```

One thing to note is that in *main()*, we have to use *Pair<char *,int>* to invoke the constructors and as an argument for *sizeof*. That's because *Pair<char *,int>* and not *Pair* is the class name. Also, *Pair<String,ArrayDb>* would be the name of an entirely different class.

Here's the program output:

```
Rating:    Eatery
5:         The Purple Duke
4:         Jake's Frisco Cafe
5:         Mont Souffle
3:         Gertie's Eats
Oops! Revised rating:
6:         Gertie's Eats
```

Template Specializations

Sometimes you may need or want to modify a template to behave differently when instantiated for a particular type. For instance, suppose you defined a template along these lines:

```
template <class T>
class SortedArray
{
        ...// details omitted
};
```

This template sorts items as they are added to the array. Suppose the template uses the > operator to compare values. This works well for numbers. It won't work for class objects, however, unless you've defined that operator for the class. Suppose you haven't done so for the (hypothetical) *Flames* class. Then you might be able to rewrite the template definition using some *Flames* method to do the comparison. Or suppose you wanted a sorted array of strings as represented by the *char* * type. You would need to modify the template code so that it used *strcmp()* instead of >. Or perhaps you have a type in mind for which the existing template works but for which there's a more efficient algorithm you can use. In all these cases you can provide a *template specialization*. This takes the form of a template defined for one specific type instead of for a general type. When faced with the choice of a specialized template and a general template that both match an instantiation request, the compiler will use the specialized version.

A specialized class template definition has the following form:

```
class Classname<specialized-type-name> { ... };
```

For example, to provide a *SortedArray* template specialized for the *char* * type, you would use code like the following:

```
class SortedArray<char *>
{
        ...// details omitted
};
```

Here the omitted code would use *strcmp()* instead of > to compare array values. Now, requests for a *SortedArray* of *char* * will use this specialized definition instead of the more general template definition:

```
SortedArray<int> scores;      // use general definition
SortedArray<char *> dates;    // use specialized definition
```

 # Multiple Inheritance

Multiple inheritance describes a class that has more than one immediate base class. As with single inheritance, public multiple inheritance should express an *is-a* relationship. For example, if you have a *Waiter* class and a *Singer* class, you could derive a *SingingWaiter* class from the two:

```
class SingingWaiter : public Waiter, public Singer {...};
```

Note that you have to qualify each base class with the keyword *public*. That's because the compiler assumes private derivation unless instructed otherwise:

```
class SingingWaiter : public Waiter, Singer {...}; // Singer is a private base
```

As discussed earlier in this chapter, private and protected MI can express a *has-a* relationship. We'll concentrate on public inheritance now.

Multiple inheritance can introduce new problems for the programmer. The two chief problems are inheriting different methods of the same name from two different base classes and inheriting multiple instances of a class via two or more related immediate base classes. Meeting these problems involves introducing a few new rules and syntax variations. Thus, using multiple inheritance can be more difficult and problem-prone than using single inheritance. For this reason, many in the C++ community object strongly to MI; some want it removed from the language. Others love MI and argue that it's very useful, even necessary, for particular projects. Still others suggest using MI cautiously and in moderation.

Let's explore a particular example and see what the problems and solutions are. We'll use a variation on the *Worker* class example. In particular, assume we have a *Worker* class from which we've directly derived a *Waiter* class and a *Singer* class and that we wish to use MI to derive a *SingingWaiter* class from the *Waiter* and *Singer* classes. (See Figure 13-3.) Tentatively, assume we're starting with the class declarations in Listing 13-16. They are based on the single inheritance example of Listing 13-12. At this point, we won't worry about the details. Instead, let's look at two general problems raised by this first draft:

❧ How many workers?

❧ Which method?

 ## Listing 13-16 *workerfd.h*

```
// workerfd.h  -- working classes, first draft
#include "strng2.h"
```

continued on next page

continued from previous page

```
class Worker
{
private:
        String fullname;
        long id;
protected:
        virtual void data() const;
public:
        Worker() : fullname("no one"), id(0L) {}
        Worker(const String & s, long n)
                        : fullname(s), id(n) {}
        virtual void set();
        virtual void show() const;
};

class Waiter : public Worker
{
private:
        int panache;
protected:
        void data() const;
public:
        Waiter() : Worker(), panache(0) {}
        Waiter(const String & s, long n, int p = 0)
                        : Worker(s, n), panache(p) {}
        Waiter(const Worker & wk, int p = 0)
                        : Worker(wk), panache(p) {}
        void set();
        void show() const;
};

class Singer : public Worker
{
public:
        enum {Vtypes = 7};
protected:
enum {other, alto, contralto, soprano,
                                bass, baritone, tenor};
private:
        static char *pv[Vtypes];        // string equivs of voice types
        int voice;
protected:
        void data() const;
public:
        Singer() : Worker(), voice(other) {}
        Singer(const String & s, long n, int v = other)
                        : Worker(s, n), voice(v) {}
        Singer(const Worker & wk, int v = other)
                        : Worker(wk), voice(v) {}
        void set();
        void show() const;
};
```

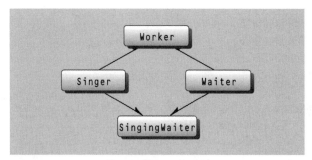

Figure 13-3 Multiple inheritance with a shared ancestor

How Many Workers?

Suppose we start out by publicly deriving *SingingWaiter* from *Singer* and *Waiter:*

```
class SingingWaiter: public Singer, public  Waiter {...};
```

Since both *Singer* and *Waiter* inherit a *Worker* component, a *SingingWaiter* winds up with two *Worker* components. See Figure 13-4.

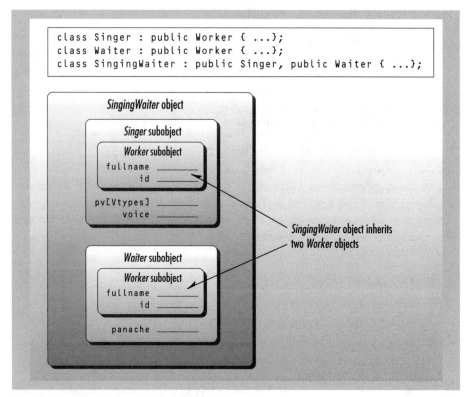

Figure 13-4 Inheriting two base objects

As you might expect, this raises problems. For example, ordinarily you can assign the address of a derived class object to a base class pointer, but this becomes ambiguous now:

```
SingingWaiter ed;
Worker * pw = &ed;     // ambiguous
```

Normally, such an assignment sets a base class pointer to the address of the base class object within the derived object. But *ed* contains two *Worker* objects, hence there are two addresses from which to choose. You could specify which object by using a type cast:

```
Worker * pw1 = (Waiter *) &ed;     // the Worker in Waiter
Worker * pw2 = (Singer *) &ed;     // the Worker in Singer
```

This certainly complicates the technique of using an array of base class pointers to refer to a variety of objects (polymorphism).

Having two copies of a *Worker* object causes other problems, too. However, the real issue is why should we have two copies of a *Worker* object at all? A singing waiter, like any other worker, should have just one name and one ID. When C++ added multiple inheritance to its bag of tricks, it added a new technique, the *virtual base class,* to make this possible.

Virtual Base Classes

Virtual base classes allow an object derived from multiple bases that themselves share a common base to inherit just one object of that shared base class. For our example, we would make *Worker* a virtual base class to *Singer* and *Waiter* by using the keyword *virtual* in the class declarations:

```
class Singer : virtual public Worker {...};
class Waiter : virtual public Worker {...};
```

Then we would define *SingingWaiter* as before:

```
class SingingWaiter: public Singer, public  Waiter {...};
```

Now a *SingingWaiter* object will contain a single copy of a *Worker* object. In essence, the inherited *Singer* and *Waiter* objects share a common *Worker* object instead of each bringing in its own copy. See Figure 13-5. Since *SingingWaiter* now contains but one *Worker* subobject, we can use polymorphism again.

Let's look at some questions you may have:

❧ Why the term *virtual?*

❧ Why not dispense with declaring base classes virtual and make virtual behavior the norm for multiple inheritance?

❧ Are there any catches?

First, why the term *virtual?* After all, there doesn't seem to be an obvious connection between the concepts of virtual functions and virtual base classes. It turns out that

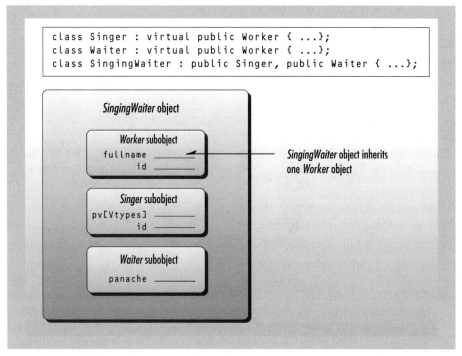

```
class Singer : virtual public Worker { ...};
class Waiter : virtual public Worker { ...};
class SingingWaiter : public Singer, public Waiter { ...};
```

SingingWaiter object

Worker subobject
fullname _____
id _____

SingingWaiter object inherits
one *Worker* object

Singer subobject
pv[Vtypes] _____
id _____

Waiter subobject
panache _____

Figure 13-5 Inheritance with a virtual base class

there is strong pressure from the C++ community to resist the introduction of new keywords. It would be awkward, for example, if a new keyword corresponded to the name of some important function or variable in a major program. So C++ merely recycled the keyword *virtual* for the new facility—a bit of keyword overloading.

Next, why not dispense with declaring base classes virtual and make virtual behavior the norm for multiple inheritance? First, there are cases for which one might want multiple copies of a base. Second, making a base class virtual requires that a program do some additional accounting, and you shouldn't have to pay for that facility if you don't need it. Third, see the next paragraph.

Third, are there catches? Yes. Making virtual base classes work requires adjustments to C++ rules, and you have to code some things differently. Also, using virtual base classes may involve changing existing code. For instance, adding the *SingingWaiter* class to the *Worker* hierarchy required that we go back and add the *virtual* keyword to the *Singer* and *Waiter* classes.

New Constructor Rules

Having virtual base classes requires a new approach to class constructors. With non-virtual base classes, the only constructors that can appear in an initialization list are constructors for the immediate base classes. But these constructors can, in turn, pass information on to their bases. For example, the single inheritance class declarations in Listing 13-12 included this constructor:

```
SingingWaiter(const Worker & wk, int p = 0, int v = other)
                    : Waiter(wk,p), voice(v) {}
```

Here the *Waiter(wk,p)* constructor uses the *p* value to initialize the *Waiter::panache* member and passes the *wk* argument back to the implicit *Worker(const Worker &)* constructor.

This automatic passing of information doesn't work if *Worker* is a virtual base class. For instance, consider the following possible constructor for the multiple inheritance example:

```
SingingWaiter(const Worker & wk, int p = 0, int v = Singer::other)
                    : Waiter(wk,p), Singer(wk,v) {}
```

The problem is that automatic passing of information would pass *wk* to the *Worker* object via two separate paths (*Waiter* and *Singer*). To avoid this potential conflict, C++ disables the automatic passing of information through an intermediate class to a base class if the base class is virtual. Thus, the above constructor will initialize the *panache* and *voice* members, but the information in the *wk* argument won't get to the *Waiter* subobject. However, the compiler must construct a base object component before constructing derived objects; in the above case, it will use the default *Worker* constructor.

If you want to use something other than the default constructor for a virtual base class, you need to invoke the constructor explicitly. Thus, the constructor should look like this:

```
SingingWaiter(const Worker & wk, int p = 0, int v = Singer::other)
                    : Worker(wk), Waiter(wk,p), Singer(wk,v) {}
```

Here the code explicitly invokes the *Worker(const Worker &)* constructor. Note that this call is legal and often necessary for virtual base classes and illegal for nonvirtual base classes.

TIP

If a class has an indirect virtual base class, a constructor for that class should explicitly invoke a constructor for the virtual base class unless all that is needed is the default constructor for the virtual base class.

Listing 13-17 shows a complete set of class declarations for the *Worker* hierarchy of classes.

Listing 13-17 *workermi.h*

```
// workermi.h  -- working classes
#include "strng2.h"
```

```
class Worker
{
private:
        String fullname;
        long id;
protected:
        virtual void data() const;
        virtual void get();
public:
        Worker() : fullname("no one"), id(OL) {}
        Worker(const String & s, long n)
                        : fullname(s), id(n) {}
        virtual void set();
        virtual void show() const;
};

class Waiter : virtual public Worker
{
private:
        int panache;
protected:
        void data() const;
        void get();
public:
        Waiter() : Worker(), panache(0) {}
        Waiter(const String & s, long n, int p = 0)
                        : Worker(s, n), panache(p) {}
        Waiter(const Worker & wk, int p = 0)
                        : Worker(wk), panache(p) {}
        void set();
        void show() const;
};

class Singer : virtual public Worker
{
protected:
        enum {other, alto, contralto, soprano,
                        bass, baritone, tenor};
        enum {Vtypes = 7};
        void data() const;
        void get();
private:
        static char *pv[Vtypes];        // string equivs of voice types
        int voice;
public:
        Singer() : Worker(), voice(other) {}
        Singer(const String & s, long n, int v = other)
                        : Worker(s, n), voice(v) {}
        Singer(const Worker & wk, int v = other)
                        : Worker(wk), voice(v) {}
        void set();
        void show() const;
};
```

continued on next page

609

continued from previous page

```
class SingingWaiter : public Singer, public Waiter
{
protected:
        void data() const;
        void get();
public:
        SingingWaiter()  {}
        SingingWaiter(const String & s, long n, int p = 0,
                                        int v = Singer::other)
                    : Worker(s,n), Waiter(s, n, p), Singer(s, n, v) {}
        SingingWaiter(const Worker & wk, int p = 0, int v = Singer::other)
                    : Worker(wk), Waiter(wk,p), Singer(wk,v) {}
        SingingWaiter(const Waiter & wt, int v = other)
                    : Worker(wt),Waiter(wt), Singer(wt,v) {}
        SingingWaiter(const Singer & wt, int p = 0)
                    : Worker(wt),Waiter(wt,p), Singer(wt) {}
        void set();
        void show() const;
};
```

In addition to requiring that we alter class constructor rules, MI requires other coding adjustments. For instance, you may have noticed the addition of a *get()* function to the original versions of Listing 13-12 and 13-16. Let's look at this and other changes next.

Which Method?

Note that *SingingWaiter* defines new *show()* and *data()* methods. Because a *SingingWaiter* has no new data members, you might think we could dispense with them and just use the inherited methods. This brings up the first problem. Suppose we do omit new versions of these methods and create a *SingingWaiter* object and use it to invoke the *show()* method:

```
SingingWaiter newhire("Elise Hawks", 2005, 6, soprano);
newhire.show();        // ambiguous
```

With single inheritance, failing to redefine *show()* results in using the most recent ancestral definition. In this case, each direct ancestor has a *show()* function, making this call ambiguous.

TIP

Multiple inheritance can result in ambiguous function calls. For instance, a *BadDude* class could inherit two quite different *draw()* methods from a *Gunslinger* class and a *PokerPlayer* class.

You can use the scope resolution operator to clarify what you mean:

```
SingingWaiter newhire("Elise Hawks", 2005, 6, soprano);
newhire.Singer::show();        // use Singer version
```

However, a much better approach is to redefine *show()* for *SingingWaiter* and to have it specify which *show()* to use. For instance, if you want a *SingingWaiter* object to use the *Singer* version, do this:

```
void SingingWaiter::show()
{
        Singer::show();
}
```

In practice, however, we want *SingingWaiter::show()* to display data from all its ancestor classes, so the code has to be a bit different. For instance, we could try this:

```
void SingingWaiter::show()
{
        Singer::show();
        Waiter::show();
}
```

This could easily lead to displaying a person's name and ID twice, once with *Singer::show()* and once with *Waiter::show()*. To avoid this, we have to take some care in designing these methods. One scheme is to define methods that display information pertaining only to one class. For instance, have a *Worker::data()* method that displays only name and ID information, have a *Waiter::data()* method that displays only panache information, and so on. Make these methods protected so that they are invisible to the outside world but are accessible to derived classes. The various *data()* methods then can be used as building blocks for constructing *show()* methods.

For instance, *Waiter::show()* can call *Worker::data()* and *Waiter::data()*:

```
void Waiter::show() const
{
        cout << "Category: waiter\n";
        Worker::data();
        data(); // Waiter::data()
}
```

Similarly, *SingingWaiter::show()* can call upon methods for all its subobjects:

```
void SingingWaiter::data() const
{
        Singer::data();
        Waiter::data();
}

void SingingWaiter::show() const
{
        cout << "Category: singing waiter\n";
        Worker::data();
        data();
}
```

Here the *data()* method displays data specifically about waiters and singers, and *show()* displays the more general worker information. The earlier single inheritance example of Listings 13-12 and 13-13 took a similar approach, but there each *data()* invoked the *data()* of its parent class so that, for example, *Waiter::data()* displayed both *Waiter* information and *Worker* information. That way, *Waiter::show()* had to invoke just one *data()* method instead of two. That approach, however, fails for multiple inheritance, for it would result in both *Singer::data()* and *Waiter::data()* displaying *Worker* information. Instead, we have to make each *data()* method more restrictive and shift more work to *show()*. This adjustment is much the same as that made for constructors. That is, instead of having methods of a derived class invoke methods of an intermediate base class, which then invoke methods of its base class, we have the class invoke methods of the top base class directly.

We face a similar problem with the *set()* functions, which solicit data for setting object values. We want *SingingWaiter::set()*, for example, to ask for *Worker* information once, not twice. Because all the class data is private, *SingingWaiter* methods can't access *Worker* data directly but have to use *Worker* methods. We can use the same solution as we did for information display: provide protected methods for each class that solicit just the information needed for the noninherited component. Use those methods (call them *Worker::get()*, and so on) as programming building blocks. Listing 13-18 shows the code for the various class methods.

COMPATIBILITY NOTE

The version of g++ available to the author (2.0) required replacing

```
char * Singer::pv[] = {"other", "alto", "contralto",
                       "soprano", "bass", "baritone", "tenor"};
```

in Listing 13-18 with the following:

```
char * Singer::pv[Singer::Vtypes] = {"other", "alto", "contralto",
                       "soprano", "bass", "baritone", "tenor"};
```

It also required making *Vtypes* a *public enum* in the *Singer* class instead of *protected*. Metrowerks CodeWarrior required the form used in the listing. The other compilers tested accepted either form.

Listing 13-18 *workermi.cpp*

```
// workermi.cpp -- working class methods
#include "workermi.h"
#include <iostream.h>
// Worker methods
void Worker::set()
{
        cout << "Enter worker's name: ";
        get();

}

void Worker::show() const
```

```
{
        cout << "Category: worker\n";
        data();
}

// protected methods
void Worker::data() const
{
        cout << "Name: " << fullname << "\n";
        cout << "Employee ID: " << id << "\n";
}

void Worker::get()
{
        cin >> fullname;
        cout << "Enter worker's ID: ";
        cin >> id;
        while (cin.get() != '\n')
                continue;
}

// Waiter methods
void Waiter::set()
{
        cout << "Enter waiter's name: ";
        Worker::get();
        get();
}


void Waiter::show() const
{
        cout << "Category: waiter\n";
        Worker::data();
        data();
}

// protected methods
void Waiter::data() const
{
        cout << "Panache rating: " << panache << "\n";
}

void Waiter::get()
{
        cout << "Enter waiter's panache rating: ";
        cin >> panache;
        while (cin.get() != '\n')
                continue;
}

// Singer methods

char * Singer::pv[] = {"other", "alto", "contralto",
```

continued on next page

continued from previous page

```
                                  "soprano", "bass", "baritone", "tenor"};

void Singer::set()
{
        cout << "Enter singer's name: ";
        Worker::get();
        get();
}

void Singer::show() const
{
        cout << "Category: singer\n";
        Worker::data();
        data();
}

// protected methods
void Singer::data() const
{
        cout << "Vocal range: " << pv[voice] << "\n";
}

void Singer::get()
{
        cout << "Enter number for singer's vocal range:\n";
        for (int i = 0; i < Vtypes; i++)
        {
                cout << i << ": " << pv[i] << "    ";
                if ( i % 4 == 3)
                        cout << '\n';
        }
        if (i % 4 != 0)
                cout << '\n';
        cin >>  voice;
        while (cin.get() != '\n')
                continue;
}

// SingingWaiter methods
void SingingWaiter::data() const
{
        Singer::data();
        Waiter::data();
}

void SingingWaiter::get()
{
        Waiter::get();
        Singer::get();
}

void SingingWaiter::set()
{
```

```
        cout << "Enter singing waiter's name: ";
        Worker::get();
        get();
}

void SingingWaiter::show() const
{
        cout << "Category: singing waiter\n";
        Worker::data();
        data();
}
```

Of course, curiosity demands we test these classes, and Listing 13-19, based on Listing 13-14, provides code to do so. Note that the program makes use of the polymorphic property by assigning the addresses of various kinds of classes to base class pointers. Compile it along with *workermi.cpp* and *strng2.cpp*. Also make sure the *arraytp.h* header file (the one containing our array template definition) is present.

COMPATIBILITY NOTE

If your system doesn't support templates, you can use a regular array instead. Just make the minor changes suggested in the listing.

Listing 13-19 *workmi.cpp*

```
// workmi.cpp -- multiple inheritance
// compile with workermi.cpp, strng2.cpp
#include <iostream.h>
#include <string.h>
#include "workermi.h"
#include "arraytp.h"  // omit if no template support
const int SIZE = 5;
int main(void)
{
        ArrayTP<Worker *, (int) SIZE> lolas;
        // if no template support, omit the above and use the following:
        // Worker * lolas[SIZE];

        for (int ct = 0; ct < SIZE; ct++)
        {
                char choice;
                cout << "Enter the employee category:\n"
                        << "e: worker  w: waiter   s: singer   "
                        << "t: singing waiter   q: quit\n";
                cin >> choice;
                while (strchr("ewstq", choice) == NULL)
                {
                        cout << "Please enter an e, w, s, t, or q: ";
                        cin >> choice;
                }
                if (choice == 'q')
```

continued on next page

continued from previous page

```
                                break;
                    switch(choice)
                    {
                            case 'e':        lolas[ct] = new Worker;
                                                 break;
                            case 'w':        lolas[ct] = new Waiter;
                                                 break;
                            case 's':        lolas[ct] = new Singer;
                                                 break;
                            case 't':        lolas[ct] = new SingingWaiter;
                                                 break;
                    }
                    cin.get();
                    lolas[ct]->set();
            }

            cout << "\nHere is your staff:\n";
            for (int i = 0; i < ct; i++)
            {
                    cout << '\n';
                    lolas[i]->show();
            }
            for (i = 0; i < ct; i++)
                    delete lolas[i];
            return 0;
}
```

Here is a sample run:

```
Enter the employee category:
e: worker  w: waiter  s: singer  t: singing waiter  q: quit
e
Enter worker's name: Wilmot Snipside
Enter worker's ID: 2004
Enter the employee category:
e: worker  w: waiter  s: singer  t: singing waiter  q: quit
t
Enter singing waiter's name: Natasha Gargalova
Enter worker's ID: 2005
Enter waiter's panache rating: 6
Enter number for singer's vocal range:
0: other   1: alto   2: contralto   3: soprano
4: bass    5: baritone   6: tenor
3
Enter the employee category:
e: worker  w: waiter  s: singer  t: singing waiter  q: quit
q

Here is your staff:

Category: worker
Name: Wilmot Snipside
Employee ID: 2004
```

```
Category: singing waiter
Name: Natasha Gargalova
Employee ID: 2005
Vocal range: soprano
Panache rating: 6
```

Let's look at a few more matters concerning multiple inheritance.

Mixed Virtual and Nonvirtual Bases

Consider again the case of a derived class that inherits a base class by more than one route. If the base class is virtual, the derived class contains one subobject of the base class. If the base class is not virtual, the derived class contains multiple subobjects. What if there is a mixture? Suppose, for example, that class B is a virtual base class to classes C and D and a nonvirtual base class to classes X and Y. Furthermore, suppose, class M is derived from C, D, X, and Y. In this case, class M contains one class B subobject for all the virtually derived ancestors (that is, classes C and D) and a separate class B subobject for each nonvirtual ancestor (that is, classes X and Y). So, all told, it would contain three class B subobjects.

Virtual Base Classes and Dominance

Using virtual base classes alters how C++ resolves ambiguities. With nonvirtual base classes the rules are simple. If a class inherits two or more members (data or methods) from different classes but having the same name, using that name without qualifying it with a class name is ambiguous. If virtual base classes are involved, however, such a use may or may not be ambiguous. In this case, if one name *dominates* all others, it can be used unambiguously without a qualifier.

So how does one member name dominate another? A name in a derived class dominates the same name in any ancestor class, direct or indirect. For example, consider the following definitions:

```cpp
class B
{
public:
        short q();
        ...
};

class C : virtual public B
{
public:
        long q();
        int omb()
        ...
};

class D : public C
{
```

continued on next page

continued from previous page

```
            ...
};

class E : virtual public B
{
private:
        int omb();
        ...
};

class F:  public D, public E
{
        ...
};
```

Here the definition of $q()$ in class C dominates the definition in class B because C is derived from B. Thus, methods in F can use $q()$ to denote $C::q()$. On the other hand, neither definition of $omb()$ dominates the other because neither C nor E is a base class to the other. Therefore, an attempt by F to use an unqualified $omb()$ would be ambiguous.

The virtual ambiguity rules pay no attention to access rules. That is, even though $E::omb()$ is private and hence not directly accessible to class F, using $omb()$ is ambiguous. Similarly, even if $C::q()$ were private, it would dominate $D::q()$. In that case, you could call $B::q()$ in class F, but an unqualified $q()$ for that would refer to the inaccessible $C::q()$.

Multiple Inheritance Synopsis

First, let's review multiple inheritance without virtual base classes. This form of MI imposes no new rules. However, if a class inherits two members of the same name but from different classes, you need to use class qualifiers in the derived class to distinguish between the two members. That is, methods in the *BadDude* class, derived from *Gunslinger* and *PokerPlayer*, would use *Gunslinger::draw()* and *PokerPlayer::draw()* to distinguish between *draw()* methods inherited from the two classes. Otherwise the compiler should complain about ambiguous usage.

If one class inherits from a base class by more than one route, then the class inherits one base class object for each nonvirtual instance of the base class. In some cases this may be what you want, but more often multiple instances of a base class are a problem.

Next, let's look at MI with virtual base classes. A class becomes a virtual base class when a derived class uses the keyword *virtual* when indicating derivation:

```
class marketing : virtual public reality { ... };
```

The main change, and the reason for virtual base classes, is that a class that inherits from one or more instances of a virtual base class inherits just one base class object. Implementing this feature entails other requirements:

> A derived class with an indirect virtual base class should have its constructors invoke the indirect base class constructors directly, something which is illegal for indirect nonvirtual base classes.

❧ Name ambiguity is resolved by the dominance rule.

As you can see, multiple inheritance can introduce programming complexities. However, most of these complexities arise when a derived class inherits from the same base class by more than one route. If you avoid that situation, about the only thing you need to watch for is qualifying inherited names when necessary.

Summary

C++ provides several means for reusing code. Public inheritance, described in Chapter 12, enables you to model *is-a* relationships, with derived classes being able to reuse the code of base classes. Private and protected inheritance also let you reuse base class code, this time modeling *has-a* relationships. With private inheritance, public and protected members of the base class become private members of the derived class. With protected inheritance, public and protected members of the base class become protected members of the derived class. Thus, in either case, the public interface of the base class becomes an internal interface for the derived class. This sometimes is described as inheriting the implementation but not the interface, for a derived object can't explicitly use the base class interface. Thus, you can't view a derived object as a kind of base object. Because of this, a base class pointer or reference is not allowed to refer to a derived object without an explicit type cast.

You also can reuse class code by developing a class with members that are themselves objects. This approach, called containment, layering, or composition, also models the *has-a* relationship. Containment is simpler to implement and use than private or protected inheritance, so it usually is preferred. However, private and protected inheritance have slightly greater capabilities. For instance, inheritance allows a derived class access to protected members of a base class. Also, it allows a derived class to redefine a virtual function inherited from the base class. Since containment is not a form of inheritance, neither of these capabilities are options when you reuse class code by containment. On the other hand, containment is more suitable if you need several objects of a given class. For instance, a *State* class could contain an array of *County* objects.

Multiple inheritance (MI) allows you to reuse code for more than one class in a class design. Private or protected MI models the *has-a* relationship, while public MI models the *is-a* relationship. Multiple inheritance can create problems with multi-defined names and multi-inherited bases. You can use class qualifiers to resolve name ambiguities and virtual base classes to avoid multi-inherited bases. However, using virtual base classes introduces new rules for writing initialization lists for constructors and for resolving ambiguities.

Class templates let you create a generic class design in which a type, usually a member type, is represented by a type parameter. A typical template looks like this:

```
template <class T>
class Ic
{
```

continued on next page

continued from previous page

```
        T v;
        ...
public:
        Ic(const T & val) : v(val) { }
        ...
};
```

Here the *T* is the type parameter and acts as a stand-in for a real type to be specified at a later time. (This parameter can have any valid C++ name, but *T* and *Type* are common choices.)

Class definitions (instantiations) are generated when you declare a class object, specifying a particular type. For instance, the declaration

```
class Ic<short> sic;
```

causes the compiler to generate a class declaration in which every occurrence of the type parameter *T* in the template is replaced by the actual type *short* in the class declaration. In this case the class name is *Ic<short>*, not *Ic*.

You can provide specialized class declarations that override a template definition. Just define the class, using the template name followed by angle brackets containing the type for which you want a specialization. For example, you could provide a specialized *Ic* class for character pointers as follows:

```
class Ic<char *>.
{
        char * str;
        ...
public:
        Ic(const char * s) : str(s) { }
        ...
};
```

Then a declaration of the form

```
class Ic<char *> chic;
```

would use the specialized definition for *chic* rather than using the general template.

The goal of all these methods is to allow you to reuse tested code without having to copy it manually. This simplifies the programming task and makes programs more reliable.

Review Questions

1. For each of the following sets of classes, indicate whether public or private derivation is more appropriate for the second column:

class Bear	class PolarBear
class Kitchen	class Home
class Person	class Programmer
class Person	class HorseAndJockey
class Person, class Automobile	class Driver

2. Suppose we have the following definitions:

```
class Frabjous {
private:
        char fab[20];
public:
        Frabjous(const char * s = "C++") : fab(s) { }
        virtual void tell() { cout << fab; }
};

class Gloam {
private:
        int glip;
        Frabjous fb;
public:
        Gloam(int g = 0, const char * s = "C++");
        Gloam(int g, const Frabjous & f);
        void tell();
};
```

Given that the *Gloam* version of *tell()* should display the values of *glip* and *fb*, provide definitions for the three *Gloam* methods.

3. Suppose we have the following definitions:

```
class Frabjous {
private:
        char fab[20];
public:
        Frabjous(const char * s = "C++") : fab(s) { }
        virtual void tell() { cout << fab; }
};

class Gloam : private Frabjous{
private:
        int glip;
public:
        Gloam(int g = 0, const char * s = "C++");
        Gloam(int g, const Frabjous & f);
        void tell();
};
```

Given that the *Gloam* version of *tell()* should display the values of *glip* and *fab*, provide definitions for the three *Gloam* methods.

4. Suppose we have the following definition, based on the *Stack* template of Listing 13-7 and the *Worker* class of Listing 13-17:

```
Stack<Worker *> sw;
```

Write out the class declaration that will be generated. Just do the class declaration, not the non-inline class methods.

5. Use the template definitions in this chapter to define the following:

   ◀ An array of *String* objects

> A stack of arrays of *double*

> An array of stacks of pointers to *Worker* objects

6. Describe the differences between virtual and nonvirtual base classes.

Programming Exercises

1. The *Wine* class has a *String* class object (Chapter 11) holding the name of a wine and a *LimitArr* class object (Chapter 12) holding the number of available bottles for each of several years. Implement the *Wine* class using containment and test it with a simple program. The program should prompt you to enter a wine name, the size of the array, the first year for the array, and the number of bottles for each year. The program should use this data to construct a *Wine* object, then display the information stored in the object.

2. The *Wine* class has a *String* class object (Chapter 11) holding the name of a wine and a *LimitArr* class object (Chapter 12) holding the number of available bottles for each of several years. Implement the *Wine* class using private inheritance and test it with a simple program. The program should prompt you to enter a wine name, the size of the array, the first year for the array, and the number of bottles for each year. The program should use this data to construct a *Wine* object, then display the information stored in the object.

3. Define a *QueueTp* template. Test it by creating a queue of pointers-to-*Worker* (as defined in Listing 13-17) and using the queue in a program similar to that of Listing 13-19.

4. A *Person* class holds the first name and the last name of a person. In addition to its constructors, it has a *show()* method that displays both names. A *Gunslinger* class derives virtually from the *Person* class. It has a *draw()* member that returns a type *double* value representing a gunslinger's draw time. The class also has an *int* member representing the number of notches on a gunslinger's gun. Finally, it has a *show()* function that displays all this information.

   A *PokerPlayer* class derives virtually from the *Person* class. It has a *draw()* member that returns a random number in the range 1 through 52 representing a card value. (Optionally, you could define a *Card* class with suit and face value members and use a *Card* return value for *draw()*). The *PokerPlayer* class uses the *Person show()* function. The *BadDude* class derives publicly from the *Gunslinger* and *PokerPlayer* classes. It has a *gdraw()* member that returns a bad dude's draw time and a *cdraw()* member that returns the next card drawn. It has an appropriate *show()* function. Define all these classes and methods, along with any other necessary methods (such as methods for setting object values), and test them in a simple program similar to that of Listing 13-19.

5. Here are some class declarations:

```
// emp.h -- header file for employee class and children
#include <string.h>
#include <iostream.h>

const int SLEN = 20;
class employee
{
protected:
        char fname[SLEN];       // employee's first name
        char lname[SLEN];       // employee's last name
        char job[SLEN];
public:
        employee();
        employee(char * fn, char * ln, char * j);
        employee(const employee & e);
        virtual void showall() const; // labels and shows all data
        virtual void setall();                  // prompts user for values
        friend ostream & operator<<(ostream & os, const employee & e);
        // just displays first and last name
};

class manager:  virtual public employee
{
protected:
        int inchargeof;                 // number of employees managed
public:
        manager();
        manager(char * fn, char * ln, char * j, int ico = 0);
        manager(const employee & e, int ico);
        manager(const manager & m);
        void showall() const;
        void setall();
};

class fink: virtual public employee
{
protected:
        char reportsto[SLEN];           // to whom fink reports
public:
        fink();
        fink(char * fn, char * ln, char * j, char * rpo);
        fink(const employee & e, char * rpo);
        fink(const fink & e);
        void showall() const;
        void setall();
};

class highfink: public manager, public fink // management fink
{
public:
        highfink();
```

continued on next page

623

continued from previous page

```
        highfink(char * fn, char * ln, char * j, char * rpo, int ico);
        highfink(const employee & e, char * rpo, int ico);
        highfink(const fink & f, int ico);
        highfink(const manager & m, char * rpo);
        highfink(const highfink & h);
        void showall() const;
        void setall();
};
```

Provide the class method implementations and test the classes in a program. Here is a minimal test program. You should add at least one test of a *setall()* member function.

```
// useemp1.cpp -- use employee classes
#include <iostream.h>
#include "emp.h"

int main(void)
{
        employee th("Trip", "Harris", "Thumper");
        cout << th << '\n';
        th.showall();

        manager db("Deb", "Bates", "Twigger", 5);
        cout << db << '\n';
        db.showall();

        cout << "Press a key for next batch of output:\n";
        cin.get();

        fink mo("Matt", "Oggs", "Oiler", "Juno Barr");
        cout << mo << '\n';
        mo.showall();
        highfink hf(db, "Curly Kew");
        hf.showall();

        cout << "Using an employee * pointer:\n";
        employee * tri[4] = {&th, &db, &mo, &hf};
        for (int i = 0; i < 4; i++)
                tri[i]->showall();

        return 0;
}
```

COMPATIBILITY NOTE

Symantec C++ requires that the elements of the *tri* array be assigned object addresses individually rather than through an initialization statement.

Why is no assignment operator defined?

Why are *showall()* and *setall()* virtual?

Why is *employee* a virtual base class?

Why does the *highfink* class have no data section?

Why is only one version of *operator<<()* needed?

What would happen if the end of the program were replaced with this code?

```
employee  tri[4] = {th, db, mo, hf};
for (int i = 0; i < 4; i++)
        tri[i].showall();
```

CHAPTER 14

FRIENDS, EXCEPTIONS, AND MORE

You will learn about the following in this chapter:

- ◇ Friend classes
- ◇ Friend class methods
- ◇ Nested classes
- ◇ Throwing exceptions, try blocks, and catch blocks
- ◇ Exception classes
- ◇ RTTI (runtime type information)

- ◇ *dynamic_cast* and *typeid*
- ◇ Namespaces

This chapter ties up some loose ends, then ventures into some of the most recent additions to the C++ language. The loose ends include friend classes, friend member functions, and nested classes, which are classes declared within other classes. The recent additions discussed here are exceptions, RTTI, and namespaces. C++ exception handling provides a mechanism for dealing with unusual occurrences that otherwise would bring a program to a halt. RTTI, or runtime type information, is a mechanism for identifying object types. C++'s new namespace mechanisms provide ways to avoid name conflicts. These last three facilities are new to C++, and many compilers do not yet support them. Also, these facilities may change a bit between the draft versions described here and final versions.

Friends

Several examples in this book have used friend functions as part of the extended interface for a class. Such functions are not the only kinds of friends a class can have. A class also can be a friend. In that case, any method of the friend class can access private and protected members of the original class. Also, you can be more restrictive and designate just particular member functions of a class to be friends to another class. A class defines which functions, member functions, or classes are friends; friendship cannot be imposed from the outside. Thus, although friends do grant outside access to a class's private portion, they don't really violate the spirit of object-oriented programming. Instead, they provide more flexibility to the public interface.

Friend Classes

When might you wish to make one class a friend to another? Let's look at an example. Suppose you need to program a simple simulation of a television and a remote control. You decide to define a *Tv* class representing a television and a *Remote* class representing a remote control. Clearly, there should be some sort of relationship between these classes, but what kind? A remote control is not a television and vice versa, so the *is-a* relationship of public inheritance doesn't apply. Nor is either a component of the other, so the *has-a* relationship of containment or of private or protected inheritance doesn't apply. What is true is that a remote control can modify the state of a television, and this suggests making the *Remote* class a friend to the *Tv* class.

First, let's define the *Tv* class. We can represent a television with a set of state members, that is, variables that describe various aspects of the television. Here are some of the possible states:

❧ On-off

❧ Channel setting

❧ Volume setting

❧ Cable or antenna tuning mode

❧ TV tuner or VCR input

The tuning mode reflects the fact that the spacing between channels for channels 14 and up is different for cable reception than it is for UHF broadcast reception. The input selection chooses between TV, which could be either cable or broadcast TV, and a VCR. Some sets may offer more choices, but this list is enough for our purposes.

Also, a television has some parameters that aren't state variables. For instance, televisions vary in the number of channels they can receive, and we can include a member to track that value.

Next, we need to provide the class with methods for altering these settings. Many television sets these days hide their controls behind panels, but it's still possible with most televisions to change channels, and so on, without a remote control. However, often you can go up or down one channel at a time but can't select a channel at random. Similarly, there's usually a button for increasing the volume and one for decreasing the volume.

A remote control should duplicate the controls built into the television. Many of its methods can be implemented by using *Tv* methods. In addition, however, a remote control typically provides random access channel selection. That is, you can go directly from channel 2 to channel 20 without going through all the intervening channels. Also, many remotes can work in two modes—as a television controller and as a VCR controller.

These considerations suggest a definition like that shown in Listing 14-1. The definition includes several constants defined as enumerations. The statement making *Remote* a friend class is this:

```
friend class Remote;
```

A friend declaration can appear in a public, private, or protected section; the location makes no difference. Because the *Remote* class mentions the *Tv* class, the compiler has to know about the *Tv* class before it can handle the *Remote* class. The simplest way to accomplish this is to define the *Tv* class first. Alternatively, you can use a forward declaration; we'll discuss that option soon.

COMPATIBILITY NOTE

Recall that some compilers may have already defined *Bool*, *True*, and *False*, in which case you can try alternative spellings, such as *BooL*.

Listing 14-1 *tv.h*

```
// tv.h -- Tv and Remote classes
#ifndef _TV_H_
#define _TV_H_
enum Bool {False, True};        // or use built-in Boolean type, if available

class Tv
{
public:
        friend class Remote;    // Remote can access Tv private parts
        enum State{Off, On};
        enum {MinVal,MaxVal = 20};
        enum {Antenna, Cable};
        enum {TV, VCR};

        Tv(State s = Off, int mc = 100) : state(s), volume(5),
                maxchannel(mc), channel(2), mode(Cable), input(TV) {}
```

continued on next page

continued from previous page

```
        void onoff() {state = (state == On)? Off : On;}
        Bool ison() {return state == On ? True : False;}
        Bool volup();
        Bool voldown();
        void chanup();
        void chandown();
        void set_mode() {mode = (mode == Antenna)? Cable : Antenna;}
        void set_input() {input = (input == TV)? VCR : TV;}
        void settings();         // display all settings
private:
        State state;          // on or off
        int volume;           // assumed to be digitized
        int maxchannel;
        int channel;
        int mode;                  // broadcast or cable
        int input;                 // TV or VCR
};

class Remote
{
private:
        int mode;        // controls TV or VCR
public:
        Remote(int m = Tv::TV) : mode(m) {}
        Bool volup(Tv & t) { return t.volup();}
        Bool voldown(Tv & t) { return t.voldown();}
        void onoff(Tv & t) { t.onoff(); }
        void chanup(Tv & t) {t.chanup();}
        void chandown(Tv & t) {t.chandown();}
        void set_chan(Tv & t, int c) {t.channel = c;}
        void set_mode(Tv & t) {t.set_mode();}
        void set_input(Tv & t) {t.set_input();}
};
#endif
```

Most of the class methods are defined inline. Note that each *Remote* method other than the constructor takes a reference to a *Tv* object as an argument. That reflects that a remote has to be aimed at a particular TV. Listing 14-2 shows the remaining definitions. The volume-setting functions change the volume member by one unit unless the sound has reached its minimum or maximum setting. The channel selection functions use wraparound, with the lowest channel setting, taken to be 1, immediately following the highest channel setting, *maxchannel*.

Listing 14-2 *tv.cpp*

```
// tv.cpp -- methods for the Tv class (Remote methods are inline)
#include <iostream.h>
#include "tv.h"

Bool Tv::volup()
{
```

```
        if (volume < MaxVal)
        {
                volume++;
                return True;
        }
        else
                return False;
}
Bool Tv::voldown()
{
        if (volume > MinVal)
        {
                volume--;
                return True;
        }
        else
                return False;
}

void Tv::chanup()
{
        if (channel < maxchannel)
                channel++;
        else
                channel = 1;
}

void Tv::chandown()
{
        if (channel > 1)
                channel--;
        else
                channel = maxchannel;
}

void Tv::settings()
{
        cout << "TV is " << (state == Off? "Off\n" : "On\n");
        if (state == On)
        {
                cout << "Volume setting = " << volume << "\n";
                cout << "Channel setting = " << channel << "\n";
                cout << "Mode = "
                        << (mode == Antenna? "antenna\n" : "cable\n");
                cout << "Input = "
                        << (input == TV? "TV\n" : "VCR\n");
        }
}
```

Next, Listing 14-3 is a short program that tests some of the features. The same controller is used to control two separate televisions.

Listing 14-3 *use_tv.cpp*

```
//use_tv.cpp
#include <iostream.h>
#include "tv.h"

int main(void)
{
        Tv s20;
        cout << "Initial settings for 20\" TV:\n";
        s20.settings();
        s20.onoff();
        s20.chanup();
        cout << "\nAdjusted settings for 20\" TV:\n";
        s20.settings();

        Remote grey;

        grey.set_chan(s20, 10);
        grey.volup(s20);
        grey.volup(s20);
        cout << "\n20\" settings after using remote:\n";
        s20.settings();

        Tv s27(Tv::On);
        s27.set_mode();
        grey.set_chan(s27,28);
        cout << "\n27\" settings:\n";
        s27.settings();

        return 0;
}
```

Here is the program output:

```
Initial settings for 20" TV:
TV is Off

Adjusted settings for 20" TV:
TV is On
Volume setting = 5
Channel setting = 3
Mode = cable
Input = TV

20" settings after using remote:
TV is On
Volume setting = 7
Channel setting = 10
Mode = cable
Input = TV

27" settings:
```

```
TV is On
Volume setting = 5
Channel setting = 28
Mode = antenna
Input = TV
```

The main point to this exercise is that class friendship is a natural idiom in which to express some relationships. Without some form of friendship we would either have to make the private parts of the *Tv* class public or else construct some awkward, larger class that encompasses both a television and a remote control. And that solution wouldn't reflect the fact that a single remote control can be used with several televisions.

Friend Member Functions

Looking at the code for the last example, you may notice that most of the *Remote* methods are implemented using the public interface for the *Tv* class. This means that those methods don't really need friend status. Indeed, the only *Remote* method that accesses a private *Tv* member directly is *Remote::set_chan()*, so that's the only method that needs to be friend. Making selected class members friends to another class is an option, but, it's a bit more awkward. You need to be careful about the order in which you arrange the various declarations and definitions. Let's see why.

The way to make *Remote::set_chan()* a friend to the *Tv* class is to declare it as a friend in the *Tv* class declaration:

```
class Tv
{
        friend void Remote::set_chan(Tv & t, int c);
        ...
};
```

However, for the compiler to process this statement, it needs to have already seen the *Remote* definition. Otherwise, it won't know that *Remote* is a class and that *set_chan()* is a method of that class. That suggests putting the *Remote* definition above the *Tv* definition. But the fact that *Remote* methods mention *Tv* objects means that the *Tv* definition should come above the *Remote* definition. Part of the way around the circular dependence is to use a forward declaration. That means inserting the statement

```
class Tv;        // forward declaration
```

above the *Remote* definition. This provides the following arrangement:

```
class Tv;                                  // forward declaration
class Remote { ... };
class Tv { ... };
```

Could we use the following arrangement instead?

```
class Remote;                              // forward declaration
class Tv { ... };
class Remote { ... };
```

The answer is no. The reason, as mentioned earlier, is that when the compiler sees that a *Remote* method is declared as a friend in the *Tv* class declaration, the compiler needs to have already viewed the *Remote* definition.

Another difficulty remains. In Listing 14-1, the *Remote* declaration contained inline code such as the following:

```
void onoff(Tv & t) { t.onoff(); }
```

Because this calls a *Tv* method, the compiler needs to have seen the *Tv* class declaration at this point so that it knows what methods *Tv* has. But, as we've seen, that declaration necessarily follows the *Remote* declaration. The solution to this problem is to restrict *Remote* to method declarations and to place the actual definitions *after* the *Tv* class. This leads to the following ordering:

```
class Tv;                // forward declaration
class Remote { ... }; // Tv-using methods as prototypes only
class Tv { ... };
// put Remote method definitions here
```

The prototypes look like this:

```
void onoff(Tv & t);
```

All the compiler needs to know when inspecting this prototype is that *Tv* is a class, and the forward declaration supplies that information. By the time the compiler reaches the actual method definitions, it has already read the *Tv* class declaration and has the added information needed to compile those methods. By using the *inline* keyword, we can still make the methods inline methods. Listing 14-4 shows the revised header file.

Listing 14-4 *tvfm.h*

```
// tvfm.h -- Tv and Remote classes using a friend member
#ifndef _TVFM_H_
#define _TVFM_H_

enum Bool {False, True};

class Tv;        // forward declaration

class Remote
{
public:
        enum State{Off, On};
        enum {MinVal,MaxVal = 20};
        enum {Antenna, Cable};
        enum {TV, VCR};
private:
        int mode;
public:
```

```
        Remote(int m = TV) : mode(m) {}
        Bool volup(Tv & t);                    // prototype only
        Bool voldown(Tv & t);
        void onoff(Tv & t) ;
        void chanup(Tv & t) ;
        void chandown(Tv & t) ;
        void set_mode(Tv & t) ;
        void set_input(Tv & t);
        void set_chan(Tv & t, int c);

};

class Tv
{
public:
        friend void Remote::set_chan(Tv & t, int c);
        enum State{Off, On};
        enum {MinVal,MaxVal = 20};
        enum {Antenna, Cable};
        enum {TV, VCR};

        Tv(State s = Off, int mc = 100) : state(s), volume(5),
                maxchannel(mc), channel(2), mode(Cable), input(TV) {}
        void onoff() {state = (state == On)? Off : On;}
        Bool ison() {return state == On ? True : False;}
        Bool volup();
        Bool voldown();
        void chanup();
        void chandown();
        void set_mode() {mode = (mode == Antenna)? Cable : Antenna;}
        void set_input() {input = (input == TV)? VCR : TV;}
        void settings();
private:
        State state;
        int volume;
        int maxchannel;
        int channel;
        int mode;
        int input;
};

// Remote methods as inline functions
inline Bool Remote::volup(Tv & t) { return t.volup();}
inline Bool Remote::voldown(Tv & t) { return t.voldown();}
inline void Remote::onoff(Tv & t) { t.onoff(); }
inline void Remote::chanup(Tv & t) {t.chanup();}
inline void Remote::chandown(Tv & t) {t.chandown();}
inline void Remote::set_mode(Tv & t) {t.set_mode();}
inline void Remote::set_input(Tv & t) {t.set_input();}
inline void Remote::set_chan(Tv & t, int c) {t.channel = c;}
#endif
```

This version behaves the same as the original. The difference is that just one *Remote* method is a friend to the *Tv* class instead of all the *Remote* methods. Figure 14-1 illustrates this difference.

By the way, making the entire *Remote* class a friend doesn't need a forward declaration because the friend statement itself identifies *Remote* as a class:

```
friend class Remote;
```

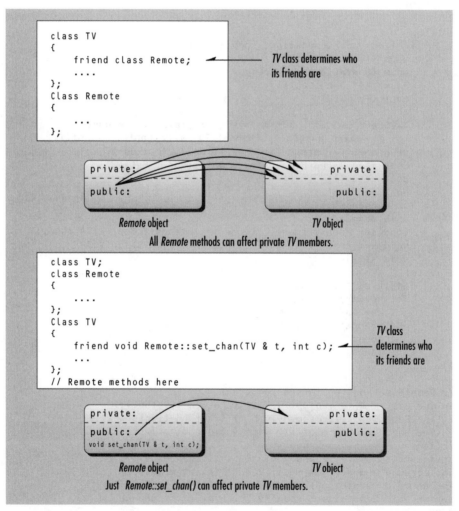

Figure 14-1 Class friends versus class member friends

Other Friendly Relationships

Other combinations of friends and classes are possible. Let's take a brief look at some of them now. Suppose the advance of technology brings interactive remote controllers. For instance, an interactive remote control unit might let you enter a response to some question posed on a television program, and the television might activate a buzzer in your controller if your response was wrong. Ignoring the possibility of television using such facilities to program the viewers, let's just look at the C++ programming aspects. The new setup would benefit from mutual friendship, with some *Remote* methods being able to affect a *Tv* object, as before, and with some *Tv* methods being able to affect a *Remote* object. This can be accomplished by making the classes friends to each other. That is, *Tv* will be a friend to *Remote* in addition to *Remote* being a friend to *Tv*. One point to keep in mind is that a *Tv* method that uses a *Remote* object can be prototyped before the *Remote* class declaration but must be defined after the declaration so that the compiler will have enough information to compile the method. The setup would look like this:

```
class Tv
{
friend class Remote;
public:
        void buzz(Remote & r);
        ...
};
class Remote
{
friend class Tv;
public:
        void Bool volup(Tv & t) { t.volup(); }
        ...
};
inline void Tv::buzz(Remote & r)
{
        ...
}
```

Because the *Remote* declaration follows the *Tv* declaration, *Remote::volup()* can be defined in the class declaration. The *Tv::buzz()* method, however, has to be defined outside the *Tv* declaration so that the definition can follow the *Remote* declaration. If you don't want *buzz()* to be inline, define it in a separate method definitions file.

Another use for friends is when a function needs to access private data in two separate classes. Logically, such a function should be a member function of each class, but that's impossible. It could be a member of one class and a friend to the other, but sometimes it's more reasonable to make the function friends to both. Suppose, for example, that we have a *Probe* class representing some sort of programmable measuring device and an *Analyzer* class representing some sort of programmable analyzing device. Each has an internal clock, and we would like to be able to synchronize the two clocks. We could do something along the following lines:

```
class Analyzer;  // forward declaration
class Probe
{
friend void sync(Analyzer & a, const Probe & p); // sync a to p
friend void sync(Probe & p, const Analyzer & a);  // sync p to ap
    ...
};
class Analyzer
{
friend void sync(Analyzer & a, const Probe & p); // sync a to p
friend void sync(Probe & p, const Analyzer & a);  // sync p to ap
    ...
};

// define the friend functions
inline void sync(Analyzer & a, const Probe & p)
{
    ...
}
inline void sync(Probe & p, const Analyzer & a)
{
    ...
}
```

The forward declaration enables the compiler to know that *Analyzer* is a type when it reaches the friend declarations in the *Probe* class declaration.

Templates and Friends

Template class declarations can have friends, too. We can classify friends to templates as follows:

◀ Nontemplate friends

◀ Bound template friends, meaning the type of the friend is determined by the type of the class when a class is instantiated

◀ Unbound template friends, meaning that all instantiations of the friend are friends to each instantiation of the class

Let's look at examples of each.

First, here's an example of a template with nontemplate friends:

```
template <class Type>
class HasFriend
{
    friend void date();            // friend to all HasFriend instantiations
    ...
};
```

The *date()* function will be a friend to all possible instantiations of the template. For instance, it would be a friend to the *HasFriend<int>* class and the *HasFriend<String>* class.

Suppose we want to provide a class argument to the friend. Can we alter the friend declaration to look like this, for example:

```
friend void date(HasFriend &);         // possible?
```

The answer is no. The reason is that there is no such thing as a *HasFriend* object. There are only particular instantiations, such as *HasFriend<short>*. To provide a class argument, then, we have to indicate an instantiation. For instance, we can do this:

```
template <class Type>
class HasFriend
{
        friend void date(HasFriend<Type> &); // bound template friend
        ...
};
```

This would require that a template function be defined:

```
template <class A>
void date(A &) { ... };
```

This combination of code results in *date<short>()* being a friend to *HasFriend<short>*, and so on. Each class instantiation has one corresponding friend function instantiation. This is an example of bound template friendship. The same technique can be used to create bound template friend classes.

Now suppose we alter the class declaration slightly:

```
template <class Type>
class HasFriend
{
        friend void date(HasFriend<T> &); // unbound template friend
        ...
};
```

The original used the same generic type name (*Type*) in the class heading and in the friend prototype. This time we use a different generic type name (*T*) for the prototype. The effect of this format is to make *all* instantiations of *date()* friends to each *HasFriend* instantiation. That is, *date<int>()*, *date<double>()*, and *date<HasFriend<String> >()* all are friends to *HasFriend<char *>*. This is an example of unbound template friendship. The same technique can be used to create unbound template friend classes.

Can templates be friends to nontemplate classes? No, they can't, but specific instantiations can be:

```
class Pal
{
        friend class HasFriend<long>; // ok
        friend class HasFriend;                // not allowed
};
```

The reason is that uninstantiated template names like *HasFriend* can only appear in templates. Regular code can only use specific instantiations such as *HasFriend<Complex>*.

Nested Classes

In C++, you can place a class declaration inside another class. The class declared within another is called a *nested class,* and it helps avoid name clutter by giving the new type class scope. Member functions of the class containing the declaration can create and use objects of the nested class. The outside world can use the nested class only if the declaration is in the public section and if you use the scope resolution operator. (Older versions of C++, however, don't allow nested classes or else implement the concept incompletely.)

Nesting classes is not the same as containment. Containment, recall, means having a class object as a member of another class. Nesting a class, on the other hand, does not create a class member. Instead, it defines a type that is known just locally to the class containing the nested class declaration.

The usual reasons for nesting a class are to assist the implementation of another class and to avoid name conflicts. The *Queue* class example (Chapter 11, Listing 11-11) provided a disguised case of nested classes by nesting a structure definition:

```
class Queue
{
// class scope definitions
        // Node is a nested structure definition local to this class
        struct Node {Item item; struct Node * next;};
        ...
};
```

Because a structure is a class whose members are public by default, *Node* really is a nested class declaration. However, this definition doesn't take advantage of class abilities. In particular, it lacks an explicit constructor. Let's remedy that now.

First, let's find where *Node* objects are created. Examining the class declaration (Listing 11-11) and the methods definitions (Listing 11-12) reveals that the only place in which *Node* objects are created is in the *enqueue()* method:

```
Bool Queue::enqueue(const Item & item)
{
        if (isfull())
                return False;
        Node * add = new Node;          // create node
        if (add == NULL)
                return False;           // quit if none available
        add->item = item;               // set node pointers
        add->next = NULL;
        ...
}
```

Here the code explicitly assigns values to the *Node* members after creating a *Node*. This is the sort of work that more properly is done by a constructor.

Now that we've found where and how a constructor should be used, we can provide an appropriate constructor definition:

```
class Queue
{
// class scope definitions
        // Node is a nested class definition local to this class
        class Node
        {
public:
                Item item;
                Node * next;
                Node(const Item & i) : item(i), next(0) { }
        };
        ...
};
```

This constructor initializes the node to item value *i* and sets the *next* pointer to *0*, which is one way of writing the null pointer in C++. (Using *NULL* would require including a header file that defines *NULL*.) Because all nodes created by the *Queue* class have *next* initially set to the null pointer, this is the only constructor we need.

Next, we rewrite *enqueue()* using the constructor:

```
Bool Queue::enqueue(const Item & item)
{
        if (isfull())
                return False;
        Node * add = new Node(item); // create, initialize node
        if (add == NULL)
                return False;           // quit if none available
        ...
}
```

This makes the code for *enqueue()* a bit shorter and a bit safer, for it automates initialization rather than requiring that we remember correctly what should be done.

This example defined the constructor in the class declaration. Suppose we wanted to define it in a methods file, instead. The definition must reflect that the *Node* class is defined within the *Queue* class. This is accomplished by using the scope resolution operator twice:

```
Queue::Node::Node(const Item & i) : item(i), next(0) { }
```

Nested Classes and Access

Two kinds of access pertain to nested classes. First, where a nested class is declared controls the scope of the class, that is, it establishes which parts of a program can create objects of that class. Second, as with any class, the public, protected, and private sections of a nested class provide access control to class members. Where and how a nested class can be used depends upon both scope and access control. Let's examine these points further.

Scope

If the nested class is declared in a private section of a second class, it is known only to that second class. This applies, for instance, to the *Node* class we just nested in the *Queue* declaration. (It may appear that *Node* was defined before the private section, but remember that private is the default access for classes.) Hence, *Queue* members can use *Node* objects and pointers to *Node* objects, but other parts of a program won't even know that the *Node* class exists. If we were to derive a class from *Queue*, *Node* would be invisible to that class, too, since a derived class can't directly access the private parts of a base class.

If the nested class is declared in a protected section of a second class, it is visible to that class but invisible to the outside world. However, in this case, a derived class would know about the nested class and could directly create objects of that type.

If a nested class is declared in a public section of a second class, it is available to the second class, to classes derived from the second class, and, since it's public, to the outside world. However, because the nested class has class scope, it has to be used with a class qualifier in the outside world. For example, suppose we have this declaration:

```
class Team
{
public:
        class Coach { ... };
        ...
};
```

Now suppose we have an unemployed coach, one who belongs to no team. To create a *Coach* object outside of the *Team* class, we can do this:

```
Team::Coach forhire;   // create a Coach object outside the Team class
```

These same scope considerations apply to nested structures and enumerations, too. Indeed, many programmers use public enumerations to provide class constants that can be used by client programmers. For instance, the classes defined in *iostream.h* use this technique to provide various formatting options, as we've touched upon earlier and will explore more fully in Chapter 15. Table 14-1 summarizes scope properties for nested classes, structures, and enumerations.

Where declared in nesting class	Available to nesting class	Available to classes derived from the nesting class	Available to the outside world
private section	yes	no	no
protected section	yes	yes	no
public section	yes	yes	yes, with class qualifier

Table 14-1 Scope properties for nested classes, structures, and enumerations

Access Control

Once a class is in scope, access control comes into play. The same rules govern access to a nested class that govern access to a regular class. Declaring the *Node* class in the *Queue* class declaration does not grant the *Queue* class any special access privileges to the *Node* class, nor does it grant the *Node* class any special access privileges to the *Queue* class. Thus a *Queue* class object can access only the public members of a *Node* object explicitly. For that reason, our example made all the members of the *Node* class public. This violates our usual practice of making data members private, but the *Node* class is an internal implementation feature of the *Queue* class and is not visible to the outside world. That's because the *Node* class is declared in the private section of the *Queue* class. Thus, although *Queue* methods can access *Node* members directly, a client using the *Queue* class cannot do so.

In short, the location of a class declaration determines the scope or visibility of a class. Given that a particular class is in scope, the usual access control rules (public, protected, private, friend) determine the access a program has to members of the nested class.

Nesting in a Template

You've seen that templates are a good choice for implementing container classes such as the *Queue* class. You may be wondering if having a nested class poses any problems to converting our definition to a template. The answer is no. Listing 14-5 shows how this conversion can be made. As usual for class templates, the header file includes the class template along with method function templates.

Listing 14-5 *queuetp.h*

```
// queuetp.h -- queue template with a nested class
#include "booly.h"

template <class Item>
class QueueTP
{
private:
        enum {Q_SIZE = 10};
        // Node is a nested class declaration
        class Node
        {
        public:
                Item item;
                Node * next;
                Node(const Item & i):item(i), next(0){ }
        };
        Node * front;           // pointer to front of Queue
        Node * rear;            // pointer to rear of Queue
        int items;              // current number of items in Queue
        const int qsize;        // maximum number of items in Queue
```

continued on next page

continued from previous page

```
        QueueTP(const QueueTP & q) : qsize(0) {}
        QueueTP & operator=(const QueueTP & q) { return *this; }
public:
        QueueTP(int qs = Q_SIZE);
        ~QueueTP();
        Bool isempty() const
        {
                return items == 0 ? True : False;
        }
        Bool isfull() const
        {
                return items == qsize ? True : False;
        }
        int queuecount() const
        {
                return items;
        }
        Bool enqueue(const Item &item);      // add item to end
        Bool dequeue(Item &item);    // remove item from front
};

// QueueTP methods
template <class Item>
QueueTP<Item>::QueueTP(int qs) : qsize(qs)
{
        front = rear = NULL;
        items = 0;
}

template <class Item>
QueueTP<Item>::~QueueTP()
{
        Node * temp;
        while (front != NULL) // while queue is not yet empty
        {
                temp = front;          // save address of front item
                front = front->next;// reset pointer to next item
                delete temp;           // delete former front
        }
}

// Add item to queue
template <class Item>
Bool QueueTP<Item>::enqueue(const Item & item)
{
        if (isfull())
                return False;
        Node * add = new Node(item); // create node
        if (add == NULL)
                return False;              // quit if none available
        items++;
        if (front == NULL)                 // if queue is empty,
                front = add;               // place item at front
```

```
        else
                rear->next = add;     // else place at rear
        rear = add;                   // have rear point to new node
        return True;
}

// Place front item into item variable and remove from queue
template <class Item>
Bool QueueTP<Item>::dequeue(Item & item)
{
        if (front == NULL)
                return False;
        item = front->item;           // set item to first item in queue
        items--;
        Node * temp = front;          // save location of first item
        front = front->next;          // reset front to next item
        delete temp;                  // delete former first item
        if (items == 0)
                rear = NULL;
        return True;
}
```

One interesting thing about this template is that *Node* is defined in terms of the generic type *Item*. Thus, a declaration like

```
QueueTp<double> dq;
```

leads to a *Node* defined to hold type *double* values, while

```
QueueTp<char> cq;
```

leads to a *Node* defined to hold type *char* values. These two *Node* classes are defined in two separate *QueueTP* classes, so there is no name conflict between the two. That is, one node is type *QueueTP<double>::Node* and the other is type *QueueTP<char>::Node*.

Listing 14-6 offers a short program for testing the new class. It creates a queue of *String* objects, so it should be compiled in conjunction with *strng2.cpp* (Chapter 11).

Listing 14-6 *nested.cpp*

```
// nested.cpp -- use queue having a nested class
// compile along with strng2.cpp
#include <iostream.h>
#include "strng2.h"
#include "queuetp.h"

int main(void)
{
        QueueTP<String> cs(5);
        String temp;

        while(!cs.isfull())
```

continued on next page

continued from previous page

```
        {
                cout << "Please enter your name. You will be "
                        "served in the order of arrival.\n"
                        "name: ";
                cin >> temp;
                cs.enqueue(temp);
        }
        cout << "The queue is full. Processing begins!\n";

        while (!cs.isempty())
        {
                cs.dequeue(temp);
                cout << "Now processing " << temp << "...\n";
        }
        return 0;
}
```

Here is a sample run:

```
Please enter your name. You will be served in the order of arrival.
name: Kinsey Millhone
Please enter your name. You will be served in the order of arrival.
name: Adam Dalgliesh
Please enter your name. You will be served in the order of arrival.
name: Andrew Dalziel
Please enter your name. You will be served in the order of arrival.
name: Kay Scarpetta
Please enter your name. You will be served in the order of arrival.
name: Richard Jury
The queue is full. Processing begins!
Now processing Kinsey Millhone...
Now processing Adam Dalgliesh...
Now processing Andrew Dalziel...
Now processing Kay Scarpetta...
Now processing Richard Jury...
```

Exceptions

Programs sometimes encounter runtime problems that prevent the program from continuing normally. For example, a program may try to open an unavailable file, or it may request more memory than is available, or it may encounter values it cannot abide. Usually, programmers try to anticipate such calamities. C++ *exceptions* provide a powerful and flexible tool for dealing with these situations. Exceptions were added to C++ recently, and not all compilers have implemented them yet.

Before examining exceptions, let's look at some of the more rudimentary options available to the programmer. As a test case, we'll take a function that calculates the harmonic mean of two numbers. The harmonic mean of two numbers is defined as the inverse of the average of the inverses. This can be reduced to the following expression:

$$2.0 * x * y / (x + y)$$

Note that if *y* is the negative of *x*, this formula results in division by zero, a rather undesirable operation. One way to handle this is to have the function call the *abort()* function if one argument is the negative of the other. The *abort()* function has its prototype in the *stdlib.h* header file. A typical implementation, if called, sends a message like "abnormal program termination" to the standard error stream (the same as the one used by *cerr*) and terminates the program. It also returns an implementation-dependent value indicating failure to the operating system or, if the program was initiated by another program, to the parent process. Whether *abort()* flushes file buffers depends upon the implementation. If you prefer, you can use *exit()*, which does flush file buffers. Listing 14-7 shows a short program using *abort()*.

Listing 14-7 *error1.cpp*

```
//error1.cpp -- use the abort() function
#include <iostream.h>
#include <stdlib.h>
double hmean(double a, double b);

int main(void)
{
        double x, y, z;

        cout << "Enter two numbers: ";
        while (cin >> x >> y)
        {
                z = hmean(x,y);
                cout << "Harmonic mean of " << x << " and " << y
                        << " is " << z << "\n";
                cout << "Enter next set of numbers <q to quit>: ";
        }
        cout << "Bye!\n";
        return 0;
}

double hmean(double a, double b)
{
        if (a == -b)
        {
                cout << "untenable arguments to hmean()\n";
                abort();
        }
        return 2.0 * a * b / (a + b);
}
```

Here's a sample run:

```
Enter two numbers: 3 6
Harmonic mean of 3 and 6 is 4
Enter next set of numbers <q to quit>: 10 -10
untenable arguments to hmean()
abnormal program termination
```

Note that calling the *abort()* function from *hmean()* terminates the program directly without returning first to *main()*.

The program could avoid aborting by checking the values of *x* and *y* before calling the *hmean()* function. However, it's not safe to rely upon a program to know (or care) enough to perform such a check.

A more flexible approach than aborting is to use a function's return value to indicate a problem. For example, the *get()* member of the *ostream* class ordinarily returns the ASCII code for the next input character, but it returns the special value EOF if it encounters the end of a file. This approach doesn't work for *hmean()*. Any numeric value could be a valid return value, so there's no special value available to indicate a problem. In this kind of situation, you can use a pointer argument or reference argument to get a value back to the calling program and use the function return value to indicate success or failure. The *istream* family of overloaded >> operators use a variant of this technique. By informing the calling program of the success or failure, you give the program the option of taking actions other than aborting. Listing 14-8 shows an example of this approach. It redefines *hmean()* as a *Bool* function whose return value indicates success or failure. It adds a third argument for obtaining the answer.

Listing 14-8 *error2.cpp*

```
//error2.cpp __ return an error code
#include <iostream.h>
#include <float.h>
#include "booly.h"

Bool hmean(double a, double b, double * ans);

int main(void)
{
        double x, y, z;

        cout << "Enter two numbers: ";
        while (cin >> x >> y)
        {
                if (hmean(x,y,&z))
                        cout << "Harmonic mean of " << x << " and " << y
                                << " is " << z << "\n";
                else
                        cout << "One value should not be the negative "
                                << "of the other - try again.\n";
                cout << "Enter next set of numbers <q to quit>: ";
        }
        cout << "Bye!\n";
        return 0;
}

Bool hmean(double a, double b, double * ans)
{
```

```
        if (a == -b)
        {
                *ans = DBL_MAX;
                return False;
        }
        else
        {
                *ans = 2.0 * a * b / (a + b);
                return True;
        }
}
```

Here's a sample run:

```
Enter two numbers: 3 6
Harmonic mean of 3 and 6 is 4
Enter next set of numbers <q to quit>: 10 -10
One value should not be the negative of the other - try again.
Enter next set of numbers <q to quit>: 1 -19
Harmonic mean of 1 and 19 is 1.9
Enter next set of numbers <q to quit>: q
Bye!
```

Program Notes

Here, the program design allowed us to continue, bypassing the effects of bad input. Of course, the design does rely upon the user to check the function return value, something that programmers don't always do. For instance, to keep the sample programs short, most of the listings in this book don't check to see if *new* returns the null pointer or if *cout* was successful in handling output.

We could use either a pointer or a reference for the third arguments. Many programmers prefer using pointers for arguments of the built-in types, for it makes it obvious which argument is being used for the answer.

The Exception Mechanism

Now let's see how we can handle problems with the exception mechanism. A C++ exception is a response to an exceptional circumstance that arises while a program is running, such as an attempt to divide by zero. Exceptions provide a way to transfer control from one part of a program to another. Handling an exception has three components:

- Throwing an exception
- Catching an exception with a handler
- Using a try block

You *throw an exception* when a problem shows up. For instance, we'll modify *hmean()* in Listing 14-7 to throw an exception instead of calling the *abort()* function. A throw statement, in essence, is a jump; that is, it tells a program to jump to statements at another location. The *throw* keyword indicates the throwing of an exception. It's followed by a value, such as a character string or an object, indicating the nature of the exception.

You *catch an exception* with an *exception handler* at the place in a program where you wish to handle the problem. The *catch* keyword indicates the catching of an exception. A handler begins with the keyword *catch* followed, in parentheses, by a type declaration indicating the type of exception to which it responds. That, in turn, is followed by a brace-enclosed block of code indicating the actions to take. The *catch* keyword, along with the exception type, serves as a label identifying the point in a program to which execution should jump when an exception is thrown. An exception handler also is called a *catch block*.

A *try block* identifies a block of code for which particular exceptions will be activated. It's followed by one or more catch blocks. The try block itself is indicated by the keyword *try* followed by a brace-enclosed block of code indicating the code for which exceptions will be noticed.

The easiest way to see how these three elements fit together is to look at a short example, such as that provided in Listing 14-9.

Listing 14-9 *error3.cpp*

```
//error3.cpp
#include <iostream.h>
#include <stdlib.h>
double hmean(double a, double b);

int main(void)
{
        double x, y, z;

        cout << "Enter two numbers: ";
        while (cin >> x >> y)
        {
                try {
                        z = hmean(x,y);
                }       // end of try block
                catch (const char * s)          // start of exception handler
                {
                        cout << s << "\n";
                        cout << "Enter a new pair of numbers: ";
                        continue;
                }       // end of handler
                cout << "Harmonic mean of " << x << " and " << y
                        << " is " << z << "\n";
                cout << "Enter next set of numbers <q to quit>: ";
        }
        cout << "Bye!\n";
        return 0;
```

```
}

double hmean(double a, double b)
{
        if (a == -b)
                throw "bad hmean() arguments: a = -b not allowed";
        return 2.0 * a * b / (a + b);
}
```

Here's a sample run:

```
Enter two numbers: 3 6
Harmonic mean of 3 and 6 is 4
Enter next set of numbers <q to quit>: 10 -10
bad hmean() arguments: a = -b not allowed
Enter a new pair of numbers: 1 -19
Harmonic mean of 1 and 19 is 1.9
Enter next set of numbers <q to quit>: q
Bye!
```

Program Notes

The try block looks like this:

```
try {
        z = hmean(x,y);
}       // end of try block
```

If any statement in this block leads to an exception being thrown, the catch blocks after this block will handle the exception. If the program called *hmean()* somewhere else outside this (or any other) try block, it wouldn't have the opportunity to handle an exception.

Throwing an exception looks like this:

```
if (a == -b)
        throw "bad hmean() arguments: a = -b not allowed";
```

In this case, the thrown exception is the string *"bad hmean() arguments: a = -b not allowed"*. Executing the throw is a bit like a executing a return statement in that it terminates function execution. However, instead of returning control to the calling program, a throw causes a program to back up through the sequence of current function calls until it finds the function containing the try block. In Listing 14-9, that function is the same as the calling function. Soon we'll look at an example involving backing up more than one function. Meanwhile, in this case, the throw passes program control back to *main()*. There, the program looks for an exception handler (following the try block) that matches the type of exception thrown.

The handler, or catch block, looks like this:

```
catch (const char * s)          // start of exception handler
{
        cout << s << "\n";
```

continued on next page

continued from previous page

```
        cout << "Enter a new pair of numbers: ";
        continue;
}       // end of handler
```

It looks a bit like a function definition, but it's not. The keyword *catch* identifies this as a handler, and the *const char * s* means that this handler matches a thrown exception that is a string. This declaration of *s* acts like a function argument definition in that a matching thrown exception is assigned to *s*. Also, if an exception does match this handler, the program executes the code within the braces.

If a program completes executing statements in a try block without any exceptions being thrown, it skips the catch block or blocks after the try block and goes to the first statement following the handlers. So when the sample run processed the values 3 and 6, program execution went directly to the output statement reporting the result.

Let's trace through the events in the sample run after the values *10* and *-10* are passed to the *hmean()* function. The *if* test causes *hmean()* to throw an exception. This terminates execution of *hmean()*. Searching back, the program determines that *hmean()*

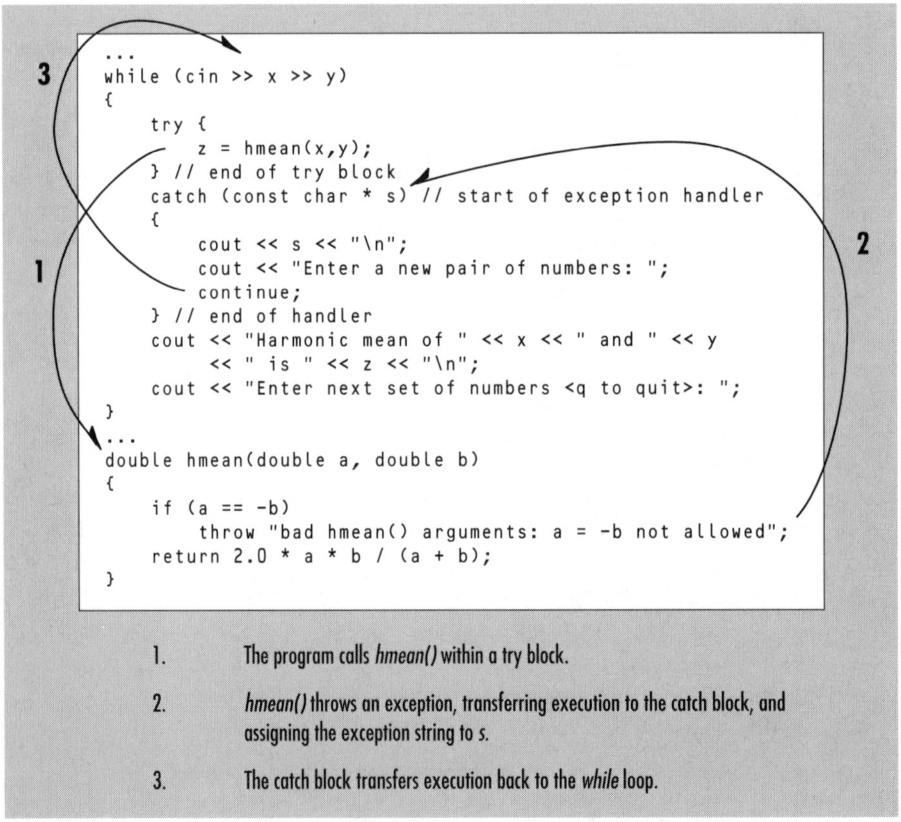

```
3   ...
    while (cin >> x >> y)
    {
        try {
            z = hmean(x,y);
        } // end of try block
        catch (const char * s) // start of exception handler
        {
            cout << s << "\n";
            cout << "Enter a new pair of numbers: ";
            continue;
        } // end of handler
        cout << "Harmonic mean of " << x << " and " << y
             << " is " << z << "\n";
        cout << "Enter next set of numbers <q to quit>: ";
    }
    ...
    double hmean(double a, double b)
    {
        if (a == -b)
            throw "bad hmean() arguments: a = -b not allowed";
        return 2.0 * a * b / (a + b);
    }
```

1.   The program calls *hmean()* within a try block.

2.   *hmean()* throws an exception, transferring execution to the catch block, and assigning the exception string to *s*.

3.   The catch block transfers execution back to the *while* loop.

Figure 14-2 Program flow with exceptions

was called from within a try block in *main()*. It then looks for a catch block with a type matching the exception type. The single catch block that is present does match, for you can assign type *char* * to *const char* *. Detecting the match, the program assigns the string *"bad hmean() arguments: a = -b not allowed"* to the variable *s*. Next, the program executes the code in the handler. First, it prints *s*, which is the caught exception. Then it prints instructions to the user to enter new data. Finally, it executes a *continue* statement, which causes the program to skip the rest of the *while* loop and jump to its beginning again. The fact that the *continue* takes the program to the beginning of the loop illustrates the fact that handler statements are part of the loop and that the *catch* line acts like a label directing program flow. See Figure 14-2.

Uncaught Exceptions

You may be wondering what happens if a function throws an exception and there's no try block or else no matching handler. In that case, the program calls a function called *terminate()*. By default, *terminate()* calls the *abort()* function. In short, throwing an exception without catching it, by default, aborts the program.

You can modify the behavior of *terminate ()* by registering a function that *terminate()* should call. To do this, call the *set_terminate()* function, which has the following prototype:

```
typedef void (*PFV)(); // PFV points to a function returning void
PFV set_terminate(PFV);
```

The *set_terminate()* function takes, as its argument, the name of a function with no arguments and the *void* return type. If you call the *set_terminate()* function more than once, *terminate()* calls the function set by the most recent call to *set_terminate()*.

Let's look at an example. Suppose you want an uncaught exception to cause a program to print a message to that effect and then call the *exit()* function, providing an exit status value of 5. First, design a function that does these two things and has the proper prototype:

```
void my_quit()
{
        cout << "Terminating due to uncaught exception\n";
        exit(5);
}
```

Next, at the start of your program, designate this function as your chosen termination action:

```
set_terminate(myquit);
```

Exception Versatility

C++ exceptions offer a lot of versatility, for the try block lets you select which code gets checked for exceptions and the handlers let you specify what gets done. For example, in Listing 14-9, the try block was inside the loop, so program execution continued inside the loop after the exception was handled. By placing the loop inside the try block, we can make an exception transfer execution to outside the loop, thus terminating the loop. Listing 14-10 illustrates that. It also demonstrates two more points:

❧ You can qualify a function definition to indicate which kinds of exceptions it throws.

❧ A catch block can handle more than one source of exceptions.

Here's how to qualify a function prototype to indicate the kinds of exceptions it throws:

```
double hmean(double a, double b) throw(const char *);
```

This accomplishes two things. First, it tells the compiler what sort of exception or exceptions a function throws. If the function then throws some other type of exception, the compiler will catch the faux pas. Second, it alerts anyone who reads the prototype that this particular function throws an exception, reminding the reader that he or she may want to provide a try block and a handler. Functions that throw more than one kind of exception can provide a comma-separated list of exception types; the syntax imitates that of an argument list for a function prototype. For example, the following prototype indicates a function that can throw either a *const char* * exception or a *double* exception:

```
double multi_err(double z) throw(const char *, double);
```

The same information that appears in a prototype, as you can see in Listing 14-10, also should appear in the function definition.

Listing 14-10, as mentioned earlier, places the entire *while* loop inside the try block. It also adds a second exception-throwing function, *gmean()*. This function returns the geometric mean of two numbers, which is defined as the square root of their product. This function isn't defined for negative arguments, which provides grounds for throwing an exception. Like *hmean()*, *gmean()* throws a string-type exception, so the same catch block will catch exceptions from either of these two functions.

Listing 14-10 *error4.cpp*

```
//error4.cpp
#include <iostream.h>
#include <stdlib.h>
#include <math.h> // for sqrt(); unix users may need -lm flag
double hmean(double a, double b) throw(const char *);
double gmean(double a, double b) throw(const char *);

int main(void)
{
        double x, y, z;
```

```
                cout << "Enter two numbers: ";
                try {
                        while (cin >> x >> y)
                        {
                                z = hmean(x,y);
                                cout << "Harmonic mean of " << x << " and " << y
                                        << " is " << z << "\n";
                                cout << "Geometric mean of " << x << " and " << y
                                        << " is " << gmean(x,y) << "\n";
                                cout << "Enter next set of numbers <q to quit>: ";
                        }
                } // end of try block
                catch (const char * s)        // start of catch block
                {
                        cout << s << "\n";
                        cout << "Sorry, you don't get to play any more. ";
                }       // end of catch block
                cout << "Bye!\n";
                return 0;
        }

double hmean(double a, double b) throw(const char *)
{
        if (a == -b)
                throw "bad hmean() arguments: a = -b not allowed";
        return 2.0 * a * b / (a + b);
}

double gmean(double a, double b) throw(const char *)
{
        if (a < 0 || b < 0)
                throw "bad gmean() arguments: negative values not allowed";
        return sqrt(a * b);
}
```

Here's a sample run that gets terminated by bad input for the *hmean()* function:

```
Enter two numbers: 1 100
Harmonic mean of 1 and 100 is 1.9802
Geometric mean of 1 and 100 is 10
Enter next set of numbers <q to quit>: 10 -10
bad hmean() arguments: a = -b not allowed
Sorry, you don't get to play any more. Bye!
```

Because the exception handler is outside the loop, bad input terminates the loop. After the program finishes the code in the handler, it proceeds to the next line in the program, which prints *Bye!*.

For comparison, here's a sample run that gets terminated by bad input for the *gmean()* function:

```
Enter two numbers: 1 100
Harmonic mean of 1 and 100 is 1.9802
Geometric mean of 1 and 100 is 10
```

continued on next page

continued from previous page

```
Enter next set of numbers <q to quit>: 3 -15
Harmonic mean of 3 and -15 is 7.5
bad gmean() arguments: negative values not allowed
Sorry, you don't get to play any more. Bye!
```

The message reveals which exception was handled.

Multiple Try Blocks

You have many choices about setting up try blocks. For example, you could handle the two function calls individually, placing each within its own try block. That allows you to program a different response for the two possible exceptions, as the following code shows:

```
while (cin >> x >> y)
{
    try {   // try block #1
        z = hmean(x,y);
    }       // end of try block
    catch (const char * s)      // start of catch block #1
    {
        cout << s << "\n";
        cout << "Enter a new pair of numbers: ";
        continue;
    }       // end of catch block #1
    cout << "Harmonic mean of " << x << " and " << y
        << " is " << z << "\n";
    try {   // try block #2
        z = gmean(x,y);
    }       // end of try block #2
    catch (const char * s)      // start of catch block #2
    {
        cout << s << "\n";
        cout << "Data entry terminated!\n";
        break;
    }       // end of catch block #2
    cout << "Enter next set of numbers <q to quit>: ";
}
```

Another possibility is to nest try blocks, as the next sample shows:

```
try {   // outer try block
    while (cin >> x >> y)
    {
    try {   // inner try block
        z = hmean(x,y);
    }               // end of inner try block
    catch (const char * s)
    {
        cout << s << "\n";
        cout << "Enter a new pair of numbers: ";
        continue;
    }       // end of inner catch block
```

```
            cout << "Harmonic mean of " << x << " and " << y
                    << " is " << z << "\n";
            cout << "Geometric mean of " << x << " and " << y
                    << " is " << gmean(x,y) << "\n";
            cout << "Enter next set of numbers <q to quit>: ";
        }
} // end of outer try block
catch (const char * s)
{
        cout << s << "\n";
        cout << "Sorry, you don't get to play any more. ";
}       end of outer catch block
```

Here an exception thrown by *hmean()* gets caught by the inner exception handler, which allows the loop to continue. But an exception thrown by *gmean()* gets caught by the outer exception handler, which terminates the loop.

Unwinding the Stack

Suppose a try block doesn't contain a direct call to a function throwing an exception but that it calls a function that calls a function that throws an exception. Execution still jumps from the function in which the exception is thrown to the function containing the try block and handlers. Doing so involves *unwinding the stack,* which we'll discuss now.

First, let's look at how C++ normally handles function calls and returns. C++ typically handles function calls by placing information on a stack (Chapter 8). In particular, a program places a return address in the calling function on the stack along with any function arguments, which are treated as automatic variables. If the called function creates any new automatic variables, they, too, are added to the stack. If a called function calls another function, its information is added to the stack, and so on. When a function terminates, program execution passes to the address stored when the function was called, and the top of the stack is freed. Thus a function normally returns to the function that called it, and so on, with each function liberating its automatic variables as it terminates. If an automatic variable is a class object, then the class destructor, if any, is called.

Now suppose a function terminates via an exception throw instead of via a return call. Again, the program frees memory from the stack. But instead of stopping at the first return address on the stack, the program continues freeing the stack until it reaches a return address that resides in a try block. See Figure 14-3. Control then passes to the exception handlers at the end of the block rather than to the first statement following the function call. This is the process called unwinding the stack. One very important feature is that, just as with function returns, the class destructors are called for any automatic class objects on the stack.

Listing 14-11 provides an example of unwinding the stack. In it, *main()* calls *details()*, and *details()* calls *hmean()*. When *hmean()* throws an exception, control

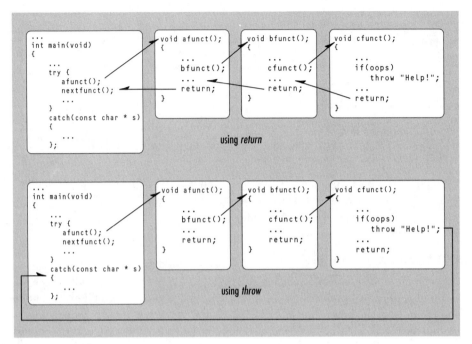

Figure 14-3 *throw* versus *return*

returns all the way to *main()*, where it is caught. In the process, the automatic variables representing the arguments to *hmean()* and *details()* are freed.

Listing 14-11 *error5.cpp*

```
//error5.cpp
#include <iostream.h>
#include <stdlib.h>
double hmean(double a, double b);
void details(double a, double b);

int main(void)
{
        double x, y;

        cout << "Enter two numbers: ";
        try {
                while (cin >> x >> y)
                        details(x,y);

        }
        catch (const char * s)
        {
                cout << s << "\n";
                cout << "Sorry, you can't play anymore. ";
```

```
        }
        cout << "Bye!\n";
        return 0;
}

double hmean(double a, double b)
{
        if (a == -b)
                throw "bad hmean() arguments: a = -b not allowed";
        return 2.0 * a * b / (a + b);
}

void details(double a, double b)
{
        cout << "Harmonic mean of " << a << " and " << b
                << " is " << hmean(a,b) << "\n";
        cout << "Enter next set of numbers <q to quit>: ";
}
```

Here's a sample run:

```
Enter two numbers: 3 15
Harmonic mean of 3 and 15 is 5
Enter next set of numbers <q to quit>: 20 -20
bad hmean() arguments: a = -b not allowed
Sorry, you don't get to play any more. Bye!
```

More Options

You can set up a handler to catch any kind of exception. Also, if a try block is nested, you can have its handlers pass control on up to the handlers for the containing try block.

To catch any exception, use the ellipses for the exception type:

```
catch (...) { // statements }
```

To pass control to a containing try block, use *throw* without a following exception:

```
catch (const char * s)
{
        cout << "Exception caught in inner loop.\n";
        throw;
}
```

This sample, for instance, prints a message, then passes control to the containing try block, where the program once again will look for a handler matching the original thrown exception.

Note that there is more than one way for one try block to contain another. One way is to nest one within another, as we discussed earlier. Another way is for one try block to contain a function call that invokes a function containing a try block. In the first case, the sample code above would pass control to the outer try block. In the second case, the sample code would cause the program to unwind the stack to find the next try block.

Exceptions and Classes

Exceptions aren't just for handling error conditions in regular functions. They also can be part of a class design. For example, a constructor could throw an exception if a call to the *new* operator fails. Or the overloaded [] operator for an array class can throw an exception if an index is out of range. Often it's useful if the exception can carry information with it, such as the value of an invalid index. One could use, say, a type *int* exception in that case, but it's more useful to throw an exception that's an object. The type of object will help identify the source of the exception, and the object itself can carry the needful information.

When exceptions refer to class processes, it's particularly useful if the exception type is defined as a nested class. Not only does this make the exception type indicate the class originating an exception, it helps prevent name conflicts. For instance, suppose we have a class called *ArrayDbE* in which we publicly declare another class called *BadIndex*. If the [] operator finds a bad index value, it can throw an exception of type *BadIndex*. Then a handler for this exception would look like this:

```
catch (const ArrayDbE::BadIndex &) { ...}
```

The *ArrayDbE::* qualifier identifies *BadIndex* as being declared in the *ArrayDbE* class. It also informs a reader that this handler is intended for exceptions generated by *ArrayDbE* objects. The *BadIndex* name gives the reader a pretty good idea as to the nature of the exception. This sounds rather attractive, so let's develop the idea. In particular, let's add exceptions to the *ArrayDb* class first developed in Chapter 12.

To the header file, we'll add two exception classes, that is, classes defining objects to be thrown as exceptions. One, as outlined above, will be a *BadIndex* class. It will be used for bad index values, and it will hold the value of the bad index. The second will be a *NoRoom* class. It will be used when a constructor can't obtain the desired amount of memory, and it will hold the size of the request. Note that these nested class declarations just describe the class; they don't create objects. The class methods will create objects of these classes if they throw exceptions of those types. Also note that the nested classes are public. This allows the catch blocks to have access to the types. Listing 14-12 shows the new header file. The rest of the definition, aside from changing the class name, is the same as the second definition of *ArrayDb* in Chapter 12. However, you could qualify the method prototypes to indicate which exceptions they can throw. That is, you could replace

```
ArrayDbE(const ArrayDbE &a);
```

with

```
ArrayDbE(const ArrayDbE &a) throw(const NoRoom &);
```

and so on. (As with ordinary function arguments, it's usually better to pass references instead of objects when throwing exceptions.)

Listing 14-12 *arraydbe.h*

```
// arraydbe.h -- define array class with exceptions
#ifndef _ARRAYDBE_H_
#define _ARRAYDBE_H_
#include <iostream.h>

class ArrayDbE
{
private:
        unsigned int size;              // number of array elements
protected:
        double * arr;                           // address of first element
public:
        class NoRoom            // exception class for insufficient memory
        {
        public:
                int asked;              // bytes requested
                NoRoom(int i) : asked(i) {}
        };
        class BadIndex          // excepton class for indexing problems
        {
        public:
                int badindex; // problematic index value
                BadIndex(int i) : badindex(i) {}
        };
        ArrayDbE();                             // default constructor
        // create an ArrayDbE of n elements, set each to val
        ArrayDbE(unsigned int n, double val = 0.0);
        // create an ArrayDbE of n elements, initialize to array pn
        ArrayDbE(const double * pn, unsigned int n);
        ArrayDbE(const ArrayDbE & a);           // copy constructor
        virtual ~ArrayDbE();                    // destructor
        unsigned int arsize() const;            // returns array size
// overloaded operators
                // array indexing, allowing assignment
        virtual double & operator[](int i);
                // array indexing (no =)
        virtual const double & operator[](int i) const;
        ArrayDbE & operator=(const ArrayDbE & a);
        friend ostream & operator<<(ostream & os, const ArrayDbE & a);
};

#endif
```

Next, we have to provide the class methods. These are the same methods used in Chapter 12 with the addition of some exception throwing. Because the overloaded [] operators throw exceptions instead of calling the *exit()* function, we no longer need to include the *stdlib.h* file. Listing 14-13 shows the result.

661

Listing 14-13 *arraydbe.cpp*

```cpp
// arraydbe.cpp -- ArrayDbE class methods
#include <iostream.h>
#include "arraydbe.h"

// default constructor -- no arguments
ArrayDbE::ArrayDbE()
{
        arr = NULL;
        size = 0;
}

// constructs array of n elements, each set to val
ArrayDbE::ArrayDbE(unsigned int n, double val)
{
        arr = new double[n];
        if (arr == 0)
                throw NoRoom(n);
        size = n;
        for (int i = 0; i < size; i++)
                arr[i] = val;
}

// initialize ArrayDbE object to a non-class array
ArrayDbE::ArrayDbE(const double *pn, unsigned int n)
{
        arr = new double[n];
        if (arr == 0)
                throw NoRoom(n);
        size = n;
        for (int i = 0; i < size; i++)
                arr[i] = pn[i];
}

// initialize ArrayDbE object to another ArrayDbE object
ArrayDbE::ArrayDbE(const ArrayDbE & a)
{
        size = a.size;
        arr = new double[size];
        if (arr == 0)
                throw NoRoom(size);
        for (int i = 0; i < size; i++)
                arr[i] = a.arr[i];
}

ArrayDbE::~ArrayDbE()
{
        delete [] arr;
}

// return array size
```

```
unsigned int ArrayDbE::arsize() const
{
        return size;
}

// let user access elements by index (assignment allowed)
double & ArrayDbE::operator[](int i)
{
        // check index before continuing
        if (i < 0 || i >= size)
                throw BadIndex(i);
        return arr[i];
}

// let user access elements by index (assignment disallowed)
const double & ArrayDbE::operator[](int i) const
{
        // check index before continuing
        if (i < 0 || i >= size)
                throw BadIndex(i);
        return arr[i];
}

// define class assignment
ArrayDbE & ArrayDbE::operator=(const ArrayDbE & a)
{
        if (this == &a)        // if object assigned to self,
                return *this;  // don't change anything
        delete arr;
        size = a.size;
        arr = new double[size];
        if(arr==0)
            throw NoRoom(size);
        for (int i = 0; i < size; i++)
                arr[i] = a.arr[i];
        return *this;
}

// quick output, 5 values to a line
ostream & operator<<(ostream & os, const ArrayDbE & a)
{
        for (int i = 0; i < a.size; i++)
        {
                os << a.arr[i] << " ";
                if (i % 5 == 4)
                        os << "\n";
        }
        if (i % 5 != 0)
                os << "\n";
        return os;
}
```

Note that the exceptions now are objects instead of strings. Also note that these exception throws use the exception class constructors to create and initialize the exception objects:

```
if (arr == 0)
        throw NoRoom(size);    // create, initialize a NoRoom object
...
if (i < 0 || i >= size)
        throw BadIndex(i);     // create, initialize a BadIndex object
```

Next, let's test the new class. There are two new features. First, the exceptions are objects, not character strings, so the catch blocks have to reflect that fact. Second, we have two distinct types of exceptions to catch, so we'll need two catch blocks. The simplest way to handle this is to place all the uses of an *ArrayDbE* object inside a single try block and to append two catch blocks at the end:

```
try {
        ...
}
catch(const ArrayDbE::NoRoom &) {
        ...
}
catch(const ArrayDbE::BadIndex &) {
        ...
}
```

When there is a sequence of catch blocks, a program attempts to match a thrown exception to the first catch block, then the second catch block, and so on. As soon as there's a match, the program executes that catch block. Providing the code in the catch block doesn't terminate the program or generate another throw; the program jumps to the statement following the final catch block after completing any one catch block in the sequence. Listing 14-14 follows this plan.

Listing 14-14 *exceptar.cpp*

```
// exceptar.cpp -- use the ArrayDbE class
// Compile with arraydbe.cpp
#include <iostream.h>
#include "arraydbe.h"

const int Players = 5;
int main(void)
{
        try {
                ArrayDbE Team(Players);
                cout << "Enter free-throw percentages for your 5 "
                        "top players as a decimal fraction:\n";
                for (int player = 0; player < Players; player++)
                {
                        cout << "Player " << (player + 1) << ": % = ";
```

```
                cin >> Team[player];
        }
        cout.precision(1);
        cout.setf(ios::showpoint);
        cout.setf(ios::fixed,ios::floatfield);
        cout << "Recapitulating, here are the percentages:\n";
        for (player = 0; player <= Players; player++)
                cout << "Player #" << (player + 1) << ": "
                              << 100.0 * Team[player] << "%\n";
    }        // end of try block
    catch (const ArrayDbE::NoRoom & nr)  // 1st handler
    {
        cout << "ArrayDbE exception: "
              << "Insufficient memory for " << nr.asked << "objects\n";
    }
    catch (const ArrayDbE::BadIndex & bi)        // 2nd handler
    {
        cout << "ArrayDbE exception: "
              << bi.badindex << " is a bad index value\n";
    }
    cout << "Bye!\n";
    return 0;
}
```

Note the second *for* loop deliberately exceeds the array bounds, triggering an exception. Here is a sample run:

```
Enter free-throw percentages for your 5 top players as a decimal fraction:
Player 1: % = 0.923
Player 2: % = 0.858
Player 3: % = 0.821
Player 4: % = 0.744
Player 5: % = 0.697
Recapitulating, here are the percentages:
Player #1: 92.3%
Player #2: 85.8%
Player #3: 82.1%
Player #4: 74.4%
Player #5: 69.7%
ArrayDbe exception: 5 is a bad index value
Bye!
```

Because the loop is inside the try block, throwing the exception terminates the loop as control passes to the second catch block following the try block.

The code for throwing a *NoRoom* exception depends upon *new* returning a *0* value (the null pointer) if it can't allot sufficient space. Some newer C++ implementations provide *new* with its own exception throwing. In that case, you would place calls to *new* within try blocks instead of testing for a null pointer value.

By the way, remember that variables defined in a block, including a try block, are local to the block. For example, the variable *player* is undefined once program control passes beyond the try block in Listing 14-14.

Exceptions and Inheritance

Inheritance interacts with exceptions in a couple of ways. First, if a class has publicly nested exception classes, a derived class inherits those exception classes. Second, you can derive new exception classes from existing ones. We'll look at both these possibilities in the next example.

In Chapter 12, we derived a *LimitArr* class from the *ArrayDb* class. Let's parallel that derivation now, deriving a *LimitArE* class from the *ArrayDbE* class. Like the original *LimitArr* class, the *LimitArE* class will allow for array indexing to begin with values other than 0. The *BadIndex* exception declared in the *ArrayDbE* class stored the offending index value. With variable index limits, it would be nice if the exception also stored the correct range for indices. We can accomplish this by deriving a new exception class from *BadIndex*:

```
class SonOfBad : public BadIndex
{
public:
        int l_lim;
        int u_lim;
        SonOfBad(int i, int l, int u) : BadIndex(i),
                                l_lim(l), u_lim(u) {}
};
```

Since the inherited *BadIndex* declaration is in scope in the *LimitArE* class, we can nest the *SonOfBad* declaration in the *LimitArE* declaration. Listing 14-15 shows the result.

Listing 14-15 *limarre.h*

```
// limarre.h -- LimitArE class with exceptions

#ifndef _LIMARRE_H_
#define _LIMARRE_H_

#include "arraydbe.h"

class LimitArE : public ArrayDbE
{
protected:
        unsigned int low_bnd;                   // new data member
        virtual void ok(int i) const;// handle bounds checking
public:
        class SonOfBad : public BadIndex
        {
        public:
                int l_lim;
                int u_lim;
                SonOfBad(int i, int l, int u) : BadIndex(i),
                                        l_lim(l), u_lim(u) {}
```

```
        };
// constructors
        LimitArE() : ArrayDbE(), low_bnd(0) {}
        LimitArE(unsigned int n, double val = 0.0)
                            : ArrayDbE(n,val), low_bnd(0) {}
        LimitArE(unsigned int n, int lb, double val = 0.0)
                            : ArrayDbE(n, val), low_bnd(lb) {}
        LimitArE(const double * pn, unsigned int n)
                            : ArrayDbE(pn, n), low_bnd(0) {}
        LimitArE(const ArrayDbE & a) : ArrayDbE(a), low_bnd(0) {}
// new methods
        void new_lb(int lb) {low_bnd = lb;} // reset lower bound
        int lbound() {return low_bnd;}      // return lower bound
        int ubound() {return arsize() + low_bnd - 1;} // upper bound
// redefined operators
        double & operator[](int i);
        const double & operator[](int i) const;
};

#endif
```

An *ArrayDbE* class constructor throws a *NoRoom* exception if it can't allocate sufficient memory. The *LimitArE* class constructors use the *ArrayDbE* constructors for
memory management, so the *LimitArE* methods don't have to attend to throwing
NoRoom exceptions. However, we do have to arrange for the *LimitArE::ok()* method to
throw a *SonOfBad* exception. Listing 14-16 shows the class methods.

Listing 14-16 *limarre.cpp*

```
// limarre.cpp
#include "limarre.h"
#include <iostream.h>

// private method
        // lower bound for array index is now low_bnd, and
        // upper bound is now low_bnd + size - 1
void LimitArE::ok(int i) const  // variable lower bound
{
        unsigned long size = arsize();
        if (i < low_bnd || i >= size + low_bnd)
                throw SonOfBad(i, low_bnd, low_bnd + size - 1);
}

// redefined operators
double & LimitArE::operator[](int i)
{
        ok(i);
        return arr[i - low_bnd];
}

const double & LimitArE::operator[](int i) const
```

continued on next page

continued from previous page

```
{
        ok(i);
        return arr[i - low_bnd];
}
```

Suppose we have a program with both *ArrayDbE* and *LimitArE* objects. Then we would want a try block that catches the three possible exceptions: *NoRoom*, *BadIndex*, and *SonOfBad*. Here we encounter an interesting new property—a catch block with a *BadIndex* reference can catch either a *BadIndex* exception or a *SonOfBad* exception. That's because a base class reference can refer to a derived object. However, a catch block with a *SonOfBad* reference can't catch a *BadIndex* object. That's because a derived object reference can't refer to a base class object without an explicit type cast. This state of affairs suggests placing the *SonOfBad* catch block above the *BadIndex* catch block. That way, the *SonOfBad* catch block will catch a *SonOfBad* exception while passing a *BadIndex* exception on to the next catch block. The program in Listing 14-17 illustrates this approach.

Listing 14-17 *excptinh.cpp*

```
// excptinh.cpp -- use the ArrayDbE and LimitArE classes
// Compile with arraydbe.cpp
#include <iostream.h>
#include "arraydbe.h"
#include "limarre.h"

const int Years = 4;
const int FirstYear = 1990;
int main(void)
{
        int year;
        double total = 0;
        try {
                LimitArE income(Years, FirstYear);
                ArrayDbE busywork(Years);
                cout << "Enter your income for the last " << Years
                            << " years:\n";
                for (year = FirstYear; year < FirstYear + Years; year++)
                {
                        cout << "Year " << year << ": $";
                        cin >> income[year];
                        busywork[year - FirstYear] = 0.2 * income[year];
                }
                cout.precision(2);
                cout.setf(ios::showpoint);
                cout.setf(ios::fixed,ios::floatfield);
                cout << "Recapitulating, here are the figures:\n";
                for (year = FirstYear; year <= FirstYear + Years; year++)
                {
                        cout << year << ": $" << income[year] << "\n";
                        total += income[year];
                }
```

668

```
        cout << "busywork values: " << busywork;
    }       // end of try block
    catch (const ArrayDbE::NoRoom & nr)  // 1st handler
    {
        cout << "ArrayDbE exception: "
            << "Insufficient memory for " << nr.asked << "objects\n";
    }
    catch (const LimitArE::SonOfBad & bi)       // 2nd handler
    {
        cout << "LimitArE exception: "
            << bi.badindex << " is a bad index value\n";
        cout << "Index should be in the range " << bi.l_lim
            << " to " << bi.u_lim << ".\n";
    }
    catch (const LimitArE::BadIndex & bi)       // 3rd handler
    {
        cout << "ArrayDbE exception: "
            << bi.badindex << " is a bad index value.\n";
    }
    cout << "Total income for " << (year - FirstYear)
        << " years is $" << total << ".\n";
    cout << "Bye!\n";
    return 0;
}
```

Here is a sample run:

```
Enter your income for the last 4 years:
Year 1990: $35000
Year 1991: $34000
Year 1992: $33000
Year 1993: $38000
Recapitulating, here are the figures:
1990: $35000.00
1991: $34000.00
1992: $33000.00
1993: $38000.00
LimitArE exception: 1994 is a bad index value.
Index should be in the range 1990 to 1993.
Total income for 4 years is $140000.00.
```

The *SonOfBad* exception terminated execution of the try block and transferred execution to the second catch block. Once the program finished processing the catch block, it jumped to the first statement following the catch blocks.

The following tip summarizes this example's main lesson.

TIP

If you have an inheritance hierarchy of exception classes, arrange the order of the catch blocks so the most derived class exception is caught first and the base class exception is caught last.

Exceptions and the Future

The main intent for C++ exceptions is to provide language-level support for designing fault-tolerant programs. That is, exceptions make it easier to incorporate error handling into a program design rather than tacking on some more rigid form of error handling as an afterthought. The flexibility and relative convenience of exceptions should encourage programmers to integrate fault handling into the program design process. In short, exceptions are the kind of feature that, like classes, can modify your approach to programming.

Expect new class libraries to incorporate exceptions. Already, the draft version of the ANSI/ISO C++ standard calls for many C++ library functions and some operators, such as *new*, to throw exceptions. Also, the draft standard describes an *exception* header file declaring exception classes to be used by these functions and operators.

Finally, keep in mind that we have described a draft version of exceptions. Several compilers have already implemented exceptions, and the programming community's experiences with them may well lead to modifications before the final standard for exceptions is ready.

RTTI

RTTI is short for *Runtime type* information. It's one of the most recent additions to C++ and, at the time of this writing, isn't supported by many implementations. The intent of RTTI is to provide a standard way for a program to determine the type of object during run time. Many class libraries have already provided ways to do so for their own class objects, but, in the absence of built-in support in C++, each vendor's mechanism typically is incompatible with those of other vendors. Creating a language standard for RTTI should allow future libraries to be compatible with each other.

What's It For?

Suppose you have a hierarchy of classes descended from a common base. You can set a base class pointer to point to an object of any of the classes in this hierarchy. Next, you call a function that, after processing some information, selects one of these classes, creates an object of that type, and returns its address, which gets assigned to a base class pointer. How can you tell what kind of object it points to?

Before answering this question, let's think about why you would want to know the type. Perhaps you want to invoke the correct version of a class method. If that's the case, you don't really need to know the object type as long as that function is a virtual function possessed by all members of the class hierarchy. But it could be that a derived object has an uninherited method. In that case, only some objects could use the method. Or maybe, for debugging purposes, you would like to keep track of which kinds of objects were generated. For these last two cases, RTTI provides an answer.

How Does It Work?

C++ has three components supporting RTTI:

❧ The *dynamic_cast* operator generates a pointer to a derived type from a pointer to a base type, if possible. Otherwise, the operator returns 0, the null pointer.

❧ The *typeid* operator returns a value identifying the exact type of an object.

❧ A *type_info* structure holds information about a particular type.

(Note: These operator and structure names are deemed likely to be the final names, but they are just draft names.) You can use RTTI only with a class hierarchy having virtual functions. The reason for this is that these are the only class hierarchies for which you *should* be assigning the addresses of derived objects to base class pointers.

RULE

RTTI works only for classes with virtual functions.

Let's examine the three components of RTTI.

The *dynamic_cast* Operator

The *dynamic_cast* operator is intended to be the most heavily used RTTI component. It doesn't answer the question of what type of object a pointer points to. Instead, it answers the question of whether you can safely convert a base pointer to a derived class pointer. Let's see what that means. Suppose we have the following hierarchy:

```
class Grand { // has virtual methods};
class Superb : public Grand { ... };
class Magnificent : public Superb { ... };
```

Next, suppose we have the following pointers:

```
Grand * pg = new Grand;
Grand * ps = new Superb;
Grand * pm = new Magnificent;
```

Finally, consider the following type casts:

```
Magnificent * p1 = (Magnificent *) pm;       // #1
Magnificent * p2 = (Magnificent *) pg;       // #2
Superb * p3 = (Magnificent *) pm;            // #3
```

Which of the above type casts are safe? Depending upon the class declarations, all of them *could* be safe, but the only ones *guaranteed* to be safe are the ones in which the pointer is the same type as the object or else a direct or indirect base type for the object. For example, type cast #1 is safe because it sets a type *Magnificent* pointer to point to a type *Magnificent* object. Type cast #2 is not safe because it assigns the address of a base object (*Grand*) to a derived class (*Magnificent*) pointer. Thus the program would expect the base class object to have derived class properties, and that, in general, is false. A *Magnificent* object, for instance, might have data members that a *Grand* object would lack. Type cast #3, however, is safe, because it assigns the address of a derived object to a base class pointer. That is, public derivation promises that a *Magnificent* object also is a *Superb* object (direct base) and a *Grand* object (indirect base). Thus, it's safe to assign its address to pointers of all three types. Virtual functions ensure that using pointers of any of the three types to a *Magnificent* object will invoke *Magnificent* methods.

Note that the question of whether a type conversion is safe is both more general and more useful than the question of what kind of object is pointed to. The usual reason for wanting to know the type is so that you can know if it's safe to invoke a particular method. You don't necessarily need an exact type match to invoke a method. The type can be a base type for which a virtual version of the method is defined. The next example will illustrate this point.

First, however, let's look at the *dynamic_cast* syntax. The operator is used like this, where *pg* points to an object:

```
Superb pm = dynamic_cast<Superb *>(pg);
```

This asks the question, can the pointer *pg* be type cast safely (as described above) to the type *Superb* *? If it can, the operator returns the address of the object. Otherwise it returns 0, the null pointer.

RULE

In general, the expression

```
dynamic_cast<Type *>(pt)
```

converts the pointer *pt* to a pointer of type *Type* * if the pointed-to object (**pt*) is of type *Type* or else derived directly or indirectly from type *Type*. Otherwise, the expression evaluates to 0, the null pointer.

Listing 14-18 illustrates the process. First, it defines three classes, coincidentally named *Grand*, *Superb*, and *Magnificent*. The *Grand* class defines a virtual *speak()* function, which each of the other classes redefines. The *Superb* class defines a virtual *say()* function, which *Magnificent* redefines. See Figure 14-4. The program defines a *getone()* function that randomly creates and initializes an object of one of these three types, then returns the address as a type *Grand* * pointer. A loop assigns this pointer to a type *Grand* * variable called *pg*, then uses *pg* to invoke the *speak()* function. Since this function is virtual, the code correctly invokes the *speak()* version appropriate to the pointed-to object:

```
for (int i = 0; i < 5; i++)
{
    pg = getone();
    pg->speak();
    ...
}
```

However, we can't use this exact approach to invoke the *say()* function, for it's not defined for the *Grand* class. However, we can use the *dynamic_cast* operator to see if *pg* can be type cast to a pointer to *Superb*. This will be true if the object is either type *Superb* or *Magnificent*. In either case, we can invoke the *say()* function:

```
if( ps = dynamic_cast<Superb *>(pg))
    ps->say();
```

Recall that the value of an assignment expression is the value of its left-hand side. Thus, the value of the *if* condition is *ps*. If the type cast succeeds, *ps* is nonzero, or true. If the type cast fails, which it will if *pg* points to a *Grand* object, *pm* is zero, or false. Listing 14-18 shows the full code.

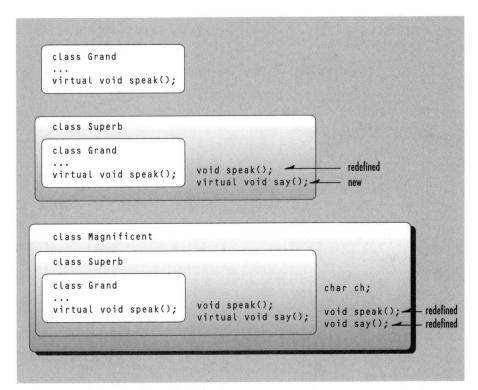

Figure 14-4 The *Grand* family of classes

Listing 14-18 *rtti1.cpp*

```cpp
// rtti1.cpp -- use the RTTI dynamic_cast operator
#include <iostream.h>
#include <stdlib.h>
#include <time.h>
#include <typeinfo.h>

class Grand
{
private:
      int hold;
public:
      Grand(int h = 0) : hold(h) {}
      virtual void speak() { cout << "I am a grand class!\n";}
      virtual int value() { return hold; }
};

class Superb : public Grand
{
public:
      Superb(int h = 0) : Grand(h) {}
      void speak() {cout << "I am a superb class!!\n"; }
      virtual void say()
              { cout << "I hold the superb value of " << value() << "!\n";}
};

class Magnificent : public Superb
{
private:
      char ch;
public:
      Magnificent(int h = 0, char c = 'A') : Superb(h), ch(c) {}
      void speak() {cout << "I am a magnificent class!!!\n";}
      void say() {cout << "I hold the character " << ch << " and the integer "
                                          << value() << "!\n"; }
} ;

Grand * getone();
int main(void)
{
      srand(time(0));
      Grand * pg;
      Superb * ps;
      for (int i = 0; i < 5; i++)
      {
              pg = getone();
              pg->speak();
              if( ps = dynamic_cast<Superb *>(pg))
                      ps->say();
      }
```

```
        return 0;
}

Grand * getone()        // generate one of three kinds of objects randomly
{
        Grand * p;
        switch( rand() % 3)
        {
                case 0: p = new Grand(rand() % 100);
                                break;
                case 1: p = new Superb(rand() % 100);
                                break;
                case 2: p = new Magnificent(rand() % 100, 'A' + rand() % 26);
                                break;
        }
        return p;
}
```

This program illustrates an important point. You should use virtual functions when possible and RTTI only when necessary. Here is a sample output:

```
I am a magnificent class!!!
I hold the character L and the integer 13!
I am a grand class!
I am a magnificent class!!!
I hold the character Y and the integer 88!
I am a superb class!!
I hold the superb value of 57!
I am a grand class!
```

As you can see, the *say()* methods were invoked just for the *Superb* and the *Magnificent* classes.

You can use *dynamic_cast* with references, too. The usage is slightly different, for there is no reference value corresponding to the null-pointer type, hence there's no special reference value that can be used to indicate failure. Instead, *dynamic_cast* throws a type *bad_cast* exception, which is defined in the *exception* header file. Thus, the operator can be used like this, where *rg* is a reference to a *Grand* object:

```
#include <exception> // for bad_cast
...
try {
        Superb & rs = dynamic_cast<Superb &>(rg);
}
catch(bad_cast){
        ...
};
```

The *typeid* operator and *type_info* Class

The *typeid* operator lets you determine if two objects are the same type. Somewhat like *sizeof*, it accepts two kinds of arguments:

◀ The name of a class

◀ An expression that evaluates to an object

The *typeid* operator returns a reference to a *type_info* object, where *type_info* is a class defined in the *type_info.h* header file. The *type_info* class overloads the == and != operators so that you can use these operators to compare types. For example, the expression

```
typeid(Magnificent) == typeid(*pg)
```

evaluates to *1* (true) if *pg* points to a *Magnificent* object and to *0* (false) otherwise.

The implementation of the *type_info* class will vary among vendors, but it will include a *name()* member that returns the name of the class. For instance, the statement

```
cout << "Now processing type " << typeid(*pg).name() << ".\n";
```

displays the name of the class of the object to which the pointer *pg* points.

Listing 14-19 modifies Listing 14-18 so that it uses the *typeid* operator and the *name()* member function. Note that they are used for situations that *dynamic_cast* and virtual functions don't handle. The *typeid* test is used to select an action that isn't even a class method, so it can't be invoked by a class pointer. The *name()* method statement shows how the method can be used in debugging. Note that the program includes the *typeinfo.h* header file.

Listing 14-19 *rtti2.cpp*

```
// rtti2.cpp  -- use dynamic_cast, typeid, and type_info
#include <iostream.h>
#include <stdlib.h>
#include <time.h>
#include <typeinfo.h>

class Grand
{
private:
        int hold;
public:
        Grand(int h = 0) : hold(h) {}
        virtual void speak() { cout << "I am a grand class!\n";}
        virtual int value() { return hold; }
};

class Superb : public Grand
{
public:
        Superb(int h = 0) : Grand(h) {}
        void speak() {cout << "I am a superb class!!\n"; }
        virtual void say()
                { cout << "I hold the superb value of " << value() << "!\n";}
};

class Magnificent : public Superb
```

```
{
private:
        char ch;
public:
        Magnificent(int h = 0, char c = 'A') : Superb(h), ch(c) {}
        void speak() {cout << "I am a magnificent class!!!\n";}
        void say() {cout << "I hold the character " << ch << " and the integer "
                                                << value() << "!\n"; }
} ;

Grand * getone();
int main(void)
{
        srand(time(0));
        Grand * pg;
        Superb * ps;
        for (int i = 0; i < 5; i++)
        {
                pg = getone();
                cout << "Now processing type " << typeid(*pg).name() << ".\n";
                pg->speak();
                if( ps = dynamic_cast<Superb *>(pg))
                        ps->say();
                if (typeid(Magnificent) == typeid(*pg))
                        cout << "Yes, you're really magnificent.\n";
        }
        return 0;
}

Grand * getone()
{
        Grand * p;

        switch( rand() % 3)
        {
                case 0: p = new Grand(rand() % 100);
                                break;
                case 1: p = new Superb(rand() % 100);
                                break;
                case 2: p = new Magnificent(rand() % 100, 'A' + rand() % 26);
                                break;
        }
        return p;
}
```

Here's a sample run:

```
Now processing type Magnificent.
I am a magnificent class!!!
I hold the character P and the integer 52!
Yes, you're really magnificent.
Now processing type Superb.
I am a superb class!!
I hold the superb value of 37!
```

continued on next page

continued from previous page

```
Now processing type Grand.
I am a grand class!
Now processing type Superb.
I am a superb class!!
I hold the superb value of 18!
Now processing type Grand.
I am a grand class!
```

Misusing RTTI

RTTI has many vocal critics within the C++ community. They view RTTI as unnecessary, a potential source of program inefficiency, and as a possible contributor to bad programming practices. Without delving into the debate over RTTI, let's look at the sort of programming that you should avoid.

Consider the core of Listing 14-18:

```
Grand * pg;
Superb * ps;
for (int i = 0; i < 5; i++)
{
        pg = getone();
        pg->speak();
        if( ps = dynamic_cast<Superb *>(pg))
                ps->say();
}
```

By using *typeid* and ignoring *dynamic_cast* and virtual functions, we can rewrite this code as follows:

```
Grand * pg;
Superb * ps;
Magnificent * pm;
for (int i = 0; i < 5; i++)
{
        pg = getone();
        if (typeid(Magnificent) == typeid(*pg))
        {
                pm = (Magnificent *) pg;
                pm->speak();
                pm->say();
        }
        else if (typeid(Superb) == typeid(*pg))
        {
                ps = (Superb *) pg;
                ps->speak();
                ps->say();
        }
        else
                pg->speak();
}
```

Not only is this uglier and longer than the original, it has the serious flaw of naming each class explicitly. Suppose, for example, that we find it necessary to derive an

Insufferable class from the *Magnificent* class. The new class redefines *speak()* and *say()*. With the version that uses *typeid* to test explicitly for each type, we would have to modify the *for* loop code, adding a new *else if* section. The original version, however, requires no changes at all. The

```
pg->speak();
```

statement works for all classes derived from *Grand,* and the

```
if( ps = dynamic_cast<Superb *>(pg))
        ps->say();
```

statement works for all classes derived from *Superb.*

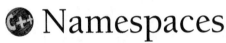

TIP

If you find yourself using *typeid* in an extended series of *if else* statements, check to see whether you should have been using virtual functions and *dynamic_cast*.

Namespaces

Names in C++ can refer to variables, functions, structures, enumerations, classes, and class and structure members. When programming projects grow large, the potential for name conflicts increases. When you use class libraries from more than one source, you can get name conflicts. For instance, two libraries might both define classes named *List, Tree,* and *Node,* but in incompatible ways. You might want the *List* class from one library, the *Tree* from the other, and each might expect its own version of *Node.* Such conflicts are termed *namespace* problems.

C++ storage classes and the class scope concept in particular can help avoid some of these problems. For instance, if the *Node* definitions were nested in the *List* and *Tree* classes, then the qualified names would be *List::Node* and *Tree::Node.* However, the experience of those developing extensive libraries is that class scope isn't a powerful enough tool. The demand for better tools led the ANSI/ISO committee to develop namespace facilities to provide greater control over the scope of names. At the time of this writing, the new namespace facilities haven't yet found their way into the market-place, but the next generation of C++ compilers probably will support them. Meanwhile, we'll take a brief overview of namespaces.

Traditional C++ Namespaces

Before looking at the new facilities, let's review the namespace properties that already exist in C++. This may help make the idea of namespaces seem more familiar. Consider the following code sample:

```
long enough = 93000000;
class Less
```

continued on next page

continued from previous page

```
{
private:
      int ears;
      ...
};
void unless(int imate)
{
      char full;
      Less ismore;
      int ears;
      short enough;
      ...
}
int erior(void)
{
      ...
}
```

You probably recall that names declared outside of any block, that is, outside of any braces, have file scope. Such names are termed external names. The external names *enough, Less, unless,* and *erior* would be recognized anywhere within the file containing this code unless hidden by more localized definitions. Thus, we can define a *Less* object in the *unless()* function, for example. We can't, however, define a function called *enough()* because its name would conflict with the external variable of the same name. We describe this conflict by saying that external names belong to the same namespace, the global namespace.

Names defined within braces, along with names of function formal arguments, have block scope. Thus the variables *imate, full,* and *enough* are known only within the *unless()* function. The *enough* in *unless()* hides the external *enough*. You can, however, use the expression *::enough* to refer to the external variable. We can describe this situation by saying that the two *enough* variables reside in different namespaces and hence don't conflict with one another. Each set of paired braces, then, defines a namespace.

Names defined within a class declaration have class scope and are only known within the class. Thus, the *ears* member of the *ismore* object doesn't conflict with the *ears* variable in *unless()*. Each class defines its own namespace. Therefore the *ears* member of a *corn* class doesn't conflict with the *ears* member of a *jug* class.

Note that namespace is not quite the same thing as scope. Scope describes where in a program a name can be used, while namespace describes when name conflicts arise. One could imagine, for example, designing a language in which function names don't conflict with variable names. That is, you could have an external variable *hubble* and a function *hubble()* in the same file. Both names would have the same scope (file scope), but since they can coexist, we would say they reside in separate namespaces.

New Namespace Features

What C++ is adding is the ability to create named namespaces. The following code, for instance, uses the new keyword *namespace* to create two namespaces, *Jack* and *Jill*.

```
namespace Jack {
    double pail;
    void fetch();
    class List { ... };
};
namespace Jill {
    double bucket() { ... }
    double fetch;
    class Queue { ... };
};
```

The names in any one namespace can't conflict with names in another namespace. Thus the *fetch* in Jack can coexist with the *fetch* in *Jill*, and the *Queue* in *Jill* can coexist with an external *Queue*. The rules governing declarations and definitions in a namespace are the same as the rules for global declarations and definitions.

Namespaces are open, meaning you can add names to existing namespaces. For instance, the statement

```
namespace Jill {
    char * goose(const char *);
};
```

adds the name *goose* to the existing list of names in *Jill*.

Of course, you need a way to access names in a given namespace. The simplest way is to use ::, the scope resolution operator, to qualify a name with its namespace:

```
Jack::pail = 12.34;     // use a variable
Jill::Queue waiting;    // create a Queue object
Jack::fetch();          // use a function
```

Having to qualify names every time they are used is not an appealing prospect, so C++ provides two mechanisms to simplify using namespace names. The first is called a *using-declaration*, which consists of preceding a qualified name with the new keyword *using*:

```
using Jill::fetch;      // a using-declaration
```

A using-declaration adds a particular name to the local scope. For instance, a using-declaration of *Jill::fetch* in *main()* would add *fetch* to the block scope defined by *main()*. After making this declaration, you can use the name *fetch* instead of *Jill::fetch*.

```
namespace Jill {
    double bucket() { ... }
    double fetch;
    class Queue { ... };
};
char fetch;
int main(void)
{
    using Jill::fetch;   // put fetch into local namespace
    cin >> fetch;        // read a value into Jill::fetch
    cin >> ::fetch;      // read a value into global fetch
    ...
}
```

Because a using-declaration adds the name to the local scope, this example would preclude creating another local variable by the name of *fetch* or using a using-declaration to add *Jack::fetch()* to the same scope. Also, like any other local variable, *fetch* would override a global variable by the same name. Placing a using-declaration at the external level adds the name to the global namespace.

The second new mechanism is called a *using-directive*. It consists of preceding a namespace name with the keywords *using namespace,* and it makes all the names in the namespace available without using the scope resolution operator:

```
using namespace Jack; // make all the names in Jack available
```

Unlike the using-declaration, the using-directive does not add the names to the local namespace; it merely makes them available.

```
namespace Jill {
        double bucket() { ... }
        double fetch;
        class Queue { ... };
};
char fetch;
int main(void)
{
        using namespace Jill; // make all Jill names available
        Queue pals;           // create a Jill::Queue object
        cin >> fetch;         // ambiguous
        cin >> ::fetch;       // read a value into global fetch
        cin >> Jill::fetch;   // read a value into Jill::fetch
        ...
}
```

Here, because *fetch* is not added to the local namespace, it does not override the global *fetch*. However, both *fetch* variables are available if you use the scope resolution operator.

Generally speaking, the using-declaration is safer to use because it adds names to the local scope and it shows exactly what names you are adding. The using-directive adds all names, even ones you may not need. Also, the open nature of namespaces means that the complete list of names in a namespace may be spread over several locations, making it difficult to know exactly which names you are adding.

You can create an alias for a namespace. For example, suppose you have a namespace defined as follows:

```
namespace my_very_favorite_things { ... };
```

You can make *mvft* an alias for *my_very_favorite_things* with the following statement:

```
namespace mvft = my_very_favorite_things;
```

You can nest namespace declarations, provided that the nested declarations come at the beginning of the containing declaration:

```
namespace elements
{
        namespace fire
```

```
        {
                int flame;
                ...
        };
        ...
};
```

In this case, you would refer to the *flame* variable as *elements::fire::flame*. Similarly, you could make the inner names available with this using-directive:

```
using namespace elements::fire;
```

Namespaces and the Future

As programmers become familiar with namespaces, common programming idioms will emerge. In particular, many hope that using the global namespace will wither away and that class libraries will be designed using the namespace mechanisms. Indeed, the draft ANSI/ISO C++ standard already calls for placing standard library functions in a namespace called *iso_standard_library*, which has the aliased name of *std*. This namespace would contain various nested namespaces corresponding to specific libraries.

To maintain compatibility with old code, C++ will use new names for the standard header files. The current proposal is to use the *ns* suffix to denote headers using namespaces. For instance, *iostream.ns* will be the new header file for using the *iostream* family of functions. ANSI C (as opposed to C++) headers will also have a *c* prefix added, so *cstring.ns* will succeed *string.h*. These new header files (both C and C++) are termed the *primary* header files. However, C++ will continue to support non-namespace versions of the standard libraries with *secondary* header files. For ANSI C library functions, the secondary header files will have the same names they always did: *string.h, stdlib.h,* and so on. For C++ libraries, however, the draft standard proposes dropping the extension. That is, *iostream.h* will be renamed *iostream*. Thus, the name of the header file will tell you if it is a C or C++ header and whether it uses namespaces or not.

Again, remember that recent additions to the draft standard, such as namespaces, are those most likely to undergo change before the final version of the standard emerges.

Summary

Friends allow you to develop a more flexible interface for classes. A class can have other functions, other classes, and member functions of other classes as friends. In some cases, you may need to use forward declarations and to exert care in the ordering of class declarations and methods in order to get friends to mesh properly.

Nested classes are classes declared within other classes. Nested classes facilitate the design of helper classes that implement other classes but needn't be part of a public interface.

The C++ exception mechanism provides a flexible way to deal with awkward programming events such as inappropriate values, failed I/O attempts, and the like. Throwing an exception terminates the function currently executing and transfers control to a matching catch block. Catch blocks immediately follow a try block, and for an exception to be caught, the function call that directly or indirectly led to the exception must be in the try block. The program then executes the code in the catch block. This code may attempt to fix the problem or it can terminate the program. Uncaught exceptions, by default, terminate a program. A class can be designed with nested exception classes that can be thrown when problems specific to the class are detected.

The RTTI (runtime type information) features allow a program to detect the type of an object. The *dynamic_cast* operator is used to cast a derived class pointer to a base class pointer; its main purpose is to ensure that it's okay to invoke a virtual function call. The *typeid* operator returns a *type_info* object. Two *typeid* return values can be compared to determine if an object is of a specific type, and the returned *type_info* object can be used to obtain information about an object.

The new namespace facility enables programmers to create named namespaces that can hold the names of variables, functions, and classes. Names in one namespace don't conflict with identical names in other namespaces. The scope operator, using-declarations, and using-directives can be used to access names in a given namespace.

Review Questions

1. What's wrong with the following attempts at establishing friends?

a.

```
class snap {
      friend clasp;
      ...
};
class clasp { ... };
```

b.

```
class cuff {
public:
      void snip(muff &) { ... }
      ...
};
class muff {
      friend void cuff::snip(muff &);
      ...
};
```

c.

```
class muff {
      friend void cuff::snip(muff &);
      ...
};
```

```
class cuff {
public:
        void snip(muff &) { ... }
        ...
};
```

2. You've seen how to create mutual class friends. Can you create a more restricted form of friendship in which only some members of class *B* are friends to class *A* and some members of *A* are friends to *B?* Explain.

3. What problems might the following nested class declaration have?

```
class Ribs
{
private:
        class Sauce
        {
                int soy;
                int sugar;
        public:
                Sauce(int s1, int s2) : soy(s1), sugar(s2) { }
        };
        ...
};
```

4. How does *throw* differ from *return?*

5. Suppose you have a hierarchy of exception classes derived from a base exception class. In what order should you place catch blocks?

6. Consider the *Grand, Superb,* and *Magnificent* classes defined in this chapter. Suppose *pg* is a type *Grand ** pointer assigned the address of an object of one of these three classes and that *ps* is a type *Superb ** pointer. What is the difference in how the following two code samples behave?

```
if (ps = dynamic_cast<Superb *>(pg))
        ps->say();       // sample #1
if (typeid(*pg) == typeid(Superb))
        (Superb *) pg)->say();                  // sample #2
```

7. Describe the differences between the actions of a using-declaration and a using-directive.

 # Programming Exercises

1. Modify the *Tv* and *Remote* classes as follows:

    a. Make them mutual friends.

    b. Add a state variable member to the *Remote* class that describes whether the remote control is in normal or interactive mode.

    c. Add a *Remote* method that displays the mode.

      d. Provide the *Tv* class with a method for toggling the new *Remote* member. This method should work only if the *Tv* is in the on state.

Write a short program testing these new features.

2. Modify Listings 14-12, 14-13, and 14-14 to use a template version of the array.

CHAPTER 15

INPUT, OUTPUT, AND FILES

You will learn about the following in this chapter:

- The C++ view of input and output
- The *iostream* family of classes
- Redirection
- *ostream* class methods
- Formatting output
- *istream* class methods
- Stream states
- File I/O

- Using the *ifstream* class for input from files
- Using the *ofstream* class for output to files
- Command-line processing
- Binary files
- Random file access
- Incore formatting

*D*iscussing C++ input and output (I/O, for short) poses a problem. On the one hand, practically every program uses input and output, and learning how to use them is one of the first tasks facing someone learning a computer language. On the other hand, C++ uses many of its more advanced language features to implement input and output, including classes, derived classes, function overloading, virtual functions, and multiple inheritance. Thus, to really understand C++ I/O, you need to know a lot of C++. To get you started, the early chapters outlined the basic ways for using the *istream* class object *cin* and the *ostream* class object *cout* for input and output. Now we'll take a longer look at C++'s input and output classes, seeing how they are designed and learning how to control the output format. (If you've skipped a few chapters just to learn advanced formatting, you can skim the sections on that topic, noting the techniques and ignoring the explanations.)

The C++ facilities for file input and output are based on the same basic class definitions that *cin* and *cout* are, so this chapter uses the discussion of console I/O (keyboard and screen) as a springboard to investigating file I/O.

The draft ANSI/ISO C++ standard includes a description of how the various I/O methods should behave. In some cases the draft standard differs from traditional C++ practices, and this chapter points out those differences. For the most part, the changes instituted by the draft standard serve to make C++ I/O more compatible with ANSI C I/O.

An Overview of C++ Input and Output

Most computer languages build input and output into the language itself. For instance, if you look through the lists of keywords for languages like BASIC or Pascal, you'll see that *PRINT* statements, *writeln* statements, and the like, are part of the language vocabulary. But neither C nor C++ have built input and output into the language. If you look through the keywords for these languages, you find *for* and *if,* but nothing relating to I/O. C originally left I/O to compiler implementors. One reason for this was to give implementors the freedom to design I/O functions that best fit the hardware requirements of the target computer. In practice, most implementors based I/O on a set of library functions originally developed for the UNIX environment. ANSI C formalized recognition of this I/O package, called the Standard Input/Output package, by making it a mandatory component of the standard C library. C++ also recognizes this package, so if you're familiar with the family of C functions declared in the *stdio.h* file, you can use them in C++ programs.

C++, however, relies upon a C++ solution rather than a C solution to I/O, and that solution is a set of classes defined in the *iostream.h* and *fstream.h* header files. This class library is not part of the formal language definition (*cin* and *istream* are not keywords); after all, a computer language defines rules for *how* to do things, such as create classes, and doesn't define *what* you should create following those rules. But, just as C implementations come with a standard library of functions, C++ comes with a standard library of classes. At first, that standard class library was an informal standard consisting solely of the classes defined in the *iostream.h* and *fstream.h* header files. The ANSI/ISO C++ committee has decided to formalize this library as a standard class library and to add a few more standard classes, such as a *String* class. (Most implementations also provide additional, but nonstandard, class libraries.) This chapter discusses standard C++ I/O. But first, let's examine the conceptual framework for C++ I/O.

Streams and Buffers

A C++ program views input or output as a *stream* of bytes. On input, a program *extracts* bytes from an input stream, and on output, a program *inserts* bytes into the output stream. For a text-oriented program, each byte can represent a character. More generally, the bytes can form a binary representation of character or numeric data. The bytes in an input stream can come from the keyboard, but they also can come from a storage device, such as a hard disk, or from another program. Similarly, the bytes in an output stream can flow to the screen, to a printer, to a storage device, or to another program. A stream acts as an intermediary between the program and the stream's source or destination. This approach enables a C++ program to treat input from a keyboard in the same manner it treats input from a file; the C++ program merely examines the stream of bytes without needing to know from where the bytes come. Similarly, by using streams, a C++ program can process output in a manner independent of where the bytes are going. Managing input, then, involves two stages:

- Associating a stream with an input to a program

- Connecting the stream to a file

In other words, an input stream needs two connections, one at each end. The file-end connection provides a source for the stream, and the program-end connection dumps the stream outflow into the program. (The file-end connection can be to a file, but it also can be to a device, such as a keyboard.) Similarly, managing output involves connecting an output stream to the program and associating some output destination with the stream. It's like plumbing with bytes instead of water. See Figure 15-1.

Usually, input and output can be handled more efficiently by using a *buffer*. A buffer is a block of memory used as an intermediate, temporary storage facility for the transfer of information from a device to a program or from a program to a device. Typically,

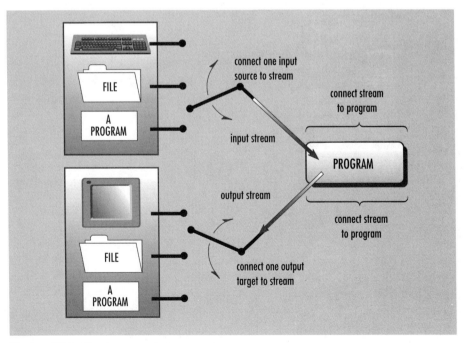

Figure 15-1 C++ input and output

devices like disk drives transfer information in blocks of 512 bytes or more, while programs often process information 1 byte at a time. The buffer helps match these two disparate rates of information transfer. For instance, suppose a program is supposed to count the number of dollar signs in a hard-disk file. The program could read one character from the file, process it, read the next character from the file, and so on. Reading a file a character at a time from a disk requires a lot of hardware activity and is slow. The buffered approach is to read a large chunk from the disk, store the chunk in the buffer, then read the buffer one character at a time. Because it is much quicker to read individual bytes of data from memory than from a hard disk, this approach is much faster as well as easier on the hardware. Of course, once the program reaches the end of the buffer, the program then should read another chunk of data from the disk. The principle is similar to that of a water reservoir that collects megagallons of runoff water during a big storm, then feeds water to your home at a more civilized rate of flow. See Figure 15-2. Similarly, on output, a program can first fill the buffer, then transfer the entire block of data to a hard disk, clearing the buffer for the next batch of output. This is called *flushing* the buffer. Perhaps you can come up with your own plumbing-based analogy for that process.

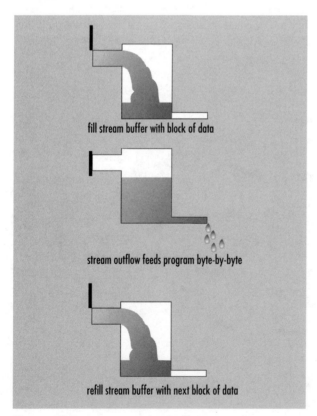

fill stream buffer with block of data

stream outflow feeds program byte-by-byte

refill stream buffer with next block of data

Figure 15-2 A stream with a buffer

Keyboard input provides a character at a time, so in that case a program doesn't need a buffer to help match different data transfer rates. However, buffered keyboard input allows the user to back up and correct input before transmitting it to a program. A C++ program normally flushes the input buffer when you press (ENTER). That's why the examples in this book don't begin processing input until you press (ENTER). For output to the screen, a C++ program normally flushes the output buffer when you transmit a newline character. Depending upon the implementation, a program may flush input on other occasions, too, such as impending input. That is, when a program reaches an input statement, it flushes any output currently in the output buffer. C++ implementations that are consistent with ANSI C should behave in that manner.

Streams, Buffers, and the *iostream.h* File

The business of managing streams and buffers can get a bit complicated, but including the *iostream.h* file brings in several classes designed to implement and manage streams and buffers for you. (Note: The draft ANSI/ISO C++ standard calls for changing the header file name to *iostream* or, for the namespace version, to *iostream.ns*.) Here are some of those classes (also see Figure 15-3):

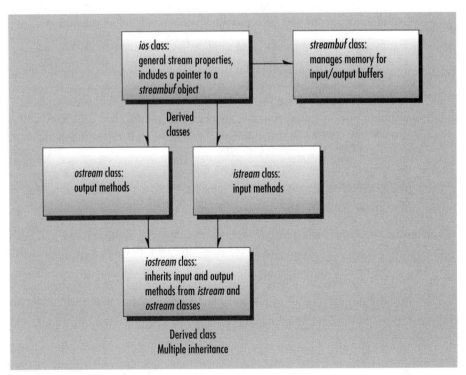

Figure 15-3 Some I/O classes

◀ The *streambuf* class provides memory for a buffer along with class methods for filling the buffer, accessing buffer contents, flushing the buffer, and managing the buffer memory.

◀ The *ios* class represents general properties of a stream, such as whether it's open for reading and whether it's a binary or a text stream, and it includes a pointer member to a *streambuf* object.

◀ The *ostream* class derives from the *ios* class and provides output methods.

◀ The *istream* class also derives from the *ios* class and provides input methods.

◀ The *iostream* class is based on the *istream* and *ostream* classes and thus inherits both input and output methods.

To use these facilities, you use objects of the appropriate classes. For example, use an *ostream* object such as *cout* to handle output. Creating such an object opens a stream, automatically creates a buffer, and associates it with the stream. It also makes the class member functions available to you.

The C++ *iostream* class library takes care of many details for you. For instance, including the *iostream.h* file in a program creates four stream objects automatically:

◀ The *cin* object corresponds to the standard input stream. By default, this stream is associated with the standard input device, typically a keyboard.

◀ The *cout* object corresponds to the standard output stream. By default, this stream is associated with the standard output device, typically a monitor.

◀ The *cerr* object corresponds to the standard error stream, which you can use for displaying error messages. By default, this stream is associated with the standard output device, typically a monitor, and the stream is unbuffered. That means information is sent directly to the screen without waiting for a buffer to fill or for a newline character.

◀ The *clog* object also corresponds to the standard error stream. By default, this stream is associated with the standard output device, typically a monitor, and the stream is buffered.

What does it mean to say an object represents a stream? Well, for example, when the *iostream.h* file creates a *cout* object for your program, that object will have data members holding information relating to output, such as the field widths to be used in displaying data, the number of places after the decimal to use, what number base to use for displaying integers, and the address of a *streambuf* object describing the buffer used to handle the output flow. A statement such as

```
cout << "Bjarne free";
```

places the characters from the string *"Bjarne free"* into the buffer managed by *cout* via the pointed-to *streambuf* object. The *ostream* class defines the *operator<<()* function used in this statement, and the *ostream* and *ios* classes also support the *cout* data members with a variety of other class methods, such as the ones this chapter discusses later. Furthermore, C++ sees to it that the output from the buffer is directed to the standard output, usually a monitor, provided by the operating system. In short, one end of a stream is connected to your program, the other end is connected to the standard output, and the *cout* object, with the help of a type *streambuf* object, manages the flow of bytes through the stream.

Redirection

The standard input and output streams normally connect to the keyboard and the screen. But many operating systems, including UNIX and MS DOS, support *redirection*, a facility that lets you change the associations for the standard input and the standard output. Suppose, for example, you have an executable DOS C++ program called *counter.exe* that counts the number of characters in its input and reports the result. A sample run might look like this:

```
C>counter
Hello
and goodbye!
Control-Z                    ← simulated end-of-file
Input contained 19 characters.
C>
```

Here, input came from the keyboard, and output went to the screen.

With input redirection (<) and output redirection (>), you can use the same program to count the number of characters in the *oklahoma* file and to place the results in the *cow_cnt* file:

```
C>counter <oklahoma >cow_cnt
C>
```

The <*oklahoma* part of the command line associates the standard input with the *oklahoma* file, causing *cin* to read input from that file instead of the keyboard. In other words, the operating system changes the connection at the inflow end of the input stream, while the outflow end remains connected to the program. The >*cow_cnt* part of the command line associates the standard output with the *cow_cnt* file, causing *cout* to send output to that file instead of to the screen. That is, the operating system changes the outflow end connection of the output stream, leaving its inflow end still connected to the program. Both DOS (2.0 and later) and UNIX automatically recognize this redirection syntax. (UNIX and DOS 3.0 and later also permit optional space characters between the redirection operators and the file names.)

The standard output stream, represented by *cout*, is the normal channel for program output. The standard error streams (represented by *cerr* and *clog*) are intended for a program's error messages. By default, all three typically are sent to the monitor. But redirecting the standard output doesn't affect *cerr* or *clog*; thus if you use one of these objects to print an error message, a program will display the error message on the screen even if the regular *cout* output is redirected elsewhere. For instance, consider this code fragment:

```
if (success)
        cout << "Here come the goodies!\n";
else
{
        cerr << "Something horrible has happened.\n";
        exit(1);
}
```

If redirection is not in effect, whichever message is selected is displayed onscreen. If, however, the program output has been redirected to a file, the first message, if selected, would go to the file but the second message, if selected, would go to the screen. By the way, some operating systems permit redirecting the standard error, too. In UNIX, for example, the 2> operator redirects the standard error.

Actually, the *istream* and *ostream* classes don't necessarily provide for redirection. The Borland C++ implementation, for example, derives an *istream_withassign* class from the *istream* class for handling redirection, and *cin* is an *istream_withassign* object. Similarly, the *cout, cerr,* and *clog* objects belong to the *ostream_withassign* class, which is derived from *ostream* in a manner that allows output redirection. Otherwise, these standard objects use the same methods as their respective base classes. For simplicity, we'll refer to *cin* as an *istream* object and *cout* as an *ostream* object.

Output with *cout*

C++, we've said, considers output to be a stream of bytes. But many kinds of data in a program are organized into larger units than a single byte. An *int* type, for example, may be represented by a 2- or 4-byte binary value. And a *double* value may be represented by 8 bytes of binary data. But when you send a stream of bytes to a screen, you want each byte to represent a character value. That is, to display the number -2.34 on the screen, you should send the five characters -, 2, ., 3, and 4 to the screen, and not the internal 8-byte floating-point representation of that value. Therefore, one of the most important tasks facing the *ostream* class is converting numeric types, such as *int* or *float,* into a stream of characters that represents the values in text form. That is, the *ostream* class translates the internal representation of data as binary bit patterns to an output stream of character bytes. (Some day we may have bionic implants to enable us to interpret binary data directly. We leave that development as an exercise for the reader.) To perform these translation tasks, the *ostream* class provides several class methods. We'll look at them now, summarizing methods used throughout the book and describing additional methods that provide a finer control over the appearance of the output.

The Overloaded << Operator

Most often, this book has used *cout* with the << operator, also called the insertion operator:

```
int clients = 22;
cout << clients;
```

In C++, as in C, the default meaning for the << operator is the bitwise left-shift operator (see Appendix E). An expression such as *x<<3* means to take the binary representation of *x* and shift all the bits 3 units to the left. Obviously, this doesn't have a lot to do with output. But the *ostream* class redefines the << operator through overloading to output for the *ostream* class. In this guise, the << operator is called the insertion operator instead of the left-shift operator. (The left-shift operator earned this role through its visual aspect, which suggests a flow of information to the left.) The insertion operator is overloaded to recognize all the basic C++ types:

- *unsigned char*
- *signed char*
- *char*
- *short*
- *unsigned short*
- *int*
- *unsigned int*
- *long*
- *unsigned long*
- *float*
- *double*
- *long double*

The *ostream* class provides a definition for the *operator<<()* function for each of the above types. (Functions incorporating *operator* into the name are used to overload operators, as discussed in Chapter 10.) Thus if you use a statement of the form

```
cout << value;
```

and if *value* is one of the preceding types, a C++ program can match it to an operator function with the corresponding signature. For example, the expression *cout << 88* matches the following method prototype:

```
ostream & operator<<(int);
```

This prototype, recall, indicates that the *operator<<()* function takes one type *int* argument. That's the part that matches the *88* in the previous statement. The prototype also indicates that the function returns a reference to an *ostream* object. That property, as we'll discuss soon, makes it possible to concatenate output, as in the following old rock hit:

```
cout << "I'm feeling sedimental over " << boundary << "\n";
```

If you're a C programmer who has suffered through C's multitudinous % type specifiers and the problems that arise when you mismatch a specifier type to a value, using *cout* is almost sinfully easy. (And C++ input, of course, is *cinfully* easy.)

The *ostream* class also defines insertion operator functions for the following pointer types:

◀ *const signed char **

◀ *const unsigned char **

◀ *const char **

◀ *void **

C++ represents a string, don't forget, by using a pointer to the location of the string. The pointer can take the form of the name of an array of *char* or of an explicit pointer-to-*char* or of a quoted string. Thus all of the following *cout* statements display strings:

```
char name[20] = "Dudly Diddlemore";
char * pn = "Violet D'Amore";
cout << "Hello!";
cout << name;
cout << pn;
```

The methods use the terminating null character in the string to determine when to stop displaying characters.

C++ matches a pointer of any other type with type *void ** and prints a numerical representation of the address. If you want the address of the string, you have to type cast it to another type.

```
int eggs = 12;
char * amount = "dozen";
cout << &eggs;              // prints address of eggs variable
cout << amount;            // prints the string "dozen"
cout << (void *) amount;   // prints the address of the amount
                           // variable
```

Note: Not all current C++ implementations have a prototype with the *void ** argument. In that case, you have to type cast a pointer to *unsigned* or, perhaps, *unsigned long,* if you wish to print the value.

Output Concatenation

All the incarnations of the insertion operator are defined to return type *ostream &.* That is, the prototypes have this form:

```
ostream & operator<<(typename);
```

(Here, *typename* is the type to be displayed.) The *ostream &* return type means that using this operator returns a reference to an *ostream* object. Which object? The function definitions say that the reference is to the object used to evoke the operator. In other words, an operator function's return value is the same object that evokes the operator. For example, *cout* << *"potluck"* returns the *cout* object. That's the feature that lets us concatenate output using insertion. For instance, consider the following statement:

```
cout << "We have " << count << " unhatched chickens.\n";
```

The expression *cout* << *"We have "* displays the string and returns the *cout* object, reducing the statement to the following:

```
cout << count << " unhatched chickens.\n";
```

Then the expression *cout* << *count* displays the value of the *count* variable and returns *cout,* which then can handle the final argument in the statement. Also see Figure 15-4.

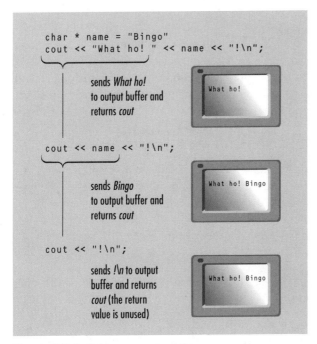

Figure 15-4 Output concatenation

This design technique really is a nice feature, which is why our examples of overloading the << operator in the previous chapters shamelessly imitate it.

The Other *ostream* Methods

Besides the various *operator<<()* functions, the *ostream* class provides the *put()* method for displaying characters and the *write()* method for displaying strings.

The *put()* method seems to be evolving. Traditionally it had the following prototype:

```
ostream & put(char);
```

You invoke it using the usual class method notation:

```
cout.put('W');        // display the W character
```

Here *cout* is the invoking object and *put()* is the class member function. Like the << operator functions, this function returns a reference to the invoking object, so you can concatenate output with it:

```
cout.put('I').put('t');       // displaying It with two put() calls
```

The function call *cout.put('I')* returns *cout*, which then acts as the invoking object for the *put('t')* call.

However, at the time of this writing, the draft standard calls for the following prototype:

```
int put(char);
```

In this incarnation, it returns the value of the displayed value instead of an *ostream* object, so it can't be concatenated.

You can use *put()* with arguments of numeric types other than *char*, such as *int*, and let function prototyping automatically convert the argument to the correct type *char* value. For instance, you once could do the following:

```
cout.put(65);                 // display the A character
cout.put(66.3);               // display the B character
```

The first statement converted the *int* value 65 to a *char* value, then displayed the character having 65 as its ASCII code. Similarly, the second statement converted the type *double* value 66.3 to a type *char* 66 and displayed the corresponding character.

This behavior came in handy prior to Release 2.0 C++, for then the language represented character constants with type *int* values. Thus, a statement such as

```
cout << 'W';
```

would interpret 'W' as an *int* value, hence display it as the integer 87, the ASCII value for the character. But the statement

```
cout.put('W');
```

worked fine. Because current C++ represents *char* constants as type *char*, you now can use either method.

COMPATIBILITY NOTE

Some current compilers, including Microsoft Visual C++ 1.0 and Borland C++ 4.0, overload *put()* for three argument types: *char, unsigned char,* and *signed char.* This makes using *put()* with an *int* argument ambiguous, for an *int* could be converted to any one of those three types.

The *write()* method writes an entire string and has the prototypes shown in Listing 15-1. The first argument to *write()* provides the address of the string to be displayed, and the second argument indicates how many characters to display. Listing 15-1 shows how this works.

Listing 15-1 *write. cpp*

```
// write.cpp -- use cout.write()
#include <iostream.h>
#include <string.h>

int main(void)
{
        char * state1 = "Ohio";
        char * state2 = "Utah";
        char * state3 = "Euphoria";

        int len = strlen(state2);
        cout << "Increasing loop index:\n";
        for (int i = 1; i <= len; i++)
        {
                cout.write(state2,i);
                cout << "\n";
        }

// concatenate output
    cout << "Decreasing loop index:\n";
    for (i = len; i > 0; i--)
                cout.write(state2,i) << "\n";

// exceed string length
    cout << "Exceeding string length:\n";
    cout.write(state2, len + 5) << "\n";

    return 0;
}
```

Here is the output:

```
U
Ut
Uta
Utah
Utah
```

continued on next page

continued from previous page

```
Uta
Ut
U
Utah Euph
```

Note that the *cout.write()* call returns the *cout* object. That's because the *write()* method returns a reference to the object that invokes it, and in this case, the *cout* object invokes it. This makes it possible to concatenate output, for *cout.write()* is replaced by its return value, *cout:*

```
cout.write(state2,i) << "\n";
```

Also, note that the *write()* method doesn't stop printing characters automatically when it reaches the null character. It simply prints how many characters you tell it to, even if that goes beyond the bounds of a particular string! In this case, we bracketed the string *Utah* with two other strings so that adjacent memory locations would contain data. We put strings on both sides because compilers differ in the order in which they store data in memory.

The *write()* method can also be used with numeric data. It doesn't translate a number to the correct characters; instead it transmits the bit representation as stored in memory. For instance, a 4-byte *long* value such as 560031841 would be transmitted as 4 separate bytes. An output device such as a monitor would then try to interpret each byte as if it were ASCII (or whatever) code. So 560031841 would appear onscreen as some 4-character combination, most likely gibberish. However, *write()* does provide a compact, accurate way to store data in a file. We'll return to this possibility later this chapter.

Flushing the Output Buffer

Consider what happens as a program uses *cout* to send bytes on to the standard output. Because the *ostream* class buffers output handled by the *cout* object, output isn't sent to its destination immediately. Instead, it accumulates in the buffer until the buffer is full. Then the program flushes the buffer, sending the contents on and clearing the buffer for new data. Typically, a buffer is 512 bytes or an integral multiple thereof. Buffering is a great time-saver when the standard output is connected to a file on a hard disk. After all, you don't want a program to access the hard disk 512 times to send 512 bytes. It's much more effective to collect 512 bytes in a buffer, then write them to a hard disk in a single disk operation. For screen output, however, filling the buffer first is less critical. Indeed, it would be inconvenient if you had to reword, say, the message *Press any key to continue* so that it consumed the prerequisite 512 bytes to fill a buffer. Fortunately, the program doesn't necessarily wait until the buffer is full. Sending a newline character to the buffer, for example, normally flushes the buffer. Also, as mentioned before, most implementations flush the buffer when input is pending. That is, suppose you have the following code:

```
cout << "Enter a number: ";
float num;
cin >> num;
```

The fact that the program expects input causes it to display the *cout* message (that is, flush the *Enter a number:* message) immediately, even though the output string lacks a newline. Without this feature, the program would wait for input without having prompted the user with the *cout* message.

If your implementation doesn't flush output when you want it to, you can force flushing by using one of two *manipulators*. The *flush* manipulator flushes the buffer, and the *endl* manipulator flushes the buffer and inserts a newline. You use these manipulators the way you would use a variable name:

```
cout << "Hello, good-looking! " << flush;
cout << "Wait just a moment, please." << endl;
```

Manipulators are, in fact, functions. For instance, you can flush *cout*'s buffer by calling the *flush()* function directly:

```
flush(cout);
```

However, the *ostream* class overloads the << insertion operator in such a way that the statement

```
cout << flush;
```

gets replaced with the *flush(cout)*; function call. Thus you can use the more convenient insertion notation to flush with success.

Formatting with *cout*

The *ostream* insertion operators convert values to text form. By default, they format values as follows:

- ◀ A type *char* value, if it represents a printable character, is displayed as a character in a field one character wide.

- ◀ Numerical integer types are displayed as decimal integers in a field just wide enough to hold the number and, if present, a minus sign.

- ◀ Strings are displayed in a field equal in width to the length of the string.

The default behavior for floating-point has changed. With older implementations it worked as follows:

- ◀ (Old Style) Floating-point types are displayed with six places to the right of the decimal, except that trailing zeros aren't displayed. (Note that the number of digits *displayed* has no connection with the precision to which the number is *stored*.) The number is displayed in fixed-point notation or else in

E notation (see Chapter 3), depending upon the value of the number. Again, the field is just wide enough to hold the number and, if present, a minus sign.

Newer implementations and the draft standard call for the following behavior:

❧ (New Style) Floating-point types are displayed with a total of six digits, except that trailing zeros aren't displayed. (Note that the number of digits *displayed* has no connection with the precision to which the number is *stored*.) The number is displayed in fixed-point notation or else in E notation (see Chapter 3), depending upon the value of the number. In particular, E notation is used if the exponent is 6 or larger or -5 or smaller. Again, the field is just wide enough to hold the number and, if present, a minus sign. The default behavior corresponds to using the standard C library function *fprintf()* with a %g specifier.

Because each value is displayed in a width equal to its size, you have to provide spaces between values explicitly; otherwise, consecutive values would run together.

There are several small differences between traditional C++ formatting and the draft standard; we'll summarize them in Table 15-3 later.

Listing 15-2 illustrates the output defaults. It displays a colon (:) after each value so you can see the width field used in each case. The program uses the expression *1.0 / 9.0* to generate a nonterminating fraction so you can see how many places get printed, and it shows the draft standard defaults.

COMPATIBILITY NOTE

Not all compilers generate output formatted in accordance with the draft standard.

Listing 15-2 *defaults.cpp*

```
// defaults.cpp -- cout default formats
#include <iostream.h>

int main(void)
{
        cout << "12345678901234567890\n";
        char ch = 'K';
        int t = 273;
        cout << ch << ":\n";
        cout << t << ":\n";
        cout << -t <<":\n";

        double f1 = 1.200;
        cout << f1 << ":\n";
        cout << (f1 + 1.0 / 9.0) << ":\n";
```

```
        double f2 = 1.67E2;
        cout << f2 << ":\n";
        f2 += 1.0 / 9.0;
        cout << f2 << ":\n";
        cout << (f2 * 1.0e4) << ":\n";


        double f3 = 2.3e-4;
        cout << f3 << ":\n";
        cout << f3 / 10 << ":\n";

        return 0;
}
```

Here is the output:

```
12345678901234567890
K:
273:
-273:
1.2:
1.31111:
167:
167.111:
1.67111e+006:
0.00023:
2.3e-05:
```

Each value fills its field. Note that the trailing zeros of *1.200* are not displayed but that floating-point values without terminating zeros have six places to the right of the decimal displayed. Also, this particular implementation (Microsoft Visual C++ 1.0) displays three digits in the exponent.

Changing the Number Base Used for Display

The *ios* class, from which *ostream* derives, stores information describing the format state. For instance, certain bits in one class member determine the number base used, while another member determines the field width. By using manipulators, you can control the number base used to display integers. By using *ios* member functions, you can control the field width and the number of places displayed to the right of the decimal. Because the *ios* class is a base class for *ostream*, you can use its methods with *ostream* objects (or descendants), such as *cout*.

Let's see how to set the number base to be used in displaying integers. To control whether integers are displayed in base 10, base 16, or base 8, you can use the *dec, hex*, and *oct* manipulators. For instance, the function call

```
hex(cout);
```

sets the number base format state for the *cout* object to hexadecimal. Once you do this, a program will print values in hexadecimal form until you set the format state to another choice. Note that the manipulators are not member functions, hence they don't have to be invoked by an object.

Although the manipulators really are functions, you normally see them used this way:

```
cout << hex;
```

The *ostream* class overloads the << operator to make this usage equivalent to the function call *hex(cout)*. Listing 15-3 illustrates using these manipulators. It shows the value of an integer and its square in three different number bases. Note that you can use a manipulator separately or as part of a series of insertions.

Listing 15-3 *manip.cpp*

```cpp
// manip.cpp -- using format manipulators
#include <iostream.h>

int main(void)
{
        cout << "Enter an integer: ";
        int n;
        cin >> n;

        cout << "n      n*n\n";
        cout << n << "      " << n * n << " (decimal)\n";
// set to hex mode
        cout << hex;
        cout << n << "      ";
        cout << n * n << " (hexadecimal)\n";

// set to octal mode
    cout << oct << n << "      " << n * n << " (octal)\n";

// alternative way to call a manipulator
    dec(cout);
        cout << n << "      " << n * n << " (decimal)\n";

        return 0;
}
```

Here is some sample output:

```
Enter an integer: 13
n      n*n
13      169 (decimal)
d      a9 (hexadecimal)
15      251 (octal)
13      169 (decimal)
```

Adjusting Field Widths

You probably noticed that the columns in the preceding example don't line up; that's because the numbers have different field widths. You can use the *width* member function to place differently sized numbers in fields having equal widths. The function has these prototypes:

```
int width();
int width(int i);
```

The first form returns the current setting for field width. The second sets the field width to *i* spaces and returns the previous field width value. That allows you to save the previous value in case you wish to restore the width to that value later.

The *width()* method affects only the next item displayed, and the field width reverts to the default value afterwards. For example, consider the following statements:

```
cout << '#';
cout.width(12);
cout << 12 << "#" <<  24 << "#\n";
```

Because *width()* is a member function, you have to use an object (*cout,* in this case) to invoke it. The output statement produces the following display:

```
#           12#24#
```

The *12* is placed in a field 12 characters wide at the right end of the field. This is called *right-justification*. After that, the field width reverts to the default, and the two # characters and the *24* are printed in fields equal to their own size.

C++ never truncates data, so if you attempt to print a seven-digit value in a field width of 2, C++ expands the field to fit the data. (Some languages just fill the field with asterisks if the data doesn't fit. C++ feels that showing all the data is more important than keeping the columns neat; C++ puts substance before form.) Listing 15-4 shows how the *width()* member function works.

Listing 15-4 *width.cpp*

```
// width.cpp -- use the width method
#include <iostream.h>

int main(void)
{
        int w = cout.width(30);
        cout << "default field width = " << w << ":\n";

        cout.width(5);
        cout << "N" <<':';
        cout.width(8);
        cout << "N * N" << ":\n";

        for (long i = 1; i <= 100; i *= 10)
        {
                cout.width(5);
                cout << i <<':';
                cout.width(8);
```

continued on next page

continued from previous page

```
                    cout << i * i << ":\n";
        }

        return 0;
}
```

Here is the output for Microsoft Visual C++ 1.0:

```
        default field width = 0:
    N:    N * N:
    1:        1:
   10:      100:
  100:    10000:
```

And here is the output for CodeWarrior 4.0:

```
default field width =          0:
N     :N * N    :
1     :1        :
10    :100      :
100   :10000    :
```

The first sample output displays values *right-justified* in their fields. The output is *padded* with spaces. That is, *cout* achieves the full field width by adding spaces. With right-justification, the spaces are inserted to the left of the values. The character used for padding is termed the *fill* character. Right-justification is the default in traditional C++.

The second sample output is *left-justified,* meaning the spaces needed to fill each field are added to the right of the value. At the time of this writing, the draft proposes left-justification as the default.

In either case, note that the program applies the field width of 30 to the string displayed by the first *cout* statement but not to the value of *w*. That's because the *width()* method affects only the next single item displayed. Also, note that *w* has the value 0. This is because *cout.width(30)* returns the previous field width, not the one to which it was just set. The fact that *w* is zero means that zero is the default field width. Because C++ always expands a field to fit the data, this one size fits all. Finally, the program uses *width()* to align column headings and data by using a width of five characters for the first column and a width of eight characters for the second column.

COMPATIBILITY NOTE

The Symantec C++ 6.0 version of *width()* returns the new value rather than the previous value of the field width.

Fill Characters

By default, *cout* fills unused parts of a field with spaces. You can use the *fill()* member function to change that. For instance, the call

```
cout.fill('*');
```

changes the fill character to an asterisk. That can be handy for, say, printing checks so that recipients can't easily add a digit or two. Listing 15-5 illustrates using this member function.

Listing 15-5 *fill.cpp*

```
// fill.cpp -- change fill character for fields
#include <iostream.h>

int main(void)
{
        cout.fill('*');
        char * staff[2] = { "Waldo Whipsnade", "Wilmarie Wooper"};
        long bonus[2] = {900, 1350};

        for (int i = 0; i < 2; i++)
        {
                cout << staff[i] << ": $";
                cout.width(7);
                cout << bonus[i] << "\n";
        }

        return 0;
}
```

Here's the output for a system using right-justification as the default:

```
Waldo Whipsnade: $****900
Wilmarie Wooper: $***1350
```

Note that, unlike the field width, the new fill character stays in effect until you change it.

Setting Floating-Point Display Precision

Traditionally, in C++, floating-point *precision* means the maximum number of digits displayed to the right of the decimal point. At the time of this writing, the draft standard describes precision as meaning the total number of digits displayed, at least for the default modes. The precision default for C++, as you've seen, is 6. (Recall, however, that trailing zeros are dropped.) The *precision()* member function lets you select other values. For instance, the statement

```
cout.precision(2);
```

causes *cout* to set the precision to 2. Unlike the case with *width()*, but like the case for *fill()*, a new precision setting stays in effect until reset. Listing 15-6 demonstrates precisely this point.

Listing 15-6 *precise.cpp*

```
// precise.cpp -- set the precision
#include <iostream.h>
```

continued on next page

continued from previous page

```
int main(void)
{
        float price1 = 20.40;
        float price2 = 1.9 + 8.0 / 9.0;

        cout << "\"Furry Friends\" is $" << price1 << ".\n";
        cout << "\"Fiery Fiends\" is $" << price2 << ".\n";

        cout.precision(2);
        cout << "\"Furry Friends\" is $" << price1 << ".\n";
        cout << "\"Fiery Fiends\" is $" << price2 << ".\n";

        return 0;
}
```

Here is the output in the traditional mode (Borland C++ 3.1):

```
"Furry Friends" is $20.4.
"Fiery Fiends" is $2.788889.
"Furry Friends" is $20.4.
"Fiery Fiends" is $2.79.
```

Note that setting the precision to 2 causes the program to round the value displayed for *price2* to 2.79 (that is, to the nearest cent) instead of merely truncating it to 2.78. Also note that the output still truncates trailing zeros.

Here is output as described in the draft standard (Borland C++ 4.0):

```
"Furry Friends" is $20.4.
"Fiery Fiends" is $2.78889.
"Furry Friends" is $20.
"Fiery Fiends" is $2.8.
```

Note that the third line doesn't print a trailing decimal point. (The dot there is the period at the end of the sentence.)

Printing Trailing Zeros and Decimal Points

Certain forms of output, such as prices or numbers in columns, look better if trailing zeros are retained. For instance, the output to Listing 15-6 would look better as *$20.40* than as *$20.4*. The *iostream* family of classes doesn't provide a function whose sole purpose is accomplishing that. However, the *ios* class provides a *setf()* (for *set flag*) function that controls several formatting features. The class also defines several constants that can be used as arguments to this function. For instance, the function call

```
cout.setf(ios::showpoint);
```

causes *cout* to display trailing decimal points. Traditionally, but not under the draft standard, it also causes trailing zeros to be displayed. That is, instead of displaying *2.00* as *2*, *cout* will display it as *2.000000* (traditional C++ formatting) or *2.* (draft standard formatting) if the default precision of 6 is in effect. Listing 15-7 adds this statement to Listing 15-6.

In case you're wondering about the notation *ios::showpoint*, *showpoint* is a nested enumerated constant (see Chapter 4) defined in the *ios* class declaration. Such constants have class scope, which means that you have to use the scope operator (::) with the constant name if you use the name outside a member function definition. So *ios::showpoint* names an *enum* constant defined in the *ios* class.

Listing 15-7 *showpt.cpp*

```
// showpt.cpp -- set the precision, show decimal point
#include <iostream.h>

int main(void)
{
        float price1 = 20.40;
        float price2 = 19.0 + 8.0 / 9.0;

        cout.setf(ios::showpoint);
        cout << "\"Furry Friends\" is $" << price1 << ".\n";
        cout << "\"Fiery Fiends\" is $" << price2 << ".\n";

        cout.precision(2);
        cout << "\"Furry Friends\" is $" << price1 << ".\n";
        cout << "\"Fiery Fiends\" is $" << price2 << ".\n";

        return 0;
}
```

Here is the output using the traditional formatting (Symantec C++ 6.0). Note that trailing zeros are shown.

```
"Furry Friends" is $20.400000.
"Fiery Fiends" is $2.788889.
"Furry Friends" is $20.40.
"Fiery Fiends" is $2.79.
```

Here is the output using the draft formatting (Microsoft Visual C++ 1.0). Note that trailing zeros are not shown, but the trailing decimal point for the third line is shown.

```
"Furry Friends" is $20.4.
"Fiery Fiends" is $2.78889.
"Furry Friends" is $20..
"Fiery Fiends" is $2.8.
```

How, then, can you display trailing zeros under the draft standard? To answer that question, we have to discuss the *setf()* function in more detail.

More About *setf()*

The *setf()* method controls several other formatting choices, so let's take a closer look at it. The *ios* class has a protected data member in which individual bits (called *flags* in this context) control different formatting aspects such as the number base or whether trailing zeros are displayed. (If you've ever had to set DIP switches to configure computer hardware, bit flags are the programming equivalent.) The *hex, dec,* and *oct* manipulators, for example, adjust the three flag bits that control the number base. The *setf()* function provides another means of adjusting flag bits.

The *setf()* function has two prototypes. The first is this:

```
fmtflags setf(fmtflags);
```

Here *fmtflags* is a *typedef* name for the type (typically *long*) used to hold the format flags. This version of *setf()* is used for setting format information controlled by a single bit. The argument is a *fmtflags* value indicating which bit to set. The return value is a type *fmtflags* number indicating the former value of that bit. You then can save that value if you later wish to restore the original settings. What value do you pass to *setf()*? If you want to set bit number 11 to 1, then you pass a number having its number 11 bit set to 1. The return value would have its number 11 bit set to the prior setting for that bit. Keeping track of bits sounds (and is) tedious. However, you don't have to do that job, for the *ios* class defines constants representing them. Table 15-1 shows some of these definitions.

Constant	Meaning
ios::showbase	use C++ base prefixes (0,0x) on output
ios:: showpoint	show trailing decimal point
ios::uppercase	use uppercase letters for hex output, E notation
ios::showpos	use + before positive numbers

Table 15-1 Formatting constants

Because these formatting constants are defined within the *ios* class, you must use the scope resolution operator with them. That is, use *ios::uppercase,* not just *uppercase.* Changes remain in effect until overridden. Listing 15-8 illustrates using some of these constants.

Listing 15-8 *setf.cpp*

```
// setf.cpp -- use setf() to control formatting
#include <iostream.h>

int main(void)
{
        int temperature = 63;

        cout << "Today's water temperature: ";
        cout.setf(ios::showpos);     // show plus sign
        cout << temperature << "\n";
```

```
        cout << "For our programming friends, that's\n";
        cout << hex << temperature << "\n"; // use hex
        cout.setf(ios::uppercase);    // use uppercase in hex
        cout.setf(ios::showbase);     // use OX prefix for hex
        cout << "or\n";
        cout << temperature << "\n";

        return 0;
}
```

Here is the output:

```
Today's water temperature: +63
For our programming friends, that's
3f
or
OX3F
```

Note that the plus sign is used only with the base 10 version. C++ treats hexadecimal and octal values as unsigned, hence no sign is needed for them. (However, some implementations may still display a + sign.)

The second *setf()* prototype takes two arguments and returns the prior setting:

```
fmtflags setf(fmtflags , fmtflags );
```

This overloaded form of the function is used for format choices controlled by more than one bit. The first argument, as before, is a *fmtflags* value containing the desired setting. The second argument is a value that first clears the appropriate bits. For instance, suppose setting bit 3 to 1 means base 10, setting bit 4 to 1 means base 8, and setting bit 5 to 1 means base 16. Suppose output is in base 10 and you want to set it to base 16. Not only do you have to set bit 5 to 1, you also have to set bit 3 to 0—this is called clearing the bit. The clever *hex* manipulator does both tasks automatically. The *setf()* requires a bit more work, for you use the second argument to indicate which bits to clear, then use the first argument to indicate which bit to set. This is not as complicated as it sounds, for the *ios* class defines constants (shown in Table 15-2) for this purpose. In particular, you should use the constant *ios::basefield* as the second argument and *ios::hex* as the first argument if you're changing bases. That is, the function call

```
cout.setf(ios::hex, ios::basefield);
```

has the same effect as using the *hex* manipulator.

Second argument	First argument	Meaning
ios::basefield	*ios::dec*	use base 10
	ios::oct	use base 8
	ios::hex	use base 16

continued on next page

continued from previous page

Second argument	First argument	Meaning
ios::floatfield	*ios::fixed*	use fixed-point notation
	ios::scientific	use scientific notation
	0	use default (mixed notation)
ios::adjustfield	*ios::left*	use left-justification
	ios::right	use right-justification
	ios::internal	left-justify sign or base prefix, right-justify value

Table 15-2 Arguments for *setf(long, long)*

The *ios* class defines three sets of formatting flags that can be handled this way. Each set consists of one constant to be used as the second argument and two to three constants to be used as a first argument. The second argument clears a batch of related bits, then the first argument sets one of those bits to 1. Table 15-2 shows the names of the constants used for the second *setf()* argument, the associated choice of constants for the first argument, and their meanings. For instance, to select left-justification, use *ios::adjustfield* for the second argument and *ios::left* as the first argument. Left-justification means starting a value at the left end of the field, and right-justification means ending a value at the right end of the field. Internal justification means placing any signs or base prefixes at the left of the field and the rest of the number at the right of the field. (Unfortunately, C++ does not provide a self-justification mode.) Fixed-point notation means using the 123.4 style for floating-point values regardless of the size of the number, and scientific notation means using the 1.23e04 style regardless of the size of the number. Note: You can use a first argument of 0 to restore the default mixed notation.

Under the draft standard, both fixed and scientific notation have the following two properties:

❧ Precision means the number of digits to the right of the decimal rather than the total number of digits.

❧ Trailing zeros are displayed.

Under the traditional usage, trailing zeros are not shown unless *ios::showpoint* is set. Also, under traditional usage, precision always meant the number of digits to the right of the decimal.

To show trailing zeros, use *setf(ios::showpoint)* in older implementations and *setf(ios::fixed, ios::floatfield)* or *setf(ios::scientific, ios::floatfield)* in draft-compliant systems.

The *setf()* function is a member function of the *ios* class. Because that's a base class for the *ostream* class, you can invoke the function using the *cout* object. For example, to request left-justification, use this call:

```
long old = cout.setf(ios::left, ios::adjustfield);
```

To restore the previous setting, do this:

```
cout.setf(old, ios::adjustfield);
```

Listing 15-9 illustrates further examples of using *setf()* with two arguments.

COMPATIBILITY NOTE

This program uses a math function, and some C++ systems don't automatically search the math library. For instance, some UNIX systems require that you do the following:

```
$ CC iomanip.C -lm
```

The *-lm* option instructs the linker to search the math library.

Listing 15-9 *setf2.cpp*

```
// setf2.cpp -- use setf() with 2 arguments to control formatting
#include <iostream.h>
#include <math.h>

int main(void)
{
        // use left justification, show the plus sign, show trailing
        // zeros, with a precision of 3
        cout.setf(ios::left, ios::adjustfield);
        cout.setf(ios::showpos);
        cout.setf(ios::showpoint);
        cout.precision(3);
        // use e-notation and save old format setting
        long old = cout.setf(ios::scientific, ios::floatfield);

        cout << "Left Justification:\n";
        for (long n = 1; n <= 41; n+= 10)
        {
                cout.width(4);
                cout << n << "|";
                cout.width(12);
                cout << sqrt(n) << "|\n";
        }

        // change to internal justification
        cout.setf(ios::internal, ios::adjustfield);
        // restore default floating-point display style
        cout.setf(old, ios::floatfield);

        cout << "Internal Justification:\n";
        for (n = 1; n <= 41; n+= 10)
        {
                cout.width(4);
                cout << n << "|";
```

continued on next page

continued from previous page

```
                      cout.width(12);
                      cout << sqrt(n) << "|\n";
          }

          // use right justification, fixed notation
          cout.setf(ios::right, ios::adjustfield);
          cout.setf(ios::fixed, ios::floatfield);
          cout << "Right Justification:\n";
          for (n = 1; n <= 41; n+= 10)
          {
                      cout.width(4);
                      cout << n << "|";
                      cout.width(12);
                      cout << sqrt(n) << "|\n";
          }

          return 0;
}
```

Here is the output using traditional formatting (Borland C++ 3.1):

```
Left Justification:
+1   |+1.000e+00  |
+11  |+3.317e+00  |
+21  |+4.583e+00  |
+31  |+5.568e+00  |
+41  |+6.403e+00  |
Internal Justification:
+   1|+      1.000|
+  11|+      3.317|
+  21|+      4.583|
+  31|+      5.568|
+  41|+      6.403|
Right Justification:
  +1|      +1.000|
 +11|      +3.317|
 +21|      +4.583|
 +31|      +5.568|
 +41|      +6.403|
```

(Symantec C++ 6.0 interprets internal justification differently. It left-justifies the sign and centers the number in the field.)

Here is the output using draft standard formatting (Metrowerks CodeWarrior CW 3.5):

```
Left Justification:
+1   |+1.000e+00  |
+11  |+3.317e+00  |
+21  |+4.583e+00  |
+31  |+5.568e+00  |
+41  |+6.403e+00  |
Internal Justification:
+   1|+      1.00|
+  11|+      3.32|
```

```
+ 21|+        4.58|
+ 31|+        5.57|
+ 41|+        6.40|
Right Justification:
   +1|       +1.000|
  +11|       +3.317|
  +21|       +4.583|
  +31|       +5.568|
  +41|       +6.403|
```

Note how a precision of 3 causes the default floating-point display (used for internal justification in this program) to display a total of three digits, while the fixed and scientific modes display three digits to the right of the decimal.

The *iomanip.h* Header File

Setting some format values, such as the field width, can be awkward using the *iostream.h* tools. To make life easier, C++ supplies additional manipulators in the *iomanip.h* header file. They provide the same services we've discussed, but in a notationally more convenient manner. The two most commonly used are *setprecision()* for setting the precision and *setw()* for setting the field width. Unlike the manipulators discussed previously, these take arguments. The *setprecision()* manipulator takes an integer argument specifying the precision, and the *setw()* manipulator takes an integer argument specifying the field width. Because they are manipulators, they can be concatenated in a *cout* statement. This is particularly convenient when displaying several columns of values. Listing 15-10 illustrates this by changing the field width several times for one output line.

COMPATIBILITY NOTE

This program uses a math function, and some C++ systems don't automatically search the math library. For instance, some UNIX systems require that you do the following:

```
$ CC iomanip.C -lm
```

The *-lm* option instructs the linker to search the math library.

Listing 15-10 *iomanip.cpp*

```cpp
// iomanip.cpp -- use manipulators from iomanip.h
// some systems require explicitly linking the math library
#include <iostream.h>
#include <iomanip.h>
#include <math.h>

int main(void)
{
        cout.setf(ios::showpoint);
```

continued on next page

continued from previous page

```
        cout.setf(ios::fixed, ios::floatfield);
        cout.setf(ios::right, ios::adjustfield);

        cout << setw(6) << "N" << setw(14) << "square root"
              << setw(15) << "fourth root\n";

        double root;
        for (int n = 10; n <=100; n += 10)
        {
                root = sqrt(n);
                cout << setw(6) << n
                      << setw(12) << setprecision(3) << root
                      << setw(14) << setprecision(4) << sqrt(root)
                      << "\n";
        }

        return 0;
}
```

Here is the output:

```
     N   square root    fourth root
    10        3.162        1.7783
    20        4.472        2.1147
    30        5.477        2.3403
    40        6.325        2.5149
    50        7.071        2.6591
    60        7.746        2.7832
    70        8.367        2.8925
    80        8.944        2.9907
    90        9.487        3.0801
   100       10.000        3.1623
```

Now you can produce neatly aligned columns. Note that this program produces the same formatting with either the traditional or draft implementations. Using *ios::showpoint* causes trailing zeros to be displayed in traditional implementations, and using *ios::fixed* causes trailing zeros to be displayed in draft-compliant implementations. Using *ios::right* makes the output right-justified, overriding the default left-justification of the draft standard. Using *ios::fixed* makes the display fixed-point in either system, and in draft-compliant systems it makes precision refer to the number of digits to the right of the decimal. In traditional systems, precision always has that meaning, regardless of the floating-point display mode.

Table 15-3 summarizes some of the differences between traditional C++ formatting and the formatting described in the January 25, 1994 draft standard. Keep in mind that this is not the final draft, so things may change. One moral of this table is that you shouldn't feel baffled if you run an example program you've seen somewhere and the output format doesn't match what is shown for the example.

Feature	Traditional C++	Draft Standard C++
put()	*ostream* & return value	*int* return value
precision(n)	display *n* digits to the right of the decimal point	display a total of *n* digits in the default mode, and display *n* digits to the right of the decimal point in fixed and scientific modes
width()	right-justified by default	left-justified by default
ios::showpoint	display trailing decimal point and trailing zeros	display trailing decimal point
ios::fixed, ios::scientific		show trailing zeros (also see comments under *precision()*)

Table 15-3 Formatting changes

Input with *cin*

Now it's time to turn to input and getting data into a program. The *cin* object represents the standard input as a stream of bytes. Normally, you generate that stream of characters at the keyboard. If you type, say, the character sequence **1992**, the *cin* object extracts those characters from the input stream. You may intend that input to be part of a string, to be an *int* value, to be a *float* value, or to be some other type. Thus extraction also involves type conversion. The *cin* object, guided by the type of variable designated to receive the value, must use its methods to convert that character sequence into the intended type of value.

Typically, you use *cin* as follows:

```
cin >> value_holder;
```

Here *value_holder* identifies the memory location in which to store the input. It can be the name of a variable, a reference, a dereferenced pointer, a member of a structure or of a class, perhaps a pointer. How *cin* interprets the input depends on the data type for *value_holder*. The *istream* class, defined in the *iostream.h* header file, overloads the >> extraction operator to recognize the following basic types:

- *signed char &*
- *unsigned char &*
- *char &*
- *short &*
- *unsigned short &*

◀ *int &*

◀ *unsigned int &*

◀ *long &*

◀ *unsigned long &*

◀ *float &*

◀ *double &*

◀ *long double &*

A typical operator function has a prototype like the following:

```
istream & operator>>(int &);
```

Both the argument and the return value are references. A reference argument (see Chapter 9) means that a statement such as

```
cin >> staff_size;
```

causes the *operator>>()* function to work with the variable *staff_size* itself rather than with a copy, as would be the case with a regular argument. Because the argument type is a reference, *cin* is able to modify directly the value of a variable used as an argument. The statement above, for example, directly modifies the value of the *staff_size* variable. We'll get to the significance of a reference return value in a moment. But first, let's examine the type conversion aspect of the extraction operator. For arguments of each type in the preceding list of types, the extraction operator converts the character input to the indicated type of value. For instance, suppose *staff_size* is type *int*. Then the compiler matches the

```
cin >> staff_size;
```

to the following prototype:

```
istream & operator>>(int &);
```

The function corresponding to that prototype then reads the stream of characters being sent to the program, say, the characters 2, 3, 1, 8, and 4. For a system using a 2-byte *int,* the function then converts these characters to the 2-byte binary representation of the integer 23184. If, on the other hand, *staff_size* had been type *double, cin* would use the *operator>>(double &)* to convert the same input into the 8-byte floating-point representation of the value 23184.0.

The *istream* class also overloads the >> extraction operator for character pointer types:

◀ *signed char **

◀ *char **

◀ *unsigned char **

For this type of argument, the extraction operator reads the next word from input and places it at the indicated address, adding a null character to make a string. For instance, suppose you have this code:

```
cout << "Enter your first name:\n";
char name[20];
cin >> name;
```

If you respond to the request by typing *Hilary,* then the extraction operator places the characters *Hilary\0* in the *name* array. (As usual, *\0* represents the terminating null character.) The *name* identifier, being the name of a *char* array, acts as the address of the array's first element, making *name* type *char* * (pointer-to-*char*).

The fact that each extraction operator returns a reference to the invoking object lets you concatenate input, just as you can concatenate output:

```
char name[20];
float fee;
int group;
cin >> name >> fee >> group;
```

Here, for example, the *cin* object returned by *cin >> name* becomes the object handling *fee.*

How *cin* >> Views Input

The various versions of the extraction operator share a common way of looking at the input stream. They skip over white space (blanks, newlines, and tabs) until they encounter a nonwhite-space character. This is true even for the single-character modes (those in which the argument is type *char, unsigned char,* or *signed char*), which is not true of C's input functions. See Figure 15-5. In the single-character modes, the >> operator reads that character and assigns it to the indicated location. In the other modes, the operator reads in one unit of the indicated type. That is, it reads everything from the initial nonwhite-space character up to the first character that doesn't match the destination type.

For example, consider the following code:

```
int elevation;
cin >> elevation;
```

Suppose you type the following characters:

```
-123Z
```

The operator will read the -, *1, 2,* and *3* characters, since they are all valid parts of an integer. But the *Z* character isn't valid, so the last character accepted for input is the *3.* The *Z* remains in the input stream, and the next *cin* statement will start reading at that point. Meanwhile, the operator converts the character sequence *-123* to an integer value and assigns it to *elevation.*

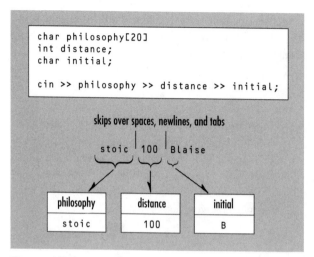

Figure 15-5 *cin* >> skips over white space

It can happen that input fails to meet a program's expectation. For example, suppose you entered *Zcar* instead of *-123Z*. In that case, the extraction operator leaves the value of *elevation* unchanged and returns the value zero. (More technically, an *if* or *while* statement evaluates an *istream* object as zero if it's had an error state set—more on that later.) The zero return value allows a program to check whether input meets the program requirements, as Listing 15-11 shows.

Listing 15-11 *check_it.cpp*

```
// check_it.cpp -- validate input
#include <iostream.h>

int main(void)
{
        cout.precision(2);
        cout.setf(ios::showpoint);
        cout.setf(ios::fixed, ios::floatfield);
        cout << "Enter numbers: ";

        double sum = 0.0;
        double input;
        while (cin >> input)
        {
                sum += input;
        }

        cout << "Last value entered = " << input << "\n";
        cout << "Sum = " << sum << "\n";
        return 0;
}
```

Here's the output when some inappropriate input (-123Z) sneaks into the input stream:

```
Enter numbers: 200.0
1.0E1 −50 −123Z 60
Last value entered = −123.00
Sum = 37.00
```

Because input is buffered, the second line of keyboard input values didn't get sent to the program until we typed *W* at the end of the line. But the loop quit processing input at the *Z* character, since it didn't match any of the floating-point formats. The failure of input to match the expected format, in turn, caused the expression *cin>> input* to evaluate to zero, or false, thus terminating the *while* loop.

Stream States

Let's take a closer look at what happens for inappropriate input. A *cin* or *cout* object contains a data member (inherited from the *ios* class) that describes the *stream state*. A stream state (defined as type *iostate* in the draft standard) consists of the three *ios* elements: *eofbit*, *badbit*, or *failbit*. Each element is a single bit that can be 1 (*set*) or 0 (*cleared*). When a *cin* operation reaches the end of a file, it sets the *eofbit*. When a *cin* operation fails to read the expected characters, as in the example above, it sets the *failbit*. You can determine or modify the stream state with the six *ios* member functions listed in Table 15-4.

Member function	What it does
good()	returns true if the stream can be used (all bits are cleared)
eof()	returns true if the end-of-file (more generally, the end of the input sequence) has been reached (*eofbit* is set)
bad()	returns true if the stream may be corrupted, for instance, there could have been a file read error (*badbit* is set)
fail()	returns true if an input operation failed to read the expected characters or an output operation failed to write the expected characters (*failbit* is set)
rdstate()	returns the stream state
clear(iostate s)	sets the stream state to *s*; the default for *s* is *0* (good)

Table 15-4 Stream states

An *if* or *while* test such as this:

```
while (cin >> input)
```

should test true only if the stream state is good (all bits cleared). If a test fails, you can use the member functions in Table 15-4 to discriminate among possible causes. For example, you could modify the central part of Listing 15-11 to look like this:

```
while (cin >> input)
{
        sum += input;
}
if (cin.eof())
        cout << "Loop terminated because EOF encountered\n";
```

Setting any of these bits has a very important consequence: the stream is closed for further input or output. For instance, the following code won't work:

```
while (cin >> input)
{
        sum += input;
}
cout << "Last value entered = " << input << "\n";
cout << "Sum = " << sum << "\n";
cout << "Now enter a new number: ";
cin >> input;  // won't work
```

If you want a program to read further input after a stream state bit has been set, you have to reset the stream state to good. This can be done by calling the *clear()* method:

```
while (cin >> input)
{
        sum += input;
}
cout << "Last value entered = " << input << "\n";
cout << "Sum = " << sum << "\n";
cout << "Now enter a new number: ";
cin.clear();   // reset stream state
while (!isspace(cin.get()))
        continue;       // get rid of bad input
cin >> input;  // will work now
```

Note that it is not enough to reset the stream state. The mismatched input that terminated the input loop still is in the input queue, and the program has to get past it. One way is to keep reading characters until reaching white space. The *isspace()* function (Chapter 6) is a *ctype.h* function that returns true if its argument is a white space character. Or you can discard the rest of the line instead of just the next word:

```
while (cin.get() != '\n')
        continue;       // get rid rest of line
```

This example assumes that the loop terminated because of inappropriate input. Suppose, instead, the loop terminated because of end-of-file or because of a hardware failure. Then the new code disposing of bad input makes no sense. We can fix matters by using the *fail()* method to test whether our assumption was correct:

```
while (cin >> input)
{
```

```
            sum += input;
    }
    cout << "Last value entered = " << input << "\n";
    cout << "Sum = " << sum << "\n";
    cout << "Now enter a new number: ";
    if (cin.fail())          // failed because of mismatched input
    {
            cin.clear();   // reset stream state
            while (!isspace(cin.get()))
                    continue;      // get rid of bad input
    }
    else    // else bail out
    {
            cout << "I cannot go on!\n";
            exit(1);
    }
    cout << "Now enter a new number: ";
    cin >> input;  // will work now
```

Other *istream* Class Methods

Chapters 3, 4, and 5 discuss the *get()* and *getline()* methods. As you may recall, they provide the following additional input capabilities:

◀ The *get(char &)* and *get(void)* methods provide single-character input that doesn't skip over white space.

◀ The *get(char *, int, char)* and *getline(char *, int, char)* functions provide string input that reads entire lines by default rather than single words.

Let's look at these two groups of *istream* class member functions.

Single-Character Input

When used with a *char* argument or no argument at all, the *get()* methods fetch the next input character, even if it is a space, tab, or newline character. The *get(char &)* version assigns the input character to its argument, while the *get(void)* version uses the input character, converted to type *int*, as its return value.

Let's try *get(char &)* first. Suppose you have the following loop in a program:

```
int ct = 0;
char ch;
cin.get(ch);
while (ch != '\n')
{
        cout << ch;
        ct++;
        cin.get(ch);
}
cout << ct << '\n';
```

Next, suppose you type the following optimistic input:

```
I C++ clearly.<enter>
```

Pressing the (ENTER) key sends this input line to the program. The program fragment will first read the *I* character, display it with *cout,* and increment *ct* to *1.* Next, it will read the space character following the *I,* display it, and increment *ct* to *2.* This continues until the program processes the (ENTER) key as a newline character and terminates the loop. The main point here is that, by using *get(ch),* the code reads, displays, and counts the spaces as well as the printing characters.

Suppose, instead, that the program had tried to use >>:

```
int ct = 0;
char ch;
cin >> ch;
while (ch != '\n')      // FAILS
{
        cout << ch;
        ct++;
        cin >> ch;
}
cout << ct << '\n';
```

First, the code would skip the spaces, thus not counting them and compressing the corresponding output to this:

```
IC++clearly.
```

Worse, the loop would never terminate! Because the extraction operator skips newlines, the code would never assign the newline character to *ch,* so the *while* loop test would never terminate the loop.

The *get(char &)* member function normally returns a reference to the *istream* object used to invoke it. This means you can concatenate other extractions following *get(char):*

```
char c1, c2, c3;
cin.get(c1).get(c2) >> c3;
```

First, *cin.get(c1)* assigns the first input character to *c1* and returns the invoking object, which is *cin.* This reduces the code to *cin.get(c2) >> c3,* which assigns the second input character to *c2.* The function call returns *cin,* reducing the code to *cin >> c3.* This, in turn, assigns the next nonwhite-space character to *c3.* Note that *c1* and *c2* could wind up being assigned white space, but *c3* can't.

If *cin.get(char &)* encounters the end of a file, either real or simulated from the keyboard ((CONTROL)-(Z) for DOS, (CONTROL)-(D) at the beginning of a line for UNIX), it does not assign a value to its argument. This is quite right, for if the program has reached the end of the file, there is no value to be assigned. Furthermore, instead of returning the invoking object *(cin), cin.get(char &)* returns zero upon detecting the end of a file. Hence you can use the following loop to read characters up to the end of a file:

```
char ch;
while (cin.get(ch))
```

```
{
        // process input
}
```

As long as there's valid input, the return value for *cin.get(ch)* is *cin,* which is nonzero, so the loop continues. Upon reaching end-of-file, the return value becomes zero, terminating the loop.

The *get(void)* member function also reads white space, but it uses its return value to communicate input to a program. So you would use it this way:

```
int ct = 0;
char ch;
ch = cin.get();                // use return value
while (ch != '\n')
{
        cout << ch;
        ct++;
        ch = cin.get();
}
cout << ct << '\n';
```

Some C++ implementation functions don't provide this member function.

The *get(void)* member function returns type *int.* This makes the following invalid:

```
char c1, c2, c3;
cin.get().get() >> c3;        // not valid
```

Here *cin.get()* returns a type *int* value. Because that return value is not a class object, you can't apply the membership operator to it. Thus you get a syntax error. However, you can use *get()* at the *end* of an extraction sequence:

```
char c1;
cin.get(c1).get();    // valid
```

The fact that *get(void)* returns type *int* means you can't follow it with an extraction operator. But, because *cin.get(c1)* returns *cin,* it makes it a suitable prefix to *get().* This particular code would read the first input character, assign it to *c1,* then read the second input character and discard it.

Upon reaching the end-of-file, real or simulated, *cin.get(void)* returns the value *EOF,* which is a symbolic constant defined in the *iostream.h* header file. This design feature allows the following construction for reading input:

```
int ch;
while ((ch = cin.get()) != EOF)
{
        // process input
}
```

You should use type *int* for *ch* instead of type *char* here because the value *EOF* may not be expressed as a *char* type.

Chapter 5 describes these functions in a bit more detail, and Table 15-5 summarizes the features of the single-character input functions.

Property	cin.get(ch)	ch = cin.get()
method for conveying input character	assign to argument *ch*	use function return value to assign to *ch*
function return value for character input	reference to a class *istream* object	code for character as type *int* value
function return value at end-of-file	0	EOF

Table 15-5 *cin.get(ch)* versus *cin.get()*

Which Form of Single-Character Input?

Given the choice of >>, *get(char &)*, and *get(void)*, which should you use? First, decide whether you want input to skip over white space or not. If skipping white space is more convenient, use the extraction operator >>. For instance, skipping white space is convenient for offering menu choices:

```
cout    << "a. annoy client         b. bill client\n"
        << "c. calm client          d. deceive client\n"
        << "q.\n";
cout    << "Enter a, b, c, d, or q: ";
char ch;
cin >> ch;
while (ch != 'q')
{
        switch(ch)
        {
              . . .
        }
        cout << "Enter a, b, c, d, or q: ";
        cin >> ch;
}
```

To enter, say, a *b* response, you type *b* and press (ENTER), generating the two-character response of *b*\n. If you used either form of *get()*, you would have to add code to process that \n character each loop cycle, but the extraction operator conveniently skips it. (If you've programmed in C, you've probably encountered the situation in which the newline appears to the program as an invalid response. It's an easy problem to fix, but it is a nuisance.)

If you want a program to examine every character, use one of the *get()* methods. For instance, a word-counting program could use white space to determine when a word came to an end. Of the two *get()* methods, the *get(char &)* method has the classier interface. Also, it's more widely supported, although both are part of the draft standard. The main advantage of the *get(void)* method is that it closely resembles the standard C *getchar()* function, letting you convert a C to a C++ program by including *iostream.h* instead of *stdio.h,* globally replacing *getchar()* with *cin.get()*, and globally replacing C's *putchar(ch)* with *cout.put(ch).*

String Input: *getline(), get(), and ignore()*

Next, let's review the string input member functions, which Chapter 4 introduced. The *getline()* member function and the third version of *get()* both read strings, and both have the same function signature:

```
istream & get(char *, int, char = '\n');
istream & getline(char *, int, char = '\n');
```

The first argument, recall, is the address of the location to place the input string. The second argument is one greater than the maximum number of characters to be read. (The additional character leaves space for the terminating null character used in storing the input as a string.) If you omit the third argument, each function reads up to the maximum characters or until a newline character, whichever comes first.

For example, the code

```
char line[50];
cin.get(line, 50);
```

reads character input into the character array *line.* The *cin.get()* function quits reading input into the array after encountering 49 characters or, by default, after encountering a newline character, whichever comes first. The difference between *get()* and *getline()* is that *get()* leaves the newline character in the input stream, making it the first character seen by the next input operation, while *getline()* extracts and discards the newline character from the input stream. Not all C++ implementations include *getline()*, but it is part of the draft standard.

Chapter 4 illustrated using the default form for these two member functions. Now let's look at the final argument, which modifies the function's default behavior. The third argument, which has a default value of '\n', is the termination character. Encountering the termination character causes input to cease even if the maximum number of characters hasn't been reached. So, by default, both methods quit reading input if they reach the end of a line before reading the allotted number of characters. The difference between *get()* and *getline()* is that *get()* leaves the termination character in the input queue, while *getline()* doesn't. (The first Turbo C++ implementation of *getline()* included the termination character in the destination string, but most implementations, including Borland C++ and newer releases of Turbo C++, simply read and discard the termination character.)

Listing 15-12 demonstrates how *getline()* and *get()* work. It also introduces the *ignore()* member function. It takes two arguments: a number specifying a maximum number of characters to read and a character that acts as a terminating character for input. For example, the function call

```
cin.ignore(80, '\n');
```

reads and discards the next 80 characters or up through the first newline character, whichever comes first. The prototype provides defaults of 1 and *EOF* for the two arguments, and the function return type is *istream &*:

```
istream & ignore(int = 1, int = EOF);
```

The function returns the invoking object. This lets you concatenate function calls, as in the following:

```
cin.ignore(80, '\n').ignore(80, '\n');
```

Here the first *ignore()* method reads and discards one line, and the second call reads and discards the second line. Together the two functions read through two lines.

Now check out Listing 15-12.

COMPATIBILITY NOTE

Early releases of Turbo C++ implemented *ignore()* so that it read up to, but not through, the terminating character. Thus, with those versions, you have to use *cin.ignore(80, '\n').get(ch)* to read and discard an entire line.

Listing 15-12 *get_fun.cpp*

```cpp
// get_fun.cpp -- using get() and getline()
// note: some C++ implementations don't support getline ()
#include <iostream.h>

const int Limit = 80;
int main(void)
{
        char input[Limit];

        cout << "Enter a string for getline() processing:\n";
        cin.getline(input, Limit, '#');
        cout << "Here is your input:\n";
        cout << input << "\nDone with phase 1\n";

        char ch;
        cin.get(ch);
        cout << "The next input character is " << ch << "\n";

        if (ch != '\n')
                cin.ignore(Limit, '\n');        // discard rest of line

        cout << "Enter a string for get() processing:\n";
        cin.get(input, Limit, '#');
        cout << "Here is your input:\n";
        cout << input << "\nDone with phase 2\n";

        cin.get(ch);
        cout << "The next input character is " << ch << "\n";
```

```
        return 0;
}
```

Here is a sample program run:

```
Enter a string for getline() processing:
Please pass
me a #3 melon!
Here is your input:
Please pass
me a
Done with phase 1
The next input character is 3
Enter a string for get() processing:
I still
want my #3 melon!
Here is your input:
I still
want my
Done with phase 2
The next input character is #
```

Note that the *getline()* function discards the # termination character in the input, while the *get()* function doesn't.

Unexpected String Input

Some forms of input for *get(char *, int)* and *getline()* affect the stream state. As with the other input functions, encountering end-of-file sets the *eofbit,* and anything that corrupts the stream, such as device failure, sets the *badbit.* Two other special cases are no input and input that meets or exceeds the maximum number of characters specified by the function call. Let's look at those cases now.

If the user responds by pressing (ENTER) without entering any other characters, both methods place a null character into the input string. This provides an easy way to terminate a loop that's reading a series of strings:

```
char temp[80];
while (cin.getline(temp,80) && temp[0] != '\0')
      ...
```

The draft standard adds a hitch to this, stating that reading no characters also sets *failbit.* This requirement may yet be altered, but if it stands, that means you would have to clear the stream state before accepting further input:

```
char temp[80];
while (cin.getline(temp,80) && temp[0] != '\0')
      ...
if (cin.fail())
      cin.clear();
```

Traditional C++ implementations, however, don't set *failbit* if no characters are read.

If you used *get(char *, int)* instead of *getline()* in this circumstance, you also would need to read and dispose of the end-of-line character remaining in the input queue.

Now suppose the number of characters in the input queue meets or exceeds the maximum specified by the input method. First, consider *getline()* and the following code:

```
char temp[30];
while (cin.getline(temp,30) && temp[0] != '\0')
```

According to the draft standard, *getline()* will read consecutive characters from the input queue, placing them in successive elements of the *temp* array, until 29 characters have been stored or until the next character to be read is the newline character or until EOF is encountered. If EOF is encountered, *eofbit* is set. If the next character to be read is a newline character, that character is read and discarded. And if 29 characters were read, *failbit* is set. Thus, according to the draft, an input line of 29 characters or more will terminate the input loop. With traditional C++ implementations, however, reaching the input limit does not set *failbit*.

Now consider the *get(char *, int)* method. It does not set the *failbit* flag if it reads the maximum number of characters. Also, with this method, you can tell if too many input characters caused the method to quit reading. You can use *peek()* (see the next section) to examine the next input character. If it's a newline, then *get()* read the entire line. If it's not a newline, then *get()* stopped before reaching the end. This technique doesn't necessarily work with *getline()* because *getline()* reads and discards the newline, so looking at the next character doesn't tell you anything. But if you use *get()*, you have the option of doing something if less than an entire line is read. The next section includes an example of this approach. Meanwhile, Table 15-6 summarizes some of the differences between traditional C++ input methods and the draft standard. Keep in mind that the draft standard is subject to change.

Method	Traditional C++	Draft C++
getline()	doesn't set *failbit* if no characters read	sets *failbit* if no characters read
	doesn't set *failbit* if maximum number of characters read	sets *failbit* if maximum number of characters read
get(char *, int)	doesn't set *failbit* if no characters read	sets *failbit* if no characters read

Table 15-6 Input changes

Other *istream* Methods

Other *istream* methods include *read()*, *peek()*, *gcount()*, and *putback()*. The *read()* function reads a given number of bytes, storing them in the specified location. For instance, the statement

```
char gross[144];
cin.read(gross, 144);
```

reads 144 characters from the standard input and places them in the *gross* array. Unlike *getline()* and *get()*, *read()* does not append a null character to input, so it doesn't convert input to string form. The *read()* method is not primarily intended for keyboard input. Instead, it most often is used in conjunction with the *ostream write()* function for file input and output. The method's return type is *istream &*, so it can be concatenated as follows:

```
char gross[144];
char score[20];
cin.read(gross, 144).read(score, 20);
```

The *peek()* function returns the next character from input without extracting from the input stream. That is, it lets you peek at the next character. Suppose you wanted to read input up to the first newline or period, whichever comes first. You can use *peek()* to peek at the next character in the input stream in order to judge whether to continue or not:

```
char great_input[80];
char ch;
int i = 0;
while ((ch = cin.peek()) != '.' && ch != '\n')
        cin.get(great_input[i++]);
great_input [i] = '\0';
```

The call to *cin.peek()* peeks at the next input character and assigns its value to *ch*. Then the *while* loop test condition checks that *ch* is neither a period nor a newline. If this is the case, the loop then reads the character into the array, and updates the array index. When the loop terminates, the period or newline character remains in the input stream, positioned to be the first character read by the next input operation. Then the code appends a null character to the array, making it a string.

The *gcount()* method returns the number of characters read by the last unformatted extraction method. That means characters read by a *get()*, *getline()*, or *read()* method but not by the extraction operator (>>), which formats input to fit particular data types. For instance, suppose you've just used *cin.get(myarray, 80)* to read a line into the *myarray* array and want to know how many characters were read. You could use the *strlen()* function to count the characters in the array, but it would be quicker to use *cin.gcount()* to report how many characters were just read from the input stream.

The *putback()* function inserts a character back in the input string. The inserted character then becomes the first character read by the next input statement. The *putback()* method takes one *char* argument, which is the character to be inserted, and it returns type *istream &*, which allows the call to be concatenated with other *istream* methods. Using *peek()* is like using *get()* to read a character, then using *putback()* to place the character back in the input stream. However, *putback()* gives you the option of putting back a character different from the one just read.

Listing 15-13 uses two approaches to read and echo input up to, but not including, a # character. The first approach reads through the # character, then uses *putback()* to insert the character back in the input. The second approach uses *peek()* to look ahead before reading input.

Listing 15-13 *peeker.cpp*

```
// peeker.cpp -- some istream methods
#include <iostream.h>
#include <stdlib.h>              // for exit()

int main(void)
{

// read and echo input up to a # character
    char ch;

        while(cin.get(ch))              // terminates on EOF
        {
                if (ch != '#')
                        cout << ch;
                else
                {
                        cin.putback(ch);       // reinsert character
                        break;                 // terminates if ch == '#'
                }
        }

        if (!cout.eof())
        {
                cin.get(ch);
                cout << '\n' << ch << " is next input character.\n";
        }
        else
        {
                cout << "End of file reached.\n";
                exit(0);
        }

        while(cin.peek() != '#')                // look ahead
        {
                cin.get(ch);
                cout << ch;
        }
        cin.get(ch);
        cout << '\n' << ch << " is next input character.\n";

        return 0;
}
```

Here is a sample run:

I used a #3 pencil when I should have used a #2.
I used a
is next input character.

Chapter Fifteen • INPUT, OUTPUT, AND FILES

```
3 pencil when I should have used a
# is next input character.
```

Program Notes

Let's look more closely at some of the code. The first approach uses a *while* loop to read input. The expression *(cin.get(ch))* returns 0 on reaching the end-of-file condition, so simulating end-of-file from the keyboard terminates the loop. If the # character shows up first, the program puts the character back in the input stream and uses a *break* statement to terminate the loop.

```
while(cin.get(ch))                    // terminates on EOF
{
        if (ch != '#')
                cout << ch;
        else
        {
                cin.putback(ch);      // reinsert character
                break;
        }
}
```

The second approach is simpler in appearance:

```
while(cin.peek() != '#')       // look ahead
{
        cin.get(ch);
        cout << ch;
}
```

The program peeks at the next character. If it is not the # character, the program reads the next character, echoes it, and peeks at the next character. This continues until the terminating character shows up.

Now let's look, as promised, at an example (Listing 15-14) that uses *peek()* to determine whether or not an entire line has been read. If only part of a line fits in the input array, the program discards the rest of the line.

Listing 15-14 *truncate.cpp*

```
// truncate.cpp -- use get() to truncate input line, if necessary
#include <iostream.h>
const int SLEN = 10;
int main(void)
{
        char name[SLEN];
        char title[SLEN];
        cout << "Enter your name: ";
        cin.get(name,SLEN);
        if (cin.peek() != '\n')
                cout << "Sorry, we only have enough room for "
                        << name << endl;
```

continued on next page

733

continued from previous page

```
        while (cin.get() != '\n')
                continue;
        cout << "Dear " << name << ", enter your title: \n";
        cin.get(title,SLEN);
        cout << " Name: " << name
                << "\nTitle: " << title << endl;

        return 0;
}
```

Here is a sample run:

```
Enter your name: El Magnifico
Sorry, we only have enough room for El Magnif
Dear El Magnif, enter your title:
Poet
 Name: El Magnif
Title: Poet
```

Note that the following code makes sense whether or not the first input statement read the entire line:

```
while (cin.get() != '\n')
        continue;
```

If *get()* reads the whole line, it still leaves the newline in place, and this code reads and discards the newline. If *get()* reads just part of the line, this code reads and discards the rest of the line. If we didn't dispose of the rest of line, the next input statement would begin reading at the beginning of the remaining input on the first input line. With our example, that would have resulted in the program reading the string *ico* into the *title* array.

File Input and Output

Most computer programs work with files. Word processors create document files. Database programs create and search files of information. Compilers read source code files and generate executable files. A file itself is a bunch of bytes stored on some device, perhaps magnetic tape, perhaps an optical disk, floppy disk, or hard disk. Typically, the operating system manages files, keeping track of their locations, their sizes, when they were created, and so on. Unless you're programming on the operating system level, you normally don't have to worry about those things. What you do need is a way to connect a program to a file, a way to have a program read the contents of a file, and a way to have a program create and write to files. Redirection (as discussed earlier this chapter) can provide some file support, but it is more limited than explicit file I/O from within a program. Also, redirection comes from the operating system, not from C++, so it isn't available on all systems. We'll look now at how C++ deals with explicit file I/O from within a program.

The C++ I/O class package handles file input and output much as it handles standard input and output. To write to a file, you create a stream object and use the *ostream* methods, such as the << insertion operator or *write()*. To read a file, you create a stream object and use the *istream* methods, such as the >> extraction operator or *get()*. Files require more management than the standard input and output, however. For instance, you have to associate a newly opened file with a stream. You can open a file in read-only mode, write-only mode, or read-and-write mode. If you write to a file, you may wish to create a new file, replace an old file, or add to an old file. Or you may wish to move back and forth through a file. To help handle these tasks, C++ defines several new classes in the *fstream.h* file, including an *ifstream* class for file input and an *ofstream* class for file output. Traditionally, C++ also has defined an *fstream* class for simultaneous file I/O, but the draft standard drops this class; instead, it uses file-opening modes to achieve the same end. These classes are derived from the classes in the *iostream.h* file, so objects of these new classes will be able to use the methods you've already learned.

Simple File I/O

Suppose you want a program to write to a file. You need to do the following:

- Create an *ofstream* object to manage the output stream.
- Associate that object with a particular file.

To accomplish this, begin by including the *fstream.h* header file. (Under the draft standard, you would include *fstream* instead, or, if you want the namespace version, *fstream.ns*.) Including this file automatically includes the *iostream.h* file for most, but not all, implementations, so you may not have to include *iostream.h* explicitly. Then declare an *ofstream* object and initialize it using the name of the file to be opened.

For example, to open the *cookies* file for output, do the following:

```
ofstream fout("cookies");  // create fout object
```

We named the object *fout* (for file *out*put) but you can use any valid C++ name, such as *outfile, cgate,* or *didi*. We chose the name *fout* for the *ofstream* object as a reminder that you can use it much as you use *cout*. For instance, if you want to put the words Dull Data into the file, you can do the following:

```
fout << "Dull Data";
```

Indeed, because *ostream* is a base class for the *ofstream* class, you can use all the *ostream* methods, including the various insertion operator definitions and the formatting methods and manipulators. The *ofstream* class uses buffered output, so the program allocates space for an output buffer when it creates an *ofstream* object like *fout*. If you create two *ofstream* objects, the program creates two buffers, one for each object. An *ofstream* object like *fout* collects output byte-by-byte from the program, then, when the buffer is filled, transfers the buffer contents en masse to the destination file. Because disk drives are designed to transfer data in larger chunks, not byte-by-byte, the buffered approach greatly speeds up the transfer rate of data from a program to a file.

Opening a file for output this way creates a new file if there is no file of that name. If a file by that name exists prior to opening it for output, the act of opening it truncates it so that output starts with a clean file. Later you'll see how to open an existing file and retain its contents.

The requirements for reading a file are much like those for writing to a file:

❧ Create an *ifstream* object to manage the input stream.

❧ Associate that object with a particular file.

The steps for doing so are similar to those for writing to a file. First, of course, include the *fstream.h* header file. Then declare an *ifstream* object, initializing it with the file name. For example, to read the *cookies* file, you can do the following:

```
ifstream fin("cookies");      // open cookies for reading
```

This calls an *ifstream* class constructor that accepts a string argument. We've used the name *fin* for the *ifstream* object to remind you that you can use *fin* much like *cin*. For instance, you can do the following:

```
char ch;
fin >> ch;          // read a character from the file
char buf[80];
fin >> buf;         // read a word from the file
fin.getline(buf, 80); // read a line from the file
```

Input, like output, is buffered, so creating an *ifstream* object like *fin* creates an input buffer which the *fin* object manages. As with output, buffering moves data much faster than byte-by-byte transfer.

The connections with a file are closed automatically when the input and output stream objects expire, for example, when the program terminates. Also, you can close a connection with a file explicitly by using the *close()* method:

```
fout.close(); // close output connection to file
fin.close();  // close input connection to file
```

Closing such a connection does not eliminate the stream; it just disconnects it from the file. However, the stream management apparatus remains in place. For instance, the *fin* object still exists along with the input buffer it manages. As you'll see later, you can reconnect the stream to the same file or to another file.

Meanwhile, let's look at a short example. The program in Listing 15-15 asks you for a file name. It creates a file having that name, writes some information to it, and closes the file. Closing the file flushes the buffer, guaranteeing that the file is updated. Then the program opens the same file for reading and displays its contents. Note that the program uses *fin* and *fout* in the same manner as *cin* and *cout*.

Listing 15-15 *file.cpp*

```
// file.cpp -- save to a file
#include <iostream.h> // not needed for many systems
#include <fstream.h>

int main(void)
{
        char filename[20];

        cout << "Enter name for new file: ";
        cin >> filename;

// create output stream object for new file and call it fout
        ofstream fout(filename);

        fout << "For your eyes only!\n";              // write to file
        cout << "Enter your secret number: ";         // write to screen
        float secret;
        cin >> secret;
        fout << "Your secret number is " << secret << "\n";
        fout.close();                     // close file

// create input stream object for new file and call it fin
        ifstream fin(filename);
        cout << "Here are the contents of " << filename << ":\n";
        char ch;
        while (fin.get(ch))               // read character from file and
                cout << ch;               // write it to screen
        cout << "Done\n";

        return 0;
}
```

Here is a sample run:

```
Enter name for new file: pythag
Enter your secret number: 3.14159
Here are the contents of pythag:
For your eyes only!
Your secret number is 3.14159
Done
```

Opening Multiple Files

You may require that a program open more than one file. The strategy for opening multiple files depends upon how they will be used. If you need two files open simultaneously, then you need to create a separate stream for each file. For instance, a program that collates two sorted files into a third file would create two *ifstream* objects for the two input files and an *ofstream* object for the output file. The number of files you can open simultaneously depends on the operating system, but it typically is on the order of 20.

However, you may plan to process a group of files sequentially. For instance, you may wish to count how many times a name appears in a set of ten files. Then you can open a single stream and associate it with each file in turn. This conserves computer resources more effectively than opening a separate stream for each file. To use this approach, declare a stream object without initializing it, then use a second statement to associate the stream with a file. For instance, this is how you could handle reading two files in succession:

```
ifstream fin;            // create stream using default constructor
fin.open("fat.dat");     // associate stream with fat.dat file
...                      // do stuff
fin.close();             // terminate association with fat.dat
fin.open("rat.dat");     // associate stream with rat.dat file
...
fin.close();
```

We'll look at an example shortly, but first, let's examine a technique for feeding a list of files to a program in a manner that allows the program to use a loop to process them.

Command-Line Processing

File-processing programs often use command-line arguments to identify files. Command-line arguments are arguments that appear on the command line when you type a command. For example, to count the number of words in some files on a UNIX system, you would type this command at the UNIX prompt:

```
wc report1 report2 report3
```

Here *wc* is the program name, and *report1*, *report2*, and *report3* are file names passed to the program as command-line arguments.

C++ has a mechanism for letting a program access command-line arguments. Use the following alternative function heading for *main()*:

```
int main(int argc, char *argv[])
```

The *argc* argument represents the number of arguments on the command line. The count includes the command name itself. The *argv* variable is a pointer to a pointer to a *char*. This sounds a bit abstract, but you can treat *argv* as if it were an array of pointers to the command-line arguments, with *argv[0]* being a pointer to the first character of a string holding the command name, *argv[1]* being a pointer to the first character of a string holding the first command-line argument, and so on. That is, *argv[0]* is the first string from the command line, and so on. For instance, suppose you have the following command line:

```
wc report1 report2 report3
```

Then *argc* would be *4*, *argv[0]* would be *wc*, *argv[1]* would be *report1*, and so on. The following loop would print each command-line argument on a separate line:

```
for (int i = 1; i < argc; i++)
        cout << argv[i] << "\n";
```

Starting with *i = 1* just prints the command-line arguments; starting with *i = 0* would also print the command name.

Command-line arguments, of course, go hand-in-hand with command-line operating systems like DOS and UNIX. Other setups may still allow you to use command-line arguments. Here's a list of some options.

❧ If you are using the Borland 3.1 integrated environment or its predecessors, you can supply command-line arguments via the Arguments selection in the Run menu.

❧ If you are using a Windows-based Borland compiler, such as 4.0, you can provide command-line arguments by selecting the Debugger topic under the Environment choice under the Options menu.

❧ Microsoft Visual C++ lets you provide command-line arguments for a program if you select Debug from the Options menu.

❧ Under Symantec C++ for the PC, you can provide command-line arguments by selecting Arguments in the Run menu.

❧ Under Symantec C++ for the Macintosh and under Metrowerks CodeWarrior for the Macintosh, you can simulate command-line arguments by placing the following code in your program:

```
...
#include <console.h> // for emulating command-line arguments
int main(int argc, char * argv[])
{
        argc = ccommand(&argv); // yes, ccommand, not command
        ...
```

❧ CodeWarrior additionally requires that you add *MacOS.lib* to the project list. When you run the program, the *ccommand()* function places a dialog box onscreen with a box in which you can type the command-line arguments. It also lets you simulate redirection.

Listing 15-16 combines the command-line technique with file stream techniques to count characters in those files listed on the command line.

Listing 15-16 *count.cpp*

```
// count.cpp -- count characters in a list of files
#include <iostream.h>
#include <fstream.h>
```

continued on next page

continued from previous page

```
#include <stdlib.h>             // for exit()

int main(int argc, char *argv[])
{
        if (argc == 1)         // quit if no arguments
        {
            cerr << "Usage: " << argv[0] << " filename[s]\n";
            exit(1);
        }

        ifstream fin;          // open stream
        long count;
        long total = 0;
        char ch;

        for (int file = 1; file < argc; file++)
        {
            fin.open(argv[file]);    // connect stream to argv[file]
            count = 0;
            while (fin.get(ch))
                count++;
            cout << count << " characters in " << argv[file] << "\n";
            total += count;
            fin.close();                         // disconnect file
        }
        cout << total << " characters in all files\n";

        return 0;
}
```

On a DOS system, for example, you could compile Listing 15-16 to an executable file called *count.exe*. Then sample runs could look like this:

```
C>count
Usage: c:\count.exe filename[s]
C>count paris rome
3580 characters in paris
4886 characters in rome
8466 characters in all files
C>
```

Note that the program uses *cerr* for the error message. A minor point is that the message uses *argv[0]* instead of *count.exe*:

```
cerr << "Usage: " << argv[0] << " filename[s]\n";
```

This way, if you change the name of the executable file, the program will automatically use the new name.

Suppose you pass a bogus file name to the *count* program. Then the input statement *fin.get(ch)* will fail, terminating the *while* loop immediately, and the program will report 0 characters. But you can modify the program to test whether it succeeded in linking the stream to a file. That's one of the matters we'll take up next.

Stream Checking

The C++ file stream classes inherit a stream-state member from the *ios* class. This member, as discussed earlier, stores information reflecting the stream status: all is well, end-of-file has been reached, I/O operation failed, and so on. If all is well, the stream state is zero (no news is good news). The various other states are recorded by setting particular bits to 1. The file stream classes also inherit the *ios* methods that report about the stream state and that were summarized earlier in Table 15-4. You can monitor conditions with these stream-state methods. For instance, you can modify the program in Listing 15-16 so that it reports bogus file names, then skips to the next file. Just add a call to *fin.good()* to the *for* loop as follows:

```
for (int file = 1; file < argc; file++)
{
        fin.open(argv[file]);

// Add this
    if (!fin.good())    // or if (!fin), for short
    {
            cerr << "Couldn't open file " << argv[file] << "\n";
            continue;
    }
// End of addition

    count = 0;
    while (fin.get(ch))
            count++;
    cout << count << " characters in " << argv[file] << "\n";
    total += count;
    fin.close();                        // disconnect file
}
```

The *fin.good()* call returns zero, or false, if the *fin.open()* call fails. In that case, the program warns you of its problem, and the *continue* statement causes the program to skip the rest of the *for* loop cycle and start with the next cycle.

The *fin* object, when used in a test condition, is converted to 0 if *fin.good()* is false and to nonzero otherwise. Therefore, you can use

```
if (!fin)
    ...
```

instead of:

```
if(!fin.good())
    ...
```

Similarly, constructions such as

```
while (fin.get(ch))
```

work because the *get()* family of member functions, as well as *getline()* and the extraction operators, return *fin*. Thus a loop of this sort may terminate for a variety of reasons, including reaching the end of a file, a hardware failure, or attempting to use a stream that hasn't been associated with a file. You can use the *eof()* method after such a loop to verify that it terminated because of reaching end-of-file rather than because of some abnormal condition.

File Modes

The *file mode* describes how a file is to be used: read it, write to it, append it, and so on. When you associate a stream with a file, either by initializing a file stream object with a file name or by using the *open()* method, you can provide a second argument specifying the file mode:

```
ifstream fin("banjo", mode1);
ofstream fout();
fout.open("harp", mode2);
```

The draft standard defines an *openmode* type to represent the mode; formerly, it was type *int*. In either case, you can choose from several constants defined in the *ios* class to specify the mode. Table 15-7 lists the constants and their meanings. Note that the draft standard drops two constants commonly available in traditional C++ implementations. The draft standard has made several changes in file I/O in order to make it compatible with ANSI C file I/O.

Constant	Meaning
ios::in	open file for reading
ios::out	open file for writing
ios::ate	seek to end-of-file upon opening file
ios::app	append to end-of-file
ios::trunc	truncate file if it exists
ios::binary	binary file
The following two constants are part of the traditional C++ interface but not of the draft standard.	
ios::nocreate	open fails if file does not exist
ios::replace	open fails if file does exist

Table 15-7 File mode constants

If the *ifstream* and *ofstream* constructors and the *open()* methods each take two arguments, how have we gotten by using just one in the previous examples? As you probably have guessed, the prototypes for these class member functions provide default values for the second argument (the *file mode argument*). For instance, the *ifstream open()* method and constructor use *ios::in* (open for reading) as the default value for the mode argument, while the *ofstream open()* method and constructor use *ios::out* (open for writing) as the default. The *fstream* class (traditional C++) doesn't provide a mode default, so you have to provide a mode explicitly when creating an object of that class.

Opening a file in the *ios::out* mode also opens it in the *ios::trunc* mode by default. That means an existing file is truncated when opened to receive program output; that is, its previous contents are discarded. While this behavior commendably minimizes the danger of running out of disk space, you probably can imagine situations in which you don't want to wipe out a file when you open it. C++, of course, provides other choices. If, for instance, you wish to preserve the file contents and add (append) new material to the end of the file, you can use the *ios::app* mode:

```
ofstream fout("bagels", ios::out | ios::app);
```

The | operator is the C++ bitwise OR operator (Appendix E). What you need to know here is that you use it to combine modes. So *ios::out | ios::app* means to invoke both the *out* mode and the *app* mode. See Figure 15-6.

Expect to find some differences among implementations. For instance, some allow you to omit the *ios::out* in the above example, and some don't. If you aren't using the default mode, the safest approach is to provide all the mode elements explicitly. Some don't support all the choices in Table 15-7, and some may offer choices beyond those

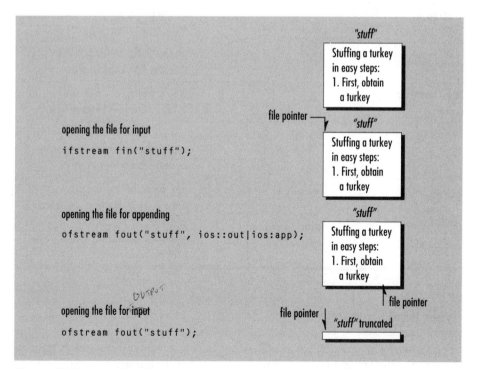

Figure 15-6 Some file-opening modes

in the table. One consequence of these differences is that you may have to make some alterations in the following examples to do them on your system. We'll offer some guidelines, but we can't cover all possible variations. Presumably, the final version of the C++ standard will create greater uniformity. The draft standard defines parts of file I/O in terms of ANSI C standard I/O. A C++ statement like

```
ifstream fin(filename, c++mode);
```

is implemented using the C *fopen()* function:

```
fopen(filename, cmode);
```

Here *c++mode* is an *ios* mode, such as *ios::in*, and *cmode* is the corresponding C mode string, such as *"r"*. Table 15-8 shows the correspondence between C++ modes and C modes.

C++ mode	C mode	Meaning
ios::in	*"r"*	open for reading
*ios::out	ios::trunc*	*"w"*	open for writing, truncating file if it already exists
*ios::out	ios::app*	*"a"*	open for writing, append only
*ios::in	ios::out*	*"r+"*	open for reading and writing, with writing permitted anywhere in the file
*ios::in	ios::out	ios::trunc*	*"w+"*	open for reading and writing, first truncating file if it already exists
*ios::in	ios::out	ios::app*	*"a+"*	open for reading and writing, with writing permitted only by appending to file
*c++mode	ios::binary*	*"cmodeb"*	open in *c++mode* or corresponding *cmode* and in binary mode; for example, *ios::in	ios::binary* becomes *"rb"*
*c++mode	ios::ate*	*"cmode"*	open in indicated mode and go to end of file. C uses a separate function call instead of a mode code. For example, *ios::in	ios::ate* translates to the mode *"r"* and the C function call *fseek(file, 0, SEEK_END)*

Table 15-8 C++ and C file-opening modes

Note that both *ios::ate* and *ios::app* place you (or, more precisely, a file pointer) at the end of the file just opened. The difference between the two is that the *ios::app* mode allows you to add data to the end of the file only, while the *ios::ate* mode lets you write data anywhere in the file, even over old data. One of the later examples demonstrates this technique.

Clearly, there are many possible combinations of modes. We'll look at a few representative ones.

Appending to a File

Let's begin with a program that appends data to the end of a file. We'll have the program maintain a file containing a guest list. When the program begins, it will display the current contents of the file, if it exists. It can use the *good()* method after attempting to open the file to check if the file exists. Next, the program will open the file for output using the *ios::app* mode. Then it will solicit input from the keyboard to add to the file. Finally, the program will display the revised file contents. Listing 15-17 illustrates how to accomplish these goals. Note how the program uses the *good()* and the *fail()* methods to test if the file has been opened successfully.

COMPATIBILITY NOTE

Some compilers, including Symantec C++ 6.0 and Microsoft Visual C++ 1.0, require users to replace the first

```
fin.open(file);
```

with

```
fin.open(file, ios::in | ios::nocreate);
```

The reason is that these compilers do not consider it an error to attempt to open a nonexistent file for reading unless the *nocreate* mode is invoked. The other compilers tested for this book, on the other hand, do consider it an error to attempt to open a nonexistent file for reading; they require the *nocreate* mode only if you want to prevent opening a nonexistent file for writing. And the draft standard doesn't even support *nocreate*.

Also, only some compilers require the *fin.clear()* call before opening the same file a second time for reading. The need occurs when the first attempt fails. In general, the file I/O methods appear to be the least standardized aspects of the language at this time.

Listing 15-17 *append.cpp*

```
// append.cpp -- append information to a file
#include <iostream.h>
#include <fstream.h>
#include <stdlib.h>              // for exit()

const char * file = "guests1.dat";
const int Len = 40;
int main(void)
{
        char ch;
```

continued on next page

continued from previous page

```
// show initial contents
   ifstream fin;
   fin.open(file);
   // fin.open(file, ios::in | ios::nocreate); //Symantec, MS VC
   if (fin.good())     // or if (fin)
   {
           cout << "Here are the current contents of the "
                   << file << " file:\n";
           while ((ios &)fin.get(ch))
                   cout << ch;
   }
   fin.close();

// add new names
   ofstream fout(file, ios::out | ios::app);
   if (!fout.good())  // or if (!fin)
   {
           cerr << "Can't open " << file << " file for output.\n";
           exit(1);
   }

   cout << "Enter guest names (enter a blank line to quit):\n";
   char name[Len];
   cin.getline(name, Len);
   while (name[0] != '\0')
   {
           fout << name << "\n";
           cin.getline(name, Len);
   }
   fout.close();

// show revised file
   fin.clear();          // not necessary for some compilers
   fin.open(file);
   if (fin.good())
   {
           cout << "Here are the new contents of the "
                   << file << " file:\n";
           while ((ios &)fin.get(ch))
                   cout << ch;
   }
   fin.close();

   return 0;
}
```

Here's a sample first run. At this point the *guests.dat* file hasn't been created, so the program doesn't preview the file.

```
Enter guest names (enter a blank line to quit):
Sylvester Ballone
Phil Kates
Bill Ghan
```

```
Here are the new contents of the guests.dat file:
Sylvester Ballone
Phil Kates
Bill Ghan
```

Next time, however, the *guests.dat* file does exist, so the program does preview the file. Also, note that the new data is appended to the old file contents rather than replacing them.

```
Here are the current contents of the guests.dat file:
Sylvester Ballone
Phil Kates
Bill Ghan
Enter guest names (enter a blank line to quit):
Greta Greppo
LaDonna Mobile
Fannie Mae

Here are the new contents of the guests.dat file:
Sylvester Ballone
Phil Kates
Bill Ghan
Greta Greppo
LaDonna Mobile
Fannie Mae
```

You've already read about the major features of the program, but there's one more point meriting review. The program uses this line to read in the guest's name:

```
cin.getline(name, Len);
```

If you have a C++ version that doesn't support *getline()*, you can do this instead:

```
cin.get(name, Len).get(ch);
```

The *get(name, Len)* portion reads up to, but not including, the newline character. The *get(ch)* part reads the newline so that the next input begins at the beginning of the next line. (The code assumes the name doesn't exceed the *Len* limit.) Otherwise, the next input statement would begin at the terminating newline character, read it as a blank line, and thus terminate the loop.

Binary Files

When you store data in a file, you can store the data in text form or in binary format. Text form means you store everything as text, even numbers. For instance, storing the value -2.324216e+07 in text form means storing the 13 characters used to write this number. That requires converting the computer's internal representation of a floating-point number to character form, and that's exactly what the << insertion operator does. Binary format, however, means storing the computer's internal representation of a value. That is, instead of storing characters, store the 8-byte *double* representation of the value. For a character, the binary representation is the same as the text representation—the binary representation of the character's ASCII code. For numbers, however, the binary representation is much different from the text representation. See Figure 15-7.

Each format has its advantages. The text format is easy to read. You can use an ordinary editor or word processor to read and edit a text file. You easily can transfer a text file from one computer system to another. The binary format is more accurate for numbers, for it stores the exact internal representation of a value. There are no conversion errors or round-off errors. Saving data in binary format can be faster because there is no conversion and because you may be able to save data in larger chunks. And the binary format usually takes less space, depending upon the nature of the data. Transferring to another system can be a problem, however, if the new system uses a different internal representation for values. In that case, you (or someone) may have to write a program to translate one data format to another.

Let's look at a more concrete example. Consider the following structure definition and declaration:

```
struct planet
{
        char name[20];          // name of planet
        double population;      // its population
        double g;               // its acceleration of gravity
};
planet pl;
```

To save the contents of the structure *pl* in text form, you can do this:

```
ofstream fout("planets.dat", ios::app);
fout << pl.name << " " << pl.population << " " << pl.g << "\n";
```

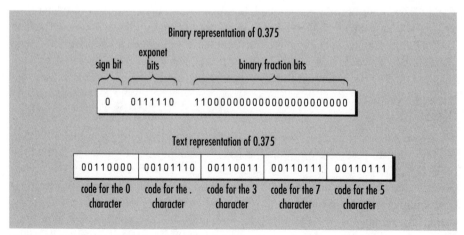

Figure 15-7 Binary and text representation of a floating-point number

Note that you have to provide each structure member explicitly by using the membership operator, and you have to separate adjacent data for legibility. If the structure contained, say, 30 members, this could get tedious.

To save the same information in binary format, you can do this:

```
ofstream fout("planets.dat", ios::app | ios::binary);
fout.write( (char *) &pl, sizeof pl);
```

This code saves the entire structure as a single unit, using the computer's internal representation of data. You won't be able to read the file as text, but the information will be stored more compactly and precisely than as text. And it certainly is easier to type the code. The two changes are using a binary file mode and using the *write()* member function, so let's examine them.

Some systems, such as DOS, support two file formats: text and binary. If you want to save data in binary form, you'd best use the binary file format. In C++ you do so by using the *ios::binary* constant in the file mode. If you want to know why you should do this on a DOS system, check the discussion in the note on Binary Files and Text Files.

BINARY FILES AND TEXT FILES

Using a binary file mode causes a program to transfer data from memory to a file, or vice versa, without any hidden translation taking place. Such is not necessarily the case for the default text mode. For instance, consider DOS text files. They represent a newline with a two-character combination—carriage return, linefeed. Macintosh text files represent a newline with a carriage return. UNIX files represent a newline with a linefeed. C++, which grew up on UNIX, also represents a newline with a linefeed. For portability, a DOS C++ program automatically translates the C++ newline to a carriage return, linefeed when writing to a text mode file; and a Macintosh C++ program translates the newline to a carriage return when writing to a file. When reading a text file, these programs convert the local newline back to the C++ form. The text format can cause problems with binary data, for a byte in the middle of a *double* value could have the same bit pattern as the ASCII code for the newline character. Also there are differences in how end-of-file is detected. So you should use the binary file mode when saving data in binary format. (UNIX systems have just one file mode, so on them the binary mode is the same as the text mode.)

To save data in binary form instead of text form, you can use the *write()* member function. This method, recall, copies a specified number of characters from memory to a file. We used it earlier to copy text, but it will copy any type data byte-by-byte *with no conversion*. For instance, if you pass it the address of a *long* variable and tell it to copy 8 characters, it will copy the 8 bytes constituting the *long* value verbatim to a file and not convert it to text. The only bit of awkwardness is that you have to type cast the address to type pointer-to-*char*. You can use the same approach to copy an entire *planet* structure. To get the number of bytes, use the *sizeof* operator:

```
fout.write( (char *) &pl, sizeof pl);
```

This statement goes to the address of the *pl* structure and copies the 36 bytes (the value of *sizeof pl* expression) beginning at this address to the file being managed by *fout*.

To recover the information from a file, use the corresponding *read()* method with an *ifstream* object:

```
ifstream fin("planets.dat", ios::binary);
fin.read((char *) &pl, sizeof pl);
```

This copies *sizeof pl* bytes from the file to the *pl* structure. This same approach can be used with classes that don't use virtual functions. In that case, just the data members are saved, not the methods. (Also, see the note in Programming Exercise 4.)

TIP

The *read()* and *write()* member functions complement each other. Use *read()* to recover data that has been written to a file with *write()*.

Listing 15-18 uses these methods to create and read a binary file. In form, the program is similar to Listing 15-17, but it uses *write()* and *read()* instead of the insertion operator and the *get()* method. It also uses manipulators to format the screen output.

COMPATIBILITY NOTE

Although the binary file concept is part of ANSI C, many UNIX-based C and C++ implementations do not provide support for the binary file mode. For instance, a UNIX-based C++ compiler may not recognize the *ios::binary* constant. The reason for this oversight is that UNIX systems only have one file type in the first place, so you can use binary operations such as *read()* and *write()* with the standard file format. Therefore, if your UNIX implementation rejects *ios::binary* as a valid constant, just omit it from your program. Symantec C++, on the other hand, has a special mode, *ios::translated*, for DOS text files and uses binary mode as a default. Indeed, it doesn't even have an *ios::binary* mode option.

Microsoft Visual C++ users should replace the first

```
fin.open(file, ios::binary);
```

with

```
fin.open(file, ios::in | ios::nocreate | ios::binary);
```

Symantec C++ users should replace the first

```
fin.open(file, ios::binary);
```

with

```
        fin.open(file, ios::in | ios::nocreate);
```

Beta versions of Metrowerks CodeWarrior don't yet support the manipulators of *iomanip.h,* but users of that product can use *cout.precision()* and
cout.width() member functions instead.

Listing 15-18 *binary.cpp*

```cpp
// binary.cpp -- append information to a binary file
#include <iostream.h>          // not required by most systems
#include <fstream.h>
#include <iomanip.h>
#include <stdlib.h>            // for exit()

struct planet
{
        char name[20];        // name of planet
        double population;    // its population
        double g;             // its acceleration of gravity
};

const char * file = "planets.dat";

int main(void)
{
        planet pl;
        cout.setf(ios::fixed, ios::floatfield);

// show initial contents
    ifstream fin;
    fin.open(file, ios::in | ios::binary);                // binary file
    //NOTE: some systems don't accept the ios::binary mode
    if (fin.good())
    {
        cout << "Here are the current contents of the "
            << file << " file:\n";
        while (fin.read((char *) &pl, sizeof pl))
            {
            cout << setw(20) << pl.name << ": "
                    << setprecision(0) << setw(12) << pl.population
                    << setprecision(2) << setw(6) << pl.g << "\n";
            }
    }
    fin.close();

// add new data
    ofstream fout(file, ios::out | ios::app | ios::binary);
    //NOTE: some systems don't accept the ios::binary mode
    if (fout.fail())
    {
            cerr << "Can't open " << file << " file for output:\n";
            exit(1);
```

continued on next page

continued from previous page

```
        }

        cout << "Enter planet name (enter a blank line to quit):\n";
        cin.getline(pl.name, 20);
        while (pl.name[0] != '\0')
        {
                cout << "Enter planetary population: ";
                cin >> pl.population;
                cout << "Enter planet's acceleration of gravity: ";
                cin >> pl.g;
                while (cin.get() != '\n')
                        continue;
                fout.write((char *) &pl, sizeof pl);
                cout << "Enter planet name (enter a blank line "
                        "to quit):\n";
                cin.getline(pl.name, 20);
        }
        fout.close();

// show revised file
        fin.clear();        // not required for some implementations, but won't hurt
        fin.open(file, ios::in | ios::binary);
        if (fin.good())
        {
            cout << "Here are the new contents of the "
                << file << " file:\n";
            while (fin.read((char *) &pl, sizeof pl))
                {
                cout << setw(20) << pl.name << ": "
                        << setprecision(0) << setw(12) << pl.population
                        << setprecision(2) << setw(6) << pl.g << "\n";
                }
        }
        fin.close();

        return 0;
}
```

Here is a sample initial run:

```
Enter planet name (enter a blank line to quit):
Earth
Enter planetary population: 5333000000
Enter planet's acceleration of gravity: 9.81
Enter planet name (enter a blank line to quit):

Here are the new contents of the planets.dat file:
            Earth:   5333000000  9.81
```

And here is a sample follow-up run:

```
Here are the current contents of the planets.dat file:
            Earth:   5333000000  9.81
Enter planet name (enter a blank line to quit):
```

```
Bill's Planet
Enter planetary population: 23020020
Enter planet's acceleration of gravity: 8.82
Enter planet name (enter a blank line to quit):

Here are the new contents of the planets.dat file:
                    Earth:      5333000000      9.81
            Bill's Planet:        23020020      8.82
```

We've already explained the major features of the program, but let's reexamine an old point. The program uses this code after reading the planet's *g* value:

```
while (cin.get() != '\n')
      continue;
```

This reads and discards input up through the newline character. The statement

```
cin.getline(pl.name, 20);
```

reads the newline so that the next input begins at the beginning of the next line. The next input statement reads the planet name, which then is checked to see if the first character is the null character. For this test to work correctly, it is essential that input extraction begin at the start of the line and not at the end of the previous line.

If your system doesn't support *getline()*, you can use *cin.get(pl.name,20).get(ch)*.

Random Access

For our last example, let's look at random access. That means moving directly to any location in the file instead of moving through it sequentially. The random access approach is often used with database files. A program will maintain a separate index file giving the location of data in the main data file. Then it can jump directly to that location, read the data there, and perhaps modify it. This approach is done most simply if the file consists of a collection of equal-sized *records*. Each record represents a related collection of data. For instance, in the preceding example, each file record would represent all the data about a particular planet. A file record corresponds rather naturally to a program structure or class.

The draft standard differs significantly from traditional C++ in its handling of random access. At the time of this writing, only a few compilers support the draft approach, so we'll present the traditional approach. But because the ANSI/ISO C++ standard is the future, we'll present that approach, too.

Traditional C++ Approach to Random Access

We'll base our example on the binary file program in Listing 15-18, for the *planet* structure provides a template for a file record. To add to the creative tension of programming, the example will open the file in a read-and-write mode so that it can both read and modify a record. You can do this by creating an *fstream* object. The *fstream* class derives from the *iostream* class, which, in turn, is based on both *istream* and *ostream* classes, so it inherits the methods of both. It also inherits two buffers, one for input and one for output, and synchronizes the handling of the two buffers. That is, as the program reads the file or writes to it, it moves both an input pointer in the input buffer and an output pointer in the output buffer in tandem.

The example will do the following:

❧ Display the current contents of the *planets.dat* file

❧ Ask which record you wish to modify

❧ Modify that record

❧ Show the revised file

A more ambitious program would use a menu and a loop to let you select from this list of actions indefinitely, but our version will perform each action just once. This simplified approach allows you to examine several aspects of read-write files without getting bogged down in matters of program design.

The first question to answer is what file mode to use. In order to read the file, you need the *ios::in* mode. For binary I/O, you need the *ios::binary* mode. (Again, on some systems you can omit, indeed, you may have to omit, this mode.) In order to write to the file, you need the *ios::out* or the *ios::app* mode. However, the append mode allows a program to add data to the end of the file only. The rest of the file is read-only; that is, you can read the original data, but not modify it. So you have to use *ios::out*. However, by default, using that mode truncates a file, discarding the data. You can negate that aspect by also using the *ios::ate* mode. This moves the file pointer to the end of the file, preserving the file data. As mentioned earlier, you use the | operator to combine modes. Thus you need the following statement to set up business:

```
finout.open(file,ios::in | ios::out | ios::ate | ios::binary);
```

Next, you need a way to move through a file. The *fstream* class inherits two methods for this: *seekg()* moves the input pointer to a given file location, and *seekp()* moves the output pointer to a given file location. (Actually, since the *fstream* class uses buffers for intermediate storage of data, the pointers point to locations in the buffers, not in the actual file.) You also can use *seekg()* with an *ifstream* object and *seekp()* with an *ostream* object. Here are the *seekg()* prototypes:

```
istream & seekg(streamoff, seek_dir);
istream & seekg(streampos);
```

The first prototype represents locating a file position measured, in bytes, as an offset from a file location specified by the second argument. The second prototype represents locating a file position measured in bytes from the beginning of a file.

Let's take a look at the arguments to the first prototype of *seekg()*. The *streamoff* type is an integer type defined by a *typedef,* and it's used to measure offsets, in bytes, from a particular location in a file. The *streamoff* argument represents the file position in bytes measured as an offset from one of three locations. The *seek_dir* argument is another integer type defined in *iostream.h*. It can be set to one of three constants defined in the *ios* class. The constant *ios::beg* means measure the offset from the beginning of the file. The constant *ios::cur* means measure the offset from the current position. The constant *ios::end* means measure the offset from the end of the file. Here are some sample calls, assuming *fin* is an *ifstream* object:

```
fin.seekg(30, ios::beg);      // same as the above
fin.seekg(-1, ios::cur);      // back up one byte
fin.seekg(0, ios::end);       // go to the end of the file
```

Now let's look at the second prototype. The *streampos* type is an integer type in some implementations, but it's a class in the draft standard. However, the *streampos* class includes a constructor with a *streamoff* argument, providing a path to convert integer values to *streampos* values. It represents an absolute location in a file measured from the beginning of the file. For many current implementations, you can treat a *streampos* position as if it measures a file location in bytes from the beginning of a file, with the first byte being byte 0. So the statement

```
fin.seekg(112);
```

locates the file pointer at byte 112, which would be the 113th byte in the file. If you want to check the current position of a file pointer, you can use the *tellg()* method for input streams and the *tellp()* methods for output streams. Each returns a *streampos* value representing the current position, in bytes, measured from the beginning of the file. When you create an *fstream* object, the input and output pointers move in tandem, so *tellg()* and *tellp()* return the same value. But if you use an *istream* object to manage the input stream and an *ostream* object to manage the output stream to the same file, then the input and output pointers move independently of one another, and *tellg()* and *tellp()* can return different values.

Because our example uses the *ios::ate* mode, the program goes to the end of the file when opening it. (Using *ios::ate*, recall, prevents the program from truncating the file.) But you can then use *seekg()* to go to the file beginning. Here is a section of code that opens the file, goes to the beginning, and displays the file contents:

```
fstream finout;                    // read and write streams
finout.open(file,ios::in | ios::out | ios::ate | ios::binary);
//NOTE: Some systems require omitting | ios::binary
if (finout.good())
{
        finout.seekg(0, ios::beg);    // go to beginning
        cout << "Here are the current contents of the "
                << file << " file:\n";
        int ct = 0;
        while (finout.read((char *) &pl, sizeof pl))
        {
                cout << ct++ << ": " << setw(20) << pl.name << ": "
                        << setprecision(0) << setw(12) << pl.population
                        << setprecision(2) << setw(6) << pl.g << "\n";
```

continued on next page

continued from previous page

```
        }
        if (finout.eof())
                finout.clear();        // clear eof flag
        else
        {
                cerr << "Error in reading " << file << ".\n";
                exit(1);
        }
}
else
{
        cerr << file << " could not be opened-- bye.\n";
        exit(2);
}
```

This is similar to the start of Listing 15-18, but there are some changes and additions. First, as just described, the program uses an *fstream* object with a read-write mode, and it uses *seekg()* to position the file pointer at the start of the file. Next, the program makes the minor change of numbering the records as they are displayed. Then it makes the following important addition:

```
if (finout.eof())
        finout.clear();        // clear eof flag
else
{
        cerr << "Error in reading " << file << ".\n";
        exit(1);
}
```

The problem is that once the program reads and displays the entire file, it sets the *eof* flag on. This convinces the program that it's finished with the file and disables any further reading of or writing to the file. Using the *clear()* method resets the stream state, turning off the *eof* flag. Now the program can once again access the file. The *else* part handles the possibility that the program quit reading the file for some reason other than reaching the end-of-file, such as a hardware failure.

The next step is to identify the record to be changed, then change it. To do this, the program asks the user to enter a record number. Multiplying the number by the number of bytes in a record yields the byte number for the beginning of the record. If *record* is the record number, the desired byte number is *record * sizeof pl*:

```
cout << "Enter the record number you wish to change: ";
long rec;
cin >> rec;
while (cin.get() != '\n')
        continue;              // get rid of newline
if (rec < 0 || rec >= ct)
{
        cerr << "Invalid record number -- bye\n";
        exit(3);
}
streampos place = rec * sizeof pl;   // convert to streampos type
finout.seekg(place);
```

The variable *ct* represents the number of records; the program exits if you try to go beyond the limits of the file. The *streampos* type originally was defined as an integer type, but in more recent C++ versions, it's defined as a class object that can be initialized with an integer position. The code above works for both cases.

Next, the program displays the current record:

```
finout.read((char *) &pl, sizeof pl);
cout << "Your selection:\n";
cout << rec << ": " << setw(20) << pl.name << ": "
        << setprecision(0) << setw(12) << pl.population
        << setprecision(2) << setw(6) << pl.g << "\n";
if (finout.eof())
        finout.clear();                                 // clear eof flag
finout.seekp(place);  // go back
```

After displaying the record, the program resets the file pointer to the beginning of the record. Then it lets you change the record:

```
cout << "Enter planet name: ";
cin.get(pl.name, 20).get(ch);
cout << "Enter planetary population: ";
cin >> pl.population;
cout << "Enter planet's acceleration of gravity: ";
cin >> pl.g;
finout.write((char *) &pl, sizeof pl) << flush;
if (finout.fail())
{
        cerr << "Error on attempted write\n";
        exit(5);
}
```

The program flushes the output to guarantee that the file is updated before proceeding to the next stage.

Finally, to display the revised file, the program uses *seekg()* to reset the file pointer to the beginning. Listing 15-19 shows the complete program.

COMPATIBILITY NOTE

Symantec C++ 6.0 and some UNIX systems require that you omit the binary mode setting. Metrowerks CodeWarrior, following the draft standard, doesn't support the *fstream* class. Symantec C++ 6.0 (PC) and 7.0 (Mac) print the final line twice. Symantec C++ 7.0 (Mac) appends the data instead of replacing the specified record. (Version 6.0 for the Mac worked properly in this respect, however.) GNU C++ 2.0 required paring

```
if (finout.eof())
        finout.clear();              // clear eof flag
else
{
        cerr << "Error in reading " << file << ".\n";
        exit(1);
}
```

down to the following:

```
finout.clear();            // clear eof flag
```

Listing 15-19 random.cpp

```
// random.cpp -- random access to a binary file (traditional C++)
#include <iostream.h> // not required by most systems
#include <fstream.h>
#include <iomanip.h>
#include <stdlib.h>              // for exit()

struct planet
{
        char name[20];          // name of planet
        double population;      // its population
        double g;               // its acceleration of gravity
};

const char * file = "planets.dat";

int main(void)
{
        planet pl;
        cout.setf(ios::fixed, ios::floatfield);

// show initial contents
    fstream finout;                         // read and write streams
    finout.open(file,ios::in | ios::out | ios::ate |
                      ios::binary);
    //NOTE: Some systems require omitting | ios::binary
    int ct = 0;
    if (finout.good())
    {
            finout.seekg(0);            // go to beginning
            cout << "Here are the current contents of the "
                    << file << " file:\n";
            while (finout.read((char *) &pl, sizeof pl))
            {
                cout    << ct++ << ": " << setw(20) << pl.name << ": "
                        << setprecision(0) << setw(12) << pl.population
                        << setprecision(2) << setw(6) << pl.g << "\n";
            }
            if (finout.eof())
                finout.clear();             // clear eof flag
            else
            {
                cerr << "Error in reading " << file << ".\n";
                exit(1);
            }
    }
    else
    {
            cerr << file << " could not be opened -- bye.\n";
```

```
        exit(2);
    }

// change a record
    cout << "Enter the record number you wish to change: ";
    long rec;
    cin >> rec;
    while (cin.get() != '\n')
        continue;                    // get rid of newline
    if (rec < 0 || rec >= ct)
    {
        cerr << "Invalid record number -- bye\n";
        exit(3);
    }
    streampos place = rec * sizeof pl;       // convert to streampos type
    finout.seekg(place);
    if (finout.fail())
    {
        cerr << "Error on attempted seek\n";
        exit(4);
    }

    finout.read((char *) &pl, sizeof pl);
    cout << "Your selection:\n";
    cout << rec << ": " << setw(20) << pl.name << ": "
        << setprecision(0) << setw(12) << pl.population
        << setprecision(2) << setw(6) << pl.g << "\n";
    if (finout.eof())
        finout.clear();                      // clear eof flag
    finout.seekp(place);        // go back

    cout << "Enter planet name: ";
    cin.getline(pl.name, 20);
    cout << "Enter planetary population: ";
    cin >> pl.population;
    cout << "Enter planet's acceleration of gravity: ";
    cin >> pl.g;
    finout.write((char *) &pl, sizeof pl) << flush;
    if (finout.fail())
    {
        cerr << "Error on attempted write\n";
        exit(5);
    }

// show revised file
    ct = 0;
    finout.seekg(0);                        // go to beginning of file
    cout << "Here are the new contents of the " << file
        << " file:\n";
    while (finout.read((char *) &pl, sizeof pl))
    {
        cout << ct++ << ": " << setw(20) << pl.name << ": "
            << setprecision(0) << setw(12) << pl.population
```

continued on next page

continued from previous page

```
                      << setprecision(2) << setw(6) << pl.g << "\n";
    }
    finout.close();

    return 0;
}
```

Here's a sample run based on a *planets.dat* file that has had a few more entries added since you last saw it:

```
Here are the current contents of the planets.dat File:
0:                Earth:       5333000000         9.81
1:         Bill's Planet:       23020020         8.82
2:              Trantor:     58000000000        15.03
3:              Trellan:         4256000         9.62
4:            Freestone:      3845120000         8.68
5:            Taanagoot:       350000002        10.23
6:                Marin:          232000         9.79
Enter the record number you wish to change: 2
Your selection:
2:              Trantor:     58000000000        15.03
Enter planet name: Trantor
Enter planetary population: 59500000000
Enter planet's acceleration of gravity: 10.53
Here are the new contents of the planets.dat file:
0:                Earth:       5333000000         9.81
1:         Bill's Planet:       23020020         8.82
2:              Trantor:     59500000000        10.53
3:              Trellan:         4256000         9.62
4:            Freestone:      3845120000         8.68
5:            Taanagoot:       350000002        10.23
6:                Marin:          232000         9.79
```

Using the techniques in this program, you can extend it to allow you to add new material and delete records. If you were to expand the program, it would be a good idea to reorganize it by using classes and functions. For example, you could convert the *planet* structure to a class definition, then overload the << insertion operator so that *cout << pl* displays the class data members formatted as in the example.

Draft Standard Approach to Random Access

The main differences between traditional C++ and draft C++ are that the draft standard doesn't define the *fstream* class for simultaneous I/O and it doesn't define the *seekg()* and *seekp()* member functions. So we have to find alternate approaches. Again, keep in mind that the standard is still under development at the time of this writing. First, we can replace

```
fstream finout;                        // read and write streams
finout.open(file,ios::in | ios::out | ios::ate |
                ios::binary);
```

with the following:

```
// associate input stream with a file
ifstream fin(file,ios::in | ios::out | ios::ate | ios::binary);
ostream fout(fin.rdbuf());    // associate output stream with same file
```

The first statement opens a file for both input and output. However, because *fin* is an *ifstream* object, it has a member function for input but not for output. The second statement creates a stream for output, but using the same buffer as the input stream. The *rdbuf()* member function returns a pointer to the *ifstream*'s object's buffer, as represented by a *streambuf* object. We use an *ostream* object instead of an *ofstream* object for two reasons. First, we just want to add output capabilities to an existing stream, not create an entire new stream. Second, there's an *ostream* constructor that takes a *streambuf* * argument, but there's no corresponding *ofstream* constructor, so using *ofstream* is not an option. Anyway, the upshot is that we can use *fin* to invoke input methods and *fout* to invoke output methods, with both sharing the same buffer.

The alternative to *seekg()* is a bit ugly. We can replace

```
finout.seekg(0);
```

with the following:

```
fin.rdbuf()->pubseekoff(0,ios::beg, ios::in | ios::out | ios::ate |
     ios::binary)
```

The *pubseekoff()* function takes three arguments. The first is an offset, in bytes. It's of type *streamoff,* which is a *typedef* name for an integer type, such as *long.* The second is a value indicating from where the offset is measured. Table 15-9 shows the possible choices. The third argument is the file mode.

Mode · Meaning

Mode	Meaning
ios::beg	from the beginning of a file
ios::cur	from the current position in the file
ios::end	from the end of the file

Table 15-9 Seek modes

The *pubseekoff()* function isn't a class member of the *ifstream* class, but it is a member function of a private member object of that class. The member object does inherit the *pubseekoff()* function, and the *rdbuf()* function returns a pointer to that member. Thus, *fin.rdbuf()* returns a pointer to an object that can invoke the *pubseekoff()* function.

The *pubseekoff()* function returns a *streampos* object that describes the current position in a file. You can use that fact to control an input loop like this, where *end* and *now* are *streampos* variables and *fmode* represents the file mode:

```
end = fin.rdbuf()->pubseekoff(0,ios::end, fmode);   // locate file end
now = fin.rdbuf()->pubseekoff(0,ios::beg, fmode);   // go to beginning
while (now != end)
{
```

continued on next page

continued from previous page

```
        fin.read((char *) &pl, sizeof pl);   // read a block
        now = fin.rdbuf()->pubseekoff(0,ios::cur, fmode);
        ...
}
```

Listing 15-20 puts these ideas together to create an alternative version of Listing 15-19. It uses *precision()* and *width()* instead of the corresponding manipulators because the only implementation (Metrowerks CodeWarrior CW 3.5) of the draft standard available to the author hadn't yet implemented the *iomanip.h* methods.

Listing 15-20 *randomds.cpp*

```
// randomds.cpp -- draft standard random access to a binary file
#include <iostream.h>          // not required by most systems
#include <fstream.h>
#include <stdlib.h>            // for exit()

struct planet
{
        char name[20];         // name of planet
        double population;     // its population
        double g;              // its acceleration of gravity
};

const char * file = "planets.dat";

int main(void)
{
        planet pl;
        cout.setf(ios::fixed, ios::floatfield);
        cout.setf(ios::right, ios::adjustfield);

// show initial contents
    ios::openmode fmode = ios::in | ios::out | ios::ate | ios::binary;
    ifstream fin(file,fmode); // associate input stream with a file
    ostream fout(fin.rdbuf());// associate output stream with same file
    streampos end;
    streampos now;
    int ct = 0;
    if (fin.good())
    {
            end = fin.rdbuf()->pubseekoff(0,ios::end, fmode);  // locate file end
            now = fin.rdbuf()->pubseekoff(0,ios::beg, fmode);  // go to beginning
            cout << "Here are the current contents of the "
                    << file << " file:\n";
            while (now != end)
            {
                    fin.read((char *) &pl, sizeof pl);        // read a block
                    now = fin.rdbuf()->pubseekoff(0,ios::cur, fmode);
                    // now is new location
                    cout << ct++ << ": " ;
                    cout.width(20);
```

```
                    cout << pl.name << ": ";
                    cout.precision(0);
                    cout.width(12);
                    cout << pl.population;
                    cout.precision(2);
                    cout.width(6);
                    cout << pl.g << "\n";
            }
            if (fin.eof())
                    fin.clear();                    // clear eof flag
    }
    else
    {
            cerr << file << " could not be opened -- bye.\n";
            exit(2);
    }

// change a record
    cout << "Enter the record number you wish to change: ";
    long rec;
    cin >> rec;
    while (cin.get() != '\n')
            continue;                       // get rid of newline
    if (rec < 0 || rec >= ct)
    {
            cerr << "Invalid record number -- bye\n";
            exit(3);
    }
    streamoff offset = rec * sizeof pl;
    now = fin.rdbuf()->pubseekoff(offset,ios::beg, fmode);
    if (fin.fail())
    {
            cerr << "Error on attempted seek\n";
            exit(4);
    }

    fin.read((char *) &pl, sizeof pl);
    cout << "Your selection:\n";
    cout << rec << ": ";
    cout.width(20);
    cout << pl.name << ": ";
    cout.precision(0);
    cout.width(12);
    cout << pl.population;
    cout.precision(2);
    cout.width(6);
    cout << pl.g << "\n";
    if (fin.eof())
            fin.clear();                            // clear eof flag

    cout << "Enter planet name: ";
    cin.getline(pl.name, 20);
    cout << "Enter planetary population: ";
```

continued on next page

continued from previous page

```
    cin >> pl.population;
    cout << "Enter planet's acceleration of gravity: ";
    cin >> pl.g;
    fout.rdbuf()->pubseekoff(offset, ios::beg, fmode);        // go back
    fout.write((char *) &pl, sizeof pl) << flush;
    if (fout.fail())
    {
            cerr << "Error on attempted write\n";
            exit(5);
    }

// show revised file
    ct = 0;
    now = fin.rdbuf()->pubseekoff(0,ios::beg,fmode); // go to beginning
    cout << "Here are the new contents of the " << file
            << " file:\n";
    while (now != end)
    {
            fin.read((char *) &pl, sizeof pl);
            now =fin.rdbuf()->pubseekoff(0, ios::cur, fmode);
            cout << ct++ << ": " ;
            cout.width(20);
            cout << pl.name << ": ";
            cout.precision(0);
            cout.width(12);
            cout << pl.population;
            cout.precision(2);
            cout.width(6);
            cout << pl.g << "\n";
    }
    fin.close();

    return 0;
}
```

The draft standard approach seems more awkward than the traditional C++ approach, but perhaps the standard will evolve into something more lovely.

Incore Formatting

The *iostream* family supports I/O between the program and a terminal. The *fstream* family uses the same interface to provide I/O between a program and a file. The C++ library also provides a *strstream* family that uses the same interface to provide I/O between a program and a *char* array. That is, you can use the same *ostream* methods we've used with *cout* to write formatted information into an array, and you can use *istream* methods like *getline()* to read information from an array. The process of reading formatted information from a *char* array or of writing formatted information to such an array is termed *incore formatting*. Let's take a brief look at these facilities.

The *strstream.h* header file (*strstream* or *strstream.ns* in the draft standard) defines an *ostrstream* class derived from the *ostream* class. If you create an *ostrstream* object, you can write information to it, which it stores in a *char* array. You can use the same methods with an *ostrstream* object that you can with *cout*. That is, you can do something like the following:

```
ostrstream outstr;
double price = 55.00;
char * ps = " for a copy of the draft C++ standard!";
outstr.precision(2);
outstr.setf(ios::fixed, ios::floatfield);
outstr << "Pay only $" << price << ps << end;
```

The formatted text goes into a *char* array, and the object uses dynamic memory allocation to expand the array size as needed. The *ostrstream* class has a member function, called *str()*, that returns the address of the array:

```
char * pstr = outstr.str();    // returns address of formatted information
```

Using the *str()* method "freezes" the object, and you no longer can write to it. Also, once you freeze the object, it's your responsibility to free the allocated memory when you no longer need it:

```
delete pstr;             // free memory when you are done
```

Listing 15-21 provides a short example. Note that it explicitly writes a null character to the *outstr* object. That's because *ostrstream* objects maintain a *char* array, and a *char* array is not in itself a string. So if you want to treat the contents as a string, as this example does, you have to supply the terminating null character explicitly. Incidentally, including the null character as part of a quoted string, and in " *megabytes.\n\0*", doesn't work necessarily, for string output functions typically don't output null characters.

Listing 15-21 *strout.cpp*

```
// strout.cpp -- incore formatting (output)
#include <iostream.h>
#include <strstream.h>
const int LIM = 20;
int main(void)
{
        ostrstream outstr;     // manages a char array

        char hdisk[LIM];
        cout << "What's the name of your hard disk? ";
        cin.getline(hdisk, LIM);
        int cap;
        cout << "What's its capacity in MB? ";
        cin >> cap;
        // write formatted information to array
        outstr << "The hard disk " << hdisk << " has a capacity of "
```

continued on next page

continued from previous page

```
                          << cap << " megabytes.\n";
        outstr.put('\0');                    // make it a string
        char * po = outstr.str();      // get address of array
        cout << po;                    // show contents
        delete po;                     // free memory
        return 0;
}
```

Here's a sample run:

```
What's the name of your hard disk? Athena
What's its capacity in MB? 425
The hard disk Athena has a capacity of 425 megabytes.
```

Instead of having an *ostrstream* object use anonymous dynamic memory, you can have it use a named array in your program. Just provide the array address and size as arguments to the *ostrstream* constructor. For instance, you can alter the beginning of Listing 15-21 to look like this:

```
#include <iostream.h>
#include <strstream.h>
const int LIM = 20;
const int ARLIM = 256;
int main(void)
{
        char ar[ARLIM];
        ostrstream outstr(ar, sizeof ar);    // manages a char array
```

Now the formatted output will be placed in the *ar* array and you can examine the contents directly. For instance, if you add a terminating null character to the array, you can display it as a string:

```
cout << ar;
```

More generally, the *ostrstream* constructor, like the *ofstream* constructor, accepts a third argument specifying the mode. The default value is *ios::out*.

The *istrstream* class lets you use the *istream* family of methods to read data from a *char* array. Suppose *buf* is an array of *char*. To create an *istrstream* object associated with this array, do the following:

```
istrstream instr(buf, sizeof buf);    // use buf for input
```

Then you use *istream* methods to read data from the array. For instance, if the array contained a bunch of integers in character format, you could read them as follows:

```
int n;
int sum = 0;
while (instr << n)
        sum += num;
```

Listing 15-22 uses the overloaded >> operator to read the contents of an array one word at a time.

Listing 15-22 *strin.cpp*

```
// strin.cpp -- formatted reading from a char array
#include <iostream.h>
#include <strstream.h>
const int LIM = 20;
int main(void)
{
        char buf[] = "It was a dark and stormy day, and "
                           " the full moon glowed brilliantly.";
        istrstream instr(buf, sizeof buf);      // use buf for input
        char word[LIM];
        while ((instr >> word).good())           // read a word at a time
                cout << word << endl;
        return 0;
}
```

Here is the program output:

```
It
was
a
dark
and
stormy
day,
and
the
full
moon
glowed
brilliantly.
```

In short, *istrstream* and *ostrstream* classes give you the power of the *istream* and *ostream* class methods to manage character data stored in arrays.

⚙ What Now?

If you have worked your way through this book, you should have a good grasp of the rules of C++. However, that's just the beginning in learning this language. The second stage is learning to use the language effectively, and that is the longer journey. The best situation to be in is a work or learning environment that brings you into contact with good C++ code and programmers. Also, now that you know C++, you can read books that concentrate on more advanced topics and upon object-oriented programming. Appendix F lists some of these resources.

In addition to increasing your understanding of C++ in general, you may wish to learn about specific class libraries. Microsoft, Borland, and Symantec, for example, offer extensive class libraries to facilitate programming for the Windows environment, and Symantec and Metrowerks offer similar facilities for Macintosh programming.

Summary

A stream is a flow of bytes into or out of a program. A buffer is a temporary holding area in memory that acts as an intermediary between a program and a file or other I/O devices. Information can be transferred between a buffer and a file using large chunks of data of the size most efficiently handled by devices like disk drives. And information can be transferred between a buffer and a program in a byte-by-byte flow that often is more convenient for the processing done in a program. C++ handles input by connecting a buffered stream to a program and to its source of input. Similarly, C++ handles output by connecting a buffered stream to a program and to its output target. The *iostream.h* and *fstream.h* files constitute an I/O class library that defines a rich set of classes for managing streams. C++ programs that include the *iostream.h* file automatically open four streams, managing them with four objects. The *cin* object manages the standard input stream, which, by default, connects to the standard input device, typically a keyboard. The *cout* object manages the standard output stream, which, by default, connects to the standard output device, typically a monitor. The *cerr* and *clog* objects manage unbuffered and buffered streams connected to the standard error device, typically a monitor.

The I/O class library provides a variety of useful methods. The *istream* class defines versions of the extraction operator (>>) that recognize all the basic C++ types and that convert character input to those types. The *get()* family of methods and the *getline()* method provide further support for single-character input and for string input. Similarly, the *ostream* class defines versions of the insertion operator (<<) that recognize all the basic C++ types and that convert them to suitable character output. The *put()* method provides further support for single-character output.

You can control how a program formats output by using *ios* class methods and by using manipulators (functions that can be concatenated with insertion) defined in the *iostream.h* and *iomanip.h* files. These methods and manipulators let you control the number base, the field width, the number of decimal places displayed, the system used to display floating-point values, and other elements.

The *fstream.h* file provides class definitions that extend the *iostream.h* methods to file I/O. The *ifstream* class derives from the *istream* class. By associating an *ifstream* object with a file, you can use all the *istream* methods for reading the file. Similarly, associating an *ofstream* object with a file lets you use the *ostream* methods to write to a file. And associating an *fstream* object with a file lets you employ both input and output methods with the file.

To associate a file with a stream, you can provide the file name when initializing a file stream object or you can first create a file stream object, then use the *open()* method to associate the stream with a file. The *close()* method terminates the connection between a stream and a file. The class constructors and the *open()* method take an optional second argument that provides the file mode. The file mode determines such things as whether the file is to be read and/or written to, whether opening a file for writing truncates it or not, whether attempting to open a nonexistent file is an error or not, and whether to use the binary or text mode.

A text file stores all information in character form. For instance, numeric values are converted to character representations. The usual insertion and extraction operators, along with *get()* and *getline()*, support this mode. A binary file stores all information using the same binary representation the computer uses internally. Binary files store data, particularly floating-point values, more accurately and compactly than text files, but they are less portable. The *read()* and *write()* methods support binary input and output.

The *seekg()* and *seekp()* functions provide traditional C++ random access for files. These class methods let you position a file pointer relative to the beginning of a file, relative to the end, or relative to the current position. The *tellg()* and *tellp()* methods report the current file position. The draft standard offers *pubseekoff()* to seek and report file positions.

Review Questions

1. What role does the *iostream.h* file (or *iostream* or *iostream.ns*) play in C++ I/O?

2. Why does typing a number such as **121** as input require a program to make a conversion?

3. What's the difference between the standard output and the standard error?

4. Why is *cout* able to display various C++ types without being provided explicit instructions for each type?

5. What feature of the output method definitions allows you to concatenate output?

6. Write a program that requests an integer and then displays it in decimal, octal, and hexadecimal form. Display each form on the same line in fields that are 15 characters wide, and use the C++ number base prefixes.

7. Write a program that requests the information shown below and that formats it as shown:

```
Enter your name: Billy Gruff
Enter your hourly wages: 12
Enter number of hours worked: 7.5
First format:
                    Billy Gruff: $      12.00:  7.5
Second format:
Billy Gruff                   : $12.00    :7.5
```

8. Consider the following program:

```cpp
//rq15-8.cpp
#include <iostream.h>

int main(void)
{
 char ch;
 int ct1 = 0;

 cin >> ch;
 while (ch != 'q')
 {
        ct1++;
        cin >> ch;
 }

 int ct2 = 0;
 cin.get(ch);
 while (ch != 'q')
 {
        ct2++;
        cin.get(ch);
 }
 cout << "ct1 = " << ct1 << "; ct2 = " << ct2 << "\n";

 return 0;
}
```

What does it print, given the following input:

```
I see a q (ENTER)
I see a q (ENTER)
```

Here (ENTER) signifies pressing the (ENTER) key.

9. Both of the following statements read and discard characters up to and including the end of a line. In what way does the behavior of one differ from that of the other?

```cpp
while (cin.get() != "\n")
        continue;
cin.ignore(80, "\n");
```

 # Programming Exercises

1. Write a program that counts the number of characters up to the first $ in input and that leaves the $ in the input stream.

2. Write a program that copies your keyboard input (up to simulated end-of-file) to a file named on the command line.

3. Write a program that copies one file to another. Have the program take the file names from the command line. Have the program report if it cannot open a file.

4. Consider the class definitions of programming exercise 13-5. If you haven't yet done that exercise, do so now. Then do the following:

Write a program that uses standard C++ I/O and file I/O in conjunction with data of types *employee, manager, fink,* and *highfink,* as defined in programming exercise13-5. The program should be along the general lines of Listing 15-17 in that it should let you add new data to a file. The first time through, the program should solicit data from the user, then show all the entries, then save the information in a file. On subsequent uses, the program should first read and display the file data, then let the user add data, then show all the data. One difference is that data should be handled by an array of pointers to type *employee.* That way, a pointer can point to an *employee* object or to objects of any of the three derived types. Keep the array small to facilitate checking the program:

```
const int MAX = 10;   // no more than 10 objects
...
employee * pc[MAX];
```

For keyboard entry, the program should use a menu to offer the user the choice of which type of object to create. The menu will use a switch to use *new* to create an object of the desired type and to assign the object's address to a pointer in the *pc* array. Then that object can use the virtual *setall()* function to elicit the appropriate data from the user:

```
pc[i]->setall();       // invokes function corresponding to type of object
```

To save the data to a file, devise a virtual *writeall()* function for that purpose:

```
for (i = 0; i < index; i++)
        pc[i]->writeall(fout);// fout ofstream connected to output file
```

Note: Use text I/O, not binary I/O, for this exercise. (Unfortunately, virtual objects include pointers to tables of pointers to virtual functions, and *write()* copies this information to a file. An object filled by using *read()* from the file gets weird values for the function pointers, which really messes up the behavior of virtual functions.) Use a newline to separate each data field from the next; this makes it easier to identify fields on input.

The tricky part is recovering the data from the file. The problem is, how can the program know whether the next item to be recovered is an *employee* object, a *manager* object, a *fink* type, or a *highfink* type? One approach is, when writing the data for an object to a file, precede the data with an integer indicating the type of object to follow. Then, on file input, the program can read the integer, then use a switch to create the appropriate object to receive the data:

```
enum classkind{Employee, Manager, Fink, Highfink}; // in class header
...
while((fin >> classtype).get(ch)){ // newline separates int from data
        switch(classtype) {
                case Employee  : pc[i] = new employee;
                               : break;
```

Then you can use the pointer to invoke a virtual *getall()* function to read the information:

```
pc[i++]->getall();
```

APPENDIX A

Number Bases

Our method for writing numbers is based on powers of 10. For instance, consider the number 2468. The 2 represents 2 thousands, the 4 represents 4 hundreds, the 6 represents 6 tens, and the 8 represents 8 ones:

$$2468 = 2 \times 1000 + 4 \times 100 + 6 \times 10 + 8 \times 1$$

One thousand is $10 \times 10 \times 10$, which can be written as 10^3, or 10 to the 3rd power. Using this notation, we can write the preceding relationship this way:

$$2468 = 2 \times 10^3 + 4 \times 10^2 + 6 \times 10^1 + 8 \times 10^0$$

Because our number notation is based on powers of 10, we refer to it as *base 10,* or *decimal,* notation. One can just as easily pick another number as a base. C++ lets you use *base 8 (octal)* and *base 16 (hexadecimal)* notation for writing integer numbers. (Note: 10^0 is 1, as is any nonzero number to the zero power.)

Octal Integers

Octal numbers are based on powers of 8, so base 8 notation uses the digits 0–7 in writing numbers. C++ uses a 0 prefix to indicate octal notation. Thus, 0177 is an octal value. You can use powers of 8 to find the equivalent base 10 value:

$$0177 \text{ (octal)} = 1 \times 8^2 + 7 \times 8^1 + 7 \times 8^0 = 1 \times 64 + 7 \times 8 + 7 \times 1 = 127 \text{ (decimal)}$$

The UNIX operating system often uses octal representation of values, which is why C++ and C provide octal notation.

Hexadecimal Numbers

Hexadecimal numbers are based on powers of 16. That means 10 in hexadecimal represents the value $16 + 0$, or 16. To represent the values between 9 and hexadecimal 16, we need a few more digits. Standard hexadecimal notation uses the letters a–f for that purpose. C++ accepts either lowercase or uppercase versions of these characters, as shown in Table A-1.

Hexadecimal digits	Decimal value	Hexadecimal digits	Decimal value
a or A	10	d or D	13
b or B	11	e or E	14
c or C	12	f or F	15

Table A-1 Hexadecimal digits

C++ uses a 0x or 0X notation to indicate hexadecimal notation. Thus 0x2B3 is a hexadecimal value. To find its decimal equivalent, you can evaluate the powers of 16:

0x2B3 (hex) = $2 \times 16^2 + 11 \times 16^1 + 3 \times 16^0 = 2 \times 256 + 11 \times 16 + 3 = 691$ (decimal)

Hardware documentation often uses hexadecimal notation to represent values such as memory locations and port numbers.

Binary Numbers

Whether you use decimal, octal, or hexadecimal notation for writing an integer, the computer stores it as a *binary,* or base 2, value. Binary notation uses just two digits, 0 and 1. As an example, 10011011 is a binary number. Note, however, that C++ doesn't provide for writing a number in binary notation. Binary numbers are based on powers of 2:

$$10011011 = 1 \times 2^7 + 0 \times 2^6 + 0 \times 2^5 + 1 \times 2^4 + 1 \times 2^3 + 0 \times 2^2 + 1 \times 2^1 + 1 \times 2^0$$
$$= 128 + 0 + 0 + 16 + 8 + 0 + 2 + 0$$
$$= 154$$

Binary notation makes a nice match to computer memory, in which each individual unit, called a *bit*, can be set to off or on. Just identify the off setting with 0 and the on

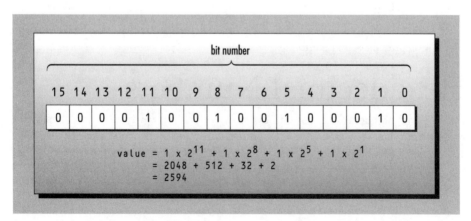

Figure A-1 A 2-byte integer value

setting with 1. Memory commonly is organized in units called *bytes,* with each byte being 8 bits. The bits in a byte are numbered corresponding to the associated power of 2. Thus the rightmost bit is bit number 0, the next bit is bit 1, and so on. Figure A-1, for example, represents a 2-byte integer.

APPENDIX B

C++ Keywords

Keywords are identifiers that form the vocabulary of a programming language. They may not be used for other purposes, such as serving as a variable name. The following list shows C++'s keywords; not all of them are currently implemented. Keywords shown in boldface are also keywords in ANSI C.

asm	**auto**	bool	**break**	**case**
catch	**char**	class	**const**	const_cast
continue	**default**	delete	**do**	**double**
dynamic_cast	**else**	**enum**	**extern**	false
float	**for**	friend	**goto**	**if**
inline	**int**	**long**	mutable	namespace
new	operator	private	protected	public
register	reinterpret_cast	**return**	**short**	**signed**
sizeof	**static**	static_cast	**struct**	**switch**
template	this	throw	true	try
typedef	typeid	**union**	**unsigned**	virtual
void	**volatile**	wchar_t	**while**	

APPENDIX C

The ASCII Character Set

Computers store characters using a numeric code. The ASCII code is the most commonly used code in the United States. C++ lets you represent most single characters directly, by including the character in single quotation marks, as in *'A'* for the A character. You can also represent a single character by using the octal or hex code preceded by a backslash; for instance, *'\012'* and *'\0xa'* both represent the linefeed (LF) character. Such *escape sequences* can also be part of a string, as in *"Hello,\012my dear"*.

When used as a prefix in the following table, the ^ character denotes using a (CONTROL) key.

Decimal	Octal	Hex	Binary	Character	ASCII Name
0	0	0	00000000	^@	NUL
1	01	0x1	00000001	^A	SOH
2	02	0x2	00000010	^B	STX
3	03	0x3	00000011	^C	ETX
4	04	0x4	00000100	^D	EOT
5	05	0x5	00000101	^E	ENQ
6	06	0x6	00000110	^F	ACK
7	07	0x7	00000111	^G	BEL
8	010	0x8	00001000	^H	BS
9	011	0x9	00001001	^I	HT
10	012	0xa	00001010	^J	LF
11	013	0xb	00001011	^K	VT
12	014	0xc	00001100	^L	FF
13	015	0xd	00001101	^M	CR
14	016	0xe	00001110	^N	SO
15	017	0xf	00001111	^O	SI

continued on next page

continued from previous page

Decimal	Octal	Hex	Binary	Character	ASCII Name
16	020	0x10	00010000	^P	DLE
17	021	0x11	00010001	^Q	DC1
18	022	0x12	00010010	^R	DC2
19	023	0x13	00010011	^S	DC3
20	024	0x14	00010100	^T	DC4
21	025	0x15	00010101	^U	NAK
22	026	0x16	00010110	^V	SYN
23	027	0x17	00010111	^W	ETB
24	030	0x18	00011000	^X	CAN
25	031	0x19	00011001	^Y	EM
26	032	0x1a	00011010	^Z	SUB
27	033	0x1b	00011011	^esc	ESC
28	034	0x1c	00011100	^\	FS
29	035	0x1d	00011101	^]	GS
30	036	0x1e	00011110	^^	RS
31	037	0x1f	00011111	^_	US
32	040	0x20	00100000	space	SP
33	041	0x21	00100001	!	
34	042	0x22	00100010	"	
35	043	0x23	00100011	#	
36	044	0x24	00100100	$	
37	045	0x25	00100101	%	
38	046	0x26	00100110	&	
39	047	0x27	00100111	'	
40	050	0x28	00101000	(	
41	051	0x29	00101001	)	
42	052	0x2a	00101010	*	
43	053	0x2b	00101011	+	

Decimal	Octal	Hex	Binary	Character	ASCII Name
44	054	0x2c	00101100	,	
45	055	0x2d	00101101	-	
46	056	0x2e	00101110	.	
47	057	0x2f	00101111	/	
48	060	0x30	00110000	0	
49	061	0x31	00110001	1	
50	062	0x32	00110010	2	
51	063	0x33	00110011	3	
52	064	0x34	00110100	4	
53	065	0x35	00110101	5	
54	066	0x36	00110110	6	
55	067	0x37	00110111	7	
56	070	0x38	00111000	8	
57	071	0x39	00111001	9	
58	072	0x3a	00111010	:	
59	073	0x3b	00111011	;	
60	074	0x3c	00111100	<	
61	075	0x3d	00111101	=	
62	076	0x3e	00111110	>	
63	077	0x3f	00111111	?	
64	0100	0x40	01000000	@	
65	0101	0x41	01000001	A	
66	0102	0x42	01000010	B	
67	0103	0x43	01000011	C	
68	0104	0x44	01000100	D	
69	0105	0x45	01000101	E	
70	0106	0x46	01000110	F	
71	0107	0x47	01000111	G	

continued on next page

continued from previous page

Decimal	Octal	Hex	Binary	Character	ASCII Name
72	0110	0x48	01001000	H	
73	0111	0x49	01001001	I	
74	0112	0x4a	01001010	J	
75	0113	0x4b	01001011	K	
76	0114	0x4c	01001100	L	
77	0115	0x4d	01001101	M	
78	0116	0x4e	01001110	N	
79	0117	0x4f	01001111	O	
80	0120	0x50	01010000	P	
81	0121	0x51	01010001	Q	
82	0122	0x52	01010010	R	
83	0123	0x53	01010011	S	
84	0124	0x54	01010100	T	
85	0125	0x55	01010101	U	
86	0126	0x56	01010110	V	
87	0127	0x57	01010111	W	
88	0130	0x58	01011000	X	
89	0131	0x59	01011001	Y	
90	0132	0x5a	01011010	Z	
91	0133	0x5b	01011011	[	
92	0134	0x5c	01011100	\	
93	0135	0x5d	01011101	]	
94	0136	0x5e	01011110	^	
95	0137	0x5f	01011111	_	
96	0140	0x60	01100000	'	
97	0141	0x61	01100001	a	
98	0142	0x62	01100010	b	
99	0143	0x63	01100011	c	

Decimal	Octal	Hex	Binary	Character	ASCII Name
100	0144	0x64	01100100	d	
101	0145	0x65	01100101	e	
102	0146	0x66	01100110	f	
103	0147	0x67	01100111	g	
104	0150	0x68	01101000	h	
105	0151	0x69	01101001	i	
106	0152	0x6a	01101010	j	
107	0153	0x6b	01101011	k	
108	0154	0x6c	01101100	l	
109	0155	0x6d	01101101	m	
110	0156	0x6e	01101110	n	
111	0157	0x6f	01101111	o	
112	0160	0x70	01110000	p	
113	0161	0x71	01110001	q	
114	0162	0x72	01110010	r	
115	0163	0x73	01110011	s	
116	0164	0x74	01110100	t	
117	0165	0x75	01110101	u	
118	0166	0x76	01110110	v	
119	0167	0x77	01110111	w	
120	0170	0x78	01111000	x	
121	0171	0x79	01111001	y	
122	0172	0x7a	01111010	z	
123	0173	0x7b	01111011	{	
124	0174	0x7c	01111100			
125	0175	0x7d	01111101	}	
126	0176	0x7e	01111110	~	
127	0177	0x7f	01111111	del, rubout	

APPENDIX D

Operator Precedence

Operator precedence determines the order in which operators are applied to a value. C++ operators come in 16 precedence groups, which are presented in Table D-1. Those in group 1 have the highest precedence, and so on. If two operators apply to the same operand (something upon which an operator operates), the operator with the higher precedence applies first. If the two operators have the same precedence, C++ uses associativity rules to determine which operator binds more tightly. All operators in the same group have the same precedence and the same associativity, which is either left to right (L-R in the table) or right to left (R-L in the table). Left-to-right associativity means to apply the left-hand operator first, while right-to-left associativity means to apply the right-hand operator first.

Some symbols, such as * and &, are used for more than one operator. In such cases, one form is unary (one operand) and the other form is binary (two operands), and the compiler uses the context to determine which is meant. The table labels operator groups unary or binary for those cases in which the same symbol is used two ways.

Here are some examples of precedence and associativity:

```
3 + 5 * 6
```

The * operator has higher precedence than the + operator, so it is applied to the 5 first, making the expression 3 + 30, or 33.

```
120 / 6 * 5
```

Both / and * have the same precedence, but these operators associate from left to right. That means the operator to the left of the shared operand (6) is applied first, so the expression becomes 20 * 5, or 100.

```
char * str = "Whoa";
char ch = *str++;
```

Both the unary * and the ++ operators have the same precedence, but they associate right to left. This means the increment operator operates upon *str* and not **str*. That is, the operation increments the pointer, making it point to the next character, rather than altering the character pointed to. However, because ++ is the postfix form, the pointer is incremented after the original value of **str* is assigned to *ch*. Therefore this expression assigns the character W to *ch,* then moves *str* to point to the *h* character.

Precedence	Operator	Assoc.	Meaning
1	::		scope resolution operator
	(expression)		grouping
2	()	L-R	function call, type cast
	[]		array subscript
	->		indirect membership operator
	.		direct membership operator
	const_cast		specialized type cast
	dynamic_cast		specialized type cast
	reinterpret_cast		specialized type cast
	static_cast		specialized type cast
	typeid		type identification
	++		increment operator, postfix
	--		decrement operator, postfix
3 (all unary)	!	R-L	logical negation
	~		bitwise negation (one's complement)
	+		unary plus (positive sign)
	-		unary minus (negative sign)
	++		increment operator, prefix
	--		decrement operator, prefix
	&		address
	*		dereference (indirect value)
	sizeof		size in bytes
	new		dynamically allocate storage
	delete		dynamically free storage
4	.*	L-R	member dereference
	->*		indirect member dereference
5 (all binary)	*	L-R	multiply
	/		divide

	^		modulus (remainder)
6 (all binary)	+	L-R	addition
	-		subtraction
7	<<	L-R	left shift
	>>		right shift
8	<	L-R	less than
	<=		less than or equal to
	>=		greater than or equal to
	>		greater than
9	==	L-R	equal to
	!=		not equal to
10 (binary)	&	L-R	bitwise AND
11	^	L-R	bitwise XOR (exclusive OR)
12	|	L-R	bitwise OR
13	&&	L-R	logical AND
14	||	L-R	logical OR
15	:?	R-L	conditional
16	=	R-L	simple assignment
	*=		multiply and assign
	/=		divide and assign
	%=		take remainder and assign
	+=		add and assign
	-=		subtract and assign
	&=		bitwise AND and assign
	^=		bitwise XOR and assign
	|=		bitwise OR and assign
	<<=		left shift and assign
	>>=		right shift and assign
17	,	L-R	combine two expressions into one

Table D-1 C++ operator precedence and associativity

APPENDIX E

Other Operators

In order to avoid terminal obesity, the main text of this book doesn't cover two groups of operators. The first group consists of the bitwise operators, which let you manipulate individual bits in a value; these operators were inherited from C. The second group consists of two-member dereferencing operators; they are C++ additions. This appendix briefly summarizes these operators.

 Bitwise Operators

The bitwise operators operate upon the bits of integer values. For example, the left-shift operator moves bits to the left, and the bitwise negation operator turns each one to a zero, and each zero to a one. Altogether, C++ has six such operators: <<, >>, ~, &, |, and ^.

The Shift Operators

The left-shift operator has the following syntax:

value << *shift*

Here *value* is the integer value to be shifted, and *shift* is the number of bits to shift. For example

```
13 << 3
```

means shift all the bits in the value *13* three places to the left. The vacated places are filled with zeros, and bits shifted past the end are discarded. See Figure E-1.

Since each bit position represents a value twice that of the bit to the right (see Appendix A), shifting one bit position is equivalent to multiplying the value by 2. Similarly, shifting two bit positions is equivalent to multiplying by 2^2, and shifting *n* positions is equivalent to multiplying by 2^n.

The left-shift operator provides a capability often found in assembly languages. However, an assembly left-shift operator directly alters the contents of a register, while the C++ operator produces a new value without altering existing values. For instance, consider the following:

```
int x = 20;
int y = x << 3;
```

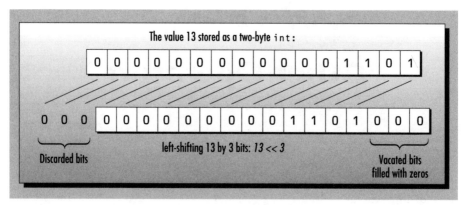

Figure E-1 Left-shift operator

This code doesn't change the value of *x*. The expression *x* << *3* uses the value of *x* to produce a new value, much as *x* + *3* produces a new value without altering *x*.

If you want to use the left-shift operator to change the value of a variable, you also have to use assignment. You can use regular assignment or the <<= operator, which combines shifting with assignment.

```
x = x << 4;        // regular assignment
y <<= 2;           // shift and assign
```

The right-shift operator (>>), as you might expect, shifts bits to the right. It has the following syntax:

value >> *shift*

Here *value* is the integer value to be shifted, and *shift* is the number of bits to shift. For example

```
17 >> 2
```

means shift all the bits in the value *17* two places to the right. For unsigned integers, the vacated places are filled with zeros, and bits shifted past the end are discarded. For signed integers, vacated places may be filled with zeros or else with the value of the original leftmost bit. The choice depends upon the implementation. See Figure E-2.

Shifting one place to the right is equivalent to integer division by 2. In general, shifting *n* places to the right is equivalent to integer division by 2^n.

C++ also defines a shift-and-assign operator if you wish to replace the value of a variable by the shifted value:

```
int q = 43;
q >>= 2;          // replace 43 by 43 >> 2, or 10
```

On some systems, using left- and right-shift operators may produce faster integer multiplication and division by 2 than using the division operator, but as compilers get better at optimizing code, such differences are fading.

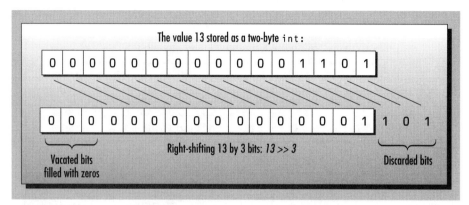

Figure E-2 Right-shift operator

The Logical Bitwise Operators

The logical bitwise operators are analogous to the regular logical operators, except they apply to a value on a bit-by-bit basis rather than to the whole. For instance, consider the regular negation operator (!) and the bitwise negation operator (~). The ! operator converts a true value (nonzero) to false (zero) and a false value (zero) to true (1). The ~ operator converts each individual bit to its opposite (1 to 0 and 0 to 1). For instance, consider the *unsigned char* value of 3:

```
unsigned char x = 3;
```

The expression !x has the value 0. To see the value of ~x, write it in binary form: 00000011. Then convert each 0 to 1, each 1 to 0. This produces the value 11111100, or in base 10, the value 252. See Figure E-3.

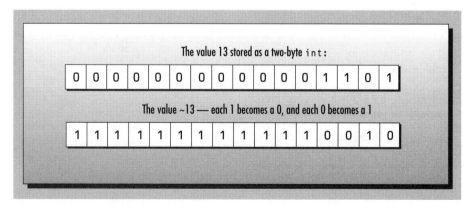

Figure E-3 Bitwise negation operator

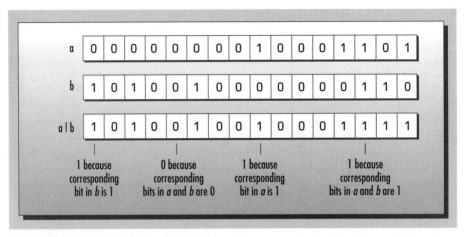

Figure E-4 The bitwise OR operator

The bitwise OR operator (|) combines two integer values to produce a new integer value. Each bit in the new value is set to 1 if one or the other, or both, of the corresponding bits in the original values is set to 1. If both corresponding bits are 0, then the final bit is set to 0. See Figure E-4.

Table E-1 summarizes how the | operator combines bits.

Bit values	b1 = 0	b1 = 1
b2 = 0	0	1
b2 = 1	1	1

Table E-1 Value of b1 | b2

The bitwise XOR operator (^) combines two integer values to produce a new integer value. Each bit in the new value is set to 1 if one or the other, but not both, of the corresponding bits in the original values is set to 1. If both corresponding bits are 0 or both are 1, then the final bit is set to 0. See Figure E-5.

Table E-2 summarizes how the ^ operator combines bits.

Bit values	b1 = 0	b1 = 1
b2 = 0	0	1
b2 = 1	1	0

Table E-2 Value of b1 ^ b2

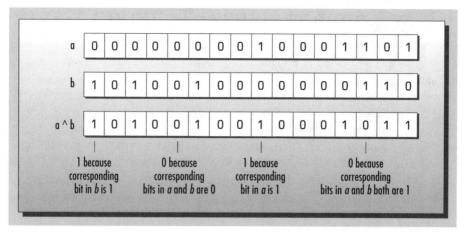

Figure E-5 The bitwise XOR operator

The bitwise AND operator (&) combines two integer values to produce a new integer value. Each bit in the new value is set to 1 only if both of the corresponding bits in the original values are set to 1. If either or both corresponding bits are 0, then the final bit is set to 0. See Figure E-6.

Table E-3 summarizes how the & operator combines bits.

Bit values	b1 = 0	b1 = 1
b2 = 0	0	0
b2 = 1	0	1

Table E-3 Value of b1 & b2

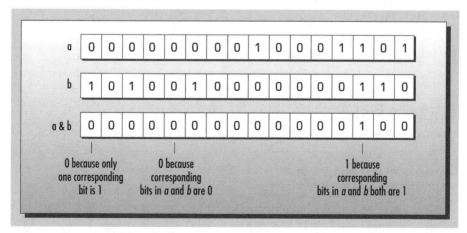

Figure E-6 The bitwise AND operator

A Few Common Bitwise Techniques

Often, controlling hardware involves turning particular bits on or off or checking their status. The bitwise operators provide the means to perform such actions. We'll go through the methods quickly.

In the following examples, *lottabits* represents a general value, and *bit* represents the value corresponding to a particular bit. Bits are numbered from right to left, beginning with bit 0, so the value corresponding to bit position n is 2^n. For example, an integer with only bit number 3 set to 1 has the value 2^3 or 8. In general, each individual bit corresponds to a power of 2, as described for binary numbers in Appendix A. So *bit* will be a power of 2 corresponding to a particular bit being set to 1 and all other bits set to 0.

Turning a Bit On

The following two operations each turn on the bit in *lottabits* corresponding to the bit represented by *bit*:

```
lottabits = lottabits | bit;
lottabits |= bit;
```

Each sets the corresponding bit to 1 regardless of the former value of the bit. That's because ORing 1 with either 0 or 1 produces a 1. All other bits in *lottabits* remain unaltered. That's because ORing 0 with 0 produces a 0, and ORing 0 with 1 produces a 1.

Toggling a Bit

The following two operations each toggle the bit in *lottabits* corresponding to the bit represented by *bit*. That is, they turn the bit on if it was off, and they turn it off if it was on:

```
lottabits = lottabits ^ bit;
lottabits ^= bit;
```

XORing 1 with 0 produces 1, turning an off bit on, and XORing 1 with 1 produces 0, turning an on bit off. All other bits in *lottabits* remain unaltered. That's because XORing 0 with 0 produces a 0, and XORing 0 with 1 produces a 1.

Turning a Bit Off

The following two operations each turn off the bit in *lottabits* corresponding to the bit represented by *bit*:

```
lottabits = lottabits & ~bit;
lottabits &= ~bit;
```

These statements turn the bit off regardless of its prior state. First, the operator *~bit* produces an integer with all its bits set to 1 *except* the bit that originally was set to 1;

that bit becomes a 0. ANDing a 0 with any bit results in 0, thus turning that bit off. All other bits in *lottabits* are unchanged. That's because ANDing a 1 with any bit produces the value that bit had before.

Testing a Bit Value

Suppose we wish to determine whether the bit corresponding to *bit* is set to 1 in *lottabits*. The following test does not necessarily work:

```
if (lottabits == bits)        // no good
```

That's because even if the corresponding bit in *lottabits* is set to 1, so might other bits be set to 1. The equality above is true only when *only* the corresponding bit is 1. The fix is to first AND *lottabits* with *bit*. That produces a value that is 0 in all the other bit positions, because 0 AND any value is 0. Only the bit corresponding to the *bit* value is left unchanged, since 1 AND any value is that value. Thus the proper test is this:

```
if (lottabits & bit == bits)        // testing a bit
```

Member Dereferencing Operators

Before discussing the member dereferencing operators, we need to provide a bit of background. C++ lets you define pointers to members of a class, but the process is not simple. To see what's involved, let's look at an example class. Listing E-1 presents a class definition.

Listing E-1

```
class example
{
private:
        int feet;
        int inches;
public:
        example();
        example(int ft);
        ~example();
        void show_in();        // display inches member
        example operator+(example &ex);
};
```

Now suppose that you wish to define a pointer to the *inches* member of this class. The following attempt fails:

```
int * pi = &inches;    // not valid C++
```

It fails because *inches* is not type *int*. That's because the type for a class member must also specify the class to which the member belongs. To make the declaration valid, we have to use the scope operator to identify the class for the pointer and for the member:

```
int example::* pi = &example::inches;       // valid C++
```

In this declaration the phrase *int example::** is the type "pointer-to-*int* member of *example* class." The expression *&example::inches* means "the address of the *inches* member of the *example* class."

You can use this form of declaration in member functions or in friend functions. The *pi* pointer acts like a class member in that it must be invoked with a class object. This is where the member dereferencing operators come in. For example, suppose *ex* is an *example* object declared in a member function. To access the *inches* member of *ex*, you can use the standard *ex.inches* notation. But you can also use the .* operator with the *pi* pointer:

```
cout << ex.inches;        // display the inches member
cout << ex.*pi;           // ditto
```

That is, the . operator accesses a member using the member name, while the .* member accesses a member using a pointer to that member.

Similarly, suppose *px* is a pointer to an *example* object. Then you can use the -> operator to access the *inches* member by name or by using the ->* dereferencing operator to access *inches* via a pointer to a member:

```
px = &ex;                 // px a pointer to an example object
cout << px->inches;       // display the inches member
cout << px->*pi;          // ditto
```

Note that *px* is a pointer to an entire object, while *pi* is a pointer to a class member.

To see how these new operators work in practice, let's use them in a slightly roundabout way of implementing the *operator+()* function. The function adds two objects. One object is an argument to the function. Since it is an object, not a pointer, we can use the .* to access the *inches* member. The other object is the invoking object, which, you recall, is represented by the pointer *this*. Hence we can use the -> operator with it. Listing E-2 shows the result.

Listing E-2

```
example example::operator+(example &ex)
{
        example sum;

        int example::*pi = &example::inches;
        // point to an inches member of example class

        sum.inches = ex.*pi + this->*pi;
        sum.feet = 12 * sum.inches;
        return sum;
}
```

Here *ex.*pi* represents the *inches* member of *ex* and *this->*pi* represents the *inches* member of the object to which *this* points. Note that **pi* is used like a member name.

Listing E-3 provides the rest of the method definitions and a *main()* function that uses the class.

Listing E-3 *memb_pt.cpp*

```
// memb_pt.cpp -- dereferencing pointers to class members
#include <iostream.h>

class example
{
private:
        int feet;
        int inches;
public:
        example();
        example(int ft);
        ~example();
        void show_in();
        example operator+(example &ex);
};

example::example()
{
        feet = 0;
        inches = 0;
}

example::example(int ft)
{
        feet = ft;
        inches = 12 * feet;
}

example::~example()
{
}

void example::show_in()
{
        cout << inches << " inches\n";
}

example example::operator+(example &ex)
{
        example sum;

        int example::*pi = &example::inches;
        // point to an inches member of example class

        sum.inches = ex.*pi + this->*pi;
```

continued on next page

continued from previous page

```
        sum.feet = 12 * sum.inches;
        return sum;
}

int main(void)
{
        example car(15);
        example van(20);
        example garage;

        garage = car + van;
        car.show_in();
        van.show_in();
        garage.show_in();

        return 0;
}
```

Here is a sample run:

```
180 inches
240 inches
420 inches
```

Type Cast Operators

The draft ANSI/ISO C++ standard proposes four type cast operators designed to make type casting safer:

```
dynamic_cast
const_cast
static_cast
reinterpret_cast
```

Chapter 14 discusses *dynamic_cast*. It's part of the RTTI (runtime type information) mechanism. Suppose *High* and *Low* are two classes, that *ph* is type *High* * and *pl* is type *Low* *. Then the statement

```
pl = dynamic_cast<Low *> ph;
```

assigns a *Low* * pointer to *pl* only if *Low* is an accessible base class (direct or indirect) to *High*. Otherwise, the statement assigns the null pointer to *pl*. In general, the operator has this syntax:

dynamic_cast < *type-name* > (*expression*)

The *const_cast* operator is for making a type cast with the sole purpose of changing whether a value is *const* or *volatile* or not. It has the same syntax as the *dynamic_cast* operator:

const_cast < *type-name* > (*expression*)

The result of making such a cast is an error if any other aspect of the type is altered. That is, *type–name* and *expression* must be of the same type, except they can differ in the presence or absence of *const* or *volatile*. Again, suppose *High* and *Low* are two classes:

```
const High bar;
...
High * pb = const_cast<High *> &bar; // valid
Low * pl = const_cast<Low *> & bar;  // invalid
```

The first type cast makes **pb* a pointer that can be used to alter the value of the bar object; it removes the *const* label. The second type cast is invalid, for it also attempts to change the type from *High ** to *Low **.

The *static_cast* operator has the same syntax as the others:

```
static_cast < type-name > (expression)
```

It's valid only if *type–name* can be converted implicitly to the same type *expression* has or vice versa. Otherwise, the cast is an error. Suppose *High* is a base class to *Low*. Then the following conversions are valid:

```
const High bar;
const Low blow;
...
High * pb = static_cast<High *> &blow;    // upcast
Low * pl = static_cast<Low *> &bar;       // downcast
```

The first conversion is valid because an upcast can be down explicitly. The second conversion, from a base class pointer to a derived class pointer, can't be done without an explicit type conversion. But because the type cast in the other direction can be made without a type cast, it's valid to use a *static_cast* for a downcast.

The *reinterpret_cast* operator is for inherently risky type casts. It won't let you cast away *const,* but it will do other unsavory things. Sometimes a programmer has to do implementation-dependent things, and using the *reinterpret_cast* operator makes it simpler to keep track of such acts. It has the same syntax as the other three:

```
reinterpret_cast < type-name > (expression)
```

Here is a sample use:

```
char dat[20];
int * pi = reinterpret_cast< int > &char;
```

Typically, such casts would be used for low-level, implementation-dependent programming.

APPENDIX F

Selected Readings

Booch, Grady. *Object-Oriented Analysis and Design.* Second Edition. Redwood City, CA: Benjamin/Cummings, 1994.

This book presents the concepts behind OOP, discusses OOP methods, and presents sample applications. The examples are in C++.

Ellis, Margaret A., and Bjarne Stroustrup. *The Annotated C++ Reference Manual.* Reading, MA: Addison-Wesley, 1990.

This book, usually called the ARM, serves as a base document for the ANSI/ISO C++ standard committee. It's not a book for learning the language, but it answers most technical questions about how the language works. Also, the last chapter, periodically updated with new printings, summarizes differences between the ARM and the draft standard.

Meyers, Scott. *Effective C++.* Reading, MA: Addison-Wesley, 1992.

The subtitle is *50 Specific Ways to Improve Your Programs and Designs.* It's aimed at programmers who already know C++, and it provides 50 rules and guidelines. Some are technical, such as explaining when you should define copy constructors and assignment operators. Others are more general, such as discussing *is-a* and *has-a* relationships.

Murray, Robert B. *C++ Strategies and Tactics.* Reading, MA: Addison-Wesley, 1993.

This book aims to help a new or intermediate C++ programmer learn to use the language effectively. It discusses classes, inheritance, templates, exceptions, and a few other topics, offering practical advice and describing common techniques.

Stroustrup, Bjarne. *The C++ Programming Language.* Second Edition. Reading, MA: Addison-Wesley, 1991.

Stroustrup created C++, so this is the definitive text. However, it's most easily digested if you already have some knowledge of C++. It not only describes the language, it also provides many examples of how to use it as well as discussions of OOP methodology. It includes template examples of a linked list implemented using a friend iterator class and of an associative array, that is, an array that can use arbitrary types as indices.

Stroustrup, Bjarne. *The Design and Evolution of C++*. Reading, MA: Addison-Wesley, 1994.

If you're interested in learning how C++ evolved and why it is the way it is, read this book.

Working Paper for Draft Proposed International Standard for Information Systems — Programming Language C++.

The draft standard is available for $55 from the following address:

CBEMA
1250 Eye Street, Suite 200
Washington, DC 20005

Its preface warns that the "document is a working draft and is known to be incorect, incomplet, and inCONsiSteNt."

APPENDIX G

Answers to Review Questions

Chapter 2

1. They are called functions.

2. It causes the contents of the *iostream.h* file to be substituted for this directive before final compilation.

3. `cout << "Hello, world\n";`

4. `int cheeses;`

5. `cheeses = 32;`

6. `cin >> cheeses;`

7. `cout << "We have " << cheeses << " varieties of cheese\n";`

8. It tells us that the function *froop()* expects to be called with one argument, which will be type *double,* and that the function will return a type *int* value.

9. You don't use *return* in a function when the function has return type *void.*

Chapter 3

1. Having more than one integer type lets you choose the type best suited to a particular need.

2.
```
short rbis = 80;              // or short int rbis = 80;
unsigned int q = 42110;       // or unsigned q = 42110;
unsigned long ants = 3000000000;
```

   Note: Don't count on *int* being large enough to hold 3000000000.

3. C++ provides no safeguards to keep you from exceeding integer limits.

4. The constant *33L* is type *long,* while the constant *33* is type *int.*

5. The two statements are not really equivalent. Most important, the first statement assigns the letter A to *grade* only on a system using the ASCII code, while the second statement also works for other codes. Second, *65* is a type *int* constant, while *'A'* is a type *char* constant.

```

6. Here are three ways:

```cpp
char c = 88;
cout << c << "\n";      // char type prints as character

cout.put(char(88));              // put() prints char as character

cout << char(88) << "\n";  // type cast value to char
```

7. The answer depends upon how large the two types are. If *long* is 4 bytes, there is no loss. That's because the largest *long* value would be about 2 billion, which is 10 digits. Since *double* provides at least 15 significant figures, no rounding would be needed.

8.   a. 8 * 9 + 2 is 72 + 2 is 74

     b. 6 * 3 / 4 is 18 / 4 is 4

     c. 3 / 4 * 6 is 0 * 6 is 0

     d. 6.0 * 3 / 4 is 18.0 / 4 is 4.5

     e. 15 % 4 is 3

9. Either of the following work:

```cpp
int pos = (int) x1 + (int) x2;
int pos = int(x1) + int(x2);
```

Chapter 4

1.   a. `char actors[30];`

     b. `short betsie[100];`

     c. `float chuck[13];`

     d. `long double dipsea[64];`

2. `int oddly[5] = {1, 3, 5, 7, 9};`

3. `int even = oddly[0] + oddly[4];`

4. `cout << ideas[1] << "\n";`

5. `char lunch[13] = "cheeseburger"; // number of characters + 1`

or

`char lunch[] = "cheeseburger";  // let the compiler count elements`

6.
```cpp
struct fish {
        char kind[20];
        int weight;
        float length;
};
```

7.
```cpp
fish petes =
    {
```
```

```
        "trout",
        13,
        12.25
  };
```

8. `enum Boolean {False, True};`

9. ```
   double * pd = &ted;
   cout << *pd << "\n";
   ```

10. ```
    float * pf = treacle; // or = &treacle[0]
    cout << pf[0] << " " << pf[9] << "\n";
                          // or use *pf and *(pf + 9)
    ```

11. ```
    unsigned int size;
    cout << "Enter a positive integer: ";
    cin >> size;
    int * dyn = new int [size];
    ```

12. Yes, it is valid. The expression *"Home of the jolly bytes"* is a string constant, hence it evaluates as the address of the beginning of the string. The *cout* object interprets the address of a *char* as an invitation to print a string, but the type cast *(int *)* converts the address to type pointer-to-*int,* which is then printed as an address. In short, the statement prints the address of the string.

13. ```
    struct fish
    {
            char kind[20];
            int weight;
            float length;
    };

    fish * pole = new fish;
    cout << "Enter kind of fish: ";
    cin >> pole->kind;
    ```

14. Using *cin>> address* causes a program to skip over white space until it finds nonwhite space. It then reads characters until it encounters white space again. Thus, it will skip over the newline following the numeric input, avoiding that problem. On the other hand, it will read just a single word, not an entire line.

Chapter 5

1. An entry-condition loop evaluates a test expression before entering the body of the loop. If the condition initially is false, the loop never executes its body. An exit-condition loop evaluates a test expression after processing the body of the loop. Thus the loop body is executed once even if the test expression initially is false. The *for* and *while* loops are entry-condition loops, while the *do while* loop is an exit-condition loop.

2. It would print the following:

   01234

Note that the *cout* << "\n"; is not part of the loop body (no braces).

3. It would print the following:

0369

12

4. It would print the following:

6

8

5. It would print the following:

k = 8

6. It's simplest to use the *= operator:
```
for (int num = 1; num <= 64; num *= 2)
        cout << num << " ";
```

7. You enclose the statements within paired braces to form a single compound statement, or block.

8. Yes, the first statement is valid. The expression *1,024* consists of two expressions—*1* and *024*—joined by a comma operator. The value is the value of the right-hand expression. This is *024*, which is octal for *20*, so the declaration assigns the value *20* to *x*. The second statement also is valid. However, operator precedence causes it to be evaluated as follows:
```
(y = 1), 024;
```
That is, the left expression sets *y* to *1*, and the value of the entire expression, which isn't used, is *024*, or *20*.

9. The *cin* >> *ch* form skips over spaces, newlines, and tabs when it encounters them. The other two forms read these characters.

Chapter 6

1. Both versions give the same answers, but the *if else* version is more efficient. Consider what happens, for instance, when *ch* is a space. Version 1, after incrementing *spaces*, then tests to see if the character is a newline. This wastes time because the program already has established that *ch* is a space and hence could not be a newline. Version 2, in the same situation, skips the newline test.

2. Both ++*ch* and *ch* + *1* have the same numerical value. But ++*ch* is type *char* and prints as a character, while *ch* + *1*, because it adds a *char* to an *int*, is type *int* and prints as a number.

3. Because the program uses *ch* = '*$*' instead of *ch* == '*$*', the combined input and output looks like this:

```
Hi!
H$i$!$
$Send $10 or $20 now!
S$e$n$d$ $ct1 = 9, ct2 = 9
```

Each character is converted to the $ character before being printed the second time. Also, the value of the expression *ch* = $ is the code for the $ character, hence nonzero, hence true; so *ct2* is incremented each time.

4. a. `weight >= 115 && weight < 125`

 b. `ch == 'q' || ch == 'Q'`

 c. `x % 2 == 0 && x != 26`

 d. `donation >= 1000 && donation <= 2000 || guest == 1`

 e. `(ch >= 'a' && ch <= 'z') ||(ch >= 'A' && ch <= 'Z')`

5. Not necessarily. For instance, if *x* is *10*, then *!x* is *0* and *!!x* is *1*.

6. `(x < 0)? -x : x`

7.
```
switch (ch)
{
        case 'A':       a_grade++;
                        break;
        case 'B':       b_grade++;
                        break;
        case 'C':       c_grade++;
                        break;
        case 'D':       d_grade++;
                        break;
        default :       f_grade++;
                        break;
}
```

8. If we use integer labels and the user types a noninteger such as **q**, the program hangs up because integer input can't process a character. But if we use character labels and the user types an integer such as **5**, character input will process 5 as a character. Then the *default* part of the *switch* can suggest entering another character.

9. Here is one version:
```
int line = 0;
char ch;
while (cin.get(ch) && ch != 'Q')
{
        if (ch == '\n')
                line++;
}
```

Chapter 7

1. The three steps are defining the function, providing a prototype, and calling the function.

2.   a. `void igor(void);`

   b. `float tofu(int n);`   or   `float tofu(int);`

   c. `double mpg(double miles, double gallons);`

   d. `long summation(long harray[], int size);`

   e. `double doctor(const char * str);`

   f. `void ofcourse(boss dude);`

   g. `char * plot(map *pmap);`

3. ```
void set_array(int arr[], int size, int value)
{
        for (int i = 0; i < size; i++)
                arr[i] = value;
}
```

4. ```
double biggest (const double foot[], int size)
{
        double max;
        if (size < 1)
        {
                cout << "Invalid array size of " << size << "\n";
                cout << "Returning a value of 0\n";
                return 0;
        }
        else    // not necessary because return terminates program
        {
                max = foot[0];
                for (int i = 1; i < size; i++)
                        if (foot[i] > max)
                                max = foot[i];
                return max;
        }
}
```

5. We use the *const* qualifier with pointers to protect the original pointed-to data from being altered. When a program passes a fundamental type such as an *int* or *double,* it passes it by value so that the function works with a copy. Thus the original data is already protected.

6. ```
int fill_array(double ar[], int limit)
{
        double temp;
        for (int i = 0; i < limit; i++)
        {
                cout << "Enter value #" << i + 1 << ": ";
                if (!(cin >> temp))   // non-numeric input
                {
```
```

```
                    cin.clear();   // reset input
                    while (cin.get() != '\n')
                            continue;     // get rid of old input
                    break;
            }
            ar[i] = temp;
        }
        return i;
}
```

7. A string can be stored in a *char* array, it can be represented by a string constant in double quotation marks, and it can be represented by a pointer pointing to the first character of a string.

8.
```
int replace(char * str, char c1, char c2)
{
        int count = 0;
        while (*str)    // while not at end of string
        {
                if (*str == c1)
                {
                        *str = c2;
                        count++;
                }
                str++;          // advance to next character
        }
        return count;
}
```

9. Because C++ interprets *"pizza"* as the address of its first element, applying the * operator yields the value of that first element, which is the character *p*. Because C++ interprets *"taco"* as the address of its first element, it interprets *"taco"[2]* as the value of the element two positions down the line, that is, as the character *c*. In other words, the string constant acts the same as an array name.

10. To pass it by value, just pass the structure name *glitz*. To pass its address, use the address operator *&glitz*. Passing by value automatically protects the original data, but it takes time and memory. Passing by address saves time and memory but doesn't protect the original data unless you use the *const* modifier for the function parameter. Also, passing by value means you can use ordinary structure member notation, but passing a pointer means you have to remember to use the indirect membership operator.

11.
```
int judge (int (*pf)(const char *));
```

Chapter 8

1. Short functions that can fit in one line of code.

2.   a.
```
void song(char * name, int times = 1);
```
      b. None. Only prototypes contain the default value information.

c. Yes, providing you retain the default value for *times:*

```
void song(char * name = "O, My Papa", int times = 1);
```

3. You can use either the string "\"" or the character '"' to print a quotation mark. The following functions show both methods.

```
#include <iostream.h>
void iquote(int n)
{
        cout << "\"" << n << "\"";
}

void iquote(double x)
{
        cout << '"' << x << '"';
}

void iquote(const char * str)
{
        cout << "\"" << str << "\"";
}
```

4.   a. This function shouldn't alter the structure members, so use the *const* qualifer.

```
void show_box(const box & container)
{
        cout << "Made by " << container. maker << "\n";
        cout << "Height = " << container.height << "\n";
        cout << "Width = " << container.width << "\n";
        cout << "Length = " << container.length << "\n";
        cout << "Volume = " << container.volume << "\n";
}
```

   b.
```
void set_volume(box & crate)
{
        crate.volume = crate.height * crate.width * crate.length;
}
```

5.   a. This can be done using a default value for the second argument:

```
double mass(double d, double v = 1.0);
```

It can also be done by overloading:

```
double mass(double d, double v);
double mass(double d);
```

   b. You can't use a default for the repeat value because you have to provide default values from right to left. You can use overloading:

```
void repeat(int times, char * str);
void repeat(char * str);
```

   c. You can use function overloading:

```
int average(int a, int b);
double average(double x, double y);
```

   d. You can't do this one because both versions would have the same signature.

e. At least one version must be defined as a *static* function in one of the files:

```
static int average(int a, int b);      // definition in file 1
static double average(int a, int b);   // definition in file 2
```

6.
```
template<class T>
T max(T t1, T t2)
{
        return t1 > t2? t1 : t2;
}
```

7. a. *homer* is automatically an automatic variable.

b. *secret* should be defined as an external variable in one file and declared using *extern* in the second file.

c. *topsecret* should be defined as a static external variable by prefacing the external definition with the keyword *static*.

d. *beencalled* should be defined as a local static variable by prefacing a declaration in the function with the keyword *static*.

Chapter 9

1. A class is a definition of a user-defined type. A class declaration specifies how data is to be stored, and it specifies the methods (class member functions) that can be used to access and manipulate that data.

2. A class represents the operations one can perform on a class object with a public interface of class methods; this is abstraction. The class can use *private* visibility (the default) for data members, meaning that the data can be accessed only through the member functions; this is data hiding. Details of the implementation, such as data representation and method code, is hidden; this is encapsulation.

3. The class defines a type, including how it can be used. An object is a variable or other data object, such as that produced by *new,* created and used according to the class definition. The relationship is much the same as that between a standard type and a variable of that type.

4. If you create several objects of a given class, each object comes with storage for its own set of data. But all the objects use the one set of member functions.

5. Note: The program uses *cin.get(char *, int)* instead of *cin >>* to read names because *cin.get()* reads a whole line instead of just one word (see Chapter 4).

```
#include <iostream.h>

// class definition
class BankAccount
{
private:
```

continued on next page

continued from previous page

```
            char name[40];
            char acctnum[25];
            double balance;
public:
            void set(void);
            void show(void) const;
            void deposit(double cash);
            void withdraw(double cash);
};

// member function definitions
void BankAccount::set(void)
{
        cout << "Enter depositor's name: ";
        cin.get(name, sizeof(name)).get();
        cout << "Enter depositor's account number: ";
        cin.get(acctnum, sizeof(acctnum)).get();
        cout << "Enter the starting balance: ";
        cin >> balance;
}

void BankAccount::show(void) const
{
        cout << "Depositor: " << name << "    Account Number: ";
        cout << acctnum << "    Balance: " << balance << "\n";
}

void BankAccount::deposit(double cash)
{
        balance += cash;
}

void BankAccount::withdraw(double cash)
{
        balance -= cash;
}

// test program
int main(void)
{
        BankAccount keating;
        keating.set();
        keating.show();
        keating.deposit(2000.00);
        keating.show();
        keating.withdraw(20000000.00);
        keating.show();
        return 0;
}
```

6. A class constructor is called when you create an object of that class or when you explicitly call the constructor. The class destructor is called when the object expires.

7. First, add a class constructor prototype to the class definition:

```
class BankAccount
{
private:
        char name[40];
        char acctnum[25];
        double balance;
public:
        BankAccount(char * client, char * num, double bal = 0.0);
        void set(void);
        void show(void) const;
        void deposit(double cash);
        void withdraw(double cash);
};
```

Then add the function definition to the methods. Note that you need to include *string.h* in order to use *strcpy()*.

```
BankAccount::BankAccount(char * client, char * num, double bal)
{
        strcpy(name, client);
        strcpy(acctnum, num);
        balance = bal;
}
```

Keep in mind that default arguments go in the prototype, not in the function definition.

8. A default constructor is one with no arguments or else with defaults for all the arguments. Having one enables you to declare objects without initializing them, even if you've already defined an initializing constructor.

9. ```
// stock3.h
#ifndef _STOCK3_H_
#define _STOCK3_H_

class Stock
{
private:
        char company[30];
        int shares;
        double share_val;
        double total_val;
        void set_tot() { total_val = shares * share_val; }
public:
        Stock();   // default constructor
        Stock(const char * co, int n, double pr);
        ~Stock() {}   // do-nothing destructor
        void buy(int num, double price);
        void sell(int num, double price);
        void update(double price);
        void show() const;
        const Stock & topval(const Stock & s) const;
        int numshares() { return shares; }
```

*continued on next page*
```

continued from previous page

```
        double shareval() { return share_val; }
        double totalval() { return total_val; }
        char * co_name();
};

#endif

#include <string.h>
#include "stock3.h"
char * Stock::co_name()
{
        char * ps = new char[strlen(company) + 1];
        strcpy(ps, company);
        return ps;
}
```

10. The *this* pointer is a pointer available to class methods. It points to the object used to invoke the method. Thus *this* is the address of the object, and **this* represents the object itself.

Chapter 10

1. Here's a prototype for the class definition file and a function definition for the methods file:

```
// prototype
Stonewt operator*(double mult);
// definition -- let constructor do the work
Stonewt Stonewt::operator*(double mult)
{
        return Stonewt(mult * pounds);
}
```

2. A member function is part of a class definition and is invoked by a particular object. The member function can access members of the invoking object implicitly, without using the membership operator. A friend function is not part of a class, so it's called as a straight function call. It can't access class members implicitly, so it has to use the membership operator applied to an object passed as an argument.

3. It has to be a friend to access *private* members, but it doesn't have to be a friend to access *public* members.

4. Here's a prototype for the class definition file and a function definition for the methods file:

```
// prototype
friend Stonewt operator*(double mult, const Stonewt & s);
// definition -- let constructor do the work
Stonewt operator*(double mult, const Stonewt & s)
{
        return Stonewt(mult * s.pounds);
}
```

5. The following five operators cannot be overloaded:

    sizeof . .* :: ? :

6. These operators must be defined by using a member function.

7. Here is a possible prototype and definition:

```
// prototype and inline definition
operator double () {return mag;}
```

Chapter 11

1.   a. This constructor leaves the *str* pointer uninitialized. The constructor should either set the pointer to *NULL* or use *new []* to initialize the pointer.

     b. This constructor does not create a new string; it merely copies the address of the old string. It should use *new []* and *strcpy()*.

     c. It copies the string without allocating the space to store it. It should use *new char[len + 1]* to allocate the proper amount of memory.

2. First, when an object of that type expires, the data pointed to by the object's member pointer remains in memory, using space and remaining inaccessible because the pointer has been lost. That can be fixed by having the class destructor delete memory allocated by *new* in the constructor functions. Second, once the destructor deletes such memory, it may wind up trying to delete it twice if a program initialized one such object to another. That's because the default initialization of one object to another copies pointer values but does not copy the pointed-to data, producing two pointers to the same data. The solution is to define a class constructor that causes initialization to copy the pointed-to data. Third, assigning one object to another can produce the same situation of two pointers pointing to the same data. The solution is to overload the assignment operator so that it copies the data, not the pointers.

3. C++ automatically provides the following member functions:

   ❧   A default constructor if you define no constructors

   ❧   A copy constructor if you don't define one

   ❧   An assignment operator if you don't define one

   ❧   An address operator if you don't define one

   The default constructor does nothing. The default copy constructor and the default assignment operator use memberwise assignment. The implicit address operator returns the address of the invoking object (that is, the value of the *this* pointer).

4. The *personality* member should be declared either as a character array or as a pointer-to-*char*. Or you could make it a *String* object. Here are two possible solutions, with changes (other than deletions) in boldface.

```
#include <iostream.h>
#include <string.h>
class nifty
{
private: // optional
        char personality[40]; // provide array size
        int talents;
public: // needed
// methods
        nifty();
        nifty(const char * s);
        friend ostream & operator<<(ostream & os, const nifty & n);
};      // note closing semicolon

nifty::nifty()
{
        personality[0] = '\0';
        talents = 0;
}

nifty::nifty(const char * s)
{
        strcpy(personality, s);
        talents = 0;
}

ostream & operator<<(ostream & os, const nifty & n)
{
        os << n.personality << '\n';
        os << n.talent << '\n';
        return os;
}
```

Or you could do this:

```
#include <iostream.h>
#include <string.h>
class nifty
{
private: // optional
        char * personality;   // create a pointer
        int talents;
public: // needed
// methods
        nifty();
        nifty(const char * s);
        nifty(const nifty & n);
        ~nifty() { delete personality; }
        nifty & operator=(const nifty & n) const;
        friend ostream & operator<<(ostream & os, const nifty & n);
};      // note closing semicolon

nifty::nifty()
{
        personality = NULL;
```

```
            talents = 0;
}

nifty::nifty(const char * s)
{
        personality = new char [strlen(s) + 1];
        strcpy(personality, s);
        talents = 0;
}

ostream & operator<<(ostream & os, const nifty & n)
{
        os << n.personality << '\n';
        os << n.talent << '\n';
        return os;
}
```

5.   a. Golfer nancy; // default constructor
         Golfer lulu(Little Lulu); // Golfer(const char * name, int g)
         Golfer roy(Roy Hobbs, 12); // Golfer(const char * name, int g)
         Golfer * par = new Golfer; // default constructor
         Golfer next = lulu; // Golfer(const Golfer &g)
         Golfer hazzard = "Weed Thwacker"; // Golfer(const char * name, int g)
         *par = nancy; // default assignment operator
         nancy = "Nancy Putter";// Golfer(const char * name, int g), then
                                  // the default assignment operator

Note: Some compilers will additionally call the default assignment operator for statements #5 and #6.

      b. The class should define an assignment operator that copies data rather than
         addresses.

Chapter 12

1. The public members of the base class become public members of the derived class.
   The protected members of the base class become protected members of the derived
   class. The private members of the base class are inherited, but cannot be accessed
   directly. The answer to review question 2 provides the exceptions to these general
   rules.

2. The constructors methods are not inherited, the destructor is not inherited, the
   assignment operator is not inherited, and friends are not inherited.

3. You would still be able use the value of an element, but you no longer could assign to it:
```
ArrayDb tosanjose[4];
double n = tosanjose[2];      // ok
tosanjose[1] = 68.8;          // no longer valid
```

4. Constructors are called in the order of derivation, with the most ancestral constructor
   called first. Destructors are called in the opposite order.

5. Yes, every class requires its own constructors. If the derived class adds no new members, the constructor may have an empty body, but it must exist.

6. Only the derived class method is called. It supersedes the base class definition. A base class method is called only if the derived class does not redefine the method. However, you really should declare as *virtual* any functions that will be redefined.

7. The default assignment operator is all that is needed. Memberwise assignment works for the new *LimitArr* data members, and the default *LimitArr* assignment operator will use the user-defined *ArrayDb* assignment operator for those members inherited from *ArrayDb*.

8. Yes, you can assign the address of an object of a derived class to a pointer to the base class. You can assign the address of a base object to a pointer to a derived class (downcasting) only by making an explicit type cast, and it is not necessarily safe to use such a pointer.

9. Yes, you can assign an object of a derived class to an object of the base class. Any data members new to the derived type are not passed to the base type, however. The program will use the base class assignment operator. Assignment in the opposite direction (base to derived) is possible only if the derived class defines a conversion operator, which is a constructor having a reference to the base type as its sole argument.

10. It can do so because C++ allows a reference to a base type to refer to any type derived from that base.

11. Passing an object by value invokes the copy constructor. Since the formal argument is a base class object, the base class copy constructor is invoked. The copy constructor has as *its* argument a reference to the base class, and this reference can refer to the derived object passed as an argument. The net result is producing a new base class object whose members correspond to the base class portion of the derived object.

12. Passing an object by reference instead of by value enables the function to avail itself of virtual functions. Also, passing an object by reference instead of value may use less memory and time, particularly for large objects. The main advantage of passing by value is that it protects the original data, but you can accomplish the same end by passing the reference as a *const* type.

13. If *head()* is a regular function, then *ph->head()* invokes *corporation::head()*. If *head()* is a virtual function, then *ph->head()* invokes *department::head()*.

14. The definition of *area()* in *House* hides the *Kitchen* version of *area()* because the two methods have different signatures.

Chapter 13

1. class Bear   class PolarBear   public, a polar bear is a kind of bear

   class Kitchen   class Home   private, a home has a kitchen

   class Person   class Programmer   public, a programmer is a person

   class Person   class HorseAndJockey private, a horse and jockey team contains a person

   class Person,   class Driver   public *Person* because a driver is a person, private
   class Automobile   *Automobile* because a driver has an automobile

2.
```
Gloam::Gloam(int g, const char * s) : glip(g), fb(s) { }
Gloam::Gloam(int g, const Frabjous & f) : glip(g), fb(f) { }
// note: the above uses the default Frabjous copy constructor
void Gloam::tell()
{
        fb.tell();
        cout << glip << '\n';
}
```

3.
```
Gloam::Gloam(int g, const char * s)
                     : glip(g), Frabjous(s) { }
Gloam::Gloam(int g, const Frabjous & f)
                         : glip(g), Frabjous(f) { }
// note: the above uses the default Frabjous copy constructor
void Gloam::tell()
{
        Frabjous::tell();
        cout << glip << '\n';
}
```

4.
```
class Stack<Worker *>
{
private:
        enum {MAX = 10};        // constant specific to class
        Worker * items[MAX];    // holds stack items
        int top;                // index for top stack item
public:
        Stack();
        Boolean isempty();
        Boolean isfull();
        Boolean push(const Worker * & item); // add item to stack
        Boolean pop(Worker * & item);// pop top into item
};
```

5.
```
ArrayTP<String> sa;
StackTP< ArrayTP<double> > stck_arr_db;
ArrayTp< StackTP<Worker *> > arr_stk_wpr;
```

6. If two lines of inheritance for a class share a common ancestor, the class winds up with two copies of the ancestor's members. Making the ancestor class a virtual base class to its immediate descendants solves that problem.

Chapter 14

1. a. The friend declaration should be as follows:
   ```
   friend class clas;
   ```
   b. This needs a forward declaration so that the compiler can interpret
   void snip(muff &):
   ```
   class muff;        // forward declaration
   class cuff {
   public:
           void snip(muff &) { ... }
           ...
   };
   class muff {
           friend void cuff::snip(muff &);
           ...
   };
   ```
   c. First, the *cuff* class declaration should precede the *muff* class so that the
   compiler can understand the term *cuff::snip()*. Second, the compiler needs a
   forward declaration of *muff* so that it can understand *snip(muff &)*.
   ```
   class muff;        // forward declaration
   class cuff {
   public:
           void snip(muff &) { ... }
           ...
   };
   class muff {
           friend void cuff::snip(muff &);
           ...
   };
   ```

2. No. For *A* to have a friend that's a member function of *B*, the *B* declaration must precede the *A* declaration. A forward declaration is not enough, for it would tell *A* that *B*
   is a class, but it wouldn't reveal the names of the class members. Similarly, if *B* has a
   friend that's a member function of *A*, the complete *A* declaration must precede the *B*
   declaration. These two requirements are mutually exclusive.

3. The only access to a class is through its public interface, which means the only thing
   you can do with a *Sauce* object is to call the constructor to create one. The other members (*soy* and *sugar*) are private by default.

4. Suppose function *f1()* calls function *f2()*. A *return* statement in *f2()* causes program execution to resume at the next statement following the *f2()* function call in function *f1()*.
   A *throw* statement causes the program to back up through the current sequence of
   function calls until it finds a try block that directly or indirectly contains the call
   to *f2()*. This might be in *f1()* or in a function that called *f1()*, and so on. Once there,
   execution goes to the next matching catch block, not to the first statement after the
   function call.

5. You should arrange the catch blocks in the order of most derived class to least derived.

6. For sample #1, the *if* condition is true if *pg* points to a *Superb* object or to an object of any class descended from *Superb*. In particular, it is also true if *pg* points to a *Magnificent* object. In sample #2, the *if* condition is true *only* for a *Superb* object, not for objects derived from *Superb*.

7. A using-declaration imports a particular name into the current namespace so that it can be used without a namespace qualifier. A using-directive makes all the names in a particular namespace available without making them part of the current namespace.

Chapter 15

1. The *iostream.h* file defines the classes, constants, and manipulators used to manage input and output. These objects manage the streams and buffers used to handle I/O. The file also creates standard objects (*cin, cout, cerr,* and *clog*) used to handle the standard input and output streams connected to every program. The ANSI/ISO C++ standard uses *iostream* instead of *iostream.h,* or *iostream.ns* if you wish to use namespaces.

2. Keyboard entry generates a series of characters. Typing **121** generates three characters, each represented by a 1-byte binary code. If the value is to be stored as type *int*, these three characters have to be converted to a single binary representation of the value *121*.

3. By default, both the standard output and the standard error send output to the standard output device, typically a monitor. If you have the operating system redirect output to a file, however, the standard output connects to the file instead of to the screen, but the standard error continues to be connected to the screen.

4. The *ostream* class defines a version of the *operator<<()* function for each basic C++ type. The compiler interprets an expression like
```
cout << spot
```
as the following:
```
cout.operator<<(spot)
```
It then can match this method call to the function prototype having the same argument type.

5. You can concatenate output methods that return type *ostream &*. This causes the invoking of a method with an object to return that object. The returned object can then invoke the next method in a sequence.

6.
```
//rq15-6.cpp
#include <iostream.h>
#include <iomanip.h>

int main(void)
{
```
continued on next page

continued from previous page

```
                cout << "Enter an integer: ";
                int n;
                cin >> n;
                cout << setw(15) << "base ten" << setw(15)
                        << "base sixteen" << setw(15) << "base eight" << "\n";
                cout.setf(ios::showbase);
                cout << setw(15) << n << hex << setw(15) << n
                        << oct << setw(15) << n << "\n";

                return 0;
        }
```

7.
```
    //rq15-7.cpp
    #include <iostream.h>
    #include <iomanip.h>

    int main(void)
    {
            char name[20];
            float hourly;
            float hours;

            cout << "Enter your name: ";
            cin.get(name, 20).get();
            cout << "Enter your hourly wages: ";
            cin >> hourly;
            cout << "Enter number of hours worked: ";
            cin >> hours;

            cout.setf(ios::showpoint);
            cout.setf(ios::fixed, ios::floatfield);
            cout.setf(ios::right, ios::adjustfield);
            cout << "First format:\n";
            cout << setw(30) << name << ": $" << setprecision(2)
                    << setw(10) << hourly << ":" << setprecision(1)
                    << setw(5) << hours << "\n";
            cout << "Second format:\n";
            cout.setf(ios::left, ios::adjustfield);
            cout << setw(30) << name << ": $" << setprecision(2)
                        << setw(10) << hourly << ":" << setprecision(1)
                        << setw(5) << hours << "\n";

            return 0;
    }
```

8. Here is the output:

   ```
   ct1 = 5; ct2 = 9
   ```

   The first part of the program ignores spaces and newlines, the second part doesn't.
   Note that the second part of the program begins reading at the newline character following the first *q*, and it counts that newline as part of its total.

9. The *ignore()* form falters if the input line exceeds 80 characters. In that case it only skips the first 80 characters.

INDEX

! (factorial), 157
! logical NOT operator, 201, 207-209
! negation operator, 791
!= operator, 167
" " double quotes, 28, 67, 69, 99, 319
directives, 27
#define directive, 60-61, 73-74, 178, 284, 368
#endif, 368
#ifndef directive, 367-368
#include, 27, 319
$ UNIX prompt, 185
% modulus operator, 80, 84, 519
% type specifiers, 696
%= operator, 162
& address operator, 118, 120, 133, 259, 285-286, 291, 456
& bitwise AND operator, 789, 793-795
& reference operator, 285-286, 295
&& logical AND operator, 201, 203-207, 209
() function call operator, 413
() parentheses. *See* parentheses
* dereferencing operator, 120
    dereferencing operators, 795-798
    dereferencing pointers, 133-134
    and pointers, 120-121, 124, 132, 133, 291, 477
    and reference variables, 286, 291
    and this pointer, 377
* indirect value operator, 120, 133
* multiplication operator, 80
*= operator, 162
+ addition operator, 80
++ increment operator, 150, 160-161, 172
+= operator, 162
, comma operator, 164-167
, comma separator, 38, 97, 164-166, 239
- subtraction operator, 80
-- decrement operator, 152, 159-161, 172

-= operator, 162
-> arrow membership operator, 138, 267, 376, 383, 477, 796
-> class member access by pointer operator, 413
->* dereferencing operator, 796
-lm option, 43, 408, 713, 715
. direct membership operator, 383
. dot membership operator, 68
    and member functions, 357, 361
    and member name, 796
    and overloading, 413
    and structures, 110, 138, 261, 264, 267
.* dereferencing operator, 796
.* pointer-to-member operator, 413
... ellipses, 659
.h suffix, 27
/ division operator, 80, 82-83
/* */ comments, 26
// comments, 22, 26
/= operator, 162
: colon, 484, 524
:: scope resolution operator, 330
    and class member name, 383, 796
    and external variables, 330
    and function calls, 610
    and initialization, 447-448
    and member functions, 353-354, 361
    and namespaces, 682
    and nested classes, 641
    and overloading, 413
; semicolon. *See* semicolons
< > angle brackets, 309, 314, 319
< input redirection operator, 167, 184, 207, 693
<< insertion operator, 28, 68, 298, 695-698, 747
<< left-shift operator, 28, 695, 789
<<= left-shift-and-assign operator, 790
<= operator, 167, 207

= assignment operator
    and == operator, 168
    and assignment statements, 34, 41
    and classes, 513, 552, 556-558
    combined, 162
    default, 530
    and enumerations, 116
    implicit, 456, 462-465, 467, 530
    and inheritance, 513, 552, 556-558
    with new, 472, 479, 556
    and overloading, 413, 462-465, 467, 479,
        518-519
    and structures, 113
== operator, 167
> output redirection operator, 167, 693
>= operator, 159, 167
>> extraction operator, 37, 266, 717-718
>> right-shift operator, 789-790
>>= right-shift-and-assign operator, 790
?: conditional operator, 212-213, 413
[] brackets
    in arrays, 95, 97, 128, 134, 245
    with new & delete, 141, 449, 453, 466, 471-
        472, 479
[] index operator, 298, 413, 510
[] subscript operator, 298, 413, 510
\ backslash, 29, 779
\0 null character, 98-102, 134, 171, 256, 719
\n newline character, 28-30
^ bitwise XOR operator, 789, 792, 794
^ CONTROL key symbol, 779
^D, 184-185, 724
^Z, 184-185, 724
_ underscore, 43, 54
' ' single quotes, 67, 69, 99, 779
{ } paired curly braces, 23, 32
    and arrays, 97
    and blocks, 144, 163, 176, 199
    and structures, 109-110, 113
| bitwise OR operator, 743, 789, 792, 794
| operator, 743, 754
|| logical OR operator, 201-203, 209
~ bitwise negation operator, 789, 791, 794
~ destructor indicator, 366, 374
0 prefix (octal), 64, 213, 773
0 to start, 94-95, 117, 205, 516, 540
0x or 0X prefix (hex), 64, 774

A

abstract base class (ABC), 550
abstract data types (ADTs), 384-388, 479
abstraction, 347-348, 351, 361
access control, 350-351, 354, 404, 510, 641-643
access declaration, 579
access, protected, 596
actual argument, 237
address assignment, 670
address operator, 118, 120, 133, 259, 285-286,
    291, 456
address and strings, 170
addresses, function, 271-272
addresses, passing, 266-268
addresses of values, 118-119, 123
algorithm concept, 3, 5
alias, 177-178, 285, 288, 291, 297, 682
ambiguity, 317, 430, 434-435, 553, 606, 610,
    617-619
angles in radians, 263, 408
ANSI (American National Standards Institute), 8
ANSI C
    compatibility, 18
    conversion, 88
    initialization, 144
    keywords, 777
    names, 54-55
    prototyping, 235-236
    standard, 8
ANSI++ library, 16-17
ANSI/ISO committee, 8
ANSI/ISO draft standard, 8
    bool type, 168, 466
    enumerations, 117
    exceptions, 670
    failbit, 107-108
    floating-point format, 702
    formatting, 716-717
    header files, 683
    input, 730
    input/output, 688
    iostream, 22, 27, 691
    mutable qualifier, 336
    namespace, 679, 683
    obtaining copy, 802
    precision, 707

ANSI/ISO draft standard *(continued)*
    random access, 753, 760-764
    specializations, 313-314, 316
    string class, 445, 465
    templates, 580
    type cast operators, 798-799
appending, 745-747
argc, 738
argument, defined, 25, 38
argument, function, 237-243
argument list, 24, 49, 303
argument passing, 88, 326-327
argv, 738
ArithArr class, 524-536
arithmetic operators, 79-84
ARM *(Annotated C++ Reference Manual)*, 8, 293, 316, 560, 580, 801
ARM C++, 18-19
array of addresses, 546
array base class, 506-522
array declaration, 94-96
array, defined, 63
array display, 249-250
array, external, 206
array filling, 248-249
array functions, 246-252
array modification, 250
array names, 133, 170, 243-244
    and pointers, 129, 131, 133
array notation, 134, 245, 257
array of objects, 380-382
array protection, 249-250
array size, 507, 590-592
array subscripts, 245
array template, 590-592
ArrayDb class, 508-522
ArrayDbE class, 660-665, 668
arrays, 93-98
    as arguments, 245-248
    and const, 249-252
    dynamic, 127-129, 134, 245
    and pointers, 129-134, 244-245
    two-dimensional, 189-192
ArrayTP class, 591
artificial intelligence, 268
ASCII character set, 66, 779-783
ASCII code, 170, 175, 748, 779

assembly language, 3
assigning addresses, 670
assigning value to function, 298
assigning values, arrays, 95-96
assignment, and conversion, 85-86
assignment, class object, 371-372, 462
assignment, default, 426
assignment, memberwise, 114
assignment operator. *See* = assignment operator
assignment statements, 32, 34-35, 41
associativity, 81-82, 154, 209-210, 785-787
AT&T C++, 10-11
automatic storage, 143
automatic storage class, 366
automatic type conversion, 236, 427, 437
automatic variables, 143-144, 322-327, 453

B

backslash (\), 29, 779
bad magic number message, 10
badbit, 721, 729
bang (exclamation point), 207
base 2 numbers, 35, 65, 774-775
base 8 numbers, 64, 773
base 10 numbers, 64, 773
base 16 numbers, 64, 773
base class, array, 506-522
base class, defined, 506
base class methods, 574-576
base constructors, 528-529
BASIC, 4, 33, 231
batch file, 47
Bell Laboratories, 3, 6, 8
binary files, 747-753
binary notation, 774-775
    ASCII characters, 779-783
binary numbers, 35, 65, 774-775
binary operator, 402, 785
binding, 543-545, 559
bit control, 794-795
bit, defined, 56, 774
bit manipulation operators, 414
bitwise operators, 789-795
bitwise techniques, 794-795
black box (function), 49
blank line, use of, 32

block, defined, 144
block scope, 322, 337, 382
blocks, 162-164, 176
boldface, use of, 18
books on C++, 801-802
books on OOP, 801
bool type, 72-73, 152, 168, 384
Boole, George, 72
Boolean variable, 72
booly.h file, 465
Borge, Victor, 157
Borland C++, xvi, 11, 13-14, 19, 71, 319, 739
bottom-up programming, 5-6, 252
bound template friends, 638-639
bounds checking, 507, 522, 538-539
break statement, 215-216, 219-221, 471
buffer, defined, 689
buffer flushing, 647, 690-691, 700-701, 736
buffering, 700, 735-736
buffers, 181, 688-693
byte, defined, 56, 775

C

C input/output, 22
C language, 3-4, 8
C++ described, 6
C++ history, 2-6
C++ standard. *See* ANSI/ISO draft standard
called function, 37, 41
calling function, 37, 41
carriage return, 30-31, 749
case label, 214, 218
case sensitivity, 10-11, 22, 25, 54, 65, 201-202
catch block, 650-654, 659
catching an exception, 649-650, 659
cerr, 356, 517, 692-694, 740
cfront program, 11, 18, 381
char type, 64, 66-72
cin, 27, 40, 180-182
cin >>, 266, 719-721
cin >> ch, 240
cin input, 717-734
cin object, 36-37, 266, 692, 694, 717
circular dependence, 633
class, basics, 348-361
class constructors. *See* constructors
class data members, 349-350, 361

class declaration, 349, 361
class, defined, 5, 39-40
class design review, 550-560
class destructors. *See* destructors
class function members, 350, 361
class functions, properties, 560
class inheritance, 506, 522-542
class libraries, 6, 40, 506, 688, 692, 767-768
class member functions, 349-350, 353-357, 361, 406-407
class members, 357
class method, defined, 41
class method definition, 349
class methods, 5, 350, 353-357, 361
class operators, 266
class scope, 354, 382-384, 483-484, 679-680
class specification, 349
class and structure, 353
class templates, 580-603
classes
    and dynamic memory, 444-454
    and exceptions, 660-666
    and friends, 628-633, 636-640
    and multiple representations, 399
    nested, 640-646
    with object members, 566-572
classic (K&R) C, 8, 88, 144, 327
clearing the bit, 711
client-server model, 360
clock_t, 177
CLOCKS_PER_SEC, 177
clog object, 692-694
coin toss, 587, 589
colon, 484, 524
combined assignment operators, 162
comma operator, 164-167
comma separator, 38, 97, 164-166, 239
command-line arguments, 738-740
command-line processing, 738-740
comments, 22, 26
comparison method, 375
comparisons, strings, 170-172
compatibility notes
    \a alert character, 71
    \a escape sequence, 215
    array initialization, 206
    binary file mode, 750-751
    bool, 629, 466

compatibility notes (*continued*)
 Boolean types, 385
 cin.get(), 186
 clock(), 177
 design flaws, 455
 draft standard, 22
 EOF, simulated, 184, 196-197
 explicit type cast, 575
 file opening, 745
 flaws, 450, 455
 float.h file, 77
 floating-point numbers, 77-78, 82
 g++ 2.0, 575, 587, 594, 612
 get(), 107
 getline(), 104
 ignore(), 728
 initializing arrays, 96, 327
 initializing structures, 111, 327
 INT_MAX, 495
 iostream, 22
 limits.h file, 58, 61
 math library, 713, 715
 memory, freeing, 339
 Metrowerks CodeWarrior, 594, 612
 output format, 702
 pointer stack, 587
 pointers, 118
 put(), 186, 699
 RAND_MAX, 494-495
 random access, 757
 stream.h, 22
 String class flaws, 450
 Symantec C++, 624, 706
 templates, 309, 597, 615
 time-delay loop, 177
 Turbo C++, 104
 type long double, 242
 width(), 706
compilation, separate, 318-321
compile time decisions, 119, 134, 443-444
compiler, defined, 3
compiler error, 199
compiling, 9, 11-17
complex.h file, 440
complex number, 440
composition (containment), 565-572, 578, 640
compound statements, 162-164
concatenate, defined, 100

concatenation, 39
 input, 719, 724
 operator, 298
 output, 697-698
 strings, 100, 106, 202
conditional expressions, 212-213
connections (streams), 689
const
 and arrays, 249-252
 external variables, 331
 keyword, 60, 73-74, 249, 253-255, 295,
  336-337, 372
 member functions, 372-373
 modifier, 257, 267
 and overloading, 517-518
 pointers, 253-255
 qualifier, 206, 312, 376
 references, 293-295, 300
 use of, 295, 555
 value (array size), 158
const_cast operator, 798-799
constant object, 253-254
constants
 char, 69-71
 character, 99
 file mode, 742
 floating-point, 78
 formatting, 710
 integer, 64-65
 setf(), 711-712
 string, 98-99
 symbolic, 58-60, 115
constructor approach, 591-592
constructor, default, 364-366
constructor definition, 363
constructor prototype, 362-363
constructors
 basics, 362-366, 371, 373-374
 and inheritance, 513-515, 528-529, 552, 556
 one-argument, 373, 429, 431, 435, 467, 530,
  552
 virtual base class, 607-610
 virtual function, 548
container classes, 580
containment (composition), 565-572, 578, 640
continue statement, 219-221, 653
conventions. *See* style conventions
conversion checklist, 87-88

conversion functions, 432-435, 467, 478, 552-553

conversions, 67, 316-318, 552-553

    automatic, 84-89

    and friends, 435-438

    trivial, 316, 599

    type. *See* type conversions

coordinates, 262-263, 398-400, 408, 417-418

coordinates program, 319-321

copy constructor, 456-462, 472, 479, 513-515, 522, 531, 551

count.exe file, 740

counting elements, 97-99

counting loop, 158-159, 162, 175, 305-307

cout, 35-36, 39-40, 414-417

cout facility, 22, 27-30

cout formatting, 701-703

cout object, 28, 692-694

cout output, 694

CplusLib library, 16

CPlusPlus.lib, 17

cpp extension, 22

ctype.h file, 210-212

ctype.h function, 722

cursor position, 29

Customer class, 490-493

D

data alteration, 246, 249, 295, 299-300

data component, 349

data concept, 3, 5

data hiding, 5, 350-353, 361, 362, 510

data integrity, 351, 361

data object, 125

data protection, 246, 249, 295, 299-300, 331

debuggers, 13-17

debugging, 670, 676

decimal notation, 773

    ASCII characters, 779-783

decimal points, 708-709

declaration, 330, 333

declaration, forward, 633-636

declaration statements, 32-34, 41

declaration-statement expression, 156

decrement operator, 152, 159-161, 172

deep copying, 460-462, 472, 489, 551

default arguments, 300-303, 308, 363

default constructor, 364-366, 456-457, 551

default label, 214

default visibility, 353

defining declaration, 34, 330, 333

definition, 34, 330, 333

delete operator, 128, 140

    delete statement, 449

    and destructors, 471, 478

    and memory, 299, 322, 449, 453-454, 464

dequeuing, 486-488

dereferencing. *See* * dereferencing operator

derivations, 524-525

derived class, 506, 524-542

derived constructors, 528-529

derived types. *See under* types

destructors

    basics, 362, 366, 374

    and classes, 448-449, 513-515, 552

    and inheritance, 513-515, 552, 556, 560

    and memory, 448-449, 453-454, 460

    and new, 471, 474, 478

    virtual function, 548

direction (vector), 396, 398

directives, 27, 60-61

displacement vector, 397-398

divide-and-conquer strategy, 270

divide-by-0 error, 210, 647, 649

division, floating-point, 82

division, integer, 82

division operator, 80, 82-83

do while loop, 178-180

dominance, 617-619

DOS, 10, 11, 184-185

double quotes (" "), 28, 67, 69, 99, 319

double slash (//), 22, 26

double type, 42, 76-78

downcasting, 537, 556

draft standard. *See* ANSI/ISO draft standard

drunkard's walk, 423

dynamic allocation, 338-339

dynamic arrays, 127-129, 134, 245

dynamic binding, 127, 134, 543-546, 559

dynamic_cast operator, 671-675, 798

dynamic memory, 322, 338-339, 444-454

E

E or e notation, 75, 702

early binding, 543-544

EasyWin, 14, 71
EBCDIC code, 66, 69
echoing, 180-181
element, array, 94
ellipses, 659
employee class, 623-624
encapsulation, 351, 361
end-of-file. *See* EOF
enqueuing, 486-487
entry-condition loop, 152, 173, 179
enum, 217-218, 428
enum constant, 709
enum facility, 115-117
enumerations, 115-117, 383, 465, 629
enumerators, 115-117, 217-218
EOF (end-of-file), 183-188, 196-197
eofbit, 721, 729-730
error handling, 224, 235-236, 257, 660, 670
error messages, 356, 418, 692-694, 740
error stream, 647
escape sequences, 69-71, 779
exceptions, 532, 646-670
    catching, 649-650, 659
    and classes, 660-666
    defined, 649
    handler, 649-654, 659
    header file, 670, 675
    and inheritance, 666-669
    mechanism, 649-653
    throwing, 649-651, 657-658
    uncaught, 653
    versatility, 653-660
executable code, 9
executable programs, 282
exercises
    Chapter 2, 51
    Chapter 3, 91
    Chapter 4, 147
    Chapter 5, 194
    Chapter 6, 227-228
    Chapter 7, 277-279
    Chapter 8, 342-343
    Chapter 9, 390-391
    Chapter 10, 440-441
    Chapter 11, 501-503
    Chapter 12, 563-564
    Chapter 13, 622-625
    Chapter 14, 685-686
    Chapter 15, 770-772

EXIT_FAILURE, 356
EXIT_SUCCESS, 356
exit values, 47
exit-condition loop, 178-179
exponent, 75
expression arguments, 590-592
expression, defined, 79, 154
expression values, 154-155
expressions and conversions, 86-88
expressions and statements, 154-156
extensibility, 36
extensions, cpp, 22
extensions, file, 10-12
external array, 206
external declaration, 112, 157-158
external identifiers, 55
external linkage, 322, 332, 336-337
external names, 680
external variables, 328-335
extraction, explained, 688

F

f or F suffix, 78, 82
factorials, 157-158, 241
failbit, 107, 721, 729-730
family of classes, 592-600
field widths, 704-706
file extensions, 10-12, 22
file input, 734-737
file mode argument, 742
file modes, 742-753
file output, 734-737
file scope, 322, 338, 382
file-opening modes, 743-744
files, multiple, 737-740
fill characters, 706-707
fin, 761
fin object, 736
first in-first out (FIFO), 479
fixed-point notation, 712
flags, format, 709-710, 712
flaws, design, 454-465
float.h file, 76
float type, 76-78
floating-point format, 701-702, 707-708
floating-point numbers, 74-79
fmtflags, 710-711
for loop, 150-160, 175-176, 189-192, 220

formal argument, 237
formal parameter, 237
format in C++, 527
formatting, 200
formatting changes, 716-717
formatting commands, 360
formatting constants, 710
formatting, cout, 701-703
formatting flags, 709-710, 712
formatting, incore, 764-767
formatting options, 642
FORTRAN, 4, 231
forward declaration, 633-636
fout, 761
fout object, 735
free store, 144, 366
friend classes, 404, 628-633
friend functions, 404-407, 414-416, 435-437
friend member functions, 404, 633-637
friendless approach, 416-417, 419-420
friends
    and conversions, 435-438
    and data hiding, 407
    mutual friendship, 637
    and operator overloading, 404-412
    and templates, 638-640
    and virtual functions, 548
fstream class, 743, 753-754
fstream.h family, 40
fstream.h file, 688, 735
function
    abort(), 647, 653
    acquire(), 355
    ArithArr(), 528
    arsize(), 510, 515
    atan(), 264
    average(), 531, 567, 569, 574
    bad(), 721
    buildstr(), 258
    buy(), 355
    c_int_str(), 257
    cin.clear(), 185, 266
    cin.get(), 106, 182-188, 210, 224, 240,
        724-727
    cin.get(ch), 182-184, 188, 196, 240, 725-726
    cin.get(char &r), 724
    cin.get(void), 725
    cin.getline(), 103, 106

function (continued)
    clear(), 221, 224, 722, 756
    clear(iosate s), 721
    clock(), 177
    clone(), 299
    close(), 736
    cout.put(), 68-69, 186, 188
    cout.setf(), 77-78, 82
    cout.write(), 699-700
    cube(), 234, 237, 291-292
    data(), 596, 610-611
    dequeue(), 489
    details(), 657-658
    display(), 431, 522
    enqueue(), 641
    eof(), 721, 742
    estimate(), 271-275
    exit(), 355-356, 517, 647
    fail(), 721-723, 745
    fill(), 706-707
    fill_array(), 249
    gcount(), 730-731
    get(), 103-108, 610, 612, 723, 727-730
    get(ch), 724
    getchar(), 185, 188, 724
    get(char &r), 723-726
    get(void), 723-726
    getall(), 772
    getline(), 103-108, 723, 727-730
    getname(), 143
    gmean(), 654-655, 657
    good(), 721, 745
    hmean(), 648, 651-652, 657-658
    ignore(), 727
    is_int(), 209
    isempty(), 385
    isfull(), 385
    isspace(), 721
    lbound(), 539
    left(), 300-303, 305-307
    length(), 471
    local(), 330
    main(), 23-25, 44
    malloc(), 125, 338
    n_chars(), 239-240
    name(), 676
    new_lb(), 539
    odds(), 242-243

function (*continued*)
 ok(), 539-541
 open(), 742
 operator typename(), 432, 435
 operator*(), 404-405
 operator+(), 400-402, 796
 operator-(), 403
 operator<(), 471
 operator<<(), 414-415, 419-420, 451, 519,
  695-696
 operator=(), 518-519
 operator[](), 511, 515-518, 521, 539-541,
  579-580
 peek(), 730-733
 pop(), 385-386, 586-587
 precision(), 707, 762
 print(), 304
 printf(), 22, 35-36
 pubseekoff(), 761
 push(), 385-386
 put(), 698-699
 putback(), 730-732
 putchar(), 185-186, 188
 puts(), 36, 37
 rand(), 423-426, 474, 494, 589
 rdbuf(), 761
 rdstate(), 721
 read(), 730-731, 750
 reassess(), 250
 rect_to_polar(), 264, 267
 recurs(), 269
 refcube(), 291-294
 remote_access(), 334
 scanf(), 22
 seekg(), 754-757
 seekp(), 754
 sell(), 355
 set(), 491, 599, 612
 set_ang(), 399
 set_by_polar(), 399, 408
 set_mag(), 399
 set_terminate(), 653
 set_tot(), 355
 setall(), 771
 setf(), 77, 82, 708-715
 setprecision(), 715
 setw(), 715
 show(), 536, 543-544, 596, 599, 610-611

function (*continued*)
 show_array(), 250, 255
 show_polar(), 263, 266-268, 400
 show_time(), 260-261
 showmenu(), 215
 simon(), 44-46
 sqrt(), 41-44
 square(), 282
 srand(), 423-426, 474, 589
 stonetolb(), 48-49
 str(), 765
 strchr(), 599
 strcmp(), 170-171, 465
 strcpy(), 135-138, 143, 363, 448
 strlen(), 100-101, 135-137, 159, 303, 448
 strncpy(), 363
 subdivide(), 270-271
 sum(), 260-261, 531
 sum_arr(), 244-247
 swap(), 308-314
 swapp(), 288-291
 swapr(), 288-291, 294
 swapv(), 288-291
 tellg(), 755
 tellp(), 755
 terminate(), 653
 time(), 423-426, 474, 589
 time(0), 425
 ubound(), 539
 update(), 330, 354
 use(), 295-297
 width(), 704-706, 762
 write(), 698-700, 731, 749-750
 writeall(), 771
function addresses, 271-272
function arguments, 237-243
function basics, 230-236
function body, 23
function call, 24, 37-38, 41, 230, 232-236
function decision strategy, 316-318
function definition, 23, 42, 230, 232
function form, 45
function heading, 24-25, 45-47
function interface, 234, 243
function, invoking with pointer, 273-274
function libraries, 37, 44, 229, 505-506
function location in C++, 338
function matching, 304-305, 313, 316-318

function name as address, 272
function overloading, 107, 183, 236, 303-308, 364-365, 373
function polymorphism, 303-308
function prototype, 42-44, 49, 230, 232-236
function signature, 303-304, 311
function syntax, 45
function templates, 308-318
function type, 49
functions
    and arrays, 243-255
    basics, 41-49
    character, 210-212
    conversion, 432-435
    defined, 4, 9, 23
    features, 49
    friend, 404-407, 414-416, 435-437
    friend member, 404, 633-637
    inline, 281-285
    library, 37, 230
    nonmember, 405
    and pointers, 271-275
    recursive, 268-271
    return values, 41-44, 231-233
    and storage classes, 337-338
    and strings, 256-259
    and structures, 259-268
    type void, 231
    user-defined, 44-49
    virtual member, 542-550

G

g++, 12, 19, 177
genericity, 580, 583
geometric mean, 654
global namespace, 680, 682-683
global variables, 328-335
GNU C++ 2.0, xvi, 10-12, 19, 757
goto statement, 221

H

h suffix, 27
harmonic mean, 646
has-a relationship, 522-523, 566-567, 572, 578, 603
header files, 43, 319, 367-368, 683

heap memory, 591
heterogeneous elements, 592, 599
hexadecimal notation, 64, 119, 773-774
    ASCII characters, 779-783
hidden members, 546, 549
hiding, data, 5, 350-353, 361, 362, 510
hiding, and scope, 323
high-level language, 3
hint, 327
homogeneous elements, 592, 599

I

IDE (integrated development environment), 10
if else if else, 200-201, 205-206, 210, 214
if else statement, 197-201, 218-219
if statement, 195-201, 269
ifstream class, 735
implementation
    derived class, 527-534
    inheritance, 566-567, 572
    queue, 481-483
    virtual functions, 545-546
implicit upcasting, 579
in scope, 322-323
incore formatting, 764-767
index, in arrays, 94-95
index out-of-bounds error, 559
indirect membership operator, 267, 383
infinite loop problem, 174-176
inheritance, 5, 445, 506, 522-542
    and exceptions, 666-669
    multiple, 565-566, 572, 575, 603-619
    private, 522
    protected, 522, 578-579
    public, 522-523, 536-537, 555-560
    varieties of, 579
initialization, 44, 57, 59, 552
    class objects, 372
    constructors, 373
initialization list, 97, 529-530, 551
initialization list syntax, 529-530, 556, 568-569
initializer list, 484-485
initializing
    2-D arrays, 190-191
    array of pointers, 191
    ArrayDb objects, 513-514
    arrays, 95-98

initializing *(continued)*
    base class components, 573-574
    class objects, 362, 364-365, 431
    contained objects, 568-569
    loops, 150-151
    objects, with new, 474
    objects to objects, 530-531
    pointers, 121-124
    reference variables, 286-287, 291
    structures, 113
inline facility, 284-285
inline functions, 338, 356
inline qualifier, 356
input, 687-694, 717-734
    concatenation, 719, 724
    defined, 27
    mixing, 108-109
    single-character, 723-727
    string, 723, 727-730
insertion, explained, 688
instance variable, 39
instances, 350, 361. *See* objects
instantiation, 582-583, 639
instructors, note to, xx
int, in function headings, 45-46
int &, 285
int*, 121-122
INT_MAX, 57-58, 209
INT_MIN, 209
int type, 33, 56-57, 62
integer division, 306
integer function, 305
integer types, 55-73
integral promotion, 87
interface
    contained object, 569-570
    function heading, 24-25
    function interface, 49
    inheritance, 566-567, 572
    public, 349, 351, 360, 361
    queue, 481
internal declaration, 112
internal justification, 712, 715
internal linkage, 322, 332, 336-337
iomanip.h file, 715-716
ios class, 692
ios member functions, 721
iostate, 721

iostream class, 692
iostream.h family, 40
iostream.h file, 27, 182-183, 186, 688, 691-693, 717
iostream methods, 266
IOStreams library, 16
is-a relationship, 522-542, 555-558, 567, 592, 603
is-implemented-as-a relationship, 523
is-like-a relationship, 523
ISO (International Standards Organization), 8
iso_standard_library, 683
istream class, 40, 692, 694, 717-718
istream methods, 721-734
istrstream class, 766-767
italics, use of, 17-18
Item type, 385, 481-482

J

jump (throw statement), 650
justification, 705-706, 712

K

K (kilobyte), defined, 127
K&R C (Kernighan & Ritchie), 8, 88, 144, 327
keyword
    auto, 325
    catch, 650, 652
    class, 309, 350, 581
    const, 60, 73-74, 249, 253-255, 295, 336-337, 372
    double, 42, 47
    enum, 115
    extern, 328-330, 332-335, 337-338
    for, 153
    friend, 405-406
    inline, 282, 356, 634
    int, 25
    mutable, 336-337
    namespace, 680, 682
    private, 350, 353, 510, 572
    protected, 351, 510, 578
    public, 350, 603
    register, 327
    return, 24, 25, 46, 47-48, 377
    static, 96, 98, 111, 144, 206, 322, 336, 338
    struct, 109-110

keyword *(continued)*
>   template, 309, 581
>   throw, 650, 658
>   try, 650
>   typedef, 178
>   unsigned, 60
>   using, 681-682
>   virtual, 543-544, 546, 606, 618
>   void, 25, 45-47, 235
>   volatile, 336-337
keywords
>   defined, 47
>   list of, 777
>   and names, 54
>   overloading, 607
>   qualifiers, 336-337

L

l or L suffix, 65, 78
L for wide characters, 72
labels, 214-218
language divergence, 7-8
last in-first out (LIFO), 326, 339, 387, 479
late binding, 543-544, 546, 559
layering, 565. *See* containment
left-justification, 706, 712
level variable (recursion), 271
libraries, 6, 8, 9, 16, 17
library files, 43
library functions, 43, 338
LimitArE class, 666-669
LimitArr class, 538-542
limits.h file, 57-60, 209, 495
line feed, 749, 779
line-oriented input, 103-108
linkage, 322, 332-335, 356
linking, 9, 11-17, 37
list, linked, 481-482, 489
list, simple, 391
listings
>   addpntrs.cpp, 130
>   address.cpp, 118
>   and.cpp, 204
>   append.cpp, 745-746
>   arith.cpp, 80
>   aritharr.cpp, 532-534
>   aritharr.h, 526-527

listings *(continued)*
>   arraydb.cpp, 511-512
>   arraydb.h, 508-509, 544
>   arraydbe.cpp, 662-663
>   arraydbe.h, 661
>   arraynew.cpp, 129
>   arrayone.cpp, 95-96
>   arraytp.h, 591
>   arrfun1.cpp, 244
>   arrfun2.cpp, 246-247
>   arrfun3.cpp, 251-252
>   assgn_st.cpp, 113-114
>   assign.cpp, 86
>   auto.cpp, 324
>   bank.cpp, 495-496
>   bigstep.cpp, 159
>   binary.cpp, 751-752
>   block.cpp, 163
>   bondini.cpp, 71
>   booly.h, 385
>   calling.cpp, 230
>   chartype.cpp, 66
>   check_it.cpp, 720
>   cinfish.cpp, 222
>   cingolf.cpp, 223
>   compstr.cpp, 171
>   condit.cpp, 212-213
>   convert.cpp, 48
>   coordin.h, 319-320
>   count.cpp, 739-740
>   ctypes.cpp, 210-211
>   cubes.cpp, 291-292
>   defaults.cpp, 702-703
>   delete.cpp, 142
>   derived.cpp, 534-535
>   divide.cpp, 82
>   dowhile.cpp, 180
>   E-1 (example class), 795
>   E-2 (example class), 796
>   E-3 (memb_pt.cpp), 797-798
>   emp.h, 623-624
>   enum.cpp, 217-218
>   equal.cpp, 169
>   error1.cpp, 647
>   error2.cpp, 648-649
>   error3.cpp, 650-651
>   error4.cpp, 654-655
>   error5.cpp, 658-659

listings *(continued)*

exceed.cpp, 61
exceptar.cpp, 664-665
excptinh.cpp, 668-669
express.cpp, 155
external.cpp, 329
file.cpp, 737
file1.cpp, 321
file2.cpp, 321
fill.cpp, 707
firstref.cpp, 285-286
fleas.cpp, 32
floatnum.cpp, 77
fltadd.cpp, 79
forloop.cpp, 150
formore.cpp, 157
forstr1.cpp, 160
forstr2.cpp, 165
fun_ptr.cpp, 274-275
funtemp.cpp, 309-310
get_fun.cpp, 728-729
hexoct.cpp, 64
if.cpp, 197
ifelse.cpp, 198-199
ifelseif.cpp, 201
init_ptr.cpp, 123
inline.cpp, 283-284
instr1.cpp, 102
instr2.cpp, 104
instr3.cpp, 105
instr4.cpp, 106-107
iomanip.cpp, 715-716
jump.cpp, 220
left.cpp, 301-302
leftover.cpp, 306-307
limarr.cpp, 539-540
limarr.h, 538
limarre.cpp, 667-668
limarre.h, 666-667
limits.cpp, 57-58
lotto.cpp, 242-243
manip.cpp, 704
modulus.cpp, 84
more_and.cpp, 206
morechar.cpp, 67
myfirst.cpp, 22
nested.cpp, 191-192, 645-646
newstrct.cpp, 139-140

listings *(continued)*

not.cpp, 208
num_test.cpp, 152
numstr.cpp, 108
or.cpp, 202-203
ourfunc.cpp, 44-45
pairs.cpp, 600-601
pe11_1.cpp, 501-502
peeker.cpp, 732
plus_one.cpp, 160-161
pntstr.cpp, 135-136
pointer.cpp, 120
precise.cpp, 707-708
problem1.cpp, 455
problem2.cpp, 455-456
protos.cpp, 233-234
queue.cpp, 492-493
queue.h, 491-492
queuetp.h, 643-645
random.cpp, 758-760
randomds.cpp, 762-764
randwalk.cpp, 424
recur.cpp, 269
rq15-6.cpp, 821-822
rq15-7.cpp, 822
rq15-8.cpp, 770
rtti1.cpp, 674-675
rtti2.cpp, 676-677
ruler.cpp, 270-271
sayings1.cpp, 470-471
sayings2.cpp, 475-476
secref.cpp, 287
setf.cpp, 710-711
setf2.cpp, 713-714
showpt.cpp, 709
sqrt.cpp, 43
stack.cpp, 386
stack.h, 385-385
stacker.cpp, 387-388
stacktem.cpp, 584-585
stacktp.h, 582-583
static.cpp, 331-332
stcktp1.h, 588
stkoptr1.cpp, 589
stock1.cpp, 368-370
stock1.h, 367
stock2.cpp, 378-379
stock2.h, 378

listings (*continued*)

stocks.cpp, 349-350, 354-355, 358-360
stone.cpp, 430-431
stone1.cpp, 434
stonewt.cpp, 428-429
stonewt.h, 427-428
stonewt1.cpp, 433-434
stonewt1.h, 433
strctfun.cpp, 264-265
strctptr.cpp, 267-268
strgback.cpp, 258
strgfun.cpp, 256-257
strin.cpp, 767
strings.cpp, 100-101
strng1.h, 445
strng2.cpp, 468-470
strng2.h, 467-468
strngs1.cpp, 446-447
strout.cpp, 765-766
strtref.cpp, 296
structur.cpp, 111
studentc.cpp, 570
studentc.h, 568
studenti.cpp, 576
studenti.h, 573-574
swaps.cpp, 288-289
switch.cpp, 215-216
textin1.cpp, 181
textin2.cpp, 182
textin3.cpp, 184-185
textin4.cpp, 187
tinsel.cpp, 520-521
travel.cpp, 260-261
truncate.cpp, 733-734
tv.cpp, 630-631
tv.h, 629-630
tvfm.h, 634-635
twoarg.cpp, 239-240
twofile1.cpp, 335
twofile2.cpp, 335
twoswap.cpp, 314-316
twotemps.cpp, 311-312
typecast.cpp, 88-89
use_lim.cpp, 541
use_new.cpp, 126
use_stuc.cpp, 570-571
use_stui.cpp, 576-577
use_tv.cpp, 632
use_vect.cpp, 411-412

listings (*continued*)

useemp1.cpp, 624
usestok1.cpp, 370-
usestok2.cpp, 380-381
vector0.h, 398
vector1.cpp, 409-411
vector1.h, 407-408
vector2.cpp, 420-423
vector2.h, 419
vegnews.cpp, 449-450
waiting.cpp, 177-178
while.cpp, 173-174
width.cpp, 705-706
workarr.cpp, 597-598
worker.cpp, 594-596
worker.h, 593-594
workerfd.h, 603-604
workermi.cpp, 612-615
workermi.h, 608-610
workmi.cpp, 615-616
write.cpp, 699
yourcat.cpp, 36
lm option, 43, 408, 713, 715
local declaration, 112
local scope, 323
local variables, 238, 328, 330-332
logical bitwise operators, 791-793
logical expressions, 201-210
logical operators, 201-210
long double type, 75-78
long integer type, 56-57, 63
loop body, 150-151
loop initialization, 150-151
loop parts, 150-151
loop problems, 174
loop test, 150-151
loop update, 150-151
loops
    counting, 158-159, 162, 175, 305-307
    do while loop, 178-180
    for loop, 150-160, 175-176, 189-192, 220
    nested, 189-192
    number-reading, 221-224
    and text input, 180-188
    while loop, 172-178, 220, 224
Lotto odds, 241-243
lowercase/uppercase, 10-11, 170-171, 201-202, 217
low-level language, 3
Lvalue, 73, 293, 295

M

machine language, 9
macros, 284-285
magnitude (vector), 396, 398
main() function, 23-25, 44
make program, 318-319
manipulators, 703-704, 711-712, 715-716
mantissa, 75
math.h file, 42-43, 264
math library, 408
McConnell, Mark, 157
mean, geometric, 646
mean, harmonic, 646
member dereferencing operators, 795-798
member functions
    defined, 68
    friend, 404, 633-637
    implicit, 456-465
    properties of, 560
    public, 550-552
    virtual, 542-550
membership operators. *See . and ->*
memberwise assignment, 114
memberwise copying, 458
memory address, 123-124, 282
memory allocation
    and compilers, 33-34, 327
    and declarations, 33-34, 447
    dynamic, 338-339
    and function call, 237
    and new, 125-127, 338-339
    runtime decision, 444
    and static variables, 327
memory freeing, 140-143, 464
memory leak, 454
memory management, 140, 143-144, 465, 473,
    515, 559
memory mismanagement, 460, 463
memory, named, 125, 133
memory pool, 144
memory returning, 140-143, 464
memory space, 127
memory, unnamed, 125, 133
message sending, 40-41, 357
methods. *See* function
Metrowerks CodeWarrior, xvi, 11, 17, 19, 71,
    319, 739

MI. *See* multiple inheritance
Microsoft Visual C++, xvi, 11, 14-15, 19, 739
    and \a, 71, 215
mixed base classes, 617
mixed notation, 712
mode member, 417-418
multifile programs, 318-321, 332-335, 520
multiple inheritance, 565-566, 572, 575, 603-619
mutual friends, 637
mv command, 12

N

name conflicts, 640, 660, 679-680
name length, 54
name, qualified (full), 354, 361
names, external, 680
names, source file, 10-11
namespace facility, 383
namespaces, 679-683
naming rules, 54-55, 73, 309
need-to-know policy, 417
nested classes, 483-484, 640-646
nested conditional expressions, 213
nested enumerations, 484
nested function calls, 298
nested loops, 189-192
nested namespaces, 682-683
nested structures, 483-484
nested try blocks, 659
nesting in a template, 643-646
new operator
    and constructors, 471-474, 478-479
    and dynamic arrays, 127-129, 134, 508
    and dynamic structures, 138-140
    and exception throwing, 665
    and memory, 125-127, 133, 322, 449,
        453-454
    and object initialization, 474
    and storage, 299
newline character, 28-30
nodes, 481
non-numeric input, 221-224
nonexpressions, 156
nonmember functions, 405
nontemplate friends, 638
nonzero (true), 72-73, 170, 196, 198
nonzero argument, 356

nonzero exit value, 47
notation (format), 712
null character, 98-102, 134, 171, 256, 719
null pointer, 127, 466, 472, 479, 513
    0 as, 641, 665, 672
null pointer assignment, 455, 460, 462
null statement, 176
number bases, 64, 703-704, 773-775
number-reading loops, 221-224
numbers and pointers, 124
numbers, size and type, 65
numeric input loop, 266

O

object-oriented programming, 5-6, 252
    approach, 346-347, 352
    features, 1, 5, 345
    philosophy, 119
object code, 9
object, defined, 5, 28, 39-40
object instance, 39
object type, 39
objects, 350, 361
    array of, 380-382
    and classes, 357
    initializing to objects, 530-531
octal notation, 773
    ASCII characters, 779-783
octal numbers, 64
odds calculation, 241-243
offset (address), 119
ofstream class, 735
OOP. See object-oriented programming
openmode type, 742
operands, defined, 79
operating system, defined, 3
operator, defined, 57
operator function, defined, 395
operator order reversal, 405-406
operator overloading, 28, 83, 298, 394-404,
    412-413
operator precedence, 81-82, 785-787
    and comma operator, 166
    and logical operators, 202-203, 209-210
    and overloading, 412
    and parentheses, 81, 131, 138, 209, 273
    and relational operators, 167

operator redefinition, 298
operators
    arithmetic, 79-84
    bitwise, 789-795
    delete. See delete operator
    dereferencing, 795-798
    list of, 786-787
    logical, 201-210
    logical bitwise, 791-793
    member dereferencing, 795-798
    new. See new operator
    prefix, 160
    redirection, 167, 184, 207, 693
    relational, 167
    shift, 789-790
    sizeof. See sizeof operator
    table of, 413
    type cast, 798-799
    See also under symbols at start of Index
ordering, 633-634
os reference, 414-415
ostream & return type, 697
ostream class, 40, 419, 692, 694
ostream methods, 415, 695-700
ostrstream class, 765, 767
out of scope, 323, 325
output, 27, 192, 687-694
overflow, 62
overloading
    + operator, 400-402
    - operator, 402-403
    << operator, 413-417, 478, 695-698
    = operator, 462-465, 467, 479, 518-519
    >> operator, 470, 717-718
    [] operator, 510, 515-518
    functions, 183, 303-308
    keywords, 607
    operators, 28, 83, 298, 394-404
    overloaded operator, 402-403
    templates, 310-312

P

padding, 706
Pair class, 600-601
parameter, formal, 237
parameterized types, 580

parentheses
    and cin.get(), 188
    and constructors, 365
    and function address, 272
    in function heading, 24-25
    and function prototype, 235
    and loops, 151, 153-154
    and pointer to function, 273
    and precedence, 81, 131, 138, 209, 273
    and sizeof operator, 58
    and white space, 31-32
Pascal procedures, 231
passing a reference, 293, 299-300, 458, 553
passing by reference, 260, 288-292, 553
passing by value, 237-238, 259-261, 288-292,
    300, 458, 553
pause, 14, 16
philosophy of C, 3-4
philosophy of C++, 119
pointed-to values, 133
pointer addition, 130-133, 161, 245
pointer arguments, 299-300
pointer arithmetic, 129-134
pointer notation, 134, 245, 257
pointer value assignment, 133
pointers
    and arrays, 127-134, 244-245
    basics, 117-124, 133-134
    to class members, 795-798
    and const, 253-255
    dangers, 124, 135-137, 144
    declaring, 121-124, 133
    defined, 93, 118, 120
    and delete, 140-143
    to functions, 271-275
    and inheritance, 531, 536-537
    and is-a relationships, 536-537
    and new, 125-129, 138-143
    and numbers, 124
    to objects, 364, 474-478
    and passing by value, 288
    returning, 298-299
    stack of, 586-590
    and strings, 109, 134-138
    this pointer, 374-379
    and typedef, 178
pointer-to-char, 135-136, 206, 256, 301, 445
pointer-to-const, 253-255
polar coordinates. *See* coordinates

polymorphism, 5, 303-308, 394, 599, 606
pop (stack), 384-386
portability, 7-8, 115-116, 356, 749
postfix operators, 160
precedence. *See* operator precedence
precision, 78, 79, 85, 707-708, 712
prefix operators, 160
preprocessor, 22, 60-61, 178, 284, 367-368
preprocessor program, 27
primary header files, 683
private class components, 352-353, 361, 362,
    509-510, 524
private derivation, 525
private inheritance, 572-580
private members, 558-559
probability theory, 425
procedural language, 3-4
procedural programming, 252, 346-347
program, defined, 3
program flow, 652-653
program language history, 2-6
programming basics, 9-11
programming exercises. *See* exercises
Project menus, 318-319
promotion, 317
protected access, 596
protected class components, 509-510, 524
protected derivation, 525
protected inheritance, 578-579
protected members, 558-559
prototype syntax, 234-235
prototypes, constructor, 362-363
prototypes, function, 42-44, 49, 230, 232-236
prototypes, pointer to function, 272-273
public class components, 352-353, 361, 509, 524
public derivation, 524, 555
public inheritance, 522-523, 536-537, 555-560,
    567, 579
public interface, 349, 351, 360, 361, 481
punctuation, and loops, 176
pure virtual functions, 550, 567
push (stack), 384-386
Pythagorean theorem, 264

Q

qualified name, 354, 361
qualifier, const, 73-74
qualify array, 206

qualifying function definitions, 654
Queue class, 479-498, 640, 645
queues, 479-498
QuickWin, 15, 71, 177, 215
quotation marks
    double (" "), 28, 67, 69, 99, 319
    single (' '), 67, 69, 99, 779
quoted (" ") strings, 67, 69, 98-99, 135, 256

R

radians, 263, 408
RAND_MAX, 494
random access, 753-764
random numbers, 425, 589
random walk problem, 411, 423-426
range, enumeration, 117
range tests, 207
range of values, 205-207
read-only data, 137
real numbers, 42
records, 753
rectangles, filled, 71
rectangular coordinates. *See* coordinates
recursion, 268-271, 282, 574-575, 600
redefining access, 579-580
redefining operators, 41
redefinition, 547-549, 578
redirection, 184, 356, 693-694, 734
reference arguments, 288-295, 299-300, 718
reference declarations, 34
reference oddities, 291-295
reference properties, 291-295
reference, returned, 401
reference variables, 285-300
references, 531, 536-537
    defined, 182
    as function parameters, 288-291
    returning, 295-299, 554
reference-to-an-int, 285
referencing declaration, 330, 333
register variable, 327
reinterpret_cast operator, 798-799
relational expressions, 151, 152, 167-172
relational operators, 167
relationships, 522-523, 555-558
Remote class, 628-637
representations, multiple, 399

request, 327
result vector, 426
return 0; statement, 25
return call, 657-658
return key, 18
return mechanism, 377
return statement, 23, 47-49, 231-232
return type, 24
return value, 25, 41-44, 46-49, 231-233
returned reference, 401
returning an object, 554
returning a pointer, 298-299
returning a reference, 295-299, 554
reusable code, 5, 505-506, 524
reverse-order problem, 405-406
reversibility, 537
review questions
    answers, 803-822
    Chapter 2, 50-51
    Chapter 3, 90-91
    Chapter 4, 146
    Chapter 5, 193
    Chapter 6, 225-227
    Chapter 7, 276-277
    Chapter 8, 340-342
    Chapter 9, 389-390
    Chapter 10, 439-440
    Chapter 11, 499-501
    Chapter 12, 561-562
    Chapter 13, 620-622
    Chapter 14, 684-685
    Chapter 15, 769-770
rewrite rule, 356
right-justification, 705-706, 712
Ritchie, Dennis, 3, 8
rounding, 86, 433
RTTI, 670-679
rules
    -> arrow operator, 138
    . dot operator, 138
    array initilization, 97-98
    array numbering, 94-95
    assigning value to function, 298
    assignment, object, 371
    associativity, 81-82
    class, 40
    const member functions, 372-373
    constructors, 373

rules *(continued)*
    conversion, 85-89
    delete and new, 140-141
    derived class, 526, 531
    downcasting, 537
    dynamic_cast syntax, 672
    E notation, 76
    enumerations, 116-117
    expressions, 155-156
    external variable definition, 334
    formatting, 30-31
    function prototype, 42
    inheritance, 528
    initialization, 60, 528
    initializing reference variables, 287
    iostream.h file, 27
    is-a relationship, 536-537
    member function, 357
    membership operators, 138
    memory freeing, 140-141
    namespaces, 681
    naming, 54-55, 73, 309
    new, 140-141, 471-472, 478-479
    null character, 99
    object, 40
    operator overloading, 403
    operator precedence, 81-82
    pointer addition, 131
    pointer arithmetic, 161
    pointer initialization, 124
    pointers, 124
    precedence, 81-82
    protected class members, 510
    returning a reference, 297-298
    rewrite rule, 356
    RTTI, 671
    scoping, 73-74, 453
    static data member, 448
    string address, 137
    strings and pointers, 135
    style. *See* style conventions
    syntax, 412
    type conversion, 429
    type mismatch, 295
    upcasting, 536
    virtual member functions, 544
runtime decisions, 119, 134, 443-444, 543, 545, 670

runtime problems, 646
runtime type information, 670-679

S

scientific notation, 712
scope, 322-323, 325, 328, 641-643
    block, 322, 337, 382
    class, 354, 382-384, 483-484, 679-680
    file, 322, 338, 382
scope operator. *See* :: scope resolution operator
scoping rules, 73-74, 453
search-and-replace, 308
secondary header files, 683
seek modes, 761
segment (address), 119
self-assignment, 464, 472
semicolons
    as expression separators, 156
    and function calls, 234
    and function prototype, 235, 239
    and loops, 151, 175-176
    and statements, 23-24, 30, 155-156
sending a message, 40-41, 357
sentinel character, 180
sequence point, 202-203
setf(), 77, 82, 708-715
shell script, 47
shift operators, 789-790
short integer type, 56-57, 63
showpoint constant, 709
side effect, 155
signed types, 55
significant figures, 76-78, 81
Simula67, 6
sizeof operator, 57-58, 97, 101, 128, 750
    and array name, 132, 245
    and overloading, 413
smart linkers, 356
smart objects, 35-37, 44, 68, 414
SonOfBad class, 666-669
source code, 9-11, 44
source code file, 319, 367
source code formatting, 30-32
source code style, 32
specializations, 312-316
speed, 281-282, 299, 546, 690, 736
spelling sensitivity, 22, 25

stack
    and automatic variables, 325-327
    basics, 384-388
    defined, 282, 479
    example, 384-388
    of pointers, 586-590
    unwinding, 657-659
Stack class, 384-388, 580-581, 583-584
standard. *See* ANSI/ISO draft standard
standard C library, 8, 36
standard class library, 688
Standard Input/Output, 688
standards, 7-8
start at 0, 94-95, 117, 205, 516, 540
startup code, 9
state members, 417-418
statement separator, 23-24
statement terminator, 24
statements, 23-24, 32-41, 154-156
static binding, 127, 134, 543-544
static_cast operator, 798-799
static class members, 444-448, 458
static modifier, 331-336
static storage, 144
static storage class, 327-332, 366, 444-445
static type checking, 236
static variables, 322, 327-332, 453
stddef.h file, 426
stdio.h file, 22, 37, 185, 688
stdlib.h file, 494
step size, 159
Stock class, 349, 358-360, 366-371
stone (weight), 48-49, 84, 427-432
Stonewt class, 427-434
stopping execution, 215
storage, 143-144
storage classes, 322-339, 679
    and dynamic allocation, 338-339
    features, 328
    and functions, 337-338
stream, 28, 688-693
stream checking, 741-742
stream.h file, 27
stream states, 721-723
streambuf class, 692, 761
streamoff, 754-755, 761
streampos, 754-755, 757
String class, 444-448, 454-456, 465-470
    flaws, 450, 454-465

string constant, 98-99, 256
string.h file, 100, 135, 171
string input, 102-108, 723, 727-730
string literal, 98, 137, 256
string size, 302
strings, 98-109
    in arrays, 100-102
    comparing, 170-172
    defined, 28, 93, 256
    and for loops, 159-160
    and functions, 256-259
    and pointers, 134-138
    quoted, 67, 69, 98-99, 135, 256
Stroustrup, Bjarne, 6, 394, 545, 558, 801-802
strstream family, 764
strstream.h file, 765
structure addresses, passing, 266-268
structure assignment, 113-115
structure data object, 109
structure declaration, 112
structure description, 109
structure member, 110
structure references, 295-300
structure variable, 109
structured programming, 2-4
structures, 93, 109-115
    and functions, 259-268
    passing, 260-266
    returning, 260-266
Student class, 568-577
style conventions
    arrays, 191
    book, 17-18
    class names, 349
    constant names, 73
    functions, 154
    if else statements, 200
    loops, 153-154
    main(), 235
    source code, 32
    text, 17-18
subobject, defined, 472
subscript, in arrays, 94-95
subscripts (indices), 190
subtraction operator, 80
suffix, file, 10
suffix, for types, 65
swapping functions, 288-291
switch statement, 214-219, 599

Symantec C++, xvi, 11, 15-16, 19, 319, 739
symbolic constants, 58-60, 115
syntax
    error, 199, 298, 412
    function prototype, 234-235
    functions and pointers, 274
    initialization list, 529-530, 556, 568-569
    initializer list, 484-485
    pure virtual function, 550
    tricks, 162-167

T

table of addresses, 546
tag (name), 109, 114-115
template class, 580-590, 600
template matching, 312
template overloading, 310-312
template specializations, 602-603
template versatility, 600
templates, 580-603
    and class family, 592-600
    and friends, 638-640
    function templates, 308-318
temporary objects, 366, 371-372, 458, 467
temporary variables, 204, 293-295
terminating null character, 98-102, 134, 171, 256, 719
termination, 356
test-condition, 173
test-expression, 151
text files, 747-749
text input, and loops, 180-188
Think C compiler, 16
this pointer, 374-379, 518
throwing an exception, 649-651, 657-658
time.h file, 177, 426
time-delay loop, 176-178
tokens, defined, 31
top-down programming, 4, 252
trailing zeros, 78, 82, 707-709, 712
translation, 694
translators, 11, 18, 96, 327
trivial conversions, 316, 599
true/false literals, 168
truncation, 85-86, 208, 433, 708
try block, 649-650, 656-657
Turbo C++, 13, 319

Tv class, 628-637
type alias, 177-178
type cast, 88-89, 427, 536-537, 671
    enumerations, 116-117
    explicit, 434-435, 555, 575
type cast operators, 798-799
type conversions, 84-89, 407, 426-438, 530, 717-718
    automatic, 236, 427, 437
type_info class, 671, 675-678
type mismatch, 294
type parameters, 583
typedef, 385, 481
typeid operator, 671, 675-678
typeinfo.h file, 676
types
    abstract data types, 384-388, 479
    bool, 72-73, 152, 168, 384
    built-in, 53
    char integer, 64, 66-72
    choosing, 62-64
    defined, 33, 347-348
    derived types
        arrays, 93-98
        defined, 93
        enumerations, 115-117
        pointer-to-int, 121-122
        pointers, 93, 109, 117-144
        reference, defined, 182, 285
        strings, 93, 98-109
        structures, 93, 109-115
    double, 42, 76-78
    float, 76-78
    floating-point, 76-78
    int, 33, 56-57, 62
    integer, 55-73
    long, 56-57, 63
    long double, 76-78
    openmode, 742
    parameterized, 580
    register, 327
    short integer, 56-57, 63
    signed, 55
    size limits, 56-58, 62, 76
    unsigned, 55, 60-62
    user-defined, 40, 347-348
    wchar_t (wide char), 72

U

u or U suffix, 65
ul suffix, 65
unary operator, 402, 785
unbound template friends, 638-639
undefined external, 43, 408
underflow, 62
UNIX, 3, 6, 10-12, 19, 184-185, 319
unsigned types, 55, 60-62
unwinding the stack, 657-659
upcasting, 536, 540, 559, 579
update-expression, 151-152, 159
uppercase/lowercase, 10-11, 170-171, 201-202, 217
user interface, 347
user-defined functions, 44-49
user-defined types, 40, 347-348
uses-a relationship, 523
using-declaration, 681-682
using-directive, 682

V

variable, level (recursion), 271
variables, 32-34, 41, 54-55
variables, local, 238
Vector class, 398, 407-412, 419-423
vector, defined, 396
virtual base class, 529, 606-608, 617-618
virtual functions, 550, 578, 592, 771-772
virtual member functions, 542-550
virtual methods, 543-545, 559-560
visibility. *See* scope
visibility of class objects, 353
void, in function heading, 25, 45-46

W

while loop, 172-178, 220, 224
white space, 31, 32, 102, 719
wide char type, 72
working classes, 593-600, 603-604, 608-610, 612-617
wraparound, 630

X

x coordinate, 417-418

Y

y coordinate, 417-418

Z

zero (false), 72-73, 196, 198
zero argument, 356
zero exit value, 47
zero return value, 720
Zortech C++ compiler, 15-16

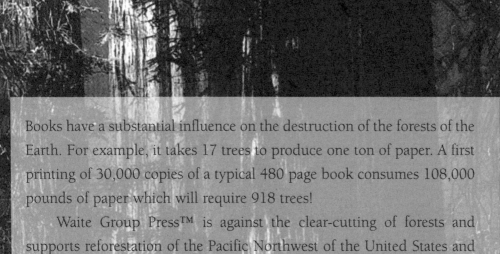

Books have a substantial influence on the destruction of the forests of the Earth. For example, it takes 17 trees to produce one ton of paper. A first printing of 30,000 copies of a typical 480 page book consumes 108,000 pounds of paper which will require 918 trees!

Waite Group Press™ is against the clear-cutting of forests and supports reforestation of the Pacific Northwest of the United States and Canada, where most of this paper comes from. As a publisher with several hundred thousand books sold each year, we feel an obligation to give back to the planet. We will therefore support organizations which seek to preserve the forests of planet Earth.

WAITE GROUP PRESS™

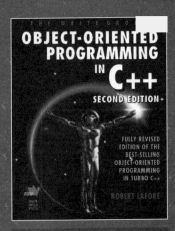

OBJECT-ORIENTED PROGRAMMING IN C++, Second Edition

Robert Lafore

How do you make the best-selling OOP programming book even better? Incorporate the suggestions from an extensive survey of instructors—updated chapters on objects, classes, overloading, constructors, inheritance, and virtual functions. Add a chapter on the newest features of the C++ programming language including templates and exceptions. Make the book fully compatible with the newest Borland C++ 4.0 compilers and add a disk with all the programs and source code. Completely revised from the ground up, this book is now better than ever.

Available Now • 800 pages
ISBN: 1-878739-73-5
$34.95 US/$48.95 Canada
1—3.5" disk

SIMPLE C++

Jeffrey Cogswell

Use POOP (Profound Object-Oriented Programming) to learn C++! Write simple programs to control ROBODOG in this entertaining, beginner-level programming book.

Available Now • 240 pages
ISBN:1-878739-44-1
$16.95 US/$23.95 Canada

MASTER C++

Rex Woollard, Harry Henderson, Robert Lafore

No background in C is required to learn to program in C++ with this computer-based training system. Covers Turbo C++ and Borland C++, and is compatible with AT&T C++.

Available now • 390 pages
ISBN: 1-878739-07-7
$39.95 US/$55.95 Canada
2—5.25" disks

SEND FOR OUR UNIQUE CATALOG TO GET MORE INFORMATION ABOUT THESE BOOKS, AS WELL AS OUR OTHER OUTSTANDING AND AWARD-WINNING TITLES.

WAITE GROUP PRESS™

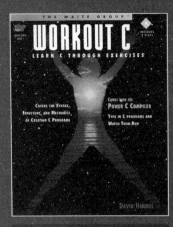

WORKOUT C
David Himmel
MIX Software's Power C Compiler and hundreds of exercises teach you C programming. Enter examples into the text editor, compile the code, and watch your programs run.

Available now • 800 pages
ISBN: 1-878739-14-X
$39.95 US/$55.95 Canada
2–5.25" disks

SIMPLE INTERNET
Jeffrey Cogswell
Simple Internet is an unique approach to learning the internet: a detective story parody that actually leads you through the Internet. Assuming the identity of Archie Finger, a normal, bagel-eating, technophobic private eye, you'll unravel a mystery embedded into the Net. Once you've solved the mystery, you'll have a solid understanding of what the Net is all about.

Available now • 175 pages
ISBN: 1878739-79-4
$16.95 US/$23.95 Canada

INTERNET HOW-TO
Harry Henderson
Are you cruising down the information superhighway in a Ferrari or are you just another hitchiker? Whether you're a beginner interested in learning to use electronic mail, an experienced "info-surfer" seeking to acquire more Unix expertise, or a power user ready to learn the details of compressing and decompressing files, this definitive guide will teach you everything you need to know to use the Internet.

Available now • 400 pages
ISBN: 1878739-68-9
$34.95 US/$48.95 Canada

TO ORDER TOLL FREE CALL 1-800-368-9369
TELEPHONE 415-924-2575 • FAX 415-924-2576
OR SEND ORDER FORM TO: WAITE GROUP PRESS, 200 TAMAL PLAZA, CORTE MADERA, CA 94925

Qty	Book	US/Can Price	Total
___	OOP in C++, Second Edition	$34.95/48.95	___
___	Simple C++	$16.95/23.95	___
___	Master C++	$39.95/55.95	___
___	Workout C	$39.95/55.95	___
___	Simple Internet	$16.95/23.95	___
___	Internet How-To	$34.95/48.95	___

Calif. residents add 7.25% Sales Tax

Shipping
USPS ($5 first book/$1 each add'l)
UPS Two Day ($10/$2)
Canada ($10/$4)
International ($30)
TOTAL

Ship to
Name _____
Company _____
Address _____
City, State, Zip _____
Phone _____

Payment Method
☐ Check Enclosed   ☐ VISA   ☐ MasterCard

Card#_____ Exp. Date _____
Signature _____

SATISFACTION GUARANTEED OR YOUR MONEY BACK.

SOFTWARE LICENSE AGREEMENT

This is a legal agreement between you, the end user and purchaser, and The Waite Group®, Inc., and the authors of the programs contained in the disk. By opening the sealed disk package, you are agreeing to be bound by the terms of this Agreement. If you do not agree with the terms of this Agreement, promptly return the unopened disk package and the accompanying items (including the related book and other written material) to the place you obtained them for a refund.

SOFTWARE LICENSE

1. The Waite Group, Inc. grants you the right to use one copy of the enclosed software programs (the programs) on a single computer system (whether a single CPU, part of a licensed network, or a terminal connected to a single CPU). Each concurrent user of the program must have exclusive use of the related Waite Group, Inc. written materials.

2. The program, including the copyrights in each program, is owned by the respective author and the copyright in the entire work is owned by The Waite Group, Inc. and they are therefore protected under the copyright laws of the United States and other nations, under international treaties. You may make only one copy of the disk containing the programs exclusively for backup or archival purposes, or you may transfer the programs to one hard disk drive, using the original for backup or archival purposes. You may make no other copies of the programs, and you may make no copies of all or any part of the related Waite Group, Inc. written materials.

3. You may not rent or lease the programs, but you may transfer ownership of the programs and related written materials (including any and all updates and earlier versions) if you keep no copies of either, and if you make sure the transferee agrees to the terms of this license.

4. You may not decompile, reverse engineer, disassemble, copy, create a derivative work, or otherwise use the programs except as stated in this Agreement.

GOVERNING LAW

This Agreement is governed by the laws of the State of California.

LIMITED WARRANTY

The following warranties shall be effective for 90 days from the date of purchase: (i) The Waite Group, Inc. warrants the enclosed disk to be free of defects in materials and workmanship under normal use; and (ii) The Waite Group, Inc. warrants that the programs, unless modified by the purchaser, will substantially perform the functions described in the documentation provided by The Waite Group, Inc. when operated on the designated hardware and operating system. The Waite Group, Inc. does not warrant that the programs will meet purchaser's requirements or that operation of a program will be uninterrupted or error-free. The program warranty does not cover any program that has been altered or changed in any way by anyone other than The Waite Group, Inc. The Waite Group, Inc. is not responsible for problems caused by changes in the operating characteristics of computer hardware or computer operating systems that are made after the release of the programs, nor for problems in the interaction of the programs with each other or other software.

THESE WARRANTIES ARE EXCLUSIVE AND IN LIEU OF ALL OTHER WARRANTIES OF MERCHANTABILITY OR FITNESS FOR A PARTICULAR PURPOSE OR OF ANY OTHER WARRANTY, WHETHER EXPRESS OR IMPLIED.

EXCLUSIVE REMEDY

The Waite Group, Inc. will replace any defective disk without charge if the defective disk is returned to The Waite Group, Inc. within 90 days from date of purchase.

This is Purchaser's sole and exclusive remedy for any breach of warranty or claim for contract, tort, or damages.

LIMITATION OF LIABILITY

THE WAITE GROUP, INC. AND THE AUTHORS OF THE PROGRAMS SHALL NOT IN ANY CASE BE LIABLE FOR SPECIAL, INCIDENTAL, CONSEQUENTIAL, INDIRECT, OR OTHER SIMILAR DAMAGES ARISING FROM ANY BREACH OF THESE WARRANTIES EVEN IF THE WAITE GROUP, INC. OR ITS AGENT HAS BEEN ADVISED OF THE POSSIBILITY OF SUCH DAMAGES.

THE LIABILITY FOR DAMAGES OF THE WAITE GROUP, INC. AND THE AUTHORS OF THE PROGRAMS UNDER THIS AGREEMENT SHALL IN NO EVENT EXCEED THE PURCHASE PRICE PAID.

COMPLETE AGREEMENT

This Agreement constitutes the complete agreement between The Waite Group, Inc. and the authors of the programs, and you, the purchaser.

Some states do not allow the exclusion or limitation of implied warranties or liability for incidental or consequential damages, so the above exclusions or limitations may not apply to you. This limited warranty gives you specific legal rights; you may have others, which vary from state to state.

SATISFACTION REPORT CARD

Please fill out this card if you wish to know of updates to
C++ Primer Plus, Second Edition, or to receive our catalog.

Company Name: _____

Division/Department: _____ Mail Stop: _____

Last Name: _____ First Name: _____ Middle Initial: _____

Street Address: _____

City: _____ State: _____ Zip: _____

Daytime telephone: ( ) _____

Date product was acquired: Month _____ Day _____ Year _____ Your Occupation: _____

Overall, how would you rate *C++ Primer Plus, Second Edition*?
- ☐ Excellent
- ☐ Very Good
- ☐ Good
- ☐ Fair
- ☐ Below Average
- ☐ Poor

What did you like MOST about this book? _____
_____
_____

What did you like LEAST about this book? _____
_____
_____

How did you use this book (problem-solver, tutorial, reference...)?
_____
_____

How did you find the pace of this book ? _____
_____
_____

What version of C++ are you using? _____

What computer languages are you familiar with? _____
_____

What is your level of computer expertise?
- ☐ New
- ☐ Dabbler
- ☐ Hacker
- ☐ Power User
- ☐ Programmer
- ☐ Experienced Professional

Where did you buy this book?
- ☐ Bookstore (name): _____
- ☐ Discount store (name): _____
- ☐ Computer store (name): _____
- ☐ Catalog (name): _____
- ☐ Direct from WGP   ☐ Other _____

What price did you pay for this book? _____

What influenced your purchase of this book?
- ☐ Recommendation
- ☐ Advertisement
- ☐ Magazine review
- ☐ Store display
- ☐ Mailing
- ☐ Book's format
- ☐ Reputation of Waite Group Press
- ☐ Other _____

How many computer books do you buy each year? _____

How many other Waite Group books do you own? _____

What is your favorite Waite Group book? _____
_____

Is there any program or subject you would like to see Waite Group Press cover in a similar approach? _____
_____

Additional comments? _____
_____

Please send to: Waite Group Press
Attn: *C++ Primer Plus, Second Edition*
200 Tamal Plaza
Corte Madera, CA 94925

☐ **Check here for a free Waite Group catalog**

C++ Primer Plus, Second Edition

SATISFACTION REPORT CARD

BEFORE YOU OPEN THE DISK OR CD-ROM PACKAGE ON THE FACING PAGE, CAREFULLY READ THE LICENSE AGREEMENT.

Opening this package indicates that you agree to abide by the license agreement found in the back of this book. If you do not agree with it, promptly return the unopened disk package (including the related book) to the place you obtained them for a refund.